PEACE AGAINST WAR

A SERIES OF BOOKS IN INTERNATIONAL RELATIONS

Bruce M. Russett, *Editor*

PEACE AGAINST WAR

The Ecology of International Violence

FRANCIS A. BEER
University of Colorado

W. H. FREEMAN AND COMPANY
San Francisco

Project Editor: Pearl C. Vapnek
Manuscript Editor: Stephen McElroy
Interior Designer: Marie Carluccio
Cover Designer: Sharon Helen Smith
Production Coordinator: Bill Murdock
Illustration Coordinator: Audre W. Loverde
Permissions Coordinator: Ruth J. Allen
Compositor: Graphic Typesetting Service
Printer and Binder: The Maple-Vail Book Manufacturing Group

Library of Congress Cataloging in Publication Data

Beer, Francis A
    Peace against war.

    (A Series of books in international relations)
    Bibliography: p.
    Includes index.
    1. Peace. 2. War. I. Title. II. Series:
Series of books in international relations.
JX1952.B39   327.1'72   80-27214
ISBN 0-7167-1250-4
ISBN 0-7167-1251-2 (pbk.)

Printed in the United States of America

2 3 4 5 6 7 8 9 10   MP   0 8 9 8 7 6 5 4 3 2

To Omar, Marie, and Jeremy

CONTENTS

FIGURES

TABLES

PREFACE

At the beginning I should say a few words about this book's scope and method—its purpose, intended audience, guiding values, and approach to theory and fact.

My major ambition has been to pull together contemporary knowledge about peace and war and express it in a systematic and readable way, so that anybody who is interested can understand what we know and what we don't.

I have aimed at a wide and diverse audience that includes professional social scientists, graduate students, undergraduates, and perhaps some policymakers, political activists, and the general public.

The book attempts to provide meaning and coherence for the professional social scientist who is not a specialist in peace and war. It is a guide to the library of writings on peace and war. The book also represents a translation of modern statistical research that is often difficult even for the specialist to understand.

Students have been a very important group. The book has evolved out of graduate and undergraduate courses I have taught for the last fourteen years. There are, finally, many people in government, politics, or the general public who search for a better understanding of peace and war or who wish to be aware of contemporary work in the field.

A book that aims at such different audiences runs the risk of falling between them. It may be too general and abstract, lacking in vital historical detail, for specialists. More general readers may find it too complex, the argument too tightly packed to make gripping bedtime reading. It may seem dry. There are few real people doing violent deeds, fighting for victory or against defeat, struggling to survive or dying. There may be too few numbers for some, too many tables and figures for others. I ask the members of each group to be tolerant and think kindly of the others.

The book begins from a very explicit value position. First, it defines science broadly, as the search for truth, rather than narrowly in terms of a particular philosophy or method. Second, it assumes that peace is good and war is bad, not only in an obvious absolute sense, but also relative to other values. In other words, we should be willing to sacrifice substantial amounts of security, welfare, and liberty in order to achieve peace and avoid war. This perspective has introduced an inevitable bias, influencing my approach to the subject, the evaluation of theories and data, and the ordering of materials.

Many people do not agree with this position. Nevertheless, it seems consistent with the spirit of an important tradition that has bound together many eminent social scientists. The most massive and best-known reference work of this tradition is Quincy Wright's *A Study of War*.

Wright's major contribution lay in the compilation of existing knowledge about war two generations ago. His work distilled the essence of many disciplines. Since Wright, social scientists whose names will be found within these covers have added to our knowledge in different disciplines and at different levels of analysis. They have studied the global system as a whole; partial international groupings, including regions, nation-states, domestic foreign policy groups; and the psychodynamics and psychostructures of individual decisionmakers. They have used different methods. Some of them have been relatively theoretical, emphasizing different verbal and mathematical models. Others have been empirical, with a heavier reliance on facts. Some have produced numerous examples to illustrate their points. Others have undertaken case studies in depth, surveys of larger numbers of cases, or statistical analyses of different geographical or social samples over different time periods.

I have tried to pull all of this work together by focusing on four major questions:

1. Description. What do we know about the historical occurrence and casualties of war?
2. Explanation. What are the major causes of peace and war and how are they related?
3. Prediction. What is the likely future of peace and war?
4. Prescription. What can we do to create more peace and less war for ourselves, our children, and our grandchildren?

In trying to answer these questions, I have concentrated mainly on the international and national levels of the world system, leaving the dynamics of secondary and primary groups, as well as individual decisionmakers, for a later time. Space limitations imposed by the economics of publishing have prevented complete development of many aspects that I originally hoped to discuss more fully. The notes, and particularly the bibliography, provide a passageway for those who wish to pass through to the wonderland of further reading.

Social science draws heavily from the evidence of the historical past. This book is, however, not a book of history. It is, rather, a book about the patterns and dynamics that will produce international violence of varying scope in the future. In this sense, it is a book about possible underlying causes of World War III.

I hope that this work will help us move a step closer to a general theory of peace and war. If it succeeds, it will contribute to subsequent research, scholarship, teaching, and general knowledge about peace and war—to the discovery of new knowledge, the recombination of elements in the body of existing knowledge, and the expansion of the community that is aware of this knowledge.

All of us have a great deal to be modest about. Our knowledge is still more a point of departure than a preliminary to arrival. Yet each of us can contribute, in a different way, to help solve what is probably the largest and most threatening problem confronting humankind today.

November 1980   Francis A. Beer

ACKNOWLEDGMENTS

My family has been at the very center of my life, thought, and feeling. Diana, my wife, over fifteen years of our marriage has given seemingly inexhaustible resources, while still retaining her self. Omar, Marie, and Jeremy, our children, have provided the deepest personal incentive for the completion of this study. Their coming and growth have been primary causes of the book, coinciding with its own conception and development. The magic they have brought into each day has helped transform the dross of work into the gold of meaning. This book, in its very deepest sense, is for them.

Friends, teachers, colleagues, and students at all stages of my life and career have contributed in some way to the shaping of the material in these pages. Some have been particularly generous with their time and resources. Much of the work was done during eight years I spent at the University of Texas at Austin. I would like to express particular gratitude to Gideon Sjoberg, whose understanding of systemic and countersystemic dynamics helped me to bring theoretical order to the subject. Carol Lukin Carl was a constant friend and critic.

The project has received financial assistance from a number of sources, including the University Research Institute of the University of Texas, the National Endowment for the Humanities, the Earhart Foundation, and the Council on Research and Creative Work of the University of Colorado. The Institute for World Order provided encouragement and crucial financial resources, both for the development of general undergraduate teaching along related lines and for research and writing. Michael Washburn gave a gentle and important personal support.

Some of the writing was done at the University of California at San Diego, where The Program on Science, Technology, and Public Policy opened its facilities to me for several months. During the last few years, I have been associated with the Conflict and Peace Studies Program, the Institute of Behavioral Science, and the Political Science Department at the University of Colorado, Boulder, first as a visitor and then in a more permanent way.

Georgialee Furniss, a dear and long-standing friend, edited the next to last version of the manuscript with the highest professional skill and personal care. Berenice Capoot and Judy Fukuhara typed different drafts. Elizabeth Farrell, Lisa Fieldman, Susan and Michelle Hall, Patricia Kenny, Sylvia Labrucherie, and Gloria Lund did additional typing, helped to compute tables, get library books, send letters requesting reprint permission, copy secondary material, and check bibliographical references.

Bruce Russett, years ago, suggested a careful rereading of Quincy Wright. At a later stage his critical evaluation encouraged me to reorganize, tighten, and polish the work; and his editorial support has helped it finally to reach its intended audience.

November 1980   Francis A. Beer

PEACE AGAINST WAR

Chapter 1

EPIDEMIOLOGY

This book aims to provide an epidemiology of peace and war.[1] It rests on two central assumptions: (1) war is like a disease, for example, cancer or heart disease; and (2) we can develop a scientific knowledge of war, similar to the knowledge we have about disease, that will allow us better to describe, explain, predict, and control it.

DISEASE

The historical development of our perception of peace and war has been similar to our view of health and disease.[2] In earlier stages of human history, disease was viewed as a supernatural event, an instrument of divine wrath or intervention. Often it was dealt with through the rituals of a shaman, medicine man, witch doctor, or prophet. Gradually, however, a more scientific outlook developed and took hold. This approach underlies the modern biological and health sciences as well as medical practice (cf. Malinowski, 1948).

The traditional view of war, like that of disease, related the supernatural and natural orders. In primitive societies war and magic were closely connected. Wives and relatives of warriors were expected to undertake certain rituals and observe complicated rules. Warriors themselves entered into a semidivine state. Thus, Frazer observed that primitive warriors

> move, so to say, in an atmosphere of spiritual danger which constrains them
> to practice a variety of superstitious observances quite different in their nature
> from those rational precautions which, as a matter of course, they adopt against

foes of flesh and blood. The general effect of these observances is to place the warrior, both before and after victory, in the same state of seclusion or spiritual quarantine in which, for his own safety, primitive man puts his human gods and other dangerous characters (1961:12–13; cf. Wilson, 1975:Ch. 8; Thompson and Jacobs, 1973; Bonaparte, 1947).

In classical Greece and Rome, the gods were thought to exercise an effect on wars. Statesmen and military men consulted oracles and sooth-sayers and undertook prescribed rituals. In the medieval Christian world, prayer was an important component of military behavior. Religious fervor partly inspired the Crusades and the holy wars. Even today, divine provi-dence and judgment are elements in the perspectives of war held by dif-ferent peoples. The need to oppose infidels and godless atheists is still strongly felt in the Islamic, Jewish, and Christian communities. Modern African warfare still incorporates traditional war charms, rites of passage, and sorcery; and it involves the spirit of a mystical community. Thus, in a symbolic novel about the Biafran war of secession, the Court of the Here-After hears that, millions of men have died

> in the dignity of kinship. . . . "Yes," said the prosecuting Counsel for Dam-nation . . . , "death is indeed an exercise in pan-Africanism. We have been known to kill each other partly because we belong to each other. We kill each other because we are neighbors" (Mazrui, 1971, cited in Bozeman, 1976:216, 224).

A new scientific perspective on war, similar to that on disease, gradually emerged from this foundation. Modern social scientific theory and research developed the idea that the causes of war lie not with the gods, but in the nature of social systems and human beings. Scientific studies concentrated on in-depth clinical analysis of selected cases of peace and war as well as on statistical associations between peace, war, and various aspects of the environment.

The parallel growth of scientific knowledge about disease and war revealed patterns of coincidence. The two often occurred together, and each seemed, under certain circumstances, to contribute to the other. War promoted disease and disease could be a cause of war. Disease and war were also similar. Both threatened, damaged, and terminated human life on a massive scale; and the two seemed to develop in similar ways.

Coincidence

Disease and war occur in similar populations. Not only humans, but also ants, rats, frogs, and numerous other species exhibit collective fighting behavior (cf. Gale and Eaves, 1975; Schneirla, 1971; Ardrey, 1970; Lorenz, 1967).

Human wars, with their dislocation and damage, help foster disease.

Specific battles produce massive direct physical damage. General wartime dislocations help cause more widespread disorders. These include general malnutrition as well as particular nutritional deficiencies, historically, for example, scurvy. War contributes to fatigue and anxiety and has been associated with increased rates of alcoholism, cholera, diphtheria, gonorrhea, hepatitis, influenza, meningitis, plague, smallpox, typhus, typhoid, and tuberculosis. Modern war also implies radiation diseases, most particularly congenital abnormalities and cancers (cf. Crosby, 1976; Curlin et al., 1976; Kay, 1976; McNeill, 1976:344; Cartwright and Biddiss, 1972; Concannon, 1967; Cattell and Gorsuch, 1965; Reinhard and Armengaud, 1961:495–96; Beebe and deBakey, 1952; Major, 1941; Zinsser, 1935; Prinzing, 1916).

Conversely, disease can also be a factor that contributes to war and other violence. In primitive societies and early extended politics, McNeill notes that

> lassitude and chronic malaise . . . of the kind induced by blood fluke and similar parasitic infections, conduces to successful invasion by the only kind of large-bodied predators human beings have to fear: their own kind, armed and organized for war and conquest (1976:172).

In more modern societies, such as Northern Europe, he continues,

> the absence of well-defined public quarantine regulations and administrative routines—religious as well as medical—with which to deal with plague and rumors of plague, gave scope for violent expression of popular hates and fears provoked by the disease. In particular, long-standing grievances of poor against rich often boiled to the surface. Local riots and plundering of private houses sometimes put the social fabric to a severe test (1976:45).

Disease may aggravate aggressive tendencies in more specific ways. Deficiencies in general health, rest, or nutrition may contribute to belligerence. Thus, Sorokin believed that "hunger, or the threat of it," may give "rise to war when there are no other means of satisfying it" (1975:201; cf. Haas and Harrison, 1977). Biological imbalances among decisionmakers may predispose them to violence, particularly in crisis situations (cf. Halsted, 1974; Wiegele, 1973). Some forms of mental strain, neurosis, and psychosis are associated with high levels of aggressive behavior (cf. Häfner and Böker, 1972). These, in turn, may have a foundation in some physiological malady, perhaps a slow virus, that allows the victim to continue functioning, but in a condition that deviates from the norm to a greater and greater degree. For example, neurosyphilis may produce paranoid cruelty concomitant with the disintegration of the central nervous system. Caesar, Charlemagne, Mussolini, Hitler, and perhaps Winston Churchill may have been so affected (Rosebury, 1971:Ch. 13; cf. Waite, 1977). More recently the hypomanic brutality of Ugandan leader Idi Amin was diagnosed as having a syphilitic base (Legum, 1977).

Similarities

War not only occurs together with disease, but in many ways seems *like* a disease itself. Such a comparison is not new. War has been compared to disease, and peace to health, in a number of major analyses (see Nettleship et al., 1975:189; Alcock, 1972; K. Boulding, 1965, 1962:Ch. 7; Penrose, 1963; Richardson, 1960a; Sorokin, 1937:383; cf. Singer and Small, 1974; Rosenau, 1964:52; Huntington, 1962:45–46).[3] But it is necessary to note that there are important differences between war and disease. Wars are supposed to result from rational human decision rather than forces of nature. Further, in war, the same biological species is both host and agent, attacker and attacked. If war is like a disease, human beings—individuals and groups—are macroparasites on their own kind. Finally, we must make it clear that we are defining war, not conflict, as a disease. War is a very specific kind of conflict that involves direct, obvious, physical injury to life. Conflict in general does not necessarily imply such physical damage.

War is, nevertheless, similar to disease in the threat it poses to life and in possible cycles and stages of its occurrence.

Threat to Life

War resembles disease primarily because it has threatened or brought physical damage or death to large populations. Thus the World Health Statistics Annual, published by the World Health Organization, includes "injury resulting from operations of war" in its list of 150 causes of death. War's opposite—peace—is like the opposite of disease—health—in the sense that it implies the preservation and extension of human life.

Cycles and Stages

Diseases and wars seem to show similar cycles and stages of development. As the first stage in the ontogeny of disease, the host may be assumed to exist in "good health"; that is, it has survived up to that point. The disease enters the host, expands, and, as the host's body begins to fight it, some weakening occurs. If the host is not successful in stopping the disease at this point, the disease accelerates its growth in the host's body. It passes from a relatively invisible or latent stage to one that is more easily observed and diagnosed. At this point we may perceive the "outbreak" of the disease in the patient. Though the disease may have been present for a long time, only at this point, in many cases, is the disease sufficiently advanced so that it can be medically treated. The disease spreads more widely among other members of the population who get it from the original host. By this time, if the host is still alive and is to continue so, we presume that the tide of affairs turns, and that a growing "resistance" gradually beats back the tide of the disease. As this happens, the host achieves "immunity," at least for the time being. This immunity may never fully develop, or it may gradually diminish. The disease again invades the host, and the whole cycle is ready to be repeated.

In the same way Richardson suggested that "some people are naturally immune" to war. Continuing the analogy to disease, he suggested that war has comparable patterns of incubation, outbreak, and contagion. Those who are susceptible will undergo "something in war analogous to the rise of temperature in fever." War contagion comes next. "Fighting is infectious," Richardson believed. "The infection is borne by sights and sounds, by rumor, by newspapers, by cinema shows, and by radio" (1960a:232; see also 233–36, 285–86). The process finally comes around full circle again to resistance and immunity.

> A long and severe bout of fighting confers immunity on most of those who have experienced it; so that they no longer readily join in fights. . . . this acquired immunity is not permanent but fades out after a decade or two. Also there arises a new generation, not rendered immune by experience (Richardson, 1960a:285–86).

SCIENCE AND TECHNOLOGY

Modern science has helped us to a better understanding of both war and disease, but scientific knowledge of war has increased less quickly than knowledge of disease. Differences in knowledge about disease and war come from differences in research possibilities. Social scientists cannot easily conduct carefully controlled experiments to test their theories. While medical scientists can try out their ideas on mice or monkeys, social scientists have no prospect for conducting large-scale wars of animal species under carefully controlled conditions. Eventually, when tests on animals establish a high likelihood of success, tests on voluntary human subjects can be made; but it is difficult to think of humans who would volunteer for comparable studies relating to war and peace. Controlled experiments have been conducted on various aspects of conflict between animals and individuals, but such conflict is only distantly related to the violence of whole societies involved in international war. Social scientists, furthermore, have nothing like the microscopic technology that allows biological science to investigate elements invisible to ordinary human observation (cf. DeWitt, 1977).

Another crucial difference between health science and peace science is in the area of professional status and action. Modern medicine gradually broke its theocratic ties and became thoroughly secular. Academic degrees are awarded in a variety of fields many of which lead to practice. Peace science has not yet advanced to the point of professional practice. Although some in the military claim that "peace is our profession," the primary emphasis of the contemporary peace movement is still religious; and its leaders have been figures like Gandhi and Martin Luther King, Jr. The profession, like the science, of peacemaking is still a hope rather than a reality (see Chatfield, 1979).

The scientific revolution, particularly in the last few years, has, nevertheless, produced a good deal of innovative and constructive work on the subject of war. Much micro or middle-range research has focused on particular times, geographical locations, or aspects of war in order to attain greater depth or precision.

This rapid development has made it extremely difficult to get a composite picture of the whole subject. Instead of a clear view of our cumulative knowledge about war, we have had a series of vignettes, some overlapping, some contradictory, all partial. Our knowledge of war is dispersed. The information we have is confusing and contradictory, even for professional analysts.

We hope to lay out here, in the most succinct possible form, the extent and limits of our contemporary knowledge. We shall try to make clear what we know and what we don't know about the incidence and causes of war, and to develop a theory which seems consistent with this knowledge. By clarifying what we already know, we may also clarify what we need to learn in the future if we are to achieve a more peaceful world.

Describing War

We must first isolate and describe war.

We shall adopt a relatively narrow definition. _War, for our purposes, is the presence of direct international violence._ This definition is to some extent arbitrary; yet it serves to direct the subject of discussion, and it accords with general usage and past research.

Our definition includes a political condition, the distinction between international and domestic violence. War is defined to include only violence between states. Violence within states, between groups or individuals, is excluded. For example civil war, revolution, class war, labor war, race war, gang war, range war, street war are all outside our boundaries unless they are part of a larger international pattern of violence.

Our definition also includes a casualty condition. It makes a distinction between direct and indirect violence. We define war to include only direct violence—in which people kill or harm each other immediately. Indirect violence kills slowly and often anonymously. Whereas direct violence can be measured by numbers of deaths, indirect violence must be measured more circuitously by "avoidable deprivation of life, in lost man-years" (Galtung and Høivik, 1971:73). The instruments of indirect violence include poverty, disease, and repression. All lack the specifying characteristic, the actual physical, direct, and brutal act of killing. Indirect violence is extremely important, not only in its own right, but also as it is related to war. Yet to include it in our definition of war would be to construe war so widely that it would come to include virtually everything painful or of an unpleasant nature (cf. Alcock and Köhler, 1979; Gurr and Bishop, 1976; Köhler and Alcock, 1976).

By contrast, we define *peace* as the absence of war, or what Galtung has called "negative peace" (1969:183). This is obviously an extremely narrow usage. The term peace is commonly employed in much broader ways. It often covers various levels below international relations and contains specifications for substantive justice or processes of political order based on previously articulated general laws. Peace may also include an affective or emotional component, and even a mystical one—for example, when we talk of eternal peace or the peace which passeth all understanding or even peace of mind (see Newcombe and Newcombe, 1972). Nevertheless, to define peace more broadly once again risks an expansion, this time to include everything that is pleasant or that we admire and love. Such a definition is pertinent in developing a general morphology of peace and violence, but it is inappropriate for the scope of our present concerns.

In the discussion that follows, we shall apply this definition to historical experience, asking ourselves how much war has occurred in history, and what trends and patterns in war incidence and casualties history has produced.

Explaining War

We must isolate war analytically in order to describe it, but we are hardly interested in it as an isolated phenomenon. We are concerned with explaining war, in drawing out conditions that are associated with it and that contribute to its existence. Such conditions are found in the world system and its two major components, the environment and decisionmakers.

The Environment

We noted previously that an understanding of the environment contributes to the explanation of disease. It seems reasonable to hope that it can also contribute to our understanding of war.

If we accept the idea that the environment is a legitimate place in which to look for causes of war, there is still the question of which aspect of the environment is likely to be most important.

Natural Environment

We know relatively little about the influence of the natural environment on war, but what we do know provides little basis for the conclusion that it is a major direct contributory factor. The natural environment, with its germs and viruses, has provided major explanations for many diseases. Given the coincidence and similarities between disease and war, one is tempted to think that the same kind of prior natural causes might be responsible for both. If certain bacteria or viruses produced not only the organic damage of disease, but also the violent behavior of war—if, like rabies, for example, the disease drove the host crazy—this would be a parsimonious explanation of the coincidence and developmental similarities between disease and war.

Unfortunately for scientific elegance, it is too long a step to suggest that viral or bacterial infections are the major direct causes of most of the collective violent behavior we know as war. The eminent Richardson was enticed, but even he drew back from such a possible link. "You will not, I hope, suggest me of being so crazy," he wrote, "as to suggest that war is due to bacteria or to a filterable virus, when I put down for discussion the thesis that fighting resembles measles, influenza, or typhoid fever" (1960a:232).

There are only tenuous connections between war and the natural environment. As we have already noted, certain diseases may occur concurrently with violent behavior. Climatic conditions, for example, temperature, may also have some influence.[4] In spite of such possible natural links, the weight of contemporary knowledge suggests that the aspect of the environment most relevant to war is the social part.

Social Environment

The social environment is that part of the environment related to human beings.

HUMAN NATURE   The simplest way of expressing this idea is to say that human nature is the cause of war. Why do human beings prey upon each other? A recurrent answer has been that it is simply our nature, or a part of it. This idea has been expressed in different metaphors. *Homo homini lupus* ("Man is a wolf to men"), said Hobbes. Freud referred to a human death instinct in terms of the mythical destructive forces of Kratos or Thanatos. He held that:

> Men are not gentle creatures who want to be loved, and who at the most can defend themselves if they are attacked; they are, on the contrary, creatures among whose instinctual endowments is to be reckoned a powerful share of aggressiveness. As a result, their neighbour is for them not only a potential helper or sexual object, but also someone who tempts them to satisfy their aggressiveness on him, to exploit his capacity for work without compensation, to use him sexually without his consent, to seize his possessions, to humiliate him, to cause him pain, to torture and to kill him (1962:58).[5]

On the other hand, Freud also identified a more positive side of human nature, a life instinct that he associated with Eros. Others have used this as a basis for a more positive view of human nature and man's subconscious.

Many people still think of "the unconscious," of regression, and of primary process cognition as necessarily unhealthy, or dangerous or bad. Psychotherapeutic experience is slowly teaching us otherwise. Our depths can also be good, or beautiful or desirable. This is also becoming clear from the general findings from investigations of the sources of love, creativeness, play, humor, art, etc. Their roots are deep in the inner, deeper self, i.e., in the unconscious. To recover them and to be able to enjoy and use them we must be able to "regress" (Maslow, 1968:196; cf. Ornstein, 1972; Brown, 1959; Menninger, 1942).

A more naturalistic view links intrahuman violence to tendencies found in other species. We find this in the social Darwinism of Herbert Spencer, emphasizing the survival of the fittest, or in the territorial instinct identified by modern ethology. This territoriality, in turn, is linked to collective fighting behavior in ants, rats, frogs, and numerous other species (cf. Leakey and Lewin, 1977:Ch. 9; Fox and Fleising, 1976; Harrison, 1975; Wilson, 1975:50–51, Ch. 11; Smith and Price, 1973; Schneirla, 1971; Ardrey, 1970; Lorenz, 1967; Nicolai, 1919). Hunting behavior and territorial defense are, however, not the same as more general aggression. General human nature does not help explain why some people are consistently peaceful and others have a relatively high level of belligerency. It seems reasonable that particular genetic endowment plays an important role in setting the scope and limits of such differential behavior. Nevertheless, even genetics only goes part of the way in explaining why the same people are peaceful and violent at different times (cf. Eibl-Eibesfeldt, 1979; 1974; Fabbro, 1978; Montagu, 1976; 1973; Nance, 1975; Melko, 1973; Mitchell, 1972; Lloyd, 1958).

TECHNOLOGY Human beings interact in specific structured social patterns that we shall identify as technology. When we think of technology, we are likely to have in mind applied science, the products of scientific research brought to bear, practically, on human needs. Or we may think of material implements, machines, or automation. The development of such devices for military use has an obvious relationship to modern warfare (cf. Wright, 1965:1501; Nef, 1950).

Technology is, however, much broader than crude material tools. Human conquest of nature—human technology—has resulted in an almost entirely artificial environment. We are less and less in contact with the primal natural environment, and more and more we interact solely with surroundings of our own making. We participate in and manipulate nature. Thus, we seed clouds, oceans, forests, and lawns to conform to our will. Technology, in its widest sense, is "the system by which society provides its members with those things needed or desired" (Webster, 1970). The modern world environment, in this light, is an immense machine—a world machine. Each of us, whether we struggle against it or not, is a part of it.

The effects of technology are not easy to perceive because they are contradictory. They cut in several directions at the same time. Humanity is unable to refine or control technology completely. Technology performs important functions in modern society; but it also carries with it particular dysfunctions as well. Collective goods imply collective bads. In many ways this technology, this new environment, is an improvement upon nature. It brings us new comforts, what we like to call a higher standard of living. In other ways, technology is much worse than nature. It brings depletion, pollution, and above all a profound sense of unreality and loss. To pass through a busy city at noon is to be in a different world from the ocean at midnight or the mountains at dawn. If we wish to take a religious or evolutionary tack, we may well call the positive, constructive dynamic of technology technogenesis. It is the technological act of creation, providing new beginnings for humanity. The negative, destructive tendency might be termed technoschismosis, technology casting humanity out of nature's Eden and setting brother against brother (cf. Richardson, 1960a:65–66; Bateson, 1936).[6]

Technology has long been recognized as having a two-edged effect on health and disease. Modern medical science has helped conquer many diseases, for example, tuberculosis, polio, and smallpox. Longer life is not, however, an unmixed blessing. Increased human populations in some ways can reduce the general quality of life when space and resources are limited.

Technology also has contradictory effects on peace and war. In some ways human technology serves to create and maintain peace, to prevent and reduce warfare. In other ways it helps to encourage and augment violence. Figure 1-1 and Table 1-1 attempt to outline in a very general way some technological factors and variables that help produce this mixed result.[7]

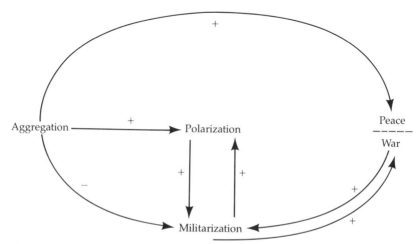

Figure 1-1
An Ecological Model of Peace and War.

Table 1-1
Ecological Variables.

Aggregation	Polarization	Militarization
Bureaucracy		
International law	Legal blocs	Law of war
International organization	Organizational coalitions	Alliances
Domestic government	Government centralization	Military regimes
Exchange		
International transactions	Transaction networks	Military trade and aid
Domestic markets	Market concentration	Military complexes Armaments
Language		
International communications	Exclusivist ideologies	Hostility
Domestic communities	Myths	Militance

1. Aggregation

Aggregation is the logic of technology that makes larger, relatively integrated units out of smaller elements. It helps produce order, structure, symmetry, regulation, and the incremental growth of the world system. We may define aggregation in terms of general superordinate structures and processes of modern bureaucracy, exchange, and language. Bureaucracy incorporates international and domestic political organization, the arrangement of relations between and within nations by international law and organization and domestic governments. Exchange comprehends complex mechanisms for the exchange of goods and services, including international transactions and domestic markets. Finally, modern language has helped bind together values and ideas in patterns of international communications and domestic communities.

It would be nice if we could specify that peace and war have reliable, direct, short- or long-term positive or negative effects on aggregation—that they have had a decisive influence on the construction or destruction of human civilization. Unfortunately, as we shall see, the evidence is very mixed, and we cannot, in good faith, draw such a conclusion. Aggregation appears to have developed independently and according to its own dynamics. Peace and war have had important short-term effects but limited long-term impact on it.

Once aggregation is in place, however, it tends to support peace and to limit or reduce violence and militarization. Aggregation allows people to coordinate their activities and ideas, to work cooperatively in larger groups. Aggregation increases the machinery available for limiting conflict. It contributes to the preservation or enhancement of life during peacetime situations, and the protection of large populations during difficult and even catastrophic conditions, including war itself.

2. Polarization

Another aspect of aggregation is at cross-purposes with this constructive influence. Aggregation helps create polarization. Polarization encompasses three cleavages occurring in aggregated structures and processes. The first such cleavage involves *differentiation*. Aggregation does not occur uniformly in space; it is not evenly distributed in the system. As Table 1-1 emphasizes, societies are separated by the boundaries of international legal blocs, organizational coalitions, and trade groups; national and subnational central governments; socioeconomic concentrations; and exclusivist ideologies and myths.

Differentiation occurs together with *inequality*, a second cleavage in aggregated structure and processes. Differentiated groups are unequal in power, wealth, and community feeling.

The third dimension of polarization is *instability*. Aggregation does not occur uniformly. World technology grows at different rates and with different rhythms in different places and times.

There have been many attempts to show that these cleavages, taken together as polarization, cause peace or war. The evidence, however, is very weak. Much stronger evidence suggests that polarization's major effect is to encourage militarization.

3. Militarization

Militarization includes international legal justification for war, alliances, military trade and aid, and militance; dominance of military elites and militaristic behavior in domestic government, economy, society, and culture.

Militarization and polarization tend to reinforce one another. The more differentiated, unequal, and unstable a society, the more it is likely to show a high military content in its various sectors. The more militarized the society, the lower its ability to overcome the forces of polarization.

Militarization, finally, is directly related to war. War implies the need for militarization. The existence of militarized structures and processes suggests that they will be put to warlike use; and, the more militarized the subgroups, the greater the damage seems likely to be.

Foreign Policymakers

Traditional analysts do not agree with our assumption that war is like a disease, caused by environmental forces.[8] They believe that the free choices of individual policymakers explain a significant part, most, or all of war activity. Peace and war are part of the statesman's inventory of methods or techniques. Thus the Greek historian, Thucydides, tells us that the strong do as they will. The great German military analyst, Carl von Clausewitz, writes that "war is an instrument of policy; . . . The conduct of war . . . is . . . policy itself which takes up the sword in place of the pen" (Clausewitz, 1968:410; cf. Gallie, 1978; Lider, 1978; Wight, 1978; Morgenthau, 1974; Aron, 1966; Kaplan, 1957; Gulick, 1955).[9]

In this view wars are not *caused* by the ecology of an interrelated environment as we have suggested. Rather, wars are *chosen* because of the subsequent beneficial effects they are likely to produce for those who wage them. Wars are a product of instrumental rationality, based on the calculation of "expected utility"—achieved by computing the values of alternative proposed actions and the probabilities of their success, comparing them, and choosing the course of action with the highest projected benefit or lowest cost. Wars are undertaken in order to reach certain clearly defined ends. The benefits of wars are calculated, balanced against their costs, and found to be generally superior to them. When the costs outweigh the benefits, the participants stop fighting (cf. Altfeld and Bueno de Mesquita, 1979; Randle, 1973; Larsen, 1973a; S. Rosen, 1972; Starr, 1972; Kecskemeti, 1964; Whiting, 1960). Modern diplomacy and intelligence supply up-to-the-minute information about all aspects of the environment. The technical tools of modern systems analysis, operations research, statistical decision theory, and mathematical game theory contribute to the rational calculation of the costs and benefits, means and ends, of belligerent activity. Modern military science supplies strategy and tactics appropriate for military activity under different circumstances. Economic, social, cultural, and psychological resources are orchestrated and applied where they will do the most good (cf. Brewer and Shubik, 1979; Snyder and Diesing, 1977).

Even if wars were chosen rather than caused, our analogy would still be valid. Disease can be chosen as well. We are not used to thinking of disease as an instrument of rational policy, while war has long been an accepted means to achieve what are seen as legitimate ends. Yet this difference is illusory. Doctors arrive at the treatment of choice after estimating the relative strengths of alternative diagnoses, treatments, and the patient; and, indeed, medical treatment can involve the use of disease. We innoculate with mild forms of disease to bolster immunities, and we break bones in order to reset them. We also use disease in biological warfare.

Wars, on the other hand, are hardly ever chosen in the simple and straightforward manner the traditional view suggests. Formal accounts of rational decisionmaking are often at odds with more informal reports. These informal accounts need not be accepted at face value. Yet the popularity of breathless narratives that reconstruct the "true story" from "inside dope," or "kiss and tell" memoirs by participants themselves, clearly suggest the deficiencies of purely rationalistic accounts and models of decisionmaking.

The rational calculation of national interest is extremely difficult. We would not go so far as to identify free will as a random force in environmental dynamics. Nevertheless, the traditional view gives foreign policymakers qualities that they may not possess, capabilities of rational processing that may be absent, particularly in the difficult conditions of wartime choice. The formal model of rationality ignores the independent effects of the environment; the lack of policymaker understanding of environmental dynamics, both generally and in relation to war; important prior environmental influences on policymakers; disagreement and confusion about the definition and importance of values, including peace and war; and the high degree of constraint, uncertainty, and emotion that typically surround decisions to go to war.

The environment exerts an influence independent of the actions or beliefs of individual policymakers. From this perspective, foreign policymakers are not so much heroes as victims. War seems less like something decisionmakers choose than something that somehow happens to them and that they do not really understand. Thus, at the outbreak of World War I, the ex-chancellor of Germany, Prince von Bülow, said to his successor, "How did it all happen?" "Ah, if only we knew," was the reply. According to Robert Kennedy's account, this exchange had an important impact on President John Kennedy's thinking at the time of the Cuban missile crisis. The exchange of the German chancellors had been reported in Barbara Tuchman's book, *The Guns of August,* which had made a great impression on the President. "I am not going to follow a course which will allow anyone to write a comparable book about this time, *The Missiles of October,*" he said.

To some extent, President Kennedy was thinking wishfully. Over half a century has passed since the outbreak of World War I. We have gained some additional understanding of the causes of war that has helped us to eliminate some conflicts. Yet our own country has been involved in international violence through the last 35 years—World War II, Korea, and Vietnam; crises in Europe (Berlin), Latin America (Cuba), and the Middle East. Obviously, statesmen's understanding of international violence does not yet enable them to avoid it entirely.

Environmental forces are so complex that policymakers may glimpse only their shadows. Thus one student of formal rationality in decisions for war, states that "in my opinion, gain (or avoidance of loss) is the common reason for undertaking warfare." Yet he recognizes that not all, but only

> some wars were undertaken for perfectly rational reasons. [And that even in these cases,] the people making the decisions may have miscalculated. Businessmen frequently make investments that turn out badly. This is not because they are not motivated by a desire for gain or because they are irrational, but simply that the problems are very difficult and it is easy to make a mistake. The problems of war and peace are equally difficult and mistakes are equally likely (Tullock, 1974:87).

Political leaders conceive, or at least justify, prospective action on the environment through different policies that unfold to reveal various programs and projects. These policies are like chess strategies. They may be clearly defined a few moves ahead. Beyond that, as alternative choices become vastly more complex, they are specified only in a general way if at all. The ultimate consequences of any particular move are difficult or impossible to foresee (cf. Stoessinger, 1978; Handel, 1977; Kinnard, 1977; Milstein, 1974; Iklé, 1971; Russett, 1962). Very often, decisions have unintended consequences, and events turn out differently than policymakers might have hoped or imagined. Military engagement is like taking the first step down a slippery slope (Schelling, 1960: 199–200). When war is joined, "the length and bloodiness of the war" are often surprises, and "defeat too is unintended" (Blainey, 1973:249). According to one estimate, "3/5 of war initiations since 1910 have been based on errors of perception, judgment and expectation of outcome" (Deutsch and Senghaas, 1975:201, cited in Alker, 1977:6).

Policymakers, in order to make good decisions, should have as much information as possible. Unfortunately, the environment rarely provides the perfect information that is most consistent with formal rationality. Policymakers may not recognize information when they see it. A good part of the messages that policymakers receive may appear to have no meaning. The messages are perceived not as important signals but as confusing noise, and this noise may further dull the attention of the decisionmaker and drown out subsequent messages (cf. Wohlstetter, 1962). Policymakers may distort the information they do receive, drawing false lessons about the past, inaccurate conclusions about the present, and false projections of the future (cf. Bonham et al., 1979; Betts, 1978; Jervis, 1976; May, 1973; Janis, 1972; Rivera, 1968; White, 1968; Frank, 1967).

Wars not only happen *to* policymakers, they also happen *through* them. Statesmen do make decisions, but the choices may be like those made by a person in the grip of a serious illness—epiphenomena reflecting the underlying the environmental forces.

The environment does not produce war by itself. It influences and limits political decisionmakers. We may describe these environmental influences on decisionmakers in colorful ways. We can say, with Hegel, that history, or destiny, works its way through individuals. Or we may see decisionmakers, like the early British Fabian socialists, as puppets controlled by outside strings. Or we may envision humanity, as Einstein did, riding on a beam of light (Bronowski, 1973:247–56).

We may also be more precise about environmental pressures to make war, to continue fighting, and finally to make peace. Objective conditions in the external environment—for example, armaments, energy, food, population—or in the decisionmakers' domestic societies will be important. Capabilities and perceived intentions of other foreign and domestic decisionmakers will also be relevant. For example, electoral politics, bureaucratic politics, or the standard operating procedures of administrative routines can help explain the actions of peace and war (cf. East et al., 1978; Hughes, 1978; Tanter, 1974; Allison, 1971). Box 1-1 summarizes how a mood change in the American government and bureaucracy exerted an independent momentum for war in Vietnam.

Foreign policymakers are people like the rest of us, and the environment also influences them in a general, personal, and private way. A growing body of psychohistorical theory and research shows that the child is parent to the adult. It illuminates how past environments, for example, the setting of childhood or other learning experiences, exert a continuing presence in decisionmakers' memories and affect their general attitudes and relations to the world, and their particular view of violence and conflict. Such theory and research suggest that decisions flow partly from springs of subconscious motivation, that public policy can result from the external projection of internal drives (cf. Hermann and Milburn, 1977; Etheredge, 1975; Friedländer and Cohen, 1975).

In order to make rational decisions, the statesman should be clear about the identities and relative importance of major values—including life, liberty, property, happiness, equality, fraternity—as well as how war will affect those values. Yet different groups and individuals in society have different priorities. War may be a good in itself or at least a lesser evil for "hawks." "Doves" have a much higher repugnance to it, no matter what the promised benefits. Further, the relationship between war and other values is not necessarily clear. To some, the failure to fight may seem to involve sacrifices. For others, however, war may appear inconsistent with desired goals (cf. Welch, 1970; Rapoport, 1969; Green, 1968; Levine, 1963).

Decisions are made under varying conditions. Formal rationality may be approached most closely when there is a wide range of alternative options, accurate information, and plenty of time. The decision for war, however, typically tends to rank low on such measures. War decisions involve relatively high degrees of forced choice. The onset of war is often seen in the context of a restricted range of choice, rather than an expanded one. Statements of lack of choice often appear in explanations of war: "We did not want war"; "we were forced to act"; "we had no choice but to . . ." While one's enemies appear free to do as they please, one's own side seems to operate in a much more necessary and closed decisionmaking context. Table 1-2 shows that leaders of major European states typically saw their own range of choice before World War I as relatively closed and less significant than the forces of necessity or the choices of their enemies.

Finally, decisions to go to war are ones in which judgment is quite likely to be infused with emotion. Even though it may seem that confrontation with danger or death clears the mind wonderfully, the decision to go to war involves considerable confusion and stress. Information is inadequate, and time and tempers tend to be shorter than usual. Panic is

Box 1-1

THE MOMENTUM OF VIETNAM

Very subtly in the late winter and into the early spring of 1964 a change began to take place within the government and the bureaucracy. It was something which was not announced, but Vietnam gradually became a more sensitive, more delicate, and more dangerous subject. As such it became something spoken about less and less, the decisions become more and more closely held, and the principals became even more guarded with whom they spoke on the subject. They did not want to be seen with known, identified doves; they did not want to be considered soft. If they had to meet with, say, a reporter known as a dove, they would let friends know that it had to happen, as Bill Bundy did, but with an inflection in his voice of what-else-can-I-do, and a pleasure in telling aides that he was keeping the dove journalist waiting, which was what a dove deserved. Or at the White House, where the subject became more and more sensitive, Chester Cooper, a former CIA analyst who was extremely knowledgeable about Indochina, found that it was more and more difficult to reach McGeorge Bundy on the subject as the questions became graver and the failures more apparent. Cooper began to write memos to his boss expressing his grave doubts about the situation in Vietnam, but he soon found that the subject was so delicate that it was better to write them by hand so that Bundy, reading them, would know that not even a secretary had seen these words and these thoughts; such doubts did not exist except in the most private sense between two men.

Actually, changes and nuances like these were indications of which way they were going, although they were not signals that the outside public, or for that matter, the men involved themselves, could read. Part of this was the growing sense of failure over Vietnam and part of it was the new style that Lyndon Johnson had brought to the White House and the government at large, a sharp contrast to the Kennedy style which was post-Bay of Pigs to ventilate an issue as much as possible within the government. Above all, Johnson believed in secrecy. He liked to control all discussions; the more delicate the subject, the more he liked to control it. Thus by his very style Johnson limited the amount of inner governmental debate, partly because debate went against his great desire for consensus, whether a good policy or not, a wise one or not. The important thing was to get everyone aboard; if there was consensus there was no dissent and this was a comforting feeling, it eased Johnson's insecurities.

So the reins of debate began to tighten and be limited and the bureaucracy began to gear up for war. Individual doubters began to be overwhelmed by the force of the bureaucracy, the increasing thrust of it, mounting day by day, like the current of a river as it nears the ocean.

SOURCE: Halberstam (1972:440–41). Reprinted by permission of International Creative Management. Copyright © 1969, 1971, 1972 by David Halberstam.

Table 1-2

Perceived Freedom of Choice: World War I. (Perceptions of alternatives: frequency of "Choice," "Necessity," and "Closed" alternatives for own nation and enemies.)[a]

	Choice	Necessity		Choice	Closed
Germany					
Self	10	110	Self	10	20
Enemies	25	2	Enemies	25	0
$X^2 = 85.8, p < .001$			$X^2 = 26.2, p < .001$		
Austria-Hungary					
Self	13	80	Self	13	7
Enemies	1	1	Enemies	1	0
Fisher exact p = n.s.[a]			Fisher exact p = n.s.[b]		
Russia					
Self	7	20	Self	7	7
Enemies	6	2	Enemies	6	0
Fisher exact p = .02			Fisher exact p = .04		
France					
Self	1	13	Self	1	5
Enemies	12	2	Enemies	12	2
$X^2 = 17.8, p < .001$			Fisher exact p = .008		
Great Britain					
Self	7	20	Self	7	23
Enemies	21	2	Enemies	21	0
$X^2 = 21.6, p < .001$			$X^2 = 29.3, p < .001$		
Dual Alliance					
Allies	13	20	Allies	13	3
Enemies	26	3	Enemies	26	0
$X^2 = 17.6, p < .001$			Fisher exact p = .05		
Triple Entente					
Allies	30	17	Allies	30	7
Enemies	39	6	Enemies	39	2
$X^2 = 6.4, p = .02$			$X^2 = 3.75, .10 > p > .05$		

[a]Perceptions of leading national decisionmakers, derived by content analysis of all documents written between June 27 and August 4, 1914.

[b]n.s. = not significant or $p < .05$.

Source: Holsti (1972a:67). Reprinted with permission of Macmillan Publishing Co., Inc., from *International Crisis: Insights from Behavioral Research*, by Charles F. Hermann. Copyright © 1972 by The Free Press, a Division of the Macmillan Company.

both a threat and a possibility (cf. Holsti, 1972a, 1972b; Janis, 1972; Kennedy, 1969; North et al., 1963; see also Hallstrom, 1973; Paige, 1968).

Whatever the case for policymakers, war for most individuals is not something they choose. It is given, often against their will, as part of the environment in which they live—or die.

Predicting and Controlling War

The description of war and an explanation of its environmental ecology should educate our guesses and improve our probabilities of being correct when we try to forecast the missing data of the future. It should upgrade the quality of our forecasts about the natural course of wars and help us recognize other developments, germane to warfare, in the world environment. It should tell us more about the external influences on decisions for or against war.

Such knowledge should help make future decisions more rational, more in tune with our real interests; by showing us likely consequences of our own decisions and actions. With this knowledge we should be more capable of interventions to alter the natural course of wars in a constructive way and to limit future war outbreaks and casualties.

Increased knowledge of the ecology of international violence provides no certainty that we shall achieve perfect peace, but we hope that it will improve the chances that we shall make things marginally better rather than drastically worse.

Chapter 2

VIOLENCE

Our first important questions about peace and war center on historical description. How much peace and war have occurred in history? How many casualties? Have there been historical trends? Are there similar patterns in domestic order and violence? Do peace and war occur in regular cycles? What is the evidence that peace and war have regular stages, that they spread contagiously or are limited by resistance?

HOW MUCH PEACE AND WAR IN HISTORY?

We ask first how much peace and war have there been in history?[1] Superficially, this seems an easy question, one that should produce a simple answer. We should be able to say that there have been so many years of peace, so many years of war, and so many people killed or wounded.

Norman Cousins, chairman of the editorial board of *Saturday Review*, is the only person who has been brave enough to try to answer this question independently. He suggests that between 3600 BC and the present day, there have been only 292 years of peace—without a war of some kind. Further, he asserts that more than 14,500 wars have taken place in which more than 3½ billion people perished, either directly or through famine or epidemics. The estimated historical war dead thus come close to equaling the total population of the contemporary world.[2]

Many other analysts have used Cousins' estimates, and so they have passed into the body of accepted collective knowledge. Unfortunately, however, Cousins has never explained publicly how he arrived at his figures. If we wish to try and answer the question, therefore, we must ourselves look at the record of historical statistics.

Measurements

Table 2-1 gives some examples of different ways that wars may be measured. At the outset, we can distinguish three categories of wars, according to political scope and the number of people involved and killed—*world major wars, regional major wars,* and *world major international and domestic violence.* Four important studies help provide a shared body of detailed knowledge about these wars. The most up-to-date of these is Singer and

Table 2-1
Measurement of Major Violence.

Study	Political Conditions	Casualty Conditions
World: Major Wars		
Wright	Legal recognition of war: "political groups, especially sovereign states"	"Considerable magnitude": troops $\geq 50,000$
Singer and Small, intensive	International, at least one independent nation-state, population $\geq 500,000$; diplomatic missions from two major international powers 1920–1965 (member of League of Nations or U.N. at any time)	Direct and substantial battle-connected deaths ≥ 1000
Regions: Major Wars		
Sorokin	Nation-wars, involving one of 12 major European states	None specified
Singer and Small	Nation-wars, involving at least one state in the specified region; region-wars, fought in the specified region	Direct and substantial battle-connected deaths ≥ 1000
World: Major International and Domestic Violence		
Richardson	Human quarrels, "malice aforethought"	Lethal result (≥ 317)
Singer and Small, comprehensive	Inclusion in at least one of the four studies listed here	

Small's study (1972), which gives a comprehensive summary of the other three major studies—Richardson (1960b), Wright (1965), and Sorokin (1937). In addition, Singer and Small report results of their own intensive research on war between 1816 and 1965.

World major wars have been measured by Wright (1965) and Singer and Small (1972). The principal characteristic of such wars is their global significance. Wright's measure requires the legal recognition of war by "political groups, especially sovereign states," and the use of at least 50,000 troops. Singer and Small, in their intensive study, require that at least one participant be an independent nation-state, and that there be at least 1,000 deaths in battle.[3]

Major wars in a particular geographical region have been measured using two different methods, which focus on the identification of nation-wars and region-wars. Nation-wars are counted as wars in which only one member of a given region participates. Thus, Sorokin (1937) gives us nation-war figures, separately tallying wars in the history of 12 major European states. Singer and Small's intensive study (1972) tabulates nation-wars for Africa, Asia, Europe, the Middle East, and the Western hemisphere. Region-wars are counted as wars where the main locus of fighting is in a particular area. Singer and Small's intensive study calculates these as well as nation-wars.

World major international and domestic violence is a category that is broader than the central definition of this study. It exceeds our political condition by including not only violence between states but also within them. Nevertheless, we are interested in the grouping because we wish to relate international and domestic violence. The studies that concern us include Richardson's tabulation of "deadly quarrels." These are "murders, banditries, mutinies, insurrections, and wars small and large"; but not "accidents, and calamities such as earthquakes and tornadoes." Where the dividing point is hazy, "the legal criterion of 'malice aforethought' is taken as a guide" (Richardson, 1960b:6). Singer and Small's comprehensive list (1972:Ch. 5) incorporates the results of previous studies, including Richardson's.[4]

Estimates

These measures help us to estimate the number of violent incidents and casualties that have occurred in different time periods.[5]

Incidence

Table 2-2 shows the estimates of incidents in different categories of violence. Thus, Wright counts about 200 world major wars between 1480 and 1941. Singer and Small's intensive list includes 93 world major wars from 1816 to

Table 2-2
Estimated Major Violence: Incidents, 1100–1965.

Study	From Year		No. of Incidents	To Year
World: Major Wars				
Wright	1480		200	1941
Singer and Small, intensive	1816		93[a]	1965
Regions: Major Wars				
Sorokin ca. AD 1100			862	1925
Singer and Small, intensive				
Europe	1816	144[c]	33[d]	1965
Western hemisphere	1816	35	16	1965
Africa	1816	4	8	1965
Middle East	1816	28	19	1965
Asia	1816	28	27	1965
World: Major International and Domestic Violence[e]				
Richardson	1820		317	1949
Singer and Small, comprehensive	1916		367	1965

[a]Includes interstate, colonial, and imperial wars with casualties ≥ 1,000.

[b]Nation-wars, fought *by any member* of the specified region. The total is inflated by multiple counting of wars.

[c]Nation-wars, fought *by any member* of the specified region. The nation-war total is 239. It exceeds the world total of 93 wars by 157 percent because of multiple counting of wars between nations of the same region.

[d]Region-wars, fought *within* specified area. The region-war total is 103. It exceeds the world total by 11 percent because of multiple counting of wars fought in several regions.

[e]We note, for comparative purposes, that Bouthoul and Carrère (1976) list 366 incidents between 1740 and 1974, 284 incidents between 1816 and 1965; and 245 incidents for the period 1820–1949.

SOURCE: Singer and Small (1972:59, 78, 292, 295); Richardson (1960b:Ch.2); Wright (1965:651); and Sorokin (1937:283).

1965. Sorokin finds 862 major nation-wars in Europe between AD 1100 and 1925, while Singer and Small's intensive study estimates various numbers of nation-wars and region-wars for the different continents. Singer and Small's comprehensive survey includes 367 separate incidents of world major international and domestic violence between 1816 and 1965, which is comparable with Richardson's estimate of 317 incidents for the slightly shorter period 1820–1949.

These numbers by themselves are a very abstract summary of concrete human historical experience. Tables 2-3 and 2-4 go a little bit further, giving us the names of world major wars between 1480 and 1965. Tables 2-5 and 2-6 do the same for world major domestic violence between 1509 and 1949. Tables 2-7 and 2-8, finally, give a summary of world major international and domestic violence between 1945 and 1975.

Table 2-3
World Major Wars, 1480–1815.

War	Years	Name of Treaty of Peace
War of Granada	1482–1492 .	
Italian Wars	1495–1504	Blois
Ottoman War	1492–1503	
League of Cambrai	1508–1509	
Scottish War	1510–1513	
Conquest of Goa	1510–1511	
War of Holy League	1511–1514	Orléans
Russo-Polish War	1511–1526	
Ottoman War	1512–1519	
Franco-Swiss War	1515–1515	Geneva
Dano-Swedish War	1516–1525	
Conquest of Mexico	1520–1521	
1st War against Chas. V	1521–1526	Madrid
Ottoman War	1521–1531	
Scottish War	1522–1523	
2nd War against Chas. V	1526–1529	Cambrai
Conquest of Peru	1531–1531	
Ottoman War	1532–1534	
Polish War	1532–1533	
Lübeck War	1533–1536	
Russo-Polish War	1534–1537	
3rd War against Chas. V	1536–1538	Nice
Ottoman War	1537–1547	
Algerian Expedition	1541–1541	
Scottish War	1542–1546	
4th War against Chas. V	1542–1544	Crespy
Siege of Boulogne	1544–1546	
Schmalkaldic War	1546–1547	
Ottoman War	1551–1568	Adrianople
5th War against Chas. V	1552–1559	Cateau Cambrésis
German Wars	1552–1555	Augsburg
Russo-Swedish War	1554–1557	Moscow
Russo-Swedish War	1559–1561	
Ottoman War	1559–1564	
Great Northern War	1561–1570	Stettin
Ottoman War	1565–1568	Adrianople
Ottoman War	1569–1580	
Russo-Swedish War	1572–1583	
Russo-Polish War	1572–1575	
Italian War	1575–1575	
Spanish-Portuguese War	1579–1582	
Ottoman War	1583–1590	
War of the Armada	1585–1604	

SOURCE: Reprinted from *A Study of War*, Tables 31–37, by Quincy Wright by permission of the University of Chicago Press. © 1942, 1965 by the University of Chicago. All rights reserved.

War	Years	Name of Treaty of Peace
Russo-Swedish War	1590–1595	Teusina
Swedish-Polish War	1598–1599	
Wars of Kalmar	1600–1629	Altmark
Franco-Savoian War	1600–1601	
Polish-Swedish War	1600–1609	
Russo-Swedish War	1603–1617	Slatbourg
Daghestan Expedition	1605–1605	
Russo-Polish War	1609–1618	
Ottoman War	1610–1619	
Austro-Venetian War	1615–1618	Madrid
Spanish-Savoian War	1615–1617	
Spanish-Venetian War	1617–1621	
Polish-Turkish War	1618–1621	
Spanish-Turkish War	1618–1619	
Thirty Years' War	1618–1648	Westphalia
Bohemian War	1618–1623	Nikolsburg
Protestant Union War	1618–1620	Ulm
Palatinate War	1620–1623	
Dutch-Spanish War	1621–1648	Münster
Danish War	1625–1629	Lübeck
Spanish-English War	1625–1630	
Swedish-Prussian War	1626–1629	Strohm
War of Mantuan Succession	1627–1631	Cherasco
Swedish-Imperial War	1630–1648	Osnabrück
Saxon War	1630–1635	Prague
Danish-Hamburg War	1630–1643	
French-Imperial War	1635–1648	Münster
Swedish-Danish War	1643–1645	Bromsbro
Russo-Polish War	1632–1634	Polisnovka
Pequot War	1637–1637	
Danish-Polish War	1638–1638	
Spanish-Portuguese War	1640–1668	Lisbon
Turkish-Venetian War	1644–1668	
Tatar Wars	1646–1649	
Franco-Spanish War	1648–1659	Pyrénées
Anglo-Dutch Naval War	1652–1655	Westminster
Russo-Polish War	1654–1667	Andrusovo
Great Northern War	1654–1660	Copenhagen
Dutch-Portuguese War	1657–1661	
Ottoman War	1657–1664	Temesvar
Sweden-Bremen	1665–1666	Habenhausen
Anglo-Dutch Naval War	1665–1667	Breda
Barbary States War	1666–1694	
Franco-Spanish War	1667–1668	Aix-la-Chapelle

(continued on next page)

Table 2-3 *(continued)*

War	Years	Name of Treaty of Peace
Anglo-Dutch Naval War	1672–1674	Westminster
1st Coalition against Louis XIV	1672–1678	Nijmegen
Turkish-Polish War	1673–1676	Zurawno
King Philip's War	1675–1675	
Danish-Hamburg War	1676–1679	
Russo-Turkish War	1678–1681	
Ottoman War	1682–1699	Karlowitz
Franco-Spanish War	1683–1684	Ratisbon
Franco-Imperial War	1683–1684	Regensburg
Danish-Hamburg War	1686–1686	
2nd Coalition against Louis XIV	1688–1697	Ryswick
Amour Expedition	1689–1689	Nerghinsk
Azov Expedition	1695–1696	
Second Northern War	1700–1721	Nystadt
War of Spanish Succession	1701–1713	Utrecht
Russo-Turkish War	1710–1712	Pruth
British-Swedish War	1715–1718	Stockholm
Ottoman War	1716–1718	Passowitz
Seizure of Sardinia	1717–1717	
War of Quadruple Alliance	1718–1720	London
Swedish-Hanoverian War	1719–1721	Nystadt
British-Spanish War	1726–1729	Seville
War of Polish Succession	1733–1738	Vienna
Russo-Austrian War	1735–1739	Belgrade
War of Austrian Succession	1739–1748	Aix-la-Chapelle
Russo-Swedish War	1740–1743	Abö
Seven Years' War	1754–1763	Paris
Sepoy Mutiny	1763–1765	
Russo-Turkish War	1768–1774	Kutchuk Kainarji
Seizure of Corsica	1768–1769	
Confederation of Bar	1768–1772	
Falkland Islands	1770–1770	
Spanish-Moroccan War	1775–1775	
Mahratta War	1778–1782	Salbai
War of Bavarian Succession	1777–1779	Teschen
Seizure of the Crimea	1783–1784	
Brabant Revolt	1787–1790	
Austro-Turkish War	1787–1792	Sistova
Russo-Swedish War	1788–1790	Verelii
Tippu Sahib	1792–1799	
Russo-Persian War	1795–1796	
Tripoli-U.S.	1801–1805	Tripoli
1st Mahratta War	1802–1804	Surge Angengaum
Russo-Persian War	1804–1813	Gulistan

War	Years	Name of Treaty of Peace
Napoleonic Wars	1803–1815	Vienna
Third Coalition	1805–1805	Pressburg
Franco-Prussian	1806–1807	Tilsit
Peninsular War	1807–1814	Paris
Anglo-Danish	1807–1814	Kiel
Franco-Austrian	1809–1809	Schönbrunn
Russian Expedition	1812–1813	
War of Liberation	1813–1814	Paris
Hundred Days' War	1815–1815	Paris
Russo-Turkish	1806–1812	Bucharest
Russo-Swedish	1808–1809	Frederikshavn
War of 1812	1812–1814	Ghent
Austria-Naples	1815–1815	Calvi
Algiers-U.S.	1815–1815	U.S.S. "Guerrière"

Table 2-4
World Major Wars, 1816–1965.

War	Years	War	Years
British-Maharattan	1817–1818	Second British-Sikh	1848–1849
Greek	1821–1828	Roman Republic	1849
Franco-Spanish	1823	La Plata	1851–1852
First Anglo-Burmese	1823–1826	First Turco-Montenegran	1852–1853
Javanese	1825–1830	Crimean	1853–1856
Russo-Persian	1826–1828	Anglo-Persian	1856–1857
Navarino Bay	1827	Sepoy	1857–1859
Russo-Turkish	1828–1829	Second Turco-Montenegran	1858–1859
First Polish	1831	Italian Unification	1859
First Syrian	1831–1832	Spanish-Moroccan	1859–1860
Texan	1835–1836	Italo-Roman	1860
First British-Afghan	1838–1842	Italo-Sicilian	1860–1861
Second Syrian	1839–1840	Franco-Mexican	1862–1867
Peruvian-Bolivian	1841	Second Polish	1863–1864
First British-Sikh	1845–1846	Ecuadorian-Colombian	1863
Mexican-American	1846–1848	Second Schleswig-Holstein	1864
Austro-Sardinian	1848–1849		
First Schleswig-Holstein	1848–1849		
Hungarian	1848–1849		

SOURCE: Singer and Small (1972:59). *(continued on next page)*

Table 2-4 *(continued)*

War	Years	War	Years
La Plata	1864–1870	Spanish-Moroccan	1909–1910
Spanish-Chilean	1865–1866	Italo-Turkish	1911–1912
Seven Weeks	1866	First Balkan	1912–1913
Ten Years	1868–1878	Second Balkan	1913
Franco-Prussian	1870–1871	World War I	1914–1918
Dutch-Achinese	1873–1878	Russian Nationalities	1917–1921
Balkan	1875–1877	Hungarian-Allies	1919
Russo-Turkish	1877–1878	Greco-Turkish	1919–1922
Bosnian	1878	Riffian	1921–1926
Second British-Afghan	1878–1880	Druze	1925–1926
British-Zulu	1879	Manchurian	1931–1933
Pacific	1879–1883	Chaco	1932–1935
Franco-Indochinese	1882–1884	Italo-Ethiopian	1935–1936
Mahdist	1882–1885	Sino-Japanese	1939
Sino-French	1884–1885	Russo-Japanese	1939
Central American	1885	World War II	1939–1945
Serbo-Bulgarian	1885	Russo-Finnish	1939–1940
Sino-Japanese	1894–1895	Indonesian	1945–1946
Franco-Madagascan	1894–1895	Indochinese	1945–1954
Cuban	1895–1898	Madagascan	1947–1948
Italo-Ethiopian	1895–1896	First Kashmir	1947–1949
First Philippine	1896–1898	Palestine	1948–1949
Greco-Turkish	1897	Korean	1950–1953
Spanish-American	1898	Algerian	1954–1962
Second Philippine	1899–1902	Tibetan	1956–1959
Boer	1899–1902	Russo-Hungarian	1956
Russo-Japanese	1904–1905	Sinai	1956
Central American	1906	Sino-Indian	1962
Central American	1907	Second Kashmir	1965

Table 2-5

World Major Domestic Violence, 1509–1820.

Domestic Violence	Years	Name of Treaty of Peace
Moorish Insurrection	1509–1511	
Peasants' War	1524–1525	
War of Kappel	1531–1531	Kappel
Arundel's Rebellion	1549–1550	
Wyatt's Rebellion	1554–1554	
Great Northern War	1562–1570	Stettin
1st Huguenot War	1561–1563	Amboise
War of Dutch Independence	1566–1579	

Table 2-5 *(continued)*

Domestic Violence	Years	Name of Treaty of Peace
2nd Huguenot War	1567–1568	Longjumeau
Scotch Rebellion	1567–1568	
3rd Huguenot War	1569–1570	St. Germain
4th Huguenot War	1572–1573	Edict of Boulogne
5th Huguenot War	1575–1576	Chastenoy
6th Huguenot War	1576–1577	Poitiers
Irish Rebellion	1580–1580	
7th Huguenot War	1580–1580	Fleix
War of Three Henrys	1585–1598	Vervins
Scotch Rebellion	1594–1594	
O'Neill's Rebellion	1598–1602	
Dutch Independence	1600–1609	
Russian Civil War	1604–1610	
Hungarian Revolt	1611–1615	
Conde's Rebellion	1615–1615	
Huguenot War	1621–1629	Paris
Cossack Revolt	1634–1638	
Catalonian Revolt	1639–1659	
British Civil War	1640–1649	
Irish Rebellion	1641–1643	
Andalusian Revolt	1641–1641	
Neapolitan Revolt	1646–1648	
Cossack Rebellion	1648–1654	
La Fronde	1648–1652	
Irish Rebellion	1649–1652	
Scottish War (Chas. II)	1650–1651	
Polish Civil War	1666–1666	
Cossack War	1668–1681	
Hungarian Revolt	1670–1687	
Covenanter Rising	1677–1679	
Bohemian Revolt	1680–1680	
Revolt of Strellsi	1682–1684	
English Civil War	1685–1688	
Hungarian Insurrection	1703–1711	Nagy-Majteny
Catalonian Rebellion	1705–1715	
British Civil War	1715–1716	
Scotch Civil War	1745–1746	
Orange Revolt (Netherlands)	1747–1747	
Greek Revolt	1770–1770	
Russian Revolt	1773–1774	
American Revolution	1775–1783	Paris
French Revolution	1789–1802	Amiens
First Coalition	1792–1797	Campo Formio
Vendée	1793–1796	
Franco-American War	1798–1800	Paris
Egyptian Expedition	1798–1801	
Second Coalition	1799–1802	Amiens
Polish Insurrection	1792–1795	
Haitian Revolt	1802–1803	Haut du Cap

Table 2-6
World Major Domestic Violence by Casualties, 1820–1949.

Casualty Range: 3,162,277–316,228 **Casualty Magnitude:** 6 ± ½[a]	**Years**
Taiping Rebellion	1850–1864
American Civil War	1861–1865
Russian Revolution	1917–1920
Spanish Revolution	1930–1939
1st Chinese Communist War	1929–1936
Communal Riots in India	1946–1948

Casualty Range: 316,227–31,623 **Casualty Magnitude:** 5 ± ½	**Years**
Massacre of the Janissaries	1826
Moslem Rebellions in West China	1861–1878
Cuban Revolt	1868–1878
Armenian Massacres	1894–1897
Columbian Civil War	1899–1902
Mexican Revolution	1910–1920
Moslem Rebellion in Kansu, China	1928
Chinese Civil War	1930
Greek Civil War	1946–1949

Casualty Range: 31,622–3,163 **Casualty Magnitude:** 4 ± ½	**Years**
Latin American Revolt	1810–1824
Greek Revolt	1821–1830
Revolt in Kashgaira	1822–1828
Polish Insurrection	1830–1831
Portuguese Revolution	1831–1834
Egyptian Revolt	1831–1833
Carlist Revolt	1833–1847
Montenegran War	1853
Sepoy Rebellion	1857–1859
Italian War	1859
Italian Revolution	1860–1861
Paris Commune	1871
Carlist War	1872–1876
Satsuma Rebellion	1877
Chilean Revolution	1891
Armenian Massacres	1909
Banditry and Suppression in North China	1913–1914
Old vs. New Systems in China	1913
Russian Turkestan	1916
Szechuan	1920
Riffian War	1921–1925
Chinese Civil War	1926–1928
Chinese Turkestan	1931–1934
Greek Civil War	1944–1945

[a]Casualty Magnitude is the logarithm to the base ten of casualty range.

SOURCE: Richardson (1960b:Ch. 2).

Table 2-7

World Major International and Domestic Violence, 1945–1967.

Conflict	Type[a]	Size[b]	Parties
Europe			
Greek Civil War	CI	4.65	Greece, Yugoslavia / Albania Bulgaria / U.S.
Berlin crisis	I	2.0	U.S.S.R. / NATO
Trieste question	I		Yugoslavia / Italy
Corfu channel rights	I		U.K. / Albania
Cyprus independence	C	3.0	U.K. / EOKA forces
Hungarian crisis	CI	4.0	U.S.S.R. / Hungary
Cyprus	CI	3.0	Cyprus / Greece and Turkey / U.N. intervention
Middle East			
Iran	I	NH	Iran / U.S.S.R.
Egypt independence	CI		U.K. / Egypt
Palestine question	CI	3.55	Israel / Egypt / Iraq / Transjordan / Syria / Lebanon
Arab-Israeli War I	I	3.5	Israel / Egypt / Iraq / Transjordan / Syria / Lebanon
Morocco	C	NH	France / Morocco
Tunisia	C	3.5	France / Tunisia
Iran	CI		U.K. / Iran
Algerian war of independence	CI	5.0	France / Algeria
Aden-Yemen border	BC		U.K. / Yemeni tribes
Suez invasion	I	3.0	U.K. / France / Israel / Egypt
Sinai campaign	I		Israel / Egypt
Spanish Morocco	BC		Spain / Morocco
Muscat-Oman Revolt	I		U.K. / Muscat-Oman
Lebanon	I	3.0	U.K. / U.S. / Jordan / Lebanon
Lebanon civil war	CI		
Mosul (Iraq) revolt	C		Iraq Government / rebel officers
Tunisia-Bizerte crisis	I		France / Tunisia
Iraq-Kurds	C		Civil Government / Kurds
Kuwait intervention	CI	NH	Iraq, Kuwait / U.K. / Arab League
Morocco-Algeria border	BC		Morocco / Algeria OAS intervention
Yemen Civil War	CI	3.0	Royalists, republican / UAR and Saudi Arabia

[a]C = Civil, I = International, BC = Border Conflict.

[b]This is according to Richardson's scale of numbers of deaths:

Range	7 ± ½ =	31,622,777 to 3,162,278
	6 ± ½ =	3,162,277 to 316,228
	5 ± ½ =	316,227 to 31,623
	4 ± ½ =	31,622 to 3,163
	3 ± ½ =	3,162 to 317
	2 ± ½ =	316 to 32

SOURCE: SIPRI (1969b:Table 4A.1). See also Bouthoul and Carrère (1976:Annex II), Wood (1968); Kende (1968); Carroll (1968); Wainhouse et al., (1966); Holsti (1966); Deitchman (1964); and Kellog (1964).

(continued on next page) **31**

Table 2-7 (*continued*)

Conflict	Type[a]	Size[b]	Parties
Middle East (*continued*)			
Aden Civil War	CI		U.K. / Aden / Yemen / UAR
Syrian coup d'état	C		Civil Government / military rebels
Arab-Israeli War II	I	4.5	Israel / UAR / Jordan / Syria / Iraq / Lebanon
Far East			
Indonesian War of independence	CI	3.2	Dutch Government / nationalists
Indochina War (Vietnam I)	CI	4.0	France / Indochina / Laos and Cambodia
Chinese Civil War	CI	5.0	Kuomintang / Chinese Communist Party / U.S.
Indian communal riots	CI	5.9	India / Pakistan
Taiwan (Formosa)	CI	3.2	Kuomintang / Taiwanese
Hyderabad, India	C	3.3	Indian Government / Nizam and Moslems
Kashmir	CI	3.0	India / Pakistan
Philippines Civil War	C	3.0	Philippine Government / Hukbalahap rebels
Burmese Civil War	C		Burmese Government / Karen and Shan tribesmen
Malayan insurgency	C	3.0	U.K. / Malaya and Malayan Communist Party
Burmese border conflict	BC		Burma / Kuomintang forces
Korean War	I	6.0	N. Korea / China / S. Korea / U.S. / U.N. intervention
Tibet I	CI		Tibetan Government / China
Quemoy-Matsu Islands	I	3.0	China / Kuomintang troops / U.S.
Tibet II	CI	4.0	China / Tibetan rebels
Vietnam War II	CI	5.0	N. Vietnam / S. Vietnam / U.S.
Naga revolt in India	C	3.5	Indian Government / Nagas
Burmese border conflict	BC		Burma / China
Indonesian Civil War	C	4.5	Government / Communists
Laotian Civil War	CI	4.0	Royalists / republicans
Longju and Ladutch incidents	BC		China / India
Thailand, Cambodian border	BC		Cambodia / Thailand
West Irian	I	2.0	Indonesia / Netherlands
Goa, India	I	2.0	India / Portugal
Nepal Civil War	C		Government / insurgents
Vietnam War III	CI		S. Vietnam / FNL / N. Vietnam / U.S. / Philippines / S. Korea / Thailand / Australia / New Zealand

Conflict	Type[a]	Size[b]	Parties
Far East (*continued*)			
Brunei revolt	CI		Brunei / U.K. / Sarawak / N. Borneo
Indian frontier war	BC	4.0	India / China
Malaysian confrontation	I	3.0	Indonesia / Malaysia / U.K. / Australia / New Zealand
Thailand insurgency	C		Government / insurgents / U.S.
Rann of Kutch	BC		Pakistan / India
India-Pakistan	I	4.0	Pakistan / India
Indonesian crisis	C	5.5	Government / insurgents
Latin America			
Bolivia	C	3.0	Government / insurgents
Bolivia	C	2.65	Government / insurgents
Paraguay	C	2.7	Government / insurgents
Costa Rica	CI		Costa Rica / Nicaragua
Colombia	C	6.0	Government / insurgents
Honduras	BC		Honduras / Nicaragua
Honduras	BC		Honduras / Nicaragua / Guatemala
Nicaragua	BC		Nicaragua / Costa Rica
Guatemalan intervention	CI	1.5	Guatemala / U.S.
Cuba	C	3.0	Government / Castro rebels
Venezuela	C		Venezuela / Dominican Rep.
Dominican Rep.	CI		Dominican Rep. / U.S.
Cuba (Bay of Pigs)	I		Cuba / U.S.
Cuba crisis	I		Cuba / U.S.S.R / U.S.
Cuba missile crisis	I	NH	Cuba / U.S.S.R. / U.S. / Organization of American States
Panama canal	I	1.5	Panama / U.S.
Guatemala	C		Government / insurgents
Dominican Republic	CI	3.5	Government / insurgents / U.S. / Organization of American States
Peru	C		Government / insurgents
Africa			
Madagascar	C	3.0	France / Madagascar
Kenya (Mau-Mau)	C	4.0	U.K. / Mau Mau
Cameroons	C	3.0	France / U.K. / nationalists
Ruanda-Urundi	C	5.0	Bahutus / Watusi
Congo	CI	5.0	Congo / Katanga province / U.N. forces
Angola	C	4.0	Portugal / Angolans
Somalia-Ethiopia	BC	2.5	Somalia / Ethiopia
Burundi	C	3.0	Ruanda / Burundi
Portuguese Guinea	CI		Portugal / nationalists / Congo (Kinshasa)

(continued on next page)

Table 2-7 *(continued)*

Conflict	Type [a]	Size [b]	Parties
Africa *(continued)*			
Kenya, Somalia	BC		Kenya / Somalia / U.K.
East African mutinies	I	2.5	Kenya / Uganda / Tanganyika / U.K.
Congo (Kinshasa)	CI		Government / insurgents / Belgium / U.S.
Mozambique	C		Portugal / nationalists
Nigeria	C		Coup d'état: Government / army
Ghana	C		Coup d'état: Government / army
Congo (Kinshasa)	C	2.5	Kisangani mutiny: Government / army
Nigeria	C		Government / "Biafra"
Sudan, Uganda	BC		Sudan / Uganda

If we take peace to be the total absence of war, the lists confirm Cousins' suggestion about the rarity of peace. The 52 years without world major war between 1480 and 1965 can be listed all too briefly: 1505–1507, 1548–1550, 1722–1725, 1730–1732, 1749–1753, 1766–1767, 1776, 1780–1782, 1785–1786, 1800, 1819–1820, 1834, 1837, 1843–1844, 1850, 1886–1893, 1903, 1908, 1927–1930, 1937–1938, 1963–1964. Even this short list of global periods of peace may be too long. For example, it tells us that 1776 and 1963–1964 were peaceful years; yet the American experience of the Revolution and the Vietnam war was quite violent.[6]

Casualties

The incidence of war is not its most important aspect. Casualties give wars their importance. This is the aspect of war that makes it most like a disease; this dimension unites the human beings who fight, suffer, and die.

We shall present some general casualty estimates here, but we must remember that war casualties are even more difficult to measure than war incidence. Casualty figures in major wars are subjects of debate. A good example of this is the inflated body count figures of the Vietnam war. Casualty records on minor wars, even in contemporary times, are spotty.

Table 2-9 shows some casualty estimates for different categories of violence. Wright does not provide us with detailed casualty figures, but Singer and Small's intensive study estimates almost 30 million casualties incurred directly by the combatants in world major wars between 1816 and 1965. This figure does not include civilian mortality or deaths caused by

Table 2-8
World Major International and Domestic Violence,
1967–1975.[a]

Conflict	Years
Zaire	1967
Zimbabwe (Rhodesia)	1967–(1980)
S. Yemen	1968
Chad	1968–1972
El Salvador/Honduras	1969
S. Yemen/Saudi Arabia	1969
U.K. (N. Ireland)	1969–
Cambodia	1970–1975
Sudan	1970
Philippines	1970–1976
Jordania	1970
Guinea	1970
Pakistan (Bangladesh)	1971
Sri Lanka	1971
Jordania	1971
N. Vietnam	1972–1973
Burundi	1972
Uganda/Tanzania	1972
Yemen/S. Yemen	1972
Israel/Arab countries	1973
Iraq (Kurds)	1945–1975
Cyprus	1974
Lebanon	1975–1976
E. Timor	1975–(1978)
Angola	1975–1976
W. Sahara	1975–

[a]Dash without year following indicates conflict continues.
Year in parentheses indicates conflict may have ended.
SOURCE: Kende (1977:67; 1978:239–41).

indirect and long-term effects of war. Even so, it is about 15 percent larger than total military forces of the whole contemporary world (ACDA, 1978:72).

According to Sorokin's estimates, about 35½ million people died in European wars between AD 1100 and 1925, without counting World War II or any casualties in the middle of the twentieth century. Singer and Small's figures show that about 22 million casualties occurred in European wars between 1816 and 1965. They also present casualty figures for major wars in other regions.

War casualties have been quite dramatic in our own time. The twentieth century has been characterized as "the century of total war" (Aron, 1955).

Table 2-9
Estimated Major Violence: Casualties, 1100–1965.

Study	From Year		Casualties	To Year
World: Major Wars				
Wright			Incomplete	
Singer and Small, intensive	1816		29,189,600[a]	1965
Regions: Major Wars				
Sorokin				
Europe 500 BC Incomplete	AD 1100		35,406,571[b]	1925
Singer and Small intensive	1816			1965
Europe		21,973,700[a]	22,430,100[c]	
Western Hemisphere		929,500	459,300	
Africa		29,800	8,376,200	
Middle East		783,800	10,986,700	
Asia		5,472,800	16,639,700	
World: Major and Minor Violence[d]				
Richardson			Incomplete	
Singer and Small, comprehensive			Incomplete	

[a]Total of nation-war casualties.
[b]Total of nation-war casualties (incomplete).
[c]Region-wars. The region-war casualty total is about 58,892,000. It exceeds the nation-war casualty total by 102 percent because of multiple counting of casualties in wars fought in several regions.
[d]Bouthoul and Carrère (1976:20) estimate 85 million casualties between 1740 and 1974. These include estimates of deaths of soldiers and civilians caused by famine and disease. (See also Urlanis, 1971.)

In its first 15 years probably over 100 million people—military and civilian—have been killed or died as a result of war wounds. Tables 2-10 and 2-11 show that the two world wars alone, during less than 10 years, killed over 60 million persons among the major participants, a number larger than the *entire* present population of Britain, France, or Italy. More than 8 million soldiers and 1 million civilians were killed directly in World War I. An estimated additional 18 million people died in the influenza epidemic of 1918 (cf. Crosby, 1976; Kay, 1976). Almost 17 million soldiers and 35 million civilians were killed in World War II.

In addition to world wars, a series of regional wars has gone on in Europe, Africa, Asia, the Middle East, and Latin America. In the most extreme cases, domestic violence has inflicted casualties equivalent to major international war. Between 1960 and 1970 internal wars killed an estimated 700,000 Chinese, 500,000 Indonesians, and 250,000 Nigerians (Wood, 1968). Many other domestic conflicts have also involved major military action.[7]

Table 2-10

Casualties: Major Participants, World War I.

Country[a]	Total Mobilized	Killed or Died of Wounds	Civilians Killed or Died from Injuries (Estimate)	Total Killed or Died
Austria–Hungary	7,800,000	1,200,000	180,000	1,380,000
Belgium	267,000	14,000	90,000	104,000
Bulgaria	560,000	87,000	n.a.[b]	87,000 +
France	8,410,000	1,363,000	150,000	1,513,000
Germany	11,000,000	1,774,000	225,000	1,999,000
British Empire	8,904,000	908,000	9,000	917,000
Italy	5,615,000	460,000	300,000	760,000
Rumania	750,000	336,000	170,000	506,000
Russia	12,000,000	1,700,000	n.a.	1,700,000 +
Serbia	707,000	125,000	n.a.	125,000 +
Turkey	2,850,000	325,000	250,000	575,000
U.S.	4,355,000	126,000	n.a.	126,000 +
Total	63,218,000	8,418,000	1,374,000 +	9,792,000 +

[a]This list excludes non-European belligerents such as China, Japan, Thailand, Latin American countries, and also certain smaller European belligerents such as Greece, Luxembourg, and Portugal, who all played a relatively minor role in the war.
[b]n.a. = no figures available.
SOURCE: Wood (1968:24).

Extrapolations Without Trends

We may now return to our earlier question about the total amount of peace and war in world history. Our information about war incidence and casualties provides a detailed basis for speculation. If we take Cousins' date of 3600 BC as a boundary for the historical past, we may extrapolate the results of the major studies backward to this point. In doing this we suppose that peace and war occur at about the same rate now as they did in earlier centuries. We neglect, for the time being, historical trends involving changes in rate since 3600 BC.

We begin with estimates of violence in different areas and time periods. In Table 2-12 we extrapolate these figures back to 3600 BC and forward to 1980. When we do this, we get 2,400–3,500 world major wars and various subtotals for regional wars.[8] Overall we get more than 13,600 incidents of major international and domestic violence.

The data on peace seem weaker, but we can use the same procedure to extrapolate total years without world major wars. If we do this, we get about 597 years of world major peace between 3600 BC and AD 1980.

Table 2-11
Casualties: Major Participants, World War II.

Country	Total Mobilized	Killed or Died of Wounds	Civilians Killed or Died from Injuries (estimate)	Total Killed or Died
Australia	1,000,000	27,000	nil	27,000
Britain	5,896,000	557,000	61,000	618,000
Canada	1,041,000	32,000	nil[b]	32,000
China	17,251,000	2,220,000	20,000,000	22,220,000
France	5,000,000	202,000	108,000	310,000
Germany	10,200,000	3,250,000	500,000	3,750,000
India	2,394,000	36,000	nil	36,000
Italy	3,100,000	149,000	783,000	932,000
Japan	9,700,000	1,507,000	672,000	2,179,000
Poland	1,000,000	64,000	2,000,000	2,064,000
Rumania	1,136,000	520,000	n.a.[c]	520,000
U.S.S.R.	22,000,000	7,500,000	7,500,000	15,000,000
U.S.	16,113,000	292,000	nil	292,000
Yugoslavia	3,741,000	410,000	1,275,000	1,685,000
Total	99,572,000	16,766,000	32,899,000	49,665,000
Countries not listed above[a]	8,410,000	167,000	1,406,000	1,573,000
Grand Total	107,982,000	16,933,000	34,305,000	51,238,000 +

[a]Including Belgium, Brazil, Bulgaria, Czechoslovakia, Denmark, Finland, Greece, Hungary, Netherlands, New Zealand, Norway, Philippines, and South Africa.
[b]nil = none or less than 1,000.
[c]n.a. = no figures available.
SOURCE: Wood (1968:26) and Wright (1965:1542).

Table 2-13 shows war casualty extrapolations for the same period. For world major wars, we get about 1.1 billion direct battle deaths; again, we are not counting indirectly caused or civilian deaths or assorted casualty subtotals for major wars in different regions.[9]

TRENDS

The picture of peace and war we have developed so far is like a snapshot, or perhaps an archaeological remnant, where experience is captured and frozen. We should like to get more of a moving picture, to know about changes or variations in peace and war over time. We may thus ask whether there are any clear, long-run historical trends in peace and war.

Research suggests that such long-run trends may exist. In particular,

Table 2-12

Extrapolated Major Violence, Without Trend: Incidence, 3600 BC–AD 1980[a].

Study	Total Incidents		
World: Major Wars			
Wright		2,416	
Singer and Small, intensive		3,460	
Regions: Major Wars			
Sorokin			
Europe		5,824[b]	
Singer and Small, intensive	[c]		[d]
Europe	5,358		1,228
Western Hemisphere	1,302		595
Africa	149		298
Middle East	1,042		707
Asia	1,042		1,005
World: Major International and Domestic Violence[e]			
Richardson		13,609	
Singer and Small, comprehensive		13,655	

[a]Trendless extrapolation formula:

$$W_t = \frac{W_e\,T_t}{T_e}$$

W_t = extrapolated wars for total time.
W_e = estimated number of wars in original study.
T_e = time (in years) selected for original estimate.
T_t = total time of period 5,581.
  For a more qualitative description of the earlier part of the period, see Dupuy and Dupuy (1970).
[b]Nation-wars.
[c]Nation-wars. May be normalized by taking 38.91 percent of total. See note c, Table 2-2 above.
[d]Region-wars. May be normalized by taking 90.29 percent of total. See note d, Table 2-2 above.
[e]Extrapolation of the Bouthoul and Carrère (1976) figures produces 8,683 incidents, which seems very low for this category.

peace today may be more diffused, war more concentrated, and casualties more aggravated than in the past. An early study, published near the beginning of World War I, was already sensitive to such change.

> Wars may be less frequent than formerly, yet they may be greater in magnitude, involving larger proportions of the total population. They may be more bitterly fought and subject to less interruption than in the olden times; and also the suffering may be greater even in spite of advancing knowledge and skill in the care of the wounded (Woods and Baltzly, 1915:2).

Figure 2-1 and Table 2-14 outline the specific implications of such a trend in greater detail. As we move through time from 3600 BC to AD 1980,

Table 2-13
Extrapolated Major Violence, Without Trend: Casualties, 3600 BC–AD 1980.

Study	No. of Casualties	
World: Major Wars		
Wright	—	
Singer and Small, intensive	1,086,047,700[a]	
Regions: Major Wars		
Sorokin		
Europe	239,230,110[b]	
Singer and Small, intensive		
Europe	817,568,130[a]	834,549,250[c]
Western hemisphere	17,089,022	34,583,597
Africa	1,108,759	311,650,480
Middle East	29,162,585	408,778,480
Asia	203,624,650	619,107,770
World: Major International and Domestic Violence[d]		
Richardson	—	
Singer and Small, comprehensive	—	

[a]Nation-wars.
[b]Nation-wars (incomplete).
[c]Region-wars. May be normalized by taking 49.56 percent of the total.
[d]Extrapolation of the Bouthoul and Carrère (1976) figures gives 2,016,489,300, which seems very low compared with the extrapolated estimate for world major wars. See note a, Table 2-12, for trendless extrapolation formula.

Table 2-14
Possible Historical Trends: Indicators of Peace Diffusion, War Concentration, and War Aggravation.

Peace Diffusion	War Concentration	War Aggravation
Fewer peace periods	Fewer wars	Higher casualties in absolute numbers
Longer peace periods	Shorter wars	Higher casualties relative to population
	More intense wars More nations involved More battles	

peace diffusion implies that peace periods have become longer and less frequent. Paradoxically, there are fewer peace periods because of war concentration. War is also less frequent and interrupts peace less often. When wars do occur, they are shorter, but more severe. More nations, both ab-

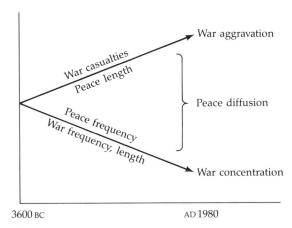

Figure 2-1
Possible Historical Trends: Peace Diffusion,
War Concentration, and War Aggravation.

solutely and in proportion to the total number of nations, take part. More
battles occur; total casualties and casualties relative to population are
larger.[10]

Some evidence from the studies of different categories of wars supports
different aspects of such a general set of trends. We shall present a part
of it here. At the same time, however, we must bear in mind that there are
many gaps and that the case supporting such trends is quite modest.

Peace Diffusion and War Concentration

World Major Wars

Figure 2-2 is a bar graph of the dates and durations of periods of general
peace and war in modern civilization. Such general wars are the most serious of world major wars. From this figure we see that the frequency of
peace and war seems to drop markedly over 3½ centuries. As we have
moved forward in time, there appear to have been fewer, but much longer
periods of general peace, fewer but shorter periods of general war.

Taking the larger, more complete sample of world major wars, Wright
finds a relative decline "in the proportion of war years to peace years,"
which we would expect when war length goes down and peace length
goes up. World major wars also seem to have become shorter. Over the
last four centuries, he observes, there has been "a decrease in the length"
of major wars.

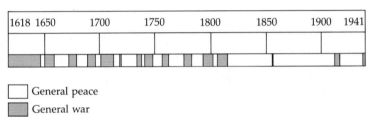

Figure 2-2
World General Peace and War Incidence, 1618–1941. (SOURCE:
Reprinted from p. 650 of *A Study of War* by Quincy Wright by
permission of the University of Chicago Press, © 1942, 1965 by
the University of Chicago. All rights reserved.)

While major wars from the sixteenth to the nineteenth centuries often lasted
over ten years, there were many short . . . wars. The average duration of a war
during these centuries was about five years compared with three years in the
nineteenth century. The average for the first forty years of the twentieth century
has been 2.6 years (Wright, 1965:235; cf. Rummel, 1967).

Singer and Small's intensive study of a more recent world major wars
also presents some evidence of the general trend. Some of their figures
suggest declining war frequency. They note that "the number of wars
. . . goes down for the second half of our 150 years," with the twentieth
century hosting less than its share (1972:189). Of 93 major wars, only 32
began in the twentieth century while 61 occurred in the nineteenth century.
Table 2-15 further supports declining war frequency. It calculates the proportion of total wars we should expect in the nineteenth and twentieth
centuries from the proportion of total years in each century. Thus, the
period 1816–1900 includes just under 57 percent of the 150 years between
1816 and 1965 while 1901–1965 includes just over 43 percent. On a purely
random basis we should expect the same distribution of wars. We observe
over 65 percent of the total number of wars in the earlier period and under
35 percent of the wars in the later one. We thus get about 9 percent fewer
wars in the twentieth century than we would expect. This difference is
reasonably significant in a statistical sense. On the basis of chance alone,
we would expect such a difference less than one out of ten times. This is
particularly relevant when we consider that the number of nations in
the international system—and therefore the mathematical possibilities
for war—substantially increased from the nineteenth to the twentieth
century."[11]

Singer and Small's data on world major wars also shows some other
evidence of war concentration. While the number of wars declined, more
twentieth-century nations were involved in more months of war, even after
adjustment for the increased number of modern nations.[12]

Table 2-15

Declining War Frequency: World Major Wars, 1816–1965.

Study	Years	Proportion of Wars Expected (Based on Time)	Proportion of Wars Observed	Difference
Singer and Small,	1816–1900	.567	.656	+ .089[a]
intensive list	1901–1965	.433	.344	− .089

[a]Significant below $p = .10$ using z test for proportion, two-tailed.

SOURCE: Singer and Small (1972:59; 82–128).

European Major Wars

European history provides a large part of our sample of world major wars. It is, therefore, not particularly surprising that the European evidence also supports the same general trend of peace diffusion and war concentration. Over time, there have tended to be fewer major European wars, and European states spent less of their time at war. Thus Wright notes that:

> The number of European wars has declined from over 30 a half-century in the sixteenth and seventeenth centuries to less than half that number in the nineteenth and twentieth centuries. . . . In the sixteenth and seventeenth centuries the major European states were formally at war about 65 per cent of the time. In the three succeeding centuries the comparable figures were 38 per cent, 28 per cent, and 18 per cent respectively (Wright, 1965:638, 235).[13]

Major European wars have tended to have greater numbers of participants and battles in modern times than in the past. Thus "the number of participants in a war has tended to increase from 2 or 3 in the sixteenth and seventeenth centuries to 3 or 4 in the nineteenth and twentieth centuries" (Wright, 1965:638–39). And there has been a general increase in the number of battles.

> In the sixteenth century less than two important battles occurred on the average in a European war; in the seventeenth century, about four; in the eighteenth and nineteenth centuries, about 20; and in the twentieth century, over 60 (Wright, 1965:237).

World Major International and Domestic Violence

When we come to comprehensive figures for total international and domestic major violence, the picture is less complete. Evidence still suggests, however, that the total number of major violent incidents has declined in recent years. Table 2-16 takes its figures from Singer and Small's comprehensive study. Like the preceding table, it compares the proportion of wars expected from the proportion of total years in the nineteenth and twentieth

Table 2-16

Declining War Frequency: World Major International and Domestic Violence, 1816–1965.

Study	Years	Proportion of Wars Expected (Based on Proportion of Years)	Proportion of Wars Observed	Difference
Singer and Small, comprehensive list				
International subset	1816–1900	.567	.708	+.141[a]
alone	1901–1965	.433	.292	−.141
Total set	1816–1900	.567	.698	+.131[a]
	1901–1965	.433	.302	−.131

[a]Significant below $p = .001$ using z test for proportion, two-tailed.

SOURCE: Singer and Small (1972:59; 82–128).

centuries with the proportion of wars actually observed. The nineteenth century again has more than its share of both international and total incidents of major violence while the twentieth century has less than we might have expected from its proportion of the total years. The differences of 14 percent and 13 percent are very significant statistically; we would expect them less than one time out of a hundred on the basis of chance.

The international component of violence in this table makes up most of the difference between the nineteenth and the twentieth century—not only does it take a sharper drop than domestic violence, but it also makes up about 70 percent of the comprehensive list.[14]

War Aggravation

War casualties—both in absolute numbers and relative to population—may also have increased in more recent times. Singer and Small's intensive study of world major wars reveals a sharp rise in raw battle deaths between the nineteenth and the twentieth century.[15]

Tables 2-17 and 2-18 present Sorokin's estimated absolute casualty figures for nine major European countries in the four centuries between 1601 and 1925, and for four countries during the eight centuries 1101–1925. These figures show a substantial and continuous rise in the absolute number of people killed in wars over the last 900 years except for a slight dip in the nineteenth century.

Table 2-17

Increasing War Casualties: Nine European Countries, Absolute Indicators, 1601–1925.[a]

Century	Casualties	Population	Army, Absolute Strength	Civilians, Absolute Strength
20th	22,035,150[b]	401,000,000[c]	60,425,000[b]	340,575,000
19th	3,645,627	238,000,000[d]	24,333,800	213,666,200
18th	4,505,990	135,000,000[d]	31,055,500	103,944,500
17th	3,711,090	100,000,000[d]	25,796,000	74,204,000
Total	33,897,857			

[a]Austria, England, France, Russia, Poland, Spain, Italy, Netherlands, Germany.
[b]For the first quarter only. The figure underestimates the indicator for the twentieth century.
[c]In 1910.
[d]About 1850, 1750, 1650.

SOURCE: Sorokin, (1937:341). (Comparative population figures in McNeill, 1969:496–97, 602–3; Thomlinson, 1965:362, 486; Borrie, 1970:19, 47–48 are generally consistent with Sorokin's population estimates.)

Table 2-18

Increasing War Casualties: Four European Countries, Absolute Indicators, 1101–1925.[a]

Century	Casualties	Population[b]	Army	Civilians
20th	16,147,550	305,000,000	41,465,000	263,535,000
19th	2,912,771	171,530,000	17,869,800	153,660,200
18th	3,622,140	90,000,000	24,849,000	65,151,000
17th	2,497,170	55,000,000	15,865,000	39,135,000
16th	573,020	35,000,000–45,000,000	9,758,000	24,242,000–35,242,000
15th	285,000	25,000,000–35,000,000	5,000,000	20,000,000–30,000,000
14th	166,729	18,000,000–25,000,000	3,867,000	14,133,000–21,133,000
13th	68,440	13,000,000–18,000,000	2,372,000	10,628,000–15,628,000
12th	29,940	10,000,000–13,000,000	1,161,000	8,839,000–11,839,000
Total	26,302,760			

[a]France, England, Austria-Hungary, Russia.
[b]In 1910 and other mid-centuries.

SOURCE: Sorokin (1937:335–45).

The absolute casualty figures for the first quarter of the twentieth century in Europe, even before World War II, exceeded

> the total casualties for all the preceding centuries taken together. . . . The curse of privilege to be the most devastating or most bloody war century belongs to the twentieth; in one quarter century it imposed upon the population a "blood tribute" far greater than that imposed by any of the whole centuries compared (Sorokin, 1937:336, 342).

The trend is even more striking if we add in the middle fifty years of the twentieth century, 1925–1975. Table 2-11 estimated that in World War II the major European states lost almost 25 million people. Colonial, postcolonial, and civil wars have also claimed large numbers of European lives. Taken together, total casualties for this period probably approached the aggregate sum of casualties for prior centuries plus the first quarter of the twentieth century, which included World War I.[16]

The rise in absolute war casualties might be a result of increases in the sizes of modern armies or populations. Unfortunately, however, casualties as proportions of armed forces, civilians, and total population have also gone up.[17] Tables 2-19 and 2-20 convert the absolute figures into estimated proportions. They show a long-term rise in casualties—relative to the size of armies, civilian population, and total population—except for some relaxation in the eighteenth and nineteenth centuries (cf. Stefflre, 1974; Alker and Bock, 1972:426; Wright, 1965:245, 656).

Table 2-21 suggests some aggravation in world major domestic violence. Here we divide Richardson's domestic incidents between 1820 and 1949 into two equal time periods, 1820–1884 and 1885–1949. The later period shows a slightly higher number of total incidents, and a higher number of violent incidents involving high casualties. Between the two periods, the number of major domestic incidents with the highest casualties—between 31,000 and 3 million—doubled, going from 5 to 10. Simultaneously the number of violent domestic events with casualties between 3,000 and 32,000 declined by almost 30 percent (cf. Taylor and Hudson, 1972:110–15).

Extrapolations with Trends

We may accept, for the time being, the hypothesis of peace diffusion, war concentration, and war aggravation. Nevertheless, we draw conclusions with considerable risk. We must be careful to remember that this hypothesis has not really been confirmed, and that there may actually be no trend at all. Unlikely as it sounds, there may have been no significant change over

Table 2-19
Increasing War Casualties: Nine European Countries, Relative Indicators, 1601–1925.[a]

Century	Army/ Population	Civilians/ Population	Casualties/ Army	Casualties/ Civilians	Casualties/ Population
20th	.151	.849	.365	.065	.055
19th	.102	.898	.150	.017	.015
18th	.230	.770	.145	.043	.033
17th	.258	.742	.144	.050	.037

[a]Austria, England, France, Russia, Poland, Spain, Italy, Netherlands, Germany.

Table 2-20

Increasing War Casualties: Four European Countries, Relative Indicators, 1101–1925.[a]

Century	Army/ Population	Civilians/ Population	Casualties/ Army	Casualties/ Civilians	Casualties/ Population
20th	.136	.864	.389	.061	.053
19th	.104	.896	.163	.019	.017
18th	.276	.724	.146	.056	.040
17th	.288	.712	.157	.064	.045
16th	.279–.217	.721–.783	.059	.023–.016	.013–.016
15th	.200–.143	.800–.857	.057	.014–.010	.008–.011
14th	.215–.155	.785–.845	.043	.012–.008	.006–.009
13th	.182–.132	.818–.868	.029	.006–.004	.004–.005
12th	.116–.089	.884–.911	.026	.003	.002–.003

[a]France, England, Austria-Hungary, Russia.

time in the incidence of peace and war and in the casualties of violence. Peace and war may occur about as frequently and last as long as they ever did; casualties may also be very comparable to what they have always been.

Our evidence is far from being complete. Estimates for world major wars are based primarily on European experience. They tend to give relatively shallow coverage to major conflict in Asia, Africa, and Latin America; and, as we have pointed out, even the European statistics are not very reliable.[18]

The lists may also be incomplete from another perspective. The level of domestic violence may be much higher than they would suggest. The *New York Times* reported well over 1,200 unequivocal examples of internal war between 1946 and 1959 (civil wars, including guerrilla wars, localized

Table 2-21

Increasing Casualties: World Major Domestic Violence, 1820–1949.

	3,162,277– 316,228	316,227– 31,623	31,622– 3,163	Total Incidents
Casualty Range:				
Casualty Magnitude:	$6 \pm \frac{1}{2}$	$5 \pm \frac{1}{2}$	$4 \pm \frac{1}{2}$	
Time Period				
1820–1884	2[a]	3	14	19
1885–1949	4	6	10	20
Total				
1820–1949	6	9	24	39

[a]Number = conflicts of a particular magnitude in given time period.

SOURCE: Richardson (1960b:Ch. 2).

rioting, widely dispersed turmoil, organized and apparently unorganized terrorism, mutinies, and coups d'état). And the *Times* certainly did not include all of the incidents that occurred (Eckstein, 1964:3; cf. Wilkinson, 1980:33–34, 120).

Finally, we have less historical information on earlier periods than later ones. Thus, the possible trend toward casualty increases may be in part the result of underreporting of earlier casualties, particularly civilian casualties of a more indirect nature. Indirect casualties are still with us. Modern medicine and logistics have probably worked to reduce indirect mortality. Yet, in contemporary times, heavy civilian casualties have resulted from modern military techniques that were not previously available. In particular, aerial bombardment has taken a significant civilian toll. In wartime modern transportation and population concentration spread lethal global epidemics almost overnight. As we have already noted, World War I helped spread the Spanish flu epidemic of 1918 that killed millions.

In earlier wars, military techniques may have provided more primitive tools for taking life. Nevertheless, civilian knowledge was also more restricted in its capabilities to support and save it. Famine and disease were particularly widespread sources of mortality. Earlier wars caused massive casualties in civilian populations, which are not reflected in our statistics. During the Thirty Years' War, for example, one estimate reports an absolute decline in the population of the German Empire from 21 million to 13.5 million between 1618 and 1648 (Leckie, 1970:12).[19]

If trends of peace diffusion, war concentration, and war aggravation have indeed taken place, they require adjustments in our extrapolations of wars and casualties since 3600 BC. The total number of peaceful years—without world major war—may be smaller than we thought. The incidence of war may be greater. The general trend of peace diffusion and war concentration implies more peace and fewer wars today—less peace and more wars yesterday. Thus, as we move back in time, we must subtract from our peace extrapolations and add to our total war figures.[20] This means probably a good deal less than 600 years of major world peace, perhaps even a number approaching zero.

The extrapolated number of wars should be revised upward. We should, therefore, take the first extrapolated total numbers of wars in Table 2-12 as lower limits. We may now estimate over 3,500 world major wars. Separate European states may have been involved in such wars over 6,000 times, and over 1,250 of the wars probably occurred in Europe. Further, more than 14,000 incidents of world major and minor violence may have occurred since 3600 BC.

The total number of casualties in history may be smaller than we extrapolated. A trend of war aggravation involves more casualties today. When we move backward in time, the trend is reversed, which implies lower casualties in past centuries and lower total casualties. The trend evidence thus suggests that we should subtract something from our figures and that the extrapolated number of casualties should be revised down-ward. From this perspective, the extrapolated total casualty figures in Table 2-13 appear as upper limits. Our evidence suggests something under 1 billion direct battle deaths in world major wars since 3600 BC, of which less than 800 million occurred in Europe.

We must again emphasize that the evidence is very incomplete. The actual number of wars may exceed our lower limits by really substantial amounts. With greater historical knowledge of non-European areas, the total number of wars might be much larger, and the European proportion of them smaller. In this case, the decline in number, length, and frequency over time may have been sharper than our more recent evidence suggests. The true number of historical casualties may really be substantially higher than our upper limits imply. More detailed empirical knowledge of earlier casualties, including indirect casualties, particularly in the non-European world, could result in enormous upward adjustments of our figures.

CYCLES, STAGES, AND CAUSES

We now shorten our focus and move from long-term trends to medium- and short-term historical cycles and stages. We are no longer interested in processes that span millennia, but rather in those that may take place within centuries, generations, decades, years, months, or weeks.

Cycles

The idea that regular cycles in peace and war exist is intuitively appealing. Some data suggest the existence of recurring periods. Figure 2-2 shows the alternating incidence of world general peace and war. The European casualty figures found in Tables 2-17 to 2-20 sketch a general rise, interrupted by a fall in the nineteenth century, which in turn gives way to another period of increase.

Length

If cycles in war and peace do exist, we should be able to specify how long they are, and how much time it takes to go through a typical rise and fall. A good deal of research has tried to answer this question; unfortunate-ly, it has not provided a single definite answer, but a number of different possibilities.

Wright's study of world major wars led him to identify four major periods of peace and war (Wright, 1965:223–32).

1. A peace period of about 50 years between major war outbreaks and con-centrations.

2. A war period of 4–5 years for the fighting of such wars.
3. A campaign period, falling most usually in spring and summer.
4. A battle period, usually during daytime.

These periods have been the subject of vigorous subsequent debate. The most extensive study has probably centered on the peace period. Sorokin's work on European major wars made him extremely skeptical about the existence of any cyclical period of general peace and of proposed lengths to such a cycle.

> None of the periods claimed, [including] . . . the 50-year period of Q. Wright, so far have been proven, and they can hardly be proven. The same is true of the much longer periods of 111, 300, 500, 600, 675 years, and so on, claimed by various authors. All that we can say is that the war–peace curve fluctuates, but in its fluctuations, with the exceptions mentioned, no regular periodicity or uniform rhythm is noticeable (Sorokin, 1937:357).

Subsequently, Richardson reanalyzed Wright's list of major international and domestic violence (1960b:Ch. 3). He found no evidence of regularity; he saw supposed regular war–peace periods as sheer chance.

More contemporary studies give us the same lesson. Singer and Small's intensive study of world major wars suggests a regular peace period, somewhat shorter than Wright's, "between 20 and 40 years in the fluctuations of the amount of war *underway* during the 150 years" that they studied (1972:212). On the other hand, their data show no regular peace periods when they consider "the intervals between the beginnings of successive wars" (1972:215). New wars seemed to begin at random intervals (cf. Singer and Cusack, 1979).[21]

Major international peace periods of nation-states that have been particularly war prone during the last 150 years appear in Table 2-22. The figures again show little regularity. The mean peace periods of different nations vary from roughly 5 to 25 years. The range of peace periods varies from 0 (China, Japan, Turkey) to about 50 (the United States).

Estimates of major international and domestic peace and violence can vary in the same way. One study of *52 Peaceful Societies* (Melko, 1975) in history has estimated the periods between major international or domestic violence. Such peace periods vary from 100 to 550 years. Median and mean peace periods for different groups range from 130 to 335 years. Other analysts suggest different periods.[22]

Wright's other periods have received less subsequent research attention than the peace period. Investigating the campaign period, Singer and Small's analysis supports a tendency to campaign in the spring (Wright's thesis), but it also implies that fall seems a propitious time.

> In sheer number of joint decisions to go to war over the past century and a half, April and October are clearly the preferred months. . . . The passage of time and associated developments in the technology of war, communications, and agriculture seem to have exercised little impact on seasonal concentrations (1972:253).

Table 2-22

Peace Periods: Intervals Between Major Wars, Belligerent Societies, 1816–1965.

Nation	No. of Wars	Interwar Intervals (In Years)[a]										Mean
U.S.	5	50.2	18.7	23.1	4.9							24.2
Salvador	3	21.1	0.6									10.8
England	7	26.4	0.6	57.4	20.8	5.0	3.3					18.9
Belgium	3	21.5	10.6									16.1
France	12	3.9	21.5	4.7	3.2	2.8	3.4	13.3	29.1	20.8	5.4 3.3	10.1
Spain	5	35.9	5.6	31.9	10.9							21.1
Germany/ Prussia	6	14.6	1.9	4.0	43.4	20.8						16.9
Austria- Hungary	6	0.1	9.8	4.6	1.9	48.0						12.9
Hungary	3	21.9	11.8									16.8
Italy/ Sardinia	10	5.8	3.2	1.2	0.0	5.4	45.2	2.6	16.9	4.1		9.4
Yugoslavia/ Serbia	4	0.2	1.0	22.4								7.9
Greece	7	15.4	0.2	3.9	0.5	18.0	9.7					8.0
Bulgaria	4	0.2	2.2	23.2								8.5
Rumania	4	3.1	1.3	21.9								8.8
Russia	10	0.5	24.1	21.1	26.1	8.9	21.4	1.8	0.0	16.6		13.4
Ethiopia	3	4.7	9.8									7.3
Turkey	11	0.5	24.1	21.1	19.1	14.4	0.0[b]	0.2	1.2	0.5	28.0	10.9
China	7	9.1	36.7	4.2	0.0[b]	5.2	9.2					10.7
Japan	7	8.9	8.9	13.1	4.2	0.0[b]	2.2					6.2

[a]Figures only include interwar intervals for nations that fought in three or more interstate wars.

[b]0.0 = A nation left one war and entered a new war on the same day (as in the cases of China and Japan), or left one war after starting a new war (as in the case of Turkey).

SOURCE: Singer and Small (1972:214).

Intervals between minor domestic violence may also occur in regular periods. For example "crimes follow a seasonal cycle in any given year" (Lunden, 1967:26). Further, most crime occurs during nonworking periods—nighttime and weekends, for example. There is little confirmation, however, that violent crimes increase during annual vacation periods, for example, summer in the United States (cf. Bloch and Geis, 1970:144–46; Lunden, 1967:Ch. 4).

We may conclude that a whole set of intersecting cycles for peace and violence may exist. Such cycles may be of different durations for different geographical regions and different levels of violence. In this case the numbers we have presented here may be the foundation of a much more solid body of knowledge about regular fluctuations in peace and war. On the other hand, it is also possible that the cycles we see are only a mirage, that our numbers are the results of chance or of other factors in the environment.

Trends

Our inability to specify the length of general cycles in peace and war limits any discussion about possible trends. If regular cycles in peace and war do exist, we should like to know whether they are becoming flatter, like easy ocean waves on a mild day; sharper, like choppy waters with many short waves on a windy day; or more severe, like long, deep, and high ocean swells during a storm.[23]

If regular cycles do exist, the hypothesis of a long-run trend toward peace diffusion and war concentration suggests that they may have become more severe. While the trough of the peace period may have gotten longer, the wave of war may tend to be higher.[24]

Stages

We have already mentioned the possibility that there may be stages in peace and war similar to stages of health and disease. If such stages exist, we should be able to identify discrete periods similar to infection and resistance.

Infection

Infection in peace and war implies the kind of process we find in epidemic disease. Acute contagion brings a bunching and acceleration of violence, or positive association of violent incidents and casualties with subsequent violent incidents and casualties—the more violence, the more violence—at least up to a certain point. Once violence breaks out, it should spread with increasing speed.[25]

Infection in peace and war also suggests a pattern similar to that of endemic or chronic disease. Groups of states or single nations may be more prone to violence than others on a relatively long-term basis.

There is considerable theoretical reason and empirical evidence to support the idea that such patterns of acute and chronic violence exist. It is difficult to know the degree to which departures from normal patterns of behavior are statistically significant; nevertheless, they have taken place in numerous historical spaces and times.

War

We can see a pattern like contagion in Figure 2-3, which outlines periods of acute belligerence. This figure shows the amount of world major war begun and under way during the last two centuries. A relatively solid peace, with a low level of endemic warfare, seems to exist most of the time. Yet sudden, high, sharp peaks rise quite suddenly from the peace valley floor.

Bunching and acceleration of violence occur in time. Some times are relatively peaceful. For example, the periods around 1840, 1890, 1930, and 1960 show low levels of world major war. Other periods—centering around World Wars I and II and the Korean conflict—are extraordinarily warlike. These periods show a very rapid movement from peace to war. The number of participants increased as the wars spread across continents and oceans. The scope of violence—reflected in the employment of available military forces and weapons, and casualties—also grew very rapidly.

Bunching and acceleration also occur in space. Once a certain threshold of nation-state involvement is reached—for example, 200 nation-months of war begun or 70 nation-months of war under way in a single year—then many other nations seem to join the conflict.

The idea of contagion suggests further that wars should spread rapidly at points of contact between states. In line with this idea, a number of studies report a strong general relationship between the number of wars and the number of borders with other nations, particularly colonial borders or borders with other warring nations (cf. Terrell, 1977:100; Soroos, 1977:89; Garnham, 1976a, 1976b; Starr and Most, 1976; Midlarsky, 1975:68–71; Richardson, 1960b:176–81 and Ch. 11).[26]

Research on world major wars reveals some evidence of chronic belligerence. Nations that participate in wars as either partners or belligerents, or that do not participate, may repeat their experiences. Thus, Richardson emphasizes revenge and retribution as possible motives for violence (1960b:197–204).

Singer and Small's analysis of their intensive data on world major wars gave them contradictory results.

> One of the more widely accepted propositions in the folklore of international politics is that war begets war, on the premise that: (a) the victorious initiator of war will seek to repeat his success; (b) that another will be encouraged by the example; or (c) that the defeated party will, alone or with others, move as soon as feasible to settle old scores (Singer and Small, 1974:274).

As expected, war years tended to follow war years during the nineteenth century. Nevertheless, this effect did not occur in the twentieth century or over the statistical expanse of the whole 150 years covered by their study. Overall, they report that "very few nations initiate[d] wars in the decades following prior war experience," though, if they were victorious in such

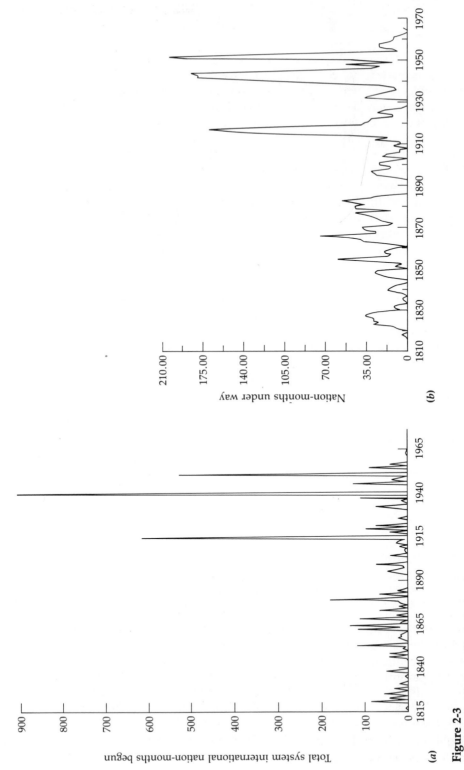

Figure 2-3
World Major War Incidence, 1816–1965. (*a*) Annual amount of international war begun. (*b*) Annual amount of international war under way. (SOURCE: Singer and Small, 1972:207, 209.)

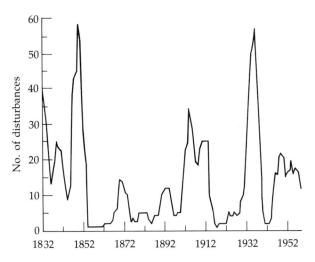

Figure 2-4
Major Domestic Violence Incidence: France, 1832–1958.
(NOTE: Five-year moving average centering
on year shown. SOURCE: Tilly, 1973:107; cf. Tilly and Tilly,
1975:57–59; Shorter and Tilly, 1974; Tilly, 1964.)

wars, the chances increased somewhat that they would go to war again
(Singer and Small, 1974:274).

Follow-up studies of world major wars during this period report more
positive findings. H. Starr notes that "the consequences of war partnership
appear to be more future partnership; the consequences of belligerency
appear to be more future belligerency; and the consequences of non-participation appear to be more future non-participation" (1975:58). Davis et
al. (1977) find that war activity twenty years in the past may help to explain
present wars.[27]

Domestic Violence

Infection may also be a stage in domestic violence. Indeed, our everyday
language reflects a perception of domestic violence as contagious or infectious when we speak of "rashes" of revolutions or "crime waves." Figure 2-4
sketches the number of violent domestic disturbances in France during
the last two centuries.[28] Again we see valleys of domestic peace and sudden,
sharp, apparently contagious spurts of acute conflict. The threshold in
France leading to the highest levels of domestic violence appears to be
around a moving average of 40 civil disturbances a year. If this barrier was
pierced, as it was during the periods before 1850 and around 1930, violence
took another quantum jump. Other categories of domestic violence also
seem to show contagious traits, for example, political assassination, indi-

vidual homicide, and suicide (cf. Li and Thompson, 1975; Berkowitz, 1973; Havens, et al., 1970:28). Different kinds of domestic violence may, furthermore, help produce contagious effects on each other. Thus one authority on crime notes that:

> Societies undergoing violent and extended periods of revolution have always displayed higher crime rates than societies devoid of revolution or with few disorders. The French Revolution of 1790 and the Russian Revolution of 1917 are examples to support this statement. The Athenian Thucydides (471 to 400 B.C.) described the Corcyraen Revolution in these words, "Death thus raged in every shape, there was no length to which violence did not go: sons were killed by their fathers. . . . Brothers rose against brothers. . . . Men were slaughtered everywhere" (Lunden, 1967:76).

War and Domestic Violence

The contagion of violence does not necessarily stay within specific international or domestic boundaries. Violence at different levels can also bunch and accelerate. The dynamic of contagion, under appropriate circumstances, may go from international to domestic, or domestic to international violence.

> Every war has two faces. It is a conflict both between and within political systems: a conflict that is both external and internal. [It is inevitable that] internal wars affect the international system [and that] the international system affects internal wars (Modelski, 1964:18, 24, 26).

The international rivalries of the contemporary world have often seemed to impel the actors to undertake a kind of miniaturization in warfare, where they fight through domestic proxies. Thus, the long-standing international struggle between the British and French for colonial domination contributed to the American Revolution. In the judgment of a prominent naval historian, the American Revolutionary War was

> a resumption of the struggle between France and England for colonial domination. The efforts of American Continental and State navies, together with privateers, had little effect on the outcome of the Revolution . . . ; it was the French navy that broke the hold of King George upon the rebellious colonies (Potter, 1955:90).

Wartime violence seems to dissolve the glue of normal domestic coexistence. World War I contributed to the Russian Revolution of 1918; to postwar violence within the newly independent states of Eastern Europe; and to the continuing violence of the 1920s and 1930s within the vanquished and the victorious states. The legacy of World War I appeared to include the post–World War I communist scare in the United States, symbolized by the trial of Sacco and Vanzetti; violent internal conflict in the Soviet, German, and Italian states; strife between groups of the left and right in Britain and France; and eventually the civil war in Spain.

World War II provided the frame within which domestic groups allied with national governments could persecute unreliable and unwanted elements within the state. In some cases, however, as in China, the dissident elements gained the upper hand and waged war not only on the external invader but also on the internal regime. Thus, the Japanese invasion of China in World War II contributed to the Chinese Communist revolution.

The ending of World War II led to violence by long-suffering resistance movements. In the Axis countries members of such movements overthrew Mussolini in 1943 and were behind the anti-Hitler coup in 1944. In Allied nations, resisters retaliated against collaborators, and this violence did not stop with the signing of peace treaties. Finally, the war experience, combined with the postwar weakness of the European states, contributed to the subsequent domestic violence of the anticolonial revolutionary movements all over the Third World. In the United States, the domestic upheaval of the McCarthy period followed World War II, the beginning of the Cold War, and the Korean conflict; and Watergate was part of the heritage of Vietnam.

In the contemporary world, the tools of unconventional war include a variety of clandestine and overt techniques aimed at subverting existing regimes and increasing the probability of domestic violence. These were a part of the German *Anschluss* in Austria; Soviet activities in Eastern Europe, particularly in Czechoslovakia in 1948; and American support for the Cuban emigrés at the Bay of Pigs in 1962. Such techniques are particularly effective when there are strong ethnic bonds between outsiders and insiders, as in the postwar struggle between Greeks and Turks over Cyprus.

Traditional theory suggests that domestic violence can also contribute to international violence in a number of different ways. First, domestic strife may be projected outward. If revolution or turmoil threatens a regime, it may undertake wars as diversions, "foreign circuses," or crusades, looking for external "targets" or "scapegoats" (Blainey, 1973:73–81). Incumbent political leaders can try to reassert their domestic dominance in the face of an external threat, real or imagined, by violent international activity. "Politicians seeking internal solidarity, stability, and order," can "use war and the preparation for war to maintain or expand the war of government class or party" (Burrowes and Spector, 1973:295 citing Wright, 1965:140, 225, 254, 727, 1016). From a psychological perspective, domestic political turmoil may increase the anxieties of elites. As levels of insecurity rise, leaders may project their fears into the international arena and act out their repressed hostilities at a distance (Rosecrance, 1963:304; cf. Haas and Whiting, 1956:62–63).

If domestic revolution is successful, it can affect international relations. Domestic turbulence has been a powerful force, helping to create a contemporary "revolution in world politics." Successful domestic insurgencies have rallied around the banners of nationalism, communism, socialism, and various religions to challenge the international status quo.[29]

Domestic differences can pull outside states into violence. The essence of this idea is expressed metaphorically in the traditional notion that vacuums of power exist into which foreign actors can be sucked. Even the possibility of domestic turbulence may tempt outside military intervention.

> The spread of civil strife within a nation often resembled the death of a king; the royal funeral bells in the eighteenth century often had the same martial echoes as the bells that rang the curfew in troubled lands in later centuries. Both bells invited an enemy to attack. . . . Civil unrest, like the death of kings, marked the crumbling of established authority and therefore affected perceptions of national power. Increasingly in Europe the royal funeral was replaced by civil strife as a dangerous disturber of the peace (Blainey, 1973:70, 86).

The state itself, faced with unrest, may call on outside governments to help. Thus "the Austrian monarchy, faced in 1849 with an insurrection in its Hungarian provinces, persuaded the tsar to help in snuffing a rebellion which could otherwise have inspired similar rebellions within Russia" (Blainey, 1973:83).

Alternatively, the rebels may seek outside help and make the violence more truly international.

> In the nineteenth century, for example, the rebels within the Turkish empire nourished strong ties with either the governments of Russia, Greece or Serbia; and those governments at times went to war against Turkey. On occasions the government and the rebels of the troubled nation each formed links with outside nations; that was true in the Spanish war of the 1930s and in South Vietnam in the 1960s. Whereas the government in Saigon had allies in Washington, the rebels had allies in Hanoi (Blainey, 1973:83).

One act of strategic violence, such as the assassination of Austrian Archduke Franz-Ferdinand at Sarajevo in 1914, can trigger global general war.

Psychological and sociological theory have traditionally assumed that increased individual violence creates predispositions to collective violence, international and domestic. Civilization implies strong repression and frustration of individual needs. During peacetime, these frustrations may be reflected in incidents of individual violence. A rise in numbers of individual crimes suggests increasing pressure within societies toward collective violence. During wartime, crime and suicide rates should go down as violent energies are shifted out of the civilian sector and into the military where they are effectively repressed, or onto the battlefield where they are disguised in the casualty statistics (cf. Dollard et al., 1967; Durkheim, 1966; Freud, 1962).

Contemporary research has provided systematic data supporting the idea that, in certain times and under certain circumstances, international and domestic violence vary together. Sorokin's research on European major wars led him to conclude that, in general, international and domestic violence each ran a course independent of the other, without either positive or negative association. He found only a slight indication that disturbances tend to occur more frequently during and around years of war, being more frequent in war years, and in the years immediately preceding and following wars, and becoming rarer as we move further in either direction from the years of war (Sorokin, 1937:487–89).

Nevertheless, his data do suggest a positive relationship between war and domestic violence during certain periods of European history. In Figure 2-5 we can see a strong covariation between war casualties and domestic disturbance in Greece during the fifth, third, and second centuries BC; in Rome during the first century BC and consistently in the 500 years following the birth of Christ; generally during the Roman Empire; and in Europe of the twelfth, thirteenth, sixteenth, seventeenth, eighteenth, and twentieth centuries.

World international and domestic major violence in the nineteenth and twentieth centuries also shows some positive relationships. Table 2-23 gives some concrete examples of instances where war and domestic disturbances occurred together. A reanalysis of Richardson's data has also revealed a positive relationship between world major international and domestic violence for 24 selected cases (Denton and Phillips, 1968).

A number of other studies have gone into more detail and focused on particular indicators of international and domestic violence. These indicators have included war and foreign clashes, revolutions, riots, and assassinations. Table 2-24 summarizes some results for the years 1837–1960. The positive numbers show some strong associations among indicators of violence at the same level. Several of the relationships across levels—war and riots, foreign clashes and riots between 1837 and 1937—are also strongly positive. Most of the other cross-level associations are also positive, though less so (cf. Kegley et al., 1978; M. Haas, 1974:221).

Statistical data on violence in Africa between 1963 and 1965, summarized in Table 2-25, also show a substantial positive association between indicators of international violence, incidents of large-scale domestic revolutionary activity, and numbers of people killed in them. There is a less substantial relationship, though still a positive one, between international violence and outbreaks of anomic violence.[30] Finally, for reasons that are not obvious, there appears to be a very slightly negative relationship between international violence and subversive activities.

Some research has connected national experience of international violence with domestic assassinations, homicide, and suicide. Different studies in this area have used different analytical methods, and relationships are not very clear. War is not necessarily correlated in all societies with either high or low rates of political assassination, general crime, homicide, or suicide. In other situations, however, war and such domestic violence do go together (cf. Farberow, 1975; Schaich, 1975; Kirkham et al., 1970:188–89; Powell, 1970; Lunden, 1967).

Sometimes domestic violence predicts international violence. One historical survey of the European international system over the last two cen-

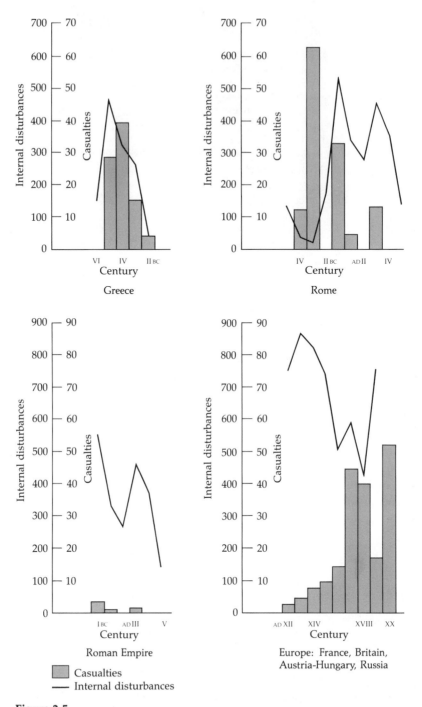

Figure 2-5

Major War Casualties and Domestic Disturbance: Greece, Rome, Europe, 600 BC–AD 1925. (NOTE: Internal disturbances are measured by a figure that gives weight to the number, duration, and severity of these events. Casualties are measured by the total number during the century divided by the average population during that century. SOURCE: Wright, 1965:597; from Sorokin, 1937:297.)

Table 2-23
War and Domestic Disturbance: 1816–1939.

Year	War	Seat of Civil Disturbance
1823	French Pyrénées Expedition	Spain
1828	Russo-Turk	Greece
1830	Belgian	Belgium, France
1830	Franco-Algerian	Paris
1848	Danish-Prussian	Berlin
1848	Sardinian-Austrian	Vienna, Milan
1849	Hungarian Expedition	Hungary
1853	Crimean	Danubian Principalities
1860	Italian	Sicily
1861	Mexican Expedition	Mexico
1862	Haiti	San Domingo
1864	Danish-Prussian	Holstein
1876	Serbo-Turk	Bosnia
1877	Russo-Turk	Balkans
1882	Egyptian Expedition	Egypt
1885	Serb-Bulgarian	E. Rumelia
1894	Sino-Japanese	Korea
1897	Greco-Turk	Crete
1898	Spanish-U.S.	Cuba
1899	Boer	Transvaal
1900	Boxer Expedition	Peking
1911	Italian-Turk	Turkish Empire
1912	First Balkan	Macedonia
1914	World War I	Bosnia
1918	White Russian	Russia
1919	Third Afghan	India, Afghanistan
1919	Greco-Turk	Turkey
1920	Russo-Polish	Russia
1931	Sino-Japanese	Japan, China
1936	Spanish	Spain
1937	Sino-Japanese	China

SOURCE: Reprinted with permission of Macmillan Publishing Co., Inc., New York, and Macmillan Press, Ltd., London and Basingstoke, from *The Causes of War*, by Geoffrey Blainey. © Geoffrey Blainey, 1973.

turies concluded that "domestic stability and internal peace are the vehicle[s] of international stability and external peace" (Rosecrance, 1963:306). Another survey of wars between 1815 and 1939, whose data appear in Table 2-23, noted a tendency of wars to be associated with civil disturbance. "Many international wars in Europe after 1800 were not preceded by civil strife; and civil strife did not always lead to war," said Blainey. Nonetheless, it is astonishing to discover how many wars had been heralded by serious

Table 2-24

World International and Domestic Violence: Selected Indicators, 1837–1960.[a]

Level	Measure	Years		
		1837–1937	1955–1957	1958–1960
Same Level				
Indicators of international violence	War, foreign clashes[b]	.58	.38	—
Indicators of domestic violence	Revolution, riots	.14	.32	.30
	Revolution, assassinations	.06	.19	.31
	Riots, assassinations	.36	.45	.51
Cross-Level				
Relation of international and domestic violence	War, revolution	.06	−.04	−.02
	War, riots	.41	.12	.01
	War, assassinations	.08	.19	.00
	Foreign clashes, revolution	.13	.12	—
	Foreign clashes, riots	.54	.08	—
	Foreign clashes, assassinations	.14	.15	—

[a]Numbers represent Pearson product–moment correlations between the two indicated measures. The higher the number—either positive or negative—the higher the statistical relationship in either a positive or negative direction. The closer the number is to zero, the lower the statistical relationship.
[b]Cattell (1949:448) defines foreign clashes as fighting incidents and political clashes not accompanied by or immediately followed by war.
SOURCE: For the years 1958–1960, Tanter (1966); 1955–1957, Rummell (1963a); 1837–1937, calculated from Cattell (1949), unrotated factor structure by Rummell (1963a). (Cf. M. Haas, 1974:219, 221, 230; Zimmerman, 1975; Wilkenfeld, 1973b:121; Rummell and Tanter, 1972; Bwy, 1971:117).

unrest in one of the warring nations (Blainey, 1973:70). In the Middle East from 1949 to 1967, violent domestic conflict in the Arab states tended to precede international conflict with Israel (Wilkenfeld, 1975, 1972:150–51). At a more individual level, there was a relatively steady rise in French and German suicide rates in the pre-war periods between 1830 and 1914, and again between 1918 and 1939 (Powell, 1970:165, from Halbwachs, 1930:323, 369).

Other statistical studies suggest that war can help produce domestic violence. War can lead to governmental violence. A study of American wars over the last 80 years concludes with the observation that U.S. wars have tended to lead to a postwar "repressive and reactionary response" (Stohl, 1976:131). Pockets of assassination have occurred after major wars as well as during periods of general domestic unrest (Havens et al., 1970:28).

A study of comparative crime rates of the twentieth century showed that wars led to substantial postwar increases in general rates of homicide.

Table 2-25
International and Domestic Violence: Africa, 1963–1965.[a]

Domestic Violence	International Violence	
	Military Violence Troop Mobilizations Official Military Violence	**Foreign Killed** Number Killed in Foreign Violence
Substantially Positive Relations		
Revolutionary activities Revolutions Civil war Antigovernment riots Political boycotts	.39	.31
Domestic killed Number killed in domestic violence	.31	.33
Less Substantial Relations		
Anomic outbreaks Riots, strikes, political clashes, intertribal conflict Antigovernment demonstrations Military	.12	.21
Subversive activities Guerrilla warfare Terroristic acts Assassinations Plots	− .04	− .09

[a]Figures represent interfactor Pearson product–moment correlations.
SOURCE: Collins (1973:274). Adapted from "Foreign Conflict Behavior and Domestic Disorder in Africa," by John N. Collins, in *Conflict Behavior and Linkage Politics,* edited by Jonathan Wilkenfeld. Copyright © 1973 by Longman Inc. Reprinted with permission of Longman Inc., New York.

In Table 2-26 we see that postwar homicide rates in a global sample of states increased after major wars of the twentieth century. The increases were primarily in nations that had relatively high ratios of battle deaths to population, regardless of whether such nations were victorious or defeated in the war.

Resistance

We have been considering the idea that violence may, like disease, have an infectious stage. The analogy between war and disease also suggests that under appropriate circumstances, war is subject to resistance. When we think of war resistance, we may think of war resisters, people who oppose

Table 2-26

World Major War and Postwar Domestic Homicide Rate Changes: Twentieth Century.[a]

		Homicide Rate Change		
		Decrease	Unchanged	Increase
>500 battle deaths per million prewar population	Victorious nations	U.S. (II)[b]	Canada (II)[b] England (I) France (I) Japan (1904 Russo-Japanese)	Australia (II) Belgium (I) England (II) France (II) Italy (I) Netherlands (II)[b] New Zealand (II) Norway (II) Portugal (I) South Africa (II) U.S. (I)
	Defeated nations	Finland (II) Hungary (I)		Bulgaria (I)[c] Germany (I) Hungary (1956 Russo-Hungarian) Italy (II) Japan (II)
<500 battle deaths per million prewar population	Victorious nations	Israel (1956 Sinai) Italy (1896 Italo-Ethiopian) Italy (1935 Italo-Ethiopian)	Japan (1932 Manchuria)	Israel (1967 6-Day) Japan (1894 Sino-Japanese) Japan (I) Pakistan (1965 2nd Kashmir)
	Defeated nations	India (1962 Sino-Indian)	Egypt (1956 Sinai) India (1965 2nd Kashmir)	Jordan (1967 6-Day)

[a]Entries in parentheses refer to World Wars I and II and other wars.
[b]Murder and manslaughter.
[c]Crimes against the person, homicide included.
SOURCE: Archer and Gartner (1976:955).

wars and refuse to fight. War resistance in this sense is a part, but only a part, of what we mean by the term here. For us, war resistance is the opposite of contagion. It suggests the process through which war is avoided or limited. It includes the bunching of peace, where there is little violence over long periods of time. It also implies the slowing of violence after it has broken out.

We can see the bunching of peace in Figure 2-3 where the great nineteenth-century valley of international tranquility is broken only by short shoots of violence. We can also see the bunching in the extraordinarily low nineteenth-century casualty statistics of Tables 2-17 to 2-20.

Resistance also implies the deceleration of violence following outbreak or contagion. Some such process is implied in classical doctrines of preventive war, where a little violence in the present presumably avoids more violence later. Resisting aggression theoretically helps to limit its expansion.

The idea of resistance suggests that protracted violence produces forces that draw it down and finally bring about peace. War is only contagious within limits and under some circumstances. After war has broken out, at a certain point its growth slackens and begins to decline. We can see this slowing in the Vietnam war statistics. Figure 2-6 shows how cumulative U.S. Department of Defense strength, battle casualties, and battle deaths rose contagiously in the early 1960s and then again in 1965. A resistance

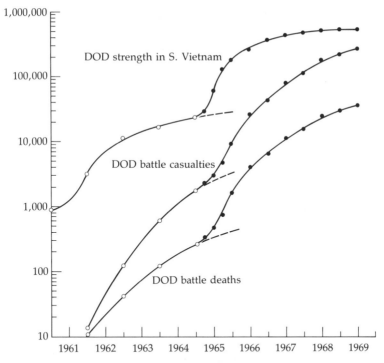

Figure 2-6

U.S. Military Strength, Battle Deaths, and Battle Casualties: Vietnam, 1961–1969. (NOTE: DOD = U.S. Department of Defense. SOURCE: Voevodsky, 1969:63; cf. SIPRI, 1976e:49; Voevodsky, 1972, 1971; Mueller, 1973:36; Alcock and Lowe, 1969:96–98; Horvath, 1968; Klingberg, 1966.)

pattern was, however, clearer in the years 1963–1964, and beginning again in 1966.

Domestic violence shows similar resistance patterns. We find the bunching of domestic peace in relatively peaceful societies (Melko, 1973). There are also relatively peaceful periods in all societies. Thus, Figure 2-4 shows the bunching of major domestic peace in France during the second half of the nineteenth century, and in periods around World Wars I and II during the twentieth century. Figure 2-7 depicts the slowing of cumulative indicators of global violence, after prior rises, between 1945 and 1966 (cf. Burbeck et al., 1978; Midlarsky, 1978).

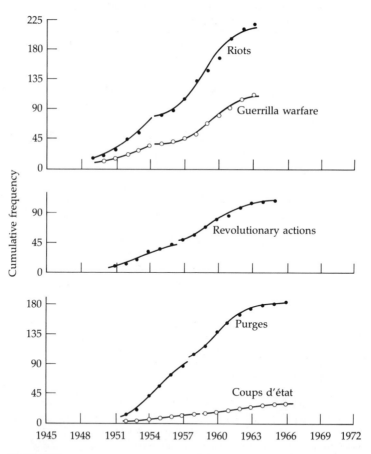

Figure 2-7
World Domestic Violence, 1945–1966. (NOTE: The figure relates political violence and change, accumulated through time on arithmetic coordinates. The lines represent least-squares logistic equations. SOURCE: Hamblin et al., 1973:126. Data from Banks, 1971.)

Some evidence also supports the idea of resistance between international and domestic levels of violence. Under appropriate circumstances violence at one level may seem to work against violence at another. The history of European major war sketched in Figure 2-5 shows inverse relationships between international and domestic violence—in Greece during the fourth century BC; in Rome during the fourth, third, and second centuries BC; and in Europe as a whole in the fourteenth, fifteenth, and nineteenth centuries.

International violence may appear to limit domestic violence. External conflict may seem to produce internal cohesion, helping domestic opponents forget their differences as they rally round the flag. In sixteenth-century Europe,[31] for example, the onset of international war helped produce domestic tranquility.

> If Germany . . . was quiet between 1555 and 1618, it was because her surplus of adventure-seeking troops had been sent abroad to Hungary, Italy and in particular to the Netherlands and France. . . . The reward of making trouble for others was peace at home.

The end of war abroad seemed to help release forces of violence at home. Some of this domestic violence took a sacred, religious form.

> In France, the massive demobilization of armies which followed the peace of Cateau-Cambrésis contributed in no small measure to the outbreak of the Wars of Religion, disturbances far more serious in the long run than foreign wars.

Some domestic violence was more obviously secular, as piracy became a "substitute for declared war."

> The suspension of major hostilities in the Mediterranean after 1574 was undoubtedly one cause of the subsequent series of political and social disturbances, including the increase in brigandage. On the water, the end of conflict between the great states brought to the forefront of the sea's history that secondary form of war, piracy. Already a force to be reckoned with between 1550 and 1574, it expanded to fill any gaps left by the slackening of official war. From 1574–1580, it increased its activities even further, soon coming to dominate the now less spectacular history of the Mediterranean. The new capitals of warfare were not Constantinople, Madrid and Messina, but Algiers, Malta, Leghorn and Pisa. Upstarts had replaced the tired giants and international conflicts degenerated into a free-for-all (Braudel, 1973:865).

Domestic violence may, conversely, seem to restrain tendencies toward international violence. Societies experiencing considerable domestic violence may be too preoccupied to undertake international conflicts. Either weariness or the pressures of domestic survival limit external aggressive behavior. One explanation of the relative peace prevailing among European nations during the nineteenth century was that "revolution had served as a kind of substitute for war" and that "civil war absorbed belligerent spirits" (Thomson, 1962, quoted in Blainey, 1973:11). "The government suffering from civil unrest— whether Denmark in 1864 or Turkey in 1897—usually preferred to avoid an international war, if war could be avoided. A troubled nation could more easily defeat its own rebels if it did not also have to fight a foreign enemy" (Blainey, 1973:86).

Societies with relatively little internal strife may more easily undertake international violence. "Opposition to one kind of war" may be useful to be better able to fight another kind, "like a government which keeps its peace with one adversary to concentrate all its force upon crushing the other" (Friedrich, 1968:68).

There is some evidence of a negative relationship between violence at different levels in the contemporary world. Figures 2-3 and 2-4 suggested that periods where the incidence of international major violence was high—like those around World Wars I and II—seemed to go together with drops in the incidence of French domestic violence. On the other hand, high levels of domestic violence in France occurred during times of relative international calm.

One study of the 1946–1965 period found an inverse relationship between prior domestic conflict and subsequent international casualty losses. The higher the level of previous domestic violence, the lower the subsequent international damage, and vice versa (Midlarsky and Thomas, 1973). Another study of Middle East conflict found that, in the case of Israel, governmental instability predicted peace with the Arabs to a small degree (Wilkenfeld, 1975; 1972:150–51).

Major collective violence—international or domestic—sometimes seems to bring a decline in individual violence. For example, under some circumstances there may be a negative relationship between war incidence and casualties, on the one hand, and the number of suicides in a population on the other. Thus, there were sharp drops in French and German suicide rates during the revolutionary period around 1848 and the international war periods around the war of 1871 and World War I (cf. O'Malley, 1975; M. Haas, 1974:230; Powell, 1970:165–66; Durkheim, 1966; Halbwachs, 1930).[32]

Causes

Up to this point, we have concerned ourselves with describing peace and war in history. We shall now turn our attention to explanation, and ask about possible deeper causes of peace and war.

Peace and War

Peace and war, according to one school of thought, may cause themselves to a considerable extent. This idea underlies much of the theory about infection and resistance. The hypothesis of infection implies that an initial small amount of violence can be at least a proximate cause of later more substantial violence. Resistance suggests that some peace may cause more peace, for example through peace learning or habituation.

Violence, at a certain point, may also be a driving force for peace, as the most belligerent segments of societies run out of enemies to vanquish or are killed, and as the less belligerent people become tired of violence. As the costs of war become more serious, people may be more resistant to war in the short run. Such resistance presumably prevents or delays the outbreak of some wars that would have occurred in earlier times. When wars do break out, resistance helps to shorten them. People undertake violence less frequently and, when they do, for shorter periods of time. Yet because of the length of time since prior serious wars, levels of resistance to later wars may wear down, and they may explode more easily.

Peace may thus eventually result in war. During the course of a long peace, war weariness fades. With the passage of time the costs of war are made up or forgotten. Opposition to violence diminishes with the passage of time, the blurring of memory, and the arrival of new, presumably non-resistant generations. War readiness increases. Violence again breaks out. If resistance is still strong, the violence does not expand; but if resistance has decayed sufficiently, contagion again occurs and the cycle repeats itself.

These explanations seem to have the virtue of being parsimonious and efficient; they appear to explain a good deal with very little. Unfortunately, however, they promise more than they deliver. Peace and violence offer very limited and partial kinds of explanations for themselves. There are some strong associations between levels and rates of peace and violence in successive time periods, but these fall very short of revealing underlying mechanisms of cause and effect.[33]

Even these associations are tenuous. A constant or regular connection between peace and violence at different times does not always and necessarily exist. Under some circumstances there seem to be strong relationships; yet in other cases these are absent or reversed. If it is correct that violence causes violence, we should expect a continuing long-term upward trend in violent incidents, of which there is no evidence. Further, we should expect violence to be infectious in all circumstances, which it is not. The infection hypothesis that violence causes violence may be true under certain circumstances. By itself, however, it is too simple an explanation. It does not tell us why violence does not spread infinitely or at least to the finite natural limits of population or geography. Pushed to its logical conclusion, the hypothesis leads us to expect the relatively rapid elimination of the human race, without explaining how it has managed its past and present survival.

The resistance hypothesis that violence inhibits violence seems true in some cases, but it also has limited applicability. It appears to apply in some circumstances, and when it does, in different ways. For example, a century of general European peace followed the end of the Napoleonic wars and preceded the outbreak of World War I while only a generation passed between World War I and World War II.

Prior peace or violence may influence the probability and seriousness of subsequent peace or violence. But they are neither necessary nor sufficient to explain themselves or each other.

Technology

To explain peace and war more fully, we need to examine additional factors that inhibit and promote international and domestic violence. This is the gist of the suggestion that "war and revolution in the concrete are always the result of the concomitance of several conditions, always the same, but appearing in different forms and in a variety of sequences" (Timasheff, 1965:283).

As we noted in Chapter 1, such factors are located in the human technology of our social environment, and we identified them as aggregation, polarization, and militarization. Chapters 3, 4, and 5 will examine them in depth.

Chapter 3

AGGREGATION

Aggregation is the constructive logic of technology. Figure 3-1 tries to show what we mean by aggregation in a graphic way. Aggregation makes larger relatively integrated units out of smaller previously unconnected parts. It includes the common links in the social environment. Aggregation implies structure, symmetry, regulation, cooperation. It is the difference between order and randomness (cf. Pusić, 1977).

Table 3-1 outlines what we mean by aggregation in more detail. Aggregation involves the great structures and processes of human civilization: bureaucracy, exchange, and language. These, in turn, include such elements as international law, organization, transaction, and communication; national and subnational governments, markets, and communities.

What are the effects of peace and war in creating or restraining aggregation? In Table 3-1 we may note that there is no causal arrow leading *to* aggregation. This suggests that peace or war does not generally make a difference in the growth of bureaucracy, exchange, and language.

From one theoretical perspective, it would seem that peace should be the best soil for the growth of aggregation. If we view aggregation as a natural, gradual process, peace provides conditions of order and predictability that should encourage regular, uninterrupted growth. Innovations occur and expand to the extent that they find a safe niche in the existing order (cf. Coleman, 1975; Hamblin et al., 1973; Rogers and Shoemaker, 1971).

Aggregation should grow during peacetime because decisionmakers perceive that it is good. Aggregation is a massive mechanism that produces

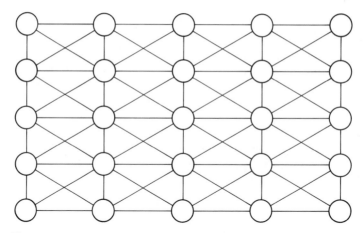

Figure 3-1
An Aggregated Environment.

enormous benefits. Bureaucracy, exchange, and language coordinate the movements of multitudes through learned routines and repertoires of co-operative action. Through aggregation collective humanity achieves new leverage and power to harness nature to its conscious will.

An opposing theory suggests that war provides a major energizing force for aggregation. To be sure war damages or destroys human social systems as well as property and lives. Nevertheless, traditional diplomatic and military analyses have implied that war generally has positive effects, even though particular wars may turn out badly. Wars, in this perspective, are like investments. They are undertaken for reasons of state, and there are many circumstances in which the benefits of war outweigh the costs. This view has been based on a broader theory of human history and evolution. The Social Darwinist theory of evolution suggests that war may be a necessary engine of natural selection, a natural and positive activity that clears away the obsolete and weak aspects of human civilization and creates needed room for stronger and better-adapted elements to develop. War, in this light, is a catalyst for many innovations that would not otherwise occur. These innovations later spill over into peacetime civilization and enrich it. Old restraints are weakened and change is accelerated as parts of the existing order are destroyed. Existing elements may be combined more rapidly into new patterns (cf. Marwick, 1974:10–11).

Such theorizing suggests that peace or war may contribute in different ways to aggregation. Unfortunately, no firm body of empirical research provides strong factual evidence to support the primacy of either peacetime incrementalism or wartime crisis in producing aggregation. Some of the particular effects of peace or war seem positive, others negative; some are short-term, others long-term; some influence collective bodies, others subgroups or individuals.

Table 3-1
Aggregation and Peace.

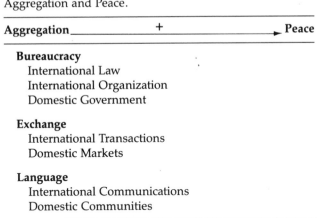

Aggregation	+	Peace

Bureaucracy
   International Law
   International Organization
   Domestic Government

Exchange
   International Transactions
   Domestic Markets

Language
   International Communications
   Domestic Communities

My own personal preference would be to lean toward the constructive influence of peace as being firmer and longer lasting. The costs of of war— to larger international, national, and subnational communities as well as to individuals—seem much higher than any possible benefits. I doubt whether war really paid even in prior times. Whatever one's judgments about past history, war's positive effects would seem particularly question-able during our lifetime because of the enormous increase in the cost side of the cost-benefit equation.

This is, however, a controversial area, where prejudices are strongly held. Much of the evidence is inconclusive, some is contradictory. In the absence of an agreed, comprehensive, precise method of social accounting, it is probably best to say that the effect of peace or war on aggregation remains unproven. For this reason I do not feel justified in including any arrow to specify the cause of aggregation.

Table 3-1 does, however, show a positive arrow *from* aggregation to peace. Bureaucracy, exchange, and language at international and domestic levels—international law, international organization, domestic government, international transactions, domestic markets, international communication, and domestic community—all work to produce fewer and shorter wars. Wars occur, to some extent, because of a failure or a lack of aggregation. To the extent that aggregation continues into the wartime situation, it helps diminish casualties.

In the sections that follow, we shall consider evidence about causal relationships between bureaucracy, exchange, and language, on the one hand—and peace and war, on the other. We must be careful to note that while aggregation has positive effects, they are not terribly strong. In spite of the fact that aggregation works directly against violence, it is unable to repress it permanently and completely. Aggregation itself, particularly at the international level, is still quite weak. Further, aggregation is only one factor in collective life. Alone, it has only a modest impact on the amount of violence.[1]

BUREAUCRACY: INTERNATIONAL LAW

Bureaucracy is the political, administrative dimension of technology. Bureaucratic institutions use general rules to control individual behavior and so direct the efforts of many people to a single purpose. If one casts a broad eye over human history, it may not be too bold to see the progressive bureaucratization of the world (Jacoby, 1973).

Global bureaucratization has not always occurred in a straight line. Particular bureaucratic organizations have risen and fallen (cf. Eisenstadt, 1963). There has, nevertheless, been measurable growth in bureaucracies from primitive times, so that today people have organized themselves into overlapping networks networks of territorial and functional structures. Human organization seems to have progressed from relatively simple, early, free-wandering families through the increasingly complex organizational forms of centrally based bands with restricted mobility; semipermanent sedentary villages; simple nuclear towns; advanced nuclear city-states; supranuclear, integrated, preindustrial empires; industrial nations and empires; and finally, global organizations like the League of Nations or the U.N.[2]

Migratory and preindustrial organizations are no longer common. Most of the other organizational forms, however, are well represented in today's world, and most people are members of several of these groupings. Figure 3-2 lists different contemporary forms and estimates their relative importance as measured by distribution of human population. The U.N., the closest facsimile we have of a global organization, comprehends most of humankind. Taken together, so do the collections of nation-states; cities, towns, and villages; extended kin groups and nuclear families.

We are particularly interested in the broadest and most complex types of organization, at the international and national levels. The most identifiable bureaucratic components are international law and organization and domestic government. When we speak of international law, we refer to the body of structures and processes involved in interpreting and applying law beyond the domain of particular national states. Similarly, international organizations are the formal institutions in which representatives meet to discuss common problems and make collective decisions affecting more than one nation. By contrast, domestic governments are the political institutions and processes operating within territorially based societies.

International law comprehends a stable and systematic set of rules to govern world relations as well as the process through which these common

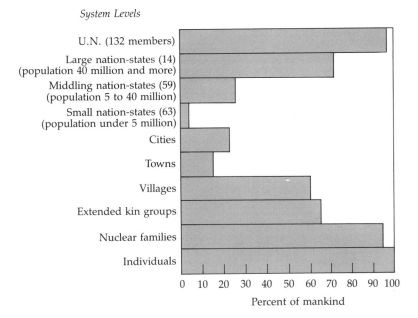

Figure 3-2
Bureaucratic Distribution of Population. (NOTE: Shaded
bars indicate estimated population included in particular
types of bureaucratic structures. SOURCE: Deutsch, 1974:153.)

rules are made, interpreted, and enforced. In recent centuries international
law has appeared to make some progress in increasing its autonomy from
the surrounding environment of national laws, in establishing its authority
in specific sectors of activity, and in increasing the kinds and numbers of
subjects who have identity and can make claims on it. The basis of international law is "the common consent of the member-states of the Family
of Nations" (Lauterpacht, 1955:25).[3] In recent times the specification of
areas of such consent has grown. It has included the identification of
authoritative sources of international law. These sources, according to Article 38(1) of the Statute of International Court of Justice, include:

(a) international conventions, whether general or particular, establishing rules
   expressly recognized by the contesting states;
(b) international custom, as evidence of a general practice accepted as law;
(c) the general principles of law recognized by civilized nations;
(d) . . . judicial decisions and the teachings of the most highly qualified pub-
   licists of the various nations, as subsidiary means for the determination
   of rules of law (Akehurst, 1977:30).

Specification has also involved efforts to codify an expanded body of international law in different areas. These areas include terrorism, human

rights, air, space, and the sea (cf. Evans and Murphy, 1978; Churchill et al., 1977; Max Planck Institute, 1975–1978; Dhokalia, 1970).

Table 3-2 sketches the development of major international institutions in the last century and a half. The right-hand column shows the establishment of important international legal structures. In 1815 the Congress of Vienna and numerous bilateral arbitration agreements made a first step in setting up international legal procedures. The next major advance occurred more than half a century later with the establishment of a nongovernmental International Law Institute; almost 30 years more elapsed before the Hague Conventions and declarations at the end of the nineteenth century. In 1901 the Permanent Court of Arbitration was created. The Permanent Court of International Justice was established under the League of Nations in 1919 and the International Court of Justice under the U.N. in 1945.

Regional international legal institutions have also grown. The Central American Court of Justice was created in 1907, but unfortunately lasted only a short while. The European Court of Human Rights was born within the Council of Europe in 1950. The Court of the European Coal and Steel Community, created in 1952, became the Court of the European Communities in 1957 (cf. Franck, 1964).

The subjects of international law have increased. Traditionally, a distinction had existed between nation-states as subjects of international law, and other actors that were designated as its objects. In the category of states, active participation has expanded beyond the Western European nations and now includes a more global representation and participation. Multilateral treaties and conventions have favored this trend because they have made possible greater and more equal participation and consent. Beyond the nation-state lie individuals. After a prolonged stage in which the predominant, not to say exclusive, concern was the regulation of the conduct of states as distinct entities, attention is now being given to "promoting the growth of a body of world law transcending states and applicable, on a footing of equality, to individuals, corporations, international organizations, states" (Corbett, 1969:13).

Causes of International Law

Has peace or war contributed more to the development of international law? History provides examples on each side. The major international legal institutions outlined in Table 3-2 began in relatively peaceful periods. The years at the turn of the twentieth century were particularly fruitful, producing the two Hague conferences and the creation of the Permanent Court of Arbitration.

Figure 3-3 shows the early popularity of nonbinding settlement procedures and of binding arbitration in major international law texts. Both techniques achieved their strongest growth and highest acceptance in the relative peace of the nineteenth century.

At the same time, war has also provided an impetus toward the growth of international law. The lessons of past wars, or the fear of future ones, have contributed strongly to the creation of major global legal institutions. We see in Table 3-2 that such institutions, after the beginning of the twentieth century, were established immediately following the two world wars.

Most wars end with the signing of treaties of peace. If the wars have been small, the treaties themselves are logically narrow, limited to the immediate participants and reasons for the conflict. The treaties that end general wars, however, often establish the foundations of a whole new international order and the framework for the law of peace in the ensuing era. Such treaties are a principal source of international law for the historical periods that follow their adoption.

Table 3-3 chronicles general European and world wars and the major international peace treaties and international organizations that followed them. The Thirty Years' War between major European powers and the Eighty Years' War between the Dutch and Spanish were both concluded in 1648. In this year, leaders of major European powers signed three treaties in the Westphalian towns of Münster and Osnabrück. The Peace of Westphalia generally governed German affairs for the following 150 years and is considered to be a major legal foundation of the modern nation-state system.[4]

In the seventeenth century, Louis XIV, King of France, undertook a series of wars to expand French boundaries. The Treaty of Utrecht, signed in 1713, formally ended the war of the Spanish succession. In addition it contained French ambitions to dominate Europe and acknowledged the existence of a balance of power among the major European states.

The French Revolution, which broke out in 1789, and the Napoleonic Wars that followed, shook the legal foundations established at Westphalia and Utrecht by threatening the continuity and integrity of existing nation-states and their rulers. The defeat of Napoleon at Waterloo led to a territorial settlement, achieved through the Final Act at the Congress of Vienna (1815), which reorganized and reconstructed Europe. The peace treaties of Westphalia and Utrecht had sought to organize Europe on the basis of nationality, but the French Revolution and Empire had shown that the nation-state itself could threaten international order. The Congress of Vienna, therefore, returned to a more feudal concept of legitimacy. Louis XVIII was put on the French throne; elsewhere the rights of rulers rather than peoples were reinforced.

The Great Powers that had defeated Napoleon—Austria, Britain, Prussia, and Russia—established the Concert of Europe, "a continuing Euro-

Table 3-2
Major International Institutions, 1800–1965.

Date	Political	Functional	Legal
1815	Congress system of periodic but ad hoc consultation between great powers established		Numerous bilateral arbitration agreements
1821		International Commission for the Elbe	
1831		International Commission for the Rhine	
1856		International Commission for the Danube with own flag and insignia	
1868		International Telegraphic Bureau (later ITU)	
1873			International Law Institute (nongovern-mental)
1874		General Postal Union (later U.P.U.)	
1875		International Bureau of Weights and Measures	
1881		International health offices set up at Havana and Vienna	
1885		Regulations for international telephone service agreed	
1890	International Union of American Republics		
1899			Hague Conventions and declarations
1901		International Labor Office (nongovernmental) at Basel	Permanent Court of Arbitration

Source: Luard (1968:230–31).

Date	Political	Functional	Legal
1902		First International Sugar Agreement	
1907		International Office of Public Health at Paris	Second Hague Conference: regular conferences agreed
1910	Pan-American Union		
1919	League of Nations	Organs of the League to deal with slavery, white slavery, drug traffic, communications, health, and financial assistance. I.L.O. established	Permanent International Court of Justice
1922		International Commission for Air Navigation	
1945	U.N. Arab League	Food and Agriculture Organization	International Court of Justice (within U.N.)
1946		UNESCO World Bank International Monetary Fund	International Law Commission (within U.N.)
1947		World Health Organization International Civil Aviation Organization	
1948	Organization of American States		
1950	Council of Europe	International Meteorological Organization	
1957		International Maritime Consultative Organization	
1959		International Atomic Energy Authority	
1963	Organization of African Unity		
1964		U.N. Conference on Trade and Development	

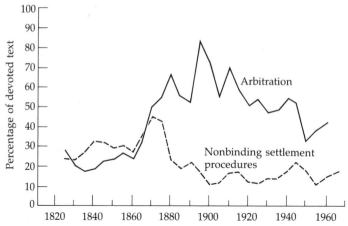

Figure 3-3

International Dispute Settlement: Nonbinding Procedures and Arbitration in International Law Texts, 1815–1969. (NOTE: The analysis rests on content analysis of 204 international law texts, including some multiple editions of the same work. "The index used to portray the perceived importance of arbitration as a method of conflict resolution was based upon the proportional space given to arbitration *vis-à-vis* other pacific methods of dispute settlement; i.e., good offices, commissions of inquiry, conciliation, mediation, and adjudication. Upon determining the percentage of textual space devoted by each author to arbitration, the mean for each five year interval between 1815 and 1970 was computed." SOURCE: Raymond, 1976:18–20; cf. Kegley and Raymond, 1980.)

pean directorate, which would meet whenever necessary to see that their settlement was not endangered" (Craig, 1961:20). The Concert was a precursor of modern international organizations.

> Russia and Austria interpreted the legitimacy principle as bestowing a right upon great powers to decide jointly upon measures for preserving the new order. The Concert of Europe was established to facilitate major power consultation whenever disturbances were perceived to threaten the Vienna settlement. The Concert, in fact, intervened to put down nationalist uprisings in Spain and in Italy, though Great Britain was reluctant to give any sign of support to either venture (M. Haas, 1974:340–41).

World Wars I and II concluded with various agreements made at Versailles, Fontainebleau, Bretton Woods, and San Francisco. These peace settlements included the establishment of universal international courts, the Permanent Court of International Justice and the International Court of

Table 3-3
General Wars, Major Peace Treaties, and International Organizations:
Seventeenth to Twentieth Centuries.

General Wars	Major Peace Treaties	International Organizations
Thirty Years' War	Westphalia (1648)	—
Louis XIV Wars	Utrecht (1713)	—
Napoleonic Wars	Vienna (1815)	Concert of Europe
World War I	Versailles (1919)	League of Nations
World War II	San Francisco (1945)	U.N.

Justice; created territorial boundaries and jurisdictions of nation-states in the new order; and established legal guidelines for the postwar international economic and monetary regime.

Such examples do not prove that either peace or war generally promotes or hinders the growth of international law. In order to draw such conclusions we would need much more systematic evidence.[5] Without such evidence we can not, in good scientific conscience, assert that peace or war are independent determinants of international legal development.

Effects of International Law

Theory and research give more support to the idea that international law contributes directly to the maintenance of peace and the limitation of war. An important element of international law has traditionally been opposed to violence. Thus Wright notes that:

> While certain branches of law have as their end the definition and regulation of permissible violence and the organization of collective violence, and while all systems of law tolerate certain kinds of violence under certain circumstances, the normal end of law, the maintenance of order and justice, is hostile to violence (1965:863).[6]

International law helps create peace and harness violence through two major segments, the law of peace and the law of war. (We find this division in Grotius' classic work on the law of peace and war, *De Jure Belli ac Pacis* and the distinction still exists in modern handbooks [cf. Lauterpacht, 1955].) The institutions and rules of the international law of peace and war help to settle some disputes and to define the scope and limits of permissible and forbidden belligerent action. Nevertheless, peace often breaks down, and wars still occur.

The Law of Peace

The international law of peace includes the definition of subjects and objects of the law of nations, the organs that nation-states use to maintain international relations, and provisions for international transactions. The law of peace helps maintain cooperative and orderly relations between states and thereby contributes to a general atmosphere that reduces the chances for violent conflict. It has been most successful in technical regulation, in helping to order less controversial matters, for example, international economic, cultural, and scientific relations. Here it has been a law "of conciliation and arbitration," rather than one of definitive judicial settlement (E. Haas, 1964:492). It has grown gradually, building on the existing body of consensus, adapting itself to the possibilities of the existing international system. Such law is "lodged in the need for reciprocal benefits received from respect to the legal rule" (Grzybowski, 1970:521; cf. Verwey, 1972).

Dispute Settlement

The international law of peace includes a variety of procedures for the amicable settlement of disputes. These involve negotiations between the parties themselves; nonbinding assistance through the good offices, inquiry, mediation, or conciliation of a third party; or binding arbitration and adjudication (cf. Fisher, 1978; Fawcett, 1977; Bar-Yaacov, 1975; Donelan and Grieve, 1973; Cot, 1972; Edmead, 1971; Northedge and Donelan, 1971; Young, 1967).

Different methods have been stressed at different times. Figure 3-3 suggested that authors of law textbooks in the early and mid-nineteenth century generally saw nonbinding techniques as more important while such methods seemed less significant in the late nineteenth and twentieth centuries. Since 1815 the emphasis on "good offices as a means of conflict resolution has been moderate and relatively stable." Mediation was relatively popular until 1860, but decreased after that. "The weight given to conciliation has steadily increased since 1920" (Raymond, 1976).

Arbitration includes binding third-party settlement of disputes outside an established legal framework. The study of international law texts shows that the importance of binding "arbitration increased from 1815 until 1900, but decreased thereafter." Nevertheless, arbitration has remained more important than nonbinding settlement procedures. The annual number of cases actually submitted to arbitration has showed a similar pattern, growing until the turn of the century, and then declining. International arbitration increased its load of violent and previolent disputes through the nineteenth century. After 1890, however, it handled fewer and fewer of these serious cases (Raymond, 1976:25–26).[7]

The relative decline in international arbitration during the twentieth century may have been due in part to the growth of international adjudication as a substitute. The structure and process of international arbitration are similar to adjudication; for example, both arbitral tribunals and international courts usually lack obligatory jurisdiction (cf. Jackson, 1975). When states choose to accept their authority, however, both arbitration and adjudication provide for collective decisionmaking and binding outcomes. A major difference between the two methods is that adjudication comprehends third-party settlement of disputes according to standard legal and judicial procedures while arbitration operates in a less formally legal way.

The World Court has included the Permanent Court of International Justice under the League of Nations, and later the International Court of Justice under the U.N. It is the most important structure of international adjudication. Its success, however, has been extremely limited. States have been reluctant to accept its jurisdiction, and it has handled a relatively small number of cases. During 38 years between 1924 and 1961, the World Court handled the 55 cases outlined in Table 3-4—24 cases for the PCIJ and 31 cases for ICJ.[8]

Table 3-5 shows that most cases handled by the PCIJ or ICJ have centered on less controversial issues such as contracts, treatment of persons, or territory, rather than more difficult issues involving hostilities or the threat of hostilities. In later years there has been a rise in the percentage of cases involving the outbreak of hostilities. The PCIJ heard no such cases while they formed 26 percent of the ICJ caseload. Nevertheless, there has also been a drop in results; 67 percent of PCIJ cases led to action with consequences, and the same proportion were settled by the PCIJ or with its help. Under the ICJ only 26 percent of the cases produced action with consequences, and only 32 percent were settled by the institution or with its help.

The development of international regional courts, like that of the World Court, has been slow and their success has been modest. A comparative study of the Central American Court of Justice, the International Court of Justice, the Court of European Communities, and the European Court of Human Rights concluded that "only the Court of the European Communities is truly supranational." None of the others was based on common interests or had real and autonomous powers. Three of the courts—the Central American Court of Justice, the Court of European Communities, and the European Court of Human Rights—"allowed access by individuals, or by entities other than nation-states, [but] only with the latter two courts has this right of individual access been given practical reality" (Grieves, 1969:172–73, 178).

Even in the European Communities, international law is a long way from achieving compulsory jurisdiction and binding verdicts enforceable by supranational agencies. The Court of the European Communities has heard and decided a substantial number of cases involving both states and private parties. It has been able to introduce "the beginnings of a body of substantive, and possibly procedural, European case law based on the

Table 3-4

International Law: Two-Party Conflicts Submitted to the World Court, 1924–1961.

Permanent Court of International Justice

Case	Participants	Year of Introduction
Mavrommatis Palestine Concessions	Greece/Great Britain	1924
Interpretation of Article 179, Annex, Paragraph 4, of the Treaty of Neuilly	Greece/Bulgaria	1924
German Interests in Polish Upper Silesia and the Factory at Chorzow	Germany/Poland	1925
Denunciation of the Treaty of November 2, 1865, Between China and Belgium	Belgium/China	1926
Lotus Case	France/Turkey	1927
Rights of Minorities in Upper Silesia (Minority Schools)	Germany/Poland	1928
Payment of Various Serbian Loans Issued in France	France/Serb-Croat-Slovene State	1928
Payment of Brazilian Federal Loans	France/Brazil	1928
Free Zones of Upper Savoy and the District of Gex	France/Switzerland	1929
Legal Status of Eastern Greenland (includes SE Greenland case)	Denmark/Norway	1931
Delimitation of the Territorial Waters between Castellorizo and Anatolia	Turkey/Italy	1929
Administration of the Prince of Pless	Germany/Poland	1932
Appeal from Judgment of Czechoslovak-Hungarian Mixed Arbitral Tribunal (Peter Pazmany University v. Czechoslovakia	Czechoslovakia/ Hungary	1933
Polish Agrarian Reform and the German Minority	Germany/Poland	1933
Lighthouse Case	France/Greece	1933
Oscar Chinn Case	U.K./Belgium	1934
Pajzs, Csaky and Eterhazy	Hungary/Yugoslavia	1935
Losinger & Co.	Switzerland/Yugoslavia	1935
Diversion of Water from the River Meuse	Netherlands/Belgium	1936
Borchgrave Case	Belgium/Spain	1937
Phosphates in Morocco	Italy/France	1936
Panevezys-Saldutiskis Railway	Estonia/Lithuania	1937
Electricity Co. of Sofia and Bulgaria	Belgium/Bulgaria	1938

International Court of Justice

Société Commerciale De Belgique	Belgium/Greece	1938
Corfu Channel Case	U.K./Albania	1947
Fisheries Case	U.K./Norway	1949
Asylum Case	Columbia/Peru	1949

SOURCE: Coplin and Rochester (1972:547–48).

Case	Participants	Year of Introduction
Rights of Nationals of the U.S. in Morocco	France/U.S.	1950
Ambatielos	Greece/U.K.	1951
Anglo-Iranian Oil Co.	U.K./Iran	1951
Minquiers and Ecrehos Case	France/U.K.	1950
Nottebohm	Liechtenstein/ Guatemala	1951
Case of Certain Norwegian Loans	France/Norway	1955
Case Concerning Right of Passage over Indian Territory	Portugal/India	1955
Case Concerning the Application of the Conv. of 1902 Governing the Guardianship of Infants	Netherlands/Sweden	1957
Interhandel Case	Switzerland/U.S.	1957
Case Concerning Sovereignty over Certain Frontier Land	Belgium/Netherlands	1957
Case Concerning Arbitral Award Made by King of Spain on 23 December 1906	Honduras/Nicaragua	1958
Case Concerning Aerial Incident of 27 July 1955	Israel/Bulgaria	1957
Case Concerning the Temple of Preah Vihear	Cambodia/Thailand	1959
Case Concerning the Protection of French Nationals and Protected Persons in Egypt	France/Egypt	1949
"Electricité de Beyrouth" Company Case	France/Lebanon	1953
Treatment in Hungary of Aircraft and Crew of U.S.	U.S./Hungary	1954
Treatment in Hungary of Aircraft and Crew of U.S. (U.S.S.R.)	U.S./U.S.S.R.	1954
Aerial Incident of March 10, 1953	U.S./Czechoslovakia	1953
Antarctica Case	U.K./Argentina	1955
Antarctica Case	U.K./Chile	1955
Aerial Incident of Oct. 7, 1952	U.S./U.S.S.R.	1955
Aerial Incident of July 27, 1955	U.S./Bulgaria	1957
Aerial Incident of July 27, 1955	U.K./Bulgaria	1957
Aerial Incident of Sept. 4, 1954	U.S./U.S.S.R.	1958
Case Concerning the Barcelona Traction, Light and Power Co.	Belgium/Spain	1958
Case Concerning the Compagnie du Port, des Quais et des Entrepots de Beyrouth and the Société Radio-Orient	France/Lebanon	1959
Aerial Incident of Nov. 7, 1954	U.S./U.S.S.R.	1959
Case Concerning the Northern Cameroons	Cameroon/U.K.	1961

Table 3-5

International Law: Two-Party Conflicts Submitted to the World Court:
Issues, Action, Outcome, 1924–1961.[a]

	Type of Issue in Cases				
	Contractual	Treatment of Persons	Territorial	Threat of Hostilities	Outbreak of Hostilities
PCIJ N = 24	42	50	8	0	0
ICJ N = 31	26	16	32	0	26

	Actions with External Consequences		Outcome of Disputes	
	Action with Consequences	No Decision or Consequential Action	Settled by or with the Help of	Unsettled or Settled Outside the Institution
PCIJ N = 24	67	33	67	33
ICJ N = 31	26	74	32	68

[a]All figures are percentages.

SOURCE: Coplin and Rochester (1972:541–44).

provisions of the Treaties" (Feld, 1964:121). The Court has participated in

> the beginnings of consensual processes crystallizing within and around the legal system. . . . The judges for their part are beginning to respond to a variety of pressures and inducements by incorporating Community rules into their decisional processes (Scheingold, 1971:48).

But these are only beginnings. "In terms of political integration," there has been no "generally strong note in the jurisprudence of the Court" (Feld, 1964:118). Even taking into account the Court's greater emphasis on economic questions,

> the judges do not appear to have been very active federalizers, and the most important controversies are seldom litigated. . . . The problem in all of this is that the legal process remains at the margins of basic public policy and therefore suspect as a potential integrator (Scheingold, 1971:48).

This historical record suggests that we should not be terribly optimistic about the role of international courts in the settlement of serious international disputes.[9] Permanent central institutions are not very strong. They have no generally recognized authority to provide third-party decisions on the merits of competing claims of justice and self-defense, or to impose sanctions for violations of international law.

Yet we must bear in mind that adjudication is just one of many methods of international dispute settlement, and perhaps not even the most effective one. Further, it is extremely difficult to know the extent to which measures for the settlement of disputes have been effective individually or in different combinations because they are applied with different degrees of seriousness in different situations, and not all activities of the concerned parties are in the public record.

It seems reasonable to assume that the machinery of dispute settlement, taken as a whole, does some good. It represents an attempt to make the law of peace more concrete through action by specific institutions on particular issues. In dealing with these issues, it outlines the areas of existing agreement, possible future agreement, and disagreement. Such action probably does make a modest contribution in helping develop international consensus and reducing international conflict (cf. Kegley and Raymond, 1980).

The Law of War

The weakness of international dispute settlement has meant that conflicts may not be settled through cooperative processes, but through trial by combat. Even when this happens, international law helps limit violence. A separate body of international law, the law of war, deals with armed conflicts, laying down a comprehensive and complex set of rules. These rules define the rights and privileges of those who fight. They also help protect the noncombatants, those who wish to remain aloof from the contest or innocent civilians (cf. Miller, 1975; Friedman, 1972; Schwarzenberger, 1962:Chs. 10, 11).[10]

Writers in the "realist school" of international law—and a good deal of public opinion—have been quite skeptical of international law. They have been particularly dubious about its effectiveness in dealing with issues of "high politics," where controversy and stakes are highest, and war often seems inevitable.

In its most cynical form, this approach suggests that the international law of war merely licenses the prince, statesman, or foreign policymaker to kill his enemies whenever or however he feels it appropriate. Once war has broken out the normal limits of civilization are removed, and humanity returns to a primitive state of nature. "Cry 'Havoc!' and let slip the dogs of war," says Shakespeare in *Julius Caesar.* A modern political philosopher describes the line of argument in more detail.

> For as long as men and women have talked about war, they have talked about it in terms of right and wrong. And for almost as long, some among them have derided such talk, called it a charade, insisted that war lies beyond (or

beneath) moral judgment. War is a world apart, where life itself is at stake, where human nature is reduced to its elemental forms, where self-interest and necessity prevail. Here men and women do what they must to save themselves and their communities, and morality and law have no place. *Inter arma silent leges:* in time of war the law is silent (Walzer, 1977:3).

While we may understand this position, and even sympathize with it, such extreme disbelief is probably overdone. As we shall see, the international law of war is a commonly agreed upon device for regulating and limiting violence. The contribution of the international law of war is limited, not always equal to its appointed task; nevertheless, it does exist and probably helps in a modest way (cf. Nardin, 1976).

Just War

The international law of war relies heavily on the doctrine of the just war, or as it was called in the Latin of the classical churchmen and lawyers, the *bellum justum*. This doctrine grew out of the shared culture and values— particularly a concern with justice—of early Greek and Roman civilization as expressed in writers like Plato and Cicero. It took root in Christian theology as developed by Augustine, Thomas Aquinas, and the body of canon law. A secular branch of just war doctrine was also part of medieval customs and concepts of civilized behavior. De Vitoria, Suarez, Gentili, Grotius, and later scholars were concerned with appropriate authority to make war and to determine objectives, intent, and mode of conduct. Such concerns have passed down to us in the expanded discussions of contemporary handbooks as well as specialized analysis (cf. Bainton, 1978; Klaassen, 1978; Walzer, 1977; Johnson, 1975; Melzer, 1975; Ramsey, 1968; Tucker, 1966; Tooke, 1965; McDougal and Feliciano, 1961:132). Finally, the doctrine of just war has taken modern form in various positive agreements—bilateral and multilateral treaties, acts of international courts and organizations.

The doctrine of the just war has two major branches: (1) justification for going to war, *jus ad bellum,* and (2) justifiable acts in wartime, *jus in bello.*

> The moral reality of war is divided into two parts. War is always judged twice, first with reference to the reasons states have for fighting, secondly with reference to the means they adopt. The first kind of judgment is adjectival in character: we say that a particular war is being fought justly or unjustly. Medieval writers made the difference a matter of prepositions, distinguishing *jus ad bellum,* the justice of war, from *jus in bello,* justice in war. These grammatical distinctions point to deep issues. *Jus ad bellum* requires us to make judgments about aggression and self-defense; *jus in bello* about the observance or violation of the customary and positive rules of engagement. The two sorts of judgment are logically independent. It is perfectly possible for a just war to be fought unjustly and for an unjust war to be fought in strict accordance with the rules (Walzer, 1977:21).

JUS AD BELLUM   The justification for going to war, *jus ad bellum,* depends on four principal elements (Johnson, 1975:26):

1. Proper authority.
2. Just cause.
3. Right intent.
4. Peaceful end.

Classical writers insisted on the *proper authority* to engage war. Cicero, in Roman times, stated that "just war must be waged under the authority of the state" (Bainton, 1978:136). Subsequently, the medieval scholars Gentili and Grotius transformed the "requirement of proper authority to wage war into the requirement that war be a public contest, solemnly declared" (Johnson, 1975:19). We find this element today in the importance that we give formal declarations of war and peace treaties to signal the beginning and ending of these contests.

The principle of proper authority also implies the validity of a decision not to wage war or join in a particular contest. Recognition of certain areas as war zones and certain states as belligerents implies that some areas may be peace zones and some states nonbelligerents.

Over the years, the legal status of neutrality has been safeguarded and developed to protect the rights of those who did not wish to become involved. International law has paid special attention to freedom of the seas, particularly with regard to neutral commerce, and the inviolability of neutral territory. Larger powers have sometimes specifically contracted, through international treaties, to guarantee the territorial integrity of smaller neutral nations. Neutral states have elaborated different shades of neutrality to fit their needs (cf. Ginther, 1975).[11]

The concept of proper authority also inhibits intervention in the domestic conflicts of other states. The sovereign alone has traditionally had proper authority on his own territory over his own subjects, a monopoly of violence within his own borders. Most states observe this norm most of the time. When they violate it, national leaders may claim that they are intervening on the side of proper authority, that there is no proper authority, or that the conflict is international rather than domestic.[12]

Proper authority withdraws the protection of international law, limited though it is, from actors who undertake unauthorized violence against duly constituted domestic governments. This principle traditionally placed brigands and pirates outside the pale of law. Today, terrorists may fall in the same category as do some activities of mercenary soldiers and multinational corporations (cf. Burmester, 1978; Evans and Murphy, 1978; Bloomfield and Fitzgerald, 1975; Mössner, 1972; Rubin, 1970).

In the modern world the principle of proper authority has come into conflict with, and lost ground to, other elements of just war such as *just cause* and *right intent.* Insurrection against established government was once the most serious of crimes. Today it has become somewhat more acceptable, with the separation of church and state, the passing of absolute rule, and the prevalence of popular democratic and socialist standards of legitimacy. Dissident subnational groups often find international support for violence in the name of basic political, social, economic, and cultural human rights. Examples range from the American Revolution, justified by the Declaration of Independence, down to contemporary Third World wars of national liberation and self-determination (cf. Schafer, 1974).

The principles of just cause and right intent, in turn, have been weakened by the requirement that a just war be consistent with and supportive of peace. As war casualties have increased, the *end of peace* has become much more important. International values have gradually developed to restrict the use of violence justified by "reason of state" (cf. Kegley, 1974).

Various international agreements have sought to maintain peace. Provisions in the Hague Conventions of 1899 and 1907, the Covenant of the League of Nations, the Kellogg–Briand Pact (Pact of Paris) of 1928, and the U.N. Charter laid down strong new regulations. In these agreements, nations promised to delay warlike activity until the processes of international law and organization had been given a chance to settle the dispute; not to engage in aggressive action against other states; and, in some instances, to abandon war altogether as a mode of national policy (cf. Žourek, 1974).

International law has implied penalties. Grotius believed that an unjust belligerent should pay reparations. In the twentieth century, this idea was reflected in provisions of the Fourth Hague Convention of 1907; in popular preoccupation with "war guilt" after both world wars; in the Treaty of Versailles' assessments on Germany after World War I; and in the Potsdam Agreement of 1945 that provided for German payments after World War II.

An international criminal law has gradually developed through which some acts of war have moved from the category of delict or offense to that of crime (Bowett, 1958:272; cf. Schafer, 1974). The Charter of the International Military Tribunal that convened at Nuremberg specified the existence of a series of international crimes, one of which was

> Crimes against Peace: Namely, planning, preparation, initiation or waging of a war of aggression, or a war in violation of international treaties, agreements or assurances, or participation in a common plan or conspiracy for the accomplishment of any of the foregoing.

Further, the Charter held individuals responsible for their actions.

> Leaders, organizers, instigators, and accomplices participating in the formulation or execution of a common plan or conspiracy to commit any of the foregoing crimes are responsible for all acts performed by any persons in execution of such plan (von Glahn, 1970:702).

Crimes against peace remain, however, rather ambiguous. Aggression, guilt, and responsibility have proved extremely difficult to define. The U.N.

did not reach a consensual definition of aggressive war until 1974. The core of the definition is "the priority principle," which establishes first action, including a first strike, as *prima facie* evidence of aggression. Nevertheless "other relevant circumstances" may mitigate the burden of priority. The international legal scholar Myres McDougal has pointed out that a state is not obliged to be "a sitting duck," and initial violence may be justified in certain contexts of clear and present danger (cf. Ferencz, 1975; Stone, 1958).

JUS IN BELLO   Once war has actually begun, international law helps define its limits. Despite claims of military necessity, the doctrine of *jus in bello* helps us say whether or not the war is being fought justly, whether the actions are legitimate, and the means are appropriate to the ends being sought.

We find early discussions of the limits on fighting in a number of places, for example, in Plato's *Republic*, which gave advice on the "usages of war," seeking to mitigate its more brutal aspects. The classic Islamic scholar Shaybānī formulated rules concerning the conduct of the army in enemy territory, the spoils of war, safe conduct, prisoners of war, peace treaties, and other related matters. The religious bonds that united Christian kings, and the secular, medieval codes of chivalry in Europe and Japan strictly prescribed appropriate and inappropriate battle conduct.

Contemporary limits on wartime violence, articulated through the doctrine of *jus in bello*, include two major elements: proportionality and discrimination (Johnson, 1975:26; cf. Schindler and Toman, 1973). The principle of *proportionality* centers on the means of violence, which are supposed to be limited by the purpose at hand. For example, proportionality suggests that the battlefield use of particularly inhumane weapons should be restricted. Early international agreements limited the use of such "conventional" weapons as expanding bullets, or dumdums, "named after a British arsenal in India in which such bullets had first been produced on a quantity basis" (von Glahn, 1970:544; cf. SIPRI, 1978a; Applegate, 1977; Dobbyn et al., 1975; Owen, 1975; DiMaio et al., 1974). The Treaty of Versailles at the end of World War I contained provisions against the use of poison gas.

Proportionality also implies that civilian injury or damage should not be disproportionate to the value of the main military target. Thus, contemporary treaties have attempted to restrict the worst modern weapons— atomic, biological, and chemical. A major argument for limiting their use is that the negative human effects of using such weapons are vastly disproportional to any military gains that a belligerent actor might hope to achieve by using them.

> In the Preamble to the 1967 Treaty of Tlatelolco it is stated "that nuclear weapons, whose terrible effects are suffered, indiscriminately and inexorably, by military forces and civilian population alike, constitute, through the persistence of the radioactivity they release, an attack on the integrity of the human species

and ultimately may even render the whole earth uninhabitable." The Preamble to the 1968 Non-Proliferation Treaty mentions "the devastation that would be visited upon all mankind by a nuclear war." The 1971 Agreement on Measures to Reduce the Risk of Outbreak of Nuclear War between the USA and the USSR takes into account "the devastating consequences that nuclear war would have for all mankind" (SIPRI, 1976c:5).

Discrimination is the second major principle of the *jus in bello*. The principle of discrimination centers on the objects of violence. It suggests that belligerents should discriminate between combatants and noncombatants and that noncombatants should be protected.

Noncombatants of a belligerent state have traditionally had a hard time of it. Invading armies historically ravaged and plundered; friendly armies lived off civilian food and shelter. Nevertheless, earlier wars were limited by available military techniques, and they were predominantly "wars between armed forces, rather than wars between peoples" (Akehurst, 1977:249).

Modern war has made life much more difficult for noncombatants because it has tended to be total. Whole societies—rather than armies or navies—now go to war; and the distinction between soldier and civilian has become blurred. Partly because of this blurring, the contemporary *jus in bello* includes new elements that seek to protect the innocent from indiscriminate slaughter.

The charter of the International Military Tribunal at Nuremberg specified two kinds of crimes in addition to crimes against peace. These were crimes against humanity and war crimes, both of which included specified actions against noncombatants.

> Crimes against Humanity: Namely, murder, extermination, enslavement, deportation, and other inhumane acts committed against any civilian population, before or during the war, or persecutions on political, racial or religious grounds in execution of or in connection with any crime within the jurisdiction of the Tribunal, whether or not in violation of the domestic law of the country where perpetrated.
>
> War Crimes: Namely, violations of the laws or customs of war. Such violations shall include, but not be limited to, murder, ill-treatment or deportation to slave labor or for any other purpose of civilian population of or in occupied territory, murder or ill-treatment of prisoners of war or persons on the seas, killing of hostages, plunder of public or private property, wanton destruction of cities, towns or villages, or devastation not justified by military necessity (von Glahn, 1970:702).

The chief allied prosecutor at Nuremberg summed up the intent:

> War consists largely of acts that would be criminal if performed in time of peace—killing, wounding, kidnapping, destroying or carrying off other people's property. Such conduct is not regarded as criminal if it takes place in the course of war, because the state of war lays a blanket of immunity over the warriors. . . . But the area of immunity is not unlimited, and its boundaries are marked by the laws of war (Taylor, 1970:19; cf. Wakin, 1979).

The principles and judgments of Nuremberg were affirmed and incorporated into international law by a U.N. General Assembly resolution in December, 1946, and the Genocide Convention of 1948.

International tribunals have assigned penalties for transgressions, and offenders have been prosecuted in a series of contemporary international proceedings. A trial at Leipzig in 1921 had preceded the Nuremberg proceedings of 1945–1949. Additional trials took place in Manila, 1946; Tokyo, 1946–1948; Jerusalem, 1961; Frankfurt, 1963–1965; Stockholm and Roskilde, 1967. Many have been found guilty and punished with imprisonment or death.

> By late November, 1948, a total of 7,109 defendants had been arrested for war crimes, including the "major cases" at Nuremberg and Tokyo. Of these, 3,686 had been convicted and 924 trials had resulted in acquittals. Of those convicted, death sentences were received by 1,019, and 33 defendants had committed suicide. Prison sentences were received by 2,667 and 2,499 cases were still pending. Numerous files remained open, however, where war crimes had been committed but the culprits had disappeared. In the intervening years, many of these, particularly in France and in Germany, have been discovered by their own governments and have been tried for violations of the laws of war. Thus by early 1964 some 5,500 individuals had been tried in West Germany, with about 1,000 cases still pending (von Glahn, 1970:705).

Red Cross conventions resulting from the Geneva Diplomatic Conference of 1949 reaffirm and expand the immunity of noncombatants. The four major conventions of the 1949 Geneva Conference attempt to provide immunity to those who were once combatants, but who have ceased to be so—prisoners of war, the sick, wounded, and shipwrecked—as well as civilians. They deal with:

> Treatment of Prisoners of War; Amelioration of the Condition of the Wounded and Sick in Armed Forces in the Field; Amelioration of the Condition of Wounded, Sick and Shipwrecked Members of Armed Forces at Sea; and Protection of Civilian Persons in Time of War (von Glahn, 1970:545).

The general principles of the *jus in bello* are reflected in an inventory of more specific war crimes. Table 3-6 presents some of the specific acts that are currently defined as war crimes.

Modern insurgency and counterinsurgency have shown the limits of the *jus in bello*. The Vietnam war, for example, included various actions that might be classified as violating the principles of proportionality and discrimination. The United States used chemical defoliants with general, negative, long-term effects on human, animal, and plant life. American leaders ordered massive bombings of North Vietnamese population centers. Both sides undertook attacks on civilians, including torture and assassination. There were violations of regulations concerning prisoners of war (cf. Rosas, 1976; Risner, 1974; Falk et al., 1971; Levie, 1969).[13]

Table 3-6
International Law: War Crimes.

---

1. Making use of poisoned or otherwise forbidden arms or munitions;
2. Treachery in asking for quarter or simulating sickness or wounds;
3. Maltreatment of corpses;
4. Firing on localities which are undefended and without military significance;
5. Abuse of or firing on a flag of truce;
6. Misuse of the Red Cross or similar emblems;
7. Wearing of civilian clothes by troops to conceal their identity during the commission of combat acts;
8. Improper utilization of privileged (exempt, immune) buildings for military purposes;
9. Poisoning of streams or wells;
10. Pillage;
11. Purposeless destruction;
12. Compelling prisoners of war to engage in prohibited types of labor;
13. Forcing civilians to perform prohibited labor;
14. Violation of surrender terms;
15. Killing or wounding military personnel who have laid down arms, surrendered, or are disabled by wounds or sickness;
16. Assassination, and the hiring of assassins;
17. Ill-treatment of prisoners of war, or of the wounded and sick—including despoiling them of possessions not classifiable as public property;
18. Killing or attacking harmless civilians;
19. Compelling the inhabitants of occupied enemy territory to furnish information about the armed forces of the enemy or his means of defense;
20. Appropriation or destruction of the contents of privileged buildings;
21. Bombardment from the air for the exclusive purpose of terrorizing or attacking civilian populations;
22. Attack on enemy vessels which have indicated their surrender by lowering their flag;
23. Attack or seizure of hospitals and all other violations of the Hague Convention for the Adaptation to Maritime Warfare of the Principles of the Geneva Convention;
24. Unjustified destruction of enemy prizes;
25. Use of enemy uniforms during combat and use of the enemy flag during attack by a belligerent vessel;
26. Attack on individuals supplied with safe-conducts, and other violations of special safeguards provided;
27. Breach of parole;
28. Grave breaches of Article 50 of the Geneva Convention for the Amelioration of the Condition of the Wounded and Sick in Armed Forces in the Field, of 1949 and Article 51 of the Geneva Convention of 1949 Applicable to Armed Forces at Sea: "wilful killing, torture or inhuman treatment, including biological experiments, wilfully causing great suffering or serious injury to body or health, and extensive destruction and appropriation of property not justified by military necessity and carried out unlawfully and wantonly";

SOURCE: Reprinted with permission of Macmillan Publishing Co., Inc., from *Law Among Nations*, 2nd ed., by Gerhard von Glahn. Copyright © 1970 by Gerhard von Glahn.

29. Grave breaches of the Geneva Convention Relative to the Treatment of Prisoners of War, of 1949, as listed in Article 130: "wilful killing, torture or inhuman treatment, including biological experiments, wilfully causing great suffering or serious injury to body or health, compelling a prisoner of war to serve in the forces of the hostile Power, or wilfully depriving a prisoner of war of the rights of fair and regular trial prescribed" in the Convention;

30. Grave breaches of the Fourth Geneva Convention of 1949, as detailed in Article 147: "wilful killing, torture or inhuman treatment, including biological experiments, wilfully causing great suffering or serious injury to body or health, unlawful deportation or transfer or unlawful confinement of a protected person, compelling a protected person to serve in the forces of a hostile Power, or wilfully depriving a protected person of the rights of fair and regular trial prescribed in the present Convention, taking of hostages and extensive destruction and appropriation of property, not justified by military necessity and carried out unlawfully and wantonly." In addition, conspiracy, direct incitement, and attempts to commit, as well as complicity in the commission of, crimes against the laws of war are punishable.

The best-known American attack on civilians occurred at the hamlet of My Lai. The report of the chief U.S. Army investigator, Lt. Gen. William R. Peers, describes the incident as follows:

> During the period 16–19 March 1968, US Army troops of TF Barker, 11th Brigade, American Division, massacred a large number of noncombatants in two hamlets of Son My Village, Quang Ngai Province, Republic of Vietnam. The precise number of Vietnamese killed cannot be determined but was at least 175 and may exceed 400.
>
> . . .
>
> On 16 March, soldiers at the squad and platoon level, within some elements of TF Barker, murdered noncombatants while under the supervision and control of their immediate superiors. A part of the crimes visited on the inhabitants of Son My Village included individual and group acts of murder, rape, sodomy, maiming, and assault on noncombatants and the mistreatment and killing of detainees. They further included the killing of livestock, destruction of crops, closing of wells, and the burning of dwellings within several subhamlets.
>
> . . .
>
> At every command level within the Americal Division, actions were taken, both wittingly and unwittingly, which effectively suppressed information concerning the war crimes committed on Son My Village (Goldstein et al., 1976:314–16; cf. Green, 1976; Bishop, 1974; Dinstein, 1965).

The final American action seems relatively mild, even laughable, given the nature of the offense. The Army tried one person, Lt. William Calley, under the Uniform Code of Military Justice. The court found Lt. Calley guilty and sentenced him to life imprisonment. This sentence was later reduced, then overturned. Lt. Calley was released after serving two years in prison.

If we can bring ourselves to look at the American legal action in a positive light, we should bear in mind that legal issues are complex. Even in domestic law, there are not necessarily remedies for all wrongs, and we find mild punishments for horrible crimes. The trial of Lt. Calley, in spite of its slim results, symbolically reaffirmed the applicability of international law, not only to national leaders, but also to ordinary soldiers. It further undercut the defenses of "military necessity" or "superior orders" as blanket justifications for battlefield actions. Finally, it has led to a stronger emphasis on the provisions of international law in armed-service field manuals and basic training.[14]

A four-year Diplomatic Conference on the Reaffirmation and Development of International Humanitarian Law in Armed Conflicts has recently produced two additional protocols to the 1949 Geneva conventions. The Conference approved these in 1977, and now they are ready for national signatures.

These protocols extend the principles of proportionality and discrimination. They include revolutionaries and guerrilla fighters in certain civil wars. They grant immunity to prisoners of war and to the sick and wounded in "armed conflicts in which peoples are fighting against colonial domination and alien occupation and against racist regimes in the exercise of their right to self-determination." They advance the protection of civilians.

> Prohibited for the first time [are] saturation bombings of cities, regardless of whether they contain military targets, and attacks designed to spread terror among civilians, such as the air raids on German and British cities during World War II.
>
> Furthermore, indirect assaults on civilians are banned. These include warfare intended, or likely, to create "widespread damage to the natural environment" and attacks on dams, dikes, nuclear plants and other facilities whose disruption would inflict harm to civilian populations.
>
> And for the first time in the long history of international law deliberate starvation of civilians [is] proscribed as a method of warfare. Presumably this would include sieges and blockades that deny vital foodstuffs to civilians as well as long-lasting crop defoliation (Forsythe and Magat, 1978. cf. Levie, 1979; Bond, 1974).

The international law of war and the doctrine of the just war operate within severe constraints. There is no detailed international agreement on all aspects of justice (see Bozeman, 1971, 1960). Rules are often badly defined, at cross-purposes, misapplied, or ignored. Yet, however primitive this body of law is, it does set some bounds to violence and stands as a foundation for future advances in international law.

BUREAUCRACY: INTERNATIONAL ORGANIZATION AND NATIONAL GOVERNMENT

World bureaucratization has also implied the development of international organizations and national governments. Early attempts at global international institutions centered in Europe. "At millennial intervals Western Civilization has made an attempt to organize itself as a world-empire, as a world-church, or as a world-federation," noted Wright (1965:1043).

Only in the twentieth century have truly global international institutions begun to appear. We have already seen in Table 3-2 how a network of international institutions with universal, regional, and specialized concerns has gradually taken form. As this network has become larger, denser, and more complex, it has also increased its resource base. There has been an absolute rise in international organization expenditures from almost nothing in the nineteenth century to about half a billion dollars per year by the mid-1960s. International organizations have also increased their resources relative to national government revenues, national income, and population.[15]

Bureaucratization has also implied the growth of domestic governments. The modern nation-state comprehends highly structured institutions dominating millions of square miles and encompassing hundreds of millions of human beings. The number of nation-states participating in the international system has increased to about 150. This growth has been particularly dramatic with the emergence of Third World nation-states after World War II. The governments of nation-states have also broadened their capabilities over time. Today they expend substantial portions of their societies' collective resources and employ millions of citizen-workers.[16]

Finally, bureaucracy includes private organizations. Many of these have international connections, assets, and operations. The economic resources of the largest of the multinational corporations—General Motors, Exxon, and Ford, for example—are equivalent to those of many developing nation-states and small powers (cf. Modelski, 1979b, 1974; Mennis and Sauvant, 1976; Gilpin, 1975; Barnet and Müller, 1974; Vernon, 1971; Kindleberger, 1970a). Religious organizations also have an important international dimension (cf. D. Hudson, 1977; Bock, 1974).

Causes of International Organization and National Government

It is unclear whether or how peace or war have contributed to the development of international organization and national government. We may try to see their influence from three data sources for the nineteenth and twentieth centuries: Table 3-2, which traces the establishment of major international institutions; Figure 3-4, which sketches the members of new international governmental organizations (IGOs) and nongovernmental organizations (NGOs); and Table 3-7, which outlines some cumulative statistics.

In general, it appears that the overall effect of either peace or war on international organization may be quite limited. Table 3-2 suggests that major new IGOs have appeared fairly regularly, with the rate increasing somewhat during our time. Figure 3-4 includes lines connecting the tops of short-term waves of new IGOs and NGOs. These lines outline the upper limits of a long-term upward trend above the peaks of short-term fluctuation.

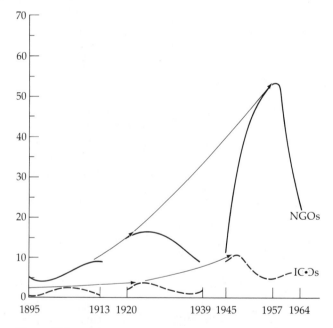

Figure 3-4

New International Organizations, 1895–1964.
(DATA PLOT: NGOs = formation of new nongovernmental organizations. IGOs = formation of new intergovernmental organizations. NOTE: ——→ = upper limits of short-term fluctuations, extrapolated secular growth trend, author's estimate. SOURCE: Pelowski, 1971:280. Reproduced from *Journal of Peace Research*, by permission of the publishers, Universitetsforlaget, Oslo, Norway.)

Table 3-7

The Growth of International Governmental Organizations, 1815–1964.[a]

Years	No. of IGOs	No. of Nations	No. of Member ships	Mean No. Nations per IGO	Mean No. IGOs per Nation	Mean No. Shared Member ships	Mean Percentage Universality
1815–19	1	23	6	6.1	.3		26.1
1820–24	1	23	6	6.1	.3		26.1
1825–29	1	25	6	6.1	.2		24.0
1830–34	1	28	6	6.1	.2		21.4
1835–39	2	31	18	9.0	.6		29.0
1840–44	2	35	18	9.0	.5		25.7
1845–49	2	38	18	9.0	.5		23.7
1850–54	2	40	18	9.0	.5		22.5
1855–59	3	42	24	8.0	.6		19.0
1860–64	3	44	21	7.0	.5		15.9
1865–69	6	39	54	9.0	1.4	.5	23.1
1870–74	7	34	65	9.3	1.9	.8	27.3
1875–79	9	34	106	11.8	3.1	1.4	34.6
1880–84	11	35	136	12.4	3.9	1.8	35.3
1885–89	17	38	203	11.9	5.3	2.6	31.4
1890–94	21	38	267	12.7	7.0	3.1	33.5
1895–99	23	41	299	13.0	7.3	3.4	31.7
1900–04	30	43	412	13.7	9.6	4.0	31.9
1905–09	44	45	639	14.5	14.2	6.8	32.3
1910–14	49	45	753	15.4	16.7	7.9	34.1
1915–19	53	51[b]	826	15.6	16.2	7.6	30.1
1920–24	72	63	1336	18.6	21.2	9.4	29.5
1925–29	83	65	1528	18.4	23.5	10.2	28.3
1930–34	87	66	1639	18.8	24.8	10.5	28.5
1935–39	86	67	1697	19.7	25.3	11.0	29.5
1940–44	82	65	1560	19.0	24.0	10.9	29.3
1945–49	123	75[c]	2284	18.6	30.5	13.0	24.8
1950–54	144	82	2684	18.6	32.7	14.2	22.7
1955–59	168	90	3338	19.9	37.1	15.7	22.1
1960–64	195	122	4436	22.7	36.4	14.3	18.6

[a]This table is composed of columns from various tables found in Singer and Wallace (1970), Wallace and Singer (1970), and Skjelsbaek (1970). There were unfortunately some minor printing errors in the earlier presentations of Singer and Wallace's data, and Skjelsbaek used a preliminary and uncleaned version of the same.
[b]Wallace and Singer (1970) do not report data for Austria after the collapse of Austria-Hungary. It is therefore not included in the table for this period.
[c]Neither do they report data for Germany and Japan from January 1, 1945, to their respective capitulations in 1945. They are therefore not included in the table for this period.
SOURCE: Skjelsbaek (1971).

Table 3-7 shows that the total numbers of IGOs, national IGO membership, average numbers of nations per IGO, and IGOs per nation all rose fairly steadily over the nineteenth and twentieth centuries, without much apparent perturbation by peace or war.

Two other measures of growth in Table 3-7 show a less continuous picture, but there is no obvious relationship to the level of international violence. The mean number of shared IGO memberships measures the number of nation-pairs that are members of the same IGO. This measure rose steadily to a high during the period 1955–1959 but then dropped off slightly in 1960–1964. The mean percentage of universality measures the extent to which all possible nations are members of all possible IGOs. This indicator has fluctuated. It declined briefly during the generation following the Napoleonic Wars; rose sharply in the period between 1835 and 1839; declined until 1864; rose till 1884; fluctuated within fairly narrow limits till the outbreak of World War I; and then went consistently down in the next half century.

Some of the data suggest that peace may be relatively good, and war harmful, for new international organizations. We see in Table 3-2 that no major organizations were created immediately preceding or during the world wars. Figure 3-4 also shows that the formation rate of IGOs and NGOs generally declined before the two world wars. Decisionmakers presumably saw the wars coming and were reluctant to build additional international institutions in a period of uncertainty.[17]

Other aspects of the data cast doubt on the efficacy of peace and harmfulness of war for international organizations. In Figure 3-4 new IGOs drop in the relatively peaceful decades before World Wars I and II and in the late 1940s. New NGOs also decline in the 1920s, 1930s, 1950s, and 1960s.

War may provide a short-term impetus for growth. Many of the major international organizations in Table 3-2 were formed directly following the two world wars. In Figure 3-4 we see that IGO- and NGO-formation rates jumped immediately after both world wars. At such times perhaps there is a mood of atonement and a desire to do better in the future than in the past, perhaps a greater international feeling of security (cf. Singer and Wallace, 1970).

Our knowledge about the effect of peace or war on the growth of national governments is also inconclusive. A good deal of theory and research suggests that war has been an important, even essential, means of building modern states and empires. Leaders of early bureaucratic empires broadened their domains through force of arms. Modern European nations expanded into the Americas, Africa, and Asia through military violence. World Wars I and II seemed to provide a catalyst for the formation of independent states in central and eastern Europe and the Third World.

We must, however, bear in mind that war has also contributed to the dissolution of governments. European colonization advanced only at the expense of preexisting indigenous political systems. World Wars I and II helped produce the dismemberment of Austria-Hungary, Germany, and the great European imperial systems (cf. Wright, 1965:257–58).

Comparative studies extending from primitive tribal society to the present suggest that peace or war has not necessarily produced long-term significant effects on the origin or growth of government (cf. Service, 1975:266–89; Linz, 1973).

Figure 3-5 provides a good modern illustration of the relative independence of general governmental growth from the influence of peace or war. It depicts the increase of U.S. federal government civilian employees between 1800 and 1965. The number of employees has risen at a relatively constant rate over the last two centuries. Periods of war may have contributed to some short-term fluctuations, but not always in the same direction. Sometimes war seems to have diminished the number of governmental civilian employees; at other times it appears to have increased their number. Over the long run these short-term fluctuations appear to have made little difference in the overall trend.

Effects of International Organization and National Government

International organization and national government contribute directly to the creation and maintenance of peace, the prevention and limitation of warfare. However, their influence, like that of international law, is modest.

International Organization

International organization, says an eminent scholar, is "fundamentally, even though not exclusively, a reaction to the problem of war" (Claude, 1964:197). Since the fourteenth century, modern political theorists have attempted to formulate comprehensive plans for international peace based on international organization. Many of these plans have been rooted in religion or philosophy, for example, proposals by Dante, Kant, Rousseau, Bentham, and the Abbé de St. Pierre. Others, like the more contemporary work by Grenville Clark and Louis Sohn (1966) have come from international legal scholars.[18]

Extensive international institutions, with the possible exception of major organized religions, did not exist until the nineteenth and twentieth centuries. As international organizations have developed in recent times, they have attempted to maintain peace and limit violence in various ways.

The charter of the U.N., for example, includes in its Preamble, Purposes and Principles:

> We the peoples of the United Nations determined
> to save succeeding generations from the scourge of war, which twice in our
> life-time has brought untold sorrow to mankind and . . . to practice tolerance

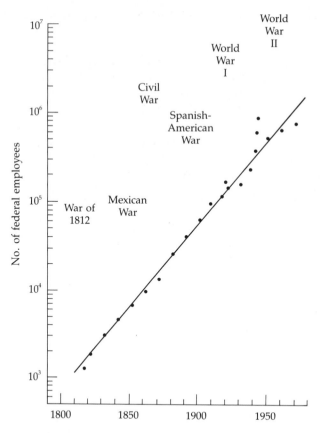

Figure 3-5

**Federal Government Civilian Employees: U.S.,
1800–1965.** (NOTES: Numbers of civilian employees
were multiplied by a constant for display purposes,
and "plotted on semilogarithmic coordinates by years.
The data are subject to fluctuations because of war and
other societal crises; however, the long-term trend is
linear, suggesting single exponential epochs. . . . The
number of civilian federal employees has increased
since 1812 in one long, regular exponential epoch;
specifically, the number has increased from 0.6 to 1.4
percent of the total population. Hence federal civilian
employees have been increasing about 2.4 times as fast
as the total population." SOURCE: Hamblin et al.,
1973:99.)

and live together in peace with one another as good neighbors, and to unite
our strength to maintain international peace and security, and to ensure, by
the acceptance of principles and the institution of methods, that armed force
shall not be used, save in the common interest . . . do hereby establish an
international organization to be known as the United Nations.

. . .

The Purposes of the United Nations are:

1. To maintain international peace and security, and to that end: to take effective collective measures for the prevention and removal of threats to the

peace, and for the suppression of acts of aggression or other breaches of the peace, and to bring about by peaceful means, and in conformity with the principles of justice and international law, adjustment or settlement of international disputes or situations which might lead to a breach of the peace;

2. To develop friendly relations among nations based on respect for the principle of equal rights and self-determination of peoples, and to take other appropriate measures to strengthen universal peace;

3. To achieve international co-operation in solving international problems of an economic, social, cultural, or humanitarian character, and in promoting and encouraging respect for human rights and for fundamental freedoms for all without distinction as to race, sex, language, or religion; and

4. To be a center for harmonizing the actions of nations in the attainment of these common ends.

The Charter also has separate chapters dealing with "pacific settlement of disputes," and "action with respect to threats to the peace, breaches of the peace, and acts of aggression."

We shall consider in some detail three of the most important types of international organization tasks involving dispute settlement, collective security and peacekeeping, and war relief. Such activities, as we shall see, have a direct, constructive impact. At the same time, we must be careful to note the limits of this influence.

Dispute Settlement

International organizations at all levels attempt to help settle disputes between their members. Table 3-8 outlines 66 major cases of 2-party international conflict submitted to the League of Nations and the U.N. between 1920 and 1966.[19] Table 3-9 gives a simple statistical analysis of these cases. The table shows that the League handled a much greater proportion of cases involving less controversial disputes over contracts, treatment of persons, and territory. Only 40 percent of the League's cases had to do with the threat or outbreak of hostilities. On the other hand, over two-thirds of the cases taken to the U.N. involved the threat or outbreak of hostilities.

The League's efforts seem to have been relatively effective. Almost three-quarters of the League's actions produced external consequences, and it helped settle almost half the disputes it took on. Unfortunately, the U.N.'s greater willingness to deal with more serious disputes has not been so successful. Less than two-thirds of the actions listed had external consequences, and it helped settle less than a fifth of the cases.

A survey of evaluations by independent experts yielded a judgment that the U.N. has done relatively well in dealing with conflicts of either a very high or very low visibility and intensity (E. Haas et al., 1972). The greatest U.N. achievements came in its earlier years, and involved decolonization and other issues not directly connected with the Cold War. The parties were generally nonaligned smaller and middle-power states. The U.N. scored "major successes" in the "three wars between Israel and the Arabs, in two wars between India and Pakistan, in ejecting the Netherlands

Table 3-8

International Organization: Two-Party Conflicts Submitted to the League of Nations and U.N., 1920–1966.

Two-Party Cases for the League of Nations		
Case	Participants	Year of Introduction
Enzeli	Iran/U.S.S.R.	1920
Aaland Islands	Sweden/Finland	1920
Vilna	Poland/Lithuania	1920
Coto	Panama/Costa Rica	1921
Upper Silesia	Poland/Germany	1921
Eastern Carelia	Finland/U.S.S.R.	1921
Tunis Nationality Decrees	U.K./France	1922
Hungarian Frontier	Hungary/Yugoslavia	1922
Burgenland	Austria/Hungary	1922
Salgo Tarsan	Hungary/Czechoslovakia	1922
Hungarian Optants	Hungary/Romania	1923
Jaworzina	Poland/Czechoslovakia	1923
Corfu	Greece/Italy	1923
Ecumenical Patriarch	Greece/Turkey	1925
Dmir Kapu	Bulgaria/Greece	1925
Albanian Minorities	Albania/Greece	1925
Mosul Territory in Iraq	Turkey/U.K.	1924
Cruiser "Salamis"	Greece/Germany	1925
Bahrein Islands	Iran/U.K.	1927
Gran Chaco I	Bolivia/Paraguay	1928
Gran Chaco II	Bolivia/Paraguay	1932
Rhodope Forest	Greece/Bulgaria	1930
Manchuria	China/Japan	1931
Bulgarian-Greek Debt	Bulgaria/Greece	1931
Finnish Vessels	Finland/U.K.	1931
Iraq-Syrian Frontier	France/U.K.	1931
Letica	Peru/Columbia	1932
Anglo-Persian Oil Co.	U.K./Iran	1932
Iraq Frontier	Iran/Iraq	1934
Hungarian Frontier	Hungary/Yugoslavia	1934
Marseilles Crimes	Hungary/Yugoslavia	1934
Ethiopia	Ethiopia/Italy	1935
Syria (Sanjak)	Turkey/France	1936
China	China/Japan	1937
Russo-Finnish War	Finland/U.S.S.R.	1939

SOURCE: Coplin and Rochester (1972:549–50).

Two-Party Cases for the U.N.		
Case	**Participants**	**Year of Introduction**
Forces in Iran	Iran/U.S.S.R.	1946
Thai Border	Thailand/France	1946
Treatment of Indians	India/S. Africa	1946
Corfu Channel	U.K./Albania	1947
Kashmir I	India/Pakistan	1948
Intervention in China	China/U.S.S.R.	1949
Threats to Yugoslavia	Yugoslavia/U.S.S.R.	1951
Anglo-Iranian Oil Co.	U.K./Iran	1951
Morocco	Egypt/France	1951
Forces in Burma	Burma/Nat. China	1953
West Irian	Indonesia/Netherlands	1954
Syria-Turkish Crisis	Syria/Turkey	1957
Cambodian Border	Cambodia/Thailand	1958
Sudanese Border	Sudan/Egypt	1958
Tunisian Border	Tunisia/France	1959
Laos Intervention	Laos/N. Vietnam	1959
Eichmann Kidnapping	Argentina/Israel	1960
South Tyrol	Austria/Italy	1960
Cuban Complaint	Cuba/U.S.	1960
U-2 Incident	U.S./U.S.S.R.	1960
Mauritania	Morocco/France	1960
Goa Invasion	Portugal/India	1961
Venezuelan Boundary	Venezuela/U.K.	1962
Cyprus	Greece/Turkey	1963
Senegal Border	Senegal/Portugal	1963
Ethiopian Border	Ethiopia/Somalia	1964
Panama	Panama/U.S.	1964
Haiti/Dominican Rep.	Haiti/Dominican Rep.	1963
Cambodian Border	Cambodia/S. Vietnam	1964
Gibraltar	U.K./Spain	1965
Mercenaries in Angola	Rep. of Congo/Portugal	1966

from Indonesia, in pacifying the Congo, in arranging the Korean armistice, and in ending the Greek civil war." It had more "limited successes in abating the major wars in Algeria and temporarily in Laos and in reducing clashes between Israel and the Arabs in the two prolonged truce periods, 1949–1956 and 1956–67" (E. Haas et al., 1972:26–27; cf. Auma-Osolo, 1976:20–23).

Regional organizations tended to be most successful in relatively low-intensity conflicts, of a local nature, with no military operations or "sporadic ill-organized fighting" that had not spread beyond the space of a bilateral dispute and that involved

Table 3-9

International Organization: Two-Party Conflicts Submitted to the League of Nations and U.N.: Issues, Action, Outcome, 1920–1966.[a]

	Type of Issue in Cases					
	Contractual	Treatment of Persons	Territorial	Threat of Hostilities	Outbreak of Hostilities	NA[b]
League N=35	14	12	34	6	34	0
U.N. N=31	3	7	16	10	58	6

	Actions with External Consequences		Outcome of Disputes	
	Action with Consequences	No Decision or Consequential Action	Settled by or with the Help of	Unsettled or Settled Outside the Institution
League N=35	74	26	49	51
U.N. N=31	64	36	19	81

[a]All figures are percentages.
[b]Other issue categories not applicable.
SOURCE: Coplin and Rochester (1972:541–44).

the smallest and weakest nations. [In larger disputes,] successes were all of the minimal variety of helping to abate and isolate confrontations, and they were monopolized by the Organization of African Unity: the Algerian-Moroccan and Somali border fighting and the case of Tutsi terrorism in Rwanda (E. Haas et al., 1972:16–17; cf. Butterworth, 1978b).[20]

The achievements of international organizations in the settlement of international disputes are important. At the same time we must be clear about the fact that they are also quite limited. Nations are not required to submit their disputes to international organizations, and states often raise preliminary objections to having their conflicts even considered. The survey of independent experts that we have just considered concludes that, in spite of their accomplishments, "international organizations as a whole did one-fourth as well as they ideally might." If international organizations succeeded 25 percent of the time, they obviously failed 75 percent. Among the higher-intensity cases,

the UN failed in Vietnam, Yemen, the Cuban missile crisis, the Hungarian intervention, and in ejecting Portugal from Africa . . . [Among the regional organizations] the OAU failed in Biafra, and in the Congolese Simba rebellion. . . ; the Arab League failed in Yemen . . . and in the Algerian-Moroccan war (E. Haas et al., 1972:17, 27; cf. Butterworth, 1978a; Raman, 1977; Ciobanu, 1975).

Some aggregate statistical studies take a more pessimistic view. Between 1815 and 1945, Singer and Wallace found that neither the number of international organizations nor the size of their membership was positively related to the reduction of war. They concluded that there was

> almost no discernible correlation between the amount of international organization existing in any period and the amount of war which began in the following (five year) period. The amount of intergovernmental organization has almost no effect on the amount of war which the system experiences (1970:540).

A study of international regions between 1951 and 1962 found that neither "common institutional membership [nor] similarity of U.N. voting behavior" made war less likely (Russett, 1967:198, 201). Instead, members of the same international organizations appeared more than twice as likely to fight each other as nonmembers. An analysis of a global sample of nations produced a similar result. The study showed that the number of wars a nation experienced and the number of its citizens killed in those wars were positively related to its absolute number of representatives and its relative financial contribution to the U.N. (Rummel, 1968:196).

There are many possible reasons for such statistical findings.[21] They do not require us to disbelieve in any achievements of international organizations. They do, however, remind us that the capabilities of international organizations for resolving international disputes are still quite modest.

Collective Security and Peacekeeping

International organization has developed an executive function for the international law of war. The logic of the *jus ad bellum* leads to the activities of collective security and peacekeeping. If war should only be undertaken for just cause, it makes sense that an international body should determine whether or not the conditions of justice have been met. This body should, further, be able to use various sanctions, including military intervention, to enforce the peace when other methods for doing so fail.

Following World War I, international relations seemed to have entered a new age, where security appeared indivisible. Violence in one place could explode into global catastrophe. A threat against any single nation seemed to be a threat against all. If one nation were successfully attacked, others might fall, like dominoes, until a whole row of states had been laid flat.

The members of the League of Nations reacted to this situation, and helped to define it, by advancing the idea of collective security. Under the doctrine of collective security, the League's founders agreed to take collective sanctions, including the possibility of military action, against an aggressor.

Collective security did not work very well under the League for a number of reasons. The League's membership was never universal; it contained only a part of the global community. In spite of Woodrow Wilson's best efforts, and the sacrifice of his health to mobilize public opinion, the United States never joined the League. The Soviet Union, Germany, Austria, Hungary, Bulgaria, and Turkey were omitted from the original list. The U.S.S.R. never entered. Germany became a member in 1926, but withdrew in 1933.

To oppose all aggression in principle was one thing, but actually to undertake military action when it occurred on somebody else's territory was another. Major test cases came in 1931 with the Japanese attack on Manchuria and in 1935 when Italy attacked Ethiopia. The League put some economic sanctions into force against Italy. But in neither case were members of the League willing to mount military opposition.

World War II strengthened earlier convictions about security's indivisibility. It also marked the final failure of the League's ambitious attempt at collective security. The survivors of World War II built the U.N. espousing the more modest ambition of "a limited collective security system" or "a selective security system" (Padelford et al., 1976:496).

U.N. practice has built on the League's experience. The U.N., like the League, did not include many nations when it was formed. The most important long-lasting omission was Communist Chinese representation in general membership and the Security Council. Gradually, however, the U.N. has filled the gaps, including Chinese representation, and come close to a truly representative national membership (cf. Kim, 1978).

In addition to achieving near-global membership, the shapers of the U.N. tried to strengthen the decisionmaking process in military situations. The U.N. Charter provides that the Security Council can reach decisions to bind all U.N. members. Article 47 of the U.N. Charter establishes a Military Staff Committee, responsible to the Security Council, and consisting of the Chiefs of Staff of the Security Council's permanent members. Article 47 also implies the possibility of a permanent central military force through which U.N. institutions might take collective action (cf. Naidu, 1975; Saksena, 1974).

The General Assembly in 1950 passed the Uniting for Peace Resolution, through which the Assembly could recommend collective military measures by two-thirds vote. The General Assembly used this procedure to identify North Korea as an aggressor against South Korea in 1950, and authorized a U.N. military force, consisting of components from the United States and a number of other nations, to fight in South Korea.

The U.N. has subsequently created limited collective military forces at lower levels to conduct particular peacekeeping operations. These have been noncoercive, nonmandatory, consent operations. Individual nations voluntarily have supplied forces for a limited period of time to help keep the conflicting parties apart without assigning guilt or blame. Major forces were sent to the Middle East (UNEF I and II) in 1956 and 1973, the Congo (ONUC) in 1960, and Cyprus (UNFICYP) in 1964. Other more limited U.N. forces of military observers have helped with disputes in Greece, various parts of the Middle East, Kashmir, and West Irian (cf. Pelcovits and Kramer, 1976:538; Rikhye et al., 1974; Wainhouse et al., 1973).

The U.N. system has achieved some substantial gains. It has reinforced the principle of common concern about any act of international violence, and it has developed the theory and practice of both military and non-military sanctions (cf. Combacau, 1974). Despite their improvements on the League's procedures, U.N. collective security and peacekeeping have still operated within severe limits. Binding decisions can only be made with the agreement of all the permanent members of the Security Council. Each permanent member has a veto. In cases of serious conflicts the U.N. Security Council has not regularly acted with collective decision to prevent or reduce violence.[22] The General Assembly has taken major responsibilities in some instances, such as in Korea; yet the political basis for continued peacekeeping has been too limited for generally effective action.

The U.N. has not developed a strong permanent central military capability. The Military Staff Committee has met in the formalistic ritual described in Box 3-1. Trygve Lie, the first U.N. Secretary General, made two attempts to expand this central U.N. capability. In 1948 he tried to create a uniformed guard and in 1952 "a UN Legion composed of volunteers but recruited on a national basis." Both attempts were "choked off by the Permanent Members of the Security Council" (Auma-Osolo, 1976:19).

Though nations have volunteered contingents for particular peacekeeping operations, no permanent military forces are available. Where forces were created, there have been significant conflicts over personnel and funding levels, as well as over national contributions. And regrettably, when mobilized, these forces have not always kept the peace.

There are many apparent reasons for the failure of international organizations to compile a more impressive record in peacekeeping and collective security. The international legal ground underneath these activities is shaky. The U.N. General Assembly has undertaken responsibilities that the Charter originally outlined for the Security Council. Further, in spite of substantial efforts, the U.N. has been unable to elaborate more than a very general definition of international aggression.

The very idea of collective security as it has been developed through the League of Nations and the U.N. is in direct opposition to the international legal right of neutrality. If states are compelled to act against a breach of the peace, they cannot simultaneously remain free of the conflict.

General collective security can conflict with more limited efforts to provide security. Article 51 of the U.N. Charter recognizes the legitimacy of initial "individual or collective self-defense if an armed attack occurs"

Box 3-1

THE U.N. MILITARY STAFF COMMITTEE

Military Meeting at U.N. Is a Ritual
By Kathleen Teltsch

UNITED NATIONS, N.Y., Jan. 18—On alternative Thursdays, a group of beribboned admirals, generals and other officers arrive at the United Nations, descend to an obscure basement conference room and hold a meeting of the Military Staff Committee that follows a ritual virtually unvaried in 20 years.

They exchange greetings. They take their seats. And they attend to their agenda of business—usually consisting of fixing the date for their next meeting, which everyone knows will be on Thursday two weeks hence. This completed, with a final round of handshakes, they file out again and go their separate ways.

Rarely does the session last longer than four or five minutes—and that includes consecutive translations into three languages. For convenience, members usually stow their officers' caps in a handy rack intended for documents but never used for that purpose.

. . .

This has been going on for years, basically because the Charter provided for the creation of such a military committee and the five nations represented on it have political as well as practical reasons for retaining the exercise.

Established in an earlier climate of big-power friendliness, the committee was made up of representatives of the Security Council's permanent members—the United States, the Soviet Union, Britain, France and Nationalist China—and, among other duties, it was supposed to organize a world police force to help the Council keep peace.

For two years, the military leaders from the five met and labored—sometimes by night as well as day—without resolving basic problems. Sample: Should the proposed force be made up of equal contingents from each nation, and what constituted equivalent land, air and sea forces.

By 1948, in the midst of a deepening cold war, the parties openly acknowledged their deadlock. But the meetings continued, gradually dwindling to the present five-minute sessions.

Only when one of the regular club members departs—usually into retirement—do the private sessions last a bit longer to provide a proper farewell. Occasionally, once the formal business is over, there is some amiable conversation.

Once Vice Adm. Andrew McB. Jackson Jr., the United States top-ranking member, idly wondered aloud how long it might be before leap year would fall in such a way that the every-other-Thursday club could squeeze three meetings into February.

against a nation or nations. This is the basis for regional security agreements and national defense programs.

Violence involving nonnational actors has remained in limbo since the U.N. is not authorized to intervene in the domestic affairs of states (cf. Arntz, 1975).

Collective security also involves important political problems. As we noted in our discussion of international law, there is no central pole of power, no authority, no referee; no final arbiter; no central and decisive institution that can enforce a final decision. Authority is distributed at various points within the international system and limited to particular issues or situations.

In order for collective security to succeed, it depends on the general security, cooperation, and trust that it is supposed to help create. All nations have to be willing to unite against any nation that has committed violence against any one of them. In the most extreme cases, the system is an all-or-nothing affair that does not function unless everybody contributes and unless there are no major defectors. But it is precisely the situation of general insecurity and mutual distrust that makes this condition almost impossible to fulfill. Assistance to others involves risks and costs to oneself, and there can be no guarantee of reward or repayment. A number of nations may bear significant costs, but if their partners renege on obligations earlier assumed, then nobody reaps any benefits. Once the danger is over, those assisted may even turn out to be future enemies.

International organizations, to some extent, do increase systemic capabilities for conflict management (see Butterworth, 1978a, 1978b). Yet growth in their capabilities has not necessarily kept up with growth in the loads that they must carry. While the absolute number of international organizations has grown impressively, such structures have barely kept pace with the remarkable increase in the number of nations whose peace they are supposed to help keep.

International organizations themselves place new loads on their members, who are not necessarily ready to assume them. Membership in international organizations does not in itself lead to cooperative behavior, nor does it necessarily imply major integrative learning (cf. Russett, 1967:201). Members of international organizations, like participants in other arenas, are reluctant to pay substantial costs and enjoy the ride better if it is free. In its most extreme form, "the idea that everything could be obtained for nothing was an important element of the pattern of thought which shaped the League of Nations and the United Nations idea" (Schiffer, 1954:301).[23]

If collective security finally fails, it can produce the global war that it is supposed to avoid. If international security really is indivisible, and if it is breached in a major way at a particular point, then a collective military response involves the very real threat of world war. This is precisely what happened in the 1930s and 1940s when the Axis powers undertook their military initiatives and the Allies collectively resisted in the name of world peace and democracy.

War Relief

When war has broken out, the international legal doctrine of *jus in bello* aims to limit injury and damage. International organization activity for war relief helps implement this goal.

Soldiers themselves, families, or camp followers have historically cared for those injured by war. In our times the Red Cross, one of the oldest and most respected international nongovernmental organizations, has helped provide such assistance.

The International Committee of the Red Cross has contributed to the development of a humanitarian law of armed conflict through the Geneva conventions of 1949 and 1977. These agreements have given the Red Cross a right of access across battle lines, and an opportunity to apply humanitarian international law on the battlefield. For these and related efforts, the Red Cross has received Nobel Peace Prizes in 1917, 1944, and 1963 (cf. Forsythe, 1977, 1976a, 1975b; Freymond, 1976; Utter, 1976; Suter, 1974). Other international nongovernmental organizations that work in the same area include the American Friends Service Committee (cf. Yarrow, 1978) and Amnesty International; each group has received the Nobel Peace Prize—the Friends in 1947 and Amnesty International in 1977.

International governmental organizations have also been concerned with humanitarian and war relief. The League of Nations created a High Commissioner for Refugees and then an International Office for Refugees that received the Nobel Peace Prize in 1938. The U.N. has had a number of such agencies over the years—the U.N. Relief and Rehabilitation Administration (UNRRA), the International Refugee Organization (IRO), the U.N. Korean Reconstruction Agency (UNKRA), and the U.N. High Commissioner for Refugees (UNHCR), which was awarded the Nobel Peace Prize in 1954. These agencies and others have dealt with refugee problems caused by World War II, Korea, the Arab–Israeli conflict, and conflicts in various other parts of the world.

These contributions are important. At the same time it is hardly necessary to point out that international organizations have hardly eliminated war-related suffering.

National Government

National institutions and practices have served as examples for international structures, both in a general way and also for maintaining peace. Thus one author states that, "from territoriality resulted the concepts and institutions which characterized the interrelations of sovereign units, the modern state system. Modern international law . . . could then develop" (Herz, 1957:480).

Early techniques for conflict management were models for later ones. Different legal systems settled disputes differently in politically centralized or decentralized societies (cf. Bohannan, 1967:51). Some techniques of primitive societies and early city- or nation-states were forerunners of contemporary international legal and organizational activities. For example:

> During the fifteenth and sixteenth centuries, when Swiss internal peacemaking reached its fullest development, two general lines of procedure were utilized: disputes were settled either "in minne," meaning literally "in love," but connoting a process of friendly compromise embracing conciliation and mediation; or "in recht" ("in law")—i.e., by arbitration under the pacts (Lloyd, 1958:68–69).

Leaders of modern nation-states today use such methods to try and moderate international conflicts. Thus, recent U.S. Secretaries of State, and even the President of the United States, have tried to mediate and conciliate disputes between Israel and the Arab states (cf. Wank, 1978).

Nations have also acted independently to try and implement various aspects of the international law of war, though often in a partisan or incomplete way. Thus the United States took the lead in applying the doctrine of collective security to the Korean conflict in 1950. It helped prosecute Axis war criminals after World War II, and it tried Lt. Calley. The United States has also contributed to war relief. Following World War I, Herbert Hoover led a relief mission to Europe and particularly the Soviet Union. After World War II the United States began extensive foreign aid programs.

National government, in traditional theory, produces peace and limits violence within its own borders. Traditional political philosophy has held the nation-state to be the highest level of organizational achievement of which humanity is capable. If one accepts the idea that culture and civilization have either developed through natural progress or have been painfully created from a situation of original barbarism or chaos, then the nation-state is the logical precondition and guarantor of civilized interaction between human beings, the achievement of the good life, and the activity of "rational man." This view of the state has existed in the Hegelian view of history; in the cooperative, voluntaristic perspective found in social contract theorists beginning with Thomas Hobbes; and, finally, in the rational–legalistic view of bureaucracy taken by Max Weber (Young, 1975).

Contemporary research tends to confirm the idea that common government can be a force for domestic tranquility. Richardson's "statistics of deadly quarrels" between 1820 and 1945 suggest that a past history of domestic political stability is a predictor of future peace (1960b:190). He found that common government seems to have an internally "pacifying influence" that increases with the government's age. His figures suggest that the more years of common government, the fewer observed pairs of belligerents inside the common boundaries (cf. Wilkinson, 1980:33–36).

The comparative study of historical integration attempts in the North Atlantic area notes that good government was an important dimension of the "core area" around which a "security community" was built. The core usually had a substantial capacity to act that was a function of efficient administrative institutions as well as "size, power, and economic strength. . . . These core areas were larger, stronger, more advanced political units around which integration developed. . . . Furthermore, not only the existing capabilities, but the growth in those capabilities, seemed important" (Deutsch et al., 1957:138).

Domestic political institutions are not, however, sufficient by themselves to eliminate conflict within state boundaries. Richardson's statistics show that even the most extensive period of common government could eventually lead to belligerency (1960b:190). The comparative historical analysis of integration in the North Atlantic area found that, by themelves, governmental institutions might bring little net benefit. New political units cutting across national boundaries did relatively little to create security and moderate conflict in the absence of other appropriate background conditions (Deutsch et al., 1957:81–83; cf. Nardin, 1971).

EXCHANGE AND LANGUAGE

In addition to bureaucracy, exchange and language are the other major aggregative strands that bind the global system together. Exchange includes socioeconomic dimensions of technology while language involves its psychocultural aspects.

Both exchange and language appear to have grown over time. Exchange relationships rely on division of labor and specialization. In the simplest human societies, these relationships are based on natural biological capabilities, for example, differentiation of roles between sexes or generations. Exchanges in modern society are much more substantial and complex. Natural human capabilities have been augmented by artificial specializations, the cumulative results of discovery or invention.[24]

In the contemporary world, we call the exchange of goods and services across national boundaries international transactions. No reliable figures exist on the volume of international transactions throughout history, but modern modes of transportation have certainly increased the flow of goods and services into a much wider and denser pattern of global exchange than was possible in earlier times. Not only have contacts developed between larger numbers of groups and individuals, but the volume of transactions between them has grown. The activities of nation-states, businesses, philanthropic foundations, religious groups, revolutionary groups, labor, science, and many other organizations cross national boundaries. They exchange increasing numbers of treaties, agreements, materials, commodities, managers, experts, workers, and tourists. One indicator of the dramatic growth in global transactions is the dollar value of world trade. Between 1938 and 1976 the volume of international trade rose from about $25 billion to $1 trillion (U.N., 1978b:466–67; 1971:12–13).[25]

Exchanges in domestic markets differ from international transactions in important ways. First, the exchanges take place within, rather than between, national boundaries. Second, national bureaucratic structures coordinate domestic activities to a much greater extent. In any event, domestic exchanges have also increased over time.[26]

Language is a very special kind of discovery or invention, less easily grasped than bureaucracy or exchange. By language we mean "imagination"—images that can be, and are, communicated. In this wide sense, language has many facets. First it comprises the process of communication of images through pictures, words, and actions. Second, language comprehends filters, codes, or symbols, endowing sounds, gestures, or material objects with commonly understood meanings. These meanings are embedded in communities. They rest on collectively agreed perceptions, beliefs, attitudes. Such agreement works within limits. The meanings are not always definitive or precise. Often there are important ambiguities and ambivalences. Yet they establish a collective basis for communication. Finally, language includes the particular messages and bits of information themselves that are communicated.

Though we have little systematic historical data, it seems clear that the absolute level of international and domestic communication has also grown over time. Modern media—satellites, television, radio, journals, magazines, newspapers, letters, telegrams, telephones—transmit increased amounts of information. The relative balance between international and domestic communication has, however, not been stable. International communication appeared to advance particularly strongly at the end of the nineteenth century and the beginning of the twentieth. Yet following World War I, it seemed to fall off relative to domestic message exchange. A study of mail flows revealed that:

> The mean share of international mail was less than 14 per cent in 1880, indicating a low to fair level of international integration at that time. This average share of international mail rose to a fair level of world integration, or at least interdependence, with almost 30 per cent in 1913, but declined again to about 25 per cent for the average of the years 1928–34, and further to about 18 per cent for the period 1946–51, while still remaining above the lower limit of the "fair" category (Deutsch, 1960:151).

Causes of Exchange and Language

We reiterate that our model suggests no causal relation from peace or war to aggregation. This does not imply that peace or war does not influence exchange or language. It means, instead, that we cannot reliably specify whether the net result of their effects will be constructive or destructive.

International Transactions and Communications

Theories of international integration suggest that peace promotes the growth of international transaction and communication. In relatively stable environments, the benefits derived from gradual steps in community building have a chance to spill over easily into new areas of potential cooperation (cf. E. Haas, 1968; Mitrany, 1966; Deutsch et al., 1957).[27]

By the same logic, war may have negative effects on international transaction and communication. In the short run, wars can disrupt the settled flow of peaceful international relations. We see the nature of the effects in Figure 3-6, which shows absolute trade levels for the major European states between 1870 and 1914. It is particularly striking that the volume of trade turns sharply down for all countries near the beginning of World War I. Figure 3-7 outlines the pattern of relative European trade from 1928 to 1963. Lines here reflect not dollars, but the proportion of each partner's trade taken by others. From this figure we can sense a premonition of World War II. Relative trade between France and Germany dropped sharply before 1938. Relative trade between the European Six—Belgium, France, Germany, Italy, Luxembourg, the Netherlands—and the two Anglo-American states also declined during this time.

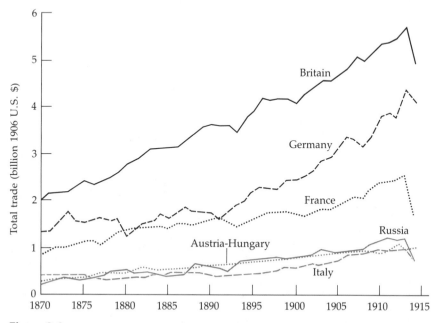

Figure 3-6

Absolute International Trade: Major European States, 1870–1915.
(SOURCE: *Nations in Conflict* by Nazli Choucri and Robert C. North. W. H. Freeman and Company. Copyright © 1975. P. 35.)

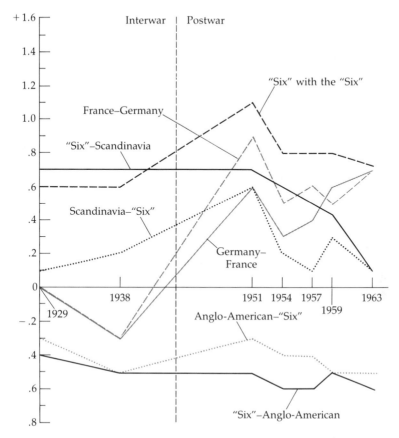

Figure 3-7
Relative Trade: Europe, 1928–1963. (NOTE: Trade figures as "indexes
of relative acceptance" that measure departure of imports from
values expected at random. SOURCE: Alker and Puchala, 1968:304.
Reprinted with permission of Macmillan Publishing Co., Inc., from
Quantitative International Politics, by J. David Singer. Copyright ©
1968 by The Free Press, a Division of the Macmillan Company.)

Wars may also have long-term destructive effects on international transaction and communication. Many analysts have suggested that the physical
damage of World War I, and the stipulations of the treaties that ended the
war, had a long lasting negative influence.[28]

Nevertheless, war need not always hinder international transaction
and communication. Other analysts believe that the general economic effects of World War I were relatively short-lived and insignificant. They take
particular issue with the assumption that World War I was a primary cause
of the Great Depression of the following decade.[29]

War may damage some economic relationships, but it also generates new ones. The coming of war may induce allies to undertake denser forms of trade, assistance, and communication than would otherwise occur. Figure 3-6 shows us that relative trade of the Scandinavian nations—Denmark, Norway, and Sweden—with the European Six increased in the 1930s.

Positive wartime transaction and communication may outlast the immediate wartime situation that created them and carry over into peacetime. Thus, the Allied cooperation in both world wars formed the skeleton for the new postwar order. We see in Figure 3-7 that while Anglo–American relative trade with the European Six had dropped during the 1930s, it bounced up in the immediate postwar period.

Even relations between enemies may have constructive implications. During wartime, negotiations occur to define hostilities and to bring them to a close (cf. Rogers, 1976; Randle, 1973; Iklé, 1971; Fox, 1970; Kecskemeti, 1964). The basis of cooperation may then carry over and expand when peace is reestablished. Following World War II, the Allies provided substantial assistance to rebuild the former Axis societies. The effect was to lay the basis for growth of relative trade among all the Western European states—allies and enemies—and to help integrate the Federal Republic of Germany, Italy, and Japan firmly into the Western postindustrial world. We see some of the result in Figure 3-7 as relative trade between France and Germany rises dramatically between 1938 and 1951.[30]

National Markets and Communities

The effects of wars on national markets and communities are also ambivalent, sometimes positive, sometimes negative.

Benefits of War

A substantial body of literature suggests that warlike societies reap important material benefits. In the Darwinist evolutionary view, war reflects the most basic dynamic of life, the struggle for species survival, and is a fundamental instrument of human progress. Through trial by combat, war encourages the reproduction of the fittest societies and of the strongest groups and individuals within them. The strongest should live and prosper; the weakest should die or suffer on the battlefield or as a result of war's outcome (cf. Naroll and Divale, 1976:100–101; Baumgartner, 1970; Davie, 1968; Goldschmidt, 1959; Nicolai, 1919).

If we review contemporary history, we can see that some states—for example, the United States, U.S.S.R, and China—seem to have drawn collective strength and identity from the suffering of war and revolution. Even countries that were recently and humiliatingly defeated in war, like Japan, or partitioned, like Germany, have reemerged very strongly in the postwar world.

From a contemporary economic perspective, war may appear at least partly functional. It requires a relatively efficient logistic support base. War brings new government planning and activity to domestic markets, coordinating existing economic activity and encouraging accelerated growth. War can be "a stimulant . . . its destruction may remove blocks to change, and . . . on rare occasions it gives rise to a discontinuity which may favor growth" (Kindleberger, 1964:319, 328–29; cf. Olsson, 1976; Huston, 1966).

War may appear to offer an incentive for the fuller utilization of resources that might otherwise have lain idle. Large national defense establishments sop up surplus unemployed labor and generate income for major segments of the population. War seems to be an important fiscal weapon in the counterrecessionary arsenal, superior even to public works.

> Only the massive military spending of World War II had ended the Great Depression of the 1930's. The 15 percent unemployment rate of the Great Depression was cured only by the enormous increase in military spending from about $1,500,000,000 in 1940 to more than $81,000,000,000 in 1945. After the early post–World War II boom, unemployment began climbing again. In 1949 it reached a postwar high of nearly 6 percent. Once again, though, the massive upsurge of Korean War military spending cured the problem and reduced unemployment to less than 3 percent of the work force (Fitzgerald, 1972:61; cf. Janeway, 1968:175).

The economy of affluence seems intricately connected with war. Peace-related arms reductions threaten workers in a whole variety of defense-related fields. At the least, if there are reductions in defense spending, there may be substantial dislocation in such industries and a good deal of individual discomfort and inconvenience, if not hardship (cf. Udis, 1973; U.S. ACDA, 1972; Berkowitz, 1970; Benoit and Boulding, 1963).

War appears to help to eliminate obsolete factories and equipment and to dispose of surplus goods. A theory of war as the disposition of surplus values depicts war as a kind of price-maintenance or price-fixing mechanism in which surplus wealth and population can be disposed of in order to keep up the value and values of those who remain (Bouthoul, 1970:232–34; Lewin, 1967).

War may encourage mechanical or electronic innovation, and defense research and development may benefit civilian society. In earlier times, war contributed to mass production, mechanization, and standardization. The innovations of modern aerospace, naval, and land warfare have also provided some benefits to the advanced consumer economy (cf. Grand-Jean, 1967:431; Nef, 1950).

In poor societies, war can imply forced development—the rapid conversion of traditional agricultural markets into industrialized ones. Military rule in Third World states is thus often justified on the grounds that the military are the most effective agents of modernization in those societies. Military elites appear in many settings as agents of constructive national change.

As we have previously noted, war can foster belief systems that promote national cohesion. The threat of danger and the shared experience of violence can help draw together the political community against outsiders.[31]

War may also have beneficial effects below the national level. For example, war may encourage greater involvement in collective cultural life and more interpersonal communication between family members (cf. Cohen and Dotan, 1976). Increased family cohesion and caring may carry over into peacetime. Thus, the end of World War II seemed to produce a renewed valuation of children, with beneficial effects. In some places adolescent delinquency rates were substantially below normal among children born between 1946 and 1947 (McKissack, 1974).

Costs of War

Despite some apparent benefits, war also has harmful effects on national markets and communities. Mumford states the argument in its most general form when he says that "the one massive cause for both industrial and social retardation that the technical historians have so far slighted, is the repeated, indeed chronic, devastations and decimations of war" (1967:249). From this point of view, war is less like investment than consumption or waste.[32]

Some war costs are direct and can be measured relatively easily. Thus, Table 3-10 estimates total direct costs for major U.S. wars by adding the total original costs for military forces, production, and other similar factors during wartime; veterans' benefits; and interest payment on war loans. By 1970 these direct costs were estimated at $352 billion for Vietnam, and two-thirds of a trillion dollars for World War II.

The direct costs, large as they are, seem puny beside possible indirect costs of war. Such indirect costs may include serious weakening, perhaps even disintegration, of political communities. The historical decline of states like Spain, Portugal, the Netherlands, England, and France over the last centuries has been attributed, in part, to the costs of the wars in which they engaged. World Wars I and II helped produce the dissolution of political structures and formal ties between most European states and their overseas components; massive domestic violence in Russia and China; and the dismemberment of Austria-Hungary and Germany.

Wars provide a substitute for demolition, but they seem a good deal less efficient. They eliminate some obsolete factories and equipment, but they also do important damage to agricultural, industrial, and infrastructural foundations of economic systems.

The development of modern armaments implies warlike damages and costs even in time of peace. For example, one of the most serious problems of nuclear weapons involves their testing. In 1945, the United States dropped nuclear weapons on Hiroshima and Nagasaki with devastating effects. Subsequently, the United States and the Soviet Union tested succeeding generations of nuclear weapons above ground. These explosions involved serious changes in the earth's atmosphere, and the fallout effects of radioactive isotopes in atmospheric testing could be expected to lead to severe genetic damage. Today, in spite of the limits imposed by the partial nuclear test ban treaty, some nations—France, China, India—continue to test above ground.

Modern armaments also produce structural damage of unknown consequence to the biosphere. For example, in the last major U.S. atmospheric testing before the signature of the partial nuclear test ban treaty, high-level nuclear devices were exploded over Johnston Island in the Pacific. These tests were partly designed to measure the effects of high-level blasts on military communications and to assess their implications for central command and control of dispersed U.S. nuclear capabilities. The Johnston Island tests accomplished substantial disruption of trans-Pacific communication. They also produced effects in the outer layer of the stratosphere—the Van Allen radiation belt—which many scientists believe to be highly dangerous.

Nations with major nuclear arsenals have subsequently done their testing underground. Such underground testing can be expected sooner or later to produce serious geological effects and damage because of increased stresses in the earth's crust. The issue was most publicly joined at the time of the "Cannikin" test in November 1971, off Amchitka Island in the Aleutians. Though the worst fears of the pessimists were not immediately realized, nobody can be certain about eventual or cumulative effects of continued underground testing, particularly if explosive yields are increased (cf. SIPRI, 1979b, 1976b; R. B. Russell, 1974).

Another negative aspect of war is that it distorts collective investment. War efforts can draw on some slack that exists in most domestic economies. Thus, the national defense expansion of World War II came partly from previously unrealized product and reduced personal consumption. Ultimately, however, defense expenditures take resources away from areas that contribute much larger multipliers to general affluence. States with higher levels of Gross National Product (GNP) tend to devote a greater proportion of it to defense (Beer, 1972b; Russett, 1970b:Ch. 4). Presumably, they do so because they can better afford it than small countries. Yet even in large states, domestic markets have finite capacities. Goods and services provided for the defense sector have to be taken, at least in part, from others.

The competition between military and civilian sectors for resources is traditionally expressed in economics as the "guns or butter" problem. One has to choose between one or the other, or the amounts of each that one is satisfied to get along with. Military products do not necessarily return to the economy. They are unlike civilian capital investment, which helps to produce future generations of goods, or consumption, which contributes to the maintenance of the working force.

Table 3-10
Direct War Costs: U.S., 1776–1970.[a]

War	Estimated Total War Costs	Original War Costs[b]	Veterans' Benefits			Estimated Interest Payments on War Loans	
			Total Costs Under Present Laws[c]	Percent of Original War Costs	Total Costs to 1970	Total	Percent of Original War Costs
Vietnam conflict[a]	352,000	110,000	220,000[e]	200[e]	2,461	22,000[f]	20[f]
Korean conflict	164,000	54,000	99,000	184	15,016	11,000	20
World War II	664,000	288,000	290,000	100	87,445	86,000	30
World War I	112,000	26,000	75,000	290	45,585	11,000	42
Spanish-American War	6,460	400	6,000	1,505	5,436	60	15
Civil War (Union only)	12,952	3,200	8,580	260	8,570	1,172	37
Mexican War	147	73	64	88	64	10	14
War of 1812	158	93	49	53	49	16	17
American Revolution	190	100	70	70	70	20	20

[a]All costs in millions of dollars, except percent columns.

[b]Based on expenditures of Departments of the Army and Navy to World War I and major national security expenditures thereafter. Usually the figures begin with the year the war began but in all cases they extend one year beyond the end of the actual conflict.

[c]To World War I, estimates are based on Veterans Administration data. For World War I, World War II, and Korean conflict, estimates are those of the 1956 report of the President's Commission on Veterans' Pensions plus 25 percent (the increase in the average value of benefits since the Commission made its report).

[a]Estimates based on assumption that war would end by June 30, 1970 (except for veterans' benefit costs to 1970). Occupation costs not included. Background data:

	Billion U.S. \$
Original cost	
a. Major national security expenditures for Vietnam conflict, 1965–70 fiscal years	108.5
b. Cost of supporting American personnel in S. Vietnam, 1954–64, at \$25,000 per man per year	1.5
Total	110.0
Veterans' benefits	
Medium estimate, 200 percent of original cost[b]	220.0
Interest on war debt	
Medium estimate, 20 percent of original cost[c]	22.0
Total, medium estimate	352.0

[b]Medium-level estimate of 200 percent (high, 300; low, 100) based on figures expressing relationship of veterans' benefits payments to original costs of other major U.S. wars.

[c]Medium-level estimate of 20 percent (high, 30; low, 10) based on figures showing interest payments on war loans as percentage of original costs of other major U.S. wars.

SOURCE: U.S. Department of Commerce, Bureau of the Census (1975:1140).

123

War does not necessarily enhance economic growth or innovation in either more or less developed national economies. For example:

> The experience of the war [World War II] was that only certain industries, in particular textiles, cement, and processed foods, were successfully started or developed in most of the poorer countries of the world. . . . Only in Canada and Australia was there a large and decisive shift towards industrialization (Milward, 1977:354–55).

Nor does defense spending necessarily produce higher employment. Modern defense production is very expensive. It is capital intensive and uses highly skilled labor. If defense expenditures take the place of other public spending, they may produce fewer jobs. The statistical relationship between war and employment is also highly questionable (M. Haas, 1974:217; cf. Nincic and Cusack, 1979).

Defense expenditure detracts from spending on public education, health, and special welfare services as well as private capital investment. To the extent that war expenditures work against or postpone personal consumption and welfare services, the present generation must bear the cost. At the same time, the preparations for international violence restrict the opportunities of future generations by reducing their inheritance in a variety of economic and social dimensions, leaving them materially poorer, worse educated, less healthy (cf. Lee, 1973; Udis, 1973; Culyer and Jacobs, 1972; Russett, 1970b:Chs. 5 and 6; Benoit and Boulding, 1963).[33]

The costs in lost opportunities of heavy defense spending may, ironically, damage ultimate military strength. Civilian capabilities and production facilities that might have been built could be converted into wartime uses; and investment in civilian health, education, and welfare and in fixed capital investment would have high payoffs, at least during conditions of mobilization for subnuclear war.

Wartime production is not necessarily efficient (see Melman, 1975; 1970b; J. R. Fox, 1974; Fitzgerald, 1972; Kaufman, 1970; Proxmire, 1970). Nor does war necessarily enhance business profits. Traditional Marxist–Leninist analysis suggests that business interests may find it profitable to use international violence, particularly to expand and maintain their access to raw materials, labor, and markets. But war in our century has not necessarily worked in this way. International violence either has been generally unrelated to business profit margins or has actually diminished profitability in some related businesses (Pearson and Baumann, 1977; Finsterbusch and Griesman, 1975).

War need not contribute to scientific progress. War stimulates natural and social scientists to improve military weapons and operations or to investigate questions of war and peace (cf. Ahmad and Wilke, 1973; Ellis, 1973). However, such research may cost dearly in lost opportunities. Scientific activity in other areas may fail to develop as rapidly as it might otherwise have done. High war casualties, moreover, may diminish the general level of scientific competence in subsequent generations (cf. Simonton, 1976a, 1976b; Melman, 1965).

War has complex demographic effects. Figure 3-8 shows the population distribution of Germany between 1910 and 1950. The 1910 graph shows the traditional normal population pyramid. The 1925 pyramid reflects the damage of World War I. It shows a strong indentation in male population between ages 25 and 40. Further, children below the age of ten are about half the expected proportion, reflecting the absence of fathers. "The relative lack of ten year olds is due to the small number of births during the war, the paucity of adult males to loss of fighting men" (Mausner and Bahn, 1974:353).

> In the pyramid of 1939, both features noted above persist. However, each of them appears at a later age. That is, the waist-like constriction has moved from age 10 to a little past age 20, and the relative paucity of men has moved upwards from ages 25 to 40 toward 40 to 55. In addition, there is a small constriction opposite ages five and six representing fewer births and, possibly, increased mortality among infants and young children, during the economic depression of the early 1930's. The decrease in births is probably due to low birth rates as well as to the paucity of young adults of reproductive age.
>
> The final pyramid (1950) continues to show all of the previous trends, but at successively later ages. Additional irregularities below age ten suggest marked fluctuations in the birth rates during the years immediately preceding the date of the pyramid. The large proportion of ten year olds may reflect pronatalist Nazi policies in the early years of World War II. The smaller percentage of children at about five years of age is due to the lowered birth rates consequent upon the continued prosecution of the war and the collapse of the Third Reich (Mausner and Bahn, 1974:353).

Figure 3-9 depicts the generational distribution of the French population in 1931. The graph of French citizens of native origin shows war-caused indentations like those of the German population. Naturalized citizens and foreigners living in France, however, are dramatically overrepresented in the middle age groups. There is a particularly large number of foreign men between ages 20 and 40.[34]

War may appear to produce the benefit of enhanced community spirit in the short run, but this solidarity may be superficial and temporary as the excitement of anticipated adventure gives way to the hard reality of casualties. In wars like Korea and Vietnam "public support declines as the length and the costs of the war grow, but the decline is steeper at the early part of the war and slower toward its end" (Mueller, 1973:266; cf. Burstein, 1979).

National communications systems can be disrupted by war, particularly if the war is carried on in home territory. Wars can sound the death knell for traditional belief systems. World War I, for example, marked the general end of the concept of monarchical legitimacy.

War may bring the destruction of the fittest societies or individuals, rather than their survival. War is not necessarily an efficient mechanism

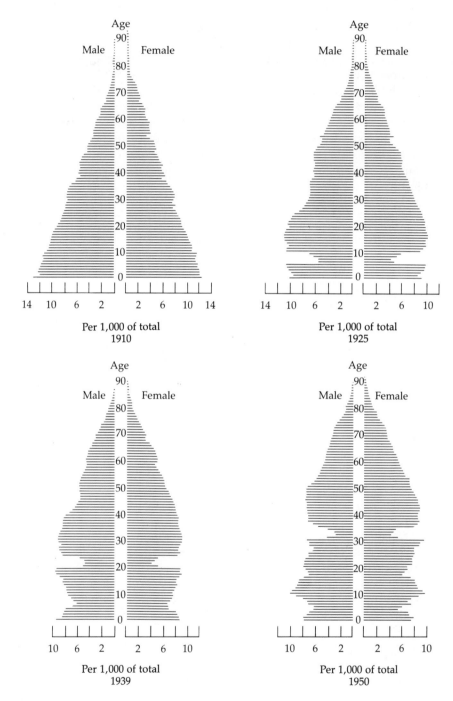

Figure 3-8
Population Distribution: Germany 1910–1950. (SOURCE: Mausner and Bahn, 1974:233.)

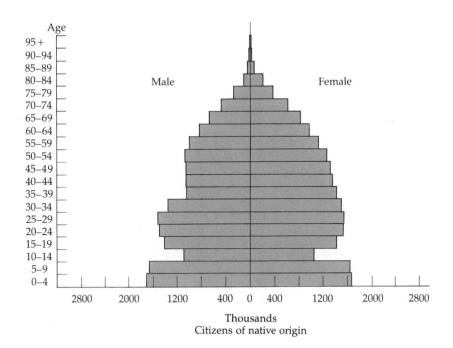

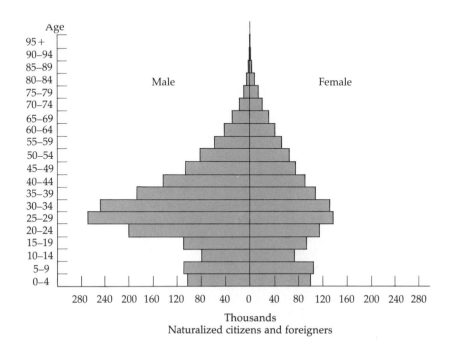

Figure 3-9
Population Distribution: France, 1931. (SOURCE: Kirk, 1946:118.)

for beneficial species selection. The parents of future generations may be those who have been found physically unfit to undertake military service. Modern war involves the indiscriminate death of masses of human beings on the sides of both the winners and the losers, and long-range delivery of atomic, biological, and chemical weapons implies mass destruction of civilian areas. Among those most likely to survive immediate effects may be the military and political leaders who have access to hardened, filtered, and well-provisioned sites. Long-term genetic consequences can vary with the strength and direction of the wind.

War leaves long-term physical and psychological problems for many of those who do survive, its human residuals. War obviously produces severe physical damage to all parts of the human body. Much of this is immediately evident in direct battle deaths and casualties. Other damage takes longer to appear. War-induced diseases have drawn out consequences for their many victims. In modern war, there may be radioactive effects from exposure to battlefield blasts, tests, or leakage of atomic weapons. There can also be long-term damage from destructive chemicals. The mustard gas used in World War I caused severe long-term disabilities as have the defoliants and herbicides used in Vietnam (cf. Norman, 1975; Koslow, 1977).

Physical injury can have harmful psychological effects. Organic damage to the brain or central nervous system—brain injuries, lesions, or indirect impacts—may contribute to pathological behavior, including anxiety, depression, and even criminality.[35]

The experience of war, even without physical injury, may produce psychoses and neuroses of varying severity. Those who go off to war often do so enfolded in the myth of the warrior. This myth may not survive the reality of combat (cf. Lifton, 1973; Gray, 1970). Combat conditions produce and exacerbate general anxiety and specific fears of separation, abandonment, disfigurement, and death. After returning from war, veterans may be depressed, apathetic, withdrawn, detached, and alienated—numbed in their emotions and memories. They may have a good deal of shame, guilt, irritability, resentment, hostility, anger, hysteria, rage. They may have difficulty in relating to other people, job instability, and loneliness. They may be more susceptible to physical disease, drug abuse, alcoholism. Finally, they may have relatively high suicidal and assaultive tendencies.[36]

Prisoners of war suffer psychological effects similar to those produced by combat. The "homecoming syndrome" of military prisoners of war[37] is similar to the "survivor syndrome" of those incarcerated in concentration or internment camps. Those people held in concentration camps experience similar "psychic traumatization" (Eitinger, 1961). Their symptoms include

> chronic anxiety states, cued off by nightmares and sleeplessness at night, and disturbing associations and screen memories during the day. [They may be]

continuously depressed, unable to enjoy themselves, and unable to establish new interpersonal contacts. [Such individuals react adversely to] any additional stress, [and have] feelings of great pessimism. [Even] many years after liberation, [survivors show] feelings of envy, suspiciousness, hostility, and mistrust toward the world and other people, the whole constituting what might be termed a paranoid personality. [There are] difficulties of functioning in everyday life: social maladjustment expressed in work and interpersonal difficulties, withdrawal from social life, and sexual and parenthood difficulties (Barocas, 1970:53–58; cf. Bolewski, 1972; Antonovsky et al., 1971; Eitinger, 1970, 1969, 1964; Koranyi, 1969).

Later personality disorders tend to be more severe for younger inmates of concentration camps. One study shows individuals who had been interned in Germany during World War II in their early 20s appeared particularly afflicted by nervousness, anxiety, asthenia, hypochondria, and neurocirculatory symptoms (Meyers et al., 1974).

Similar problems appear among those who do not fight. Thus, one study of American draft evaders in Canada during the Vietnam War found feelings of "guilt, depression, anger, anxiety, dehumanization, alienation, and shame" (Levine, 1974:24). Even among those men with high draft numbers (a low chance of being drafted) there was substantial guilt.[38]

Military wives' psychological problems center around themes of desertion, role ambiguity, ambivalence toward the return of the husband, repressed anger, sexuality, and social isolation.[39]

War neuroses extend back from the front lines in a number of other directions. Civilians may be directly exposed to violence through nuclear attack, military occupation, or guerrilla fighting. Such experience also leaves permanent marks, for example, depression, anxiety, and weakness. In Japan, the sudden postwar overthrow of the old social establishment and traditional value system appeared even to exacerbate asthma and allergic disorders (Ikemi et al., 1974).[40]

War affects subsequent generations (cf. Krystal and Niederland, 1971). Undernutrition as a result of wartime conditions can retard children's brain growth and permanently impair mental performance (Stein et al., 1975). The postwar end of food scarcity, on the other hand, may contribute to overfeeding, which in later life can produce *anorexia nervosa,* or neurotic self-starvation (Duddle, 1973).

In wartime children have to deal with a variety of stresses, including direct violence, danger, parental fear, bereavement, disruption of normal nurturant processes, and parental absence. These stresses produce such common wartime problems as general anxiety, fears of separation and abandonment, role distortion, sleep disorders, personality displacement, aggression, and suicide.

Family separation and parental absence can have permanent effects on children's emotional growth. While the institutionalization of children in a safe but distant place during war might be preferable to the risk of bodily damage or incarceration in harsher quarters with adults, children raised in such environments tend to be more withdrawn and distant and to have problems of individual and group-oriented identity and self-esteem. In extreme cases, incomplete families contribute to children's schizoid neuroses. The effects of such separation carry into adulthood. There is some evidence that a child's war experience is related to subsequent marital discord, and it may also be connected to extreme political belief and identification later in life.[41]

Some studies have found that concentration camp survivors became "parents who carried on almost desperate forced attempts to attain identifications for themselves through their children." As parents, they used their children as "transferential objects and forced the child into a destructive identification." The parents, "being terrified of their own aggression and unable to express it, [might] broadcast explicit or implicit cues for their children to act out and vicariously gratify the wishes of the parents." The children of concentration camp survivors also displayed aspects of the survival syndrome, including such symptoms as "explosive aggressive behavior" and "severe depressive reactions" (Barocas, 1970:57; cf. Davidson, 1980; Epstein, 1979; Gay et al., 1974).

These problems are not negligible. Veterans alone in the U.S. civilian population numbered almost 2 million by the end of the Civil War and almost 30 million at the end of the Vietnam War (U.S. Department of Commerce, 1975:1144).

Effects of Exchange and Language

We have been discussing the uncertain effects of peace and war, their alleged benefits and costs, for the structures and processes of exchange and language. We must now reverse the coin and ask how exchange and language affect peace and war. Traditional political theory suggests that international transactions and communications, national markets and communities help to create and maintain peace, to prevent war, to limit violence when it breaks out. Some evidence supports this theory though not so strongly as we might like. International transactions and communications, national markets and communities, do show positive direct effects. We must be careful to note, however, that these effects are weak and, in many circumstances, not distinctly visible.[42]

International Transactions and Communications

Traditional theory suggests that international transactions enhance peace and reduce war in a number of ways. They help create and maintain relationships of benefit of all parties. Thus they contribute to the development of common interests and a cooperative internationalization of outlook. Ideally, international trade contributes to prosperity. Wider exchange enhances the production of optimal amounts of goods and services. Output can be increased and costs lowered by efficient arrangement of the factors of production, by taking advantage of economies of scale and specialization (cf. Blainey, 1973:Ch. 6).[43]

The expansion of trade implies the substitution of peaceful for warlike behavior. Increased trade is a normal part of civil society that should divert effort from military activities to more constructive pursuits. Conversely, "when foreign trade is scanty, unemployment is rife, . . . governments may think the time suitable for setting more men to work on preparations for war. Hitler did that on a vast scale when he first came to power" (Richardson, 1960a:225). States should be reluctant to make war on their trading partners because of the economic costs. Interrupting the flow of goods and services can not only produce domestic hardship but also weaken any war effort.

Empirical evidence shows that international transactions may indeed have some pacifying effect. A cross-cultural survey covering 2,500 years found that, in general, trade was "more frequent in more peaceful decades than in less peaceful ones" (Naroll et al., 1974:333–34). One implication of this finding is that the trade may have contributed to the peace.

In the recent history of the North Atlantic international system, international transactions were an important element in the construction of "security communities," areas with low or nonexistent expectations of war (Deutsch et al., 1957:144). Studies of the Western European supranational communities following World War II also suggest a "spillover" dynamic through which economic cooperation and trade in a limited sphere exerted an expansive logic on other types of relations. Trade, in this situation, pointed toward international community and away from violence (see Lindberg and Scheingold, 1970; E. Haas, 1968).

Long-term trends of increasing international trade may have had a positive influence, but it has been limited. Figure 3-6 shows a general long-term growth in total European trade for the last third of the nineteenth century with acceleration in the first decade of the twentieth century. This trend may have contributed to the general European peace in the nineteenth century. It did not, however, hold up in the first part of the twentieth century and was insufficient to prevent World War I.[44]

Short-term trends in trade may also have an impact, but again, of a modest sort. Figure 3-7 suggests a decline in the relative trade between Germany and France following 1929. If trade had a powerful, immediate influence, we would expect that war would have occurred immediately. The 1930s, of course, were quite violent; yet World War II did not break out in full force until 1939 (cf. Rosecrance et al., 1977; Pelowski, 1971:280).

Other evidence casts a more serious shadow on the assumption that trade is an easy road to peace. For example, a study of a global sample of nations from 1955 to 1957 reveals no significant association between over a dozen measures of foreign trade and war incidence or casualties (Rummel, 1972:363). And another study of trade and war during the period 1954–1963 finds that clusters of nations in the same trading group are "more than twice as likely to fight each other" than chance might have predicted (Russett, 1967:198).[45]

Migration, like trade, has often been viewed as a direct bond that can link nations together. It seems plausible: migrants contribute their capital, skills, and labor to their new societies. They intermarry and have children. At the same time, we must note that there is little evidence systematically testing the assumption that all, or even most of migration's effects are good. If we are willing to accept the idea provisionally, we must bear in mind that migrants also bring problems. Attachments to their countries of origin may promote involvement in foreign wars (M. Haas, 1974:218). Further, problems in religious, ethnic, and socioeconomic assimilation may increase domestic conflict (cf. Hibbs, 1973:65–80, 173–75, 181; Choucri, 1974b; Feldstein, 1967; Kirk, 1946).

Traditional theory proposes that, in addition to trade and migration, international communication provides information and contacts, encouraging images, values and patterns of identification that help create and maintain peace and reduce the likelihood of war. Societies have traditionally conducted peaceful relations through communications that included oral and written messages as well as elaborate sets of symbols and ritual activities. These have provided the means for doing business together and a channel for showing respect (cf. Ginsberg, 1975; Ostrower, 1965; Bozeman, 1960:29–32; Numelin, 1950).

In the modern world, national leaders periodically pay visits of state to other countries to meet their decisionmakers face to face. Diplomatic practice provides accepted channels of communication at lower levels. Routine diplomacy encompasses many levels of information exchange, including representation, intelligence gathering, and the earnest of good will and good faith (cf. Nicolson, 1950; Thayer, 1959).

If conflict threatens, "hot lines" of direct communication between decisionmakers in major capitals provide additional fast and reliable communication channels.[46] Top-level officials travel quickly between national capitals. An example is U.S. "shuttle diplomacy" in the Middle East. Similar activities, though slower paced and less visible, attempted unsuccessfully to avoid World War II (cf. Burns and Bennett, 1974).

Other sectors of modern society participate in international communications. Mass media report the activities of political leaders: their articulation of symbols of peace and community and their attempts to resolve conflicts. Under some circumstances the media can enhance peace. Thus "media diplomacy" helped produce the dramatic Egyptian–Israeli peace initiatives of 1978 (cf. Davison, 1974).

Civil servants and businessmen in the international organizations of New York, Brussels, Geneva, Paris, and elsewhere exchange information and reach agreements. Presumably, they also contribute to establishing more general patterns of cooperation. Government-sponsored exchange programs of opinion leaders and private travel are symbols of trust and good will that presumably help draw states and peoples toward friendlier relations (cf. Nye and Keohane, 1972; Angell, 1969).

Social scientists have developed new tools and methods to assist in conflict management. For example, "controlled communication" projects have brought together

> representatives of nations or national [ethnic] communities involved in an active conflict, for face-to-face communication in a relatively isolated setting, free from governmental and diplomatic protocol. Discussions, following a relatively unstructured agenda, take place under the guidance of social scientists who are knowledgeable both about group process and about conflict theory. The talks are designed to produce changes in the participants' perceptions and attitudes and thus to facilitate creative problem-solving (Kelman, 1972:168, discussing Doob, 1970; Burton, 1969; cf. Doob, 1974).

Finally, professional and business colleagues, friends and relatives, write, wire, and call their counterparts in other countries.

While such international communication may do some good, its effectiveness is probably limited. The 2,500-year cross-cultural survey noted that diplomatic activity "had little if any effect on war frequency." The same study found "exchanges of culturally influential elites such as visiting teachers, students, missionaries, royal brides, entertainers, or hostages to be more frequent in peaceful decades." Such exchanges undoubtedly helped cement international friendship, but they also reflected it. Thus the authors suggest that

> perhaps cultural factors do indeed promote peace. But perhaps it is only that cultural factors are more common in time of peace than in time of war. Obviously, when two nations are at war, trade is discouraged between them. Presumably, when two nations are at war, influential elites are not so likely to visit back and forth, either (Naroll et al., 1974:332–35).

In the contemporary world, summit meetings by themselves do not necessarily produce more peaceful international relations (cf. Thompson and Modelski, 1977). Constructive international communications between belligerents typically decline before and during wars. At the level of mass behavior, a 1955–1957 global sample showed no relationship between mail and either the incidence of wars or of war deaths (Rummel, 1972:363; cf. McGowan and Shapiro, 1973:134–35).

If international communication has a substantial positive effect, it should help promote and maintain a strong "ideological loyalty to an international order" within domestic communities (Modelski, 1961:139). Different strata of contemporary society do identify to some extent with international symbols. Thus, most national political leaders pay lip service to the structures and processes of international community. Yet strong international loyalty does not generally exist. International identification is neither deep nor salient, particularly in conflict situations. Most people know very little about the U.N., much less care deeply about its fate and functions. At the regional level, the outlook is only slightly more encouraging. Thus, European opinion leaders have expressed support for the European community publicly and in surveys, and European school children are apparently more supranationally minded than in past generations (cf. Feld and Wilgen, 1977; Hero, 1977; Puchala, 1973; Lerner and Gorden, 1969; Inglehart, 1967). Yet the precise significance of such loyalties is unclear. General attitudes are not necessarily good predictors of behavior, especially if they conflict with other more deeply held values.

The evidence we have described here might be taken to contradict the theoretical position that international transactions and communications have an independent positive effect on peace and war. Such a judgment would probably be too harsh. The U.S. establishment of trade relations with the Soviet Union and China, and media diplomacy in the Middle East are particularly striking recent examples of the way in which international transactions and communications can help achieve greater cooperation. At the same time, the positive direct effects of international transactions and communications are limited. They may easily be offset by other negative factors in the environment.

National Markets and Communities

A widely accepted body of theory proposes that national markets and communities contribute to international and domestic peace in important ways. Liberal economists have long suggested that national markets help to produce higher standards of living, and good living conditions work to lessen frustrations that can lead to violence. Rich people should be more satisfied, have more to lose, or at least have better manners.[47]

Psychologists have held that identification with national communities should also help build and reinforce the skills, habits, and dispositions of general integrative learning. Freud described two kinds of emotional ties between people helping create peace. The first of these is a relatively primary bond, "relations resembling those towards a loved object, though without having a sexual aim." Today we might call this compassion (see Eckhardt, 1979, 1976, 1972; Rosenthal, 1972). The second kind of emotional tie is a more secondary bond, "by means of identification. Whatever leads men to share important interests, to undertake altruistic rather than selfish behavior, produces this community of feeling, these identifications. And the structure of human society is to a large extent based on them" (Einstein and Freud, 1971:22, cf. Doob, 1964). Piaget and Weil note that "the child's discovery of his homeland and understanding of other countries" is part of a broader "process of transition from egocentricity to reciprocity" (1951:578).[48] Guetzkow (1955) holds that feelings of identification with one level of community often go together with support for others, and there exists a "core of citizens" with loosely coupled "multiple loyalties."

Some evidence suggests that there may be an association between the level of economic well-being and international peace or violence. The historical experience of North Atlantic communities showed that peaceful behavior was fostered by "core areas" with high levels of interior transactions and standards of living (Deutsch et al., 1957:137). The experience of supranational Western European communities established following World War II has corroborated this finding. The creation of a larger domestic market here seemed to go hand in hand with peace. Some statistical research has also appeared to confirm some positive association between different levels of economic development and peace.[49]

Other studies, however, find little relationship between wealth and war. In primitive tribal societies, economic factors were not major causes of peace or violence. Often they seemed to have "little influence" (Otterbein, 1970:Preface). Over the long sweep of European history, "wars and revolutions happen[ed] in periods of impoverishment" but also in times of "enrichment" (Sorokin, 1937:253). The European experience in particular underlines the fact that wealth by itself is not sufficient to eliminate violence. In Europe both international and domestic violence have continued, and in some respects have increased, since the twelfth century. This has occurred in spite of the fact that Europe, together with North America, is the most technologically developed group of nations in the world system today. As such, it enjoys substantial material benefits to which many people in the less wealthy nations of the world aspire. Statistical data from a 1955–1957 global sample reveal no association between gross national product, national income, industrialization, capital formation, or the cost of living—and the number of wars or war casualties (Rummel, 1972:356).

As national markets contain wealth, national communities are based on language. Language is how people express not only what binds them together, but also what separates them. The continuing negotiation of the social contract and the peaceful resolution of conflict and frustration allow vast numbers of human beings to continue to live together. Deutsch et al.'s study of historical North Atlantic societies found that shared information, affection, and habits of compromise, tolerance, and trust were important pieces in an overall pattern of peacefulness. It was also important that the members had a genuine reluctance to wage war (1957:72, 129).

Other research also suggests that cultural stability and continuity help produce security and tend to increase tendencies to peace (cf. McGowan and Shapiro, 1973:126–27; Blainey, 1973:83; Sorokin, 1937:499). Further, the shared subjective bases of domestic community seem particularly likely to reduce wars when they contain idealized aspirations toward peace and prohibitions against violence (cf. Gurr, 1968; Nef, 1968; Alexander, 1975).

Language can also help represent more passive war resistance that may exist in public opinion; to present information about the costs of war, alternatives to war, and the benefits of peace; to convey information about war costs such as casualties; to affect public attitudes about the wars.[50]

Language can be a tool for active war resistance. The articulation of public opinion is an important part of the general political environment. It influences political officeholders most particularly because it affects their chances for reelection. For example, in the case of Vietnam, political speeches and lobbying, television and radio commentary, journalistic and scholarly writings, the symbolic actions of popular demonstration—all helped mobilize opponents of the war and converted or neutralized those who supported it (cf. Thompson et al., 1974; Granberg and Faye, 1972; Haavelsrud, 1972).

Chapter 4

POLARIZATION

Modern technology and aggregation imply polarization. Figure 4-1 sketches the outline of a polarized environment.[1] Table 4-1 lists some of the characteristics of polarization.

As we use the term, polarization has three dimensions: differentiation, inequality, and instability. Differentiation means that there are few actors; the boundaries that define the actors are firm; and there are few links between actors. The actors are unequal in size and resources. Some are powerful and rich, others weak and poor. The actors are, finally, unstable. They change their numbers, shapes, and other characteristics at different rates.

AGGREGATION AND POLARIZATION

Aggregation helps produce polarization. Table 4-2 suggests specific ways that bureaucracy, exchange, and language lead to this result. In this chapter we shall describe details of this process.

Differentiation

We have seen how aggregation draws large numbers of human beings together in communities. At the same time, aggregation divides people from each other. Cooperative human structures and processes have grown in

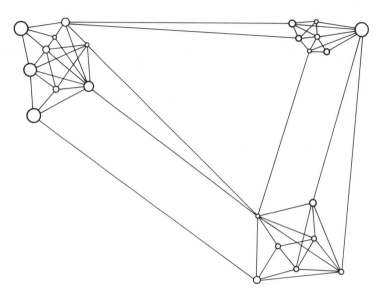

Figure 4-1
A Polarized Environment.

clusters. As the clusters have increased in size, they have become fewer. As they have bound previously separate elements more tightly, they have separated them from other clusters.[2] Major differentiation separates international and national groups.

International Differentiation

As international relations have increased, a few massive global groups have appeared, tied by relatively limited interactions and separated by relatively clear boundaries. Three major international groups can be defined, if one's geography is very loose, as the global Northwest, Northeast, and South. The Northwest includes North America; Western Europe; parts of Western Asia, for example, Japan, South Korea, Taiwan, Australia, New Zealand; and some other states such as Israel and South Africa. The Northeast comprehends the Soviet Union, Eastern Europe, perhaps some of Northern Asia—China, Tibet, Mongolia, North Korea, Vietnam. Finally, the South contains the rest of Asia, most of Latin America, the Middle East, and Africa.[3]

These major international groups have formed separate legal blocs, organizational coalitions, transaction networks, and ideologies.

Legal Blocs

The development of international law has implied the growth of international legal blocs.

Table 4-1
Polarization: Characteristics.

Characteristics	Environment	
	Unpolarized	Polarized
Differentiation		
Groups	Many	Few
Links	Many	Few
Boundaries	Flexible	Firm
	Permeable	Impermeable
Inequality		
Power, wealth, identification	Equal	Unequal
Instability		
Change	Slow	Rapid
	Even	Uneven

Table 4-2
Aggregation and Polarization.

Aggregation	+ ⟶	Polarization
Bureaucracy		**International Polarization**
International law		International legal blocs
International organization	Differentiation	International organizational coalitions
National government		
Exchange		
International transactions	Inequality	International transaction networks
National markets		International ideologies
Language		**National Polarization**
International communications		National government centralization
National communities	Instability	National market concentration
		National myths

Historically, different sets of law bound early groups of states in their relations with each other. The classical Greek city-states subscribed to a common code that went beyond the boundaries of individual city-states and separated the Greeks from others, who were labeled barbarians. Roman, Moslem, and Christian law united peoples from many different nations.

In the contemporary world a different body of international legal theory and practice has grown up in each of the three major global zones—Northwest, Northeast, and South. International legal blocs are based partly on major philosophical differences between the three major global zones. Thus,

> the disagreement between socialist and nonsocialist lawyers . . . prescinds from a disagreement about the nature of society, and ultimately about the nature of man. . . . disagreement between lawyers of new countries and lawyers of old ones . . . prescinds from the political notion of nationalism and reflects a nineteenth century philosophy of the state (O'Connell, 1970:65).

The idea of a universal international law seems to have developed most markedly in the Northwestern international sector. We have seen, in our previous discussion of the growth of the law of peace and war, that the scholars who are credited with the development of international law have been predominantly Western European and that European statesmen have been most active in promoting the structures and processes of international law.

The World Court, in spite of its universalistic name, has served mainly Northwestern states. One study found that the typical state using the World Court has been culturally and geographically East or West European (68 percent). Of 55 cases, 52 have included at least one European litigant. The three exceptions have all occurred since the end of World War II. Over time, moreover, East European participation has declined. "World Court clients have tended to have a 'constitutional government' (61 percent), a 'polyarchic' pattern of representativeness (55 percent) and a developed or intermediately developed economy (82 percent)" (Coplin, 1968:322; see also Coplin and Rochester, 1972).

A separate body of Northeastern international law began to emerge after the Russian revolution. At the current time this body of law separates the socialist states from others and binds them in a network of common treaties and practices (cf. Tunkin, 1974). And there is now a distinctively Southern international legal bloc as well that has emerged much later than the other two groups and is still partly embedded in them (cf. Anand, 1972).

Organizational Coalitions

The growth of international organizations has led to organizational coalitions. International organizations have developed most substantially in the global Northwest. The forerunner of modern international governmental organizations with general concerns was the Concert of Europe, which originally included the major Northwestern powers: Austria, Britain, Prussia, and Russia.

In the twentieth century, the great European and Atlantic powers drew up the blueprints for, and have guided the operation of, both the League of Nations and the U.N. The same states have spun most of the strands in the contemporary global web of international governmental institutions devoted to particular technical sectors or geographical areas. They have also been at the forefront in developing international nongovernmental organizations, for example, multinational corporations.

Since the end of World War II, substantial Northeastern and Southern groupings have also become apparent.[4]

Contemporary U.N. voting is an area where we may see these coalitions most clearly. U.N. voting, according to the theory of democratic pluralism, should rest upon and contribute to "a complex and fluid pattern of international relations," without differentiated groups. States should win or lose relatively equally. Nations should join different voting groups depending on their priorities, their resources, and the particular issues involved. Though nations might oppose each other in one context they should vote together in another (U Thant, cited in Alker and Russett, 1965:126; cf. Hanrieder, 1971; Mitchell, 1970; Deutsch and Singer, 1964).

U.N. voting, in fact, does not show such fluidity. Instead it rests on substantial coalitions that vote together on many issues. Figure 4-2 shows these coalitions in the U.N. General Assembly during the early 1960s. The core of the Northwestern coalition at this time consisted of Western Europe and the old British Commonwealth. A more southerly component of the western grouping included the Scandinavian and Latin American states, together with Finland, Turkey, Japan, and Israel. The Northeastern coalition seemed relatively small and isolated, comprehending the Soviet bloc and Cuba. The South was quite distant from the Northeast on this map and included most of the Afro-Asian states.[5]

Transaction Networks

The general growth of international transactions has led to transaction networks in which groups of nation-states concentrate their exchanges of goods and services. In earlier times transactions developed within local or regional boundaries. Patterns of transactions helped to separate the medieval European economy, the Arab world, China and Japan, and various other African, American, and Asian civilizations (cf. Wallerstein, 1972). The modern expansion of international transactions has supported the growth and consolidation of some of these earlier groupings while others have declined.

We can see the outline of the three major world groups in contemporary U.N. trade statistics. U.N. statisticians describe each group in terms of different economic institutions and practices: The Northwestern communities are seen as developed market economies; the Northeast as centrally planned economies; and the South as developing market economies.[6]

Table 4-3 shows the source and destination of the major networks' trade. It is clear that the Northwestern economies do most of their trading with members of their own network. In 1977 the developed market econ-

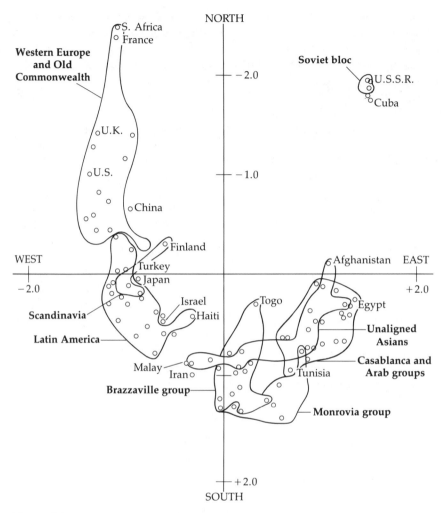

Figure 4-2
International Organization Coalitions: Voting Groups in the U.N. 16th General Assembly, 1961–1962. (NOTE: Unrotated factor scores. SOURCE: Alker, 1964.)

omies exported about $729 billion worth of goods and services to the world. Almost $518 billion of these exports, or over 71 percent of the total, were to other developed market economies.

The centrally planned economies did about $59 billion out of $107 billion, or over 55 percent of their trade, within the Northeastern network during 1977. The Eastern European COMECON (Council for Mutual Economic Aid) nations do most of their international trade with each other (cf. Loeber, 1977).

Table 4-3

World Exports, Source and Destination, 1974–1977. (Million U.S. $ F.O.B.)

Exports From	Year	World[a,b,c]	Exports To		Developing Market Economies	
			Developed Market Economies[c,d]	Centrally Planned Economies[b,c]	Total[d,e]	OPEC[f]
World[a,b,c]	1974	838212	588004	70961	173676	36558
	1975	872217	572712	90946	200595	57095
	1976	988294	666223	94441	219404	65183
	1977	1119607	748642	105311	255674	80368
Developed market economies[c,d]	1974	541660	397944	26593	113803	29044
	1975	577192	402040	33440	138318	47455
	1976	642101	458025	33910	147201	54769
	1977	729061	517741	34501	172578	67207
Centrally planned economies[b,c,e]	1974	71127	22566	36352	11625	2258
	1975	84546	23063	47573	13319	3144
	1976	92069	26672	50318	14491	3095
	1977	107303	28874	59195	17966	3608
Developing market economies[d,g]	1974	225426	167495	8016	48249	5257
	1975	210479	147610	9933	48959	6496
	1976	254124	181526	10213	57711	7318
	1977	283244	202028	11615	65130	9553
OPEC[f]	1974	125713	98431	1535	24849	530
	1975	112973	83808	2147	24154	787
	1976	136171	101267	2473	29008	932
	1977	146751	109202	2678	31201	1175

[a]Including special category exports, ships' stores, bunkers, and other exports whose destinations could not be determined.

[b]Excluding the intertrade of the centrally planned economies of Asia.

[c]Excluding the trade conducted in accordance with the Supplementary Protocol to the Treaty on the Basis of Relations between the Federal Republic of Germany (FRG) and the German Democratic Republic (GDR). These data, reported by the sender, are in the table below.

	Million U.S. $			
	1974	1975	1976	1977
FRG to GDR	1,424	1,594	1,699	1,873
GDR to FRG	865	979	—	—

[d]This classification is intended for statistical convenience and does not, necessarily, express a judgment about the stage reached by a particular country in the development process.

[e]Exports of the U.S.S.R. for which country of destination could not be attributed are included in the totals of the world, the development market economies, the developing market economies, and the centrally planned economies, but data are not available to allow their inclusion in the figures for the components of these regions.

[f]Algeria, Ecuador, Gabon, Indonesia, Iran, Iraq, Kuwait (including Neutral Zone), Libyan Arab Jamahiriya, Nigeria, Qatar, Saudi Arabia, United Arab Emirates, and Venezuela.

[g]Excluding exports of Southern Rhodesia.

SOURCE: Copyright United Nations, 1978:30. Reproduced by permission.

The Southern developing market economies are the least differentiated of the world groups, exporting most of their goods and services to Northern partners. In 1977 their internal trade included about $65 billion out of a total of $283 billion, or 23 percent.

Ideologies

The growth of international communication has helped differentiate international ideologies, showing people not only what unites, but also what divides them. The Northwest identifies itself as the free world. It places great importance on pluralistic political institutions, a relatively unrestricted market economy, and the virtues of competition. The Northeast, on the other hand, is socialist. It emphasizes the necessity for economic planning of production and distribution, social equality, the virtues of cooperation and the hope of comradeship within society. Southern peoples tend to place high importance on their own identity, but the specific content of that identity is still emerging. However, it appears to include the attainment of the material prosperity enjoyed by Northern countries, and the maintenance of unique historical cultural values (cf. Sargent, 1978; Crespigny and Cronin, 1975; Ebenstein, 1973; Gould and Truitt, 1973; Shaw, 1973).

National Differentiation

The development of modern nation-states has supported national differentiation, defined in terms of governmental centralization, market concentration, and myths. As states have grown larger, national governments have become more centralized and powerful. They have increased the size of their territories, population, and resources. Centralized national governments have become the major agents of leadership and change for their societies, achieving greater power through their control of resources, events, and other actors.[7]

National markets have become more concentrated. As the markets have grown larger, they have become more complex and dense. Large economic enterprises, governmental or private corporations, have become more important, replacing the small landholder, craftsman, or entrepreneur. Population has clustered in large cities.

The growth of national communities has supported national myths. Nations have adopted common languages and beliefs. Modern education and communications media have centralized the transmission of common symbols and information. In a modern national community "cultural and religious pluralism" is difficult to sustain. The national "symbol of identity is the culture which is shared by most of its citizens. Such a state supervises the transmission of that culture, at a literate level, from generation to generation" (Gellner, 1975:215).

Inequality

Aggregation helps produce inequality between and within international and national groups (cf. Rogers and Shoemaker, 1971:342).

International Inequality

The major international groups are unequal. The Northwest clearly dominates the others. The Northeast holds an intermediate position, and the South appears plainly subordinate. The Northwestern and Northeastern groups are better defined, more cohesive, more separate, more powerful, and richer than the South. The South is, to some extent, a residual category, formed by subtracting the first two groups from the rest of the world and incorporating the remainder. It has tended to be much poorer and weaker.

We can see the inequalities clearly in the relations of the different international legal blocs, organizational coalitions, transaction networks, and ideologies.

Legal Blocs

THE NORTHWESTERN LEGAL BLOC The Northwestern legal bloc has emerged from the historical background as the dominant contemporary legal grouping. Northwestern states have dominated the global environment partly through the system of international law. As early as the end of the fifteenth century, European international law formalized the division of the world into European spheres of influence. In 1493, following Columbus' first voyage to the New World, the Pope divided the world between Spain and Portugal. Ambassadors from the two countries signed the Treaty of Tordesillas in 1494, reaffirming the original papal division, though changing the location of the line of demarcation.

International law, as developed and interpreted by the Northwestern states, legitimated later agreements with similar purposes. Europeans and North Americans thus dominated the international treaties that were made after World Wars I and II, laying the groundwork for the relations that were to govern nations during the subsequent periods of peace. These treaties also implied the division of large parts of the world into spheres of influence dominated by the major powers.[8]

As we have already seen, the Northwestern legal bloc has played a leading role in the World Court and uses it most frequently. This does not mean that Northwestern nations necessarily abide by its decisions. World powers are least likely to accept Court rulings (Jarvad, 1968:297).[9]

THE NORTHEASTERN LEGAL BLOC Not surprisingly, Soviet international legal theory, since the Russian Revolution, has emphasized the inequality of the legal system. The Soviet perspective has formed the center of a new body of Northeastern international law that has developed over the last half century.

Early Soviet leaders found some aspects of traditional international law useful for self-protection at particular times under specific circumstances. Thus, the classical doctrine of sovereignty helped them fight off external intervention in Soviet affairs in the early postrevolutionary years.

Postrevolutionary Soviet international lawyers, however, were skeptical that international law was generally useful in defending the interests of socialism. They were suspicious of and hostile to generally accepted international legal customs, treaties, and courts. Soviet legal theorists mistrusted capitalist bias in the writings of international legal authorities and the results of collective international lawmaking as found in international organizations. They held that international law was part of the superstructure of the international capitalist system. They felt it inevitably reflected the system's class character and promoted the interests of those who had created it.[10]

For example, they saw treaties as merely another instrument in the class struggle. The Soviet approach to international treaties has generally rejected the traditional legal principle of *pacta sunt servanda*, the idea that treaties should be honored.[11] It has relied instead on other opposing doctrines, for example, *rebus sic stantibus*, the idea that circumstances may have changed. The new Soviet regime did not automatically accept treaties signed by the Czars. Even treaties explicitly agreed to by Soviet leaders were renounced if revolutionary consciousness showed that it was appropriate to do so.

In more recent times Soviet legal authorities have come to believe that general international law has emerged from a transitional configuration into a more modern one that increasingly reflects the interests of the global masses and fosters the international growth of socialism. At the same time the U.S.S.R.'s particular outlook has become more general and blended with that of a number of other states forming part of the Northeastern sector.

Contemporary Northeastern international legal theory distinguishes between two segments of international law. The first of these is the law of peaceful coexistence, which links capitalist and socialist states and attempts to regulate their relations.

The law of peaceful coexistence softens earlier opposition to some aspects of traditional international law. For example, international legal writings are more acceptable because of the contemporary contributions of socialist lawyers. Treaties are honored to a greater extent because the Soviet regime has agreed to a much greater proportion of them. According to one estimate "the Soviet state concludes over 400 treaties and agreements a year" (Blischenko, 1975:819).

International organizations have been recognized as more legitimate sources of international law, as the U.N. has come to include a greater proportion of socialist and Third World governments, and as the policies of capitalist states appear to have been increasingly influenced by socialistic forces.

The law of peaceful coexistence sets the scope and limits of capitalist and socialist cooperation—in economic and cultural relations or development of the law of space, for example—and also provides the rules for contention between the two major world groups.

The law of peaceful coexistence retains a heavy emphasis on the traditional principle of nonintervention of external powers in the socialist sphere. It maintains that the law of peaceful coexistence itself cannot be used to weaken or dissolve the socialist commonwealth; for example, it cannot be used to justify secession or revolution among its members.

At the same time, Northeastern doctrine has held that colonialism is an international crime and has upheld the socialist right to resist colonial exploitation, including the right of a third party to assist peoples struggling against imperialist governments.

Socialist international law is the second major segment of the Northeastern vision of international law. It regulates relations between socialist countries. Socialist international law theoretically represents a higher form of internationalism that is evolving in a dialectical relationship with traditional international law. It includes and justifies the agreements and political processes of the international socialist community. Socialist international law also includes the body of multilateral treaties providing economic integration in COMECON and military cooperation in the Warsaw Pact.

THE SOUTHERN LEGAL BLOC   The Southern legal bloc, like the Northeastern one, has emphasized the inequality of traditional international law, and thus Southern states have incorporated aspects of the earlier Soviet doctrine on treaties. Many Third World states have refused to recognize the validity, through any law of state succession, of earlier treaties signed between colonizers and colonized that legitimated the activities of external powers in their countries. Their refusal is based partly on the grounds that the original treaties were unequal in a number of ways, and partly on the principle of *rebus sic stantibus*. They hold that the world is a much different place today than when the treaties were signed (cf. David, 1975; Chen, 1974; Alexandrowicz, 1973).

American President Woodrow Wilson's emphasis on national self-determination as a right and as the basis of sovereignty—legally enshrined in the peace settlement that followed World War I—has encouraged and justified many emerging Third World regimes in aggressively asserting their separate identities and interests.

Contemporary Southern legal theorists have moved well beyond Wilson's vision of self-determination, which was essentially political. "All of the diverse elements of Wilson's concept of 'self-determination' were imbued with the general ideal of democracy, as then understood, and 'economic self-determination' was not generally embraced within it" (Pomerance, 1976:26). In the modern world the definitions of self-determination and sovereignty have been broadened to include various other dimensions of national existence and to limit the intervention of external powers (cf. Alexander and Friedlander, 1978; Buchheit, 1978).

Southern states have attempted to extend the principle of self-determination to include economic dimensions as well, for example, the right to exclusive control of national material resources. Thus, in a series of U.N. Conferences on the Law of the Sea (UNCLOS), they have attempted to limit traditional freedom of the seas for military purposes, and fishing and mineral exploration of offshore resources. They have favored extending a state's sovereignty over its ocean boundaries to a 12-mile limit, subject to the right of innocent passage by ships from other states. Further, they have supported the creation of

> a 200-mile economic zone in which the coastal state exercises sovereign rights over the exploration, exploitation, conservation, and management of living and nonliving resources and in which all states continue to enjoy freedoms, in particular of navigation and overflight and other uses related to navigation and communication; coastal state sovereign rights over the exploration and exploitation of the resources of the seabed and subsoil of the continental margin where it extends beyond 200 miles, coupled with a duty to contribute some international payments in respect of mineral production in the area of the margin beyond 200 miles (Stevenson and Oxman, 1975:764; cf. Miles, 1977; Johnston, 1976; H. Newcombe, 1976b:183, 220–35).

For the Southern bloc economic self-determination also implies the legitimacy of expropriating or limiting foreign ownership of resources within individual countries. This right implicitly extends to a share of global resources controlled by other wealthier peoples in other territorial settings. Thus, the right of self-determination, by implication, includes the right to the resources at home or abroad—food or energy, for example—required for survival at a decent level.

Additionally, the Southern bloc has generally favored limiting the use of the most technically advanced military capabilities over which Southern nations have little control and which could be used to their detriment.

Southern states have taken a generally similar position in the contemporary conferences on humanitarian international law in armed conflicts. They have sought to revise the Geneva Convention, trying to redefine international conflicts to include wars of liberation against colonial, racist, and occupying regimes. While they would avoid specifying who would authoritatively identify the character of such regimes, they generally would provide for the protection of civilians and prisoners of war in such cases, for example, as the struggle of the Palestinians against Israel. They would not, on the other hand, define international conflicts to include civil wars or conflicts against Third World regimes that do not seem to be colonial, racist, or occupational, for example, the Kurdish rebels against the government of Iran (cf. Forsythe and Magat, 1978).

The development of the Northeastern and Southern international legal blocs has reflected inequality in the system of international law. It is not clear, however, that the new blocs have substantially reduced Northwestern dominance over the international legal system. Further, the development of the blocs has reinforced inequality elsewhere. For example, the Soviet interpretation of socialist international law holds that it is entirely appropriate for socialist states to provide assistance to other socialist states, including military intervention against a government if the socialist character of the regime is threatened. This view may be consistent with Article 51 of the U.N. Charter and was used to justify the Soviet Union's intervention in Hungary in 1956, Czechoslovakia in 1968, and Afghanistan in 1979, to support regimes that it favored.

Organizational Coalitions

The Northwest has also dominated international organizations. Northwestern states have been able to afford membership in more international governmental organizations than have Northeastern and Southern states. Further, they have paid larger shares of international organization budgets and sent larger delegations, which have presumably given their views additional weight.[12] Table 4-4 gives an example of Northwestern support of international organizations. It lists the public international organizations to which the United States contributed in 1976.

In the U.N. Security Council, the Northwestern states and their allies have cast few vetoes, suggesting that they have had relatively good control of the proceedings. The Soviet Union, regularly outnumbered, could not hope to achieve a majority on most issues and cast about 100 vetoes in the first generation of Security Council proceedings alone (H. Newcombe, 1976b:154–55; cf. Junn, 1980; Bailey, 1968, 1969).

During the U.N.'s early years, the Northwestern coalition clearly predominated in the General Assembly. Table 4-5 shows that in 1946 the Northwestern coalition commanded a clear majority. Western European states had 17.7 percent of total General Assembly votes, and their allies in the Americas another 43.1 percent. Figure 4-3 suggests that during this early period the United States was on the winning side of most roll call votes.

Northwestern voting power in the General Assembly has declined since then. More Northeastern and Southern states have been admitted. Postcolonial independence brought a particularly large influx of new Southern members to the U.N. Some of the new members were from Europe and the Americas, but most were from Africa and Asia.

These new members have changed the U.N.'s voting structure. The Northwest has become weaker. Western Europe in 1976 only had 13.6 percent of the General Assembly votes, and the Americas another 19.7

Table 4-4
Major Public International Organizations Supported by the U.S., 1976.

U.N. and Special Programs

U.N.
   U.N. Emergency Force and U.N. Disengagement Observer Force
     (UNEF/UNDOF)
   U.N. Environment Program (UNEP)
   U.N. Force in Cyprus (UNFICYP)
   U.N. Fund for Drug Abuse Control (UNFDAC)
   U.N. Fund for Namibia
   U.N. Fund for Population Activities (UNFPA)
   U.N. Trust Fund for Development Planning and Projections
   U.N. Volunteers
U.N. Children's Fund (UNICEF)
U.N. Development Program (UNDP)
U.N. High Commissioner for Refugees Program (UNHCR)
U.N. Institute for Training and Research (UNITAR)
U.N. Relief and Works Agency for Palestine Refugees in the Near East
   (UNRWA)

Specialized Agencies and the International Atomic Energy Agency

---

Food and Agriculture Organization (FAO)
   U.N./FAO World Food Program
   U.N./FAO Sahelian Trust Fund
Intergovernmental Maritime Consultative Organization (IMCO)
International Atomic Energy Agency (IAEA)
   IAEA Operational Program
International Civil Aviation Organization (ICAO)
   ICAO Joint Financing Program
International Labor Organization (ILO)
International Telecommunication Union (ITU)
U.N. Educational, Scientific and Cultural Organization (UNESCO)
Universal Postal Union (UPU)
World Health Organization (WHO)
World Meteorological Organization (WMO)
   WMO—Voluntary Assistance Program

Inter-American Organizations

Organization of American States (OAS)
   OAS Voluntary Programs
InterAmerican Indian Institute
InterAmerican Institute of Agricultural Sciences
InterAmerican Tropical Tuna Commission
Pan American Health Organization (PAHO)
Pan American Institute of Geography and History (PAIGH)
Pan American Railway Congress Association (PARCA)
Postal Union of the Americas and Spain

SOURCE: U.S. House of Representatives, Committee on International Relations (1976).

Other Regional Organizations

North Atlantic Treaty Organization (NATO)
North Atlantic Assembly
Central Treaty Organization (CENTO)
Colombo Plan Council for Technical Cooperation in South and Southeast Asia
Indus Basin and Tarbela Development Funds
International Commission of Control and Supervision (ICCS)
Organization for Economic Cooperation and Development (OECD)
Southeast Asia Treaty Organization (SEATO)
South Pacific Commission

Other International Organizations

Bureau of International Expositions (BIE)
Consultative Group on International Agricultural Research (CGIAR)
Customs Cooperation Council
General Agreement on Tariffs and Trade (GATT)
Hague Conference on Private International Law
Intergovernmental Committee for European Migration (ICEM)
International Agency for Research on Cancer (IARC)
International Agreement Regarding the Maintenance
    of Certain Lights in the Red Sea
International Bureau of the Permanent Court of Arbitration
International Bureau for the Protection of Intellectual Property
International Bureau for the Publication of Customs Tariffs
International Bureau of Weights and Measures
International Center for the Study of the Preservation and the Restoration
    of Cultural Property (Rome Center)
International Coffee Organization
International Commission for the Conservation of Atlantic Tunas
International Commission for the Northwest Atlantic Fisheries
International Cotton Advisory Committee
International Council for the Exploration of the Seas (ICES)
International Council of Scientific Unions (ICSU) and its Associated Unions
International Criminal Police Organization (INTERPOL)
International Hydrographic Organization
International Institute for Cotton (IIC)
International Institute for the Unification of Private Law
International Lead and Zinc Study Group
International North Pacific Fisheries Commission
International Organization for Legal Metrology (IOLM)
International Rubber Study Group
International Secretariat for Volunteer Service (ISVS)
International Seed Testing Association (ISTA)
International Union of Official Travel Organizations (IUOTO)
International Whaling Commission
International Wheat Council
The Interparliamentary Union
North Atlantic Ice Patrol
North Pacific Fur Seal Commission
Permanent International Association of Navigation Congresses
West African Rice Development Association (WARDA)

Table 4-5

The Composition of the U.N. by Geographical Area, 1946, 1976.

	1946		1976	
	No. of Countries	% of Total	No. of Countries	% of Total
Africa	4	7.8	49	33.3
Americas	22	43.1	29	19.7
Asia	8	15.7	33	22.5
Eastern Europe	6	11.8	11	7.5
Western Europe	9	17.7	20	13.6
Oceania	2	3.9	5	3.4
Total	51	100.0	147	100.0

SOURCE: Jacobson (1977:61). Reprinted with permission from the *Proceedings of the Academy of Political Science*, Vol. 32, No. 4 (1977): 56–68.

percent, for one-third of the total. Figure 4-3 shows that the United States in recent years has lost more roll call votes than it has won.

The Northeast has also lost Eastern European strength, dropping from 11.8 percent in 1946 to 7.5 percent of the votes in 1976. Nevertheless, the Soviet Union has, in the last decade, tended to be on the winning side of most General Assembly roll calls. The Northeast has made common cause with the South on a substantial number of issues.

The South has been the largest vote gainer. Between 1946 and 1976, Africa increased its share of U.N. General Assembly votes from 7.8 percent to 33.3 percent, Asia from 15.7 percent to 22.5 percent.

The decline of Northwestern strength in the General Assembly suggests a weakening of Northwestern dominance. At the same time, we should note that confidence in the U.N.'s ability to resolve international problems has declined as well. Following World War II, Northwestern leaders hoped that they would be able to use the U.N. as an important international tool. As their influence there has declined, they have directed many of their efforts and activities into other channels (cf. Yeselson and Gaglione, 1974).

We should also realize that Northwestern economic influence in the U.N. still remains strong. Table 4-6 shows national contributions to U.N. budgets during 1979. Eight Northwestern states—the United States, Japan, West Germany, France, the United Kingdom, Italy, Canada, and Australia—are among the top ten contributors to the U.N. Four more Northwestern states fall in the top twenty. The leading Northwestern nation, the United States, contributes more than twice as much as its nearest competitor, the U.S.S.R.

Despite the complexity of its position in the U.N. in recent years, the Northwest continues to control many international nongovernmental or-

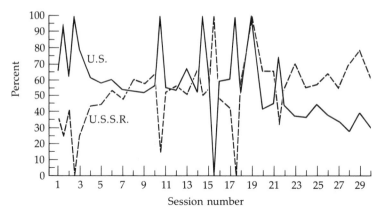

Figure 4-3
U.N. General Assembly Roll-Call Votes: U.S. and U.S.S.R.
Positions in Relation to the Winning Side, 1946–1974.
(SOURCE: Jacobson, 1977:58. Reprinted with permission from the
Proceedings of the Academy of Political Science, Vol. 32, No. 4 [1977]:
56–68.)

Table 4-6
Percentage Scales of Assessment for U.N. Budgets and Net Contributions Payable
by Member States for 1979. (U.S. $.)

Member State	Percentage Scale of Assessments	Net Contribution to U.N. Regular Budget
U.S.	25.00	143,024,903
U.S.S.R.	11.60	55,232,182
Japan	8.64	41,138,452
Germany, Federal Rep. of	7.70	36,662,741
France	5.82	27,711,319
China	5.50	26,187,673
U.K.	4.52	21,521,505
Italy	3.38	16,093,515
Canada	3.04	14,476,918
Australia	1.54	7,332,548
Spain	1.53	7,284,934
Ukrainian SSR	1.53	7,284,934
Netherlands	1.42	6,761,180
Poland	1.39	6,618,338
German Democratic Rep.	1.33	6,332,655
Sweden	1.24	5,904,130
Belgium	1.08	5,142,307
Brazil	1.04	4,951,851
Czechoslovakia	0.84	3,999,572
Argentina	0.84	3,999,572

SOURCE: Copyright United Nations, 1980. Reproduced by permission.

ganizations, for example, multinational corporations. Northwestern economic theory suggests that multinational corporations are instruments of general aggregation, providing "production and peace for all humankind, regardless of national interests" (Cockcroft, 1976:24). The most modern management techniques, combined with economies of scale and vast reserves of cash and personnel, make for efficient use of resources and delivery of the most up-to-date goods and services to all parts of the world. Multinational corporations, however, have a specifically Northwestern identity. The majority of multinational corporations are centered in the United States and owned and controlled by Americans. American standards and practices organize and control foreign affiliates (cf. Mennis and Sauvant, 1976).

Transaction Networks

The Northwest, over the last several centuries, has been the core, the central growth pole, the dominant force of the world economy. European exploration of Asia, Africa, and the Americas opened up global commerce and migration. During the imperial colonial period, migration tended to flow from Europe outward to the rest of the world, and the home country directly or indirectly administered the economies and prices of the colonies.

Contemporary Northwestern dominance of international transactions is apparent from world trade figures. Table 4-7 sketches world imports and exports between 1948 and 1977. The developed market economies in 1977 imported $796 billion and exported $730 billion worth of goods, for a total of more than $1.5 trillion or about two-thirds of total world trade.

We have already seen that a high volume of this trade is internal, and thus immune from foreign influence. Less than 30 percent of Northwestern trade takes place with the rest of the world. When they do trade outside, the developed market economies sell mainly high-prestige, high-technology industrial and electronic products and services. The Northwest has a near monopoly of knowledge at the leading edge of high technology and gets a good price for it.

Northeastern international transactions are separate but unequal. Northeastern leaders, following Marxist theory, have been highly skeptical of international transactions because of their capitalist nature. Following the revolution, the Soviet government exercised strict controls over a limited amount of foreign trade (cf. Quigley, 1974). At the end of World War II the Soviet Union did not ratify the Bretton Woods Agreements that established the postwar international financial order (see Milward, 1977:364). The imports of the centrally planned economies in 1977 totaled about $116 billion, and exports $107 billion, for a total of $223 billion or about 10 percent of total world trade.[13]

The Southern group of states has a less isolated but clearly subordinate position in the modern international transaction network. In 1977 the developing market economies imported almost $242 billion and exported

Table 4-7
World Imports and Exports, 1948–1977. (Million U.S. $.)

Imports C.I.F.

	1948	1958	1960	1965	1969	1970	1971	1972	1973	1974	1975	1976	1977
World[a,b]	63274	114360	134209	197161	286915	328772	365905	430185	591299	853656	904088	1016019	1153619
Developed market economies[b,c]	41142	74069	88767	137328	206327	237796	264638	312516	430130	612231	614522	703804	795805
Centrally planned economies[a]	3745	12774	16290	22968	30429	34667	37422	45951	62316	79600	100853	104867	115965
Developing market economies[c]	18387	27517	29152	36864	50159	56308	63846	71716	98854	161825	188714	207348	241850
OPEC[d]	2548	5392	5406	6219	5884	9856	11467	14094	20373	32842	51773	63429	80406

Exports F.O.B.

	1948	1958	1960	1965	1969	1970	1971	1972	1973	1974	1975	1976	1977
World[a,b]	57190	108504	128209	186953	273595	313423	350585	415851	576710	841021	873228	990608	1119870
Developed market economies[b,c]	36578	71353	85951	126591	194653	224908	252057	298635	408248	543355	578600	643167	730251
Centrally planned economies[a]	3642	12310	15277	22028	30126	33268	36444	43207	57897	71992	85528	93034	107318
Developing market economies[c]	16970	24640	26980	36335	48816	55248	62083	74009	110565	225674	209099	254408	282302
OPEC[d]	3116	7357	7787	11242	15161	17429	23027	27169	42029	125117	112871	137214	147010

[a]Excluding trade among each of the following countries: China, Mongolia, Democratic People's Republic of Korea, and former Democratic Republic of Vietnam (beginning 1976, Vietnam).
[b]Including trade conducted in accordance with the Supplementary Protocol to the Treaty on the Basis of Relations Between the Federal Republic of Germany and the German Democratic Republic.
[c]This classification is intended for statistical convenience and does not necessarily express a judgment about the stage reached by a particular country in the development process.
[d]Algeria, Ecuador, Gabon, Indonesia, Iran, Iraq, Kuwait, Libyan Arab Jamah., Nigeria, Qatar, Saudi Arabia, United Arab Emirates, and Venezuela.
SOURCE: Copyright United Nations, 1978:22, 23. Reproduced by permission.

about $282 billion worth of products. Total imports and exports were $524 billion or only about 23 percent of the world total. Most of the Southern bloc exports have been agricultural products or natural resources that have until recently brought relatively low prices in the world market. In addition, Southern economies send a much lower proportion of their exports to each other than the other groups. The low degree of internal trade implies that southern economies are particularly vulnerable to policy changes in the outside world.

Historically, Southern subordination to the other two trading blocs has occurred for a number of reasons, including distance from the Northwestern growth pole and the character of imperial relations. Recently, revolutionary nationalism in the Third World has challenged the direct influence of particular Northwestern states. The Southern group has been gradually formulating a coherent and complex program for a new international economic order. This program sets forth a number of major topics for negotiations, including markets for raw materials and commodities; access to markets of developing countries; targets, flows, and terms of development assistance; debt; financial transfers and reserves; and science and technology transfers (cf. Cox, 1979; Sauvant and Hasenpflug, 1977; Singh, 1977; Gosovic and Ruggie, 1976). Southern inequality and dependence have continued today partly because of continued Northwestern dominance of international trade, aid, and investment. Northwestern states have been better able to use the modern forms of international organization, like common markets and multinational corporations, to further their own interests.[14]

Southern producers of different products do not always have the same interests, nor do they act to support each other. Recently some Southern states have taken advantage of the growing Northwestern shortage of natural resources to make substantial gains. For example, the Organization of Petroleum Exporting Countries (OPEC) has dramatically raised the price of fossil fuels. Table 4-7 shows that the OPEC states in 1948 imported and exported a total of only about $5.7 billion or 4.7 percent of world trade. By 1977 this amount had increased to $227 billion or 10 percent of the global total.

Other commodity cartels, organizations composed of international producers of particular primary products, have been less effective. Producer organizations in products like copper and coffee have not had similarly good luck (cf. Krasner, 1978; Rothstein, 1978, 1977; Mingst, 1976; Park et al., 1976).

Ideologies

Northwestern states have dominated the technology of modern communication. They have used journalism and advertising particularly well to present their ideology, an image of reality consistent with their views and interests.

In earlier days European news cartels, including the British Reuters and French Havas and Wolff agencies, carried most public international information through ships and cables. These companies directly supported European imperial interests. Thus, Sir Roderick Jones of Reuters stated:

> Reuters must be preserved, strengthened and entrenched, not merely for the sake of the Agency and the newspapers, but also for the sake of the country. While fully alive to the necessity for maintaining inviolate in the eyes of foreigners Reuters' international detachment and impartiality in the service of the Press not only of the Empire but also of the rest of the world, we could not escape the fact, nor did our enemies let us, that Reuters was a purely British institution. As such, with its many links and ramifications beyond the Empire, Reuters actual and potential value in maintaining and extending British influence abroad, notably in the Far East, so important to Britain yet so neglected by our public men, was undeniable (Jones, 1951:236 in Harris, 1976:154; cf. Schiller, 1975; Cooper, 1942).

The contemporary growth of international communications has brought some division and competition between Northwestern actors. The established agencies, Reuters and Havas, for some time hindered the American companies from expanding rapidly into Western European spheres of influence. Nevertheless, American activity did expand and the Associated and United Press have gradually replaced the older European news agencies in many parts of the world. Other multinational media corporations, largely owned and operated by Americans, have come to dominate the international distribution of magazines, periodicals, radio, movies, and television (cf. Varis, 1975).

In spite of their formidable growth, Northwestern international communications agents have not penetrated very far into the Northeastern sector. The Northeast has constructed and maintained a relatively separate network of international communications. Governmental restrictions on the free flow of information have helped Eastern Europe, the Soviet Union, and China remain relatively isolated and self-contained.

Northwestern expansion of international communications beyond Western Europe and North America has occurred mainly in the global South. Figure 4-4 suggests how the media reach of the capitals of the Northwest—New York, London, Paris—extend into Asia, Latin America, and Africa. On the other hand, Moscow's reach extends mainly into Eastern Europe.

Northwestern communications penetration of the South rests on an economic base. The Northwest can provide the trained personnel for legions of reporters in Third World countries. It supports news bureaus abroad as well as facilities for news transmission and analysis, including satellites and computers.

The network of international communication brings international information home to the Northwest, and governmental intelligence services and social scientists of various kinds supplement the media in this task.

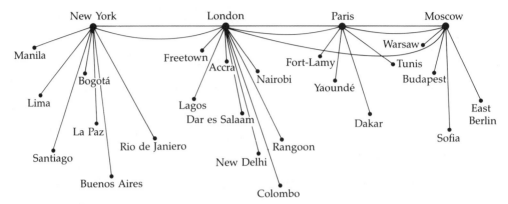

Figure 4-4

International Communication Networks. (SOURCE: M. Singer, 1972:190. Reprinted with permission of Macmillan Publishing Co., Inc., from *Weak States in a World of Power*, by Marshall R. Singer. Copyright © 1972 by The Free Press, a Division of the Macmillan Company.)

The network also disseminates Northwestern images, values, and information to the South. Cultural and information services abroad, scientific and cultural exchange programs, educational practices and materials, all broadcast the Northwestern view of reality (cf. Meyer, 1977; Carnoy, 1974; Freire, 1973; Illich, 1972).

Such activity directly enhances Northwestern interests in the South. It helps to exclude Northeastern ideology. It has

> provided a highly effective ideological club against the Soviet Union and its . . . zone of anti-capitalist influence. [It has helped to] create suspicion about an alternate form of social organization [and] to weaken thereby the enormous popular interest in Europe and Asia at war's end for one or another varieties of socialism (Schiller, 1975:78).

Southern news markets are also markets for Northwestern goods and services. "Public channels of transmission" become "private commercial conduits" as the media carry substantial private advertising that promotes the Northwestern way of life and its models of consumption (Schiller, 1976:179). Northwestern advertising agencies sell Northwestern exports. At the same time, they are themselves an important export industry, doing an increasing amount of their business abroad.

> These organizations conduct marketing research, publish controlled circulation magazines, annual reports, user handbooks, sales brochures, produce videotapes and films, handle data processing, provide public relations counsel, and measure consumer reaction to advertising and packaging (Schiller, 1976: 178).

Southern states have generally reacted to such ideological penetration on an individual basis, excluding media or programs from particular states.

Recently, they have begun to demand a new international information policy to deal with the problem collectively. So far there has been little concrete result (cf. Varis, 1976).

National Inequality

Aggregation tends to support national inequality as well as international inequality.

The idea that national governments, markets, and communities help produce and maintain inequality seems a strange one initially (cf. Jackman, 1975). Most citizens of Northwestern states enjoy a standard of living today that would have been unimaginable a hundred years ago. Northeastern political systems have undergone revolutions to reduce the amount of inequality that existed under old regimes. Southern states have adopted economic development as one of their most important goals and have made great improvements in their level of economic welfare.

From another viewpoint, however, the idea that national aggregation produces inequalities between nation-states appears quite reasonable. As states take form, their boundaries, dynamics, and use of resources will yield more or less power, wealth, and community identification. Thus some states become more powerful, richer, more cohesive. Others are weaker, poorer, more fragmented (cf. Tucker, 1977).

National aggregation also supports inequalities within states. For example, in all states, those who control the levers of government, commerce, and communication are more powerful than those who do not.

Capitalist societies, by definition, support an unequal distribution of wealth and other values. Socialist societies hope to equalize the distribution of power and wealth by reducing or eliminating the rich. Unfortunately, however, this only changes the appearance of economic concentration rather than solving the problem. The state or its bureaucrats now control the resources taken from the capitalists, and this gives rise to the post-revolutionary dilemmas of state capitalism and the "new class" of bureaucrats who administer it. The individual worker still does not control either the product of his or her labor or the work process (cf. Zaslavsky, 1980; Kohn, 1976; Parkin, 1971).

Development, which is usually defined in terms of increasing production of goods and services, does not necessarily bring more equal distribution. This is particularly apparent in nations of the Third World. One analyst states that "even countries growing in excess of UN goals, i.e., at more than 5% annually, have generally been experiencing a worsening in the distribution of income and increase in the volume of low level poverty, as well as in associated rates of unemployment or underemployment" (Ranis, 1975:558). "In the majority of developing countries," another observer notes, "the benefits of economic development accrue chiefly to the upper income groups—the highest 20 percent or 40 percent of the population—and in some countries the poorest 20 percent or even a larger percentage do not participate in the process of economic advancement at all." He continues:

> Since 1955 ample evidence has accumulated to bear out Kuznets' "speculation" that in the developing countries income is distributed even less equally than it was in the industrialized countries before the trend toward even greater inequality was reversed—in some countries before the turn of the century, in others not until after the first World War; the evidence is indeed that in most, though perhaps not in all developing countries, inequality has increased (Adler, 1973:2; cf. Chenery et al., 1974; Griffin, 1974; Adelman and Morris, 1973).

Instability

Finally, aggregation helps create instability. The general structures and processes of the world environment have developed relatively gradually. We have tried to look back in history and to discern the outlines of change. As we have done this, we have described a relatively undifferentiated and equal environment slowly giving way to the modern differentiated and unequal world.

As aggregation has developed, long-term change has also accelerated. Growth has occurred at compound rates. The major contemporary international groups we have discussed did not exist in an obvious way 200 years ago. Modern population and resource consumption have grown to astonishing levels.

Within the larger pattern of growth, sharp, short-term changes have occurred.[15] Historical city-states and empires grew rapidly to eminence and power and then, just as suddenly, declined. Experiences in the Mediterranean, particularly Greece, Rome, and North Africa inspired Plato, Polybius, Cicero, and Ibn Khaldun to develop cyclical theories of history. Later imperial experiences like those of Portugal, Spain, and the Netherlands and a broader global concern influenced the more contemporary theories of rise and decline formulated by writers like Spengler, Sorokin, and Toynbee.

These short-term changes may have grown sharper. In the twentieth century major empires have dissolved all over the world. The collapse of the czarist regime in Russia, and its replacement by the new Soviet order, laid the groundwork for the consolidation of the Northeastern group. Nationalistic revolutions in Asia, Africa, and Latin America have helped create the global South. Figure 4-5 describes the continuing pattern of domestic political instability in the 1960s.[16]

Modern markets undergo sharp expansions and contractions as they pass through economic cycles of varying lengths.[17] Table 4-8 and Figure 4-6 provide a vivid example of the sharp contraction of world trade during the global depression of the 1920s and 1930s.

Figure 4-5
National Political Instability: Global Sample, 1945–1966.
(SOURCE: Hamblin et al., 1973:126.)

The rapidity and discontinuity of such changes involve serious cultural and psychological shocks. Communities moving rapidly into the future, from traditional to industrial, or from industrial to postindustrial society, may strongly feel the loss of roots and the need to rediscover or reinvent common myths. Political moods may become volatile as old issues die and new ones are born (cf. Holmes, 1980; Lauterbach, 1974; Toffler, 1970).

POLARIZATION, PEACE, AND WAR

We have seen how the aggregative structures and processes of bureaucracy, exchange, and language lead to the differentiation, inequality, and instability of polarization. We might now expect that polarization should lead

Table 4-8
The Contracting Spiral of World Trade, 1929 to March 1933.
(Total imports in old U.S. gold $, millions.)

Month	1929	1930	1931	1932	1933
January	2,997.7	2,738.9	1,838.9	1,206.0	992.4
February	2,630.3	2,454.6	1,700.5	1,186.7	944.0
March	2,814.8	2,563.9	1,889.1	1,230.4	1,056.9
April	3,039.1	2,449.9	1,796.4	1,212.8	
May	2,967.6	2,447.0	1,764.3	1,150.5	
June	2,791.0	2,325.7	1,732.3	1,144.7	
July	2,813.9	2,189.5	1,679.6	993.7	
August	2,818.5	2,137.7	1,585.9	1,004.6	
September	2,773.9	2,164.8	1,572.1	1,029.6	
October	2,966.8	2,300.8	1,556.3	1,090.4	
November	2,888.8	2,051.3	1,470.0	1,093.3	
December	2,793.9	2,095.9	1,426.9	1,121.2	
Average	2,858.0	2,326.7	1,667.7	1,122.0	

SOURCE: Kindleberger (1973:172), from League of Nations, *Monthly Bulletin of Statistics*, February 1934, p. 51.

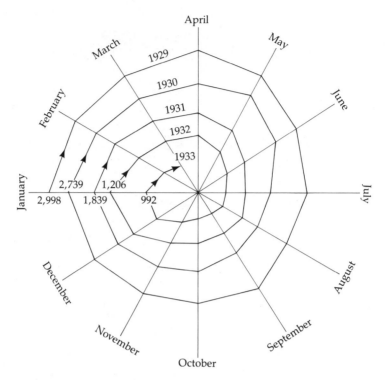

Figure 4-6
The Contracting Spiral of World Trade: 75 Countries,
1929 to March 1933. (SOURCE: Kindleberger, 1973:172. From
The World in Depression, 1929–1939 [Allen Lane / The
Penguin Press]. Copyright © Charles P. Kindleberger, 1973.
Reprinted by permission of Penguin Books Ltd., University
of California Press, and Deutscher Taschenbuch Verlag.)

directly to violence. As we shall see, a good deal of writing has centered
around the possibility of such a connection. Our original model, however,
does not include a direct link between polarization, peace, or war. Contemporary research suggests that differentiation and inequality vary independently from international violence. There is some evidence that instability
may have a more direct association with war, but the relationship is still far
from being generally confirmed.

Differentiation

We may suppose that war helps produce differentiation and that differentiation in turn contributes to violence. It may seem that war clarifies and
defines the boundaries of international and national groups. The separation

of such groups, in turn, may appear to imply independent identities and interests that lead to conflicts. Nevertheless, available evidence does not confirm such direct connections at either international or national levels.

International Differentiation

The degree of international differentiation may be defined by the number of major groups or poles in the environment. A bipolar environment is one with only two major poles, and we may consider such an environment to be highly differentiated. A multipolar environment, on the other hand, includes many different poles. It has a lower degree of cleavage (cf. Rapkin et al., 1979).

The separation between groups is more significant in bipolar environments. We might, therefore, expect bipolar environments to be relatively violent, and multipolar ones to be more peaceful. Deutsch and Singer provide what is probably the best known short formulation of this hypothesis. "As the system moves away from bipolarity toward multipolarity," they say, "the frequency and intensity of war should be expected to diminish" (1964:390).[18]

Some historical experience suggests that there is more war when the international system is divided into two opposing groups. Thus, the European environment divided between France alone, and Austria, England, Prussia, and Russia allied, at the time of the Napoleonic wars. Around World War I the world environment gradually split between England, France, Russia, and the United States; and Austria, Germany, and Italy. Before World War II, England, France, the United States, and eventually the U.S.S.R., separated themselves out from Germany, Italy, and Japan (cf. M. Haas, 1974:335–57).

In a bipolar environment aggregative structures and processes may have a harder time in keeping peace. For example, international legal blocs have disintegrative implications for the universal international system. They are not only building blocks for the larger community, but also stumbling blocks on the way to its attainment, not only partial but also opposed forms of international order. Partial legal systems are, in a sense, "competitive attempts at building rival systems for law" (Hoffmann, 1968:xvii; cf. von Glahn, 1970:724). As such, they both reflect and give coordinated force to fundamental political differences.

International organizations may also be less effective in helping to keep the peace in bipolar situations. While U.N. peacekeeping forces have been introduced more often into conflicts when great powers were involved, such attempts have not necessarily been successful (Pelcovits and Kramer, 1976). A survey of experts found that international organizations seem to do "worst in managing conflicts among parties belonging to opposing cold war blocs" (E. Haas et al., 1972:17, 27).

Another body of theory and research goes in the opposite direction, suggesting that international differentiation implies *less* violence, rather than more. War may tend to discourage differentiation; differentiation, in turn, may be a force for fewer wars, if not lower casualties.[19]

Bipolarity may heighten distrust between the major groups, but at the same time, it may tend to deter them from fighting. As the contending groups grow in size, wars between them are increasingly expensive—wars that all parties lose. Thus Rosecrance notes:

> Under bipolarity, one would expect a small number of conflicts, because the issues would be confined to those between the two major camps. Since other powers would be part of one coalition or another, they would not follow individual and separate policies. But the bipolar conflicts which did occur would be likely to be very dangerous and have far-reaching consequences. A war between bipolar camps is world war. In a multipolar system, war between two minor participants may have small impact on the system as a whole. Thus under multipolarity we would have:

$$\text{Expectation of conflict} = \underset{\text{(high)}}{\text{Probability}} \times \underset{\text{(low)}}{\text{Consequences}}$$

> Under bipolarity we would have:

$$\text{Expectation of conflict} = \underset{\text{(low)}}{\text{Probability}} \times \underset{\text{(high)}}{\text{Consequences}}$$

> (Rosecrance, 1973:118).

A number of statistical studies seem to confirm this line of reasoning. They suggest that fewer wars occur when there are a few tight international coalitions. One contemporary study, for example, correlates a number of different characteristics of wars with the number of poles. It finds that environments with more poles tend to show a number of violent characteristics. These include:

> Increasing level of disturbance. . . .
> Wars not concluded by treaties.
> Lengthy wars with major powers as participants.
> Many war victories on the part of each major power. . . .
> New wars in many years in the era. . . .
> Many years with victories by major powers.
> Members entering or departing from the subsystem primarily through violent means. . . .
> Many years containing wars started by major powers.
> Many wars won by major powers.
> Many wars occur.
> Many wars won by major powers that desire to destabilize power stratification.
> Many wars with destabilizing outcomes.
> Many wars started by major powers with nonsovereign participants (M. Haas, 1974:416–17; cf. p. 386).

The same study also relates war characteristics to the tightness of the poles. As the poles go from tight to loose, there are a number of war-related characteristics that seem to cut in different directions. Major powers, however, are involved in many wars in loose environments (M. Haas, 1974:416–17).

The study concludes that "tight polarity . . . conditions actors to think in terms of power. But foreign policy elites are less free to act, and they start wars less often; ideological considerations will enter into decision-making." On the other hand, it notes that "multipolarity [also] socializes decision-makers to think in terms of power considerations; foreign wars and interventions are common, and nearly every member of the subsystem, having a broad decision latitude, initiates at least one war" (M. Haas, 1974:385; cf. Bueno de Mesquita, 1978, 1975; Ostrom and Aldrich, 1978, Zinnes et al., 1978a:352; 1978b:43; Midlarsky, 1975:76; Pfister, 1974).

The research results on either side are not sufficiently strong for us to conclude there is a valid, reliable, direct relationship between characteristics of peace or war, on the one hand, and international differentiation, on the other. Each theoretical school has some evidence supporting the influence of bipolarity or multipolarity. This evidence, however, is still incomplete and contradictory.[20]

National Differentiation

A good deal of theory and research has also focused on aspects of national differentiation. It has attempted to relate national government centralization, market concentration, and myths to patterns of peace and war.

Government Centralization

The prehistoric landscape contained tribal societies engaged in hunting and gathering activities. Such groups were widely dispersed, according to today's standards, and did not come into much contact. Boundaries between territories were quite general. Violence between such societies occurred, but at a relatively low level. Primitive violence tended to be more personal, less institutionalized—for example, "fighting, homicide, feud." Primitive marauding and looting could be an important source of collective sustenance. Nevertheless, "organized offensive warfare to conquer people or territory, with its essentially impersonal involvement and lack of personal motivation" was not found in such societies (Lesser, 1968:95).

The subsequent historical development of national political communities and war has led some theorists to suggest a direct association between the two. The development of the state appears to have enhanced war; warfare may have also helped produce the modern state from primitive tribal society. However, other theorists disagree, believing that the development of war and the state occurred relatively independently (cf. Wright, 1977:380; Service, 1975:266–89; Wilson, 1975:574).

A comparative cross-historical study supports the second view. It reveals little statistical association between war frequency and a number of differentiating variables, including natural barriers, closeness, location of capital cities, and general centralization (Naroll et al., 1974:331–32, 336).

In modern societies, variables associated with political centralization do not appear strongly related to war. Such variables include boundaries, location of capital cities, and the concentration of power.

BOUNDARIES AND CAPITALS   Modern states share common boundaries with other nations—sometimes these imply peace, as with contemporary relations between the United States and Canada. Sometimes they suggest violence, as in the Middle East.

Statistical studies of the relationship between boundaries and wars have produced varying results. Richardson found a positive correlation between the number of frontiers and the number of external wars (1960b:176). The more frontiers a state had, the more likely it seemed to go to war (cf. Wilkinson, 1980:41–47; Wesley, 1962). More recently Starr and Most (1978) contradict Richardson. They report that there is no general relationship between the number of borders and wars. Rather the association seems to vary across different time periods, data sets, types of borders, and kinds of wars.

The quality of territorial boundaries has also been considered important. Traditional geostrategic theory has long held that war should occur less often where national physical boundaries are most clearly defined. Sharp or wide national barriers like mountain ranges or oceans can help reduce the diffusion of international violence or friction between neighbors as in the historical cases of Switzerland and the United States.

This idea is reflected in the more general New England wisdom of Robert Frost, that "good fences make good neighbors." There is, unfortunately, no systematic historical research to confirm it.

Nations are physically differentiated not only at their borders, but also from their interiors. One cross-national sample suggests a positive relationship between the number of wars and the closeness of national capitals: the closer the capitals, the more wars; the further apart the capitals, the fewer conflicts (Garnham, 1976). This finding is interesting, but the sample was quite small. The hypothesis requires more research.

POWER CONCENTRATION   Some branches of political and social theory suggest that war has encouraged the concentration of political power and that power concentration, in turn, helps produce war. The evidence again, is contradictory. Wright believed that primitive warlikeness increased the concentration of power (1965:557, 559). Otterbein's (1977, 1970) studies of early societies, on the other hand, suggest that power concentration by itself had no direct effect on the frequency of war.

Qualitative historical studies and traditional political philosophy argue in favor of the association between power concentration and war in modern nation-states. War may lead to power concentration. "The normal degree of government control of the activities of individuals varies greatly among states," says Wright, "but, however intense or loose the normal control, it becomes more intense in time of war" (1965:697). Andreski's comparative historical study of war suggests that increased governmental regulation is the major direct effect of war experience. War often, although not always, "produces the extension of state control over the economic and other aspects of social life" (Andreski, 1968:111; cf. Stein and Russett, 1980; Krehbiel, 1973; Jaurès, 1972; de Jouvenel, 1957).

In contemporary libertarian political systems, war seems to require tight administration and firm coordination in order to mobilize civilian resources for military use and to take up the slack of normal political life. A dangerous world appears to require concentrated national decisionmaking. In contemporary systems that are already concentrated, international violence provides an impetus for broadening and deepening the already extensive internal power of the state and the network of internal control.

> Not all tendencies towards the extension of the sphere of governmental regulation are the result of military factors. Nor does intensive warfare in itself necessarily produce totalitarianism. It only inevitably does so when technico-military circumstances make the cooperation of the whole adult population imperative. In conditions of industrial warfare this cooperation is, more than ever, essential (Andreski, 1968:111; see also p. 115).

If war results in the actual military conquest of a modern state, political concentration can follow during postwar reconstruction. Many contemporary central governments are, at least in part, the result of earlier wars. Central administrations in countries like France, Germany, and Italy emerged in part as a result of the violent history of unification. In the German case, Prussia and her allies wrested territory away from the feudal Germanic aristocracy as well as from Austria, Italy, France, and Denmark. In Italy, Piedmont accomplished like results with similar tactics.

States where power is broadly distributed can be a force for peace because of presumed habits of compromise, tolerance, and trust. Many Western democratic philosophers and political leaders have developed this line of argument—for example, Dante, Rousseau, Bentham, Kant, and many American presidents (see Waltz, 1959). The experience of Switzerland appears to be an object lesson in the efficacy of broad distribution of power. The Swiss with their federal, democratic institutions have led the world in the development of international law, organization, transaction, and communication; they have, too, a long history of neutrality.

Concentrated governments are supposed to be more prone to violence for a number of structural reasons. Centralization implies heavy decisional loads.

> One of the problems with imperialism is that as decision-making authority becomes centralized, the burdens on the imperialist leaders become intolerable, for along with the trappings of added power come political headaches (Barnet, 1968:265).

One aspect of such burdens is simply the restricted information flow through centralized communications channels (Friedrich and Brzezinski, 1956). Further, centralized governments put a substantial amount of distance between themselves and the population, and this distance may help make them both more able and willing to undertake wars threatening the lives of their citizens. In evaluating the costs and benefits of war, the dominant class or group may be more callous, particularly in discounting the costs of violence to other citizens.

In spite of such arguments, there are obvious historical exceptions to the association between war and political concentration. For example, the requirements of guerrilla warfare or exile often lead to the dissolution of formal central institutions of government and the dispersal of key personnel. Thus provisional governments of conquered European states during World War II—led by figures like de Gaulle or Beneš—were located in London. Often spontaneous, decentralized institutions have appeared as regular parts of revolutionary situations—French communes, Russian Soviets are examples (cf. Arendt, 1962:259–60).

Contemporary statistical studies have not really provided solid support confirming the relationship between concentration and war. One cross-national study of the 1950s found that such concentraton was not related either to the number of wars or of people killed in wars (Rummel, 1972:358; 1968:191; cf. M. Haas, 1974:203, 213, 214, 231). Another study focused on the effect of political concentration on violent contagion. It analyzed relations between domestic and foreign conflict in centralized and decentralized regimes. The results were not strong enough to be conclusive (Wilkenfeld, 1973b, 1972; cf. Kegley et al., 1978).[21]

Market Concentration

Some theories have proposed the differentiation of concentrated national markets as a dynamic force in international violence. Concentrated markets contain dense populations. Wars give such concentrated populations room to expand. This is the gist of a major theory of warfare in primitive societies (Savon, 1975; Netting, 1974; Hallpike, 1973; Vayda, 1968a, 1968b). In the 1930s it was reflected in the argument that the German state needed *Lebensraum*, or room to live.[22]

Systematic studies of contemporary societies suggest that the importance of population concentration varies in different cases and is generally limited. A study of the forces leading to World War I states that "population density was . . . a strong element in explaining expansion" (Choucri and North, 1975:188). Another analysis—by one of the same authors—of the role of population variables in a set of 45 local conflicts in the developing world since World War II has a more modest message. Size of population, measured both in absolute terms and relative to resources, appeared usually as only a background factor, or a minor irritant. It was only rarely a major irritant or centrally important, and only once the sole determinant of such conflicts. The internal distribution of national population appeared to be slightly more important, but it was usually not directly related to conflicts. Rural/urban mixture, population density, location in relation to resources, and location in relation to borders were usually background factors or minor irritants, though they were often major irritants as well. Only rarely were they of central importance and never were they the sole determinants of such conflicts (Choucri, 1974b:106–7; see also M. Haas, 1974:200; Bremer et al., 1973).[23]

Myths

It is unclear whether or not there is a direct relationship between differentiated national myths, peace, and war. One historical study found compatible main values, a distinctive way of life, and ethnic or linguistic assimilation to be important for maintaining peace between political communities (Deutsch et al., 1957).

States with substantial cultural differences between them may come into conflict (cf. Bloom, 1977; Gale and Gale, 1977). A recent cross-national study of 75 countries between 1955 and 1960 related a general measure of foreign conflict, including indicators of war frequency and casualties, to differences between a country and its neighbors. Political, linguistic, and religious differences together seemed to account for about 20 percent of the variance in foreign conflict behavior (Terrell, 1977; cf. Wilkinson, 1980:Ch. 9; Choucri, 1974b:108–9).

On the other hand, international cultural similarity can help produce violence. Thus the German *Anschluss* in Austria in 1938, the struggle between Greeks and Turks over Cyprus, and U.S. support for the Cuban emigrés at the Bay of Pigs in 1962 all relied to some extent on ethnic bonds between insiders and outsiders.

War, or external threats, may help strengthen collective national beliefs. This effect, however, depends on a complex set of preconditions.[24]

One theoretical perspective suggests that states in which myths are widely and deeply shared may be more prone to international violence. Intensely shared myths may unify different classes and groups within nations around such themes as racial supremacy, a civilizing mission, or a communal destiny. Historically, these have formed the basis for territorial expansion using various means, including violence (cf. Mattelart, 1976; McClelland, 1975; Benda, 1969). Conversely, states with limited and shallow myths may be more peaceful if only because they may not be so sure of their rectitude.

However, another body of theory suggests that this deduction is probably not true—at least in its simple form. States where the myths have a limited and shallow base in popular consciousness may also have an incentive to undertake external conflict to restore group cohesion. Thus, Simmel noted that external enemies are useful "in order for the group to remain conscious of . . . unity as its vital interest." In some situations groups "search for enemies . . . in order to help maintain and increase group cohesion" (1955:97–98). Following this theme, Wright suggests that "today, as in the past, states, especially new states, have found it difficult to organize political authority sufficient to maintain internal order unless they are in hostile relations to outside states. War or fear of war has often been used to integrate states" (1965:1516; cf. Waltz, 1959:81; Coser, 1956:104).

A statistical study of cross-national data supports the idea that national cultural unity may be a force for war. The study shows that wars and foreign clashes tend to be more frequent, and both absolute and per capita casualties higher, when societies have high religious and racial homogeneity and when the largest racial group is a large part of the total population (M. Haas, 1974:22). Furthermore, the study shows that states with well-articulated ideologies of development tend to have slightly more wars and higher absolute and per capita casualties (1974:210). Modern media are important sources articulating such ideologies. The study finds that wars tend to be more frequent in states where cinema attendance, newspaper circulation, and radio receivers are in high proportion to population (1974:224).

Most of these statistical associations are not, however, particularly strong, and some findings of the same study go in the opposite direction. Thus, states with high proportions of library book circulation and telephones per capita show low ratios of foreign killed per capita (1974:224, 243).[25]

Inequality

There are powerful arguments relating war and inequality. Violence has been associated with injustice, and injustice with inequality, in Western political theory since its beginnings. Many modern social scientists of conflict—Marx, Freud, Simmel, Pareto, Michels, Mannheim, Lasswell, Mills, Coser, Dahrendorf, Marcuse, Edelman, Galtung—have shown in detail the way that structures and processes of domination and subordination imply direct or indirect violence. It seems obvious that violence leads to inequality. There are no historical records, says Andreski, "of military victories where the conquerors acquired no privileges" (1968:40). Existing inequalities, on the other hand, provide a very powerful incentive for violence.

International Inequality

Classical political theory implies that war may increase international inequality. Early writers like Thucydides, Machiavelli, Hobbes, Clausewitz, as well as contemporary strategic thinkers, suggest that statesmen of dominant powers may see war as a useful instrument of statecraft, a means of enforcing their dominance on subordinate states. And a Marxist perspective also implies that war leads to inequality. In this view, war is a profitable enterprise, part of the international struggle for capital accumulation.[26]

Contemporary empirical research has not fully confirmed these theoretical insights. One study considered the effects of World Wars I and II on national positions in the international hierarchy of development, using a variety of socioeconomic indicators. A major finding was that later national rankings were correlated very closely with earlier national rankings regardless of war experience (Barbera, 1973).

Another study analyzed the effects of World Wars I and II on projections of GNP and population of major participants. It concluded that:

> The power levels of winners and neutrals are affected only marginally by the conflict.
> Nations defeated in war suffer intense short-term losses; the outcome makes much difference to them in the short run, especially in terms of power levels.
> In the long run (from 15 to 20 years), the effects of war are dissipated, because losers accelerate their recovery and resume antebellum rates; they may even overtake winners. Soon, the power distribution in the system returns to levels anticipated had the war not occurred (Organski and Kugler, 1977:1365–1366; cf. Organski and Kugler, 1980; SIPRI, 1978f:55–56; Kirk, 1946:66).[27]

We might expect international inequality to help make wars both more frequent and more serious. The more unequal any international environment is, the more violence we might expect. This would be particularly true from the perspective of Marxist theory. Marxism—in both traditional and contemporary forms—highlights the inclination of monopoly capitalism to export the class struggle, exploitation, and revolution on a global scale through imperialism. Marxism predicts that the expansion of monopolistic cartels will eventually produce the violent total breakdown of the international system.

Alternatively, however, inequality might work to produce fewer wars since inferiors should be cautious about fighting superiors and equals afraid of losing their rank.

Empirical research does not confirm either relationship. Data from the last two centuries yield contradictory results. In the nineteenth century, international equality correlated with more peace. In the twentieth century, however, international inequality was more closely related with peace. Less war occurred when there was a "preponderance . . . of power concentrated in the hands of a very few nations" (Singer et al., 1972:19–20).

Narrower studies of different geographical areas and time periods in the twentieth century, using different methods, have also come to different conclusions. Some suggest that war is more likely between groups of equal size and resources (Garnham, 1976a, 1976b; Weede, 1976). Some find that countries that are unequal are more likely to go to war (Wallensteen, 1973:116). Others find that general foreign conflict, including both war incidence and casualties, are unrelated to differences in size and economic development (Terrell, 1977; Ferris, 1973:115).[28]

We find no clearer relationship between war and inequality if we focus on nation-states.

National Inequality

Unequal Nation-States

As we have already suggested, one branch of theory proposes that unequal states may have more frequent and costly wars: superpowers because they can; ministates because they must. The opposite line of argument proposes that unequal states may fight less than others: dominant states because their preponderance makes it unnecessary; minor states because their weakness makes a war effort Quixotic and because they are not prizes worth combat.

Some historical statistics support the first line of argument. Imperial nations experienced more international violence during their heyday. After they lost most of their empires, they became more peaceful (Köhler, 1976, 1975). In contemporary times great powers have fought more wars than others, and the casualties of these wars have been greater (Modelski, 1978; Wallensteen, 1973; cf. Eberwein and Cusack, 1980; McGowan and Gottwald, 1975; Russett and Monsen, 1975; Wright, 1965:220–21).

Other contemporary cross-national studies to which we have already referred present a more complex picture. On the one hand, prominence in an international bloc is strongly positively related to the frequency of wars and foreign clashes as well as to total casualties. Prominence is, however, less related to casualties per capita. There is no substantial association between the simple fact of whether or not a state is a colonial power and the numbers of its foreign conflicts and casualties (M. Haas, 1974:204, 239). Finally, GNP per capita is not substantially related to most indicators of foreign conflict (Rummel, 1972:367).

Domestic Inequalities

The relationship of internal inequalities with peace and war is also ambiguous. According to one view, war is a force for social mobility. "Sorokin in his fundamental work on *Social Mobility* expressed the view, that war fosters vertical (or . . . interstratic) mobility, and I believe that on the whole he is right," says Andreski (1968:134).

During wartime minorities may be integrated into the emergency effort and appear to achieve more equal status. "Among primitive tribes where women help in wars their standing is high [and in modern] Europe, women made the greatest strides towards equality during and after the two World Wars, in which they proved to be very useful" (Andreski, 1968:73–74; cf. Lang, 1972:138).

War allows "some groups to improve their position relative to that of other groups, largely by shifts into industries and localities of labor scarcity" (Lang, 1972:139). During wartime the military structure can expand to include the whole society. In contemporary society, every person is both potentially a target and a citizen-soldier.

Even if one takes this view, social inequalities still remain. With the resumption of peace, moreover, minority gains may largely evaporate (cf. Buchanan, 1977; Fiman et al., 1975; Greenwald, 1975; Moskos, 1975; Strayer and Ellenhorn, 1975; Stevens, 1973).

Another perspective suggests that while armed conflict itself is "not a sufficient cause for the emergence of rank differences where none" exist, it operates "to institutionalize whatever rankings" are already recognized (Lang, 1972:138).

Relatively equal societies have often appeared less belligerent. Primitive societies, for example, have tended to be more peaceful when they have been more egalitarian (Fabbro, 1978; cf. Melko, 1973:114). The peaceful security communities in the North Atlantic area have been most successful where there have been relatively broad political, social, or economic elites and relatively close connections and easy mobility between social strata (Deutsch et al., 1957:148–49).

One of the contemporary cross-national studies casts doubt on any simple associations. This study finds that whether states have great internal discrepancies between rich and poor, or narrow differences, seems irrelevant for amounts of international violence. There is little significant association between most indicators of foreign conflict and indicators of inequality in land ownership, employment, or group discrimination. The major exception is for some aspects of income inequality before taxes; the more income inequality a society has, the fewer wars and absolute casualties. Per capita casualties, however, are not substantially associated with income inequality (M. Haas, 1974:217, 226, 231, 243).[29]

Instability

A number of analysts argue that peace and war are directly related to instability. War is an event that appears to break sharply from the smooth valley of peaceful behavior, a kind of catastrophe. It thus seems appropriate that it should be related to other kinds of instability (cf. Holt et al., 1978; Zeeman, 1977, 1976).

In some cases war has helped produce startling changes in international and national political systems. Table 4-9 shows how some recent wars involving major powers helped produce regime changes among the losers. In addition, modern wars have contributed to the dissolution of overseas empires of the winners.

Table 4-9

Regime Change and the Outcomes of Sustained War
Among Major Powers.

	Regime Change	No Regime Change
Winners	0	10
Losers	9	0

Major-Power War[a]	Winner	Loser
Franco-Prussian	Prussia	France
Russo-Japanese	Japan	Russia[b]
World War I	Great Britain France U.S. Italy Japan	Germany Austria-Hungary Russia
World War II	U.S. U.S.S.R. Great Britain	Germany Japan Italy France

[a]War in which there was a clear loser; that is, a nation that surrendered, was occupied, or lost territory.

[b]Classified as a regime change because of the Revolution of 1905, the writing of a new constitution, and the czar being forced to establish a Duma. This is a marginal case since the chief of state (the czar) did not change.

SOURCE: Stein and Russett (1980). Reprinted with permission of Macmillan Publishing Co., Inc., from *Handbook of Political Conflict: Theory and Research*, edited by T. R. Gurr. Copyright © 1980 by The Free Press, a Division of Macmillan Publishing Co., Inc.

War implies sharp economic changes. During wartime, a large segment of the labor force enters military service. Existing job and family patterns are disrupted. Unemployment declines. Personal income increases (Grand-Jean, 1967:204; Backman, 1952:224).

War tends to be inflationary. Prices characteristically rise rapidly during wartime. Figure 4-7 shows this rise for France and Great Britain during World Wars I and II. Figure 4-8 does the same for the United States during its history. Most recently, both the Korean and the Vietnam wars

> were accompanied by rising prices and declining unemployment, except that unemployment rose markedly in the last years of the war in Viet-nam as (but not necessarily because) United States troops were being withdrawn. There was also an unemployment effect connected with the Korean War, but this did not occur until after the truce was signed (Mueller, 1973:37–38).

The push of rising costs contributes to wartime inflation. Both material supplies and labor come into short supply as expanding military demands

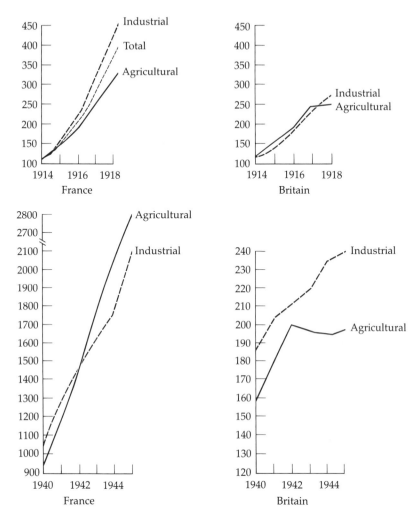

Figure 4-7
Rise in Wholesale Prices: France and Britain, World Wars I and II.
(SOURCE: Grand-Jean, 1967:186).

conflict with civilian needs. In the short run, limits exist beyond which it is extremely difficult to convert civilian resources to defense use. There are consumption boundaries beyond which defense expenditure, even during the most extreme wartime conditions, cannot go. As welfare increases within a given national society, these consumption requirements probably tend to increase with it. The requirements of war also justify higher taxes. As war budgets rise, these taxes necessarily become increasingly severe. The taxes in turn are part of the cost of products and services. As the taxes rise, prices rise with them.

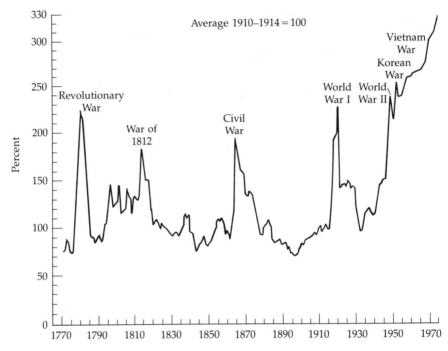

Figure 4-8
Rise in Wholesale Prices: U.S., 1770–1972. (SOURCE: Morris and Morris,
1976:749. Data since May 1920 are reproduced by permission of Harcourt
Brace Jovanovich, Inc., from *Our National Debt*, prepared by The Committee
on Public Debt Policy, copyright, 1949, 1977 by Harcourt Brace Jovanovich,
Inc., and *Statistical Abstract*, 1960; Economic Report of the President, 1973.)

The pull of increasing demand is another source of wartime inflation.
Extra money appears in the hands of the government, and then other
buyers. Wartime spending is normally not financed from current government revenue, but through borrowing in various forms—loans, bonds,
printing of currency. This money gradually filters down through the economy to corporate producers and individual consumers (cf. Machlup, 1969).

War, finally, implies changes in all other aspects of collective life—the
demographic, social, cultural, and psychological sectors.

Instability, in turn, may contribute to war. Sharp international and
national changes have often anticipated wars.

Some theorists believe that domestic political instability precedes war.
A qualitative study of diplomatic history over the last two centuries reached
the conclusion that "there tends to be a correlation between international
instability and the domestic insecurity of elites" (Rosecrance, 1963:293–96).
Another historian notes that, since 1870, "diversionary war tended to be

related to the polarization of politics, which in turn, was a function of the reality or fear of approaching internal chaos" (Mayer, 1971:145).

> Political actors who tended to favor resort to war for internal purposes looked for support to social and occupational strata, interest groups, and political formations that were anxious, if not panicky, about their life chances in the crisis-torn, modernizing world about them. . . . Starting with the Franco-Prussian War, the politics of counterrevolution and of diversionary war have repeatedly been closely tied, if not completely interlocked. They were activated by the same conservative political leaders, who, doubtful of their ability to master mounting internal dysfunctions, inclined toward the preemptive use of force, either at home or abroad. Significantly, the cadres of the bureaucracy, foreign office, army, police and church either were drawn from or had strong attachments to one or more segments of the crisis strata. For fear of losing the loyalty of these cadres and institutions that are so vital for the maintenance of law and order—let alone for preventive confrontations—otherwise self-confident and compromise-seeking conservatives became responsive to the pressures of counterrevolutionary leaders who counseled recourse to force and violence (Mayer, 1971:144).

Other scholars see economic instability as a major cause of international violence.[30] In the Mediterranean, during the Middle Ages, economic depression seemed to lead to large-scale war.

> The *Jihād* or Crusade was almost invariably encouraged by an unfavourable economic situation. . . . The great battles between Turk and Christian . . . (Prevesa, 1538, Lepanto, 1571) occur where one would logically expect to find them, in periods of recession. [At the same time,] civil wars, in which Christian fought Christian and Moslem Moslem, were . . . usually preceded by a "boom"; they come speedily to a halt when the economy takes a downward turn. In Christendom therefore, the major diplomatic treaties, the "Ladies' Peace" (Paix des Dames) (1529), Cateau Cambrésis (1559), Vervins (1598) occur either at the very peak of an upward curve or close to one (Braudel, 1973:897–98).

One study of the historical period preceding World War I concludes that economic and other growth led directly to the war. National development produced "lateral pressure" on other nation-states. "A substantially growing state is . . . likely to generate expansion, competition, rivalry, conflict, and violence. Growth can be a lethal process" (Choucri and North, 1975:1; cf. Lee, 1973).

Another study of the period before World War I reveals a number of short-term economic disruptions anticipating the conflict. Wheat prices and interest rates, important components of the general cost of living, showed an inflationary rise, as prewar hoarding began. At the same time, there was a flight from the securities of the prospective belligerents and their currencies, whose values declined. Gold became more popular (Holsti, 1972a:56–66).

Many have seen the dislocations of the Great Depression as important determinants of World War II. For example, the proletarianization of the German middle class as a result of the depression has often been blamed for the growth of aggressive fascism. Thus, one scholar states:

> In various respects the economic standard of many salaried employees, officials, engineers and members of similar groups closely approached that of the manual workers. As regards income and dependence on the business cycle, mechanization of work and division of labor, the two classes were difficult to distinguish. But the economic closeness of the two groups, under the influence of conflicting notions of self-esteem, increased the political tension between them and, as is well known, disposed the lower middle groups toward fascist attitudes (Speier, 1952b:28).

A series of studies have tried to relate international status to war. Rapid change helps produce inconsistencies between major dimensions of international status, particularly when status that has traditionally been ascribed is giving way to a status based on emerging achievement. Thus, changes in indicators of traditional international status—like the number of diplomatic missions received by a nation—often trail changes in a nation's other capabilities—population, urbanization, iron and steel production, military budgets, personnel, and so on. Status inconsistency, in turn, is empirically associated with violence. Where status inconsistency has been high, some studies suggest that war tends to be more frequent and casualties higher.[31]

Population instability has also appeared to be related to war. Studies of primitive people show that external wars were relatively infrequent when there was no migration or when migration occurred into unoccupied land. On the other hand, war was more frequent when people migrated into occupied land (Otterbein, 1977:704; cf. Divale et al., 1976). "Major movements and conquests of nomads" helped create violence in historical empires (Eisenstadt, 1963:337). European migration connected with the colonization of overseas empires also led to violence in the initial conquest and in the ultimate liberation of those territories.

In spite of such evidence the general relevance of migration to contemporary international violence is unclear. Figure 4-9 shows that gross European emigration overseas was relatively high in the 15 years before World War I. Nevertheless, it dropped off sharply in the decade before World War II.

A recent comprehensive study of the determinants of local conflicts also shows mixed results. Population movement was sometimes of central importance or a major irritant in the conflict. In most cases, however, population movements, absolute rates of growth, or differential rates of growth were only background factors or minor irritants (cf. Choucri, 1974b:106–8; M. Haas, 1974:236).

Current theorizing based on psychological literature suggests that instability may produce gaps between people's expectations and their achievements and that consequent anger and resentment may lead to violence.

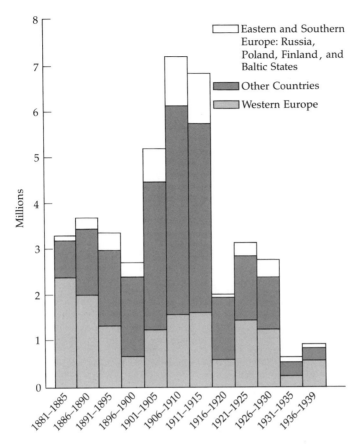

Figure 4-9
Gross Emigration Overseas: European, 1881–1939.
(SOURCE: Svennilson, 1954:65).

Figure 4-10 sketches how expectations and achievements can remain consistent in stable, improving, or declining social situations. Figure 4-11, on the other hand, shows a number of possible inconsistent patterns. Model *a* depicts how achievements can remain relatively stable, but expectations may be high for some future event, like political independence. After independence, however, there may be considerable disappointment as achievements actually change very little. Model *b* shows that rapid improvement may lead to a rise in achievements, but that expectations may increase still more quickly. This may happen with rapid growth or prosperity. Newly emerging groups and actors resent the heritage from the past that holds them back and may be frustrated because all their expectations cannot be met at once. Model *c* depicts a pattern where achievements improve rapidly for a time, but then deteriorate in an upside-down

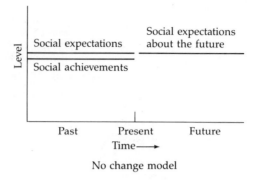

No change model

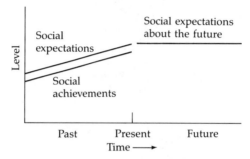

Slow change model, improvement pattern

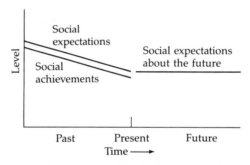

Slow change model, deterioration pattern

Figure 4-10

Consistent Expectations and Achievements. (SOURCE: Feierabend/ Feierabend/Nesvold, "Social Change and Political Violence: Cross-National Patterns" in *Anger, Violence, and Politics: Theories and Research*, edited by Feierabend/Feierabend/ Gurr, © 1972, p. 113. Reprinted by permission of Prentice-Hall, Englewood Cliffs, New Jersey.)

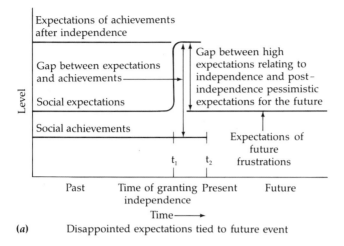

(*a*)   Disappointed expectations tied to future event

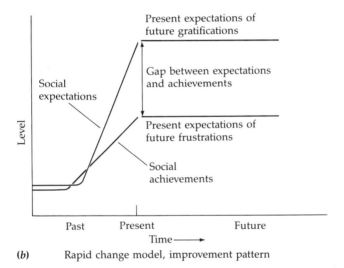

(*b*)   Rapid change model, improvement pattern

Figure 4-11

Inconsistent Expectations and Achievements. (SOURCE:
Feierabend/Feierabend/Nesvold, "Social Change and
Political Violence: Cross-National Patterns" in *Anger,
Violence, and Politics: Theories and Research*, edited by
Feierabend/Feierabend/Gurr, © 1972, pp. 111–15.
Reprinted by permission of Prentice-Hall, Englewood
Cliffs, New Jersey.)

(*continued on next page*)

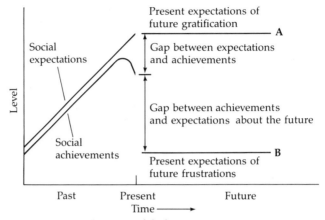

(c)   J-curve change model, deterioration pattern

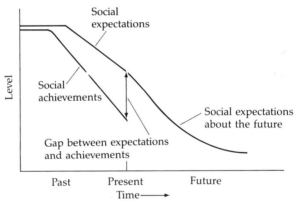

(d)   Rapid change model, deterioration pattern

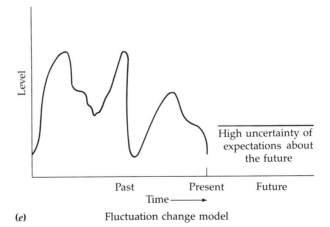

(e)   Fluctuation change model

Figure 4-11 (continued)

"J-curve" pattern. This may occur under conditions of rapid modernization. Established elites may lose ground as the newly wealthy challenge and transform traditional structures and the accepted processes of society. Or the dip may occur as part of a process of disdevelopment, where a society is forced to retrench because it loses part of its resource base. Model *d* shows achievements deteriorating rapidly, but expectations coming down in an unrealistically slow fashion. Model *e*, finally, shows a pattern of unpredictable fluctuation.

Gaps between expectations and achievements may lead to feelings of relative deprivation and frustration (see Wedderburn, 1974; Gurr, 1970; Runciman, 1966). Individuals and groups vary in their reactions to frustration. In some, the result may be fear, anxiety, or depression; in others, anger. If anger occurs, violence may be directed against an object or person in the individual's immediate environment. Crimes against persons and property, disguised "accidents," and various forms of subtle retaliation within the complicated political, economic, and social games of contemporary culture occur. Or anger may be turned inward and lead to self-destructive, masochistic behavior.

Frustration and anger may also be directed onto collective structures and processes, leading to domestic or international violence. International violence may be more likely when there is a high degree of frustration among elites who directly control collective foreign policy processes and military capabilities.[32]

In spite of such theorizing and evidence, we must say that there are not enough data to confirm that instability is directly related to war. Some work, indeed, strongly supports the idea that *no* direct connection exists. Table 4-10 summarizes findings of a cross-national study. It related the incidence and casualties of international violence to 33 variables reflecting national change. The only substantial positive relations occur with general system party instability and major government crises. Most of the other relations are negative, suggesting that instability is related to less rather than more international violence. The ambivalence and weakness of the results suggest even more strongly, however, that there is no direct association. There were "about as many negative as positive correlations between indicators of fluctuation and national aggression" and most of the correlations were low. The study, therefore, concluded "that change has no consistent relation to war incidence" (M. Haas, 1974:189–97).

Table 4-10

National Instability and War. (Figures represent Pearson product–moment correlations.)

Indicator of Fluctuation[a]	Conflicts		Foreign Killed	
	Wars	Clashes	Total	Per Capita
Annual change in national income/ annual change in population	−.11	−.28	−.09	−.18
Annual change in national income/ annual change in population[d]	.20	−.29	−.02	
Annual change in per capita electricity consumption	−.26	(−.31)	−.26	−.23
Annual change in per capita GNP	.22	−.26	.04	−.03
Annual change in per capita radios	.08	−.09	.01	.02
Annual change in per capita telephones	.00	.05	−.07	−.09
Annual change in per capita rail freight ton-kilometers	−.17	−.22	−.25	−.23
Annual change in per capita electricity production	−.16	−.04	−.21	−.14
Late increase in industrial production[c]	−.19	−.13		
Per capita electricity production annual increments[h]	(−.32)			
Annual change in population	.06	.21	.11	.18
Annual change in per capita caloric intake	.10	−.20	.09	.28
Annual change in per capita protein grammage intake	.06	−.29	−.01	.12
Annual change in per capita government budget	.09	.12	.13	.09
National income in stability	.09	.10	.00	.04
Annual change in urbanites	−.11	−.27	−.21	−.07
Annual change in agricultural employment	−.01	.17	.04	.03
Annual change in per capita literacy	−.07	−.03	−.15	−.25
Annual change in percent communist strength/population	−.11	−.20	−.18	−.16
Government instability	−.09	.03	.05	.12
Government instability[g]			.29	
System instability	.05	.21	.28	(.31)

[a]Findings from other studies are denoted by the letters following each variable number, as follows:
[b]Signs are reversed to be indicators of asymmetry.
[c]Cattell (1949).
[d]Rummel (1972).
[g]Gregg and Banks (1965).
[h]Haas (1968).
[i]Rummel (1963a).
[j]Tanter (1966).

SOURCE: M. Haas (1974:190–97). By permission of The Bobbs-Merrill Co., Inc., from *International Conflict*, by Michael Haas, copyright © 1974 by The Bobbs-Merrill Co., Inc.

Indicator of Fluctuation[a]	Conflicts		Foreign Killed	
	Wars	Clashes	Total	Per Capita
System instability[g]			(.36)	
Average age of latest 2 governments[b]	.04	−.09	−.04	.05
Average age of latest 2 governments[b,d]	.08			
Years independent/chief executives[b]	−.02	.04	.11	.20
Annual change in birth rate	−.04	−.07	−.12	−.12
Annual change in death rate	.09	−.08	.00	−.12
Annual change in marriage rate	.12	−.26	−.14	−.20
Major governmental crises	−.04	.19	.18	(.32)
Major governmental crises[r]	.09	.11	.13	
Major governmental crises[i]	.01	.06	.12	
Illegitimacy of present government	.20	.08	.10	−.02
Illegitimacy of present government[d]	.04	.11	.10	
Legality of latest 2 governmental changes[b]	.09	.17	.07	.05
Legality of latest 2 governmental changes[b,d]	−.07	.14	.09	
Annual change in per capita defense expenditures	−.16	−.24	−.21	−.09
Annual change in per capita education expenditures	−.09	(−.32)	(−.34)	−.28
Annual change in per capita welfare expenditures	.03	−.28	−.17	−.27
Annual change in per capita total government expenditures	.06	−.05	−.13	.01
Party system instability	−.07	.17	.06	.21
Party system instability[g]			(.34)	
Annual change in number of government ministries	.04	.02	−.06	−.09
Annual change in number of parliamentary parties	.04	−.03	.01	.05

Chapter 5

MILITARIZATION

Polarization may not immediately affect peace or war, but it is both a direct cause and a direct effect of militarization. Militarization brings to mind weapons and soldiers. These are a part, but only a part, of militarization. Militarization is a much broader category and includes the international law of war, alliances, military trade and aid, and hostility. It also comprehends national military regimes, military complexes, and militance.

Aggregation inhibits militarization. International arms limitation measures, for example, help to dampen arms races. Ultimately, however, militarization is the critical direct link with international violence.[1]

POLARIZATION AND MILITARIZATION

Table 5-1 outlines the relationship between the elements of polarization and militarization. The arrows go both ways suggesting that the two are broadly related and that each helps cause the other. Differentiation, inequality, and instability in international and national structures and processes are tied to various military characteristics.

Differentiation

International Differentiation

The elements of international differentiation are legal blocs, organization coalitions, transaction networks, and ideologies; and they are directly related to the law of war, alliances, military trade and aid, and hostility.

186

Table 5-1
Polarization and Militarization.

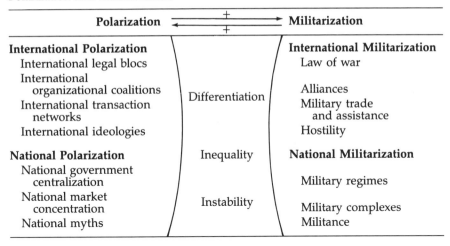

Polarization		Militarization
International Polarization		**International Militarization**
International legal blocs		Law of war
International organizational coalitions	Differentiation	Alliances
International transaction networks		Military trade and assistance
International ideologies		Hostility
National Polarization	Inequality	**National Militarization**
National government centralization		Military regimes
National market concentration	Instability	Military complexes
National myths		Militance

Law of War

As we have seen, the international law of peace and war helps limit the outbreak and conduct of war. At the same time, however, international law and its associated institutions can be used as weapons. Thus, the World Court's function is not only to settle conflict decisively, through adjudication, arbitration, or "explicit mediation" (Barkun, 1968:151–53): States also use the Court as an additional bargaining device in the game of nations (cf. Franck, 1968). Referring disputes to the Court may indicate a genuine willingness to settle differences, but it can also be an attempt to mount an international public relations campaign against an opponent or to maneuver the adversary into a setting where one's own chances of success are greater and one's opponent's position is weakened. The United States' appeal to the Court for release of the hostages taken by Iran is an example.

The doctrine of just war, as we have seen, has attempted to limit the initiation and fighting of wars. At the same time international legal blocs have adapted some doctrines—just war, self-defense, and war guilt–for military purposes.

JUST WAR Medieval transnational groups developed a legal doctrine of just war that specified that many wars were legitimate and could be undertaken with the blessings of international law and in good conscience. This doctrine implied that many wars were fought justly and that most actions undertaken by belligerents during the course of war were appropriate.

The international Islamic community helped provide a foundation for a legal doctrine of just war that included offensive violence and encouraged holy wars against infidels living within legal systems alien to Islam. Under the injunctions of Islamic law, it was the duty of Islamic rulers to bring non-Islamic territory under their civilizing jurisdiction and to use forceful means if necessary.

> The world was split into two divisions: the territory of Islam (the dār al-Islām), which may be called the *Pax Islamica*, comprising Islamic and non-Islamic

communities that had accepted Islamic sovereignty, and the rest of the world, called the dār-al-harb, or the territory of war. . . . The instrument which would transform the dār-al-harb into the dār-al-Islām was the jihād, [or crusade] (Khadduri, 1966:11–15).

The medieval international Christian community conceived that the legal doctrine of just war legitimated crusades for the Church. It "took war for religion to be the purest, holiest, most just kind of conflict imaginable" (J. G. Johnson, 1975:8). Thus Grotius devoted a chapter in *De Jure Belli ac Pacis* to the question "Is it ever right to go to war?" and concluded with a quotation on the duty of a Christian soldier, differentiating between the "ungodly enemy," and innocent fellow citizens. "We have fought always for justice, for godliness, and for the safety of the innocent," he said (Grotius, 1949:38).

Such use of the international doctrine of the just war is still important today. Modern religions, to some extent, still define issues of justice in such a way that international violence may be necessary. Some of the conflicts in the Middle East are examples.

On a global scale, secular ideology has partly replaced religion as the definer of legal justice. Northwestern leaders assert the justice of wars that preserve free institutions, "make the world safe for democracy," or preserve their people from foreign atheistic systems. Northwestern communities excuse possible injustice in the fighting and the killing of the innocent by claiming their cause is just. Thus, during World War II, the justice of the Allied cause presumably warranted saturation bombing of Axis urban population centers. And contemporary Northwestern interpretations of international law uphold the necessity of targeting urban populations in the event of nuclear war.

Northeastern and Southern international leaders, and their international legal advisers, also emphasize the justice of direct international violence when they use it. The Northeast and South have long contended that the whole structure of the international system, including international law, is really a weapon to defend Northwestern material interests. In this view, international law is part of the arsenal of the Northwestern imperialist powers to intimidate peoples who challenge them, or to keep in line those who are weaker. Such theorists and their political leaders believe that "an unjust war is one representing 'imperialist aggression'," while a just war is "one which liberates people from the injustices of capitalism or imperialism" (von Glahn, 1970:525).

SELF-DEFENSE International blocs, legal blocs, or individual states can also use the doctrine of self-defense to justify violence. Under Article 51 of the U.N. Charter, states retain the "inherent right of individual or collective self-defense," in the event of armed attack against them, "until the Security Council has taken measures necessary to maintain international peace and security." The Security Council has rarely taken such measures; and, "in the absence of a central authority for the enforcement of the law of nations, states have on occasion to take the law into their own hands," says Lauterpacht (1955, I:13–14). "Self-help, and intervention on the part of the other states which sympathize with the wronged one, are the means by which the rules of the laws of nations can be, and actually are enforced."

International blocs use the legal principle of collective self-defense to justify offensive war on a number of grounds. A narrow interpretation of the international law of self-defense includes a reply to direct attack on one's own territory. This requires the aggressor to strike first and defenders to strike back second. But a broader interpretation of the international right of self-defense permits armed intervention on the territory of other states even in the absence of direct attack on one's own state. The right of collective self-defense may implicitly include the right of a group of states to go to war to enforce international law against the perpetrators of crimes against peace. Groups of states may also be justified in going to war against others who have committed crimes against humanity or war crimes. These crimes were only explicitly defined after World War II. Nevertheless, the Allies emphasized Axis atrocities to justify violence against the Axis powers, and particularly Germany, in World War II.

The U.N. Charter does not require that states wait for prospective attackers to destroy them. They may respond to possible imminent attack. Thus, Israel has argued that Arab military buildups have justified military first-strikes in self-defense.

States may depend on certain economic conditions for survival, the defense of which may also require violence. The Germans in World War I, and the Japanese in World War II, claimed that Allied economic blockades or embargoes justified some of their actions.

WAR GUILT   International blocs can use the international legal system and the development of international criminal law to point the accusing finger of guilt, and further prosecute wars after the end of overt hostilities. The victors of past wars have used international law to brand the losers as aggressors, extract reparations from the defeated communities, and discredit and execute their leaders. The Allies invoked international law after World War I to demand heavy payments from their defeated enemies, and the Soviet Union did the same following World War II.

Following major wars, international criminal trials have been at some distance from the highest aspirations and ideals of international law. The absence of an International Criminal Court, or some international court with compulsory and binding jurisdiction in matters of war, leaves decision and enforcement in the hands of the aggrieved parties, their friends, or proxies.

It has been difficult to produce forceful legal sanctions against winners or remedies for losers. Thus in the Shimoda case, a Japanese court rejected arguments that the atomic attacks on Hiroshima and Nagasaki were justified by "military necessity" and "reached the principal conclusion that the United States had violated international law by dropping atomic bombs. . . . It also concluded, however, that [the] claimants had no legal basis for recovering damages from the Japanese government" (Falk, 1968a:374). In spite of considerable evidence of wrongdoing in the case of the massacres at My Lai, there was little legal action.

It has seemed easier to prosecute the defeated. The judicial bodies that are supposed to judge the claims and counterclaims of aggression and self-defense are to a considerable extent the instruments of one side versus another. Even in routine decisions in the International Court of Justice, judges have shown a tendency toward national bias, "a disposition to favor their own countries" (Hensley, 1968:568). In the supercharged atmosphere of trials for war crimes, the problem has been even more severe. At least initially these trials presumed guilt on the part of the defendants, and lacked many of the major safeguards of legal due process. They had many aspects of a "victor's justice," a "barely disguised revenge" (Minear, 1971:19; see also Vaughan and Sjoberg, 1970).

Claims of injustice, self-defense, and war guilt broaden and deepen international conflict. As violence expands, participants use international legal norms and symbols as tools to communicate their own intentions, to defend their interests or aspirations and actions, and as clubs to beat their opponents.

Alliances

International law is connected with international military alliances. Such alliances rest on international legal agreements to undertake certain military activity under specified circumstances in contemporary times.

International organization coalitions are also related to alliances.[2] Univeralistic international organizations have represented, in part, weapons in the game of international politics (cf. Yeselson and Gaglione, 1974). Coalitions with strong military aspects have used such international organizations to further their own interests. Thus the Grand Alliance that defeated Napoleon was the basis for the Concert of Europe, created to oversee the peace that followed. The victorious powers "established themselves as a continuing European directorate, which would meet whenever necessary to see that their settlement was not endangered" (Craig, 1961:20).

The victorious Allies of World War I dominated the League of Nations from beginning to end, in membership, official positions, and policies.

> The annex to the Covenant lists thirty-one Allied and Associated States which had signed the treaties as the original members and thirteen neutral states which had been asked to accede to the Covenant. All of the European Allies, the British Dominions, the succession states of Eastern Europe, Japan, China, and Siam in the Far East. All of the Latin American states, and Persia, the Hejaz, and Liberia had been asked to send representatives. But none of the former enemy states was included in the original list and, although Austria and Bulgaria were admitted after the first meeting of the Assembly, Hungary was not a member until 1922, Germany until 1926, and Turkey until 1932 (Craig, 1961:543).

In the League, the Allies used the language of universalistic collective security to bolster their own collective self-defense. Northwestern democracies tried to mobilize the League, without much success, to oppose the moves of the Axis powers. During the 1930s, the League censured Japan for its intervention in the Chinese province of Manchuria and voted economic sanctions against Italy for its invasion of Abyssinia.

The Allies of World War II dominated the U.N. during its early years. The symbol of this control was the fact that China, France, Great Britain, the United States, and the U.S.S.R. were permanent members of the Security Council, with veto power over all substantive matters.

The revolution in China and increasing hostility between the Soviet Union and the Western Allies dissolved the bonds of the earlier alliance. The Northwestern coalition, however, was able to continue to use the U.N. for military purposes. In 1950 the North Korean army invaded South Korea. The United States provided military support to the South Korean government. American leadership, temporary Soviet withdrawal from the Security Council, and a pro-Western majority in the General Assembly membership combined to allow the U.S. to condemn the North Korean invasion and subsequent military activity by the People's Republic of China. The U.N. supported American forces assisting the South Korean government, and many nations sent additional military assistance.

The Northwestern states have provided most of the support for subsequent U.N. peacekeeping forces. Major Northeastern states, including the Soviet Union and China, have generally been reluctant to contribute soldiers, material, or money.

More partial international organization coalitions are more obviously related to military alliances. States that cooperate at the U.N. and in other arenas also cooperate militarily to defend their interests. In the contemporary world, a ring of Northwestern alliances has included such institutions as the North Atlantic Treaty Organization (NATO), ANZUS (Australia, New Zealand, United States), the Southeast Asia Treaty Organization (SEATO), and the Central Treaty Organization (CENTO). The main element of the Northeastern alliance system is the Warsaw Treaty Organization. In the Southern world, regional organizations like the Arab League, Organization of African Unity (OAU), and Organization of American States (OAS) also have collective self-defense tasks (cf. Beer, 1970).

Military Trade and Assistance
International transaction networks have a military component. Members of the developed market economy group also tend to be members of the network of Northwestern military alliances. Similarly the centrally planned economies cooperate militarily in the Warsaw Treaty Organization and elsewhere.

The Northwestern and Northeastern networks carry not only general transactions, but also a good deal of military trade and aid (Neuman and

Harkavy, 1979; Farley et al., 1978; Harkavy, 1975). Table 5-2 suggests that the Northwestern and Northeastern networks are militarily self-contained, doing most of their arms transactions among themselves. The United States, United Kingdom, France, and the Federal Republic of Germany export most complete weapons, licenses, and components to their NATO allies. The U.S.S.R. is the major supplier for the Warsaw Pact states.

Military considerations restrict transactions outside the networks. Major alliances, like NATO, embargo strategic materials, excluding them from trade with the other side. Beyond this, general transactions between alliances are limited. Between 1974 and 1977, for example,

> the combined imports of all NATO countries from the Communist countries, as a percentage of the NATO members' total imports, remained relatively steady, while exports fluctuated. Imports ranged between 3.1 percent and 3.4 percent. Exports were 4.4 percent in 1974, rose to 5.2 percent in 1975, and decreased to 4.7 percent in 1976 and 4.2 percent in 1977.[3]

Hostility

International ideologies also imply a militaristic element. Ideologies can be weapons of consciousness, providing hostile interpretations of reality and distorting communication. They establish collective identity in opposition to other groups. They can be used to interpret others in terms of negative stereotypes. Table 5-3 provides one interpretation of international ideologies. It shows the way in which different actors—superpowers, major developed countries, minor developed countries, and developing countries—may tend to view themselves in a favorable light and others in a negative and hostile way.[4]

National Differentiation

National differentiation also involves military elements (cf. Evans et al., 1980; Skjelsbaek, 1979). National governmental centralization, market concentration, and myths are linked with national military regimes, military complexes, and militant attitudes and beliefs.

Military Regimes

National governmental centralization has developed together with military regimes. Research on primitive societies suggests a strong early relationship between political centralization and high military sophistication (Otterbein, 1970).

The centralization of governmental power in the European nation-state after the fifteenth century was both cause and effect of the introduction of gunpowder and modern armies.

> Kings alone could afford to finance the development of new technologies and armies. Taxation as a means of raising money revived methods largely unused since Roman times and kings launched an ever-accelerating process: new taxes supported new armies, new armies imposed higher taxes, and higher taxes necessitated larger armies. Kings then became the ultimate repositories of violence within their societies, and the bureaucracy—civil mercenaries anal-

ogous to those who staffed the new armies—grew in accordance with royal power. By the beginning of the sixteenth century, the French king employed approximately 12,000 civilians.

European kings effectively conquered their own societies.

. . .

The feudal nobility was dealt a severe blow. Their castles were no longer impregnable, so they became dependent on the king. The new weapons made their cavalry obsolete and they thus were of no use to the king. Their power over local inhabitants was reduced, since their role as defenders became even less credible. The gradual decline in the prestige and power of the nobles, which began in the sixteenth century, continued for several hundred years. In addition, the appearance of new weapons and infantry gave the common man an important role in warfare (Bridgman, 1978:108–9).[5]

National governmental centralization and militarization are related in modern communities too. Central governments and their agents have a near monopoly on violence. They alone can afford to pay for substantial military forces, and they alone can use most implements of violence. Central governments—not subordinate authorities or citizens—are entitled to go to war if other states seriously violate national rights under international law.

The professional soldier is tightly bound to the state.

The emergence of the military profession in the form we know it today in the countries of Europe and North America is a consequence of several major social developments, such as state centralization, creating a rationale for national armies, recruited domestically rather than internationally, and facilitating (through national legislation and central bureaucracy) the mobilization of cheap military labor for mass armies (Abrahamsson, 1971:37).

The military is the protector of the central government. "The military organization is not simply an elite of the state; it is also the state's major defender. Thus the professional is always on guard concerning the stability and sustenance of the state" (Perlmutter, 1977:25; cf. Huntington, 1957).

The connection between the soldier and the state is perhaps most evident in the contemporary Southern hemisphere, where the military seems to be a major force in modern nation-building. Cross-national statistics tend to support the relationship. A global sample for the period 1955–1957 shows that the overall level of defense expenditure and military personnel is related to political centralization. The relationship remains with controls for both GNP and population. The militarization indicators are also generally associated with a unitary form of government although this relationship is weaker (Rummel, 1972:App. 2).

Military Complexes

National governmental centralization and the concentration of national markets go together with the development of military complexes.

Central governments have historically undertaken initiatives that broadly coordinated economic activity at the same time that they developed narrow military capabilities. Early extended governments undertook "large-scale economic planning for military purposes involving several mil-

Table 5-2
Northern Arms Trade: Complete Weapons, Licenses, Components, 1975.[a]

Imports From \ Exports To	Belgium	Canada	Denmark	France	Germany, Federal Rep. of	Greece	Italy	Luxembourg	Netherlands	Norway	Portugal	Turkey	U.K.	U.S.	Bulgaria	Czechoslovakia	German Democratic Rep.	Hungary	Poland	Romania	U.S.S.R.	Albania	Austria	Finland	Ireland	Spain	Sweden	Switzerland	Yugoslavia	Australia	China	Japan	New Zealand
Belgium					3								3	3																			
Canada																																	
Denmark																															3		
France	2				123	1					1															1							
Germany, Federal Rep. of			3	3		1	3		1		1	12	13	3						2			3		1	123	3	3	23		1	3	
Greece							2				12															13	13						
Italy				3	3	1						1	3													1			3				
Luxembourg																																	
Netherlands					3		1						3	3																			
Norway				3			3		3				3	3																			
Portugal																																	
Turkey	1																																
U.K.	123		3		13									13						2						3	3	1	23	1		3	1

	U.S.																			
U.S.	3	13 13 13	123	1 123	1	3	12	1 123	1	1	12	1	1 123	1	1	13	13 13 1	23	123 13	
Bulgaria																				
Czechoslovakia																				
German Democratic Rep.																				
Hungary										1										
Poland																				
Romania									1 123	12		1	1		1		1	12		1
U.S.S.R.									1	1	(1)	1		1		(1)				
Albania																				
Austria																				
Finland																				
Ireland								1												
Spain																				
Sweden		3	1 3		2						2			3	1					
Switzerland			3	3									1		3	1				
Yugoslavia					1							1								
Australia											1			1	1					
China																				
Japan																	1			1
New Zealand																				

a 1 = trade in complete weapons; 2 = trade in licenses; 3 = trade in major components or subsystems (or in the technology for those items).

SOURCE: SIPRI (1976e:142).

Table 5-3
Hostile Ideological Stereotypes.[a]

Image from Point of View of U.S. and U.S.S.R.	Image from Point of View of a Major Developed Country	Image from Point of View of a Minor Developed Country	Image from Point of View of a Developing Country
Only we can assure world peace.	We are also a major country, entitled to participate in global government.	We are a small country, but more mature than the super countries—look how they mess things up.	This is all a conspiracy of the "haves" to continue to control the world and prolong our misery.
Because of the potential of nuclear and ultra-conventional weapons, small conflicts can damage us and even cause irreversible global damage.	What they really want is to keep us down and avoid any competition to their hegemony.	Soon technology will make us all equal in military strength. They want to preserve inequality—and hide their ambitions behind the mask of global benevolence.	The White Race enters now a new stage of global imperialism marked by obvious collusion between the white super countries—who want to perpetuate their racial oppression.
The U.N. is dominated by a mass (and mess) of countries without responsibility or power.	What ruins the U.N. is the Veto power of the big countries—and now they want to blame us.	There is a global forum available—the U.N. Only big power intrigues hinder its work. Let us make the U.N. work better—on a basis of real equality between all member states and mutual good will.	The one attempt to achieve international democracy is the U.N. This is why they want to bury it.
Problems such as pollution and overpopulation endanger us and the world. Their handling requires world leadership, which only we can supply.	They became corrupt and decadent and want all others to become the same.	We are entitled to control our own destiny.	"Pollution," "over-population"—these are all nonsense invented to keep us down. Soon they will restrict the energy we may use!
"Sovereignty" is an outdated concept, which does not fit a world of close mutual dependencies.	Sovereignty is to nations what liberty is to individuals. They want to enslave us.	For them we are just pawns to be moved as they wish.	Imperialism is not dead, it only changes its forms. Now they want to hide their aggression behind a facade of words on "mutual dependence." But we know the truth.

"Equality of states" is obviously a myth, and a dangerous one, at that.	Modern weapons serve as "equalizers." Therefore, they want to prevent us from getting and developing nuclear (and ultra-conventional) weapons.	States are equal, just as individuals are. The fact that they have more bombs does not make them any better.	This is a new fascist racism. They regard coloured nations as inferior to whites. But we will show them who is better.
Other countries do not have the necessary perspective to handle global issues. Only we can do so.	We are more objective than the two super countries and we are better equipped to handle problems than those "big brutes."	It is the struggle between big nations which ruins the world. The more power small nations get, the better for the world. If the big countries would break up into smaller ones, this would be all for the better.	Western culture is bankrupt. Artificial efforts to sustain its hegemony are doomed.
Other countries must be restrained from causing the world, their region and themselves damage.	We have heard this before, from all rulers who wanted to conquer the world.	It is true that some countries need restraint—namely the super-powers. It is really true—power corrupts, and super-power corrupts superbly.	They see the writing on the wall, but it will not help them.
A "crazy state" can cause catastrophe. The only way to prevent it is close control of the world.	All this talk about "crazy states" is just a smoke screen. They are "crazy" and want to control the world forever.	History repeats itself, and it is always the small and innocent countries which pay the price for the craziness of the big powers.	Who but a crazy nation can regard the awakening of a new world as crazy?
Others do not need large armies and should not be permitted to have nuclear weapons. We will assure to them justice.	Throughout history, power has changed. It is our turn to become a super country—but they want to stop history and perpetuate their own status.	We are able to protect ourselves; protection by them is worse than none at all.	It is now our turn. They will not stop it.
Therefore, we must establish a just and strong Pax Americana Sovietica.	Therefore, we must resist oppression of the world by the two super countries. Let us show we are also strong; let us develop our military might to defend our sovereignty and liberty.	Therefore, let us resist their domination as best we can.	Therefore, let us resist this new oppression. Let us gather strength for the day of reckoning.

197

aThese images are presented as probable reactions by opinion leaders and policymakers. Many other reactions are also possible and probable; the images in reality will be very heterogeneous.

SOURCE: Dror (1971:88–89).

lions of workers" (Speier, 1952b:10). And Wright notes that the modern bureaucratic state implies "complete organization of the state's resources, economy, opinion, and government for war even in times of peace," including the militarization of civilians (1965:248; cf. Mumford, 1967:215–23; Vagts, 1959).

European states developed the ties between general socioeconomic organization and military activity.

> The German defense ministry under Field Marshal Erich Ludendorff was the prototype of the modern military-industrial complex. "Before the First World War the officer corps and the leaders of heavy industry were mainstays of the authoritarian political and social system of the German empire." World War I demonstrated that war was no longer a matter of military prowess, of blitz, or of tactical maneuverability; in total war the outcome was determined by a nation's economic strength and its political and social stability. The mobilization of resources, human and material, and the active participation of different social groups made for an all-encompassing war machine. The military organization and war machine merged with the grand economic and capitalist corporation. Each emulated the other, consciously or otherwise. The war ministry was both a bureaucratic and a military organization. The German general staff staffed the war ministry and the war ministry patterned itself after the general staff. Several engineers who ran the raw material section of the German defense ministry during World War I, people like Richard von Moellendorff and Walter Rathenau, were devout students of scientific management and American capitalist organization. The contribution of Allgemeine Elektritizitäts Gesellschaft (the General Electric Company of Germany), which was one of Germany's greatest industrial concerns and was headed by Rathenau, was decisive in the mobilization of the economy and of labor and industry for total war. Emil Lederer, the German economist, is quoted as follows: "We can say that on the day of mobilization the *society* which existed until then was transformed into a community" (Perlmutter, 1977:11, quoting Feldman, 1966:3, 41, 27).

In contemporary societies, we refer to the military complex by various names. We talk about the "military-industrial complex," the "military establishment," or "the mil-org" (cf. Stern, 1978; Rosen, 1973; Sarkesian, 1972; Pursell, 1972; Yarmolinsky, 1970; Carey, 1969; Swomley, 1964; Boulding, 1963b).

Obviously, the military itself is a central component of the military complex. In earlier times, military activity was much more a general part of social life. Gradually, however, the military has become more specialized. Though we retain the idea of the citizen-soldier, modern society has seen the gradual development of a permanent differentiated military force that includes regular, reserve, and paramilitary components (cf. Zurcher and Harries-Jenkins, 1978). This professional military has a separate professional identity and expertise as well as its own characteristic patterns for various aspects of life, including politics, justice, education, religion, and family.[6]

Separate branches of law and administration deal with military affairs.

Table 5-4
Military and Civilian Employees: U.S. Department of Defense, 1945–1978.
(Thousands of employees, averages[a].)

Category	1945	1950	1955	1960	1965	1970	1975	1978
Total civilian employment	2,684.1	962.6	1,569.6	1,250.2	1,165.4	1,334.5	1,084.2	1,012.8
Total military employment	11,809.1	1,538.8	3,177.8	2,489.4	2,665.8	3,293.5	2,146.6	2,066.3
Civilians as Percentage of Total	18.5	38.5	33.1	33.4	30.4	28.8	33.6	32.9

[a]Actual data are shown for all fiscal years except 1978, which reflects the average number of employees for fiscal 1978 in the fiscal 1979 budget request.
SOURCE: Binkin et al. (1978:4). Published by permission from *Shaping the Defense Civilian Work Force: Economics, Politics, and National Security,* by Martin Binkin et al. Copyright © 1978 by the Brookings Institution.

Military managers must mobilize enormous resources and organize massive and complex tasks of research, development, production, and maintenance.

The military directly employs substantial numbers of civilians. Table 5-4 shows the relationship of civilian to military employees of the U.S. Department of Defense between 1945 and 1978. Defense budgets pay the salaries of workers outside government as well. One analyst estimated "that over 50 percent of the engineers and scientists engaged in research and development work in American industry were working on projects financed by defense or space programs" (Murray L. Weidenbaum, cited in Baldwin, 1967:146).

The components of the military complex outside formal government are themselves sizable adjunct bureaucracies. U.S. government military contracts may represent a very substantial percentage of defense contractors' total sales (Lapp, 1969:App. II). Table 5-5 shows the 100 corporations with the largest volume of defense contracts in 1978.

Following World War II, General Eisenhower supported an integrated U.S. military complex. He believed the war had "demonstrated more convincingly than ever before the strength our nation can best derive from the integration of all of our national resources in time of war" (Melman, 1970b:231). Following the war, Eisenhower issued a policy memorandum calling for continuation of this integration, which would provide for routine logistic support, ready reserve, and emergency back-up. Upon leaving the presidency, Eisenhower warned against the increasing influence of the military complex. Nevertheless, subsequent military management techniques have used budgetary incentives and constraints to create an even more integrated defense mechanism. "As a result of these controls, the relation between buyer and seller [is] a relationship between top management and subsidiary management" (Melman, 1970b:37, see also pp. 13–14, 21). Table 5-6 points out that in a number of cases the government actually owns a substantial number of production facilities.

Table 5-5

One Hundred Companies Which with Their Subsidiaries Received the Largest Dollar Volume of Military Prime Contract Awards, Fiscal Year 1978.

Rank	Parent Company	Rank	Parent Company
66	Aerospace[a] Corp.	46	General Telephone & Electronics Corp.
56	Agip Spa	41	General Tire & Rubber Co.
32	Amerada Hess Corp.	51	Goodyear Tire & Rubber Co.
39	American Motors Corp.	55	Gould, Inc.
21	American Telephone & Telegraph Co.	10	Grumman Corp.
89	Atlantic Richfield Co.	59	Guam Oil & Refining Co., Inc.
64	AVCO Corp.	87	Gulf Oil Corp.
78	Beech Aircraft Corp.	74	Harris Corp.
40	Bendix Corp.	44	Harsco Corp.
86	Bethlehem Steel Co.	54	Hercules, Inc.
7	Boeing Co.	92	Hewlett Packard Co.
42	Brittish Petroleum Co. Ltd.	17	Honeywell, Inc.
96	Burroughs Corp.	8	Hughes Aircraft Co.
61	Chamberlain Mfg. Corp.	27	International Business Machines Co.
81	Charles Stark Draper Labs, Inc.	95	International Harvester Co.
13	Chrysler Corp.	37	International Telephone & Telegraph Corp.
53	Coastal Corp.[b]	60	Johns Hopkins University[a]
88	Computer Sciences Corp.	28	LTV Corp.
34	Congoleum Corp.	77	Lear Siegler, Inc.
71	Control Data Corp.	6	Litton Industries, Inc.
98	Cubic Corp.	4	Lockheed Corp.
97	Day & Zimmerman, Inc.	91	Loral Corp.
82	Dupont E. I. de Nemours & Co.	19	Martin Marietta Corp.
58	E. Systems, Inc.	90	Mason & Hanger Silas Mason Co.
72	Eastman Kodak Co.	69	Massachusetts Institute of Technology[a]
68	Emerson Electric Co.	2	McDonnell Douglas Corp.
43	Engelhard Minerals & Chemical Corp.	93	Mitre Corp.[a]
33	Exxon Corp.	48	Mobil Corp.
30	FMC Corp.	65	Motorola, Inc.
20	Fairchild Industries, Inc.	99	Natomas Co.
26	Ford Motor Co.	84	Norris Industries, Inc.
63	General Cable Corp.	57	North American Phillips Corp.
1	General Dynamics Corp.		
5	General Electric Co.		
24	General Motors Corp.		

[a]Educational or other nonprofit institution.
[b]Formerly, Coastal States Gas Corp.

SOURCE: U.S. Department of Defense, Washington Headquarters Services, Directorate for Information, Operations, and Reports. *100 Companies Receiving the Largest Dollar Value of Military Prime Contract Awards, Fiscal Year, 1978*, p. 7.

Rank	Parent Company	Rank	Parent Company
15	Northrop Corp.	76	Standard Oil of Indiana
50	Ogden Corp.	62	Sun Co., Inc.
79	Pacific Resources, Inc.	83	Sverdrup & Parcel & Associates, Inc.
73	Pan American World Airways, Inc.	31	TRW, Inc.
45	Petroleos Mexicanos	36	Teledyne, Inc.
16	RCA Corp.	25	Tenneco, Inc.
9	Raytheon Co.	22	Texas Instruments, Inc.
49	Ret Ser Engineering Co.	12	Textron, Inc.
23	Reynolds R. J. Industries, Inc.	70	Thiokol Corp.
94	Rich, Marc & Co.	29	Todd Shipyards Corp.
11	Rockwell International Corp.	85	Transamerica Corp.
47	Royal Dutch Shell Group	100	United Industrial Corp.
67	Sanders Associates, Inc.	80	United States & South American Enterprises
52	Signal Companies Inc. (The)	3	United Technologies Corp.
35	Singer Co.	75	Vinnell Corp.
14	Sperry Rand Corp.	18	Westinghouse Electric Corp.
38	Standard Oil Co. of California		

Table 5-6

U.S. Government-Owned Industrial Production Plants, 1979.

Army		
Plant and Location	**Operator**	**Status**
Aircraft—GOCO[a]		
Stratford Engine Stratford, CT	AVCO Lycoming	Active
Saginaw Aircraft Saginaw, TX	Bell Helicopter Textron	Active
Ammunition—GOCO		
Riverbank AAP Riverbank, CA	Norris Industries, Inc.	Active
Joliet AAP Joliet, IL	Uniroyal, Inc.	Active
Indiana AAP Charlestown, IN	ICI Americas, Inc.	Active

[a]GOCO = Government-owned, contractor-operated.
[b]GOGO = Government-owned, government-operated.

SOURCE: U.S. Department of Defense, Washington Headquarters Services, Directorate for Information, Operations, and Reports (1979 mimeographed pages) *(continued on next page)*

Table 5-6   *(continued)*

	Army	
Plant and Location	**Operator**	**Status**
Iowa AAP Middletown, IA	Mason & Hanger	Active
Newport AAP Newport, IN	Uniroyal, Inc.	Inactive
Sunflower AAP Desoto, KS	Hercules, Inc.	Inactive
Kansas AAP Parsons, KS	Day & Zimmerman, Inc.	Active
Louisiana AAP Shreveport, LA	Thiokol Corp.	Active
Twin Cities AAP New Brighton, MN	Federal Cartridge	Inactive
Lake City AAP Independence, MO	Remington Arms Co.	Active
Gateway AAP St. Louis, MO	Voss Machinery	Inactive
Cornhusker AAP Grand Island, NB	Mason & Hanger	Inactive
Ravenna AAP Ravenna, OH	Ravenna Arsenal	Inactive
Hays AAP Pittsburgh, PA	Plant Facilities & Eng. Inc.	Inactive
Volunteer AAP Chattanooga, TN	ICI United States	Inactive
Holston AAP Kingsport, TN	Holston Defense	Active
Milan AAP Milan, TN	Martin Marietta Corp.	Active
Longhorn AAP Marshall, TX	Thiokol Corp.	Active
Lone Star AAP Texarkana, TX	Day & Zimmerman, Inc.	Active
Radford AAP Radford, VA	Hercules, Inc.	Active
Badger AAP Baraboo, WI	Olin Corp.	Inactive
St. Louis AAP St. Louis, MO	Donovan Const.	Inactive
Scranton AAP Scranton, PA	Chamberlain Mfg. Corp.	Active
Ammunition—GOGO[b]		
Alabama AAP Childersburg, AL	Government ARRCOM	Inactive Excess
Pine Bluff Arsenal Pine Bluff, AR	Government ARRCOM	Active
Rocky Mtn Arsenal Commerce City, CO	Government ARRCOM	Active

Army		
Plant and Location	**Operator**	**Status**
Phosphate Dev Sheffield, AL	Government TVA	Inactive
Hawthorne AAP Hawthorne, NV	Government ARRCOM	Active
McAlester AAP McAlester, OK	Government ARRCOM	Active
Combat Vehicles—GOCO		
Army Tank Warren, MI	Chrysler Corp.	Active
Lima Mod Center Lima, OH	Chrysler Corp.	Active
Electronics—GOCO		
Carbonyl Iron & Nickel	GAF Corp.	Active
Redstone Redstone Arsenal, AL	Raytheon Co. Thiokol Chem.	Active
Michigan Missile Sterling Hgts, MI	Vought Corp.	Active
Tarheel Missile Burlington, NC	Western Electric Co., Inc.	Active
Weapons—GOGO		
Watervliet Arsenal Watervliet, NY	Government ARRCOM	Active
Rock Island Arsenal Rock Island, IL	Government ARRCOM	Active

Navy		
Aircraft—GOCO		
Reserve Plant Columbus, OH	Rockwell International Corp.	Active
Reserve Plant Dallas, TX	LTV Aerospace, Vought Systems Division	Active
Reserve Plant Bloomfield, CT	Kaman Aerospace Corp.	Active
Reserve Plant Bethpage, NY	Grumman Aerospace Corp.	Active
Reserve Plant Calverton, NY	Grumman Aerospace Corp.	Active
Electronics—GOCO		
Reserve Plant St. Paul, MN	Univac Division of Sperry Rand Corp.	Active
Reserve Plant Rutherford Island S. Bristol, ME	Tracor Marine	Active

(continued on next page)

Table 5-6 *(continued)*

	Navy	
Plant and Location	**Operator**	**Status**
Missiles—GOCO		
Ordnance Plant Magna, UT	Hercules, Inc.	Active
Ordnance Plant Pomona, CA	General Dynamics Corp.	Active
Ordnance Plant Sacramento, CA	Aerojet Solid Propulsion Co.	Active
Reserve Plant Bedford, MA	Raytheon Co.	Active
Reserve Plant Bristol, TN	Raytheon Co.	Active
Ordnance Plant Mishawaka, IN	Bendix Corp.	Inactive Excess
Ordnance Plant Sunnyvale, CA	Lockheed Missiles & Space Co., Inc.	Active
Ordnance Station Indian Head, MD	Government NAVSEA	Active
Weapons—GOCO		
Ordnance Plant Pittsfield, MA	General Electric Co.	Active
Ordnance Plant Minneapolis, MN	FMC Corp.	Active
Ordnance Plant Rochester, NY	Eastman Kodak Co.	Active
Reserve Plant McGregor, TX	Hercules, Inc.	Active
Ordnance Plant Cumberland, MD	Hercules, Inc.	Active
Ordnance Station Louisville, KY	Government	Active

	Air Force	
Aircraft—GOCO		
Air Force Tulsa, OK	McDonnell Douglas Rockwell International Corp.	Active Excess
Air Force Ft. Worth, TX	General Dynamics Corp.	Active
Air Force Marietta, GA	Lockheed-Georgia	Active
Air Force Wichita, KS	Boeing Co.	Active

Air Force		
Plant and Location	**Operator**	**Status**
Air Force San Diego, CA	General Dynamics Corp.	Active
Air Force Toledo, OH	Teledyne, Inc.	Active
Air Force Everett, MA	General Electric Co.	Active
Air Force Lynn, MA	General Electric Co.	Active
Air Force Cincinnati, OH	General Electric Co.	Active
Air Force Palmdale, CA	Serv-Air, Inc. Rockwell International Corp. Rockwell International Corp. Lockheed Corp. Northrop Corp. McDonnell Douglas Corp.	Active
Air Force Neosho, MO	Teledyne, Inc.	Active
Air Force Albuquerque, NM	General Electric Co.	Active
Air Force St. Louis, MO	McDonnell Douglas Corp.	Active

Electronics—GOCO

Air Force Binghamton, NY	General Electric Co.	Active

Forging and Extrusion—GOCO

Forging Cleveland, OH	Alcoa	Active
Extrusion Buffalo, NY	Curtiss-Wright Corp.	Active
Extrusion Halethorpe, MD	Kaiser Aluminum	Active
Forging N. Grafton, MA	Wyman-Gordon	Active
Air Force Porter, NY	Bell-Textron, Inc.	Active
Air Force Tucson, AZ	Hughes Aircraft Co.	Active
Air Force Hill AFB, UT	Boeing Aerospace	Active
Air Force Lampo Junction, UT	Thiokol Corp.	Active
Air Force Waterton, CT	Martin Marietta Corp.	Active

The government is taking on the traditional role of the private entrepreneur while the companies are becoming less like other corporations and acquiring [many] of the characteristics of a government agency or arsenal. In a sense, the close, continuing relationship between the Department of Defense and its major suppliers is resulting in a convergence between the two, which is blurring and reducing much of the distinction between public and private activities in an important branch of the American economy (Weidenbaum, quoted in Melman, 1970b:13; cf. Kucera, 1974; Sapolsky, 1972).

Civilian enterprises directly employ military personnel. Military men frequently move into defense-related industry. Table 5-7 shows the number of former high-ranking Defense Department personnel employed by private corporations with military contracts.

Finally, direct defense expenditures and the personal outlays of individuals on defense payrolls support and influence the populations of urban centers that provide military logistic support.

Table 5-7

Private Corporations Employing Former U.S. Defense Department Personnel, Fiscal Year 1978.

Corporation	Personnel[a]				
	A	B	C	D	Total
AAI Corp.	1	0	0	1	2
AM General Corp.	1	0	0	0	1
Aerojet General Corp.	9	0	2	0	11
Aerospace Corp.	2	0	1	0	3
Airesearch Mfg. Co. of Arizona	1	0	0	0	1
American Telephone & Telegraph Co.	2	0	0	1	3
Applied Devices Corp.	1	0	1	0	2
Automation Industries, Inc.	16	0	3	1	20
AVCO Corp.	3	0	0	0	3
AVCO Everett Research Lab.	1	0	0	1	2
BDM Corp.	60	2	3	2	67
Bath Iron Works Corp.	2	0	0	0	2
Battelle Memorial Institute	6	0	3	1	10
Beech Aircraft Corp.	10	0	0	0	10
Bendix Co.	2	0	1	0	10
Boeing Co.	48	4	13	1	66
Boeing Services International, Inc.	7	0	1	0	8
Boeing Vertol Co.	0	0	1	0	1
Bolt, Beranek & Newman, Inc.	0	0	0	1	1
Booz, Allen & Hamilton, Inc.	18	1	1	0	20

[a]A: Retired military officer, Maj./Lt. Cmdr. or above.
B: Former military officer, Maj./Lt. Cmdr. or above.
C: Former civilian employee whose salary was equal to or above minimum GS–13 during three years preceding termination of service with DoD:
D: Former employee of, or consultant to, defense contractor who during last fiscal year was employed by DoD at salary equal to or above minimum GS–13 salary.
Source: U.S. Department of Defense, Washington Headquarters Services, Directorate for Information, Operations, and Reports (1979, mimeographed pages).

Corporation	Personnel[a]				
	A	B	C	D	Total
Bunker Ramo Corp.	3	0	1	0	4
Burroughs Corp.	3	0	0	0	3
California, University of	1	0	0	2	3
Calspan Corp.	6	0	0	1	7
Chamberlain Mfg. Corp.	2	1	0	0	3
Champlin Petroleum Co.	1	0	0	0	1
Chrysler Corp.	4	0	0	0	4
Coloney, Wayne H., Inc.	1	0	1	0	2
Computer Sciences Corp.	48	0	0	2	50
Comtech Laboratories, Inc.	0	0	0	1	1
Control Data Corp.	13	0	3	1	17
Cutler Hammer, Inc.	2	0	2	1	5
Data Design Laboratories	17	0	0	0	17
Dayton, University of	1	0	1	0	2
Dynalectron Corp.	4	0	0	0	4
EG&G, Inc.	5	0	1	0	6
ESL, Inc.	7	0	0	2	9
E. Systems, Inc.	29	1	2	0	32
Electrospace Systems, Inc.	3	0	0	0	3
Emerson Electric Co.	12	0	0	0	12
Exxon Corp.	1	0	0	0	1
FMC Corp.	5	0	0	0	5
Fairchild Industries, Inc.	6	0	2	1	9
Federal Electric Corp.	1	0	0	0	1
Felec Services, Inc.	2	0	0	0	2
Ford Aerospace & Communications	24	2	1	1	28
GTE Sylvania, Inc.	11	1	1	1	14
Garrett Corp.	0	0	1	0	1
General Dynamics Corp.	54	0	8	0	62
General Electric Co.	19	1	1	6	27
General Motors Corp.	3	0	1	1	5
General Research Corp.	11	0	4	2	17
Georgia Tech Research Institute	1	0	0	0	1
Goodrich BF Co.	1	0	0	0	1
Goodyear Aerospace Corp.	3	0	0	0	3
Gould, Inc.	3	0	1	0	4
Grumman Aerospace Corp.	10	0	0	0	10
Gulf Oil Corp.	3	1	0	0	4
HRB Singer, Inc.	1	0	0	0	1
Harris Corp.	8	0	0	1	9
Hewlett Packard Co.	1	0	2	0	3
Honeywell, Inc.	18	0	4	2	24
Honeywell Information Systems, Inc.	3	0	0	1	4
Hughes Aircraft Co.	41	1	7	6	55
IIT Research Institute	3	0	2	1	6
ITT Gilfillan, Inc.	1	0	0	0	1

(continued on next page)

Table 5-7   *(continued)*

Corporation	Personnel[a]				
	A	B	C	D	Total
Institute for Defense Analysis	2	0	3	4	9
International Business Machines Co.	8	0	0	0	8
International Harvester Co.	2	0	0	0	2
International Telephone & Telegraph Corp.	3	0	2	0	5
Interstate Electronics Corp.	2	0	0	0	2
Itek Corp.	1	0	1	0	2
Jacksonville Shipyards, Inc.	3	0	0	0	3
Johns Hopkins University	0	0	1	3	4
Kaman Aerospace Corp.	0	0	0	2	2
Kentron Hawaii, Ltd.	4	0	1	0	5
Kollmorgen Corp.	1	0	0	0	1
Lear Siegler, Inc.	5	0	0	0	5
Linkabit Corp.	0	0	1	0	1
Litton Industries, Inc.	4	0	0	1	5
Litton Systems, Inc.	3	0	0	0	3
Lockheed Corp.	39	1	3	2	45
Lockheed Electronics Co., Inc.	9	0	0	1	10
Lockheed Missiles & Space Co., Inc.	14	0	2	3	19
Lockheed Shipbuilding Construction	4	0	0	0	4
Logicon, Inc.	12	0	1	0	13
Loral Corp.	0	0	0	1	1
Lykes Bros. Steamship Co., Inc.	0	1	0	0	1
Magnavox Co.	1	0	0	0	1
Magnavox Government & Industrial Electronics Co.	2	0	2	0	4
Marquarot Co.	1	0	0	0	1
Martin Marietta Corp.	60	2	8	6	76
Mason & Hanger Silas Mason Co.	2	0	0	0	2
Massachusetts Institute of Technology	0	0	2	7	9
McDonnell Douglas Corp.	27	0	2	0	29
Mitre Corp.	11	1	7	5	24
Motorola, Inc.	2	0	0	0	2
Newport News Shipbuilding & Dry Dock Co.	1	0	0	1	2
Northrop Corp.	39	0	6	3	48
Northrop Worldwide Aircraft Services, Inc.	42	1	7	0	50
Olin Corp.	1	0	0	0	1
Paccar, Inc.	0	0	1	0	1
Pacific Architects & Engineers, Inc.	1	0	0	0	1
Pan American World Airways, Inc.	4	0	0	0	4
Parker Hannifin Corp.	2	0	0	0	2
Parsons Ralph M. Co., Inc.	21	0	2	0	23
Perkin Elmer Corp.	2	0	0	0	2
Phillips Petroleum Co.	1	0	0	0	1
Planning Research Corp.	21	0	1	3	25
Pride Refining, Inc.	1	0	0	0	1

Corporation	Personnel[a]				
	A	B	C	D	Total
R&D Associates	5	1	3	4	13
RCA Alaska Communications, Inc.	1	0	0	0	1
RCA Corp.	17	0	3	1	21
RCA Global Communications, Inc.	1	0	0	0	1
RAND Corp.	2	0	3	2	7
Raytheon Co.	13	1	4	2	20
Raytheon Service Co.	7	0	0	0	7
Reflectone, Inc.	0	0	0	1	1
Reynolds R. J. Industries, Inc.	1	0	0	0	1
Rochester, University of	0	0	0	1	1
Rockwell International Corp.	36	0	10	0	46
Rosenblatt M. Son, Inc.	0	0	1	0	1
SRI International	6	0	2	5	13
Sanders Associates, Inc.	2	0	4	1	7
Science Applications, Inc.	40	3	2	11	56
Sierra Research Corp.	1	0	0	0	1
Singer Co.	5	0	2	0	7
Southern California, University of	0	0	1	0	1
Southwestern Refining Co., Inc.	1	0	0	0	1
Sperry Rand Corp.	17	0	0	3	20
Summa Corp.	0	0	1	0	1
System Development Corp.	23	0	0	4	27
Systems Consultants, Inc.	17	0	0	1	18
Systems Research Lab., Inc.	6	1	0	0	7
TRW Colorado Electronics, Inc.	5	0	0	0	5
TRW, Inc.	51	0	8	4	63
Teledyne Brown Engineering	2	0	0	0	2
Teledyne CAE	2	0	0	0	2
Teledyne Firth Sterling	1	0	0	0	1
Teledyne, Inc.	2	0	0	0	2
Tesoro Petroleum Corp.	1	0	0	0	1
Texas Instruments, Inc.	13	1	2	3	19
Textron, Inc.	9	0	0	0	9
Thiokol Corp.	4	0	0	0	4
Tracor, Inc.	21	1	3	0	25
Union Carbide Corp.	1	0	0	0	1
United Technologies Corp.	8	0	3	2	13
Value Engineering Co.	12	0	2	0	14
Vought Corp.	9	1	1	1	12
Watkins Johnson Co.	1	0	0	0	1
Western Electric Co., Inc.	2	0	0	0	2
Western Union Telegraph Co.	5	1	0	0	6
Westinghouse Electric Corp.	17	0	0	1	18
Xerox Corp.	1	0	0	1	2
Totals	1319	31	184	132	1666

Militance

National myths imply national militance. National myths are generally eth-nocentric. They emphasize exclusive identification with one's country. Such identification also implies a belief in military defense of that country (cf. Ferrero, 1972; Vagts, 1959).

National militance is often projected in rhetoric that calls for the defense of cherished values and rights against uncivilized, lawless, tyrannical, and aggressive enemies (Ivie, 1974).

Militant national myths allow the projection and transference of in-dividual anxieties, insecurities, and frustrations onto the larger tableau of group life. Individuals with strong beliefs in national myths tend to be at home in, and supportive of, a militarized environment. They may identify with militarized society in a relatively dogmatic and rigid way. They often have a pessimistic, negative, or suspicious view of human nature, a belief that others can be deterred from attack only by threats of violence. In ad-dition, militaristic individuals may score high on measures of punitiveness, inflexibility, perceptions of enmity for other people and coercion by them. They may also have high degrees of competitiveness and desire for power, influence, and achievement. These characteristics, however, may be joined with feelings of low self-esteen and self-worth, inefficacy and insecurity.[7]

Military symbols are often embedded in the deeper dimensions of national mythology. Armaments are part of the secular religion. There is a sense in which a secret weapon is also a sacred weapon. The secret weapon has a sort of magical quality to it. It seems to appear through fairly unpredictable sorts of processes, and it seems to confer superhuman pow-ers upon its possessor. The naming of modern weapons systems suggests this sacred dimension. Whole series of American missiles and delivery systems are given the names of Greek and Roman gods—Nike, Hercules, Thor, Zeus, Jupiter, Saturn, Poseidon. Early exploratory programs in space carried the names of Apollo and Mercury.[8]

Inequality

Militarization is also related to international and national inequality.

International Inequality

It seems reasonable to assume that the degree of inequality in a particular historical or geographical international environment should be associated with its degree of militarization. This particular relationship has not yet been thoroughly investigated.[9] It is clear, however, that the Northwestern and Northeastern groups that dominate the global system also have the highest levels of military expenditure, trade, and assistance. Table 5-8 shows that the Northwestern NATO nations in 1957 accounted for almost two-thirds of the world military budget. By 1977 the proportion had come down, but only just below one-half. The Northeast, represented by the Warsaw Treaty Organization, spent over 21 percent of the world's military outlay in 1957, a proportion that rose to about 26 percent in 1977.[10]

Northern networks dominate the arms trade. Table 5-9 shows the major weapons exporters—Northwestern and Northeastern states. Southern nations are the world's major weapons importers.

Northern states also provide most of the world's direct and indirect military assistance. The global North supplies military equipment and advisors. It also helps Southern states develop technologies with military applications. Training and materials for the development of nuclear energy, for example, enhance possible military nuclear capabilities (cf. Ra'anan et al., 1978; SIPRI, 1971; Leiss et al., 1970).

Northern dominance of modern industrial technology encourages a preeminent international military role. The economic law of comparative advantage implies that Northern states should specialize in high technology areas where they already have an edge, and this, in fact, occurs. The benefits of knowledge and scale reduce costs and conserve resources for Northern states, while Southern states are militarily dependent on the North because of their limited industrial capabilities. Table 5-10 shows very limited domestic arms production in most Southern countries.

Northern military activity furthers Northern political and economic interests. The nuclear "umbrella" provided by the United States, Britain, and France theoretically protects Northwestern interests around the world. Soviet capabilities presumably do the same for the Northeast. More conventional forces are used for direct military intervention and indirect military activities such as "showing the flag," military alerts, and mobilization.

Northern states use military trade and aid to extract important resources from the South. In the contemporary world, exports of modern Northern weapons to the South help to assure a steady flow of Southern natural resources, including oil (cf. Ronfeldt and Sereseres, 1977; Harkavy, 1975; Bova, 1972).

Northern ideology, finally, emphasizes inequality to justify military activity. Northern states have historically stressed their own supposed superiority because of particular political, social, economic, cultural, scientific, or genetic characteristics. They have perceived differences between their own civilization and others' so-called barbarism, and undertaken crusades in the name of a white man's burden, civilizing mission, manifest destiny, the master race. More recently they have used the doctrine of development for the same purpose.

National Inequality

Unequal Nation-States

Unequal individual nations undertake disproportionate military efforts. Table 5-11 suggests in a very general way that the leading states of the international system between 1815 and 1965 tended to have the greatest

Table 5-8
World Military Expenditures, 1957–1977.[a]

	1957	1958	1959	1960	1961	1962	1963	1964	1965	1966	1967
U.S.	69,584	69,622	70,004	68,130	70,937	76,943	75,824	73,326	72,928	86,993	100,363
Other NATO	29,817	27,301	29,830	31,050	32,241	35,397	36,697	37,241	37,157	37,325	38,980
Total NATO	99,401	96,923	99,834	99,180	103,178	112,340	112,521	110,567	110,085	124,318	139,980
U.S.S.R.	31,300	30,500	33,000	32,700	40,800	44,600	48,900	46,700	44,900	47,000	50,800
Other WTO[b]	2,700	2,900	3,000	2,958	3,250	4,147	4,469	4,471	4,598	4,833	5,252
Total WTO	34,000	33,400	36,000	35,658	44,050	48,747	53,369	51,171	49,498	51,833	56,052
Other Europe	3,160	3,225	3,300	3,300	3,546	3,867	3,999	4,226	4,256	4,422	4,20
Middle East	1,025	1,225	1,325	1,340	1,450	1,620	1,810	2,090	2,400	2,875	3,735
South Asia	1,100	1,100	1,075	1,090	1,150	1,494	2,317	2,287	2,364	2,313	2,101
Far East (excl China)	2,900	3,100	3,300	3,400	3,550	3,783	3,977	4,304	4,838	4,929	5,442
China	(9,750)	(9,000)	(10,000)	(10,000)	(11,800)	(13,700)	(15,500)	(18,400)	(19,400)	(21,800)	(23,500)
Oceania	974	976	1,024	1,018	1,006	1,039	1,166	1,356	1,559	1,779	1,937
Africa (excl Egypt)	300	275	325	390	575	855	967	1,163	1,338	1,397	1,733
Central America	350	375	400	435	458	512	548	583	574	617	663
South America	2,000	2,060	1,700	1,725	1,680	1,727	1,810	1,793	2,193	2,179	2,614
World Total	154,960	151,659	158,283	157,536	172,443	189,684	197,984	197,940	198,505	218,462	241,540

	1968	1969	1970	1971	1972	1973	1974	1975	1976	1977	1976X
U.S.	103,077	98,698	89,065	82,111	82,469	78,358	77,383	75,102	71,019	76,412	91,008
Other NATO	37,795	37,633	38,381	40,412	42,619	43,326	44,577	45,683	46,854	47,047	59,891
Total NATO	140,872	136,331	127,446	122,523	125,088	121,684	121,960	120,785	117,873	123,459	150,899
U.S.S.R.	58,600	62,200	63,000	63,000	63,000	63,000	61,900	61,100	61,100	60,400	61,100
Other WTO[b]	6,387	7,012	7,498	7,974	8,240	8,808	9,444	10,263	10,848	11,300	10,848
Total WTO	64,987	69,212	70,498	70,974	71,240	71,808	71,344	71,363	71,948	71,700	71,948
Other Europe	4,560	4,740	4,864	4,983	5,288	5,382	5,752	5,967	5,907	5,970	8,264
Middle East	4,425	5,225	6,175	6,900	9,843	13,480	16,558	18,560	21,525	17,750	32,796
South Asia	2,176	2,312	2,403	2,856	3,082	2,745	2,591	2,835	3,315	3,240	3,850
Far East (excl China)	6,086	6,531	7,061	7,746	8,163	8,181	8,264	8,825	9,000	9,600	12,869
China	(25,500)	(27,500)	(29,300)	(30,000)	(27,500)	(27,500)	(27,500)	(27,500)	(27,500)	(27,500)	(27,500)
Oceania	2,101	2,129	2,125	2,125	2,131	2,102	2,177	2,174	2,158	2,124	2,749
Africa (excl Egypt)	2,012	2,422	2,567	2,843	2,996	3,362	4,728	5,223	6,210	6,500	8,621
Central America	742	724	761	783	799	820	839	974	1,150	1,200	1,396
South America	2,549	2,662	2,807	3,301	3,364	3,808	3,378	3,879	4,160	4,510	4,520
World Total	256,010	259,788	256,007	255,034	259,494	260,872	265,091	268,085	270,746	273,553	325,412

[a]Millions of U.S. $ at 1973 prices and 1973 exchange rates, except final column, X, at 1978 prices and exchange rates and therefore not comparable to the other years.
[b]At 1978 prices and Benoit–Lubell exchange rates.

SOURCE: SIPRI (1978f:142–43).

Table 5-9
Northern Arms Exports and Southern Arms Imports, 1950–1975.[a]

Values of Exports of Major Weapons[c]

Country	1950	1951	1952	1953	1954	1955	1956	1957	1958	1959	1960	1961	1962
U.S.	91	109	103	73	285	305	330	346	381	249	545	300	281
U.S.S.R.	25	43	28	176	9	66	148	256	196	111	165	391	786
U.K.	96	64	46	165	166	175	198	180	358	183	196	185	95
France	3	3	1	41	70	70	123	70	131	49	37	38	92
Canada	14	4	1	*	—	1	39	4	5	62	11	16	2
China	23	23	—	—	—	—	—	5	231	133	125	—	—
Czechoslovakia	—	—	—	—	—	43	58	6	23	58	45	5	5
Federal Rep. of Germany	*	*	—	1	4	7	9	5	7	26	23	5	2
Italy	7	29	—	2	—	2	31	29	28	*	7	—	*
Japan	—	—	—	1	15	—	9	11	23	12	—	11	18
Netherlands	35	14	6	2	1	85	1	2	1	4	1	2	2
Sweden	*	1	16	5	6	6	6	—	37	*	1	*	—
Other indus. West	—	—	—	7	*	5	*	—	—	—	1	2	1
Other indus. East	—	—	—	—	—	—	2	*	29	24	*	—	8
Third World	—	—	—	15	1	1	3	5	11	2	3	2	8
Total[d] (incl. Vietnam)	294	289	201	488	556	765	957	919	1,461	920	1,159	957	1,302

Country	1963	1964	1965	1966	1967	1968	1969	1970	1971	1972	1973	1974	1975
U.S.	393	284	413	393	367	576	954	962	916	958	885	1,200	1,769
U.S.S.R.	329	287	408	608	1,013	892	870	836	1,085	726	1,542	1,540	1,652
U.K.	135	137	203	148	155	225	266	142	300	283	242	481	503
France	148	105	74	107	52	220	131	156	211	269	411	357	477
Canada	10	9	14	9	9	36	14	28	42	30	3	*	5
China	—	39	7	36	13	4	7	17	81	120	21	80	48
Czechoslovakia	12	7	3	6	9	30	17	24	11	10	1	11	5
Federal Rep. of Germany	10	20	10	64	3	8	13	1	19	37	2	101	118
Italy	15	15	5	1	16	51	41	33	32	39	4	106	65
Japan	1	1	5	9	23	38	2	*	*	—	—	2	—
Netherlands	*	9	17	1	—	4	19	7	26	20	30	25	32
Sweden	—	—	—	1	—	—	*	—	—	4	1	5	16
Other indus. West	2	*	23	18	45	6	8	3	37	10	16	9	10
Other indus. East	*	—	*	—	1	—	1	—	4	—	13	—	2
Third World	3	2	3	19	12	7	16	6	11	14	16	211	141
Total[a] (incl. Vietnam)	1,058	914	1,192	1,553	1,885	2,059	2,126	2,247	2,835	2,673	2,909	4,070	4,843

[a]Millions of U.S. $ at constant 1973 prices.
[b]A = yearly figures. B = five-year moving averages.
[c]The values include licensed production.
[d]Items may not add up to totals because of rounding. Figures are rounded to nearest 10.
[e]Five-year moving averages are calculated from the year arms imports began, as a more stable measure of the trend in arms imports than the often erratic year-to-year figures.
* < $1 mn.

SOURCE: SIPRI (1976e:249–53).

215

(continued on next page)

Table 5-9 (continued)

Values of Imports of Major Weapons by Third World Countries: By Region[a,b]

Region		1950	1951	1952	1953	1954	1955	1956	1957	1958	1959	1960	1961	1962	1963
Far East (excl Vietnam)	A	147	152	57	209	174	222	227	211	506	396	583	153	272	237
	B[c]	—	—	148	163	178	209	268	312	385	370	382	328	309	244
South Asia	A	44	20	19	92	104	108	176	254	488	148	205	221	144	169
	B	—	—	56	69	100	147	226	235	254	263	241	178	160	152
Middle East	A	35	55	12	70	81	186	350	300	249	238	123	150	439	301
	B	—	—	51	81	140	197	233	265	252	212	240	250	262	305
North Africa	A	—	—	—	—	—	—	6	5	4	6	9	12	30	26
	B	—	—	—	—	—	—	—	—	6	7	12	17	21	32
Sub-Saharan Africa	A	—	5	4	16	18	12	1	1	3	46	27	43	36	36
	B	—	—	—	11	10	10	7	13	16	24	31	38	39	48
South Africa	A	8	—	16	15	17	15	54	22	18	17	4	3	12	118
	B	—	—	11	13	23	25	25	25	23	13	11	31	35	63
Central America	A	6	5	27	12	10	18	15	6	11	14	45	162	228	74
	B	—	—	12	14	16	12	12	13	18	48	92	105	107	101
South America	A	54	52	35	73	144	195	118	112	134	45	139	156	83	55
	B	—	—	92	100	113	128	141	121	110	117	111	96	94	83
Total (excl Vietnam)	A	294	289	201	488	547	755	947	912	1,413	911	1,135	900	1,245	1,015
	B	—	—	364	456	588	730	915	988	1,064	1,054	1,121	1,041	1,028	1,028
Vietnam	A	—	—	—	—	9	9	11	7	48	9	24	56	57	43
	B	—	—	—	—	—	—	17	17	20	29	39	38	50	57
Total[a]	A	294	289	201	488	556	765	957	919	1,461	920	1,159	957	1,302	1,058
	B	—	—	366	460	593	737	932	1,004	1,083	1,083	1,160	1,079	1,078	1,085

Region		1964	1965	1966	1967	1968	1969	1970	1971	1972	1973	1974	1975	Total[a]
Far East (excl Vietnam)	A	300	260	380	152	203	448	207	320	124	231	190	489	6,850
	B[c]	290	266	259	289	278	266	260	266	214	270	—	—	—
South Asia	A	61	163	299	207	227	239	229	381	313	221	285	136	4,953
	B	167	180	192	228	241	257	278	277	286	267	—	—	—
Middle East	A	296	337	336	813	962	927	1,118	1,350	831	1,704	2,260	2,696	16,219
	B	342	417	549	675	831	1,033	1,035	1,181	1,437	1,753	—	—	—
North Africa	A	30	62	93	103	64	67	92	94	128	111	174	582	1,698
	B	48	63	70	78	84	84	89	98	120	218	—	—	—
Sub-Saharan Africa	A	52	72	71	62	42	55	95	102	68	142	299	177	1,481
	B	53	59	60	60	65	71	72	87	135	148	—	—	—
South Africa	A	39	142	70	60	34	35	59	53	28	28	210	137	1,213
	B	76	86	69	68	52	48	40	39	74	90	—	—	—
Central America	A	26	14	16	13	6	8	4	36	27	43	90	105	1,035
	B	72	29	15	11	9	13	16	24	35	55	—	—	—
South America	A	39	84	106	98	159	121	113	170	237	367	406	482	3,777
	B	73	76	97	114	119	132	160	182	226	300	—	—	—
Total (excl Vietnam)	A	844	1,135	1,372	1,507	1,697	1,898	1,916	2,502	1,738	2,711	3,769	4,788	37,281
	B	1,122	1,175	1,311	1,522	1,678	1,877	1,923	2,126	2,500	3,074	—	—	—
Vietnam	A	70	57	181	378	362	228	331	333	917	63	142	15	3,350
	B	82	146	210	241	296	326	434	374	357	294	—	—	—
Total[a]	A	914	1,192	1,553	1,885	2,059	2,126	2,247	2,835	2,673	2,909	4,070	4,843	40,632
	B	1,204	1,320	1,521	1,763	1,974	2,230	2,385	2,527	2,884	3,395	—	—	—

Table 5-10
Domestic Arms Production in Developing Countries.[a]

	Fighter Aircraft, Jet Trainers, Aeroengines	Light Aircraft	Helicopters	Missiles, Rockets	Large Fighting Ships	Medium Fighting Ships (up to 500 ts)	Small Fighting Ships and Others (below 100 ts)	Submarines	Tanks and APC	Small Weapons, Ammunition, Guns, etc.	Electronics and Avionic
Europe											
Greece	1	1			1	1	1, n	1	1[2]	1, i	1[1], n
Spain	1	1	1	1	n	1	1		1	1	
Portugal	1[1], i	1[1], i		1	1	1	n, n	1, n	1[1], n	1	
Turkey	i	1								1	
Yugoslavia	1					1				1	
Latin America											
Argentina	i	1, i	1	1	1	1, i		1	1, i	1, i	
Brazil	i, 1	1		1, i	1	n	i	n	1, i	1, i	n[1], n
Chile						n	1			i	
Colombia						n				1	
Dominican Rep.		1				n, 1	1				
Mexico	1[1]	1			n, 1	i				i, 1	
Peru	1[1]					1, i	1			1	
Venezuela	n[2]					n				1[1], n	
Africa											
Algeria										n	
Congo										n	
Gabon											
Ghana											
Guinea						n	n				
Ivory Coast							n			1, 1	

Malagasy Rep.									
Nigeria	l[1]			l	l	l	l	l	l	n[1]
S. Africa	l	i	l	l	n	l	l	l	l	n[1]
Sudan									l	
Zaire									?	
Morocco						l		l		
Near/Middle East										
Egypt	l	i	l	l	n	l	l	l	l	l
Iran	l[2]	l[1]	l[1]	l[1]	l[1]	i	l[1]	l	l	l
Israel	l[1]		l	l	l	l	l	i	i	i
Saudi Arabia	i	i	i	i	i	i		i		
Yemen (Aden)				?	?					
Asia										
Bangladesh	i		l		l	n	n	l		
Burma	l		l	l	l	l	l	l	l	
Hong Kong	l	i	l		l[1]	i				
India	l	l	l	l	n	l	l	l	i	i
Indonesia	l	l	l	l	n	n	n	l	l	l
N. Korea	l[1]		l[1]	n		n	n	l	n	
S. Korea	l[1]	i		l		n	l		l	l
Malaysia						l		n	n	
Nepal									l	
Pakistan	l[1]	i	l	l	l	n	n	l	l	l
Philippines		l[1]	l[1]	n	l[1]	l	l	l	l	l
Singapore	l	l				l	l	l	l	n
Sri Lanka		i	l							
Taiwan	l	l	l	l	nl[2]	n	n	l	l	n
Thailand						l	l	l	l	n
Vietnam		l	l			l	n	n		

[a] i = indigenous design
l = license production and technical assistance
n = not known whether i or l
[1] = planned
[2] = only refitting, repair, etc.

219

SOURCE: Lock and Wulf (1977:131).

Table 5-11
National Alliance Memberships, 1815–1965.

No. of Memberships	No. of States	States
0	24	Jamaica, Trinidad, Ireland, Switzerland, Papal States, Two Sicilies, Malta, Cyprus, Sweden, Norway, Zanzibar, South Africa, Israel, Korea, Cambodia, Laos, N. Vietnam, S. Vietnam, Singapore, Indonesia, India, Ceylon, Maldive Islands, Nepal
1	27	Hanover, W. Germany, E. Germany, Saxony, Hesse Electoral, Hesse Grand Duchy, Mechlenburg-Schwerin, Tuscany, Iceland, Mali, Liberia, Sierra Leone, Nigeria, Congo (K), Uganda, Kenya, Tanzania, Burundi, Somalia, Zambia, Kuwait, Mongolia, Taiwan, S. Korea, Burma, Thailand, Malaya
2	53	Canada, Haiti, Dominican Rep., Cuba, Mexico, Guatemala, Honduras, Salvador, Nicaragua, Costa Rica, Panama, Venezuela, Brazil, Paraguay, Chile, Argentina, Uruguay, Holland, Luxembourg, Bavaria, Baden, Wurtembourg, Austria, Modena, Parma, Lithuania, Finland, Denmark, Gambia, Dahomey, Mauritania, Niger, Ivory Coast, Upper Volta, Togo, Cameroons, Gabon, Central African Republic, Chad, Congo (B), Rwanda, Ethiopia, Malawi, Malagasy, Morocco, Algeria, Tunisia, Sudan, Syria, Lebanon, Jordan, N. Korea, Philippines
3	10	Colombia, Bolivia, Belgium, Senegal, Libya, Saudi Arabia, Yemen, Pakistan, Australia, New Zealand
4	8	Ecuador, Peru, Portugal, Estonia, Latvia, Guinea, Ghana, UAR
5	3	Albania, Iran, Afghanistan
6–10	7	Spain (6), Iraq (6), Japan (6), China (9), U.S. (10), Hungary (10), Greece (10).
11–15	3	Poland (11), Bulgaria (12), Czechoslovakia (15)
16–20	2	Austria-Hungary (16), Rumania (18)
20–24	4	Turkey (21), Germany-Prussia (22), Yugoslavia (23), Italy (24)
25+	3	England (25), France (29), Russia (47)

SOURCE: Job (1976:80). From *Mathematical Models in International Relations,* by Dina A. Zinnes and John V. Gillespie. Copyright © 1976 by Praeger Publishers, Inc. Reproduced by permission of Praeger Publishers.

number of international alliance memberships. Less important states, on the other hand, seem to have joined fewer alliances.

Dominant states within the major contemporary international groups undertake the largest amounts of military expenditure, trade, and assistance. Larger nations have larger absolute defense budgets. Table 5-8 has shown that U.S. military expenditures in 1977 were over 60 percent of total NATO outlays. The Soviet military budget accounted for almost 85 percent of the Warsaw Pact total (cf. Rapkin et al., 1979:271).

Larger nations also have military expenditures that are disproportionate to their resources. Table 5-12 shows the military expenditures of NATO and Warsaw Pact states as percentages of national product. The United States and U.S.S.R. again lead their allies. More systematic statistical analysis confirms the point. A 1964 cross-national study reports generally high correlations between military expenditures as percentages of GNP and national populations (Dahl and Tufte, 1973).[11] Another contemporary cross-national survey presents a summary model in which bloc prominence is directly related to a nation's military–administrative budget (M. Haas, 1974:296).

Large nations undertake unequal military assistance and trade. Contemporary U.S. military activities offer a good example. The program of U.S. general economic assistance to Europe after World War II, named after General George Marshall, helped revitalize the Western European economies. It provided resources for leaders who had the vision of the European Economic Community. At the same time, however, the new Europe was an essential component of the Atlantic alliance. Western Europe was the first line of U.S. defense against the U.S.S.R. As one observer put it:

> American capital was . . . made available under the Marshall Plan for reconstruction in order to defend Europe and Asia from the threat of Soviet arms and ideology within the framework of the defences of the United States itself (Milward, 1977:364).

Other U.S. foreign aid programs to other regions followed World War II. Some of these programs have provided general aid; others have concentrated on narrower military forms of assistance, including the direct transfer of military advisers, material, training, or funds for such purposes. Such military assistance comprised over one-third of U.S. total aid to foreign nations in 1975.

Outright military assistance has gradually given way to more indirect forms of aid. Instead of giving equipment and services to foreign nations, the United States now often sells them. Figure 5-1 shows how direct aid has shrunk and military sales have expanded between 1968 and 1977.

In poorer nations, dependence on external aid may, in turn, generate pressures for additional militarization. One analyst suggests:

> The external dependence of poor nations on rich nations produces distortions in the economic structures of poor societies. These distortions create a large

Table 5-12

National Military Expenditure as a Proportion of National Product, 1954–1974.

	NATO: Military Expenditure as a Percentage									
	1954	1955	1956	1957	1958	1959	1960	1961	1962	1963
North America										
Canada	7.0	6.6	6.1	5.6	5.2	4.6	4.3	4.3	4.2	3.7
U.S.	11.6	10.0	9.8	9.9	10.0	9.4	8.9	9.1	9.3	8.8
Europe										
Belgium	4.8	3.8	3.5	3.6	3.6	3.5	3.4	3.3	3.3	3.4
Denmark	3.2	3.2	3.0	3.1	2.9	2.6	2.7	2.6	3.0	3.0
France	7.3	6.4	7.7	7.3	6.8	6.6	6.4	6.2	6.0	5.6
Germany, Federal Rep. of	4.0	4.1	3.6	4.1	3.0	4.4	4.0	4.0	4.8	5.2
Greece	5.5	5.2	6.0	5.1	4.8	4.9	4.9	4.3	4.0	3.9
Italy	4.0	3.7	3.6	3.5	3.4	3.3	3.3	3.1	3.2	3.3
Luxembourg	3.3	3.2	1.9	1.9	1.9	1.8	1.1	1.1	1.4	1.3
Netherlands	6.0	5.7	5.7	5.2	4.7	4.0	4.1	4.5	4.5	4.4
Norway	5.0	3.9	3.5	3.6	3.5	3.6	3.2	3.3	3.6	3.5
Portugal	4.2	4.2	4.0	4.0	4.0	4.3	4.2	6.4	7.0	6.5
Turkey	5.4	5.1	4.7	4.1	3.8	4.5	4.7	5.0	4.9	4.6
U.K.	8.8	8.2	7.8	7.2	7.0	6.6	6.5	6.3	6.4	6.2

	WTO: Military Expenditure as a Percentage									
	1954	1955	1956	1957	1958	1959	1960	1961	1962	1963
Bulgaria	..	..	..	4.8	5.0	3.9	4.0	4.6	5.0	5.2
Czechoslovakia	6.3	7.8	6.8	6.6	6.0	5.8	5.4	5.6	6.2	6.3
German Democratic Rep.	..	..	..	..	2.7	..	1.4	1.4	3.6	3.7
Hungary	..	..	..	1.8	..	2.0	2.2	2.3	3.1	3.9
Poland	4.2	5.6	4.8	3.4	3.5	4.1	4.0	4.1	4.3	4.5
U.S.S.R.[a]	10.9	11.4	9.1	8.6	7.4	6.9	6.4	7.6	7.7	8.2
									22.5	23.4

[a]An alternative series for the Soviet Union shows the SIPRI estimates of the dollar-equivalent of Soviet military expenditures as a percentage of official Soviet estimates of the dollar-equivalent of Soviet National Income for 1962–1973.

SOURCE: SIPRI (1976e:152–55).

potential for conflict. Under pressure from external and domestic actors, the dependent state attempts to stabilize the situation by the use of coercion to control conflict (Jackson et al., 1977:1).

Domestic Inequality

Militarization goes together with inequality *within* as well as among nations. Military affairs have historically been associated with class distinctions. Most of the military heroes in literary history—Hector, Achilles, Ulysses, Aeneas, Roland, for example—were aristocrats.

Putting the class differences in stark terms, the nineteenth century British essayist John Ruskin distinguished between two "human races." The first was a kind of super race of aristocratic warriors, remaining proudly

of Gross Domestic Product

1964	1965	1966	1967	1968	1969	1970	1971	1972	1973	1974
3.6	3.0	2.8	2.9	2.6	2.4	2.4	2.3	2.1	2.0	2.0
8.0	7.5	8.4	9.4	9.4	8.8	7.9	7.1	6.7	6.0	6.1
3.4	3.2	3.1	3.1	3.2	2.9	2.9	2.8	2.8	2.7	2.8
2.8	2.8	2.7	2.7	2.8	2.5	2.4	2.5	2.3	2.1	2.4
5.3	5.2	5.0	5.0	4.8	4.2	4.2	4.0	3.9	3.8	3.8
4.6	4.3	4.1	4.3	3.6	3.6	3.3	3.3	3.4	3.4	3.6
3.6	3.6	3.7	4.3	4.7	4.8	4.8	4.7	4.6	4.2	4.2
3.3	3.3	3.4	3.1	3.0	2.7	2.7	2.9	3.1	3.0	2.9
1.5	1.4	1.4	1.2	1.0	0.9	0.8	0.8	0.9	0.8	..
4.3	3.9	3.7	4.0	3.7	3.6	3.5	3.4	3.4	3.4	3.5
3.4	3.7	3.5	3.5	3.6	3.6	3.5	3.4	3.3	3.1	3.1
6.7	6.2	6.3	7.3	7.3	6.7	7.0	7.4	6.9	5.9	..
4.6	4.8	4.3	4.4	4.6	4.4	4.3	4.5	4.3	4.2	3.9
6.1	5.9	5.7	5.7	5.4	5.0	4.9	5.0	5.2	5.0	..

of Net Material Product

1964	1965	1966	1967	1968	1969	1970	1971	1972	1973	1974
3.1	3.5	3.3	3.1	3.1	3.2	3.1	3.4	3.5	3.5	3.7
6.1	5.9	5.5	5.3	5.1	4.9	4.8	5.0	4.9	4.7	4.5
3.6	3.7	3.7	3.9	6.2	6.1	6.2	6.3	6.3	6.5	..
3.6	3.4	2.8	2.6	2.9	3.0	3.6	3.4	3.0	2.7	2.9
4.4	4.4	4.4	4.4	4.5	4.8	4.6	4.3	3.9	3.8	3.5
7.3	6.6	6.5	6.4	6.8	6.8	6.2	5.9	5.7	5.3	5.0
20.2	18.1	..	17.3	18.0	17.4	16.5	15.4	14.8	13.1	..

idle, using the others as cattle in peacetime and as "puppets or pieces in the game of death" during war. The second race included the workers who farmed, built, manufactured, and provided the necessities of life (Huizinga, 1954:103; cf. Pettengill, 1979).

Modern military organization has maintained this class distinction to some extent. Within the armed forces, there is a rigid separation of classes. At the top are leaders, reflecting or contributing to the upper stratum of society. At the very least, they are presumed to be officers and gentlemen. Below them are the enlisted personnel. Ranks further subdivide the groups.

Rank implies privileges. Pay rates are different. There are explicit signs of deference: saluting, or the use of "Sir." Housing, eating, and recreation facilities are segregated.

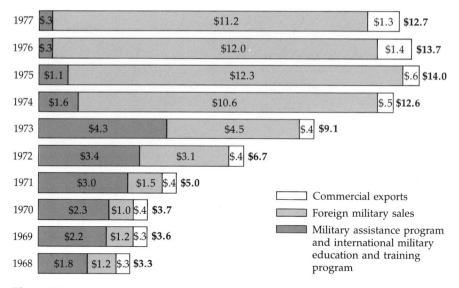

Figure 5-1

Growth and Changing Composition of Military Aid and Sales: U.S., 1968–1977.
(NOTES: Amounts are billions of $ per fiscal year. Totals may not add due to rounding. Foreign military sales data for FY 1976 exclude the transition quarter [July 1, 1976–September 30, 1976], which amounted to $1,175,222,000. Commercial exports, Military Assistance Program, and International Military Education and Training Program include the transition quarter, for which data are not separately available. Commercial exports for FY 1977 are estimated. SOURCE: Kegley and Wittkopf, 1979:84. Published by permission of St. Martin's Press, Inc., from *American Foreign Policy*, by C. W. Kegley, Jr., and E. R. Wittkopf.)

Privilege also implies rank. Officers are presumed to have better backgrounds, educations, codes of behavior, values, and goals (cf. Abrahamsson, 1971:38; Lang, 1972:73, 93).[12]

Aside from such distinctions of rank and privilege within the military itself, militarization is related to a more general inequality in communities.[13] A number of theorists have stated this relationship in strong terms. One writer states that militarization

> has comprehended the domination of the military man over the civilian, an undue preponderance of military demands, an emphasis on military considerations, spirit, ideals and scales of value, and . . . the imposition of heavy burdens on a people for military purposes, to the neglect of welfare and culture, and the waste of the nation's best manpower in unproductive army service (Kaufman, 1970:170; cf. Vagts, 1959).

Some analysts have pointed to the emergence of a new class in modern society that achieves power through control of modern bureaucracy. The military complex is an important party of this new class.

In December, 1967, Arthur I. Waskow told the American Historical Association, "The first major trend event of the last generation in America has been the emergence of what could almost be seen as a new class, defined more by its relation to the means of total destruction than by a relation to means of production" (Melman, 1970b:11; cf. Tyrrell, 1970; Mills, 1959).

The military complex in the modern state is influential in the formulation and implementation of both foreign and domestic policies. In a society with a large military sector,

> the "war establishment" is permanently active, commands considerable economic resources and can mobilize support for its objectives among its members plus—to the extent it commands normative influence—the population at large. Forces working for non-military solutions to international conflicts are less well organized, often active only on an *ad hoc* basis (i.e., come into existence only on certain occasions), have less economic resources and, as a consequence, have been less successful in mobilizing support for their objectives (Abrahamsson, 1971:128; cf. Andrews, 1974; Kucera, 1974; Wayman, 1974; Art, 1973; Smith, 1970).

The military complex controls governmental defense expenditure. This is a powerful weapon of political patronage and creates domestic political muscle. Central governmental officials can offer or withhold massive amounts of resources, and these resources are a useful means to induce or constrain, bribe or threaten, politicians to do their bidding (Melman, 1970b:11; Kaufman, 1970:28).[14]

Defense expenditure implies additional prosperity for regions that are already well off. In the United States, for example,

> the high income states tend to receive a larger than proportional share of expenditures for defense and space programs, thus reflecting the dependence of the highly industrialized areas on the design and production of weapon and space systems (Weidenbaum, 1966:37).

Table 5-13 shows the top-ranking states for various categories of defense procurement contracts. Medium- or average-income regions do not benefit equally from defense spending (cf. Sale, 1975:27; Isard and Karaska, 1961–62; Isard and Ganschow, 1961). Figure 5-2 also suggests that standard of living indicators tend to be higher in areas with greater military activities.

On the corporate level, larger companies receive a larger portion of defense contracts. Large corporate economic concentrations are theoretically well suited to military activity. They are supposed to provide the military with a stable source of essential supplies. Further, they theoretically produce at the lowest possible unit cost. One analyst believes that "prominent production economies of scale do apply with special frequency in military applications" (Hoag, 1966:23).

Contracts are awarded in lumps, and large amounts go to large contractors. Such large awards encourage already large organizations to grow still more by merging or incorporating smaller ones (cf. Nelson, 1971:104; Baldwin, 1967:27, 58; A. D. J. Kaplan, 1964:32–35).[15]

Table 5-13

Geographic Concentration of Defense Contracts, Fiscal Year 1971.[a]

Procurement Category	Amount (In Millions of $)	Calif.	N.Y.	Texas	Conn.	Mass.	Ohio	Ga.	Va.	Wash.	Ind.	Mich.	N.C.	All Other States
Aircraft assembly	4,896	3	2	1			4							
Missiles	4,634	1	4			2				3				
Electronics	3,398	1	2			4								3
Services	3,089	2	1											3,4
Ships	2,627		4		3				1					2
Ammunition	2,176	1		2										3,4
Aircraft engines	1,381				1	4	2					3		
Construction	1,283	1		2					3					4
Subsistence	883	1	3	2										4
Aircraft equipment	849	1	2	3										4
Petroleum	739	2	4	1										3
Miscellaneous supplies	633	1	2				3							4
Combat vehicles	468	3					2					1	4	
Noncombat vehicles	457	4					2				1	3		
Weapons	309	1			3	2								4
Clothing	285								4				1	2,3

[a]States are ranked 1, 2, 3, or 4.

SOURCE: Weidenbaum (1974:109), from U.S. Department of Defense, *Military Prime Contract Awards by Region and State, Fiscal years 1969, 1970, 1971* (Washington, 1971).

Large contracts imply large profits. The rate of return on defense contracts may be additionally increased by political considerations. When the military deal with the defense industry, they participate in the legitimation and award of the contracts and can refrain from too much zeal in monitoring performance efficiencies.[16]

The profits from military contracts can, in turn, find a way back into politics. They may be contributed to campaigns to elect leaders who elaborate and support the ideology of defense.[17] They may be used to pay the salaries of lobbyists. In contemporary democracies, lobbying by interest groups is accepted as a fact of political life. Insofar as it articulates different points of view and ensures pluralistic representation, lobbying is useful. But it has its dark side. The lobbyist is not merely one more participant bringing new information to rational public debate. He or she may wield powerful incentives and threats for politicians—electoral victory or defeat through financial support or opposition in the next election.

From a political point of view, Fitzgerald believes that "the process is an exceptionally effective way to control the masses of people." He continues:

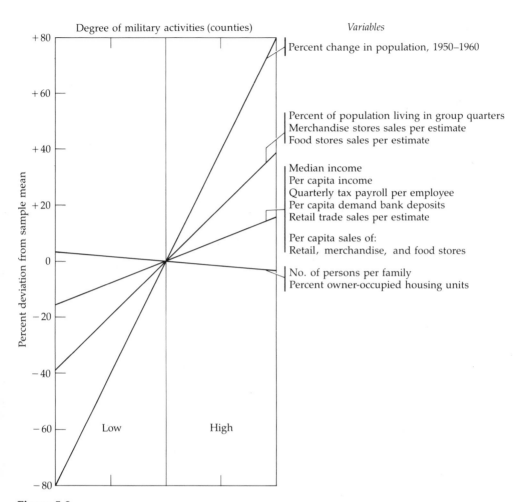

Figure 5-2
Military Activities and Socioeconomic Variables: U.S. Counties, 1950–1960.
(SOURCE: Menegakis, 1970:54. From *The Defense Economy: Conversion of Industries and Occupations to Civilian Needs*, edited by Seymour Melman. Copyright © 1970 by Seymour Melman. Reproduced by permission of Praeger Publishers.)

  Late in 1971, I had a long interview with a foreign television team that was touring the United States recording our attitudes toward military spending in general and Asian War spending in particular. I was one of the last people they interviewed, and they had heard all sorts of "Don't knock the war that feeds you" speeches and "Boondoggling makes us rich" theories. After he finished questioning me, the interviewer sat and talked for a few minutes.

  "You know," he said, "all this war economy talk is very familiar to us. Not too long ago, we had a politician who was pushing the same line. His schemes seemed to work all right for a while, but later on things sort of came apart."

  The interviewer, Herr Bitthoff, was from Germany. The name of the economic system he was referring to was Wehrwirtschaft. The promoter of the scheme was Adolf Hitler (1972:365–66).

Foreign military assistance helps support domestic inequality in other countries. Military assistance strengthens the military sector of other societies and encourages military regimes. Such regimes often claim to be agents of modernization ousting anachronistic or corrupt regimes in traditional societies; they mobilize the people and resources of nations not only militarily, but also economically and purport to bring them into the twentieth century (cf. Lang, 1972:22–23; Bienen, 1971, 1968a; Hall and Cozean, 1966; Janowitz, 1964a; Johnson, 1962). At the same time they are a kind of indirect ruling class, supported from a distance and imposed upon a much less privileged population (cf. Mazrui, 1976, 1975; Wolpin, 1973; Kolko and Kolko, 1972; De Riz, 1970; Bosch, 1968).

The costs of militarization tend to fall disproportionately on those elements of society that are already disadvantaged. The military has often been an avenue of opportunity. Military service has been an important rite of passage for many young males as they pass into manhood. It has helped those wishing to get ahead in society (cf. Cockerham, 1973). In the United States in the twentieth century, minorities have moved toward greater equality in the armed forces (cf. Binkin and Shirley, 1977; Foner, 1974; Goldman, 1973; Stillman, 1968:124).

Widespread military participation and service may help in some ways to flatten the "pyramid of social stratification" (Andreski, 1968: 73–74; cf. Lang, 1972:138). In contemporary society, a military career has been a channel of upward mobility, based on skill and achievement, for individuals of middle- and lower-class origin. Regardless of social beginnings, military men have achieved the highest levels in society. In the United States there have been a number of military presidents, including Washington, Jackson, Grant, Taylor, and Eisenhower. Men like Napoleon, de Gaulle, Mao Tsetung, Nasser, and others in the Third and Fourth Worlds rose via the military from modest beginnings to positions of great power and respect.

On the other hand, the privileged are less likely to be attracted to voluntary service. They are also better able to avoid the draft (cf. Baskir and Strauss, 1978; Davis, 1974; Gaier et al., 1972).

The disadvantaged may do better within the military than they would have in the civilian world outside, but they pay a disproportionate price. Those with lower education still concentrate in combat units, where the casualties are higher. Their lack of skills still slows movement into noncombat staffs or technical support specialties (Mellett, 1973; Moskos, 1973; Lang, 1972:89, 94–95). Minorities with equal qualifications and achievements are still not promoted as rapidly as whites (Butler, 1976:807). And Table 5-14 shows that minority veterans are less able to get jobs on their return to civilian life.

The military complex implies that the disadvantaged also pay disproportional costs in the wider community. The traditional wisdom of economics tells us that militarization comes at the expense of welfare. Guns are purchased at the cost of butter.

Table 5-14

Unemployed Men, by Age, Veteran Status, and Race, 1972–1976.

Year and Race	Unemployed Men (1,000)[a]					Unemployment Rate for Men[b]				
	Total 16 Yr. Old and Over	20–34 Years Old				Total 16 Yr. Old and Over	20–30 Years Old			
		Total U.S.	Non-veterans	Post-Korea Veterans[c]	Viet-nam Veterans[d]		Total U.S.	Non-Veterans	Post-Korea Veterans[c]	Viet-nam Veterans[d]
Total										
1972	2,635	1,075	690	54	328	4.9	5.7	5.8	2.8	6.7
1973	2,240	938	632	40	266	4.1	4.7	4.9	2.5	5.0
1974	2,668	1,159	813	35	310	4.8	5.6	6.0	2.9	5.3
1975	4,385	2,022	1,405	52	565	7.9	9.5	9.8	5.7	9.3
1976	3,968	1,810	1,277	32	501	7.0	8.2	8.5	5.0	7.9
White										
1972	2,160	871	545	49	276	4.5	5.2	5.2	2.6	6.2
1973	1,818	749	488	36	224	3.7	4.2	4.3	2.4	4.6
1974	2,146	920	641	29	249	4.3	5.0	5.4	2.5	4.7
1975	3,597	1,643	1,124	47	474	7.2	8.7	9.0	5.5	8.6
1976	3,223	1,449	1,013	29	407	6.4	7.4	7.6	4.8	7.1
Black and Other										
1972	475	204	145	6	52	8.9	9.8	9.6	5.3	11.7
1973	423	189	143	4	42	7.6	8.4	8.6	4.6	8.4
1974	521	239	172	7	61	9.1	10.3	10.1	9.4	11.3
1975	787	379	281	5	91	13.7	16.0	16.0	10.4	15.9
1976	745	361	264	3	94	12.7	14.6	14.5	8.3	15.1

[a]Annual averages.
[b]Rate is percent of male civilian labor force.
[c]Service during Feb. 1, 1955–Aug. 4, 1964.
[d]Service during Aug. 5, 1964–Apr. 30, 1975.
SOURCE: U.S. Department of Commerce (1977:375).

The tension between guns and butter reflects a struggle for scarce resources between the military complex and what has been called the welfare complex. Empirical studies of defense and welfare expenditures in Northwestern nations also show that "there does appear to be an underlying trade-off between defense and welfare expenditures" (Caputo, 1973:62; cf. Russett, 1970b:Chs. 5, 6).

The welfare complex includes government or private agencies that support social service programs. Many of these benefit poor people and minorities. Welfare cutbacks naturally work their greatest hardship on the poor. If militarization diminishes private investment, there are fewer employment opportunities. If militarization takes resources from health, education, and welfare, the burden is heaviest for those with the fewest resources to provide for themselves.

The poorer people of the poorer areas lose several times. In the United States, for example, poor states do not receive a proportionate share of defense contracts. We have already suggested that U.S. defense expenditure has worked to establish "an income redistribution effect in favor of the rich states" (Russett, 1970b:130). The poor states lose again because others' defense contracts also cut back their own welfare-oriented programs. One analyst notes that

> low income states tend to receive a larger than proportional share (in relation to a simple per capita distribution) of expenditures for the non-defense public programs. This reflects, of course, the welfare orientation implicit or explicit in so many of these programs (Weidenbaum, 1966:37).

Instability

Instability is the third dimension of polarization that is related to militarization. We find the connection at both the international and national levels.

International Instability

International instability and militarization combine in alliance races, arms races, and image races.

Alliance Races

Alliances are related to general international instability. Alliance races occur when the international environment appears likely to change. Leaders of international coalitions and particular nations may see the opportunity to mold the international system in a way favorable to their interests. Or they may fear that others may try to change it in an unfavorable way. In either case, they attempt to surround themselves with friendly allies, who may help them if the need arises. The alliance races themselves may add to international instability because they may threaten additional groups. On the other hand, if the international environment appears less likely to change, alliance races may slow.[18]

There are many examples of medium- and short-term alliance races through history. Figure 5-3 outlines national alliance commitments between 1815 and 1965. The Grand Alliance against Napoleon, and the Quadruple Alliance that followed it, capped the international alliance network at the beginning of the nineteenth century. The establishment of general peace allowed the percentage of states committed to alliances to decline dramatically. After hitting bottom around 1870, alliance commitments began to rise again, generally continuing upward until World War I. The reestablishment of general peace encouraged another decline. In the 1920s and

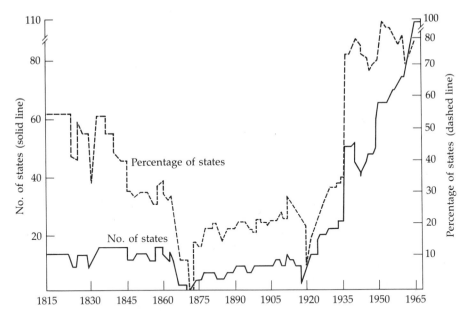

Figure 5-3
National Alliance Commitments, 1815–1965. (SOURCE: Job, 1976:84. From
Mathematical Models in International Relations, by Dina A. Zinnes and John V.
Gillespie. Copyright © 1976 by Praeger Publishers, Inc. Reproduced by
permission of Praeger Publishers.)

1930s the percentage and number of states involved in alliances rose sharply
through World War II. The subsequent peace produced another decline.
The ensuing Cold War brought another alliance increase. The new peak
in national alliance commitments was the highest in recent history, both
in the percentage of allied states and in absolute numbers.

A long-term alliance race has also occurred over the last two centuries.
As the international environment has become less secure, coalitions and
states have formed more alliances. Table 5-15 shows that 147 international
alliances were formed between 1900 and 1965, compared with only 43 for
the much longer period between 1816 and 1899. During the nineteenth
century, states formed an alliance about every other year. In the twentieth
century, the rate increased over four times, to more than two new alliances
per year.

Arms Races

Arms races have followed the same pattern as alliance races, both resulting
from international instability and contributing to it. Classical strategic theory suggests that states cannot count on their opponents' good feelings or
intentions. Nations arm themselves to provide security against their com-

Table 5-15

International Alliance Formation: Global Sample, 1816–1965.

	Years	Alliances	Alliances/Year
1816–1899	84	43	0.51
1900–1965	66	147	2.23
Total	150	190	1.27

SOURCE: Sabrosky (1980); cf. Singer and Small (1972).

petitors. National leaders are concerned at least to match, and perhaps to exceed, their opponents' capabilities.

Each international group or nation can thus become an "external pacer" in an arms race with its major competitors (Trout, 1977). The race may be run relatively slowly if the racers do not feel particularly threatened. In this case, arms levels may remain relatively constant or increase only slightly. At some point, however, the pace may begin to quicken. One side may adopt substantial arms increases, or its major competitor may feel that it is about to do so. The other side may respond by quickening its own arms activity. Both sides can be arming rapidly, but neither will achieve a substantial lead in the race, or additional security. Instead, the arms race will erode the cooperative foundations of international relations.[19]

There are many historical examples of medium- and short-term arms races. Alliances or nations do not generally compete with the whole international system or with every other member in it. Rather, there are small clusters of competitors of relatively equal rank, size, and capability.

Figure 5-4 presents two mathematical models of the arms race between the Triple Alliance (Austria, Germany, Italy) and the Triple Entente (Great Britain, France, Russia) before World War I. The line in model *a* represents the response of each alliance to changes in arms expenditures by the other in the same year. Model *b* shows the response of the Triple Entente to the Triple Alliance's arms expenditures of the previous year. Figure 5-5 separates the arms racers and suggests a similar contemporary relationship between arms expenditures by NATO and the Warsaw Pact.

International alliances are composed of individual nations. Under the umbrella of the larger arms races, these particular states undertake arms competition with particular opponents. Table 5-16 notes some of the more important arms races between particular nations for the nineteenth and twentieth centuries (cf. Wallace, 1979; Lambelet, 1975; Quester, 1966).

The last race on this list is between the United States and the Soviet Union. We are most concerned with this arms race because we are living through it and because it is a nuclear one. Figure 5-5 shows how closely the arms expenditures of NATO and the Warsaw Treaty Organization are related to those of the major superpowers. It also suggests the way in

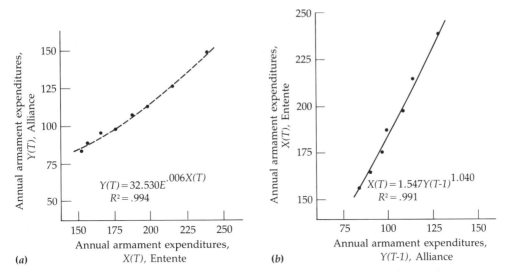

Figure 5-4
Arms Races: Triple Entente and Triple Alliance, 1906–1914. (*a*) Annual armament
expenditures for Entente and Alliance nations, 1907–1914, in millions of pounds sterling.
The dashed line represents the exponential function given in the figure. (*b*) Annual
armament expenditures for Alliance and Entente nations, 1908–1914, in millions of
pounds sterling. The line represents the nonlinear least-squares power function given in
the figure. (NOTES: Y = Triple Entente annual armament expenditure. X = Triple
Alliance annual armament expenditure. T = given year. $T − 1$ = previous year. R^2 =
% of variance explained by the equation. E = the base of the exponential function,
described by Hamblin et al., 1977:339. SOURCE: Hamblin et al., 1977:346. Data from
Richardson, 1960a.)

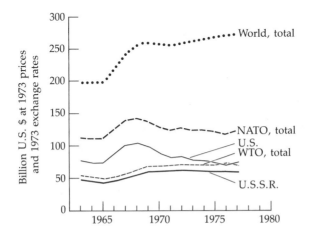

Figure 5-5
World Military Expenditure, 1963–1977.
(SOURCE: SIPRI, 1978b:10.)

Table 5-16

Arms Races, 1840–1976.

Countries	Type	Years
France vs. England	Naval	1840–1866
France vs. Germany	Land	1874–1894
England vs. France and Russia	Naval	1884–1904
Argentina vs. Chile	Naval	1890–1902
England vs. Germany	Naval	1898–1912
France vs. Germany	Land	1911–1914
England vs. U.S.	Naval	1916–1930
Japan vs. U.S.	Naval	1916–1922
France vs. Germany	Land	1934–1939
U.S.S.R. vs. Germany	Land	1934–1941
Germany vs. England	Air	1934–1939
U.S. vs. Japan	Naval	1934–1941
U.S.S.R. vs. U.S.	Nuclear	1946–

SOURCE: Huntington (1958:43).

which U.S. and U.S.S.R. arms expenditures have kept pace with each other. We must be careful to note, however, that there is an independent drop in relative U.S. expenditures beginning at the end of the 1960s. This drop coincides with the ending of the Vietnamese conflict (cf. Hollist, 1977).

Within this general pattern, the United States and the Soviet Union compete in specific military areas. Figure 5-6 outlines relatively parallel development in total arms exports between 1965 and 1974. Figure 5-7 shows operational deployment of specific military systems. It suggests a substantial relationship between most U.S. and U.S.S.R. military efforts through the late 1960s.

The relationship between deployed U.S. and Soviet military systems loosens a good deal during the 1970s. The two nations develop about two-fifths of these systems in different directions. We see this divergence in total delivery vehicles, total missile launchers, ICBM (Intercontinental Ballistic Missile) launchers, SLBM (Submarine Launched Ballistic Missile) launchers, major operational combat surface ships, tactical aircraft, and helicopters. The United States slows down, and the Soviet Union catches up, in all these areas. In the other sectors, both sides appear generally to continue the previous relationship. These include strategic offensive warheads/bombs, strategic defense missiles on launchers, bombers, strategic defense interceptors, tanks, divisions, artillery, cruise missile and attack submarines.

The loosening of the relationship between U.S. and Soviet operational capabilities has caused a good deal of debate in the United States. Some

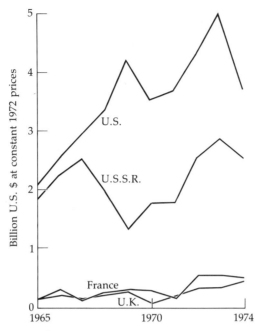

Figure 5-6
Arms Exports of Major Powers, 1965–1974.
(Source: Barton and Weiler, 1976:274.
Reprinted from *International Arms Control:
Issues and Agreements,* by the Stanford
Arms Control Group, edited by John H.
Barton and Lawrence D. Weiler, with the
permission of the publishers, Stanford
University Press. © 1976 by the Board of
Trustees of the Leland Stanford Junior
University.)

suggest that the Soviet Union has already overtaken the United States in
a number of areas and will do so in the others, that the Soviet Union will
be in a position to dominate international politics unless the United States
speeds up its own military effort (cf. Cline, 1977; Rummel, 1976).

Another line of analysis proposes that Soviet leaders have felt behind
and needed to catch up. Once they have done so, they will slow down their
military efforts.

A third tack suggests that progress in the arms race cannot be measured either by total military expenditures or deployed military systems.
Instead, one must consider overall strategic concepts, alternative capabilities, and specialized advantages. The United States does not need more
total delivery vehicles, missile launchers, including ICBM and SLBM facilities, or bombers, because it has more warheads on its missiles. The

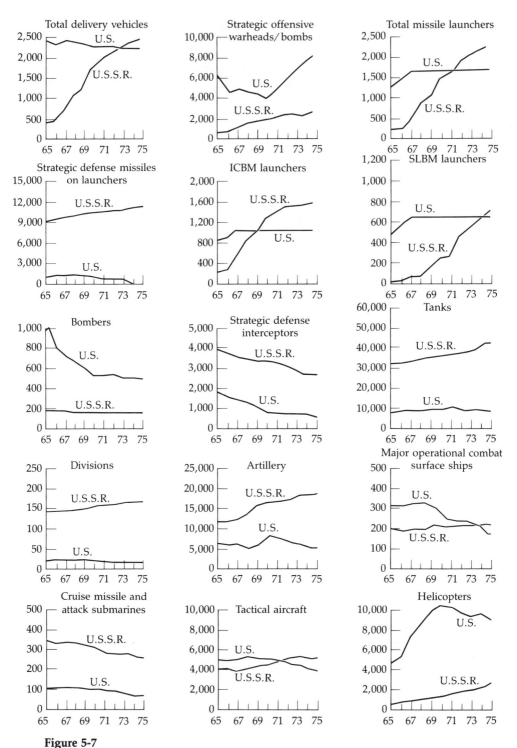

Figure 5-7

Deployed Military Systems: U.S. and U.S.S.R., 1965–1975. (Sources: U.S. Senate, Committee on Foreign Relations, Subcommittee on Arms Control, 1975:80; Brown, 1976:48.)

development of Multiple Independently Targetable Reentry Vehicles (MIRVs) has multiplied the capabilities of missile systems. Each missile can now carry a cluster of separate warheads, each of which can strike a separate target. Numbers of U.S. helicopters, used in the Vietnam War, were appropriately reduced when it ended. The Soviet Union maintains its original lead in divisions, tanks, and artillery because of its traditional role as a Eurasian land power (cf. Blechman et al., 1977).

While the debate over deployed armaments goes on, the Soviet–American arms race also extends to the area of weapons research and development. The invention of new weapons can drastically change the balance of military capability and the final outcome of the arms race. Ships that used wind power, rather than oarsmen; gunpowder; the internal combustion engine; airplanes; guided missiles; and atomic explosives have all given a military edge to those who owned them. Modern alliances and nations have tried to keep pace with or outdistance each other in discovering new means of destruction.

Contemporary frontiers of military research include space capabilities; for example, lunar, orbital, or suborbital facilities; the application of atomic particle or laser beams for missile defense; the neutron bomb, which enhances lethal atomic radiation in the immediate area of the explosion; the cruise missile, a relatively autonomous long-range missile with its own lift and propulsion system; the development of new techniques of missile propulsion, guidance, and sensing (cf. Dickson, 1976; Kemp et al., 1975; Yanarella, 1975:3; B. T. Feld et al., 1971; Schwartz, 1971; Lapp, 1970).

Arms competition, finally, includes the general economies of the competitors. The United States and the Soviet Union attempt to maintain secure international and domestic supplies of essential food, raw materials, and manufactured goods (cf. Conant and Gold, 1978; Krasner, 1978; Stanley et al., 1977; Knorr, 1975; Abrahamsson and Steckler, 1973).

Arms races occur in other countries as well. Figure 5-8 shows the dramatic rise in Third World military expenditures over the last generation, particularly in the Middle East. U.S.–U.S.S.R. competition has encouraged the buildup of Third World armaments. The superpowers and their allies have supplied most of these arms as they have struggled for political influence abroad. The United States has been particularly concerned with the fate of Israel and with maintaining secure energy supplies. The Soviet Union has tried to achieve a secure Southern border and an outlet to the Mediterranean (cf. Rattinger, 1976b; Zinnes et al., 1976).

The sum of many smaller arms races in the twentieth century has been a long-term arms race. Figure 5-9 and Table 5-17 show the dramatic long-term rise in world military expenditures during the twentieth century. World military expenditures, measured in constant dollars, increased almost 24 times from 1908 to 1975. This represents an average annual compound growth rate of just under 5 percent per year.

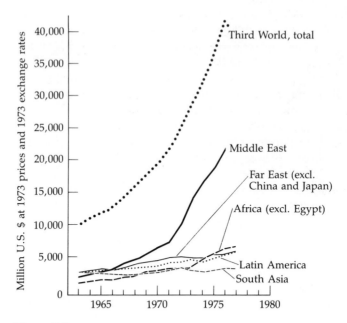

Figure 5-8
Third World Military Expenditure, 1963–1976.
(SOURCE: SIPRI, 1978b:9.)

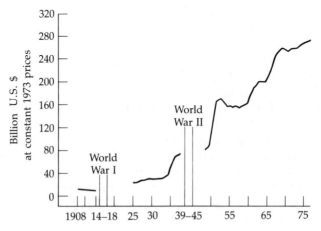

Figure 5-9
World Military Expenditure, 1908–1977.
(SOURCE: SIPRI, 1978b:11.)

Table 5-17
World Military Expenditures, 1908–1975.[a]

Year	Billion U.S. $[b]	Year	Billion U.S. $[b]
1908	9.0	1954	126.7
1913	14.5	1955	127.4
1925	(19.3)	1956	126.5
1926	(19.6)	1957	128.8
1927	(21.5)	1958	126.8
1928	21.5	1959	131.7
1929	21.7	1960	130.8
1930	23.2	1961	143.7
1931	21.9	1962	157.6
1932	20.3	1963	164.1
1933	20.1	1964	162.2
1934	23.9	1965	162.2
1935	32.6	1966	178.6
1936	47.1	1967	196.9
1937	58.8	1968	209.2
1938	61.6	1969	212.9
1948	64.7	1970	209.0
1949	67.9	1971	208.2
1950	73.5	1972	211.7
1951	107.0	1973	212.3
1952	137.2	1974	213.2
1953	140.9	1975	213.8

[a]Gaps in the table are explained as follows: Before World War I, figures exist only for 1908 and 1913. After World War I, reasonably accurate figures are available for 1928 and onwards. Figures for 1925–1927 can be adequately estimated (figures in parentheses). The post-World War II series begins in 1948 because expenditure in the first two postwar years was dominated by wartime levels of forces. Differences with Table 5-8 and Figure 5-9 exist because they use 1973 as a base year for prices.
[b]At constant 1970 prices.
SOURCE: SIPRI (1976e:96).

Image Races

International instability and militarization are joined, finally, in image races.[20] As we have already pointed out, international communities see each other in terms of ideologies that include stereotypes of others. These hostile stereotypes do not remain constant. Speeches by political figures, diplomatic communications, and media reporting give the images specific point and direction; and, of course, popular opinions and moods change (cf. Rivera, 1968:Chs. 2, 3; Farrell and Smith, 1967; Frank, 1967:Ch. 7; Stagner, 1967:Ch. 1–3; Kelman, 1965: Pt. 1; Holsti, 1962; Boulding, 1959, 1956; Almond, 1950).

Image races occur when the hostile perceptions of two opponents reflect back on each other, like mirror images. For example, one study of

U.S. and Soviet attitudes toward the Cold War shows that both groups saw their opponents in similarly dark colors (Bronfenbrenner, 1961:46–48; cf. Eckhardt and White, 1967).

1. They are the aggressors.
2. Their government exploits and deludes people.
3. The mass of their people are not really sympathetic to the regime.
4. They cannot be trusted.
5. Their policy verges on madness.

The hostility or friendliness of one nation is an important influence on another. Threats spill over into perceptions of generalized hostility. People who perceive hostility on the part of others may be more likely to be hostile toward them. After a certain point, these perceptions move with a momentum of their own. Hostility feeds upon hostility and a spiral of hostile communication is under way (cf. McGowan and Kegley, 1980; Kent, 1967; White, 1966).

The dynamics of image races involve the processes of locking in and hardening. Locking in refers to the tendency of hostile images to become increasingly important determinants, in their own right, of images held by others. Hardening refers both to the resistance of such perceptions to reversal and to the hostility of their content. Misperceptions and erroneous interpretations of the other party's intentions feed back into the system, confirming original errors (cf. Jervis, 1976, 1970; Gamson and Modigliani, 1971; Welch, 1970; Holsti et al., 1968; Holsti, 1962).

National Instability

National instability is related to military regimes, military complexes, and militance.

Military Regimes

Instability is part of a domestic environment in which the military can come to power. We see this clearly in the contemporary global South where rapid decolonization has resulted in an expanded political role for the military in Africa, Asia, Latin America, and the Middle East. Additionally, foreign countries may provide military assistance—in the form of training and resources—that strengthens the military's position relative to other domestic groups. This assistance gives the military the managerial skills, organization, and weapons to seize control of the central government. "When the authorities lack support, the chances are that the military will challenge the authorities" (Perlmutter, 1977:13; cf. Laidlaw, 1979; Väyrynen, 1979; Janowitz, 1977).

Military personnel typically come to power in one of two ways. They may conduct a relatively bloodless coup d'état through which they simply replace the politicians.[21] Alternatively, they may challenge the government—and government soldiers—through more broadly based revolutionary action.

Once in power, military regimes do not, themselves, form particularly stable governments. Military men are specialists in the use of force rather than persuasion and consensus—those invaluable tools for stable governing. The political networks and contracts that support the military are likely to be limited.

Table 5-18 compares the political stability and breadth of noncommunist governments with differing military and civilian composition. Military regimes appear less stable. The chief executive changes more rapidly, having a shorter average tenure than in civilian regimes. It is also clear that military regimes are politically narrow; they make less use of national constitutions, legislative assemblies, and political parties.

Military takeovers of previously civilian governments may involve sudden shifts in many aspects of national life. Because they operate relatively independently, "military elites are more likely than civil bureaucrats to be free of ties to the economically dominant class or classes" (Horowitz and Trimberger, 1976:228). The military in the Third World has often used this freedom to undertake rapid modernization.

Table 5-18
Military Regime Characteristics, 1951–1970.[a]

Political Variable	Regime Type			
	MR	**CRM**	**CR(900−)**	**CR(900+)**
Percent military personnel in cabinet	44.2	8.3	3.6	0.2
Mean tenure main executive	40.8	54.5	101.7	55.7
Percent years constitution not full	62.7	13.2	13.4	0.0
Percent years assembly banned	73.4	7.8	5.1	0.0
Percent years parties banned	53.5	9.3	12.1	0.0
Percent years Communist party banned	90.5	58.7	65.1	3.3

[a]Sample includes all noncommunist countries with populations over 1 million, 1951–1970.

MR: Military regimes (Armed forces have made a coup, established a government in which the main executive post is held by a military person, and have stayed in power for at least the major part of one year.)

CRM: Periods of civilian rule in countries that have experienced a military regime.

CR(900−): Low income countries that have experienced only civilian rule.

CR(900+): High income systems that have experienced only civilian rule.

SOURCE: McKinlay and Cohan (1975:9). Published by permission of Transaction, Inc., from *Comparative Politics*, Vol. 8, No. 1. Copyright © 1975 by The City University of New York.

Military regimes, finally, tend to be unstable because of their origins. The forceful methods through which they originally may have come to power are models that later challengers can imitate. Table 5-19 suggests that Third World military regimes tend to be overthrown by coups d'état more than twice as often as party states or monarchies.

Military Complexes

National instability goes together with military complexes. Rapid economic growth provides the capability for military activity, and defense expenditures help to accelerate short-term expansion.

The period before World War I provides a good historical example of the process. At this time, the general growth of the major European states was related to the expansion of enhanced military capabilities (Choucri and North, 1975:25, 245).

In contemporary times general national growth has also coincided with expansion of military activity. Table 5-20 reviews some results from a contemporary global statistical sample. It groups a number of states, mostly from the Third World, by level of defense spending and growth rate of GNP. The two seem positively associated. High levels of defense spending seem to go together with rapid growth of GNP, while low levels of GNP growth occur mostly where defense spending is also low. The author of the study reports that "the simple correlation between defense burdens and growth rates was strongly positive: countries with high growth rates tended to have high defense burdens, and vice versa" (Benoit, 1973:2).[22]

Military activity and economic growth may be related *within* nations. Figure 5-10 provides an estimate of the contribution of defense income to growth in various parts of the United States between 1952 and 1962. We can see, even at this relatively early time, the way in which military expenditure contributed to the growth of the U.S. South and West.

Defense-related growth implies natural instabilities.[23] One observer states that "of all the mid-century growth industries, none has been more phenomenal than defense" (Sale, 1975:23). Defense expenditures have inflationary implications. Foreign and domestic government expenditures

Table 5-19

Coups and Attempted Coups in Asia, Africa, and the Middle East, 1945–1972.

Political System	(1) No. of Countries	(2) No. of Coups	(2) ÷ (1)
Party state	36	63	1.75
Monarchy	12	24	2.0
Military state	27	109	4.04

SOURCE: Kennedy (1974:26). From *The Military in the Third World,* by Gavin Kennedy. Copyright © 1974 Gavin Kennedy. Used by permission of Charles Scribner's Sons and Duckworth & Co., Ltd.

Table 5-20
Defense and GNP Growth: Global Sample, 1950–1965.[a]

Defense Burden, 1950–1965

	Low	Medium Low	Medium High	High
High	Mexico (4)	Zambia (4) Venezuela (4)	Spain (3)	Greece (1) Iraq (2) Israel (1) United Arab Rep. (1) Yugoslavia (3) China (Taiwan) (1) Jordan (1)
	1	2	1	2
Medium High		Philippines (2) Sudan (3) Tunisia (1) Brazil (3)	Peru (3) Thailand (2) Turkey (1)	S. Korea (1) Burma (4) Syria (2) S. Vietnam (1)
	0	3	2	2
Medium Low	Costa Rica (2) Kenya (2) Nigeria (3) Guatemala (3) Ghana (1) S. Africa (4) El Salvador (4)	Colombia (3) Ecuador (3)	Malaysia (1) Iran (2)	
	6	2	1	0
Low	Uganda (4) Sri Lanka (4) Honduras (3)	Tanzania (4) Indonesia (4) Argentina (4)	Chile (2) India (4) Pakistan (2) Morocco (2) Dominican Rep. (3)	
	3	3	5	0

(Left axis: Rate of Growth of GNP, 1950–1965)

[a]Figures in parentheses show quartile ranks in foreign aid; (1) = High, (2) = Medium High, (3) = Medium Low, (4) = Low. Figures in squares show number in box with high foreign aid countries removed.

SOURCE: K. Boulding (1974:20), from Benoit (1973).

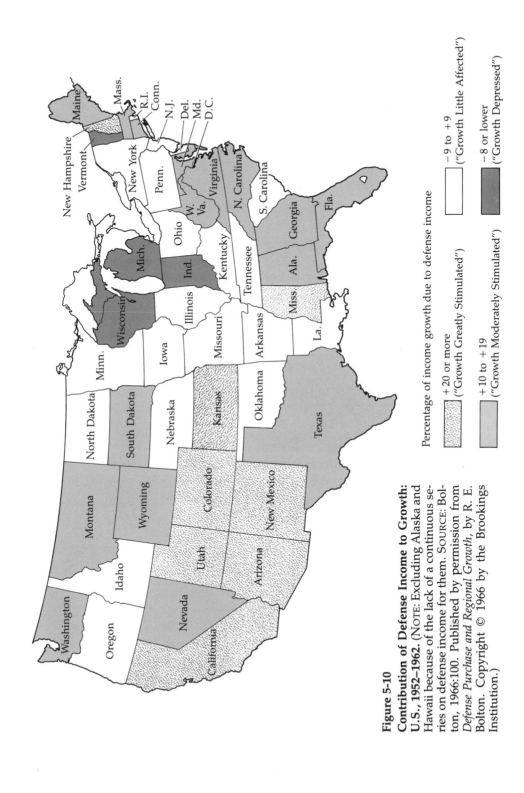

Figure 5-10

Contribution of Defense Income to Growth: U.S., 1952–1962. (NOTE: Excluding Alaska and Hawaii because of the lack of a continuous series on defense income for them. SOURCE: Bolton, 1966:100. Published by permission from *Defense Purchase and Regional Growth*, by R. E. Bolton. Copyright © 1966 by the Brookings Institution.)

Percentage of income growth due to defense income

+20 or more
("Growth Greatly Stimulated")

+10 to +19
("Growth Moderately Stimulated")

−9 to +9
("Growth Little Affected")

−8 or lower
("Growth Depressed")

provide defense. If government expenditure exceeds income, defense expenditure contributes to deficit spending. Further, weapons become obsolete increasingly fast; not only do they have to be replaced, but also the task they previously performed is taken over by more complex and, therefore, more expensive pieces of equipment. Each new generation of weapons is more sophisticated and expensive than the last.

If governmental policies change and defense expenditures are reduced, nations or regions that are highly dependent on military aid or contracts can be extremely vulnerable. The closing of large military bases or the loss of large military contracts can produce sudden massive unemployment and local economic depressions (cf. U.S. ACDA, 1972).

Militance

Finally, instability is probably associated with national militance. Little systematic research has been done on this relationship. Nevertheless, it seems consistent with what we have already discussed. We have shown how instability is related to international alliances, armaments, and image races; to national military regimes and military complexes. Cognitive consistency—the idea that behavior and attitudes go together—suggests that situations of rapid change are also likely to inspire increasingly militaristic attitudes and values. There are numerous historical examples where rapid change has produced patterns of extreme belief that in turn relied heavily on militaristic images and symbols. The interwar period in Europe in this century is only one such case (cf. Barkun, 1974).

Militance, in turn, may help produce rapid change. Militant attitudes typically focus on cutting through barriers to proceed directly to desired goals.

AGGREGATION AND MILITARIZATION: INTERNATIONAL ARMS LIMITATION

In some ways, aggregation hinders militarization. International law, organization, and communication, for example, have contributed to the limitation of armaments.[24]

Arms Limitation

Disarmament is one of humanity's oldest and fondest hopes. The prophet Isaiah (Isa. 2:4) looked forward to a day when people would "beat their swords into plowshares, and their spears into pruning hooks." In modern times a whole set of international activities has worked toward this dream.

Major international assemblies convened at The Hague in 1899 and 1907 to try and control armaments. International conferences that aimed primarily at reducing naval armaments took place in Washington during 1921 and 1922, Geneva in 1927, and London in 1930. The League of Nations sponsored a general Disarmament Conference that began in 1932 and continued until 1934 (see Goodspeed, 1959:274–81).

The U.N. has been a contemporary forum where this desire continues to be expressed. The General Assembly created the U.N. Disarmament Commission in 1952. In succeeding years the U.N. expanded membership of this Commission and created subcommittees. In 1961 the U.N. formed the 18-nation Disarmament Committee. In 1969, this became the Conference of the Committee on Disarmament, co-chaired by the United States and the Soviet Union, with enlarged membership. In May and June 1978 the U.N. General Assembly conducted a Special Session on Disarmament. In the context of the Special Session, "the World Peace Association . . . presented U.N. Secretary General Kurt Waldheim with a petition, calling for world disarmament, signed by a reported 500 million people in more than 100 countries" (Associated Press, May 24, 1978).

In spite of the grand ambition of global disarmament, most contemporary activities aim at a more limited goal that we may call arms control, or even more modestly, arms limitation.[25]

Conventional Weapons

Historical attempts at arms control aimed at what we today would call conventional weapons. Some of the weapons, however, appeared quite unconventional at the time. The international conferences at the Hague in 1899 and 1907 attempted to outlaw the use of weapons considered to be especially inhumane. These included dum-dum bullets, which expanded on impact, and poison gas (cf. von Glahn, 1970:587–90). Statesmen have also paid a good deal of attention to naval forces. The Rush–Bagot Treaty of 1817 is one of the earliest and most successful international arms limitation agreements. Under this treaty, the United States and Great Britain agreed to demilitarize the Great Lakes forever. The Washington and London naval agreements of the early interwar period, though less effective, were ambitious attempts to regulate important military capabilities.[26]

Contemporary attempts at conventional weapons limitation have been limited. Box 5-1 sketches the substantive outlines of major recent agreements, and Table 5-21 lists the nations that are parties to them. Two of the treaties—the 1959 Antarctic Treaty and the 1967 Outer Space Treaty—imply the limitation of conventional weapons. The Antarctic Treaty "denies the militarization of Antarctica and involves prohibitions against both nuclear and conventional weapons" (Foster, 1977:1). The Outer Space Treaty establishes that space is to be used exclusively for peaceful purposes. Both

Box 5-1
MAJOR ARMS LIMITATION AGREEMENTS, 1959–1978

The Antarctic Treaty has declared that Antarctica shall be used exclusively for peaceful purposes. It is an important demilitarization measure, but the question of territorial sovereignty in Antarctica has not been definitely resolved.

Signed: 1 December 1959; Entered into force: 23 June 1961.
Number of parties as of 31 December 1978: 19.

The Partial Test Ban Treaty has banned nuclear weapon tests in the atmosphere, in outer space and under water. It has helped to curb radioactive pollution caused by nuclear explosions. But testing underground has continued, making it possible for the nuclear weapon parties to the Treaty to develop new generations of nuclear warheads.

Signed: 5 August 1963; Entered into force: 10 October 1963.
Number of parties as of 31 December 1978: 109.

The Outer Space Treaty has prohibited the placing of nuclear or other weapons of mass destruction in orbit around the Earth and also established that celestial bodies are to be used exclusively for peaceful purposes. But outer space has remained open for the passage of ballistic missiles carrying nuclear weapons, and the deployment in outer space of weapons not capable of mass destruction is subject to no restrictions.

Signed: 27 January 1967; Entered into force: 10 October 1967.
Number of parties as of 31 December 1978: 78.

The Treaty of Tlatelolco has prohibited nuclear weapons in Latin America. It has thus established the first internationally recognized nuclear-weapon-free zone in a populated region of the world. Also non-Latin American states are obliged to keep their territories, which lie within the zone, free of nuclear weapons (Protocol I), while the nuclear powers undertake not to use or threaten to use nuclear weapons against the zonal states (Protocol II). But Argentina and Brazil, the only countries in the area with any nuclear potential and aspirations, are still not bound by the provisions of the Treaty.

Signed: 14 February 1967; Entered into force: 22 April 1968.
Number of parties as of 31 December 1978: 22.

The Non-Proliferation Treaty has prohibited the transfer of nuclear weapons by nuclear states and the acquisition of such weapons by non-nuclear weapon states. The latter are subject to international safeguards to prevent diversion of nuclear energy from peaceful uses to nuclear explosive devices. The Treaty grew out of the realization that the possession of nuclear weapons by many countries would increase the threat to world security. But it is being eroded because of the inconsistent policies of the nuclear-material

SOURCE: SIPRI (1979a:29–31).

(continued on next page)

suppliers, as well as the non-fulfillment of the disarmament obligations undertaken by the nuclear weapon powers.

Signed: 1 July 1968; Entered into force: 5 March 1970.
Number of parties as of March 1979: 106.

The Sea-Bed Treaty has prohibited the emplacement of nuclear weapons on the sea-bed beyond a 12-mile zone. But the Treaty permits the use of the sea-bed for facilities that service free-swimming nuclear weapon systems, and presents no obstacle to a nuclear arms race in the whole of the marine environment.

Signed: 11 February 1971; Entered into force: 18 May 1972.
Number of parties as of 31 December 1978: 66.

The Biological Weapons Convention has prohibited biological means of warfare. But chemical weapons, which are more controllable and predictable than biological weapons, and which have been used on a large scale in war, are still the subject of disarmament negotiations.

Signed: 10 April 1972; Entered into force: 26 March 1975.
Number of parties as of 31 December 1978: 80.

The SALT ABM Treaty has imposed limitations on a specific type of US and Soviet anti-ballistic missile defences. But the development of new ABMs continues.

Signed: 26 May 1972; Entered into force: 3 October 1972.

The SALT Interim Agreement has frozen the aggregate number of US and Soviet ballistic missile launchers. But it has not restricted the qualitative improvement of nuclear weapons, and the number of nuclear charges carried by each missile has been allowed to increase.

Signed: 26 May 1972; Entered into force: 3 October 1972.

The Threshold Test Ban Treaty has limited the size of US and Soviet nuclear weapon test explosions to 150 kilotons. But this threshold is so high that the parties can continue their nuclear weapon development programmes without experiencing onerous restraints.

Signed: 3 July 1974; **Not** in force by 31 December 1978.

The Document on Confidence-Building Measures contained in the Final Act of the Conference on Security and Co-operation in Europe provides for notification of major military manoeuvres in Europe, but it does not restrict these activities. Military movements, other than manoeuvres, do not have to be notified.

Signed: 1 August 1975.

The Peaceful Nuclear Explosions Treaty regulates the US and Soviet explosions carried out outside the nuclear weapon test sites and therefore presumed to be for peaceful purposes. But, apart from being a complement to the 1974 Threshold Test Ban Treaty, it has no arms control value.

Signed: 28 May 1976; **Not** in force by 31 December 1978.

The Environmental Modification Convention has prohibited the hostile use of techniques which could produce substantial environmental modifications. But manipulation of the environment with certain techniques which can be useful in tactical military operations has escaped proscription.

Signed: 18 May 1977; Entered into force: 5 October 1978.
Number of parties as of 31 December 1978: 21.

The Protocols additional to the 1949 Geneva Conventions provide for the protection of victims of international and non-international armed conflicts. They constitute a step forward in the development of the humanitarian laws of war. But they have not forbidden any specific weapon which is excessively injurious or has indiscriminate effects.

Signed: 12 December 1977; Entered into force: 7 December 1978.
Number of parties as of 31 December 1978: 2.

Current negotiations

The present bilateral, multilateral and regional arms control negotiations deal with the following subjects:

Quantitative and qualitative limitation of strategic nuclear delivery vehicles (SALT)
Control of anti-satellite weapons
Ban on all nuclear weapon tests
Prohibition of the possession of chemical weapons
Prohibition of radiological weapons
Prohibition of or restriction on certain conventional weapons which are excessively injurious or have indiscriminate effects
Reduction of forces and armaments in Central Europe.

Table 5-21

Parties to the Major Multilateral Arms Control Agreements (Ratifications, Accessions, or Successions)

State	Antarctic Treaty	Partial Test Ban Treaty	Outer Space Treaty	Treaty of Tlatelolco	Nonproliferation Treaty	Sea-Bed Treaty	BW Convention	ENMOD Convention
Afghanistan					•	•	•	
Argentina	•	•				•	•	
Australia	•	•	•		•	•	•	
Austria		•	•		•	•	•	
Bahamas		•	•	•	•		•	
Barbados			•	•	•			
Belgium	•	•	•		•	•	•	
Benin		•			•		•	
Bhutan		•					•	
Bolivia		•	•	•	•	•	•	
Botswana		•			•		•	
Brazil	•	•	•	•[a]		•	•	
Bulgaria		•	•		•	•	•	•
Burma		•	•		•			
Burundi					•			
Byelorussia		•	•		•	•	•	•
Cambodia: *see* Democratic Kampuchea								
Cameroon: *see* United Rep. of Cameroon								
Canada		•	•		•	•	•	
Cape Verde							•	
Central African Empire		•			•			
Chad		•			•			
Chile	•	•	•	•[a]	•			
China				•(Prot. II)				
Colombia				•				

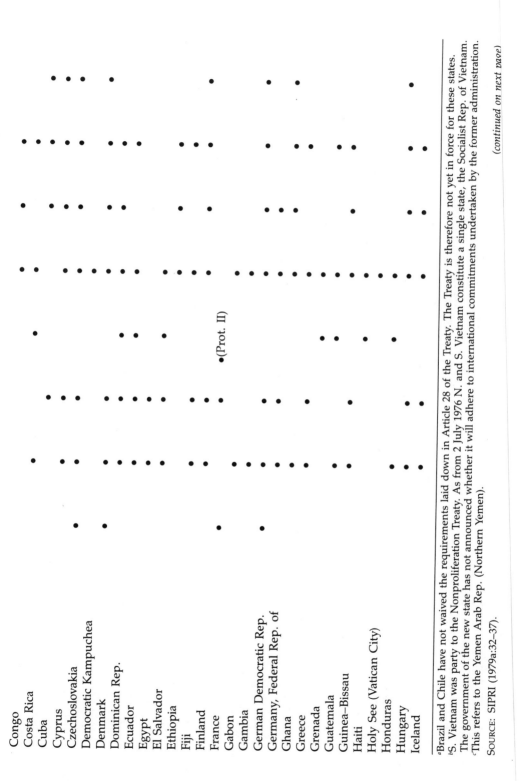

Congo
Costa Rica
Cuba
Cyprus
Czechoslovakia
Democratic Kampuchea
Denmark
Dominican Rep.
Ecuador
Egypt
El Salvador
Ethiopia
Fiji
Finland
France •(Prot. II)
Gabon
Gambia
German Democratic Rep.
Germany, Federal Rep. of
Ghana
Greece
Grenada
Guatemala
Guinea–Bissau
Haiti
Holy See (Vatican City)
Honduras
Hungary
Iceland

[a]Brazil and Chile have not waived the requirements laid down in Article 28 of the Treaty. The Treaty is therefore not yet in force for these states.
[b]S. Vietnam was party to the Nonproliferation Treaty. As from 2 July 1976 N. and S. Vietnam constitute a single state, the Socialist Rep. of Vietnam. The government of the new state has not announced whether it will adhere to international commitments undertaken by the former administration.
[c]This refers to the Yemen Arab Rep. (Northern Yemen).

SOURCE: SIPRI (1979a:32–37).

(continued on next page)

Table 5-21 (*continued*)

State	Antarctic Treaty	Partial Test Ban Treaty	Outer Space Treaty	Treaty of Tlatelolco	Nonproliferation Treaty	Sea-Bed Treaty	BW Convention	ENMOD Convention
India		•				•	•	•
Indonesia		•					•	
Iran		•	•		•	•	•	
Iraq		•	•		•	•	•	
Ireland		•	•		•	•	•	
Israel		•	•					
Italy		•			•	•	•	
Ivory Coast		•			•	•	•	
Jamaica		•		•	•			
Japan	•	•	•		•	•	•	
Jordan		•	•		•			
Kampuchea: *see* Democratic Kampuchea								
Kenya		•	•		•	•	•	
Korea, S.		•	•		•		•	•
Kuwait		•	•		•	•	•	
Lao People's Democratic Rep.		•			•			
Lebanon		•	•		•	•	•	
Lesotho					•		•	
Liberia		•			•			
Libya		•	•		•		•	
Liechtenstein		•			•			
Luxembourg		•			•		•	
Madagascar		•	•		•			
Malawi		•			•			
Malaysia		•			•			
Maldives		•			•	•		

Mali
Malta
Mauritania
Mauritius
Mexico
Mongolia
Morocco
Nepal
Netherlands
New Zealand
Nicaragua
Niger
Nigeria
Norway
Pakistan
Panama
Paraguay
Peru
Philippines
Poland
Portugal
Qatar
Romania
Rwanda
Samoa
San Marino
Saudi Arabia
Senegal
Seychelles
Sierra Leone
Singapore
Somalia
S. Africa
Spain
Sri Lanka

●(Prot. I)

(continued on next page)

Table 5-21 (continued)

State	Antarctic Treaty	Partial Test Ban Treaty	Outer Space Treaty	Treaty of Tlatelolco	Nonproliferation Treaty	Sea-Bed Treaty	BW Convention	ENMOD Convention
Sudan		•			•			
Suriname				•	•			
Swaziland		•			•			
Sweden		•	•		•	•	•	
Switzerland		•	•		•	•	•	
Syria		•	•		•	•	•	
Taiwan		•	•		•			
Tanzania: *see* United Rep. of Tanzania								
Thailand		•	•		•	•	•	
Togo		•	•		•		•	
Tonga		•	•		•			
Trinidad and Tobago		•		•	•		•	
Tunisia		•	•		•	•		•
Turkey		•	•		•	•		
Uganda		•	•		•			
Ukraine		•	•		•	•	•	•
U.S.S.R.	•	•	•	•(Prot. II)	•	•	•	•
U.K.	•	•	•	•(Prot. I&II)	•	•	•	•
United Rep. of Cameroon					•			
United Rep. of Tanzania								
U.S.	•	•	•	•(Prot. II)	•	•	•	
Upper Volta		•	•		•			
Uruguay		•	•	•	•		•	
Venezuela		•	•	•	•		•	
Vietnam[b]			•					
Yemen[c]								•
Yugoslavia		•			•	•		
Zaire		•			•	•	•	
Zambia		•	•		•	•	•	

of these agreements are somewhat tenuous because expeditions in Antarctica and outer space remain under national sovereignty and controls.

Nations with military interests in Europe have tried to achieve some conventional arms limitation. The Final Act of the Conference on Security and Cooperation in Europe, signed at Helsinki at 1975, includes a number of separate parts.[27] The Document on Conference-Building Measures is one of these parts. It requires NATO and Warsaw Pact states to notify each other before undertaking military maneuvers. It does not, however, require them to notify each other of military *movements,* or to restrict either maneuvers or movements.

NATO and Warsaw Pact nations have also undertaken talks in Vienna on the Reduction of Forces and Armaments in Central Europe. Mutual and Balanced Force Reductions (MBFR) have been a major aim. NATO allies have desired a conventional force limitation to diminish massive land force concentrations in Eastern Europe. Warsaw Pact governments have been reluctant to reduce their conventional forces because of countervailing Allied nuclear capabilities in Western Europe. The Soviet Union has been further concerned with possible resurgence of anti-Soviet sentiments in the other Warsaw Pact countries.

Some nations have made attempts to limit international trade in arms and militarily strategic materials. Supplier nations have tried to prevent recipients from retransferring arms. This effort has not been very successful. Recipient nations have continued to supply other states. Some states receiving new weapons secretly transfer their old ones to less fortunate allies and clients (cf. Burt, 1977; SIPRI, 1971; Leiss et al., 1970; Thayer, 1969).

Conventional weapons continue to be a major global problem.

> There are indications that we are on the threshold of a period of technological breakthroughs. Recent technological advances that have demonstrated particularly significant military effectiveness as compared to prior capabilities include: precision-guided antitank munitions, both ground-based and heliborne; laser-guided munitions; precision-guided standoff aerial ordnance; accurate shoulder-fired antitank weapons, using shaped-charge warheads; mobile long-range surface-to-air missiles; and man-portable precision-guided air defense weapons. The potential importance of some of these advances was dramatically brought to world attention by their use during the late stages in the U.S. involvement in Vietnam and during the Arab–Israeli war of October 1973 (Foster, 1977:4; cf. Dickson, 1976).

Nuclear Weapons

The greatest contemporary effort at arms limitation has gone into attempts to limit the testing and proliferation of nuclear weapons and production and deployment of strategic arms.

Testing

The general provisions of international law imply limitations on the testing of atomic devices. National testing is not allowed on the high seas or in the U.N. Trust Territories, which fall under international domain. General rights of national sovereignty also imply limits on some atomic testing by other nations. National atmospheric tests, for example, interrupt others' radio communications and radar controls. More importantly, they produce radioactive contamination of human populations and the ecological base of their health and livelihood. Underground tests may trigger earthquakes or volcanic eruptions (von Arx, 1974).

Particular international treaties provide additional restraints on testing. As we have already mentioned, the Antarctic Treaty of 1959 prohibits all military activity, including testing, in the Antarctic area; and the Outer Space Treaty of 1967 does the same for the cosmos.

Some treaties have specifically restricted nuclear tests. A moratorium on atmospheric nuclear testing in 1958 led to the Partial Test Ban Treaty of 1963. This treaty bans atomic weapons tests in the atmosphere, outer space, and under water (see Hopmann and King, 1976). The 1974 Threshold Nuclear Test Ban Treaty prohibits U.S. or Soviet nuclear tests under ground with explosive yields over 150 kilotons. The 1976 Peaceful Nuclear Explosions Treaty regulates Soviet and U.S. nuclear explosions for nonmilitary purposes.

These agreements appear to have accomplished some positive results. Figure 5-11 shows that the test moratorium of 1958 led to two years of no nuclear testing. Further, the limited test ban treaty of 1963 reduced the level of radioactive fallout in the atmosphere. Figure 5-12 shows that the amount of gross beta radiation in the air, tritium in water, strontium 90 and cesium 137 in milk declined substantially between 1961 and 1971.

At the same time the treaties have changed the form the testing takes rather than eliminating it. The test moratorium, the partial test ban, and the threshold test ban treaties have not abolished the testing of nuclear devices. Rather, they seem to have helped shift the timing and location of the tests. Figure 5-11 shows that the periods immediately preceding and following the moratorium included the highest number of tests during the whole period 1951–1973. There was a substantial increase in underground testing, first in 1958, and then beginning again in 1961. The 150-kiloton ceiling on underground tests does not seriously restrict most testing. The average yield of most underground testing before the 1974 Threshold Test Ban Treaty was within the 150-kiloton limit (cf. Epstein, 1975:194–95).

Nations that have not signed the test ban agreement, like France and China, have continued to explode devices in the atmosphere. The United States and the Soviet Union, which are legally bound, have simply moved their tests underground. Overall, the number of tests following the treaty was proportionately larger than before. In the 17 years between 1946 and

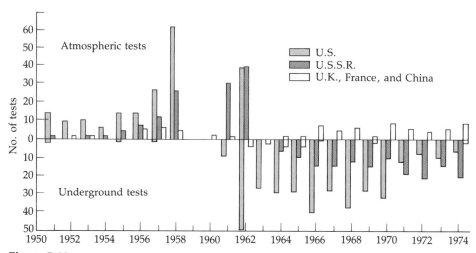

Figure 5-11

Nuclear Tests, 1951–1974. (SOURCE: Reprinted from *International Arms Control: Issues and Agreements*, by the Stanford Arms Control Group, edited by John H. Barton and Lawrence D. Weiler, with the permission of the publishers, Stanford University Press. © 1976 by the Board of Trustees of the Leland Stanford Junior University.)

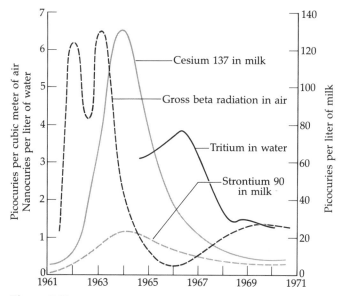

Figure 5-12

Arms Control: Atmospheric Nuclear Test Limitation Effectiveness; Radioactive Fallout, 1961–1971. (NOTE: Some of the radioactivity is natural. SOURCE: York, 1973b:300. Data from the U.S. Environmental Protection Agency.)

1963, the United States, the United Kingdom, and the Soviet Union undertook 420 nuclear tests, or just under 25 per year. In the 8 years between 1963 and 1971, they conducted 268 tests, above 33 per year, an increase in the annual rate by more than 35 percent (*Instant Research on Peace and Violence* 4 [1972]:210).

Proliferation

A whole set of international treaties and agreements has attempted to slow the proliferation of nuclear weapons around the world. Again, however, we must note that their effect has been limited.[28]

The agreements that ended World War II brought the denuclearization of the defeated Axis powers. Japan and Germany renounced direct possession of nuclear weapons in the postwar world. The United States, however, has agreed to help defend these countries with its own nuclear capabilities if necessary, and under emergency conditions it might even provide them to German and Japanese military forces.

The Antarctic, Outer Space, and Sea-Bed Treaties prohibit nuclear weapons in "new" territories. These agreements have been relatively effective because the nuclearization of such areas still presents massive problems of maintenance, command and control, and vulnerability. The question of national sovereignty is, however, still open (cf. Smith, 1979; SIPRI, 1978d; Scoville and Tsipis, 1978).

The 1962 Cuban missile crisis involved the possibility that nuclear emplacements hostile to the United States might appear in the Americas. Five years later, the Treaty of Tlatelolco established Latin America as a nuclear weapon free zone. The United States, again, defends these countries with its nuclear capabilities. Argentina, Brazil, and Chile have still not fully acceded to the treaty.

The 1968 Non-Proliferation Treaty (NPT) prohibits the dissemination of nuclear weapons by nuclear states to nonnuclear nations that are parties to it. Over 100 nations have signed the agreement. The signatories do not include the People's Republic of China, Cuba, France, India, Israel, Pakistan, or South Africa. The treaty does not remove nuclear weapons from those who already have them, nor does it prevent the nuclear "have" nations from making their weapons available to the "have nots" under agreements of alliance, in which final control lies with nuclear powers.

Furthermore, the NPT does not prohibit the dissemination of nuclear materials for peaceful uses—for example, to generate electrical energy—even though appropriate reprocessing or enrichment methods can convert waste products from nuclear energy generation into bombs. Figure 5-13 lists nations that possessed such nuclear generating capabilities in 1975 (see also Figure 6-1, p. 310).

International organizations like the International Atomic Energy Agency and Western European Union oversee the peaceful use of nuclear energy,

Figure 5-13
Nuclear Reactors, 1975. (NOTE: Nuclear reactors in operation or under construction in 48 of the 106 member states of the International Atomic Energy Agency [IAEA] are indicated on this world map. The numbers shown include both power reactors and research reactors; they are derived from the 1974 edition of *Power and Research Reactors in Member States*, published by the IAEA. In principle weapons grade material [either plutonium or uranium] can be diverted from the fuel cycle of any fission reactor. The Nonproliferation Treaty provides that the parties agree to accept the safeguard procedures set up by the IAEA to prevent the "diversion of nuclear energy from peaceful uses to nuclear weapons or other explosive devices." The IAEA safeguards apply to all fissionable materials and all peaceful nuclear activities. China does not participate in the IAEA. SOURCE: "The Proliferation of Nuclear Weapons" by William Epstein. Copyright © 1975 by Scientific American, Inc. All rights reserved.)

but their domain is limited. Nations retain sovereignty over facilities on their own territory and may convert peaceful energy resources to military purposes. And we live with the threat that nongovernmental terrorist groups may threaten such facilities or steal their nuclear materials (cf. SIPRI, 1979b; De Volpi, 1979; Rose and Lester, 1978; Blair and Brewer, 1977; Duffy, 1977; Redick, 1974; Willrich and Taylor, 1974; Willrich, 1973).

Strategic Arms Limitation

Strategic armaments include weapons that have a major role in national offense or defense. Negotiations and treaties to limit them have advanced slowly.[29] The first round of Strategic Arms Limitations Talks, SALT I, between the United States and the Soviet Union concluded with the agreements of 1972 in Moscow. The SALT I ABM Treaty prohibited each country from deploying Anti-Ballistic Missile (ABM) defense systems at more than two sites. According to the SALT I Interim Offensive Arms Agreement, the two countries further agreed to freeze the number of offensive ballistic missile launchers at their existing levels for five years.

The SALT II ABM Protocol, signed in Moscow in 1974, further restricted ABM systems, limiting each country to ABM deployment at only one site. The SALT II Interim Offensive Arms Agreement, signed in Vladivostok in 1974, committed both parties to renegotiate the earlier offensive arms agreement through 1985, with particular reference both to strategic delivery vehicles and the warheads they carry (see Barton and Weiler, 1976:172–227; Myrdal, 1974).

Figure 5-14 outlines the results of the negotiation of the late 1970s. The SALT II Agreement attempted to limit the development of long-range nuclear weapons through 1985. Under its provisions, each country agreed to an overall ceiling on total strategic nuclear delivery vehicles. The initial ceiling would be 2,400 vehicles, and this figure would decline to 2,250 before the treaty's expiration. This maximum included a number of sublimits. There would be no more than 1,320 launchers of Intercontinental Ballistic Missiles (ICBMs), Submarine-Launched Ballistic Missiles (SLBMs) equipped with Multiple Independently Targetable Reentry Vehicles (MIRVs), Air-to-Surface Ballistic Missiles (ASBMs), and airplanes equipped with long-range cruise missiles. Within this limit, 1,200 ICBMs, SLBMs, and ASBMs equipped with MIRVs and 820 launchers of ICBMs equipped with MIRVs were allowed.

The signature and ratification of the final component of SALT II would represent a substantial accomplishment in arms limitation. The agreement would help maintain a ceiling on superpowerr arms competition, perhaps preventing some extra arms expenditure, and its provisions might restrain domestic political groups in each country that wished to develop greater capabilities.

We must note, however, that some of this restraint might coincide with

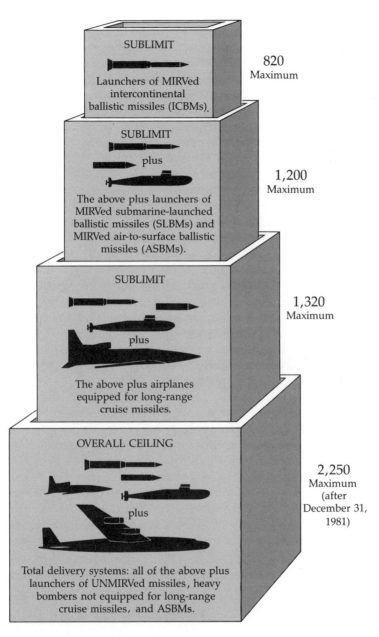

Figure 5-14
SALT II: Offensive Weapons Ceilings.
(SOURCE: U.S. Government Printing Office, 1978.)

preexisting national inclinations. If we reexamine Figure 5-7, we can see that the total number of U.S. delivery vehicles, missile launchers (including ICBM and SLBM launchers), cruise missile and attack submarines has remained relatively constant for over a decade while the number of bombers has dramatically declined. The rise in total Soviet missile launchers, especially ICBM launchers, has slowed in recent years while the number of Soviet attack submarines has also declined.

SALT II would allow some increase in the number of existing delivery systems. There is some question about whether each side would be able to verify whether the other's increase exceeded the agreed limits.[30]

SALT II would not hinder further improvement in speed, range reliability, or accuracy of strategic arms systems. It would not stand in the way of further development of the large Soviet SS-18 ICBM or new systems like the American MX ICBM or Trident submarine. SALT II would not limit the allies of either superpower.

The provisions of SALT would not neutralize the destructive implications of MIRV. MIRV means that each missile now carries many more warheads and much more destructive power than a decade ago. SALT II's ICBM quota would be high enough to inflict most possible enemy casualties. Beyond a certain point, additional numbers of delivered warheads make little difference. What remains is more than enough to all but annihilate the total populations of target nations.

SALT II would permit up to 10 MIRVs in each ICBM. If we assume that only half this potential would be realized, 820 ICBMs still imply 4,100 warheads. From Figure 5-15 it is apparent that these might kill 50 to 95 percent of the U.S. and Soviet populations. Even if one country struck first and eliminated three-quarters of another's missiles, the remaining 1,000 MIRVs could still annihilate 40 to 70 percent of the other's people. Submarine-Launched Ballistic Missiles and bombers with cruise missiles provide massive additional killing power. In the event of war, "dirty" warheads, with high levels of radioactive fallout, could be used in heavily populated zones. In a scenario of "Dirty MIRV in Europe," for example, levels of human destruction would be still further increased (cf. Lewis, 1979).

Esoteric Weapons

International agreements have also attempted to limit more esoteric weapons, again with limited effect. The Hague Convention of 1907, the 1925 Geneva Protocol, and international custom suggest that chemical and bacteriological weapons, particularly tear gas, herbicides or defoliants, and psychochemical substances are prohibited (cf. Meselson, 1978; SIPRI, 1977b, 1975c; Jaschinski, 1975; Bothe, 1973). The Biological Weapons Convention of 1972 banned the development, production, and stockpiling of biological weapons and called for the destruction of existing stockpiles.

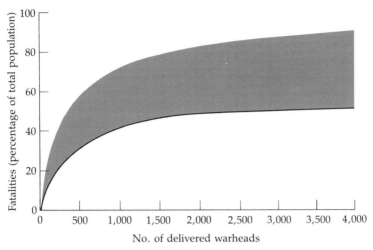

Figure 5-15
Effects on Targeted Populations: Fatalities per Delivered Warheads. (NOTE: Futility of seeking to mitigate the consequences of a full-scale nuclear exchange between the two superpowers by negotiating modest reductions in strategic-force levels or by resorting to moderately effective "damage-limiting" measures is illustrated in this graph, in which the expected fatalities in the U.S.S.R. are plotted as a function of the number of U.S. megaton-range warheads delivered. The solid curve indicates the immediate, easily calculable fatalities; the shading represents the fact that the total fatalities would probably be much larger. In either case, because of the very large number of deployed weapons, the effects of small changes in the total of delivered weapons would be negligible. The expected effects of a Russian attack against the U.S. would be similar. SOURCE: Rathjens and Kistiakowsky, 1973:206.)

Table 5-22 outlines the inventory of major biological agents and their effects. In spite of these agreements, laboratory quantities of such agents could be built into usable supplies over relatively short time periods (cf. Barton and Weiler, 1976:91, 116–22).

Other fields of physical science and engineering also have military applications. The sciences of climatology, meteorology, and geology can be used to make the air, earth, and water unfit for human beings. Volcanic eruptions, avalanches, landslides, earthquakes, clouds, fog, storms, hail, lightning, diversion and pollution of rivers, shifts in ocean currents and tides can all be artificially created (cf. Barnaby, 1976).

The U.N. Conference of the Committee on Disarmament in 1976 adopted the Convention on the Prohibition of Military or Any Other Hostile Use of Environmental Modification Techniques to inhibit the military use of such sciences. The treaty is not yet in force because the necessary number of ratifications have not yet been deposited with the U.N. Secretary General (see Juda, 1978).

Table 5-22
Biological Weapons.[a]

Agents	Diseases	Incubation Period (Days)	Effect of Treatment	Conta- giousness
Expected Causes of Death				
Viruses	Eastern Equine Encephalitis	5–15	None	By vector
	Tick-borne Encephalitis	7–14	None	By vector
	Yellow fever	3–6	None	By vector
Rickettsiae	Rocky Mountain Spotted Fever	3–10	Good	By vector
	Epidemic Typhus	6–15	Good	By vector
Bacteria	Anthrax	1–5	Moderate	Low
	Cholera	1–5	Good	High
	Pneumonic Plague	2–5	Moderate	High
	Tularemia	1–10	Good	Low
	Typhoid	7–21	Good	High
Expected Causes of Incapacitation				
Viruses	Chikungunya fever	2–6	None	By vector
	Dengue fever	5–8	None	By vector
	Venezuelan equine encephalitis	2–5	None	By vector
Rickettsiae	Q fever	10–21	Good	Low
Bacteria	Brucellosis	7–21	Moderate	None
Fungi	Coccidioi- domycosis	7–21	Poor	None

[a]Contagion "by vector" means transmission by certain species of mosquitoes or other insects.
SOURCE: Meselson (1973:307); cf. SIPRI, (1975c).

Conclusion

Arms limitation efforts have helped restrain armaments to some degree. At the same time, however, we must be clear that the success has been quite modest. By themselves, international legal and organizational efforts have not been able to control arms development and production.

One specialist has gone so far as to state that:

> Arms control as implemented in recent years . . . has not halted the arms race, but rather impelled its course. . . . Arms control has meant a retreat from disarmament. It has come to symbolize a practice of building security not on less but on more arms. Deterrence has become the main theme of arms control,

and has meant the establishment of a threat system which requires a constant augmentation of armaments, so as to enhance the retaliatory power of the adversary (Thee, 1977:95; cf. Barnaby and Huisken, 1975).

We would not dismiss the accomplishments of arms limitation so completely. Yet in spite of the proliferation of international legal agreements and the best efforts of international organizations, world military expenditures and destructive capabilities have continued to grow.

MILITARIZATION, PEACE, AND WAR

The final arrow in our original model tells us that militarization is directly related to war. War encourages militarization. If war appears imminent, militarization may seem a rational precaution. Militarization in turn leads to war. It helps broaden and deepen general distrust, anxiety, and fear as well as the extent of war itself when it occurs.

International Militarization

Law of War

There has not been a great deal of systematic study of the way in which war and the international law of war help to reinforce each other. Nevertheless, it is clear that international violence helps create the law of war. Without war there would be no need for a legal system to deal with it. And the law of war is also used to justify international violence. Thus Wright defines war as "a legal condition which equally permits two or more hostile groups to carry on a conflict by armed force" (1965:8) Another eminent legal scholar implies that the continued existence of a separate body of law for war suggests the continuing legitimacy of warlike activity. If there are discrete regimes for peace and war, national decisionmakers exercise final decision over "the choice of law governing the problems" (Jessup, 1956: Ch. 3).

The central function of the juridical term "war," is to "signify a state's choice of the laws . . . to govern its relations with other states. By declaring war, the national leadership activate[s] a different body of rights and obligations than that which [govern] its international relations in times of 'peace' " (Farer, 1971:15). International law contributes a rhetoric for "claiming and contesting various forms of external participation in internal wars; support for 'just wars of national liberation' or 'national self-determination' can thus confront various allegations of 'intervention' or 'indirect aggression and subversion' " (Falk, 1964:194).

Alliances

We have somewhat more evidence on the relationship between peace, war, and alliances. Alliances, in earlier times, do not seem to have been necessarily associated with international violence. In primitive tribal societies, extravillage alliance bonds were fragile and impermanent (Hayano, 1974). A systematic survey of historical societies over 2,000 years reveals "no relationship worth mentioning between frequency of warfare and . . . the organization of a web of defensive alliances" (Naroll et al., 1974:332–33, 339).

Modern international alliances have been more extensive and substantial. Alliances have represented an important dimension of "latent war communities" that group nations together for the purpose of armed hostilities. The major tasks of these alliances include the planning, declaration, prosecution, and termination of wars (cf. Beer, 1970, 1969).

It is interesting to return to Figure 5-3 to see the numbers and percentages of states in the international system that undertook alliance commitments over the last two centuries. This figure, and a general knowledge of modern diplomatic history, suggest that the formation of contemporary alliances appears to have preceded and coincided with general wars. Peace, on the other hand, seems to have been bad for alliances. The termination of wars has often implied the subsequent destruction of the alliances that prosecuted them.

The Napoleonic Wars at the end of the eighteenth and beginning of the nineteenth centuries brought together Austria, Britain, Prussia, and Russia as major allies against France. After their victory in 1815, they formed the Quadruple Alliance to carry their collaboration forward into peacetime. This alliance, as we have already noted, was the basis of the Concert of Europe.

The Quadruple Alliance and the Concert of Europe, however, dissolved in postwar political differences.[31] In spite of these differences, the nineteenth century was relatively peaceful. Though there were important short-term fluctuations, alliance participation generally dropped until about 1870 when the long-term decline in national alliance commitments reversed itself. Nations were again concerned with alliance building, and this trend continued until the beginning of World War I. The major diplomatic event in this pattern was the reversal of alliances that occurred around the turn of the century. Two of the allies of the Napoleonic Wars, Germany and Austria-Hungary, together with Italy, formed the Triple Alliance in 1882. Britain and Russia joined with their former enemy, France, to form the Triple Entente in 1907.

World War I changed these alliances and expanded them to include additional nations (see Sabrosky, 1975). Turkey and Bulgaria sided with Germany and Austria. Italy eventually abandoned the Triple Alliance. Together with Japan and the United States, it joined the Entente powers.

Following its victory, the winning alliance again disintegrated.[32] Two of the major powers were inactive in the League of Nations formed after the war. The leaders of the Russian revolution surrendered to the Germans in 1918 at Brest-Litovsk, and the Western allies then undertook military action against the new Soviet government. The revolutionary ideology and wartime experiences of the Soviet leaders kept the U.S.S.R. out of the League until 1934.

Though U.S. President Woodrow Wilson helped draft the peace treaty ending World War I, he was unable to carry the United States into the League that the treaty established. The United States was not ready to abandon its own postrevolutionary suspicion of entangling alliances. There was a great deal of domestic political conflict over the issue and the United States never became a member.

While alliance cohesion and commitments dropped immediately after World War I, they gradually began to rise again. The Central Powers, which had formed the defeated Triple Alliance, regrouped and emerged during the 1930s in new form, as the Axis. Germany rearmed in spite of treaty provisions and used its military forces to bring Austrian territory under German control. Italy, which had been a charter member of the Triple Alliance, was also a central actor in the Axis. Japan was a new and important addition.

World War II again brought victory to the Western powers and their allies. And again national alliance commitments dropped after the war. The victorious powers felt relatively secure. The U.N. was created to safeguard the peace. The peace terms concluding the war dissolved the Axis. Italy and Japan were not admitted to the U.N. until 1955 and 1956 respectively. Japan was not allowed to have an independent military force with international purposes, and Germany was divided into the Federal Republic and People's Democratic Republic of Germany. Neither German state was admitted to the U.N. until 1973.

This period of tranquility was, however, brief. Postwar differences between the Western powers and the U.S.S.R., together with the Chinese revolution, created serious international tensions. The U.N., burdened by the structural difficulties posed by voting in the Security Council, could not function as the postwar Allied concert it had been designed to be. During the late 1940s, the Cold War developed in full force. It involved struggle for control of various governments through clandestine or indirect means. At the same time it also raised the spectre of a third world war fought with the nuclear weapons both sides now possessed.[33]

Alliance membership began to rise again. The Western component of the Grand Alliance continued in the structure of earlier Atlantic military cooperation. SHAEF (Supreme Headquarters Allied Expeditionary Forces) quickly turned into SHAPE (Supreme Headquarters Allied Powers Europe), which was NATO's military command organization. Three of the Big Four wartime Allies—Britain, France, and the United States—were original members of NATO. And the new Western Alliance included former enemies. Italy was a charter member of NATO in 1949, and the Federal Republic of Germany joined in 1954.

The Western European Communities helped to weld the Western European states together politically and to build a strong socioeconomic foundation for Western European defense and resistance to Communist disruption and subversion. The strengthened Western European economies, the restabilization of domestic social and political structures, and the movements toward closer West European economic integration were all buttresses in the dike against Communist penetration and advance farther West.

American military and financial support helped establish the environment for Western European regional cooperation. The United States provided symbolic support by abandoning George Washington's farewell prohibition against entangling alliances. It also gave more concrete military and economic assistance. One of the most important appeals of NATO to the Western Europeans had been the guarantee that U.S. troops would be stationed in Europe. And NATO was linked with Marshall Plan aid. In the words of President Truman, NATO and the Marshall Plan were "two halves of the same walnut of Western defense" (cited in Mayne, 1970:97).

The Western Alliance came to include nations in other parts of the world. The United States, by separate treaty, agreed to provide military protection for Japan. Western alliances with Pacific states were institutionalized explicitly in organizations like ANZUS and SEATO. Member nations formed connected economic groupings like ASEAN (Association of Southeast Asian Nations). CENTO and the RCD (Regional Cooperation for Development) tied Central Asian states to the West. The OAS and various regional integration schemes in Latin America helped to support the common alliance.

In spite of their collaboration in World War II, the Soviet Union and the Allied powers had not solved their differences, which began in the middle of World War I; and it had not been certain until fairly late in World War II which side the Soviet Union would support. Following the war, the U.S.S.R. constructed its own alliance network. Events in Eastern Europe followed the trail of wartime Soviet occupation and resistance against the Germans. COMECON was created in 1949 and the Warsaw Treaty Organization in 1955. These organizations sealed the division of Germany by integrating one part of it into the socialist camp. They also reflected the desire of Soviet and Eastern European leaders to prevent penetration by Cold War rivals and to solidify internal political control.

The easing of the Cold War in subsequent years helped produce some loosening of these alliances. The Western European states broadened the membership and scope of the Common Market. To some extent they disengaged from the United States. For example, many Western European nations did not strongly support U.S. military action in Vietnam, and Western European trade policies created intracommunity commerce partly at the expense of the United States (Krause, 1968).

Similarly, Soviet and Chinese differences intensified and the Eastern European nations began to separate into discernible subregional tiers. Though the fate of the Dubček regime in Czechoslovakia showed the limits of Soviet tolerance of an independent line, the relatively independent ex-

Table 5-23 269
International Alliances and Wars: Correlations, Global Sample, 1815–1945.[a]

Frequency		Casualties	
All States			
Number of wars	07	Battle deaths for all	
Nation-months war—all	30		34
Major States			
Nation-months war—major states	28	Battle deaths for major states	31

[a]Figures show correlations between the percentage of states in alliances and indicators of war frequency and casualties beginning within three years.
SOURCE: Singer and Small (1968:278).

ample of Tito in Yugoslavia was, to some extent, adopted by others like Ceausescu in Romania.

Regional international conflicts have also encouraged more purely Southern alliances. Conflict with Israel added a sharp edge to the Arab League and the Arab Common Market and gave impetus to the formation and effectiveness of OPEC, the Organization of Petroleum Exporting Countries. Within OPEC, the "oil weapon" was forged, sharpened, and applied to the economies of the more industrialized nations.

This short sketch of the relationship between peace, war, and modern international alliances is supported to some extent by more systematic statistical analysis. Some statistical studies suggest that specific alliances are belligerent bonds or "war welds" that tend to recur over time (Richardson, 1960b:194–97; cf. Sabrosky, 1980; Siverson and King, 1980; Wilkinson, 1980:37–39; Starr, 1974; Horvath and Foster, 1963). Table 5-23 shows correlations between the percentage of states in alliances and various indicators of war frequency and casualties for all states, and for major states alone, between 1815 and 1945. A number of these correlations are relatively strongly positive.[34]

We must, however, note that there is less statistical evidence than we might like.[35] Peace does not necessarily dissolve alliances completely, nor does alliance growth always lead to war. We should be thankful that this is so, and that the alliances of the contemporary world have not so far resulted in a third world war.

Arms

Association between armaments and war is not clear in early times. The cross-national historical survey, to which we have referred several times, shows no really significant statistical associations between war frequency and a number of indicators of military capability including strength, mobility, qualilty, and prestige of the armed forces for a sample of historical periods between 2500 BC and the present (Naroll et al., 1974:329).

A study of *52 Peaceful Societies* between 2000 BC and the present also casts doubt on the assumption that early arms races contributed to war. It reports that arms tended to lead to war, not when societies reacted to each other's weapons, but rather when they developed them in relative isolation.

> Conflict is likely to occur when one side has, or believes it has, superior military techniques. This is likely to happen if two societies develop their techniques in isolation. For, although isolation contributes to peace by separating the peaceful societies from others that might attack, it also separates them from an understanding of the development of new techniques. Even if awareness of these new techniques penetrates, there is no opportunity to test them, since the society is at peace and separated from any potential enemy. Thus the Gupta failed to develop an effective heavy cavalry to protect them from Nomad attacks (Melko, 1973:154).

The empirical relationship between arms and violence is clearer in the contemporary period, though again there are anomalies. Data on national changes in armaments between 1820 and 1964 suggest that such changes in arms explain between 20 percent and 45 percent of the variance in war incidence (Wallace, 1972). Similarly, disputes preceded by "an arms race escalated to war 23 out of 28 times, while disputes *not* preceded by an arms race resulted in war only 3 out of 71 times" (Wallace, 1979:3; cf. Kemp, 1976; Smith, 1976).

Figure 5-16 sketches profiles of arms change in the twentieth century. The general pattern is similar to that of alliances. There are sharp increases before World Wars I and II; precipitous declines afterwards; a sharp rise in the late 1940s and early 1950s, coincident with the most intense part of the Cold War, and then another decline.

Figure 5-17 gives a slightly more detailed picture of the arms race leading up to World War I. Contrary to what we might expect, the sharpest general rise in total military expenditures seems to occur at the turn of the century. We see a very sharp jump in British military expenditures, particularly for the army. This rise came with the Boer War, which took place between 1899 and 1902. We may ask ourselves why none of the other major European powers apparently felt threatened enough at this time to raise their own military expenditures substantially.

After 1905 total military expenditures appear to remain pretty steady. Total French expenditures rise rapidly, as we might expect, and Austrian and Italian outlays increase moderately, just before World War I. At the same time, total military expenses of Russia and Germany actually appear to decline as war becomes imminent.

The naval race between Germany and Britain is generally assumed to have been the most important dimension of the pre–World War I arms race (cf. Pelz, 1974; Art, 1973). As we might anticipate, Figure 5-17 shows a torrid pace of naval armament leading up to World War I, with Britain far

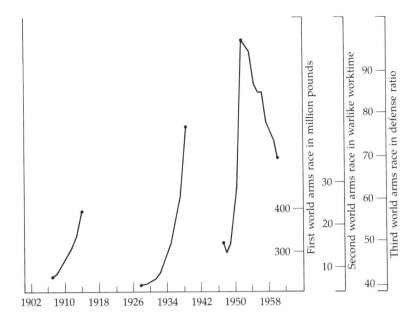

Figure 5-16
Arms Race Profiles, 1902–1958. (SOURCE: Smoker, 1967:66. Reproduced from *Journal of Peace Research*, by permission of the publishers, Universitetsforlaget, Oslo, Norway.)

outdistancing the other European nations, and Germany moving up from fourth to second place in the rankings.

There are, again, some unexpected patterns. We see a steep rise in British and German naval expenditures between 1898 and 1905. We may ask ourselves why war did not occur here. Further, between 1905 and 1910 German naval construction rose very substantially. British naval building did not follow the German lead, but declined. After 1910 German naval building slowed appreciably, but British naval expenditures rose steeply again. Finally, German naval expenditures dropped sharply just before the outbreak of the war.

Figure 5-18 shows the rate of armaments increase, in relative terms, in the years preceding World War II. It plots the differences in arms levels between successive years against the mean arms levels of those years. The pre–World War II arms race thus developed rapidly relative to the original base in its early stages, and then leveled off to some extent. The increase in annual expenditure was much greater in earlier than later years although the absolute level of armaments was much higher just before the outbreak of war. We may ask ourselves why war did not break out in 1934 when armaments were increasing most quickly.

The period following World War II raises another set of questions. The arms race profile leading up to the early 1950s is very similar to that which preceded both world wars. As the hypothesis linking arms races and wars

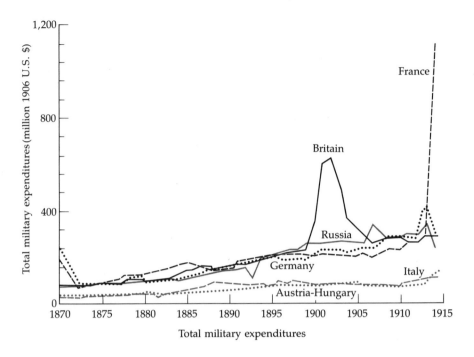

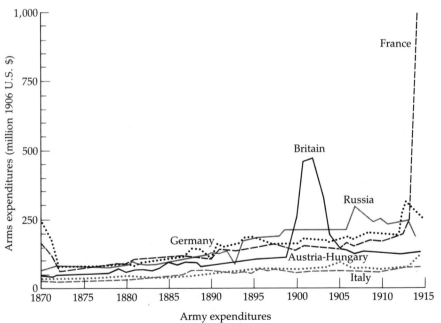

Figure 5-17
Arms Race Profiles, 1870–1914. (SOURCE: *Nations in Conflict* by Nazli Choucri
and Robert C. North. W. H. Freeman and Company. Copyright © 1975. Pp.
116–17.)

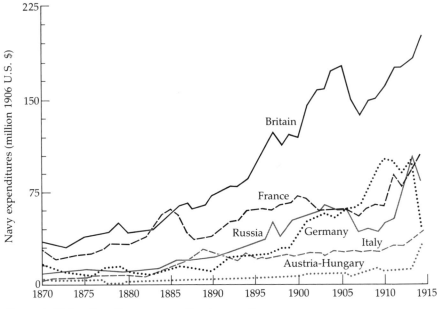

Figure 5-17 *(continued)*   Naval expenditures

would predict, war broke out, this time in Korea. Yet this war did not become a world war, and the arms race slowed. A study of the relationship between Soviet and U.S. arms expenditures between 1948 and 1960 concluded that a "mutual submissiveness effect" came into being "quite suddenly," in 1952, working "to slow the arms race when the fear experienced by both sides [became] too great" (Smoker, 1964:61–62).[36]

Figure 5-19 shows a final example that supports the relationship between armaments and war, but only for a limited period. It suggests that both arms trade and military expenditures increased dramatically in Asia, Africa, and Latin America between 1946 and 1976. War, measured in terms of time and intensity, increased through the mid-1960s, but then dramatically declined.[37]

Hostility

Wars are also related to hostile words and attitudes.

War leads to hostility in some obvious ways. Before and during war, political leaders make hostile statements against potential and actual enemies. Military leaders use modern psychological techniques in psychological warfare and propaganda (cf. Winkler, 1978; Bogart, 1976; Smirnov, 1975; Bonoma, 1974; Bobrow, 1972:36–37; Franck and Weisband, 1971; Lasswell, 1971; Lerner, 1971; Shearer, 1970; Daugherty, 1968; Dyer, 1959). Governmental agencies and the media may convey similar messages to mass audiences at home and abroad (cf. Frankel, 1966).

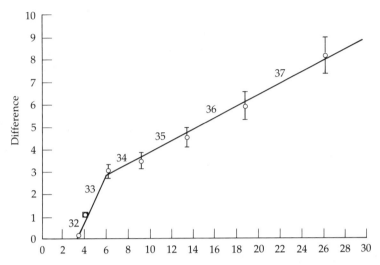

Figure 5-18
Arms Race Profile, 1932–1938. (NOTE: The graph depicts the difference in total annual expenditures between each successive pair of years, versus the mean total annual expenditures for each successive pair of years, over the time interval studied. SOURCE: Alcock and Lowe, 1969:105–7. Reproduced from *Journal of Peace Research,* by permission of the publishers, Universitetsforlaget, Oslo, Norway.)

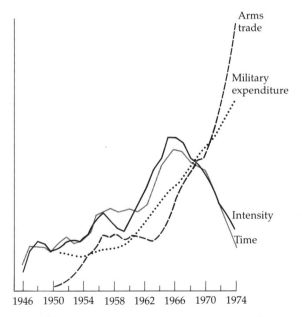

Figure 5-19
Arms Race Profile and War: Asia, Africa, Latin America, 1946–1976. (SOURCE: Kende, 1977:61.)

Information is an important weapon, a commodity that can be provided or withheld at strategic points. Language communicates the firmness of military will, the solidity of resolution and commitment. Decisionmakers tell the opponent what they intend to do before they do it. This articulation and communication of violent intentions is an important step in moving to violent actions.

Modern communications mobilize people to fight.[38] Figure 5-20 provides an example of the way this works. It shows the trend of opinion in three major American newspapers between the years 1910 and 1929. Friendliness toward France and hostility toward Germany developed in the media well before the United States committed itself to the Allied side in World War I. The shift began as early as 1911 in the *New York Times,* and 1913 in the *Chicago Tribune.* The beginning of the war itself accelerated the trend. The newspapers increased their support for France and opposition to Germany up to a peak in 1918.

Hostility contributes to war. It seems logical that people with friendly images of others should tend to have more peaceful relations. Hostile words and attitudes, on the other hand, should help produce belligerent behavior and violence.

An important dimension of psychological warfare is the dehumanization of the opponent. The aim is to suggest that one's adversary is unequal, less than human. The classical world distinguished between civilized men, who lived within the boundaries of particular political communities, and barbarians, who were outside. In the medieval world, the distinction between believers and infidels in the Christian and Moslem worlds served the same purpose.

Contemporary psychological warfare has continued to dehumanize the enemy. Militarized images include stereotypes about, or the "cartoonization" of, the enemy. Targets of recent violence have been distinguished as huns, krauts, fascists, totalitarians, capitalists, imperialists, colonizers, and gooks (Gault, 1971; cf. Bosmajian, 1974). These stereotypes help overcome normal political and cultural constraints against murder. They make it easier to kill the enemy individually or in large numbers.

Hostility from past wars may lead to future ones. World War I left an obvious residue on the popular images of the time that contributed to the outbreak of World War II. Thus, one observer believed that "nobody who lived in central Europe after the World War could have overlooked the fact that all these years were devoted to a preparation for revenge, a preparation which increased in tempo with the speed of a geometrical progression" (Alexander, 1941:506).

Legacies of World Wars I and II have also contributed to the Cold War. During World War I, Western forces invaded the Soviet Union after its surrender to the Germans at Brest-Litovsk. This military activity was supposedly aimed at denying Soviet resources to Germany. It also helped the White Russians in their resistance against the new Bolshevik regime. Similarly, American assistance to Chiang Kai-shek during and after World War

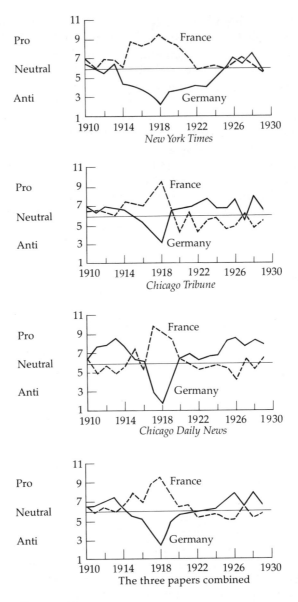

Figure 5-20
Major Newspaper Opinion: U.S., 1910–1929.
(NOTES: Graphs depict the trend of opinions
in the United States toward France and
Germany. Intensity of opinion is plotted
along the ordinate [1 = most anti and 11 =
most pro], and time by years is plotted along
the base line. SOURCE: Wright, 1965:1473.)

II aided his forces against the Communists who eventually gained control of China. Western actions in both cases produced distrust in the following years.

More recently, India and Pakistan have undertaken two wars that have been encouraged by negative stereotypes that the wars themselves have helped to generate and maintain (cf. Anant, 1974; Hague, 1973; Meade and Singh, 1973; Hague and Sabir, 1971). The series of wars in the Middle East, between Israel and the Arab states, provide another example of wars feeding on the images of past violence.

In spite of these historical cases, we must be careful to remember that hostile attitudes left over from previous wars do not always lead to future violence. In some cases the hostile images of wartime have faded rather quickly. Negative stereotypes of Germans, Italians, and Japanese, products of World Wars I and II, no longer exist in the general form they once did in the United States (cf. Stanley and Kitano, 1973). Similarly, as the Korean and Vietnam wars have passed into history, American hostility toward these former enemies seems to have decreased substantially. Military involvement in Vietnam was always a problematic and flawed activity for young people. Older people, who supported the war more strongly, have become more dovish with time (cf. Rosenbaum and Rosenbaum, 1973).

Though they fade with time, underlying images from the past do not disappear. They remain as psychological foundations for possible future wars. If political tensions reappear, a new escalation of hostile imagery builds on such bases. The hostile images produced by opposing sides, as we have seen earlier, interact to produce image races. Beyond a certain point image races seem to take on a life of their own, no longer necessarily supporting the rational purposes of the actors, but impelling them to actions they might prefer to avoid. "It is characteristic of such images that they are self confirming. That is, each party, often against its own wishes, is increasingly driven to behave in a manner which fulfills the expectations of the other" (Bronfenbrenner, 1961:51).

Image crises represent peaks in these image races. They are important thresholds of previolent and violent communication. At such peaks there tends to be a rapid and dense exchange of relatively blunt, hard messages.

Unfortunately, we do not have systematic comparative historical data that allow us to make an extensive evaluation of the association between image crises and wars, but some image crises are clearly related to war.[39] The period immediately preceding World War I was one of recurrent international crises, centering particularly in the Balkans and North Africa. The assassination of Austrian Archduke Franz-Ferdinand at Sarajevo in Serbia produced a classic image crisis where messages and information included "simple responses, gross distinctions, rigidity, and restricted information usage" (Suedfeld and Tetlock, 1977:169; cf. Suedfeld et al., 1977; Gantzel et al., 1972; North et al., 1963).

The outbreak of World War II followed a similar succession of crises in the 1930s. These crises once more involved European conflicts in Northern Africa and Central Europe. They also included conflicts in Spain and Manchuria.

Figure 5-21 presents a profile of hostile communication between Britain, France, Israel, and Egypt during 1956 and 1957. On October 29, 1956, Israel attacked Egypt in the Sinai desert. We can see that peaks in the crisis occurred during the end of October and the beginning of November.[40]

Not all image crises, however, are directly associated with the outbreak of war. Thus, the immediate post–World War II period presented an almost continuous succession of hostile verbal incidents. Hostility over access to Berlin, for instance, declined to "inactivity or extinction," only during 1954–1956, 1958, and 1963, between 1948–1963 (McClelland, 1968:179). The Cuban missile crisis also involved a large amount of hostile communication. Unlike crises that ended in war, however, the images increased in "complexity, fine distinctions, flexibility, and extensive information search and usage" as the Cuban crisis approached its climax (Suedfeld and Tetlock, 1977:169).[41]

Hostile communication does not stop at the war's edge. Hostility follows through from the prewar situation to war itself. Hostile image escalation may help expand wars that are already in progress. Thus between 1964 and 1968, President Johnson's use of symbols suggesting positive action, commitment, and the need to protect U.S. status abroad were reasonably good predictors of U.S. military escalation in the Vietnam War (Sullivan and Thomas, 1972:185–86; cf. Chan, 1978; Ivie, 1974).[42]

Escalation involves more than words. Table 5-24 presents a list of 44 escalation scenarios through which warlike decisions can expand.[43]

Political and diplomatic gestures may be important elements of hostile escalation. Table 5-25 presents the results of the cross-national survey between 1955 and 1957. It shows that accusations, threats, and protests are strongly associated with overt violence. Expulsion or recall of diplomats, antiforeign demonstrations, and negative sanctions are also likely to go together with wars and casualties. Severance of diplomatic relations and explusion or recall of ambassadors, however, appear insignificant (cf. M. Haas, 1974:237, 240, 461; Collins, 1973; Tanter, 1966).[44]

Economic gestures or policies may also be part of the escalation process used as substitutes for or adjuncts to war itself. We recognize this when we use such terms as *trade war* or *monetary war* to describe antagonistic economic behavior. International specialization brings with it substantial dangers. Wright (1965:1483) notes that "increased trade increases vulnerability to commercial retaliation and blockade and so may increase the sense of menace," and Blainey points out that "the very instruments of peace—railways and international canals and steamships and bills of lading—were conspicuous in the background to some wars" (1973:22; cf. Knorr and Traeger, 1977).

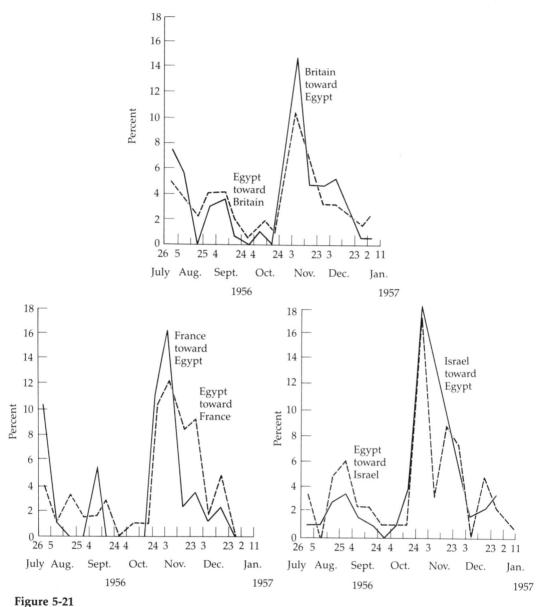

Figure 5-21

Hostile Image Interaction: Middle East, 1956–1957. (NOTE: Hostility per ten days/total hostility as a percentage from July 26, 1956, to January 11, 1957. SOURCE: These figures, drawn from "Conflict Escalation and Conflict Reduction in an International Crisis: Suez, 1956" by Edward E. Azar, are reprinted from *Journal of Conflict Resolution*, Vol. 16, No. 2 [June 1972], pp. 183–202, by permission of the publisher, Sage Publications, Inc.)

Table 5-24
An Escalation Ladder.

	Aftermaths

Civilian Central Wars	44. Spasm or Insensate War
	43. Some Other Kinds of Controlled General War
	42. Civilian Devastation Attack
	41. Augmented Disarming Attack
	40. Countervalue Salvo
	39. Slow-Motion Countercity War

	City Targeting Threshold

Military Central Wars	38. Unmodified Counterforce Attack
	37. Counterforce-with-Avoidance Attack
	36. Constrained Disarming Attack
	35. Constrained Force-Reduction Salvo
	34. Slow-Motion Counterforce War
	33. Slow-Motion Counter-"Property" War
	32. Formal Declaration of "General" War

	Central War Threshold

Exemplary Central Attacks	31. Reciprocal Reprisals
	30. Complete Evacuation (Approximately 95 percent)
	29. Exemplary Attacks on Population
	28. Exemplary Attacks Against Property
	27. Exemplary Attack on Military
	26. Demonstration Attack on Zone of Interior

	Central Sanctuary Threshold

Bizarre Crises	25. Evacuation (Approximately 70 percent)
	24. Unusual, Provocative, and Significant Countermeasures
	23. Local Nuclear War—Military
	22. Declaration of Limited Nuclear War
	21. Local Nuclear War—Exemplary

	No Nuclear Use Threshold

	20. "Peaceful" World-Wide Embargo or Blockade
	19. "Justifiable" Counterforce Attack
	18. Spectacular Show or Demonstration of Force
	17. Limited Evacuation (Approximately 20 percent)

Source: Kahn (1965:39). From *On Escalation* by Herman Kahn. Copyright © 1965 by Hudson Institute. Reproduced by permission of Praeger Publishers and Hudson Institute.

Intense	16.	Nuclear "Ultimatums"
Crises	15.	Barely Nuclear War
	14.	Declaration of Limited Conventional War
	13.	Large Compound Escalation
	12.	Large Conventional War (or Actions)
	11.	Super-Ready Status
	10.	Provocative Breaking Off of Diplomatic Relations

Nuclear War Is Unthinkable Threshold

	9.	Dramatic Military Confrontations
	8.	Harassing Acts of Violence
Traditional	7.	"Legal" Harassment—Retortions
Crises	6.	Significant Mobilization
	5.	Show of Force
	4.	Hardening of Positions—Confrontation of Wills

Don't Rock the Boat Threshold

Subcrises	3.	Solemn and Formal Declarations
Maneuver-	2.	Political, Economic, and Diplomatic Gestures
ing	1.	Ostensible Crisis

Disagreement—Cold War

National policies of embargo, economic blockade, or military actions of siege can be instruments of struggle, preceding or joining direct violence. World War I, for example, included a heavy economic element.

> The legislation of the belligerents prohibited trading with the enemy. In addition, each side endeavoured to cut the other off from the world's markets by means of an offensive economic war. The Allies encircled the Central Powers in an ever tighter blockade. For its part the German government sought, by means of a commercial war fought with U-boats, to isolate Britain economically. The longer the war went on the more both parties pinned their hopes on economic warfare. The Great War, it has been said, was as much a war of competing blockades, the surface and the submarine, as of competing armies. Behind these two blockades the economic systems of the two opposing groups of countries were engaged in a deadly struggle for existence, and at several periods of the war the pressure of starvation seemed likely to achieve an issue beyond the settlement of either the entrenched armies or the immobilized navies (Salter, 1921, cited by Hardach, 1977:11).

German submarine warfare against formally neutral merchant shipping to Britain was a major factor in bringing the United States into the war.

World War II also included an economic component. The United States in July 1940 placed an embargo on "aviation fuel and topgrade scrap iron"

Table 5-25

Hostile Communication and War: Global Sample, 1955–1957.[a]

Type of Communication	Wars	Casualties
Accusations	.56	.70
Threats	.55	.63
Protests	.51	.52
Expulsion or recall of lower diplomatic officials	.33	.32
Antiforeign demonstrations	.25	.35
Negative sanctions	.24	.30
Severance of diplomatic relations	.07	.31
Expulsion or recall of ambassadors	.01	.02

[a]Numbers are Pearson product—moment correlations.

SOURCE: Rummel (1972:457). This table, drawn from Appendix 2 by R. J. Rummel, is reprinted from *The Dimensions of Nations*, copyright 1972, p. 457, and is reprinted by permission of the publisher, Sage Publications, Inc.

to Japan. In December the United States began "unobtrusive selective licensing of . . . exports to Japan." In June there were more "unobtrusive U.S. embargoes." In July the United States froze Japanese economic assets (Snyder and Diesing, 1977:554–55). These U.S. actions helped precipitate the Japanese attack on Pearl Harbor.

In the contemporary world, the Arabs have attempted to use oil as a weapon in their continuing struggle against Israel. They have threatened to cut off petroleum shipments to Western states, bargaining for concessions on Palestinian and other related issues (see Mersky, 1978).

Finally, dramatic military mobilizations may convey hostility and warn that violence is very close. Russia, Austria, and Germany, for example, mobilized troops immediately before the outbreak of World War I. Cross-national surveys have tended to corroborate the relationship between military mobilizations and wars (M. Haas, 1974:242; Rummel, 1972:361).

National Militarization

Military Regimes

Traditional political theory has long supported the idea that peace encourages civilian governments. The institutions and processes of civil freedom seem to grow best in conditions of relative tranquility. As one eminent political philosopher observed, "constitutionalism needs peace for its survival" (Friedrich, 1968:88).

In situations where war is likely or exists, the military seems to assume a larger influence in making foreign and domestic policy. War is a dangerous business that threatens the very existence of state and society. It suggests a more forceful political form. If war lasts long enough, and is sufficiently severe, it implies martial rule, which dispenses with the safeguards of legal rights and due process. Formal "emergency powers"—including martial law, clandestine intelligence gathering and secrecy, and calls for patriotism, discipline, and obedience—vie with, and often overcome, countermovements in "bitter arguments over civil liberties" (Friedrich, 1974:91, 94).

European history seems to show the relationship of peace to civilian government, and of war to military or authoritarian rule. One analyst states that:

> The preference of Anglo-Saxon nations for democratic forms of government had owed much to the military security which the ocean provided. On the rare occasions in the last two centuries when Britain was threatened by a powerful enemy it abandoned temporarily many of its democratic procedures; thus in the Second World War Churchill and the war cabinet probably held as much power as an autocracy of the eighteenth century (Blainey, 1973:31; cf. Wolfers, 1962:Ch. 3).

The presence of more or less continual military threat in Continental Europe presumably has contributed to a more absolutist political history there.

Traditional theory and historical case studies have also suggested that civilian regimes tend to be more peaceful and that highly militarized regimes undertake more frequent and bloody wars. War may help produce a "war machine," but once it is in place, such a machine itself helps to produce further wars (cf. Schumpeter, 1951:49; Lang, 1972:16–17).

Anthropologists have seen a connection in primitive societies between military regimes and warfare. Malinowski notes that "once a strong local group developed a military machine, it would use this in the gradual subjugation of its neighbors and extension of its political control" (1941:537). Margaret Mead (1964) suggests that military activity in such societies was an invention that was used to gain competitive advantages over others.[45]

A number of important political philosophers—Kant, Rousseau, and Bentham, for example—have suggested that constitutional democratic polities tend to be more peaceful than their coercive counterparts (cf. Waltz, 1959). The peaceful ideal of democracy was perhaps expounded most forcefully by Woodrow Wilson, whose 14-point program for the post–World War I settlement showed his belief that constitutional democracy was a major precondition for a real and meaningful international peace.[46]

We argued earlier that military regimes tend to be more coercive and inegalitarian than civilian governments. It is as if the military are conquerors of their own societies. Andreski says that

> within militarized societies, it is almost always those who wield the military power who form the supreme stratum of society. . . . In all social conflicts

violence is the argument of last resort. Even where it is never used it stands in the background as the enforcement of the "rules of the game" (1968:26).

Coercive governments, in turn, appear more likely to use their military capabilities abroad. "Excess of internal authority," suggests Kennan, "leads inevitably to unsocial and aggressive conduct as a government among governments" (1951:130; cf. Spiro and Barber, 1970). It also seems logical that coercive governments can undertake international violence more quickly and easily than noncoercive governments. Waltz notes that

> in a world where military technology places a premium upon speed and opponents at times appear to be implacable, the flexibility, dispatch, coherence, and ruthlessness of authoritarian states have been thought to be decisive advantages (1967:310–11).

Military men are specialists in violence. They seem more likely to approve of going to war, and of fighting it as vigorously as possible. This assumption lies at the root of the popular perception of, and anxiety about, military thinking. Military processes of recruitment, socialization, and promotion presumably ensure that the majority of military personnel find war legitimate and justifiable. The military approach war in a special way. Thus, in Vietnam, "General Westmoreland chose and was allowed to choose (for whatever reasons) dead bodies as signs of success for the military manager" (Lammers, 1977:50).[47]

The arguments supporting the relationship between military regimes and war are intuitively persuasive, but the evidence to confirm them is largely impressionistic. Systematic statistical studies have so far presented only limited confirmation.

Some contemporary research suggests that communities with military leadership are more likely to go to war than civilian-dominated societies (McGowan and Gottwald, 1975:494; Midlarsky and Thomas, 1973). Other studies support the idea that more coercive governments may undertake more international violence. One global cross-national study covering 1955–1957 associates domestic purges with several foreign conflict indicators, including the number killed in wars between 1955 and 1957 (Rummel, 1972:360; Tanter, 1966:46). Another contemporary cross-national analysis shows a modest relationship between press censorship, restriction of political opposition, and war incidence and casualties. There is, however, little association between constitutional, authoritarian, and totalitarian regimes and war (M. Haas, 1974:214, 231).

Such results are also consistent with the idea that international violence may encourage domestic coercion. A study of governmental repression in the United States suggests that wars have provided the frame within which the national government could persecute unreliable and unwanted elements within the state. It shows that repression has increased substantially during and after major wars (Stohl, 1976).

Military Complexes

Military complexes are also linked to international violence. War obviously increases military personnel and expenditures. At the same time, the existence of such military capabilities is a precondition and an incentive for their use.

Studies of early societies show that some elements of developing military complexes were associated with war. In primitive societies military sophistication was related to the frequency with which such communities engaged in offensive external war. Military sophistication had no observable effect in deterring attacks by others—as measured by frequency of defensive war—and overall it brought higher casualty rates; but at the same time, it appeared to produce military success, and, by implication, political survival (Otterbein, 1970:70–92; cf. Turney-High, 1971).[48]

A survey of historical communities suggests that the quality of a community's armed forces was associated with war and its spoils. The authors investigated the relationship of war frequency and territorial gain to certain military characteristics, including strength, mobility, prestige, quality, defensive stance, and border fortifications. They observe:

> It is often said that God is on the side of the largest battalions. If God takes sides, it is not the side of the largest battalions, nor that of the best fortified battalions, nor that of the most renowned. Rather God if he takes sides at all, seems to stand at the side of the well-trained battalions (Naroll et al., 1974:337).

The military complex in modern times also appears to contribute to war. Military plans, for example, can trigger violent responses. A good example of this occurred at the outbreak of World War I. German military planning specified that, should war break out, it would be essential to strike rapidly to the west—through the Low Countries—and quickly eliminate France. Once this was done, German forces could turn east and deal with Russia. This plan was designed to keep Germany from fighting on both Western and Eastern fronts at the same time. The plan was not militarily successful. Its emphasis on speed, however, may have escalated the war more rapidly than would otherwise have happened.[49]

Research has found an association between war and the strength of armed forces. If we return to Tables 2-19 and 2-20, which charted the fluctuations of violence in contemporary European history, we can see that the ratio of army/population varies regularly with casualties/population. Both sets of figures generally go up through the seventeenth century, dip in the eighteenth and nineteenth centuries, and then rise again in the twentieth century.[50]

More recent data also tend to support this relationship. The absolute number of a nation's military personnel is associated with the number of its war casualties. Absolute military personnel is also strongly related to a number of other foreign conflict variables: antiforeign demonstrations, protests, expulsion or recall of diplomatic officials, accusations, threats, and troop movements. The ratio of military personnel to total national population is less strongly related to aspects of international violence. There are, however, strong correlations between military personnel/population aged 15–64, and war incidence and casualties (M. Haas, 1974:211, 242; Rummel, 1972:358; cf. Weede, 1975:Ch. 6).

War naturally leads to higher military participation. During wartime a larger proportion of national manpower goes into the military service, rather than the civilian labor pool. For example, during violent periods in American history, U.S. military employees rose dramatically while civilian government employees remained much more stable (see Figures 3-5 and 5-22).[51]

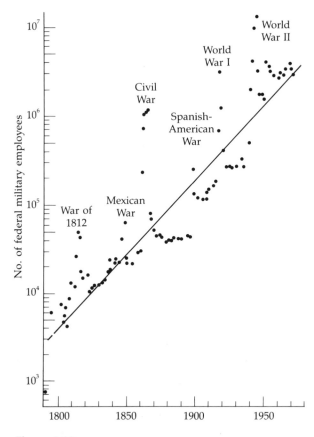

Figure 5-22
Federal Military Employees: U.S., 1800–1965.
(NOTE: Number of federal military employees, plotted on semilogarithmic coordinates by years.
SOURCE: Hamblin et al., 1973:98–99.)

Military participation, in turn, helps produce war. Andreski proposed that a primary predictor of war is the "military participation ratio," the proportion of the armed forces to the total population of a country (1968:33). Statistics covering the international system over the last century and a half suggest that the "tensions generated by . . . structural variables were translated into armed conflict primarily via increases in the size of armed forces" (Wallace, 1972:49).[52]

War is clearly related to defense expenditure. Contemporary cross-national statistics show relatively strong relationships between defense expenditure as a proportion of national income and war incidence and casualties. Indicators of strong defense expenditure are also associated with most other indicators of foreign conflict behavior.[53]

During wartime, higher proportions of GNP and government budgets go into military goods and services. Figure 5-23 shows the World War II expansion of the national defense component of U.S. GNP at the expense of civilian sectors. National defense expenditure began to grow about a year before the Japanese attack on Pearl Harbor formally brought the United States into the war. Defense expenditure reached its peak in 1944. The

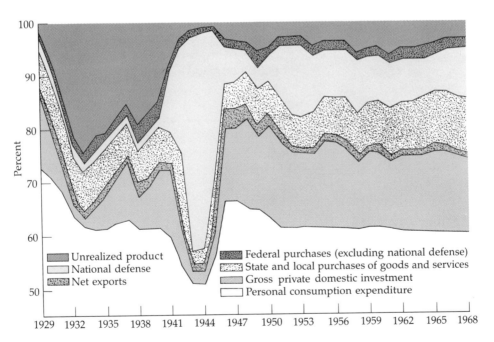

Figure 5-23
Costs of Militarization: Defense Relationship with Components of GNP, U.S., 1929–1968. (SOURCE: K. Boulding, 1970:4. Published by permission of Transaction, Inc., from *Peace and the War Industry*, edited by Kenneth E. Boulding. Copyright © 1970 by Transaction, Inc.)

beginning of its decline preceded the formal victories over Germany and Japan in 1945.[54]

High defense expenditure presumably foreshadows war. A study of the Middle East conflict reports "an upward trend in force-related activity commencing about four to five years prior to the [1967] war" (Job, 1979:53). A study of 15 Asian nations between 1946 and 1970 found that "sharp increases in military assistance tend to change decidedly the recipient nation's international conflict and cooperative behavior" after a general two-year lag, "toward increased conflict and decreased cooperation" (Sylvan, 1976:609; cf. Newcombe, 1977; Choucri and North, 1975:245; M. Haas, 1974:466).

The vast resources spent on the military complex have impelled a number of analysts to suggest that economic motives are a direct influence for war. In the earlier part of this century, munitions makers were identified as "merchants of death." Following World War I the Nye Committee investigated their role in helping to bring about and enlarge the war. It was assumed that they helped promote the war because of the profits they derived from supplying national arsenals (cf. Stromberg, 1977; Wright, 1965:1173–77).

In our own time this argument has been expanded to include the other members of the military complex: all those who gain their livelihood from providing military goods and services including not only the owners of military-related industries, but also the vast numbers of managers inside and outside of formal government, as well as ordinary defense workers.

These arguments are similar to those that identify the military mind as a cause of war. They have intuitive appeal, but they are probably too simple. Those who work in the military complex may think in more military terms and identify more strongly with defense programs, but many of them may still be against war in general or against specific wars (cf. Schevitz, 1979; Phillips, 1973).

Militance

War is both cause and effect of militance. It is intimately connected with the militarization of identities, images, values, and attitudes.

War contributes to a militarized identity of national communities. In wartime, nations appear as shelters, protecting those within against those outside.

War also helps militarize the identities of the individual citizens who make up the community. During wartime, "loyalties to church, party, or profession are subordinated to loyalty to the state" (Wright, 1965:697; cf. Krehbiel, 1973). Indeed, the militarized state takes over some of the functions previously performed by the family. For young people who serve, the military stands in loco parentis. One analyst has suggested that "armies [in this case the United States army] maintain their internal discipline by evoking and reeliciting unconscious Oedipal and pre-Oedipal anxieties and solving them regressively" (Hippler, 1971:97; cf. Saxonhouse, 1980).

Once the immediate conflict is past, war can still produce a longer-term militarization. Past military experiences become important foci of collective reference. Political leaders use military terms for civilian sectors of activity. Thus, in the Soviet Union, Stalin called

> science a "fortress" which must be "carried" by youth. The newspapers are like war communiqués. Every economic and intellectual happening becomes a "campaign" on a "front." "Armies" "fight" "battles," "brigades" "storm" "defiles," "iron battalions" take "front-line trenches" under "drum-fire" (Speier, 1969:10, quoting Klaus Mehnert).

Individuals share collective concerns of war, violence, conflict, and danger (Monaco, 1974). They are conscious of the glories of past conquests, the present injustices caused by past military defeats, the future dangers posed by possible enemies.

The wartime experience militarizes images, metaphors, analogies, and symbols as it permeates communication, art, and religion.

War enhances military control of communications. During wartime "censorship comes into effect, and important instruments of communication are taken over by the government" (Wright, 1965:697). The government mobilizes support more directly, disseminating public information or propaganda. External channels of communication convey this material with related news.

War implies the militarization of art. Violence has its own aesthetic. War itself is a kind of art form. At an earlier time, it was "the sport of kings," with rules of form and style, set criteria of grace and elegance. In the modern era, war games provide a structure for military training, testing, and rehearsal as well as popular entertainment through magazines, newspapers, books, radio, television, and movies.

The fact and fiction of war supply material for art in various other forms. Wars have inspired great music, for example, Tchaikovsky's *1812 Overture* and Beethoven's *Eroica* Symphony; great painting, El Greco's *View of Toledo*, Picasso's *Guernica*; great literature, Tolstoy's *War and Peace*. Contemporary science fiction has extended the consideration of war into the realm of the fantastic; for example, Isaac Asimov's *Foundation and Empire* trilogy and Frederick Herbert's *Dune* series present intergalactic warfare in which the future of humankind is at stake. Indeed, one of the major themes of the literature of science fiction is space war. Television and films have also used this theme: *Star Wars and* "Battlestar Galactica" are but two examples.[55]

War contributes to the militarization of religion and of mystical experience. Primitive magic and rituals included detailed interpretations of, and routines for, the conduct of wars (cf. Frazer, 1961; Malinowski, 1948). In classical Western mythology, fighting and wars among the Gods occurred, and some divinities, like Mars, were specialists in violence. In tribal societies religious prophets supported and often led military activity (see B. Wilson, 1973:Ch. 8). Wars were imbued with religious meaning. Thus, in the ancient Zoroastrian religion there was a "constant battle going on between the forces of evil and those of good, a battle whose ground extended to the limits of the universe." History was a "result of an ever-living struggle between evil and the good" (Boas, 1974:3). During the Middle Ages, the combatants attempted to achieve a "decision of holy validity," a "judgment of God" to confirm their superiority over their opponents (Huizinga, 1954:91).

In contemporary times, political ideology often appears to cast friends and enemies in terms that are close to the divine or the satanic. Humanistic socialism does battle with the devils of capitalist imperialism. Contemporary liberal democracy struggles with atheistic communism or totalitarianism.

War and religion are also joined by the meaning that they give to death. Traditional war was a situation in which a single individual could be transubstantiated through death, a rite of passage in which an adolescent could become a man or in which an older man might pass immediately and gloriously out of life. War could be a kind of existentialist attempt to come face to face with death—to meet and do battle with the dilemmas of one's existence on one's own terms; to infuse one's life with meaning by the manner of its ending; to die for a cause rather than be overtaken in the night. Organized military activity was one of the few activities that was explicitly structured to deal directly with the possibility of death. If not death oriented, it was death focused; and the central fact in the lives of military men in wartime was that they might die tomorrow.

Modern weapons of mass destruction have spread the scope of warfare and diminished whatever individual meaning may have been found in doing battle. Yet the sacred aspect of war remains. War and weapons foster feelings of omnipotent, magical, and malevolent power. It "is not 'heaven,' as formerly, that presides over battles and makes the ordeal by combat truly decisive; the possessors of the atom bomb can intervene at any moment, reverse any outcome, and erase the whole" (Jaspers, 1961:51). Advanced weapons transform war into another kind of religious vision, the Apocalypse, the Twilight of the Gods, the Day of Judgment, a kind of total theater revealing parts of man normally hidden and broadening audience participation to include the possibility of physical destruction.

Modern weapons contribute to ordinary citizens' feelings of powerlessness over their own destiny. And fears of political phenomena, including war, to some extent displace supernatural fears found in conventional early childhood development (cf. Croake and Knox, 1973; Lowther, 1973; Legras, 1970–1971). At the same time, there appears to be a desire for a benevolent magician. This helps to explain the widespread fascination with such themes as presented in J. R. Tolkien's *Lord of the Rings*, which essentially revolves around the struggle of the magical forces of Good against those of Evil for possession of the ultimate weapon—the Ring (cf. A. Wilson, 1972; Wolfenstein and Kliman, 1965).

War militarizes collective values and attitudes, implying the hardening and dehumanization of culture. Two processes occur at once: the amplification of force and desensitization to pain. Modern military capabilities contribute to the increase of pain; at the same time, changes in consciousness and perception remove preexisting moral limits to its infliction.

War requires national decisionmakers to emphasize force. Diplomacy, within the context of the game of nations, includes the translation of brute military capabilities into coercion through the threat of violence. In situations of international relations where explicit violence is not present, threat is its proxy.

The dimension of force has always existed in international relations, but it has become more acute in our time. The technology of the twentieth century has vastly expanded the scope and methods of force. Prior wars, such as the Thirty Years' War, the Hundred Years' War, and to some extent the Napoleonic and American Civil Wars, involved their civilian populations; yet the domain of direct military force probably has never extended as far and as deeply into civilian life as it does in modern times.

The expansion of force has brought with it an insensitivity to pain. Traditional political thought was not painless. Not only Machiavelli and his followers, but even nineteenth-century Liberalism found two sides in the calculus that balanced pains and pleasures. Yet pain generally occupied a rather shadowy land beyond pleasure (cf. Wolin, 1960:Ch. 11).

For modern statesmen, it can be important, relevant, functional, understandable to desensitize themselves and their audiences to the painful implications of modern warfare. U.S. presidents, in war addresses, for example, have portrayed the United States "as especially virtuous and particularly obligated to combat evil. 'Foreigners' must be held accountable and must be punished for their weaknesses" (Ivie, 1974:345). The more private worlds of presidents were not necessarily more hospitable to suffering. "Whatever humane feelings Kennedy, Johnson and Nixon had about Indo-China," said one analyst, "the sad fact is that they saw Indo-China primarily as a game board and its people primarily as pawns" (Walton, 1972:194).

An important part of a national community wants to be spared unpleasantness and is receptive to such appeals. Thus one analyst suggests the following congruent attitudes among the privileged in U.S. society:

> (a) the need to believe in a just world, (b) the Protestant Ethic, (c) a hereditarian bias, (d) authoritarianism, and (e) adherence to the ethics of personal conscience vs the ethics of social responsibility (MacDonald, 1973:37).

Similarly, revolutionary leaders, speaking to and for the disadvantaged, block out pain by emphasizing the justness of their cause, the inhuman nature of the enemy, and the need to act for the long-run collective interest, without counting immediate particular costs of life or limb (cf. Cleaver, 1968; Fanon, 1965; Memmi, 1965).

In contemporary times, the increased brutality of contemporary warfare has also been reflected in the brutalization of social science. There is an abstractness to the indicators and language used in the political and social scientific discussion of violence, including those we have used here. Although the indicators purport to describe international violence, they provide only a weak reflection of its reality. To those with no personal experience of violence, the indicators suggest that international violence is a bloodless kind of game, a mere extension of chess or checkers. The abstract description of thermonuclear devastation has relatively little substantive meaning to persons who have not actually lived through it, and very few have directly experienced the detonation of nuclear weapons on human societies.

Technical vocabulary has flattened the language of political discussion and analysis. Past, present, and future war casualties are added and projected in attempts to provide inputs for cost-benefit calculation. This procedure seems relatively simple and straightforward. It is based first on an additive assumption about human life; for example, ten lives are ten times as valuable as one life. Second, it includes an implicit transformation formula between lives and other values, particularly national territory and economic resources. Life may not necessarily be cheap, but it is certainly not priceless. In an abstract way, every man, woman, and child carries a price on his or her head. These assumptions may be egalitarian and conform fully to the cultural ordering of priorities of contemporary societies. Nevertheless, they do not reflect the very important fact that central players and their audiences may actually place unequal values on particular lives. Whose life is on the line makes a big difference.

Violence, cruelty, and pain maintain a power to fascinate those who touch them. One can easily be hypnotized by the shiny intricacies of strategic analysis—guerrilla war, counterinsurgency, conventional war, limited war, tactical nuclear war, nuclear wars of attrition, broken-back warfare, spasmic thermonuclear war, and doomsday machines; first, second, and subsequent strikes; urban, logistical, military targeting; hardening and dispersal of forces; MAD, MIRV, and ABM; and space platforms.

Since the nuclear weapons of the contemporary world offer more powerful instruments, one might hope, at the very least, that the fine edges of the new stainless steel blades of strategic analysis would be used in careful operations by skilled political surgeons. Instead the world's battlegrounds are experimental laboratories for social scientific doctors, like the medical doctors in the television series "M*A*S*H," who seem to anesthetize not their patients but themselves.

In the modern age, military and social science have achieved new heights of elegance and refinement. Contemporary strategic theorizing has gone beyond the traditional limits of the calling of arms and deep into the psychology of pain. Herman Kahn's works, *On Thermonuclear War* and *On Escalation* have joined and surpassed other better known antiutopias such as *Brave New World* and *1984*. The science of violence has attained new degrees of complexity. The outline of the first chapter of a prominent book on the subject illustrates the point (Schelling, 1966:Ch. 1):

1. The contrast of brute force with coercion
2. Coercive violence in warfare
3. The strategic role of pain and damage
4. Nuclear contribution to terror and violence
5. From battlefield warfare to the diplomacy of violence.

Metaphors are used that strongly mask the central violent dimension of the game of nations. Reasons of state are presented in lucid, clear, and compelling form with elegant turns of phrase and appealing, even ironic or jocular, images:

> Thus, in his discussion of limited strategic war, Schelling asserts our need for a "richer menu" of strategic possibilities. Kahn, who is a master of this kind of vocabulary, acknowledges that destruction is "likely to be greatly intensified at the upper end of the escalation ladder," which is a restrained way of saying that if a limited war gets out of hand it may lead to the deaths of millions and catastrophe for whole societies. However, Kahn is more interested in the "lower end" of the "escalation ladder," and here he refers to "sanitary" campaigns in which an occasional missile base may be "taken out." This last phrase, suggesting as it does the relative good humor of a clean body-block in a football game, is one of which deterrence theorists have become particularly fond (along with "cracking up" launching pads, presumably with a pneumatic drill) (Green, 1968:223).

More general literature of cruelty has shaded into the macabre. Dalton Trumbo, for example, in *Johnny Got His Gun* tells the story of the experiences of a quadruple amputee who has also lost his sight and hearing. Movies such as the *Battle of Algiers* represent the cultural avant-garde's surrogate for violent revolution. Television brought Vietnam into America's living rooms every evening. Movies like *Coming Home, The Deer Hunter,* and *Apocalypse Now* have continued American involvement in Vietnam. Black comedy has exploited the more gruesome dimensions of contemporary warfare. *Dr. Strangelove* and the work of Joseph Heller and Kurt Vonnegut match the sardonic perspective of earlier writers like Bertolt Brecht.

War accustoms individual citizens to military values and attitudes. Returning veterans are a paramilitary group within the body politic, a residue of military life within civilian society (cf. Karsten, 1978). Table 5-26 shows how different American wars have contributed to the number of veterans in civil life. The total number of returned veterans rose from less than 2 million in 1865 to over 27 million in 1970.[56]

Table 5-27 breaks the total number of veterans into age cohorts and suggests how these move through time. In 1865 the largest group of veterans, those from the Civil War, were between the ages of 20 and 24. This

Table 5-26
Veterans in Civil Life, by Period of Service: U.S., 1865–1970.[a]

Year	Total Veterans	War of 1812	Mexican War	Civil War	Indian Wars[b]	Spanish-American War	World War I	World War II	Korean Conflict Total[c]	Korean Conflict Without World War II Service	Service Between Korean Conflict and Vietnam[d,e]	Vietnam[d,f] Total[g]	Vietnam[d,f] Without Korean Conflict Service	Regular Establishment[h]
1970	27,647				Z[i]	5	1,536	14,458	5,867	4,605	3,125	4,173	3,918	185
1969	26,925				Z	6	1,647	14,592	5,847	4,590	3,134	3,169	2,956	183
1968	26,273				Z	8	1,766	14,718	5,814	4,567	3,139	2,234	2,070	180
1967	25,805				Z	10	1,888	14,832	5,797	4,563	3,142	1,493	1,370	195
1966	25,534				Z	12	2,007	14,916	5,770	4,568	3,147	962	884	175
1965	21,834				Z	15	2,121	14,969	5,718	4,568	3,152	456	434	161
1964	22,013				Z	18	2,226	15,048	5,708	4,574	3,119			147
1963	22,166				Z	22	2,343	15,100	5,663	4,567	2,617			134
1962	22,275				Z	26	2,455	15,126	5,586	4,546	2,156			122
1961	22,403				Z	31	2,565	15,156	5,531	4,538	1,760			113
1960	22,534				Z	36	2,673	15,202	5,482	4,520	1,380			103
1959	22,666			Z	Z	43	2,778	15,243	5,448	4,507	967			95
1958	22,727			Z	Z	48	2,876	15,288	5,353	4,431	569			84
1957	22,634			Z	Z	55	2,971	15,332	5,105	4,202	186			74
1956	22,372			Z	Z	63	3,061	15,370	4,686	3,812	30			66
1955	21,861			Z	Z	72	3,150	15,405	3,999	3,171	4			63
1954	20,951			Z	Z	80	3,230	15,425	2,912	2,153				63
1953	20,196			Z	Z	89	3,308	15,440	1,955	1,297				62
1952	19,338			Z	Z	99	3,382	15,369	867	428				60
1951	18,919			Z	Z	108	3,542	15,200	211	100				59
1950	19,077			Z	1	118	3,518	15,386	Z	Z				54
1949	18,945			Z	1	127	3,587	15,182						48
1948	18,745			Z	1	136	3,651	14,914						43
1947	18,262			Z	1	146	3,711	14,361						43
1946	16,655			Z	1	155	3,768	12,687						44

Year								
1945	6,498		Z	1	164	3,821	2,469	43
1944	5,689		Z	1	173	3,871	1,601	43
1943	5,002		1	1	182	3,917	858	43
1942	4,485		1	2	190	3,961	289	42
1941	4,337		2	2	198	4,002	95	38
1940	4,286		2	2	206	4,040		36
1935	4,494		13	4	244	4,201		32
1930	4,680		49	5	274	4,336		16
1925	4,894	Z	127	4	298	4,453		12
1920	5,146	Z	244	4	317	4,566		15
1915	773	1	424	1	332			15
1910	977	2	624	2	349			
1905	1,192	5	821	2	364			
1900	1,224	9	1,000	1	214			
1895	1,187	14	1,170	3				
1890	1,341	Z	1,322					
1885	1,475	3	1,449					
1880	1,593	10	1,557					
1875	1,698	16	1,654					
1870	1,802	28	1,744					
1865	1,908	46	1,830					

a In thousands.

b Includes only veterans on the benefit rolls of the Veterans Administration or predecessor agencies.

c Includes veterans who served in both World War II and the Korean conflict.

d Public Law 89–358, March 3, 1966, conferred veteran status on all persons serving on active duty in the Armed Forces after January 31, 1955. Veterans with service between the Korean conflict and Vietnam era (February 1, 1955–August 4, 1964) and Vietnam era veterans (service after August 4, 1964) included in the total veteran count beginning June 1966.

e Veterans whose only service was on active duty between January 31, 1955, and August 5, 1964. Excludes men who served on active duty for training only.

f Service after August 4, 1964.

g Includes veterans who served in both the Vietnam era and the Korean conflict or World War II.

h Former members of Regular Establishment (peacetime) receiving disability compensation from the Veterans Administration or predecessor agencies. Beginning June 1966, Regular Establishment veterans are excluded from total veterans since they are for the most part included as veterans with service between the Korean conflict and Vietnam era or as veterans of a war period.

i Z = less than 500.

SOURCE: U.S. Department of Commerce, Bureau of the Census (1975:1145).

Table 5-27
Veterans in Civil Life, by Age: U.S., 1865–1970.[a]

Year	Total, All Ages	Under 20	20–24	25–29	30–34	35–39	40–44	45–49	50–54	55–59	60–64	65–69	70 and Over	Unknown
1970	27,647	24	1,693	2,628	2,321	3,039	4,017	5,066	3,895	1,934	1,034	326	1,670	—
1969	26,925	18	1,527	2,361	2,318	3,291	4,243	5,071	3,469	1,709	894	315	1,709	—
1968	26,273	24	1,282	2,193	2,382	3,482	4,511	4,958	3,082	1,514	752	376	1,717	—
1967	25,805	31	1,095	2,149	2,541	3,580	4,791	4,785	2,680	1,374	610	466	1,703	—
1966	25,534	39	1,100	2,078	2,799	3,759	4,977	4,451	2,360	1,253	476	646	1,596	—
1965	21,834	Z[b]	13	314	2,458	3,967	5,137	4,036	2,059	1,152	387	958	1,353	—
1964	22,013	—[c]	13	580	2,930	4,222	5,148	3,596	1,823	966	378	1,200	1,127	—
1963	22,166	Z	13	906	3,316	4,508	5,025	3,189	1,614	835	451	1,365	944	—
1962	22,275	Z	20	1,426	3,502	4,773	4,839	2,765	1,461	676	555	1,478	780	—
1961	22,403	Z	98	1,976	3,715	4,955	4,494	2,429	1,333	530	772	1,461	640	—
1960	22,534	Z	281	2,425	3,962	5,127	4,060	2,115	1,219	426	1,138	1,260	521	—
1959	22,666	Z	521	2,890	4,222	5,139	3,624	1,873	1,054	418	1,423	1,091	411	—
1958	22,727	Z	857	3,195	4,498	5,023	3,227	1,665	889	503	1,617	944	309	—
1957	22,634	4	989	3,535	4,810	4,854	2,803	1,513	720	624	1,743	944	223	—
1956	22,372	17	1,446	3,526	5,008	4,528	2,469	1,380	563	866	1,720	816	158	—
1955	21,861	26	1,398	3,866	5,143	4,095	2,155	1,265	445	1,288	1,482	691	143	—
1950	19,077	1	2,196	5,023	4,064	2,154	1,280	458	1,390	1,653	650	555	136	—
1945	6,498	28	637	740	497	380	130	1,295	1,764	718	77	72	77	44

Year													
1940	4,286	—	—	—	—	16	1,287	1,848	773	86	131	72	35	38
1935	4,494	—	—	—	16	1,323	1,917	815	93	149	86	31	28	36
1930	4,680	—	—	17	1,356	1,974	849	98	162	97	37	13	56	21
1925	4,894	—	17	1,386	2,026	877	103	172	105	41	15	6	130	16
1920	5,146	17	1,416	2,075	903	107	180	112	44	18	7	3	245	19
1915	773	—	—	—	19	145	100	40	16	8	3	8	417	17
1910	977	—	—	20	150	105	42	17	8	4	11	380	238	2
1905	1,192	—	21	156	109	44	18	9	4	13	458	208	150	2
1900	1,224	12	91	64	26	11	5	3	14	521	251	121	104	1
1895	1,187	—	—	—	—	—	—	13	578	289	148	85	71	3
1890	1,341	—	—	—	—	—	14	628	321	171	105	67	35	—
1885	1,475	—	—	—	—	15	670	347	189	121	82	44	7	—
1880	1,593	—	—	—	16	710	370	203	133	93	53	5	10	—
1875	1,698	—	—	17	748	390	216	142	103	59	7	Z	16	—
1870	1,802	—	17	784	411	228	152	109	65	8	Z	Z	28	—
1865	1,908	18	820	430	239	159	116	70	9	1	Z	9	37	—

ᵃIn thousands. As of June 30. Includes all veterans of the Vietnam era, service between Korean conflict and the Vietnam era, Korean conflict, World War II, World War I, Spanish-American War, Civil War, Mexican War, and War of 1812, as well as those veterans of the Indian Wars and former members of the Regular Establishment (peacetime) who were on the benefit rolls of Veterans Administration or predecessor agencies. Veterans who served in 2 or more wars prior to the Korean conflict are included 2 or more times; veterans who served in both World War II and the Korean conflict, and in the Vietnam era, Korean conflict, and World War II are included only once.

ᵇZ = less than 500.

ᶜ—represents zero.

SOURCE: U.S. Department of Commerce, Bureau of the Census (1975:1144).

group continued to provide most veterans in civil society through the beginning of the twentieth century, but it grew constantly smaller and older, eventually passing off the scale after age 70 in 1915. At this time it was replaced by a new veteran crop, coming from World War I. This group was predominant until the arrival of veteran groups from World War II and Korea in the 1940s and 1950s. By 1970 most veterans of World War II were 50 to 54 years old, and returnees from Korea were between 45 and 49. At this time the profile of the young Vietnam veterans was just becoming visible.

Some returning veterans are antimilitaristic. The Vietnam War, for example, produced substantial resistance by soldiers, sailors, and airmen (cf. Rinaldi, 1973). Dissident Vietnam veterans formed Vietnam Veterans Against the War, with an antimilitary thrust (cf. VVAW, 1972).[57]

Veterans, nevertheless, often come home with new or reinforced militaristic attitudes. Many veterans return with a new appreciation of force, and a nostalgia for military life may appear. They may romanticize the myth of the warrior, the attitudes and skills of violence, the relationship of suffering and virtue (cf. Lifton, 1973; Janowitz, 1960).

Military service may reinforce authoritarian predispositions, including values of hierarchy and discipline: Submission is required in the service of the cause; obedience is the quality of the good soldier.

War also has important effects on different elements of the civilian population. Some of these go in an antimilitary direction, but much of the influence may be toward increased militance.

War seems to make the perceptions of political leaders more negative. Figure 5-24 sketches the balance between positive and negative symbols in U.S. Presidents' State of the Union messages since the beginning of this century. The positive symbols were highest during the relatively peaceful periods just before and just after World War I. They were quite negative during World War I, the Great Depression, World War II, the early period of the Cold War through the Korean conflict, and the Vietnam War.

Children raised in wartime environments are socialized into militant culture. A study of Irish children in Belfast, for example, found that such children were quite ethnocentric, and that other judgments were also affected by the surrounding conflict (Jahoda and Harrison, 1975).

Young people in the United States became observably more pacifistic as a result of the Vietnam War. Many of them adopted an outlook that placed a higher emphasis on love and cooperation as foundations for human relations and that opposed force, except possibly in self-defense against clear and present danger. As a generation, they were more opposed than their parents to the war in Indochina, the use of nuclear weapons, and the draft. They projected their attitudes into the political arena by demonstrations and votes against "hawks" and for "doves" (cf. Burstein and Freudenburg, 1977; Jeffries, 1974; J. M. Starr, 1974; Mueller, 1973:105; Erskine, 1972–1973; Handberg, 1972–1973; Gorsuch and Smith, 1972; Pugh et al., 1971).

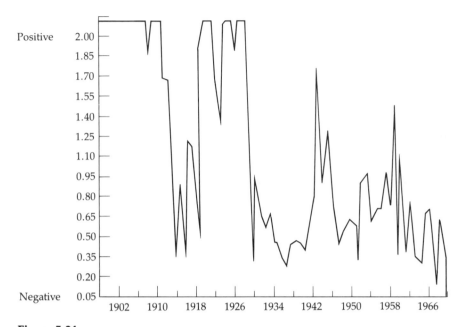

Figure 5-24
**Positive and Negative Symbols: U.S. Presidents' State of the Union
Messages, 1902–1970.** (NOTE: "An increase of negative affect [or stress] for an
individual predisposes that individual to actual physical flight. He wants to
respond behaviorally to a negatively valued situation or object by moving or
'distantiating' his body away from the stress-producing stimulus. In many
cases this behavioral response is impossible. There is 'no way out,' social
sanctions or situational sanctions preclude this possibility; for various reasons
such a behavioral response is impossible. Linguistic response does not
operate within such sanctions. Under conditions of stress, the individual can
respond linguistically by choosing to use symbolism that reflects the
directionality of the unavailable behavioral response." SOURCE: Frank, 1973:22,
42. This figure, drawn from *Linguistic Analysis of Political Elites: A Theory of
Verbal Kinesics,* Sage Professional Papers, Series/Number 02-022, by R. S.
Frank, copyright 1973, is reprinted by permission of the publisher, Sage
Publications, Inc. Cf. Stice, 1974.)

Nonetheless, such war-induced pacifism rests on shaky psychological
ground, and can easily collapse. A belief system centering on peace and
love is an ideology like others, with similar problems. Agreement on these
values does not shut out militance among true believers. In some aspects
this belief system implies a deep pessimism and an aversion to power.
Power, even in pursuit of worthy aims, is suspect because it involves domination, the possibility of error, failure, or damage to others. Yet the rejection of power to do violence may imply also a rejection of action or capability
to produce peace. Finally, to some extent, the ideology of peace and love
results from processes of unconscious reaction-formation against beliefs
and behavior of the earlier generation. It may be eroded by the psycho-

logical dynamics of repetition compulsion, through which the older belief system, believed to be vanquished, may gradually reassert itself (cf. Holsti and Rosenau, 1980, 1979; Kriesberg and Klein, 1980; Sternbach, 1974; Larsen, 1973a, 1973b; Wangh, 1972; Feuer, 1969).

War implies that many children are raised primarily by women while the men are away fighting. Children raised without fathers depend more heavily on their mothers for role models. Some may become more "feminine" adults, less tolerant of war and violence, less likely to pursue military-related careers. One study revealed a higher degree of typically feminine vocational interest among such children (Carlsmith, 1973; cf. Musgrave and Reid, 1971; Slater, 1971; Mitscherlich, 1970).

Other children growing up without fathers, however, may attempt to overcompensate in their adult masculine roles, acting out exaggerated male stereotypes. This appears more likely if the dominant female figure is highly authoritarian. Studies of particularly belligerent political leaders have revealed that such "compensatory masculinity" can help produce international violence (Friedländer and Cohen, 1975).

The absence of love and respect from both parents under wartime conditions may foster hatred for the parents and—by extension—for others. If repressed, this hostility causes neuroses. If acted out, it leads to various forms of individual and collective violence. One study found that stress on children during wartime predisposed them to suicide as young adults (Wen, 1974; cf. Saul, 1972; Fine, 1972).

The military identities, images, values, and attitudes we have discussed form "subcultures of violence" that, in turn, contribute to war (cf. Hepburn, 1971). Communities, groups, or individuals with substantial militaristic dimensions may be more belligerent. Research suggests that "primitive cultures with more militaristic attitudes engaged in more war preparations and actual warfare" (Eckhardt, 1974:75; cf. Russell, 1972; Textor, 1967; Broch and Galtung, 1966; Wright, 1965:Ch. VI). It seems reasonable that modern communities with more militaristic attitudes also engage in more war preparations. Such communities prepare for war in part because they anticipate that they will be engaged in more warfare, and they are probably correct (cf. Wilkinson, 1980:99–102).

The diffusion of military symbols in communications, art, sports, entertainment, education, and religion accustoms people to war and may imply that war has a positive value. War may seem important, meaningful, aesthetic, or even fun (cf. Comstock et al., 1978; Cater and Strickland, 1975; Manning and Taylor, 1975; Mercer, 1974; Berkowitz and Alioto, 1973; Sipes, 1973; Tolley, 1973; Aldrous and Tallman, 1972; Lang and Lang, 1972; Eron et al., 1972; Ellis et al., 1971; Feshbach and Singer, 1971; W. Weiss, 1969).

Veterans organizations can be an influence for war. Good examples of this include the combat leagues in Europe after World War I, particularly in Germany and Italy. These groups supported the violent policies of fascist regimes at home and abroad (cf. Ward, 1975; Minott, 1962).

American veterans from World Wars I and II and the Korean conflict have dominated the American Legion and Veterans of Foreign Wars. These organizations have generally supported a strong U.S. military posture, including forceful foreign intervention to defend U.S. interests.

Militaristic attitudes are often related to a number of other basic personality and attitude characteristics, which in turn provide an influence toward war. Militance, as we have already seen, implies high degrees of discipline and repression, which in turn imply collective violence.[58] Primitive societies with high degrees of discipline and sexual repression, for example, were more likely to be militaristic and warlike (Eckhardt, 1974). In modern societies firm discipline and physical punishment of children contribute to aggressive and violent behavior (Bardis, 1972). Members of religious groups, which are more traditional, orthodox, structured, and dogmatic, more easily accept the necessity of war, and the model of the soldier–saint may be particularly appealing to some of them (cf. R. A. Lewis, 1975; J. M. Starr, 1975; Granberg and May, 1972; Southard, 1969).

Authoritarianism, dogmatism, and rigidity imply strong acceptance of structure, authority, routine, discipline, obedience, and punishment together with a relatively weak self-image. Such characteristics predispose people to follow orders to inflict violence on others or themselves even if such orders run contrary to their own judgments, values, and immediate self-interest. During the Vietnam War, there appeared to be a positive association between authoritarianism and acceptance of wartime excesses like those at My Lai.

Such individuals are also more likely to undertake violent behavior on their own. One study investigated the characteristics of individuals convicted of "fragging," using explosives in assaults on superior officers during the Vietnam War. It found that such individuals tended to come from family backgrounds with high degrees of brutality and deprivation, and they tended to be insecure and have poor self-images (Bond, 1976). Another study showed that all subjects "who reported participation in personal violence had volunteered to serve in Vietnam." Further, the participants "frequently had a history of arrest prior to military service" (Yager, 1975:257).

Classic psychological theory suggests that what is repressed never disappears, but always returns in another form. War offers an outlet for the repressed concerns of modern civilization.

War can appear, in some of its dimensions, as a liberating experience. Society imposes severe limits on the natural tendencies of individuals. The frustrations of everyday life—stored as alienation, hostility, anger, hate, rage—can be relieved through external aggression and violence.

Normal taboos, prohibitions, and limits to violent behavior are lifted in wartime. Forbidden sexual activities may become possible. Death comes out into the open, allowing individuals to see it directly and deal with it face-to-face. Constraints against suicide and murder disappear. The sin and guilt of destruction can be transformed into the glory of bravery and heroism.[59]

Chapter 6

CHOICE

Our description and explanation of the dynamics of peace and war provide a basis for predicting the future and a strategy that might control it.

PROJECTIONS

Projections of the future are always risky. If we attempt to draw lessons from history, we may assume that the future will be like the past. Such extrapolations are useful only if there are no major surprises. If we suspend our doubts about continuity in history and allow ourselves to assume that the future will develop in a way consistent with our historical experience, the major factors of violence and technology—aggregation, polarization, and militarization—should tend to develop along a particular natural course.

Violence

We stated in Chapter 2 that there may be a long-run trend toward peace diffusion and war concentration and aggravation. Peaceful periods may be longer today while wars may have become less frequent and shorter. War casualties may have increased both in absolute terms and relative to population. The actual existence of such a trend is open to question. If it does exist, however, the map of future international relations will show longer, lower valleys of peace together with sharper, higher peaks of violence.

Peaceful life will become more and more the norm. Wars will become less frequent and, when they do occur, they will be shorter than in the past.

Declining general incidence of war or the termination of any particular military conflict is obviously welcome. Yet neither one necessarily implies the elimination or even reduction of the human or material costs of war. War will not go away. International violence will continue to be a problem of much more than historical interest.

Longer interwar periods will be way-stations for subsequent wars that may inflict even greater casualties than the ones that preceded them. There will be more war-related deaths both absolutely and relative to population because of the higher destruction wrought by wars when they do occur, and the chances for the average citizen to complete his or her life in peace will be reduced.

If the pattern of domestic violence follows international violence, there will be fewer civil wars. Yet again, when domestic violence does occur, it will tend to be more massive and pervasive than in the past, and it will kill and wound larger numbers of individuals and higher percentages of domestic populations.[1]

Much international violence will occur in the gray zone between peace and war. Governments will continue to intervene clandestinely in the affairs of others. Secret services and mercenaries will try to intimidate or eliminate opponents, using violence in counterinsurgency operations. Assassination and torture will be important weapons (cf. Little, 1975; Klare, 1972).

Guerrillas and terrorists will threaten organizations of all kinds—governments, cities, corporations, schools. Nuclear capabilities in the hands of terrorists will pose grave problems for highly concentrated urban or nuclear stockpile areas (cf. Beres, 1979; Norton and Greenberg, 1979; Blair and Brewer, 1977; Krieger, 1975).

Wars may be most common in the Third World, where the logic of modern technology is weaker. International violence should be relatively frequent in Southeast Asia, Africa, and Latin America. Such wars will imply relatively low casualties because they will usually center around conventional or limited nuclear capabilities.

Wars at North–South seams will be rarer but more serious. One possible area of friction is the Middle East, located at the juncture of Europe, Asia, and Africa, the center of religious conflict and energy resources. One can imagine a scenario, the early stages of which include Arab leaders raising the price of oil to new heights and using the revenues to accelerate modernization. Simultaneously, they undertake increasingly militant actions against Israel and the Western powers. These nations pay the price for oil and military defense in declining production, rising inflation, and unemployment. At some point the Palestinians, the Arab states, and their Northeastern allies attempt a final military solution to the Israeli problem. Alternatively, Israel and the Northwestern allies use military force to seize critical oil fields. Violence expands in terms of both weapons and geography. Each side undertakes nuclear strikes against the other. Fighting spreads north through Turkey and west across the Mediterranean to southern Europe and North Africa.

Unlike energy reserves, food is a problem that is geographically diffuse. If mass starvation reaches major proportions, and if the global South continues to develop military capabilities, Third World governments may threaten, provoke, or undertake nuclear war to obtain nourishment for their populations.

Wars in the Northern hemisphere should occur least often, but will carry the most dangerous implications. Possible wars in Northeast Asia include violence between the Soviet Union, China, and possibly Japan. In Northern Europe, the status of Berlin might again threaten to bring the Soviet Union and the Eastern European states to blows with the North Atlantic powers (cf. Hackett et al., 1979; Salisbury, 1970).

A portion of future organized warfare will be fought with the most advanced means of mass destruction—if only because they exist. Such wars will produce massive direct casualties as whole cities are destroyed. They will generate even larger indirect, long-term damage. The use of nuclear weapons will permanently raise global radioactivity. Nuclear effects will show up over the long term in statistics for various diseases, including genetic defects in the newborn (cf. Lewis, 1979).

If atomic, biological, and chemical warfare expands to its natural boundaries, it may cover all areas of the globe and involve the use of all weapons in national stockpiles. It may destroy large portions of existing human civilization and cause serious disabilities to that portion which remains.

Such war will be more terrible than any that humankind has ever experienced. Yet it will probably not permanently destroy global humanity. At the present time this seems technically impossible.[2]

Aggregation

Aggravated international violence, together with the exhaustion of natural resources, might destroy modern technology. Humanity might not follow the dinosaurs into extinction, but it could be thrown backward to an early industrial or preindustrial period. The world of modern global technology may end as a lost civilization like the Garden of Eden, Atlantis, or Mayan society (cf. Stavrianos, 1976; Meadows et al., 1974; Vacca, 1974).

The logic of our argument suggests, however, that aggregation will continue to grow in the future as it has in the past. International law and organization will gradually become more supranational. International legal theory and practice will include new sectors: space, the oceans, and resources are issue areas where legal growth is likely to occur. Additional international actors—supranational organizations, nation-states, various kinds of transnational groups, and individuals—will be recognized and will make use of the expanding international legal framework.

The number of international courts will grow, and with them, personnel and resources available to the international legal sector. This expanded network of international courts will help settle an increasing number of disputes within the law of peace. International court decisions will be increasingly accepted as having the authoritative force of law. International actors will find the stakes in many cases less important than the value of ongoing institutions for resolving disputes.

International courts will also act more authoritatively on the law of war. War victims in the future may seek legal redress for alleged violations of *jus ad bellum* or *jus in bello*. International criminal courts may further develop the principles of tribunals like the one convened at Nuremberg after World War II and use them more actively to punish individuals for international crimes (cf. Ferencz, 1979; Johnston, 1974; Falk, 1971b).

Other forms of international organization will continue to grow in a similar way. There may be short-run drops in support for particular institutions. Over the long run, however, existing international organizations at all levels will add to their staffs and their treasuries. New functional and regional organizations, multinational corporations and conglomerates will appear.

International organizations will contribute more extensively to dispute settlement and conflict management. They will provide more assistance to direct negotiations as well as such services as good offices, inquiry, mediation, conciliation, and arbitration. They will also supply expanded peacekeeping forces and war relief.

As international bureaucratic activities expand, they will help national governments. Many people believe that there already is too much domestic government. The future promises more rather than less.

Exchange will also continue to grow. The future will see the gradual emergence of a New International Economic Order (cf. Cline, 1979a, 1979b; Cox, 1979; Bergsten, 1975). The NIEO will include higher levels of international trade, investment, assistance, and migration. There will be an overall rise in material welfare. Global, regional, and national trade and development programs and planning will all contribute to a general increase in the standard of living. The U.N. Specialized Agencies and Regional Economic Commissions as well as various regional economic communities will continue to work to this end.

Scientific discoveries and inventions will benefit us materially. And we will increasingly find ways to deal with the critical problems of energy, pollution, food, and overpopulation. The fact that we are much more aware of these problems is itself a strong force for their amelioration and resolution (cf. Leontieff et al., 1977; Kahn et al., 1976).

The exhaustion of fossil fuels poses a short-term threat to man's energy reservoir. In the long run diverse methods will generate new energy.

Among the most promising is the development of much more efficient techniques for using solar energy. Massive solar collection stations may be built in the world's great deserts or on ocean or space platforms. A breakthrough in photovoltaic technique would allow each building and vehicle itself to generate much of the energy it requires to operate (cf. Stobaugh and Yergin, 1979; Lovins, 1977; Willrich, 1975).

Advances on these and other fronts should dissipate or transform many of the present problems of pollution. The replacement of fossil fuels must inevitably reduce the automobile exhaust fumes clouding major cities. Advanced emission control and industrial filtration systems will further protect air, earth, and water. The pollution problems of nuclear energy sources will be hard to solve. As yet, they have not been dealt with in a way that can inspire great confidence. The current state of the nuclear energy industry implies radioactive contamination and thermal pollution, and the possible impairment of life in the oceans. One hopes, however, that over time the efficiency of nuclear plants will gradually increase and their harmful emissions will substantially decline.

Agriculture will expand and diversify. New food sources will be cultivated and processed. New techniques of weather modification and water dynamics will increase agricultural yields. Desalination and the development of salt-water technology will allow people to use water resources previously inhospitable to human agriculture.

The problem of overpopulation will adapt to the solutions of technology as well. The global death rate will continue to decline—at least during peacetime, but eventually the global birth rate may level off or decline as well. The development and distribution of new and more efficient birth control devices will make family planning much easier. Child-rearing may become increasingly expensive—as a result of both market forces and government policies, including taxation—and this will also help bring overpopulation under control. State-supervised reproduction and child-rearing may even take much family planning and decisionmaking out of individual hands.

Language will continue to expand. International communications will increase. The growth of international bureaucracy and exchange implies a corresponding increase in international communications at all levels. Devices like space satellites and sensors will provide increasingly complete and sophisticated coverage of the earth's surface, allowing close monitoring of, and informed rapid intervention in, all dimensions of collective life.

Multilateral diplomacy will cover new arenas of international activity. International media, business, educational, and leisure communications will grow. Scientists and artists will improve international information transmission at all levels, from presidents and prime ministers to ordinary citizens. These international developments will feed back into domestic communities, producing some homogenization of culture as well as increasing the promulgation of the values of cooperation and peace at all levels of society.

Polarization

The direct effects of further aggregation should help to limit war and militarization. At the same time, however, continued aggregation will also work to increase polarization. Differentiation, inequality, and instability will all become more pronounced.

Major groups will become more distinct. Their boundaries will be firmer. Their connections with external groups will be weaker, their internal relations denser. The global Northwest, Northeast, and South will further develop their own separate international legal blocs, organizational coalitions, transaction networks, and ideologies. These will both bind them closer together and separate them further from each other.[3]

Nation-states will become increasingly centralized. Central national governments will dominate regional, provincial, and local political communities. National markets will become further concentrated. Populations will be more densely packed. National myths will be more pervasive as modern education and communications assimilate different ethnic and religious groups into a homogenized culture. Dissident belief systems will become rare and unpopular.

As the logic of mass politics, economics, and culture works itself out, national communities will grow at the expense of the autonomy of groups and individuals. Centralized national political systems may involve more popular participation in collective decisions and expanded formal political rights for minority groups and individuals. Advanced technology will also allow increased popular participation in decisionmaking; and such participation will increase over time—including more and more people and increasing numbers and kinds of issues—political and military as well as social, economic, and cultural. Two-way interactive television hooked into central computer facilities will allow face-to-face discussion and rapid voting (cf. Campbell, 1974).

Paradoxically, however, the application of computerized communications technology to politics may increase individual feelings of powerlessness and isolation. Many votes on many issues provide individuals with only a small portion of control. Though individuals may be increasingly included in decisionmaking about collective matters, they will also be increasingly excluded from decisionmaking about private matters. In spite of increased opportunities for participation in collective decisions, individuals may feel that their own lives are increasingly beyond their own control and subject to the arbitrary dictates of the external society. The individual will have a shrinking sector of his or her own life under his or her autonomous, private, and sole command. People will remain more and more at a physical distance, with less and less reason to leave their isolated spaces and mingle constructively with others.

Inequality will become more obvious. The powerful and rich will move further away from the weak and poor. Those who hold political power at different levels will be increasingly distant from those who do not. The rich will grow richer, and the poor will grow richer—but the rich will grow richer at a faster rate, and the poor will feel poorer.

Some presently poor states with scarce resources like oil may improve their positions through hard bargaining. Most of the world's poor, however, will travel in accommodations that are more and more distant from first class (cf. Hardin, 1977a, 1977b; Nagel, 1970).

Class inequality will advance within domestic societies as well. Bureau-technocrats will use their control of collective property to consolidate and advance their own interests (cf. Kahn et al., 1977).

Instability will become more pronounced. If growth continues, change will become more rapid as new discoveries and inventions build on each other. If growth slows, different groups will win or lose substantial amounts of cherished values (cf. Deutsch, 1975).

Militarization

The polarization of the system will be related to its further militarization. More differentiated international legal blocs and international organization coalitions will contribute to more legal justification of war and military alliances. Stronger international transaction networks will channel military transfers between nations, either through overt military trade and aid or more indirect means, including related knowledge and equipment for supposedly nonmilitary purposes.

Expanded exchange supergroups and common markets will use the boycott, embargo, and blockade in more subtle forms to exert pressure on opponents. Different sides will attempt to apply the resources they control for bargaining purposes—food, ocean and space resources, weather modification, directed pollution, energy, or perhaps the forcible exportation of surplus population (cf. Abrahamsson and Steckler, 1973; Redick, 1974). Global ideologies may expound values and plans for peace, but they will also convey hostility toward those in other camps (cf. Hsin, 1972).

National differentiation will go together with national militarization. Governmental centralization, market concentration, and mythology will keep company with more military regimes, military complexes, militant attitudes and beliefs.

As national communities become harder and more tightly bound, military regimes will become more common. Large segments of the globe will be under direct or indirect military rule.

Political communities will become more coercive, moving in the direction of garrison states. The velvet language of democracy or socialism will hide a good deal of intimidation. Repressive political regimes will rely less on prison, torture, and killing than they do today. More indirect and sophisticated methods will use the advanced technology of information gathering and persuasion to reach the end of political control more efficiently.

National military complexes will expand. The military will increasingly diversify, associating itself with widely desired social goals, including material welfare. National resources will be cultivated with an eye to their direct military application. Military managers will develop even more sophisticated political and administrative skills to generate and supervise massive budgets and personnel. Nongovernmental organizations, including business corporations, will increasingly serve military ends and use military methods.

National mythology will be increasingly militant. Individuals will be expected to identify more exclusively and completely with their nation-states than they now do. Military values, images, and attitudes will also be much more important.

Greater international and national inequality also imply the greater necessity of military capabilities. Military might will help maintain and increase such inequality. Nations with large military establishments will use them to coerce others to provide what they want. Within nation-states, the military and its allies will increasingly dominate other components of society.[4]

Instability will continue to interact with militarization. International alliance races will continue.

The growth of international aggregation implies progress in arms control. The future will see the expansion of a network of arms control treaties bringing new international actors and new areas of the arms race into the growing network of international law. Existing international organizations will expand their jurisdiction in the area of arms control. New specialized international agencies for arms control at global, regional, and bilateral levels will appear and take hold in monitoring and attempting to enforce the provisions of these agreements. Alleged violations will gradually be brought before legal tribunals.

Arms control efforts may hinder arms races, but the competitive development of weaponry will continue. The diffusion in ownership and use of atomic, biological, and chemical weapons will go forward. Third and Fourth World leaders of the future will come to possess at least the weapons of the present. If nuclear power plants are used extensively to meet future energy needs, their byproducts will accelerate the diffusion of nuclear weapons. Figure 6-1 projects that 40 countries will have nuclear capabilities by 1985 (see Gompert et al., 1977).

Weapons will gradually expand into space beyond the earth's atmosphere (cf. Salkeld, 1970). On the earth itself, there will be air, land, and sea surveillance systems with tracking ranges of thousands of miles and automatic alarms. Advanced location systems will enable decisionmakers to pinpoint geographical placement of units and individual soldiers. Spaceborne television cameras will allow zoom closeups, bringing political leaders and military staffs right down on the action (Dickson, 1976).

Automated battlefield command and control systems with computer-

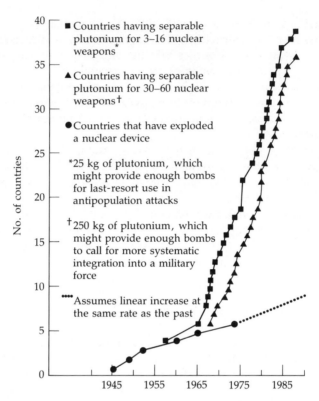

Figure 6-1
Countries with Enough Separable Plutonium
for Primitive or Small Military Forces.
(SOURCE: Wohlstetter, 1976-1977:152.)

controlled tactics will be operational. Future military arsenals will rely heavily on remote control, miniaturized electronics, and bionics. They will include remotely piloted vehicles, "smart" bombs, and self-planting land and ocean mines. There will be advanced laser designator systems for homing devices and fire control; new generations of antimissile, antiradar missiles; disintegrator lasers and follow-on "death ray" technology; as well as advanced techniques for the military modification of climate, weather, pollution, water, food, and energy supplies (cf. Barnaby, 1976; Weiss, 1975).

Civil defense may lead to the construction of vast underground living complexes. If nuclear war occurs on a substantial scale, those most susceptible to radioactively generated disease will die off in large numbers. Others with higher natural resistance may be relatively immune to high levels of radioactivity and will survive and prosper.

The rapidity and pervasiveness of communications will contribute to the maintenance of international image races and will concentrate and accentuate image crises. The simultaneity of future communications will mean that events that earlier would have taken months, weeks, or days, and whose evaluation would have been limited to a relatively small number of decisionmakers, will now take hours or minutes and involve whole populations. Escalation will occur much more rapidly.

National military regimes will turn over relatively quickly; military complexes will contribute to high rates of inflation and sudden shifts in national employment and national mood. Active policies of disdevelopment may serve as powerful political tools to defuse potential disorder. Governments may use planned recession as a political weapon against dissident segments of the population. National militance may become more volatile as advanced media help shift popular moods between hostility and friendliness.

POLICY

The preceding set of projections for the natural course of the future does not seem very desirable in terms of today's generally accepted values. While wars are fewer, casualties are higher. Though aggregation grows, so do polarization and militarization. Our analysis, however, suggests that we might produce a better tomorrow through a self-conscious policy of peace, which would include strategies aiming at war limitation and peace creation.

War Limitation

War limitation means abstaining from violence except under extreme provocation. It implies the rational management of international crises that might lead to war and of wars themselves. It suggests training in nonviolent techniques, to be used wherever possible.

Restraint

Restraint of violence is an important element of war limitation. This rules out preventive war. Waging war has often seemed like a device for creating peace. We have dealt with this idea earlier in our discussion of the theory of war resistance. Traditional analysis of international relations sees preventive war, military intervention, defense, and deterrence as processes of conflict management. A big stick may not transform wolves into lambs, but at least it helps keep them out of the fold.

Doctrines of preventive war perceive violence as a good investment: A little now avoids more later. This was the logic of those who argued the need to stand up to Hitler in the late 1930s. Similarly, the doctrine of preventive violence underlies external military intervention. It implies that international violence can work against domestic violence in other societies. Leaders of national states often see themselves in the role of world police-men. Thus, one of the justifications for U.S. intervention in the Third World during the post–World War II period was to avoid the bloodshed that would presumably occur following a Communist takeover. With intervention, it was argued, the disease of violence would not be allowed to run its course (cf. Kuehl, 1975; Kolko and Kolko, 1972; D. Horowitz, 1971; Parenti, 1971; Barnet, 1968; Williams, 1962; Fleming, 1961).

By similar reasoning, domestic violence might also limit war. Societies experiencing considerable domestic violence might be too preoccupied to undertake international conflicts. Either weariness or the pressures of do-mestic survival would limit external aggressive behavior.

While the argument for preventive war seems plausible, there is, un-fortunately, little evidence to support the belief that the cure is better than the disease. In fact it may be worse. The therapeutic benefits of violence are far from certain. At best, military intervention shores up the status quo temporarily. Thus, a recent study of the historical use of U.S. armed forces, without major war, found that they often influenced events favorably "from the perspective of U.S. decisionmakers—at least in the short term. In a very large proportion of the incidents, however, this 'success rate' eroded sharply over time." Such use of military forces "served mainly to delay unwanted developments abroad" (Blechman et al., 1978:517; cf. Stern, 1977).

If preventive war produced subsequent resistance to violence, such resistance would not logically extend beyond the geographical boundaries of prior violence. Even within those boundaries, it might be only a partial resistance. Resistance is also impermanent. Opposition to war in general would presumably fade with the passage of time, the blurring of memory, and the arrival of new, presumably nonresistant generations.

While the future benefits of violence are problematic, the immediate costs—casualties and physical damage—are much more real. People are killed and injured; limited "brushfire" wars sometimes spread out of con-trol, expanding dramatically in space, time, and weapons.

It seems more prudent to shy away from using violence as a tool and, instead, to try and prevent it from breaking out or, once it has occurred, to attempt to limit it.

Crisis Management

Crisis management is a second element of war limitation. We define a crisis as a situation that has a high probability of resulting in war. The more serious the war is likely to be, the more serious the crisis is.[5]

Crisis management implies special vigilance and attempts at control. The first step may be to identify areas or nations at high risk of violence. Figure 6-2 outlines the results of an early attempt to do this through a

Figure 6-2
Probability of War Between Pairs of States, January 1937. (Source: Reprinted from p. 1478 of *A Study of War* by Quincy Wright by permission of the University of Chicago Press. © 1965 by the University of Chicago. All rights reserved.)

survey of experts in January 1937. It ranked nations according to the estimated probabilities that they would go to war, and it appears to have been reasonably accurate.[6]

As crises evolve, high level political committees can be in charge of information gathering and analysis, elaboration of policy options, evaluation of contingency plans, and finally of actions taken (cf. Head et al., 1979; Falkowski, 1978; Frei, 1978; Belden, 1977; Janis and Mann, 1977; Janis, 1972; Hermann, 1972; R. Kennedy, 1969).

War Management

When war does occur, war limitation involves the conscious effort to prevent smaller incidents of violence from turning into larger ones, to keep limited wars limited, to prevent them from becoming total.

War limitation suggests the development of military plans that aim at combatants rather than civilians. Further, it implies the elaboration of battlefield command and control structures to contain violence in its most intense form. Remote monitoring devices, including the use of satellite surveillance, should enhance the integrity of political and military command and leadership. Training personnel in limited reaction should help strictly control firing situations. Such surveillance and training might, for example, have prevented the My Lai atrocities.

War limitation also includes the recognition that both victory and defeat may be legitimate outcomes of a given war. Some wars may only be winnable at enormous costs. Some wars may be fought for reasons other than winning, for example, to gain time. In other wars the most likely outcome may be defeat, which might be avoided by early withdrawal. A strategy of war limitation would make it easy for national leaders to cut their losses quickly in such situations (cf. Hobbs, 1979; Wolff, 1976; Mack, 1975; Wolf, 1972; Kecskemeti, 1964).

Nonviolence

War limitation finally implies a greater emphasis on nonviolence as a war-fighting technique.

Nonviolence is as old as the history of religious leaders and movements. Traditions embodied by Buddha and Christ have inspired successful modern political movements and leaders—the Indian struggle for independence under the leadership of Gandhi and the struggle of the American blacks for greater equality under the leadership of Martin Luther King, Jr., are but two modern examples.

Nonviolence cannot be used by all actors in all environments. Most human beings are different from Buddha, Christ, Gandhi, and Martin Luther King, Jr. The delayed benefits of nonviolence, coupled with the substantial discipline required and pain incurred, are likely to make it a choice immediately beyond many of us. Pacifism can also imply passivism, acquiescence, or even collaboration in violent acts by others. For example, many of the Jews incarcerated in the concentration camps of Nazi Germany during the 1930s walked docilely into the gas chambers, and in some cases even helped capture others who attempted to escape (cf. Bettelheim, 1960:Ch. 6). Pacifism in some situations, for example, the United States during World War II, may be so foreign to popular cultural ideas as to be simply unthinkable for most of the population. Nonviolent attitudes may be seen as cowardice, subversion, or even treason.

Nevertheless, nonviolence can succeed in appropriate situations. The expansion of knowledge about nonviolent methods, training in them, and their application where possible, would probably do a substantial amount to reduce both the incidence and casualties of war (cf. Reychler, 1979; Wehr, 1979; Hope and Young, 1977; R. K. Taylor, 1977; Boserup and Mack, 1975; Sharp, 1973).

Peace Creation

Beyond war limitation, we should also be interested in a broader attempt at peace creation. This attempt involves trying to shape the surrounding environment in such a way that it is stronger and less vulnerable to violence. It includes strategies that strengthen aggregation and reduce polarization and militarization.

Aggregation

Peace creation implies continued aggregation; and aggregation includes elements commonly identified by the label world order (cf. Beer, 1979b).

World Order

A strategy of world order sees the world as a developing country and continues to forge the strands of cohesion.

World order implies strong support for continued international legal codification; signature and ratification of, and compliance with, multilateral treaties, agreements, and declarations; international courts and other attempts at adjudication, arbitration, mediation, and conciliation of conflicts and disputes; participation in, contributions to, and compliance with international organizations and collective decisions reached in them; development of and participation in international transactions, including trade; the establishment of substantial global reserves of commodities in short supply such as money, food, and energy; increased international communication through such means as diplomacy, travel, media, and education; the continued efficacy of domestic governments, markets, and communities.[7]

An alternative strategy would attempt a return to nature, dismantling the existing structures and processes of global aggregation. We have discussed the global environment in terms of technology, as a great machine subject to periodic violent explosions. As the machine has gotten larger, so have the explosions.

We might think of dismantling the machine to eliminate the violence. If we could destroy technology, however, the costs would be enormous. This machine appears to provide massive benefits. Each major sector of human technology suggests a special treasure: bureaucracy, power; exchange, wealth; language, community and knowledge. Aggregated structures and processes, won through the hard discipline and sacrifice of what Marx called primitive accumulation, represent the capital of humankind. Humanity would throw away the toil and sacrifice of its ancestors, the heritage of its great-grandchildren. And violence most probably would not be eliminated but simply become more widespread—as it was in prior history.

Even if it were desirable, a return to nature is probably impossible. The historical nature from which we emerged no longer exists. Like an ancient lost continent, it has long ago dissolved. Things that have been discovered and invented are now widely known and used and cannot be disinvented or disevolved. In a very practical sense, the technology we have described is a more integral part of our own human nature than we may suspect.

Depolarization

While aggregation is valuable, it unfortunately contributes to polarization which ultimately leads to violence. If we wish to move in a more peaceful direction, we should adopt a strategy that aims at depolarization, and the creation of a world less differentiated, more equal and more stable.

Dedifferentiation

A less differentiated world would be one where there was a relatively large number of groups whose boundaries were not rigidly defined. There would be more links between groups, but not necessarily a great deal of intensive interaction within them. A strategy to achieve dedifferentiation might concentrate on three major elements—international functionalism, denationalization, and individuation.

INTERNATIONAL FUNCTIONALISM   International functionalism is the first element of dedifferentiation. It implies a more open, pluralistic society. International groups and nations cooperate in different combinations and different ways according to the logic of different issues (cf. Mitrany, 1966; E. Haas, 1964).

International functionalism means the weakening of rigid international legal blocs and organizational coalitions, for example, less consistent bloc voting across different issues in the U.N.[8]

International functionalism also implies a pattern of exchange in which international economic institutions develop in the same way as other structures, crossing rigid boundaries between exclusive international transactional networks and bringing them together. This may imply some weakening of multinational corporations and cartels.

The supergroups dominating international transactions become less important and less visible. International economic communities become more permeable. Patterns of trade and aid become more diffuse between Western and Eastern states, Northern and Southern ones. Currencies become more interconvertible. There are more open policies for migration, and for cultural, scientific, educational, and information exchange.

International functionalism finally suggests a more open pattern of communication and a weakening of the international ideologies that rigidly bind the supergroups together. Expanded communication allows a freer flow of public electronic media transmissions, journals, newspapers, as well as various forms of private correspondence. The volume of secret communication is reduced. The reduction occurs particularly between and within governments, but also in other groups such as large multinational corporations.

DENATIONALIZATION Denationalization is a second element of dedifferentiation. It implies downgrading the nation-state, at least in a relative way.

The nation-state has been, and will continue to be, a critical structural component of the global system. It aggregates subordinate groups with diverse identities and interests in a territorial framework.

National aggrandizement, however, contributes importantly to the polarization of the global system. In the international arena, some national states, like the United States, U.S.S.R., and People's Republic of China, are superpowers; and their leaders speak and act for global blocs. Domestically, the nation-state overshadows international and domestic units, and national centralization and coordination increasingly control group and individual activity.

Denationalization suggests the decentralization of government and the deconcentration of political power.

The network of international leaders should be further broadened. Historically, the political leaders of major powers have dominated international decisionmaking. In recent years the political leaders of medium-size and smaller states have begun to play a more significant role. Smaller Western and Eastern European states as well as Southern nations have participated actively in the international arena. Officials from provincial or local communities have also begun to be active in international politics.

Contact between leaders of the Canadian province of Québec and the French government is a good example. The growth of international law, organization, transaction, and communication has given important responsibilities to civil servants, business people, educators, scientists, and artists. These developments should be encouraged (cf. Alger, 1977; Bertelson, 1977; Haas et al., 1977; Keohane and Nye, 1977; Price, 1977; Mansbach et al., 1976; Nye and Keohane, 1972).

Domestically, there should be greater access to political processes and greater participation in them, with emphases on due process and group and individual rights. Such a recommendation seems to go against traditional arguments for national security in the dangerous world of interstate rivalry and violence. Nevertheless, it is in line with the deepest aspirations of traditional democratic theory, which represented a reaction to absolute rule; an attempt to limit and confine it, make it more rational, predictable, and routine.

Such a strategy may eventually even mean the dissolution of some existing nation-states. Some states, like the old Austro-Hungarian empire, or the overseas European colonial empires, may have been too large. These empires have already been dissolved; and modern movements for national self-determination may further encourage the nation-state writ small.

Denationalization suggests the deconcentration of national markets. While collective national economic policies may be required in many areas, regional and local policies are also important. Transactions between regions or cities in different countries might be relatively independent. Regional and local policies might be appropriate for dealing with problems at this level. For example, diverse energy policies might help to maximize potential and minimize costs. Neighborhood autonomy might also return advantages of smaller scale (cf. Kohr, 1978; Stavrianos, 1976; Schumacher, 1973; Arango, 1970).

Denationalization finally implies demythologizing the nation. The national interest, as a criterion for decisionmaking, might be downgraded. The concept of national interest is widely used, but its meaning is not particularly clear. Beyond its focus on the nation-state, the national interest presents no firm, objective guidelines for decisionmaking. The national interest, defined so as to support polarization, often works against interests of higher and lower levels of political communities, which are called upon to make sacrifices in its name (cf. Johansen, 1979).

Nationalism might also be diminished. The present exclusive identification with the nation-state may stand in the way of developing a broad pattern of overlapping group loyalties (cf. Beer, 1975b; Guetzkow, 1955).

INDIVIDUATION   Individuation is a third aspect of dedifferentiation. It involves the protection and development of individual human beings. Our historical view of the global system incorporates an evolution from tribal corporatism to the dignity of the individual, from concentration on rulers and aristocrats to a concern with ordinary men, women, and children. Such a view suggests that the system grows through the growth of its component parts, rather than at their expense (cf. Steiner, 1979; J. R. Clark, 1977; Kelman, 1977).

A strategy of individuation implies a number of subelements. Individuation suggests the enhancement of individual identity, that individuals have clear profiles in the global system. While this seems obvious in theory, it is less evident in fact. Only recently have nations, and the few individuals making national decisions, begun to relinquish their monopoly as subjects in international law and actors in international organizations and diplomacy. Individuals have always had clearer identities in international economic, social, cultural, and scientific endeavors, and this pattern should further be imitated in politics.

Individuation also involves the enhancement of human rights, such as those enshrined in the U.N. Universal Declaration of Human Rights and subsequent international covenants codifying civil, political, economic, social, and cultural rights (see von Glahn, 1970:Ch. 11).

Such human rights can appear in a negative light, as individual rights that cannot be infringed by larger groups, including the nation-state. But they can also be seen much more positively as encompassing rights to the means for individual security and growth, the right to a fair share of the benefits produced by the world machine, and the requirement to pay a fair share of the costs of its operation (cf. Eide, 1980; Nelson and Green, 1980; Glaser and Possony, 1979; Joyce, 1978).

Individuation suggests the importance of individual interests—even when these may be opposed to the interests of larger groups. A basic human right would seem to be the right to calculate one's own interests, whether correctly or incorrectly.

Individuation finally includes what may be the most important individual right or interest, individual survival.

Equality and Stability

The strategies we have described should also contribute to greater equality and stability.

International functionalism, denationalization, and individuation imply a more equal sharing of power, wealth, and knowledge. More groups and actors participate in various dimensions of the world environment. They contribute their resources to the common effort and, as they do so, they presumably also articulate and defend their own particular concerns.

There is also a stabilizing logic. Rapid change benefits some, but not all. As the world environment becomes more open, those who lose from rapid and discontinuous growth presumably may be able to slow or at least smooth the curve of change.

A policy such as the one we are outlining obviously cannot be implemented all at once, but only gradually over time. This is entirely appropriate. Actions can and should be undertaken incrementally, in small pieces, as experiments. Policymakers should define their expected impacts in advance and then monitor the results to see if they achieve the anticipated results. If so, additional steps can be taken; if not, little will be lost. Whether the actions succeed or fail, policymakers will have a systematic basis for learning and innovation. New and better policies aiming at the same end can be attempted.[9]

Demilitarization

Peace creation finally involves demilitarization at the international, domestic, and individual levels.

International Demilitarization

International demilitarization means downgrading the law of war, at least those aspects of it that permit violence. This means reducing the legal justifications for undertaking war and permissible wartime activities (cf. Brandt, 1972).

International organization might place less emphasis on military tasks. International military peacekeeping has sometimes seemed to be an essential condition of international peace. Provisions for it appear in the U.N. Charter, and there has been a host of U.N. peacekeeping operations in various parts of the world. This approach might receive less attention in the future. Peaceful methods of dispute settlement should become more important.

The alliance aspects of international life might gradually be reduced. Regional military activity is suggested by Articles 51–54 of the U.N. Charter. This may be the most damaging dimension of regional organization. Alliance membership, personnel, financial contributions, participation, and compliance could be diminished.

Attempts at arms limitation should obviously go forward as quickly as possible. In the absence of general controlled disarmament, it is still possible to try for the creation of particular zones—central Europe, for example—in which military forces and weapons might be drastically reduced if not totally eliminated. And there should be continuing attempts to slow escalation of the arms race at all stages: research, development, testing, production, storage, and deployment.

In addition, demilitarization means curtailing the deployment of troops or weapons outside national boundaries, sales or transfers of weapons or military equipment, technical assistance, and the transfer of nuclear materials that could be converted to weapons.

International demilitarization implies a reduction in bargaining techniques like blockades and embargoes that withhold goods and services critical to the welfare of others. In addition, it entails explicit attempts to diminish international hostility and image races. National leaders and media might try to avoid threatening gestures and words. They might work against international confrontation and personal hostility toward other leaders or peoples. Instead, they might attempt carefully to define and articulate specific issues of disagreement and reduce them.

National Demilitarization

National demilitarization involves subordinating the military sector of society. It means attempting to restrict military regimes. It implies reducing standing armies both absolutely and relative to national populations. It also means lowering military budgets, in absolute numbers as well as relative to national productivity and expenditure.[10]

National demilitarization implies downgrading paramilitary sectors of society and reducing coercion. It means replacing the military draft with voluntary military service.[11] It involves reducing secret police and clandestine intelligence activities. It includes efforts at domestic arms control, reducing armament levels of society in general. At the same time it suggests less police armament and more training in nonviolent techniques (cf. Hawkins and Ward, 1970).

National demilitarization finally means reducing the use of military metaphors, analogies, images, and symbols in communications.

Individual Demilitarization

Individual demilitarization also comprehends a number of elements. Individual demilitarization includes more comprehensive attempts to help those returning from wars and military service to readjust to civilian life (cf. O'Neill and Fontaine, 1973).

Individual demilitarization also involves support for a more widespread recognition of the history and value of conscientious objection to war and violence. It comprehends refusal to undertake military service and the performance of substitute service. It includes resistance to paying taxes for military purposes, and earmarking such funds for other uses.[12]

A strategy of individual demilitarization recognizes the aggressive dynamic of human beings. At the same time it calls for the sublimation of aggressive drives into less harmful ritualistic channels such as sports or socially constructive activities that can be a "moral equivalent of war." Such activities include the whole range of aggregative structures and processes we have described in this book under the general headings of bureaucracy, exchange, and language (James, 1973; cf. Storr, 1973; Hamblin et al., 1971; Lorenz, 1967).

Individual demilitarization accepts the necessity for conflict, struggle, and confrontation, but refuses to endorse violence as an acceptable method for social change. It insists that the means used to produce social change are as important as the ends sought and searches for alternatives to violence as ways of producing progress.

Individual demilitarization downgrades the use of violence or coercion to achieve or defend other values. It deemphasizes negative reinforcement such as punishment and threat. It stresses cooperation and consensus, with positive rewards and the promise of healthy, individual growth (cf. Milburn, 1980; Skinner, 1971; Denenberg and Zarrow, 1970; Maslow, 1968).

THE TRAGEDY OF PEACE AND WAR

At the beginning of this book, we described a mystical perspective on war prevalent in an earlier time. This mystical view suggested the close relationship between human and divine nature and the eternal, changeless, fundamental necessity of the natural order.

Such mysticism formed the framework for classical tragedy, where men and women were always ruled by fate, where the force of destiny was unavoidable and sometimes malevolent, where critical human values were often unattainable. Located in such an environment, human beings nevertheless tried to achieeve a higher destiny. Because the environment was more powerful and because of personal flaws, they failed and were destroyed.

The development of modern science seemed to promise an end to tragedy. It provided new knowledge about the natural order and gave hope that human intervention might enhance material well-being in this life. A new drama thus emerged, in which the scientist was cast as a hero, whose pride led not to destruction but redemption.

Yet tragedy still exists in the contemporary world; and this book is about such a modern tragedy. The tragedy of peace is that, while it is so desirable, it appears unattainable. The tragedy of war is that there seems to be no way quickly to diminish or eliminate it.

The major victim of the tragedy is the human race, individuals of all degrees of social importance, who have suffered or will suffer death or injury from war.

From one perspective, the tragedy is caused by a malevolent environment. Humanity is assaulted by forces beyond its control. From another viewpoint, however, humanity itself produces the tragedy. War seems to come from a fatal flaw in the technology that we ourselves have created. Though we try ever harder, we seem doomed to fail on an ever-larger scale. If we reduce the number of wars, we only increase their casualties. We try to improve the environment; but, the more we advance technological aggregation, the more we create polarization, militarization, and finally war itself.

The policy that we have suggested might help to resolve the tragedy. Unfortunately, however, the natural course projections, which include the aggravation of war, appear more likely to prevail. A policy of peace seems to have only a very slim chance of success. The same environmental dynamics that produce war also work against a policy that would reduce it.

Conventional analysis of international relations suggests that a peace policy, like the one we have outlined, is idealistic and unrealistic. Such a peace policy emerges from external observation of the international system. It relies heavily on social scientific findings. Its mood is quite different from that of decisionmakers who act closer to the center of the system. Their personal knowledge of the way the system operates tends to make them, and their historians, skeptical about the chances for improvement (cf. Heuer, 1978; Rothstein, 1972).

A policy of peace seems to threaten cherished values of the system's major actors. In the minds of many foreign policymakers, war is not the worst evil that can occur. War is justified by reasons of state. War is the continuation of diplomacy by other means, to achieve a higher strategic end.

Statesmen have traditionally used war or the threat of war to achieve strategic gains, to secure or defend political or military bases or vital resources. Soviet military interventions in Eastern Europe and Northern Asia, and U.S. actions in Cuba and Vietnam are recent examples.

Survival, liberty, and material prosperity are values that often seem more important than peace. From a Marxist perspective, war or violence is a necessary catalyst in throwing off capitalist oppression or stage in defending socialism. The Western nations have fought two great wars in the twentieth century to make the world safe for democracy. In World War II they felt they had no choice but to fight for their existence. Citizens made the same decision on an individual basis. Many of those who worked on the development of nuclear weapons saw a very limited range of choice. Nuclear weapons, to them, seemed a lesser evil than concentration camps.

If peace seems to come at the expense of national, group, or individual autonomy, some might prefer war, saying, like Patrick Henry, "Give me liberty or give me death," or more contemporarily, "Better dead than red." It may seem that a policy that places a high value on peace as an end in itself places the system at the mercy of its most ruthless member and implies unsuccessful attempts at appeasement in the short run and extinction in the long run. If peace seems to require a reordering of values, some may argue that indoctrination is incompatible with deeply held values—such as those central to the democratic ethic (see Newman, 1974). If it seems that peace can be achieved only at great material cost, many would prefer to take their chances. The expense of the great global bureaucracies of our time or the prospect of a significant redistribution of global wealth may trigger a similar reaction.[13]

These arguments represent the collective experience of international politics. They reflect the dominant tendency of the human past and present. At the same time most foreign policymakers would probably agree that this is not the best of all possible worlds.

Existing knowledge leads one to suspect that the catharsis of violence decreases the general level of important values in international or domestic society. Wars are extremely expensive. The benefits of war may be illusory when compared to the costs. Violence may produce not resistance but contagion. Strategic gains, or socioeconomic ones, may be outweighed by the resource cost of obtaining them. Societies that survive wars may have been stronger in the past. Their victories may be Pyrrhic, and they may face the future in a weaker condition (cf. Boulding and Gleason, 1965). The release of frustration, aggressive impulses, and violent fantasies may be outweighed by the general level of destruction, especially in the nuclear age (cf. Fornari, 1974; Veszy-Wagner, 1973). Polarization and militarization, which lead to violence, also imply repression, injustice, and alienation.

Peace may be more congruent than war with other key human values. Peace may be a necessary condition for liberty and welfare. More peace probably also means more liberty and more welfare, rather than less. Aggregation, which works directly to produce peace, also implies the benefits of security, liberty, and prosperity. These are the goods that technology promises and, to some extent, has already produced.[14]

In spite of the destructiveness of war and the likely benefits of peace, we cannot get from here to there quickly and easily. War is unlikely to disappear. The technology of war is a game of people against people, within the bounds set by nature and ecology. It is carried along the escalator of progress. It rests on millions of individual happenings and decisions at different levels of world society, and each advance in the technology of peace is partly canceled because of polarization and militarization of the component parts.

Today we are all prisoners of war. The technology of war encircles us and limits our freedom to lead peaceful lives. In particular situations, we find ourselves in "prisoner's dilemmas." We may clearly see the costs of war, but are not easily able to escape (cf. Axelrod, 1980; Walker, 1977; Rapoport and Chammah, 1965; Lumsden, 1973).

Our range of choice is restricted. We have only a few alternatives. We can only hope to change a small part of the system, not the whole. There are severe limits to what can be accomplished by any single society, group, or individual. If violence is like a contagious disease, then we run the risk of contracting it simply by coexisting in the same world with others, some of whom may be more susceptible than we. Communities can work to build up the resistance of their own bodies politic when extreme conditions are not present. But if a particularly virulent strain appears in one location, the preventive measures taken by others are unlikely to be completely effective. No matter how careful one's own actions, the world system is simply not yet capable of "quarantining the aggressor," and quite often cannot even identify him or her. In many cases, it is simply not possible to assign "fault"; the most one can say is that the disease has "broken out" somewhere.

We can act only with great uncertainty. We have limited information about the past and present, even less about the future. We must live with the contradictory dynamics of our ecology and of our own choices and actions. A part of the future of peace and war is necessary and predetermined. Men and women are very much creatures of their environment.

There is, however, no compelling reason to accept the idea that history is a closed and a vicious circle in which humanity is trapped in a permanent structure of violence. We need not believe that the best one may realistically hope for is some buffering of its horrors. Another part of history is open to choice. Human beings create much of their environment through purposive choice and action. Even Machiavelli, whose name has become a symbol for public cynicism, recognized that we must operate on the ideal, as well as the practical, level when dealing with world affairs (R. M. Adams, 1975; cf. Eisenberg, 1972).

We can try to improve our condition. Men and women, in groups and individually, can attempt to undertake choices and actions tending to reduce war and to create peace. Each step forward, no matter how small, opens the door to alternatives and opportunities for peaceful interaction that did not previously exist.

Modern technology has produced a situation where, if progress remains at the current rate, a little boy or girl born in 1980 may well be alive in the year 2100. If we recall the experiences of our grandparents, born in the last quarter of the nineteenth century or the first quarter of the twentieth, this is a sobering thought. We hope that if our children live through this period, they will not experience World Wars III and IV, radiation disease, totalitarian dictatorship, or mass starvation.

If our children survive until 2100, we hope that they will see a happy ending and that they will live in security, prosperity, justice, liberty—and peace.

NOTES

CHAPTER 1

1. Epidemiology can be defined broadly as "the study of the distribution and determinants of diseases and injuries in human populations," as well as the maintenance of human health and well-being (Mausner and Bahn, 1974:21–22). More narrowly, Webster (1970) defines epidemiology as "the branch of medicine that investigates" the incidence of and "all elements contributing to the occurrence of a disease in a population; ecology of a disease." Etiology is the assignment or science of causes or origins of a disease (cf. Beer 1979a; Suchman, 1968).

2. We have too little historical information to make any secure judgment about really long-run trends. We know fairly well what happened in Europe during the last 2,500 years. Behind that point in historical time, our knowledge is spotty and peters out rather quickly, based on fragmentary remains—building materials, artifacts, bones, and geological formations. Nevertheless, we can estimate trends for what we know as "history," the European period for the last 2,500 years.

3. This view of war is similar to contemporary perspectives on criminal behavior as sickness held by many sociologists, psychologists, and biologists. Heredity and nutrition alone may be important accessories to crime. In some cases their contribution is judged to be so substantial that the individual is released from responsibility and culpability for his actions. In other cases the person may be hospitalized rather than jailed. Jeffery (1979), Weisman (1971), and Jellinek (1960) provide parallel discussions of suicide and alcoholism.

The analogy is extended by those who perceive criminal justice as war (Christiansen, 1974) or "sickness as conflict" (Mitscherlich, 1969).

4. Wright's figures suggested that warlike behavior among primitive peoples increased with temperature, being highest in hot zones and lowest in cold ones. Other factors such as mountains, desert, grassland, forest, and seashore might also have an effect (1965:552–54). Starr (1977) has attempted to relate temperature to the World War I crisis. Climate may, in turn, be affected by sunspot activity. See Eddy (1977) for a sketch of the sunspot data base. Stommel and Stommel (1979) connect the explosion of an Indonesian volcano in 1816 with extraordinarily cold temperatures, crop failures, and domestic violence.

5. The relationship between sexual drives and cruelty had been more fully developed by Sade and Sacher-Masoch. A contemporary excursion along this vein is Battaille (1962). See also the discussions of necrophilia in Fromm (1973) and Maccoby (1972); incest in Rascovsky and Rascovsky (1972); as well as the relationship between sadism, war, and pacifism in Glover (1933).

A more naturalistic approach locates internal triggering stimuli for violence in muscles, glands, tissues, or the state of the central nervous system (Murphy, 1971; cf. Hartung, 1978; Thiessen, 1976; Fields and Sweet, 1975; Ehrenkranz et al., 1974; Jaffe et al., 1974; Whalen, 1974; Hawkins and Pauling, 1973; Eleftheriou and Scott, 1971; Funkenstein, 1955).

6. Marxist theory recognizes this ambivalence in its emphasis on the dialectical interplay of contradictions within advanced capitalist society, which is a mixture of conspiratorical intentions and unanticipated consequences. Even without a Marxist perspective, it is clear that modern technology provides both benefits and costs. Gideon Sjoberg's (1960) dialectical countersystem approach has been particularly valuable for broadening and clarifying my consciousness of this ambivalence (cf. Granger, 1979; Boorstin, 1978; E. B. Haas et al., 1977; Hirschman, 1977; Ferkiss, 1974, 1969; Bronowski, 1973; Müller, 1970; Wilhelmsen and Bret, 1970; Mumford, 1967–70; Ellul, 1967; Marcuse, 1964).

7. This model is tentative and speculative. It is one of many alternatives that could synthesize contemporary knowledge. It is less technically defined or specified than some might desire. It simplifies and thereby loses important detail about the nature and effects of particular variables. The causal relationships are more complex than represented. Subordinate propositions are not deduced in detail. It is not systematically tested against empirical data.

Despite its limitations, this approach has important benefits. The model serves as a flow chart helping synthesize the material of the book, organizing the argument in a single visual image that can be quickly grasped and easily understood. It combines the multiple variables of the global environment through a few major factors (cf. Andreski, 1968; Wright, 1955:564). If researchers and students find it appealing and empirically plausible, it can easily be further developed, refined, and tested against historical and contemporary reality.

8. The division between environment and policymakers is, to some extent, arbitrary. The environment is that part of the system which is given. We may think of it as a "black box," external to the decisionmakers. Its components interact as structures or processes, without personality or intentionality. It includes all systemic factors amenable to aggregate macroanalysis. Policymakers are those individuals we may single out for special attention. If they are important to us for some reason, we may try to analyze them as "white boxes," as conscious, complex individuals with particular idiosyncratic identities.

9. Contrast this view with Boulding (1978) and Curle (1971).

CHAPTER 2

1. An earlier and more technical discussion of this question appears in Beer (1974).

2. For discussion of the travels and transformations of these estimates see Haydon (1962), cited and discussed in Singer and Small (1972:11). The figures have also been attributed to N. A. Kovalsky, Vice-Director of the Institute of the International Labour Movement of the U.S.S.R. Academy of Sciences (Hecker, 1971:362–63; see also Fuller et al., 1970:18A).

3. The specifications of casualties of 1,000 or more by Singer and Small (1972:19–22), or troops of 50,000 or more by Wright (1965:636), suggest that we are talking about violence at a substantial level and that it is appropriate to give it the label of major war. Wright codes his wars by troop involvement, and it seems reasonable that the engagement of substantial bodies of troops implies direct volence.

Some judgment about the dominant boundaries of the violence is also involved in the categorizing of conflict as war. Thus, Singer and Small exclude both the American and Spanish civil wars from their list in spite of the substantial involvement of other nations in these conflicts.

4. We should also mention Bouthoul and Carrère (1976), who have recently compiled a list of major international and domestic violence. These incidents all involved significant human deaths and more than 10,000 troops in 99 percent of the cases.

All of these lists concentrate on violence between governments and against them. Government violence against its own citizens is often obscured. Amnesty International (1975) reports current governmental torture.

5. Our estimates are analogous to calculations of disease morbidity and mortality (cf. Beer, 1979a).

6. Melko (1975, 1973) gives detailed descriptions of peaceful periods in different historical societies.

7. Köhler and Alcock (1976) estimate that in 1965 alone, 11,500 to 23,000 died as a result of international war, another 92,000 from civil war, and 14 to 18 million from structural violence.

8. The extrapolation of Singer and Small's intensive estimate of world major wars is higher than Wright's. This would not be consistent with a declining secular trend of war incidence (noted on pp. 38–44 above) if all figures were complete. Nevertheless, given the vast scope of his project, it seems reasonable that Wright undercounted to some extent.

9. A comparison of the European casualty figures shows that Sorokin's research on the earlier period provides much lower extrapolations than Singer and Small's, even though Sorokin does not limit himself to direct battle deaths. This difference is consistent with and supports the rising secular trend in war casualties discussed below, though part of the difference again results from incomplete counting by Sorokin.

10. Horvath (1968) describes a curve in which the number of wars decreases with their length: a general pattern of more short wars and fewer long ones (Figure *a*). War concentration implies shifts in both number and length of wars, a general historical displacement of this curve down and to the left so that we get fewer and shorter wars as we move forward in history (Figure *b*).

(*a*)   (*b*)

Total War Incidents: War Concentration

Richardson (1960b) suggests that the number of wars and casualties are inversely related: a larger number of wars with relatively few casualties, and fewer wars with more casualties (Figure *c*). This may occur because a certain proportion of wars naturally end in a given time period, and a high rate of casualties helps stop any particular war more quickly (cf. Wilkinson, 1980:30–34; Weiss, 1963). War concentration and aggravation imply a shift of this curve downward and to the right so that we get more casualties for a smaller number of wars (Figure *d*).

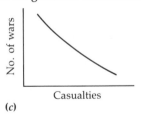

(*c*)

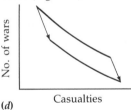

(*d*)

Total War Incidents: War Concentration

11. Singer and Small (1972:Ch. 8) are more cautious, using a complex mixture of different analytical methods and chronological cutting points. They do not feel comfortable with a conclusion that any trend exists. Their position is certainly justifiable. At the same time, however, their evidence does not necessarily disprove our trend hypothesis. There is no determinate objective way to evaluate the lessons of different methods and time periods (cf. Levy, 1980; Small and Singer, 1979; Woods and Baltzly, 1915:28–31).

12. These trends hold only for their estimate of total wars and the subset of wars among states central to the international system. Among the subset of nations more marginal to the international system, wars decline "in the total number of nation-months" (see footnote 34, Ch. 5).

Almost all of the continuous regression lines relating nation-months of war to time have an upward slope, but the correlations are not significant at the .05 level (Singer and Small, 1972:189; 196–97).

13. At the same time, Wright is careful to report that "the number of extra-European wars has increased from only 3 or 4 a half-century to 20 or 30 in that period." His figures, moreover, refer "only to recognized wars." Wright notes that "if the colonial expenditions and interventions in America, Asia, and Africa were counted, most of the great powers would have been 'at war' a large proportion of the time even in the past century" (Wright, 1965:235–36; 638).

14. The evidence that incidents of major domestic violence have declined over time is much weaker, not only from this data, but from other figures as well. Sorokin could discern no general trend in domestic disturbance, only "fluctuation" without apparent direction.

> The indicators for either quarter century or century periods show no continuous trend, either toward bigger and better "orderly progress" or toward ever-increasing disorderliness. This curve fluctuates, that is all one can say (1937:481, 487).

Visual inspection of Sorokin's data suggests that there may even be a slight upward slope in his quarter-century figures. One cannot be sure because he aggregates a number of dimensions, lumping incidence and casualties. Nevertheless, Sorokin points out that "the first quarter of the twentieth century . . . was one of the very turbulent periods" in European history (1937:487). One suspects that if Sorokin's measures were extended, the twentieth century might be one of the world's periods of high domestic violence (see Sorokin, 1937:396; 472–73).

Some other short-term contemporary data also suggest an increase in the incidence of domestic violence (cf. Taylor and Hudson, 1972:88–109).

15. Again "this holds only for all international wars and the interstate war subset. . . . Extra-systemic wars . . . decline . . . in the total number of . . . battle deaths" (Singer and Small, 1972:189). The regression coefficients linking their battle death indicators to time are all in the expected positive direction; on the other hand, the correlations are not particularly high (1972:195–97).

16. It is interesting to note that exponential growth is apparently occurring in war casualties as in other areas of modern society. Doubling time is one measure of such growth. The apparently drastic shortening of the doubling time in absolute casualties that we describe here suggests that war aggravation may exist not only as a long-term historical trend, but may also be accelerating rapidly in our own time.

17. Singer and Small (1972:198–201) report only a slight rise in battle deaths per nation-month of war.

18. The margin of error is suggested by estimates of French casualties in Napoleon's armies; they range between 400,000 and 2,500,000 (Hoedaille, 1972).

19. Reinhard and Armengaud (1961:139) give the geographical distribution of these casualties, which varied between different regions. In some parts of Germany they approached 100 percent.

20. We may imagine the historical process as a cone, filled with a certain volume of violence, of which we can observe only the contemporary part. From that observable segment we extrapolate backward. If the hypothesis of war concentration is correct, the extrapolations from observed data will be too narrow and will not include all the unobserved data, which we must add (+) (Figure *a*). If there has been peace diffusion and war aggravation, on the other hand, the extrapolations from observed data will be too large, and we must subtract from our extrapolated peace years and war casualties (−) (Figure *b*).

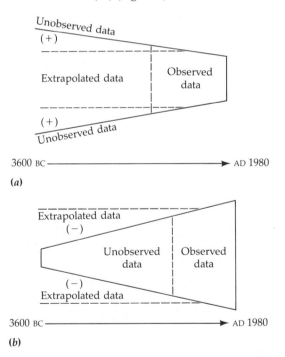

21. Other contemporary analysts propose periods of 5, 15, 17.5, 20, 25, 30–60, 100, and 200 years (see Modelski, 1979; Jouary, 1969; Denton and Phillips, 1968; Dewey, 1964; Moyal, 1949; cf. McMaster, 1978).

22. Alcock et al. suggest domestic peace periods of 4.5, 5.6, 8.6, 9.4, 17.4, 20.5, 34, and 54 years (1978:61, 65: cf. Alcock, 1978; Alcock and Young, 1973).

23. A flat cycle has a relatively long range and low amplitude. A sharp cycle has a shorter range and higher amplitude. A severe cycle has a long range and high amplitude.

24. In comparison, disease in the modern era seems generally to have moved from severe epidemic cycles to a flatter endemic configuration as hosts and parasites have come into more constant, regular contact and adapted to each other. Thus, McNeill notes a "shift from epidemic to endemic forms of infection" that coincided with and was partially responsible for the modern growth of the human population (1976:226–28). A more general incidence of disease has been associated with lower mortality. A major reason for "the decay of the force of epidemics was their increased frequency, until epidemic became merely endemic childhood disease" (McNeill, 1976:343; cf. Glass and Eversley, 1965).

25. The configuration of incidence and casualties helps make the distinction between endemic and epidemic disease. Epidemic disease shows wide swings in morbidity. Long periods where the disease is hardly in evidence are followed by sudden upsurges in prevalence and incidence rates that may seem to expand exponentially along the early part of the logistic curve (Russett, 1976). At such times mortality may be very high because the host population is under much more sudden attack. Endemic disease has a relatively stable pattern of morbidity. Prevalence and incidence rates all vary within relatively narrow limits. At the same time mortality, as reflected in case fatality, proportionate mortality, and case disability rates, tends to be low enough to allow survival and some level of well-being within the host population.

Davis et al. (1977) define what we call acute war contagion as infection, a group process involving interdependence between belligerent pairs. It occurs when one actor or group of actors taking an action changes the probability of other actors taking an action. They call chronic tendency to violence war addiction.

26. We should note that the cross-national historical study of Naroll and his associates reported that "war tended to be slightly less frequent when the Conspicuous States shared a common land boundary with their Conspicuous Rivals" (Naroll et al., 1974:332).

27. They interpret this in the light of militarization, particularly emphasizing the importance of alliances. Thus, a war 20 years in the past may contribute to subsequent militarization that will, a generation later, help produce another war.

28. Sorokin uses a different method to estimate domestic violence in Europe over the last 14 centuries (1937:396, 472).

29. "All revolutions start in principle as world revolutions," concludes Wright (1965:1110). "Starting as new symbols in local areas revolutions spread ideas of violence by contagion and opposition. . . . Their symbols and principles must, in the opinions of their initiators, become universal or nothing." Of course, the revolutionaries engender counterrevolutionaries. "Friends and foes of the new symbol . . . come into conflict and [heighten] tension levels in remote areas."

Kaplan applies these ideas to the contemporary world. He notes first "the entry onto the world stage of a large number of new nations," emerging from violent or semiviolent disintegration of the preexisting Western colonial system and its empires. Second, "the Communist challenge to the existing social and political order," arising primarily from the revolutionary triumphs achieved in the Soviet Union and China, is important in Eastern Europe and increasingly within the Third World. Third are "pre-revolutionary" conditions within "the democratic powers faced by the challenges from the Communist bloc and the new nations . . . , lacking both cohesion and conviction." Kaplan notes that within these nations, important elements of the populations are satisfied with what they have but are unwilling to take risks, except perhaps when directly threatened. Other elements of the populations of the Western nations themselves accept much of the revolutionary philosophy. They are discontented and disenchanted. They want change of a Leftist nature. There is no—or very little—support for the status quo (M. Kaplan, 1962:xiii–xiv).

30. In the United States, collective racial violence rose during World Wars I and II and the Vietnam War. During the Korean War, however, there was no major racial disturbance (Schaich, 1975).
31. The French philosopher, Bodin, suggests:

> The best way of preserving a state, and guaranteeing it against sedition, rebellion, and civil war is to keep the subjects in amity one with another, and to this end, to find an enemy against whom they can make common cause. Examples of this can be found in all commonwealths. The Romans are a specially good illustration. They could find no better antidote to civil war, nor one more certain in its effects, than to oppose an enemy to their citizens. On one occasion, when they were engaged in bitter mutual strife, the enemy found his way into the city and seized the Capitol. The citizens instantly composed their differences, and united to expel the enemy. . . . Without looking further afield, we have an example in this kingdom [France] when it was in grave peril in 1562. The English set foot in France and seized Havre de Grace, whereupon the civil war was abandoned, and the subjects united to make common cause against the enemy (Bodin, 1955:168–69; quoted in Mayer, 1971:14; see note 24, Ch. 4).

Kegley et al. (1978) propose that the degree of militarization is important in linking foreign and domestic violence in this way. (See note 53, Chapter 5.)
32. Such drops have usually been explained by a number of reasons. War offers the opportunity to transfer individual violence to the battlefield where it is transformed into the statistics of international violence and disappears from the ledgers of domestic society. At the same time war can also work against suicide because of its danger, discipline, or the creation of a sense of community or bonding with others.
33. The hypothesis of autocausation does not specify which of the two—peace or violence—may be a more important causal agent and which more an effect. It does not articulate the conditions under which the causal influence is positive or negative. It does not allow for external variables that may influence the direction, nor does it specify different effects for different time periods.

CHAPTER 3

1. As we shall see, evidence about the effects of peace and war on aggregation, and of aggregation on peace and war, is ambivalent. It is reasonable to ask why we assume that the first relationship does not exist, and that the second is positive. The answer is that peace and war seem to affect aggregation both positively and negatively in the short run, and negligibly in the long run. The effects of aggregation on peace and war are also unreliable; yet when they exist, they seem generally to be positive. More aggregation, to the extent that it has a direct effect, tends to support peace; less aggregation goes together with war.
2. Miller describes the later stages of the process in the following terms:

> *Origins*
>   Organization. The first organization was probably formed about 9000 B.C., or 11,000 (1.1×10^4) years ago. It may well have been a village or a city like Jericho or some other human activity involving groups arranged in two or more echelons.

Society. The first society was probably formed somewhat later, perhaps around 5000 B.C., or 7,000 (7×10^3) years ago, at about the beginning of history. In all likelihood there were primitive tribal "societies" before that, whose components were groups. But if organizations, in my sense, did not arise until about 9000 B.C., living systems with a preponderance of organizations as components (which is my definition of a society) did not appear until later, perhaps around 5000 B.C., or, 7,000 years ago. Much of this evolution is shrouded in prehistory. As at every level, there were probably transitional forms of systems between the early organizations and societies as I define them.

Supranational system. Finally the supranational system evolved. Probably the first empire of which there is historical and archaeological evidence was the Sumerian Empire of the Southern Mesopotamian valley. Its first dynasty ruled in the twenty-fifth century B.C., or 4,500 (4.5×10^3) years ago. It controlled a region of the world that had several cities and numerous tribes or states, which were not societies at all comparable in complexity to modern nations. In recent decades the character of supranational systems has altered markedly, and none of the present ones has the sort of absolute power and integrated decider processes of some of the early empires.

Sizes

Organization. The diameters of organizations range from about 10 m for a very small department store or factory to the diameter of a state or other major component of a nation. The largest of these is the Russian Socialist Federated Soviet Republic of the Soviet Union, with an east–west diameter only about 600 kilometers (km) less than that of the whole Soviet Union. The median organization diameter is probably that of a moderately large manufacturing organization, or about 10^2m.

Society. The smallest sovereign nation, Vatican City, is only about 1 km in diameter, and the largest, the Soviet Union, has an east–west diameter of about 11,000 km. The median modern nation has a diameter of about 10^3 km, or 10^6m.

Supranational system. The smallest supranational system was perhaps the Austrian-Hungarian Empire, which was about 300 km in diameter. The largest is perhaps the North Atlantic Treaty Organization, which is nearly 16,000 km in diameter. The median diameter of a supranational system is probably about 5×10^3 km, or 5×10^6m (Miller, 1978:1036; cf. R. N. Adams, 1975; Wilson, 1975:572).

3. There is some dispute whether states precede this body of international law or depend on it, at least in part, for their own existence (cf. Wright, 1965:App. 32).

4. One effect of the treaties was to deprive of any legitimacy the previously vague claims to overlordship on the part of the Holy Roman Empire and the papacy. The Austrian Empire, as a result of several innovations in diplomatic protocol, was no longer *primus inter pares* as a successor to the Roman Empire but, instead, merely a great power on equal footing with France, England, and Spain. The independence of smaller states was sanctioned as well—formally in the case of the United Netherlands and by implication in an agreement to respect religious choices of both Protestant and Catholic rulers (M. Haas, 1974:337).

Israel (1967) reproduces the texts of major modern peace treaties.

5. A thorough study of the question would examine various indicators of the autonomy, authority, and legitimacy of the international legal system and compare their levels and rates with levels and rates of wartime incidence and mortality, including different time leads and lags.

6. Wright has tabulated different types of legal prohibition, permission, and institutionalization of violence (1965:1394–1400).

7. A historical analysis gives us some examples of arbitration.

Two periods that have been identified are Hellenistic Greece and medieval Russia. At least 46 cases of arbitration were recorded between 300 and 100 B.C. Cities, philosophers, and even Olympic champions served as arbitrators. Ganshof (1953) believes that there was some such activity in medieval Islam. Certainly there are earlier Arabian precedents. The Kitab-al-Aghani tells us that once in Pre-Mohammedan Arabia, a bride forced her husband to make peace between two warring tribes before she would allow him conjugal relations.

One of the most eventful arbitrations of recorded history occurred in 657 in Syria, when the forces of Muawiya, being worsted in battle, placed copies of the Qur'an on their spears to signal a demand for arbitration. The pious party within the victorious army forced its leader, Ali, to accept this arbitration, which led to the founding of the Ummayad Caliphate and ultimately to the schism between Sunna and Shia.

• • •

Third party mediation and arbitration were spread over [the] entire range of thirteenth century diplomatic activity. A pope submitted to arbitration in 1244. A count of Savoy, faced with choosing his successor from among his nephews, willed the problem to arbitrators. By the end of the thirteenth century, arbitration had become the normal recourse for solving disputes which arose between mariners of different powers. What is perhaps more surprising was the frequency with which the largest powers accepted arbitration.

• • •

The Law of the March, or border, held in areas of uncertain jurisdiction between, for example, Brittany and Anjou, Gascony and Castile, Hainault and Liège, and on the Atlantic. It existed to settle grievances between private parties from different jurisdictions. Yet it was not purely private law for it allowed reprisals against the people of an offender. Conflicts were often resolved through arbitration. Each side appointed an equal number, perhaps two or three or six, arbitrators. It was common, if not universal, practice that at least one judge on each side be a trained lawyer. In cases involving mariners, one or more prominent citizens of the towns from which the ships came were often included. Hearings were held and decisions rendered. The forms and regularities of law and custom, the even number of arbiters and their competence to the task, created the confidence which was so difficult to obtain in the more purely diplomatic instances. Yet the Law of the March was dependent on the agreement of the highest authority in each political unit who must agree to participate, to appoint arbitrators, and to enforce their decisions. Thus the Law of the March was a subordinate part, a most useful tool of the larger effort at peace (Balch, 1978:33–35).

A survey of actual international arbitrations showed that arbitral tribunals handled 70 percent of arbitral cases between 1815 and 1969 while individual arbitrators dealt with 30 percent (Raymond, 1976; Stuyt, 1972).

General arbitration theory, research, and practice have continued, particularly as a means of resolving management–labor disputes, in postindustrial society (see, for example, Wetter, 1979; Subbarao, 1978; cf. Maggiolo, 1971).

8. Gamble and Fischer suggest somewhat different totals in their "overview of ICJ activity" (1976:32). Between 1946 and 1961 they tabulate a total of 41 ICJ cases, including 17 contentious judgments, 11 advisory opinions, 5 discontinued cases, and 8 cases removed by the court. Between 1962 and 1975 they find 9 contentious judgments, 3 advisory opinions, and 1 case discontinued.

9. Gamble and Fischer are particularly skeptical.

The Court has fallen far short of the role it was intended to play in the peaceful settlement of international disputes. In nearly thirty years of its existence, the Court has made judgments on only twenty-six disputes and rendered only fourteen advisory opinions. Only a handful of the disputes to reach the Court related to major international problems of the post–World War II period. None of these disputes dealing with the East–West conflict, decolonization, or control over natural resources/environmental concerns was directly settled as a result of adjudication. Most of the disputes to reach the Court and resulting in a merit or nonmerit decision have been localized and peripheral to major international problems. Although the Court's record on settlement is better in this area, it is still unimpressive; only about half of the peripheral disputes were settled or moved towards settlement by the Court.

• • •

It is clear that support for the Court is minimal. The picture emerging is bleak indeed; only thirty-four states have ever appeared in contentious proceedings resulting in merit or nonmerit decisions and only eight have appeared more than once. Most repeat users are Western European states, confirming a fact that was often demonstrated throughout the research, that is, that the strongest advocacy of the ICJ rests with Western Europe. The only other group that evidences some tendency for substantial support of the Court was Latin America, which had levels of acceptance of the Court's jurisdiction comparable to that of Western Europe but has few actual appearances before the ICJ. Some might interpret this as latent support for the Court—others would say that it is lip service not indicative of genuine national volition to use the court.

• • •

The record is clear. The Court has seldom acted and very rarely has it acted forcefully. Perhaps the peripheral benefits coming from the Court's existence are sufficient to justify the status quo. But those who accept the Court uncritically blaspheme the noble motives for creating the Court in the first place. After all, the ultimate goal is pacific settlement of disputes, not the preservation of an institution (1976:119, 123, 127).

10. International law can also help to moderate domestic violence. Its doctrine can be "invoked in attempts to limit the scope of hostilities by recognition of the applicability of international arbitral or adjudicatory procedures for peaceful settlement, or the rules of war, applying limits to belligerent action" (Falk, 1964:194; see also Bond, 1974; Luard, 1972).
11. Such provisions are similar to declaration and recognition of epidemic areas. In such areas different rules and procedures, like those of quarantine, are followed in an attempt to isolate the damage. Like quarantine, however, neutrality is not always effective.

World War II saw wholesale violations of neutral rights by belligerents on both sides in the conflict. Belgium, Luxembourg, the Netherlands, Denmark, and Norway were invaded despite their neutral status; Swiss national airspace was violated by both sides; vessels were attacked, sunk, or captured in neutral waters; and the United States became a nonbelligerent participant in the conflict long before it joined the Western Allies after the attack on Pearl Harbor (von Glahn, 1970:629).

12. Examples of such intervention include foreign activities in the American, Russian, Spanish, Chinese, and Vietnamese revolutions as well as continuing foreign military participation in various contemporary struggles in Africa, Asia, and Latin America (cf. Wilson, 1980; Little, 1975; Zorgbibe, 1975; Moore, 1974; Vincent, 1974; von Glahn, 1970; Thomas and Thomas, 1956).
13. Falk (1976, 1972a, 1969, 1968c) and Falk et al. (1971) include a comprehensive selection of articles and documents on the relationship of various aspects of international law to the Vietnam war (cf. Trooboff, 1975). Coil (1978) presents an interesting application to the American revolutionary war.
14. De Saussure (1978) discusses the relevant service publications: AFP 110–31, Army Field Manual 27–10, and NWIP 10–2 (cf. Lieber, 1875).
15. Wright (1965:1561) sketches the financial history of international organizations. SIPRI (1978f) and Sivard (1976) provide additional information on national expenditure levels and finances.
General discussions describing structures, functions, and behavior in contemporary international organization include the annual yearbooks of the Union of International Associations and the U.N; Andemicael, 1979; Jacobson, 1979; Judge, 1978; H. Newcombe, 1976b; Atherton, 1976; Feld, 1976; Goodrich, 1974; Claude,

1971; Plano and Riggs, 1967. Mansbach et al. (1976) and Nye and Keohane (1971) provide general discussions of transnational nongovernmental organizations.

16. Recent works on the development of modern nation-states include Tilly (1975), and Wallerstein (1972). Eisenstadt and Rokkan (1973) provides a good bibliography.

17. Skjelsbaek (1971) reports that states experienced a particularly sharp decline in shared organizational memberships if they were to become enemies (see also Singer and Wallace, 1970; Wallace and Singer, 1970; Smoker, 1967b).

18. General overviews of this literature appear in Wiener and Fisher (1974); Zampaglione (1973); Purves (1970); Hinsley (1967); Wynner and Lloyd (1946); and Hemleben (1943). For specific plans, see the Garland Library of Peace.

19. Methods include:

1. Bilateral negotiations: direct negotiations between the belligerents.
2. Resolution passed in either the General Assembly or Security Council, or both.
3. UN intervention either with observers or with military force.
4. UN mediation efforts
5. Mediation outside the UN.
6. Multilateral meetings or conferences—of the great powers, for example—to attempt to resolve the conflict outside the UN.
7. Decisions by the International Court of Justice, or by any ad hoc commissions for arbitration.
8. Instrument of settlement: formal termination of the conflict and/or existence of a negotiated agreement between the belligerents.

(SPIRI, 1969b:372–73; cf. Wright, 1965:1429–31, 1554–57).

20. The record of regional international organizations is similar to that of the World Court. For differences between regional organizations and the World Court, see Coplin and Rochester (1972:539).

Detailed discussions of the contributions of particular regional organizations to dispute settlement are widely scattered. Some examples are Andemicael (1976); Hassouna (1975); League of Arab States (1975); and Levin (1974). (See also Butterworth, 1976; Beer, 1969:Ch. 1.)

21. Rittberger maintains that Singer and Wallace's correlation statistics are artificially skewed in a negative direction, that they mask international organizations' positive contributions to peace. "Both the measures of international organization-building and the measures of magnitude and severity of international war are themselves positively correlated with a third variable, the advance of industrial civilization" (1973:219). The lack of observed correlation is, therefore, spurious; it shows achievement by international organizations that there is *no* correlation rather than a positive one. (See also Michalak, 1971; Nye, 1971; Sawicki, 1970.)

The findings by Russett (1967) might result from exogenous factors. Both wars and organizational membership may come from prior influences of geographical proximity. Nations in the same geographical region are bound together by shared memberships in international organizations. Neighbors tend to join together more often with each other than with more distant states. Unfortunately, neighbors may also have more to fight about than people who are separated by wide distances. On the other hand, there is also some evidence that the loads of common organizational membership, as part of a larger international integrative process, can produce important instabilities (cf. Doran, 1976; Deutsch et al., 1957:42).

22. See Bailey (1977) for a discussion of Security Council activities.

23. Collective security is like what economists have labeled a "collective good," in which the benefits are to a considerable extent indivisible, but the burdens can be parceled out in different proportions. In such a situation international groupings are held together in part by a complex system of countervailing costs, including contributions of money and personnel. Large states may carry disproportionate shares of the burden in some areas, smaller states in others. Such organizations may be able to produce more efficient and optimal conflict management than might have been possible without their structure and coordination. Yet they are far from achieving the theoretical optimality of the best of all possible worlds (cf. Beer, 1972b).

24. The number of important inventions and discoveries has increased exponentially over time, implying an analogous, augmented number of exchanges (cf. Wilson, 1975:573).

25. These figures represent a general compound growth rate of over 10 percent per year, reflecting to some extent such factors as worldwide inflation and population growth. Of course growth in particular areas varied substantially at different times during this period. (See also Kenwood and Lougheed, 1971.)

26. Discussions of interdependence and the relationship between international and domestic markets include Rosecrance and Stein (1973); Alker and Bock (1971:430); Russett (1970a); and Deutsch and Eckstein (1961). National markets with larger populations tend to have lower ratios of foreign trade to GNP (Taagepera and Hayes, 1977; Dahl and Tufte, 1973:115).

27. Durfee (1975) holds that the nature of peace requires conversation, relationship through justification, and apology. War, on the other hand, represents destruction of intersubjective relations and the ultimate separation of selves and interiority.

28. World War I produced a serious dislocation of the world economy. War loans, reparations, inflation, the vain attempts to restore pre-war exchange rates and trading patterns, hothouse manufacturing outside Europe set up during the war, much of which proved uneconomic when European manufacturing had been restored, all contributed to the depression of 1929, the breakdown of world interdependence in trade and finance, and quite possibly to the pathological political conditions in Germany and Japan which brought on World War II. In Germany, the hyperinflation of 1923–24 wiped out the middle class and helped to push it into national socialism. Large-scale unemployment in 1931 and 1932 finished the task (Kindleberger, 1970b:98; cf. Kindleberger, 1973).

•   •   •

The final effects of the war on the European economy cannot be separated from other contemporary changes and from the complicated economic process in which they formed important elements. It is possible only to indicate certain new conditions affecting development which were a direct consequence of the war. Some of these consequences, such as losses of manpower, of financial assets and of productive capacity, are accessible to quantitative measurement, while others, such as changes in technology, in contacts with overseas markets, in attitudes towards economic policy, and in business psychology, escape such measurement.

Even more important than losses of manpower or capacity was probably the dislocation in the distribution of resources between different countries or industries. Such dislocations, which appeared on a worldwide scale in agriculture, shipping and the steel industry, released cyclical processes which in some cases can be traced throughout the two inter-war decades. The typical pattern of these cycles was, in the first phase, a reduction of capacity in Europe in general, or in one European country particularly; this reduction stimulated an expansion of capacity in other parts of the world; in the meantime, European production recovered, the result being an over-expansion of some industries—as witnessed by unemployed capacity, surplus stocks or a fall in prices. National ambitions to regain lost positions often gave an extra impetus to the post-war expansion of capacity. These phases of expansion and crisis often coincided with, and were reinforced by, the general boom in the 'twenties and the depression in the 'thirties. The general business cycles during the two inter-war decades were thus interwoven with partial cycles in special industries which influenced the course of the general boom and the later depression.

The analogy of a pendulum has been used to explain the mechanisms of periodic variations in business activity; a pendulum, which is set in motion by an external shock, will continue to move in a series of swings. This analogy describes well one of the main effects of the first World War on a number of industries, and on the European economy as a whole; the dislocations created by the war meant such a shock to the economic system that great swings followed which continued over the entire inter-war period.

In other cases, the main effect of the war was not a setback in productive capacity, but a failure to keep up to date as regards new products and new methods of production. At the end of the war, the United States had taken the lead in many fields, while Europe had slid back into a weak competitive position; the motor and rubber industries exemplify this tendency. It is well known that such delays, once they have arisen, are difficult to overcome. The recognition of this difficulty forms the traditional basis for the "infant industry" argument for tariffs. A competitive disadvantage in certain fields holds back new enterprise. Further progress may in the meantime be made abroad, and the setback may in this way acquire a certain degree of permanence unless interrupted by a special effort or by national protection. This sequence of events developed in several European industries after the first World War, and in some fields the delay had not been overcome by the outbreak of the second (Svennilson, 1954:20; cf. Keynes, 1920).

29. Aldcroft states that:

The First World War and its aftermath was not the prime causal factor in the crisis that began in 1929. Certainly the repercussions of the war created maladjustments and instability within the world economy which made it more vulnerable to shocks, but the turning-point of the cycle cannot be attributed directly to the war itself. Indeed, though the war imparted a severe shock to the economic mechanism it did not, because of its timing, upset the cyclical pattern. It distorted the economic system in several ways and also aggravated the amplitude of subsequent cyclical movements but it did little, if anything, to destroy the time sequence or periodicity of cyclical activity. After the war economic systems for the most part reverted to their previous cyclical course and in all probably a downturn could have been anticipated towards the end of the 1920s even in the absence of a European war (1977:281).

30. Another interesting example of this growth of trade through war comes from the Middle East, where the Arab–Israeli conflict has had a "substantial impact on oil-related activities, accelerating the intensity of interaction between importers and exporters" (Park et al., 1976:247).

31. Mueller describes the "rally round the flag" effect in recent American history (1973:53, 58–59). Rokeach (1974) discusses the effect of the Vietnam War in heightening American collective and spiritual values, and diminishing selfish, materialist goals. Naroll and Divale, on the other hand, find "no real evidence that warfare operates as a natural selection process favoring cultural evolution" in primitive societies (1976:25; cf. Chapter 4, note 24; Stein, 1976; Linz, 1973; Deutsch et al., 1957:44–46, 156–57).

32. Classic presentations of the costs of war include Angell (1973, 1972); Jordan (1972); and Novicow (1971). See also Wheeler (1976); Lewin (1967); and Boulding and Gleason (1965).

33. Pryor notes an inverse relationship between defense and civilian expenditures for nations in which defense spending is relatively high but finds no such relationship when the ratio of defense spending is low (1969:120–24).

34. Kirk gives a detailed analysis of the effects of the war-induced migration.

The French population shows the aging attendant on long-established fertility decline. A relatively small proportion of the population was in the young working ages, a high proportion in upper middle life and old age. The war and differential mortality favoring females had resulted in an excess of two million women.

The structure of the combined foreign and naturalized population was strikingly different, concentrated as it was in the prime working ages, with few children and few old people. With its large excess of males the foreign population contributed materially to healing the wounds left by war: the reported excess of males over females in the foreign and naturalized population amounted to 544 thousand. This relationship was especially important since the excess of males was concentrated in the young adult ages. As a result of immigration many French women were enabled to marry who otherwise would have had to remain single because there were not enough native French men to go around. Since immigration tended to balance the sex ratio at the marriageable ages it probably contributed more than proportionately to the maintenance of the birth rate. It was almost certainly a factor in the relatively slow decline of the French birth rate in the interwar period.

Conversely, it seems reasonable to suppose that emigration contributed to the decline of the birth rate in the emigrating countries, since it removed a more than proportionate number of potential parents and altered the balance of the sexes.

. . .

Net increments to the labor force through immigration were certainly a source of national wealth, especially as immigration supplemented those sections of the French labor force most severely depleted by the war. The immigrants brought to France their productive capacity free of the costs of education and upbringing. At the same time immigrants suffered disadvantages in bargaining power resulting from their ignorance of French customs and language, their lack of organization, and their political disabilities. In consequence France gained the products of their labor at much lower cost than would have been necessary to induce the employment of French workers in the same capacities.

Though immigration probably contributed to the over-all prosperity of France it is obvious that particular groups suffered from foreign competition. French workers in direct competition with foreigners were probably forced to accept lower wages than they otherwise would have been able to obtain. On the other hand, foreigners were often not employed in substitution for French workers, but in jobs that Frenchmen were unwilling to take. Foreigners were characteristically employed in the less desirable occupations. Furthermore the degree of industrial activity made possible by the presence of cheap foreign labor expanded employment opportunities for Frenchmen in managerial, clerical, and service capacities.

Immigration brings greater productive capacity. It of course also brings greater demand for both consumer and capital goods. Because the immigrants are chiefly adults and because many of them establish new households, the effect on demand is probably considerably larger than that involved in the normal processes of population growth. To the extent that there was a persistent increase in demand flowing from immigration the risks of French entrepreneurs were reduced and capital investment was made more attractive than it otherwise would have been.

From the point of view of the sending country emigration has mixed implications for the economic welfare of the country. As noted above with reference to transoceanic migration, emigration characteristically draws off workers in their period of maximum productivity. The costs of raising these workers are thus lost to the country of origin, costs which are only partially balanced by emigrant remittances. The loss of productive power involved in emigration is particularly serious to those countries providing the sources of mass international migration within Europe. In these countries problems of low productivity outweigh those attendant on business cycles (1946:117–20).

Urlanis (1971:Pt. V) discusses possible compensatory increases in birthrates following wars. See also Kulischer (1948).

35. Cf. Virkkunen et al. (1976); Black (1975, 1974); Girard and Schadelle (1975); Jarho (1973); and MacRae and Brigden (1973).

36. See particularly Figley (1978). (Cf. Merbaum, 1977; Johnson, 1976; Klonoff et al., 1976; Tanay, 1976; Yager, 1976; De Fazio, 1975; Jones and Johnson, 1975; Mirin and McKenna, 1975; Perlman, 1975; Quinones, 1975; Solnit and Priel, 1975; Strayer and Ellenhorn, 1975; Adams and McCloskey, 1974; R. P. Fox, 1974; Helmer, 1974; Keehn et al., 1974; Rohrbaugh et al., 1974; Rohrbaugh and Press, 1974; Shatan, 1974, 1973; Renner, 1973; Sanders, 1973; Van Putten and Emory, 1973; Meguro, 1972; Pisztora, 1972; Braatz et al., 1971; Bloch, 1970; Bourne, 1972, 1970a; Strange and Brown, 1970; Dollard, 1944).

37. See Rutledge et al., 1979; Andersen (1975); Risner, (1974); Stenger (1973).

38. See Staw et al. (1974); Notz et al. (1971); cf. Longino (1973).

39. Cf. Rosenbaum and Najenson (1976); McCubbin et al. (1975); Cretekos (1973); and Hall and Simmons (1973).

40. Cf. Murphy (1977, 1975); Segal (1974); Lifton (1974, 1967); Brenner (1973); Fanon (1967); and Janis (1961).

41. Cf. Milgram and Milgram (1976); M. Selzer (1976); Dahl et al. (1975); Phan (1975); Baider and Rosenfeld (1974); McKissack (1974); Wen (1974); Ziv et al. (1974); Ziv and Israeli (1973); Carlsmith (1973); Freud and Burlingham (1973); Hall and Simmons (1973); Palgi (1973); Hansburg (1972); Solov'ev (1972); and Mitscherlich (1969).

42. See note 1, Chapter 3.

43. Material factors other than exchange obviously contribute to economic well-being. One of the arguments in favor of free trade has always been the prosperity of the United States, which represented a huge common market. Nevertheless, the tremendous natural wealth of the continent has also helped produce American affluence.

44. Richardson suggests one possible formula to describe the effect of mutual trade on belligerence between the Triple Alliance and the Triple Entente between 1907 and 1914; $x = U_1 - \frac{1}{4}\dot{M}$, where x = warlike attitude; U_1 = warlike expenditure in pounds sterling; $\dot{M}$ = mutual trade in pounds sterling (1960a:109–110).

45. Such evidence should make us cautious, but it does not necessarily refute the idea that trade may have a moderate pacifying effect. Other negative influences may hide the positive relationship. High levels of international cooperation and conflict often go together, and a system's increased capabilities may be masked by the loads that it has to carry. The pacifying influence of trade may be more than offset by frictions of geographical proximity or incompatible interests (cf. Soroos, 1977:89–90). Trade may help produce peace if there are appropriate institutions to manage conflict, if the rewards of trade are reasonably shared between the parties, and if there are other important social and cultural bonds.

46. McLuhan (1964) points to the use of the "hot line" as a counterproductive device. He argues that decisionmakers have destroyed invaluable dimensions of conciliatory possibility by replacing the telephone with the teletype, substituting linear for gestalt communication.

47. As it applies to national markets, the basic hypothesis can be condensed: Peace = a *(bGNP)*(cAmenities), assuming equal distribution of GNP and amenities among the population.

48. This process begins early in life as the child gradually differentiates and generalizes. The first stage would seem naturally to be the formation of a primitive ego or identity. As this occurs, other identifications presumably develop with primary groups: family and peers. Children gradually come into contact with the symbols of secondary groups, and these symbols are incorporated into the developing consciousness (cf. Beer, 1975b).

49. M. Haas reports relatively strong links between high foreign conflict and two indicators of low development: high hospital beds/physicians and low library book circulation per capita (1974:242–43; cf. McGowan and Shapiro, 1973:109; Feierabend and Feierabend, 1972:172).

There has been a great deal of research on the relationship between the general level of economic well-being and domestic peace and violence. Unfortunately, the results are not conclusive, but rather point in a number of different directions. Hibbs (1973:Ch. 3) provides a good summary and evaluation. (Cf. Eckhardt and Young, 1977.)

50. Language can also help mobilize legal and moral restraints to war (see Thompson et al., 1974; Hines et al., 1973; Eatherly, 1961).

CHAPTER 4

1. Figure 4-1 represents only the spatial elements of differentiation and inequality.
2. It may seem that the causal arrow might run from differentiation to aggregation, rather than the way we have specified it in Table 4-2. This alternative view would see that smaller communities serve as building blocks for larger ones, and that the existence of such smaller groupings is a necessary precondition for the establishment of links between them.

The view one takes depends on whether one sees the international system as a growing network of cobwebs or a collection of billiard balls (Boulding, 1977a:607–8). There is little hard empirical evidence on either side. We have chosen our own formulation because it seems to fit better with the other elements of our model. If the reader feels strongly that causality runs the other way, he or she can mentally add an arrow in Table 4-2 going from polarization to aggregation.
3. Northwestern and Northeastern groups are not of course perfectly joined. There are serious differences between many of the actors involved, for example, the Northeastern division between the Soviet Union and China, or Northwestern conflicts between Greece and Turkey. In spite of their internal conflicts, the Northwest and Northeast are each much more well defined than the Southern group of states.
4. A statistical study of common memberships in intergovernmental organizations in the nineteenth century confirms that the original core of organizations with predominantly European membership has given way to a number of clusters centering around Western and Eastern Europe, Latin America, Africa, and Asia (Wallace, 1975:80: cf. Brams, 1968:92).
5. Various studies have analyzed U.N. voting over time. (See particularly Jacobsen, 1978; Vincent, 1978, 1976a, 1976b, 1972, 1971, 1969, 1968; Harbert, 1976; Moore, 1975; H. Newcombe, 1976b; Newcombe et al., 1970; Haas and Rowe, 1973; Rowe, 1972.)
6. These labels, of course, vastly simplify the empirical mixture of central planning and market processes found within the groups, and they may imply unwarranted assumptions about the nature and direction of historical progress.
7. We should note that contemporary cross-national statistics do not confirm a simple association between today's national population or area, on the one hand, and governmental employment, expenditures, and revenues, on the other (Dahl and Tufte, 1973:38). We are talking about a more general historical tendency that may not be reflected in such statistics. For example, former imperial states, with proportionately larger governmental expenditures, are truncated versions of their former historical selves.
8. Israel (1967) provides a discussion of major historical international peace treaties.
9. Results from empirical studies of the International Court of Justice support the view that there is some bloc voting within the Court, but much less extensive or definite than in the General Assembly of the U.N. (Hensley, 1978; Newcombe, 1976b:165–70; Suh, 1969).
10. I have drawn heavily on John N. Hazard's reviews of Soviet international legal sources that have appeared in the *American Journal of International Law* during the last several years. (See also Tunkin, 1974.)
11. Soviet legal theory implies a parallel suspicion of the doctrine of *jus cogens*, rules of general international law, as a guide and limit to treatymaking (cf. Rozakis, 1976).

12. A statistical study of international organizations provides more systematic evidence of Northwestern dominance. It reports a relatively close relationship between membership in international organizations and level of economic development. Involvement in international organizations reflects "the stratification of the international system caused by different degrees of economic and technological development." Further, memberships in international organizations tend to "reinforce rather than reduce the stratification of the international system caused by great differences in economic development" (Skjelsbaek, 1972:323–25; cf. Sullivan, 1978).
13. Northwestern analysts suggest that COMECON promotes intrabloc relations of dependence and inequality (Stehr, 1977). It accommodates desires of Soviet leaders for continuing economic influence and of Eastern European leaders for assistance in economic development.
14. See particularly A. G. Frank (1978, 1977); Amin (1974); Hayter (1971). See also Gobalet and Diamond (1979); Modelski (1979b); Steiber (1979); Bornschier et al. (1978); Richardson (1978); Delacroix (1977); Caporaso (1976); Grundy (1976); Rubinson (1976); Chase-Dunn (1975); Käkönen (1975); Kaufman et al. (1975); Plaschke (1975); Tuomi (1975); Väyrynen and Herrera (1975); Beer and Wyner (1974); Wittkopf (1973).
15. We may picture the relation between long- and short-term change as follows:

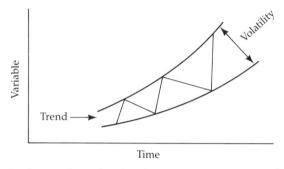

16. An increase in the number of national governments accounts for some of the increase in national political instability.
17. Alcock et al. (1978:51) outline the major alleged cycles:

Cycle	Length, in Years
Kitchin	3.3–3.4
Business	3–7
Juglar	8–11
Kuznets	15–25
Kondratieff	50–60

18. Differentiation implies that cleavages between international groups cut across many different sectors of activity. Potential conflict is more likely to result in violence because aggregative forces are relatively weak and divisive pressures strong. Furthermore, since there are few actors, decisionmakers can give more attention and resources to violent competition with their major rivals.

Relatively undifferentiated environments might help the system hold together better. Low differentiation implies a pluralistic world of cross-cutting cleavages. There should be a seamless web of countervailing loyalties, interests, and resources.

Such an environment should encourage a tendency to cooperate in peaceful change and to negotiate rather than fight.

19. A recent study investigated the relationship of major wars and major public international organizations in the nineteenth and twentieth centuries. The author expected an association between war and differentiation. He thought that, beginning about ten years before the war, shared memberships in international organizations would begin to separate out, with prospective partners joining together more densely and prospective opponents dissociating. Following the war, he believed, the pattern of shared memberships should come together again.

The data confirmed the expected separation out of prospective opponents. The data also showed a weakening of aggregative strands within the groups. Surprisingly, prospective partners also began to dissociate. Ten years after the war, neither partners nor opponents had reestablished the level of international organizational partnership that had existed before the war (Skjelsbaek, 1971).

20. All possible aspects of differentiation have not been examined. A particular difficulty is that polarity is often defined in terms of alliances, which infuses a military element. This mixture of differentiation and militarization makes it difficult to say whether differentiation has a direct influence on international violence, or whether such influence is a more indirect result of militarization. The statistical relations of those aspects of differentiation studied, with violence, are often weak. Relations are not constant over different time periods. There may be important differences, for example, between the statistical results discovered for the nineteenth and twentieth centuries.

21. A good deal of theory and research centers on the relationship of political concentration to domestic violence. On the one hand, domestic violence may contribute to political concentration. A study of historical bureaucratic empires suggests that they typically grew "during a period of unrest, turmoil, or dissolution of the existing political system (whether a patrician city-state, a tribe, a patrimonial empire, or a feudal system) or of acute strife within it" (Eisenstadt, 1963:14). In modern societies, internal turbulence, insurrection, subversion, secession have called forth counterrevolutionary forces before, during, or after the fact (see Mayer, 1971; Lipset, 1968; Meisel, 1966). Whether or not attacks have overturned the state, they have often strengthened it.

Sorokin, drawing on the European experience, observes that:

> Governmental control in the form of revolutionary or counterrevolutionary dictatorship usually increases in the periods of great revolutions. Such periods are marked by an extraordinary impoverishment and disorganization of economic life. Hence its result—an extraordinary increase of governmental control of the entire economic life of a revolutionary society. Sometimes it leads to an establishment of a "communist" or "state-socialist organization" in a revolutionary country, like the communist societies in Tabor (in revolutionary Bohemia), in Mühlhausen, in New Jerusalem, or in Paris in 1871, to mention but a few cases of that kind. In other cases it assumes other forms of totalitarianism: absolutism, dictatorship, fascism, Nazism, etc. (1937:204).

In France, the United States, Russia, and China, revolutions have contributed significantly to the growth of the power of central governments. Revolution has "left the state enlarged, better organized, more potent, and with wider areas of influence; that has been the pattern even when revolution has assaulted and attempted to diminish the state" (Ellul, 1971:160–63 cited in Johnson, 1973:105).

Governmental centralization may also help create domestic violence. A good deal of contemporary statistical research has suggested that decentralized, democratic, or "polyarchical" societies have fewer incidents of domestic violence than more centralized states (cf. Nesvold, 1971:182; Flanigan and Fogelman, 1970).

The concentration of power at the top can make centralized regimes susceptible to sudden coups.

> The growth of vast administrative networks under centralized and even largely automated direction may have the seemingly paradoxical result of making top control spots more vulnerable than before to individual and small-group strategies of power seizure (Lasswell, 1962:58; cf. Eckstein, 1970:178).

Following the same line of argument,

> revolutionary wars occur when the government is distant—politically, socially, even geographically—from a significant counterelite. Recourse to revolutionary war is a sign that the counterelite has failed to penetrate the existing political structure. . . . Divorced from the existing political system, the counterelite attempts to develop a parallel structure independent of the government. Its goal is usually the overthrow of the entire existing political and social system. . . . The decisive aspect of revolutionary war is the contest between the counterelite and the government for the support of a communal or socio-economic group that is imperfectly integrated into the existing political system (Huntington, 1962:24).

Recent work, however, casts doubt on this line of thought. A major cross-national study finds that "democratic political structures and processes apparently bear no direct relation to the cross-national incidence of mass political violence. Democratic nations experience about as much violent political conflict as do non-democratic ones" (Hibbs, 1973:130).

22. Olin (1972) applies the theory of population pressure to revolutionary movements.

Contemporary research on American cities of different sizes suggests that the size of a city is exponentially associated with the rate of violent crime. "Murder, robbery, and aggravated assault increase at an increasing rate with aggregate size" or urban population (Mayhew and Levinger, 1976:98–99).

Historical research has failed to confirm this for all kinds of violence. Thus, in France during the nineteenth century, the size of urban population was positively related to property crime, variably related to violent crime, and unreliably related to personal crime (Lodhi and Tilly, 1973).

A contemporary cross-national study, moreover, finds a high level of urbanization compared to economic development has only a modest relationship to domestic violence (Hibbs, 1973:52).

23. Considerable social theory and research has concentrated on the relationship of urbanization to domestic violence. Classical sociological theory suggests that urban centers destroy meaningful relations between individuals. Overcrowding, anonymity, and anomie provide the bases for a high rate of individual and mob violence (cf. Nye, 1975; Durkheim, 1972:Ch. 8; LeBon, 1968; Hall, 1966).

24. Stein summarizes knowledge about conflict and cohesion.

> There is a clear convergence in the literature in both the specific studies and in the various disciplines, that suggests that external conflict does increase internal cohesion under certain conditions. These conditions act as intervening variables and involve, as one could have logically expected, the nature of the external conflict and the nature of the group. The external conflict needs to involve some threat, affect the entire group and all its members equally and indiscriminately, and involve a solution (or at least there must be a useful purpose in group efforts regarding the threat). The group needs to have been an ongoing one with some pre-existing cohesion or consensus, and to have a leadership that can authoritatively enforce cohesion (especially if all the members of the group do not feel the threat). The group must be able to deal with the external conflict, and to provide emotional comfort and support to its members (1976:165).

25. Much theory and research propose that domestic violence is more frequent in societies with substantial ethnic divisions. More recent statistical modeling, however, suggests that ethnolinguistic fractionalization is related only indirectly to domestic violence (Hibbs, 1973:68–71, 181).

26. Contemporary writings on imperialism include Rosen and Kurth (1974); Hayter (1971); Baran and Sweezy (1969); Magdoff (1969); Bosch (1968); Barnet (1968). Brodie (1973: Ch. 7) critically reviews earlier historical literature. See note 14, Chapter 4.

27. We should note that these studies include military expenditure and manpower in their definitions of rank and power. Stein and Russett (1980) find some additional methodological problems.

28. Laboratory experiments and simulations also provide different results. One study states that uneven status between groups does not seem to encourage war and may help deter it. Environments with more unequal status relations have less frequent confrontations (Pfister, 1974:52). Another study, taking a game-theoretical perspective, suggests that power inequalities tend to enhance the propensity to go to war although coalition formation provides a damper (Zinnes et al., 1978a; cf. Hartman et al., 1976).

29. A large body of theory and research deals with the possible relationship between internal inequality and domestic violence.

Some work has suggested a positive association between domestic violence and inequality of land tenure (Prosterman, 1976; cf. Russett, 1964; see also Russett et al , 1964:320–31). Nevertheless, problems of statistical analysis, as well as variations in particular cases, require us to suspend judgment (cf. Nagel, 1976, 1974; Rummel, 1972:357; Russo, 1972; Mitchell, 1968).

The relationship of income inequality and domestic violence is equally obscure. In a cross-national study of 49 contemporary nations, domestic income inequality did not appreciably add to the power of other key variables in explaining internal war (Sigelman and Simpson, 1977). Intersectoral income inequality was inversely related to domestic violence in another contemporary sample of 26 Western countries (Parvin, 1973).

Other work has focused on group discrimination. One study of peaceful primitive societies found that none of them practiced discrimination (Fabbro, 1978). Discrimination has a strong intuitive appeal as an explanation for cases like the black urban riots in the United States and revolutionary movements in the Third World (cf. Feagin and Hahn, 1973). A quantitative statistical study of terrorism in societies during the 1960s has also found that discrimination was the single most important variable producing territorism (Hamilton, 1978).

Nevertheless, the relationship between discrimination and domestic violence has been very difficult to pin down using comparative statistics. Hibbs proposes that group discrimination contributes slightly to collective protest, but not directly to coups or internal war (1973:181; cf. Alcock, 1976:98).

Finally a recent study developed a number of different measures for equality that showed no direct relationship with domestic violence (Jackman, 1975:117, 196, 199).

30. Work discussing the relationship of war and economic cycles includes Blainey (1973:91–96); Flamant and Singer-Kérel (1970); Weinstock (1964); L. Wilson (1964). See also Tinbergen and Polak (1950); Schumpeter (1939); Macfie (1938); Hansen (1932:93ff.); and Sorokin (1925:376ff.).

31. Cf. Tomlin and Buhlman (1977); Midlarsky (1975); Ferris (1973:115); Wallace (1973b, 1972, 1971); East (1972); Hernes (1969); Singer and Small (1966); and Galtung (1964). Status inconsistency may have effects at all levels of society. See, for example, Hornung (1977), and Wan (1973).

32. A voluminous literature centers on the relationship between domestic violence and instability. (See, for example Lieske, 1979; Given, 1977:187; Miller et al., 1977;

Jacobson, 1976; Davies, 1974, 1973, 1972, 1971; Snyder and Tilly, 1974, 1973, 1972; Halaby, 1973; Feierabend et al., 1972; Kirkham et al., 1970:183; Gurr, 1972, 1970; and Lupsha, 1971.)

All this work has still not confirmed the relationship. Thus Hibbs' final multiequation model contains only one change variable—energy conservation 1955–1965 (1973:181). This has an extremely limited impact, and a negative one at that.

CHAPTER 5

1. Kemp sketches a causal model similar to ours, where differentiated territories, colonies, and multinational corporations help produce military alliances and arms expenditures that in turn lead to international violence (1976:75). Note also that aggregative international nongovernmental and governmental organizations, and international trade, inhibit arms expenditures:

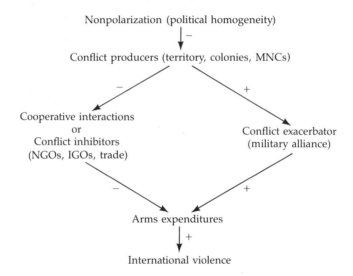

M. Haas presents and tests a number of more complex models of international systemic process and national war propensity (1974:290–97, 450–53). However, the cross-national data do not yield very satisfactory results.

2. Some attempts have been made to assess the statistical association between the differentiation of international coalitions and aspects of alliances, but the results are not conclusive. M. Haas reports limited associations between the number and tightness of poles, on the one hand, and various alliance characteristics, on the other (1974:382). Li and Thompson note "randomness and instability of alliance formation behavior in the multipolar/loosely knit periods of 1815–1914 and 1919–1939 and serial dependence and stability in the bipolar/tightly knit 1945–1965 period" (1978:1288; cf. Job, 1976; Siverson and Duncan, 1976). Such results are difficult to interpret because the poles appear to be defined partly in terms of alliance participation.

3. Department of State, Bureau of Intelligence and Research report noted in *Atlantic Community News*, February 1979.

4. These are rough characterizations of international stereotypes. An interesting empirical corroboration comes from a recent study that investigated stereotypes associated with world superpowers among students at a British university. In general the students of this major developed country rated the superpowers as strong and bad (Lawson and Giles, 1973; cf. Buchanan and Cantril, 1953).

A more traditional approach focuses on the militaristic element of world ideologies like conservatism, liberalism, and radicalism (Nelson and Olin, 1979). The U.S.S.R.'s view of war, peace, and neutrality, based on the writings of Marx, Engels, and Lenin, eerily reflects Clausewitz. It emphasizes the inevitability of war between capitalism and communism, and war as the tool and continuation of revolutionary policy (Vigor, 1975).

5. McNeill makes more general connections.

> Cannon were expensive, requiring large amounts of metal for their manufacture and rare skills for their management. Governments became fewer and more capable of maintaining domestic peace over broader regions of the earth, thanks to the global diffusion of a new weapon, the cannon (1976:232; cf. Howard, 1979).

6. The political sociology of the professional military is quite extensive. (See particularly Enloe, 1979; Sabrosky, 1979; Bienen, 1978, 1971; Margiotta, 1978; Simon, 1978; Trimberger, 1978; Abercrombie, 1977; Fitch, 1977; Kourvetaris and Dobratz, 1977; Levitan and Alderman, 1977; Perlmutter, 1977; Lissak, 1976; McCubbin et al., 1976; Moskos, 1976; Sarkesian and Gannon, 1976; Gutteridge, 1975; Janowitz, 1975, 1964, 1960; Van Doorn, 1975; Kelleher, 1974; Kennedy, 1974; Larson, 1974; Welch and Smith, 1974; Bradford and Brown, 1973; Hyman, 1973; Lang, 1972; Abrahamsson, 1971; Janowitz and Van Doorn, 1971; Little, 1971; Janowitz and Little, 1965; Finer, 1962; Huntington, 1962, 1957; Johnson, 1962; Roberts, 1962.)

7. The literature on this subject is enormous and controversial. (See especially Blong et al., 1976; Eckhardt, 1979, 1976, 1972, 1969; Eckhardt and Young, 1975; Etheredge, 1975; Granberg, 1975; Miale and Selzer, 1975; Ray, 1971; Kelman, 1973, 1972; Krauss et al., 1973; Mann, 1973; Phillips, 1973; Suedfeld and Epstein, 1973; Stinchcombe, 1973; Beit-Hallahmi, 1972; Fine, 1972; Gabbenesch, 1972; Granberg and Corrigan, 1972; Hochreich, 1972; Kelman and Lawrence, 1972; Roghmann and Sodeur, 1972; Sodeur and Roghmann, 1972; Abrahamsson, 1971:9, 78–79, 98–99, 111; Markowitz, 1971; Sniderman and Citrin, 1971; Levy, 1970. Classic works include Reich, 1971; Lasswell, 1969, 1965a; Arendt, 1963; Rokeach, 1960; Smith et al., 1956; Adorno et al., 1950; Fromm, 1941.)

8. Mailer (1970) imagines that the manned lunar landing represented a triumph of Apollonian rationality over Dionysian spontaneity, that the whole endeavor represented the flowering of the values associated with the Protestant ethic.

9. A simple way to do this would be to compare a Gini index of international inequality with military expenditure/international product or military forces/population.

10. In the early 1960s global military expenditures were "roughly equal to the income of the poorer half of mankind. . . . Because of the very large income of the rich countries, however," they represented "something less than 10 percent of the gross world product" (Boulding, 1963b:3).

11. Dahl and Tufte speculate on some of the possible reasons for this relationship:

> Since our findings run directly counter to the highly plausible conjecture that in order to maintain their independence small countries would have to spend more per capita than large countries, how do we account for the results?
>
> 1. It is possible that citizens and leaders in many smaller countries (there are notable exceptions) recognize that in a confrontation with a determined larger power they cannot maintain their independence exclusively by military means, no matter how much they might spend on defense. Suppose, for example, that an effective defense against invasion by a large country would require a small country to spend $10 billion a year. Suppose the small country's GNP is $5 billion. It could not possibly spend enough to prevent the

large country from invading, if it were determined to do so. Hence the small country would have to search for a strategy of dissuasion that would not rely on its own military resources. With a GNP of $30 billion, however, a third country could choose to spend one-third of its GNP on defense against the large country's potential aggression, for an outlay of $10 billion would provide it with a relatively high degree of insurance against invasion.

2. If small countries enter into alliances with large countries, they can take refuge under the umbrella of the large country. The total expenditures by the alliance will far exceed what would be possible for the small country. However, the large country dare not reduce total expenditures on defense; yet ordinarily it cannot coerce the small country into maintaining defense outlays; hence the small countries in an alliance may be able to get by with lower defense expenditures per capita than the large, powerful leaders of the alliance. This appears to be the case with the NATO alliance, for example.

3. Typically, the large country is more forceful, aggressive, dominant. Large states are leaders of alliances, centers of polarizing forces in the world, headquarters of empire. Their role induces them to make greater per capita expenditures on military matters in order to fulfill the requirements of the role. Where the small country concerns itself almost exclusively with countries that are on its borders, very large countries seek to defend themselves against other large countries no matter where they are located; and large countries play some part in every region of the world.

4. Some types of military goods are so inordinately costly that small countries may simply forgo them entirely; nuclear-powered submarines, intercontinental bombers, nuclear weapons, ICBMs and long-range missiles, for example.

There may be and there doubtless are any number of other explanations. But one thing is clear: smaller countries have lower costs of survival than do larger countries, as can be measured by per capita expenditures for defense (1973:126–27).

The relationship is less clear if one attempts to relate military expenditures as a percentage of GNP to GNP per capita (cf. U.S. ACDA, 1978:4; Uslaner, 1976).

12. Herrell (1972) provides an interesting sidelight to this theme. He finds that first-born males are overrepresented among military leaders (cf. Stewart, 1977).

13. One cross-national sample reveals a substantial relationship between a nation's military personnel and defense expenditure with the Gini index of inequality in land distribution. This relationship may be at least partly spurious. It still exists, but in a milder form, with controls for total population and GNP (Rummel, 1972:App. 2).

14. We should note that members of governmental agencies do not always single-mindedly pursue narrow organizational interests. One study, for example, shows that members of the National Security Council do not decide on arms transfers to Latin America primarily on the basis of the self-interest dictated by bureaucratic politics. Rather "the most important independent variable is the strategic perspective held by the members of the National Security Council" (S. S. Kaplan, 1975:399).

15. It must be noted, in the American context, that "the majority of the largest industrial corporations generally derive only a small portion of their total business from primary military contracts," though there may be substantial indirect benefits to them. A regression analysis of corporate income after taxes in relation to governmental expenditures between 1916 and 1965 shows that "corporate income is more closely linked to nonmilitary expenditures than to military spending." Thus, while a complex of corporations with an interest in high defense expenditures does exist, military procurement is not the main business of the largest corporations (Rosen, 1973:6; Lieberson, 1973).

16. Fitzgerald (1972), Kaufman (1970), and Proxmire (1970) state this argument particularly strongly.

17. We should note that U.S. business leaders, in general, are not necessarily militaristic. One study suggests that business people emphasize the values of peace and prosperity (see Russett and Hansen, 1975). However, other research finds that

American business executives, together with military officers, "provide the strongest support for Cold War positions" (Holsti and Rosenau, 1980:14; cf. Holsti and Rosenau, 1979; Holsti, 1979).

Militaristic political leaders may not be from the constituencies receiving the defense contracts. Studies of voting in the American Congress have shown that representatives and senators from districts or states with high military activity do not necessarily tend to vote for defense spending either on the floor on in committees. Nor do those from areas where there is low defense spending generally tend to vote against it. One analyst notes that:

> While for the House as a whole there was little support for the hypothesis that representatives from districts highly dependent on defense spending were more likely than representatives from nondependent districts to vote for jingoistic foreign and defense policies, certain subgroups such as the very senior members did evidence such correlation between defense spending concentrations and voting (Cobb, 1976:163; cf. Rundquist and Griffith, 1976; Bozeman and James, 1975; Cobb, 1973; Moyer, 1973; Russett, 1970b: Ch. 3; Gray and Gregory, 1968).

Recent research has begun to specify a more general pattern in which defense spending is related to the electoral cycle (see particularly Nincic and Cusack, 1979).

18. A statistical study of the last two centuries shows a strong direct positive relationship between status inconsistency and alliances (Wallace, 1972:63–65).

19. Richardson (1960a) pioneered in developing the theory of arms races. Contemporary arms race literature is voluminous (cf. Majeski and Jones, 1980; Gillespie et al., 1980; Moll and Luebbert, 1980; Wallace, 1980; Saris and Middendorp, 1980; Köhler, 1979; Lucier, 1979; Intriligator and Brito, 1978, 1977; Schrodt, 1978; Wallace and Wilson, 1978; Hamblin et al., 1977; Hilton, 1977; Kupperman and Smith, 1976; Luttwak, 1974; Rohwer, 1974; Steiner, 1973; Busch, 1970; Saaty, 1968; Wolfson, 1968; Caspary, 1967; Smoker, 1967a, 1966; Dash, 1967; Moberg, 1966; McGuire, 1965; Intriligator, 1964; Boulding, 1962; Rapoport, 1957).

20. The relationship between hostility and other aspects of international militarization may be quite complex. Goldmann (1974:202) presents an example of the intricate possibilities. His model is roughly consistent with quantitative European data between 1946 and 1970:

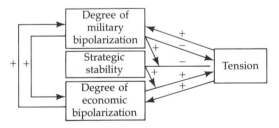

If we translate:

Tension = International hostility
Military bipolarization = International alliance differentiation
Economic bipolarization = International transaction differentiation
Strategic stability = International arms stability

21. One analyst explains the passage from civilian to military rule in terms of exchange analysis:

> As regimes and their leadership become increasingly dependent on force, the regime-military exchange process—the application of force in return for a share of the regime's

allocations of money, manpower, status, and autonomy—is likely to become asymmetrical. Regimes that lack the other essential supporting resources of government can hardly be expected to retain control over the military. Those people who do control the military in such circumstances possess an option of temporarily dissolving the exchange relationship and replacing the regime or its leadership. Possession of the option means that demands from the military will logically receive preferential treatment lest the official physical force resource be withheld or turned against the nominal incumbents. Where this political logic prevails, the regime, its leadership, and the political system are subject to increasing control by the military. Where the logic breaks down, a military coup may institute a more favorable return from the exchange process, especially if corporate and not-so-corporate interests are threatened (Thompson, 1975:485; cf. Thompson and Christopherson, 1979).

Hibbs (1973:181) confirms a positive relationship between defense expenditures as a percent of general government expenditure and coups d'état.

22. These general results parallel Brown's (1969:10) study of Latin American states.

We should note that foreign assistance may help produce both general and military growth. Thus, a statistical control for foreign aid may wash out the relationship between GNP growth and defense spending/GNP.

Some additional evidence is counter to this proposition. Another cross-national study reports conflicting influences. Change in government budget per capita predicts positively, and change in the number of government ministries predicts negatively, to military–administrative budget/GNP (M. Haas, 1974:292, 296). Further, in a sample of African states during the 1960s, GNP, both in absolute terms and relative to population, and gross domestic capital formation, increased more rapidly in civilian-ruled than in military-ruled countries.

23. A contemporary cross-national survey shows a relationship between two indicators of instability—change in government budget per capita and imbalance between energy consumption and production—and military budget as a proportion of GNP. As we suggested in note 22, however, an unchanged number of government ministries is also associated with high military budget (M. Haas, 1974:296).

24. Different analysts have suggested that militarization also has a direct effect on aggregation. The nature of this effect, however, is not clear, and the supporting evidence is weak. From one point of view, militarization has seemed to have a positive direct effect on aggregation. For example, some writers see alliances as building blocks for more universal cooperation. A study of Europe's classical balance of power noted "progress from anarchy to alliance balance to coalition equilibrium to confederation to federation" (Gulick, 1955:307). More recent research, however, suggests that alliances are weak foundation stones for expanded world order. Alliances *do* involve international cooperation, but the cooperation is a result of threats and crises. The process can be abstractly modeled as shown in the figure on the facing page. An increase in security and a decline in the level of perceived threat deprive alliances of their central defensive function. Under such conditions they tend to stagnate or wither away (cf. Beer, 1974, 1969; Kaplan, 1957:Ch. 1).

A second point of view suggests that military activities have a direct negative effect on aggregation. This perspective implies that the international law of war, alliances, military trade, and hostility—combined with national military regimes, military complexes, and militance—work against more general constructive international and national structures and processes. This perspective goes against the grain of the argument and evidence we have so far presented. We have tried to show how the development of modern technology naturally includes both constructive and destructive dimensions.

25. Burns (1977) provides a comprehensive bibliography of work in this area. See also Russett and Blair (1979); Barton and Weiler (1976); Myrdal (1976); American Academy of Arts and Sciences (1975); and the cumulative work published by SIPRI.

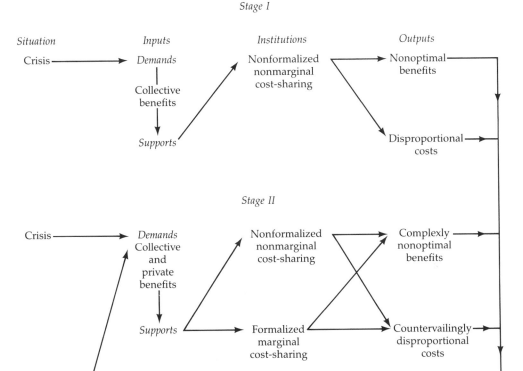

Stage I

Situation	Inputs	Institutions	Outputs
Crisis	Demands	Nonformalized nonmarginal cost-sharing	Nonoptimal benefits
	Collective benefits		
	Supports		Disproportional costs

Stage II

Crisis → Demands Collective and private benefits → Supports

Nonformalized nonmarginal cost-sharing

Formalized marginal cost-sharing

Complexly nonoptimal benefits

Countervailingly disproportional costs

Alliance Dynamics

26. One analyst discusses these agreements as follows:

> Until the United States and the Soviet Union signed the strategic arms limitation agreements in 1972, the Washington and London naval treaties of 1922 and 1930, respectively, constituted the only serious attempt in modern times to limit the development and deployment of weapons central to the military posture of the great powers. The treaties are impressive in the scope of their objectives, in their elaborate and prudent detail, and in their efforts to take account of the conflicting interests of five independent parties in several interrelated but relatively autonomous arenas. Most historians agree that they had an important effect on naval expenditures during the interwar years and, consequently, on how fast and in what way the navies expanded. Yet despite this to their credit, the overall evaluation of the treaties is still dubious. Many observers question how they affected the balance of military power and—what is more important—their long-run effect on political relations among the great powers (Blechman, 1975:14–15).

27. The final Act is divided into what has become known as three "baskets." Basket I deals with questions relating to security in Europe and comprises a Declaration on Principles Guiding Relations between Participating States, some related texts concerning implementation of the principle of abstention from the threat or use of force, and a proposal for a new system for the peaceful settlement of disputes, as well as some modest confidence-building measures entailing notification of military maneuvers and voluntary exchange of observers at such maneuvers. Basket II deals in general terms with cooperation in the fields of economics, science and technology, and the environment, and Basket III with cooperation in humanitarian and other fields (H. S. Russell, 1976:243).

28. Works on proliferation include SIPRI (1979b, 1979c); Marwah and Pollack (1978); Overholt (1977); Epstein (1976); and Quester (1973).

29. Kistiakowsky (1979) presents a lucid discussion of the arms debate over the last quarter century and of the issues of SALT II. (See also Scoville, 1977.)

30. For discussions of various aspects of verification see Kistiakowsky (1979); SIPRI (1977a); and Holzman (1975). Kissinger (1975) thoroughly discusses alleged Soviet violations of existing SALT agreements.

31. The first major difference appeared before the Quadruple Alliance was even concluded. Russian Czar Alexander I wanted to establish a new international order that would be based not on traditional diplomacy but on the principles of Christianity. Austria and Prussia joined Russia in the Holy Alliance to be based on these principles. British Foreign Secretary Viscount Castlereagh, however, "refused to have anything to do with it. 'The fact is,' he wrote to his prime minister, 'that the Emperor's mind is not completely sound' " (Craig, 1961:19).

32. One analyst describes the relationship between alliances and international tension during the interwar period as follows:

> In the international system at the time of the League's establishment in 1919, a dominant feature was the existence of a victorious alliance, which dictated the terms of the postwar settlement. But at an early stage, the withdrawal of the United States to isolation, and the consolidation of the Bolshevik regime in Russia reduced the scope and cohesiveness of the grand alliance. Simultaneously, the defeated Central Powers were the victims of domestic chaos and conflict aggravated by external pressures. A number of new states were created, with problems of legitimacy only partly solved by the support of the Allied and Associated Powers.
>
> From 1920 until 1925, the rigidity of alliances continued to decline, and the treatment of the defeated states became an increasing source of tensions. This period saw shifting patterns of influence in Europe, but also confirmed the withdrawal of the Americans and the Soviet regime. Anglo-French relations came under increasing strain, especially over Germany; and it was the German problem which acted as the focus of the diplomacy leading to the Locarno treaties in 1925. Central to these negotiations was the choice between modification and consolidation of the 1919 settlement—a choice which enabled Stresemann, the German Foreign Minister, to play on the differences between Britain and France. The eventual treaties can be seen as a victory for the more conciliatory British attitude, but were seen by the Germans themselves as only the first step in a more fundamental reorientation of European power. There followed a period of what has been termed "Locarno diplomacy," seemingly embodying the spirit of moderation and conciliation, yet during which few really important problems were solved. Increasing flexibility of alignment and orientation was accompanied by a growth of American concern for the state of Europe, but this was of an exhortatory rather than a material kind.
>
> In the early 1930s, it became clearer that the tensions arising from the peace settlement had not been resolved, and economic collapse further contributed to a revival of militant nationalism. A fluid situation arose, in which positive—often reckless—action could be profitable. The growing pervasiveness of nationalism and militarism, expressed in autarky and territorial expansion, was met in many instances by uncertainty and appeasement. Although there were attempts to re-establish or consolidate alignments, it was arguably not until 1941 that solidarity in the face of the Fascist threat was achieved (Smith, 1976:316–17).

33. Alperovitz (1965) presents an early, American revisionist interpretation of this period. Vladimirov and Teplov (1977) and Kukanov (1971) give a more purely Soviet view of NATO.

34. Nation-months of war is a measure that, as the name suggests, multiplies the number of nations involved in a war times the number of months they fight in it. The measure is justified by the idea that each large war is composed of many small wars between particular pairs of nations, and that these smaller wars go on for varying lengths of time. At the same time, absolute nation-months of war can rise not only because wars may be larger, but also because the number of states has increased (cf. Kemp, 1976; Midlarsky, 1975:76).

35. The relationship between alliances and war incidence has been further tested against more complex causal and probability models. Such testing has not produced determinate results. The association between alliance membership and war frequencies varies during different time periods. Different methods of testing also make a difference (cf. Ostrom and Hoole, 1978; Job, 1976; Siverson and Duncan, 1976; McGowan and Rood, 1975; Wallace, 1972).

36. Smoker explains cases where arms races do not lead to war by this "mutual submissiveness effect." It is a

> safety mechanism which, like a thermostat, operates when things are becoming too hot. . . . It is also my contention that when the international climate cools off sufficiently, when there is less tension, then the thermostat will switch off and the arms race will accelerate once again. This will lead to a cyclic arms race with defense ratios oscillating between maximum and minimum values (1964:579; cf. K. Boulding, 1962:33–34).

37. Kende (1977) labels this pattern a "scissors effect."

38. We should note that the demobilization of the enemy is also an important concern of modern psychological warfare. During World War II, for example, the Allies promised good treatment to Axis troops who surrendered.

39. Snyder and Diesing (1977:App.) present sketches of some major twentieth-century crises. Major work on international crises includes Hermann (1972, 1969); Holsti (1972a); and McClelland (1968, 1964).

40. Duncan and Siverson (1975) and Smoker (1969) present similar analyses of contemporary Sino-Indian conflicts. Andriole and Young (1977:127, 133) do the same for the conflict between the Soviet Union and Czechoslovakia in 1968.

41. Gamson and Modigliani see the first generation of the Cold War as a series of phases.

> The first, short phase runs from the beginning of the Cold War to the announcement of the Truman Doctrine in March, 1947. This phase is characterized by relatively belligerent Western behavior and varied or erratic Soviet behavior. While the West was uniformly refractory in its major actions and had no pattern below balanced, the Soviet coalition had a mixture of conciliatory and refractory responses and patterns ranging from fairly accommodative to extremely belligerent.
>
> The second phase bgins in 1947 and lasts until the beginning of the stalemate in Korea following the full-scale Chinese entry into the war. It is characterized by relatively belligerent behavior and refractory responses by both coalitions.
>
> The Korean stalemate begins the third phase, which ends with the almost simultaneous interventions in Suez and Hungary in October and November, 1956. It is characterized by relatively accommodative behavior and an unusually high percentage of conciliatory responses by both sides.
>
> The fourth phase begins with Suez-Hungary and ends with the Cuban missile crisis in October, 1962. We do not consider Phase IVa a genuine phase of the Cold War. . . . Both sides tended to respond in a refractory fashion to a range of patterns; however, the Soviet coalition also responded to Western belligerence in a conciliatory fashion on a number of occasions.
>
> The final phase runs from the Cuban missile crisis to . . . November, 1963. The few interaction units here, like those of the third phase, reflect mutual accommodation (1971:113; cf. Goldmann and Lagerkranz, 1977; Goldmann, 1973).

42. Data on symbolic involvement were derived from a content analysis of President Johnson's speeches on Vietnam from 1964 to 1968. The entire list of symbolic tip-off words was broken down into "positive" or highly-valued symbols (such as "democracy," "freedom," "liberty," and "justice"), and "negative" symbols (such as "terror," "anarchy," "violence," and "aggression"). Finally, more specific hypotheses from the conflict literature suggested that sub-samples of the "positive" group of symbols might be related to escalation: two of these were "commitment" symbols (such as "determination" and "commitment"), and "status" symbols (such as "honor," "will," and "status") (Sullivan and Thomas, 1972:185).

43. We should note that the metaphor of the escalation ladder has serious analytical deficiencies. First, it assumes linearity. Actually escalation may be discontinuous, going back and forth, skipping steps. Second, it assumes uniformity. Higher steps may be steeper (less probable) and also narrower (more military). Third, it suggests finitude. A ladder has a fixed number of steps. Actually the number of discrete actions that can be taken can be expanded or contracted by the actors. Finally, it suggests a high degree of rationality, that the same cognitive dynamics exist in routine and crisis situations. There may be much less rationality at higher levels as the so-called "logic" of the situation becomes overpowering. Shorter time, greater urgency, more limited-decision groups may all work to limit the range of apparent choice and to provoke further advance (cf. Smoke, 1977).

44. Hostile political and diplomatic gestures are also associated with high levels of military personnel and expenditure (Rummel, 1972:358).

45. McNeill puts the argument in epidemiological terms.

> A successful government immunizes those who pay rent and taxes against catastrophic raids and foreign invasion in the same way that a low-grade infection can immunize its host against lethally disastrous disease invasion. Disease immunity arises by stimulating the formation of antibodies and raising other physiological defenses to a heightened level of activity; governments improve immunity to foreign macroparasitism by stimulating surplus production of food and raw materials sufficient to support specialists in violence in suitably large numbers and with appropriate weaponry. Both defense reactions constitute burdens on the host populations, but a burden less onerous than periodic exposure to sudden lethal disaster.
>
> The result of establishing successful governments is to create a vastly more formidable society vis-à-vis other human communities. Specialists in violence can scarcely fail to prevail against men who have to spend most of their time producing or finding food. And . . . a suitably diseased society, in which endemic forms of viral and bacterial infection continually provoke antibody formation by invading susceptible individuals unceasingly, is so vastly more formidable from an epidemiological point of view vis-à-vis simpler and healthier human societies (1976:54–55).

46. This does not mean that democracies never have gone to war. Some of the most violent wars in history had been fought by presumably open and democratic polities such as classical Athens, Rome, or the modern United States, Britain, and France. Tocqueville would explain this away by separating democratic civilians from their armies. "Of all nations, those most fond of peace are democratic nations," he wrote. Yet the desire for advancement in an egalitarian system seems to create the paradox that "of all armies, those most ardently desirous of war are democratic armies" (Tocqueville, 1956:II; cf. Cook, 1962:38).

Moore takes a darker view. He believes that one of the hallmarks of contemporary democratic regimes is the external projection of violence that their apologists claim they avoid. His view is that "the repression by liberal society both under earlier imperialism and again now in the armed struggle against revolutionary movements in the backward areas, has been directed very heavily outward, against others" (1966:508).

47. Reality is more complex than this stereotype suggests. Military leaders do not always recommend more forceful action than civilians. Often they are more conscious of the dangers and costs. Thus, Marshal Pétain surrendered France to the Germans in World War II, partly to avoid repeating the bloodbath of World War I.

General Eisenhower refused to support forceful direct American intervention in Indochina. Generals Ridgway and Gavin publicly opposed subsequent American involvement in Vietnam, and American generals in the field in Vietnam had serious questions about whether or not the war was worthwhile (Betts, 1977; Kinnard, 1977, 1976; cf. Dixon, 1976).

48. Wright also suggests that battles were more frequent when military techniques were most advanced (1965:572–74; cf. Wesson, 1967).

49. Sherry (1977) shows how American military planning helped shape the Cold War.

50. The only exception to this pattern is a slight dip in army/population in the fifteenth century.

51. Hamblin et al. discuss the data as follows:

> The military data are not nearly as regular as the civilian data. Nevertheless, from 1794 through 1940 the diffusion of the military is characterized by one long exponential epoch. The most significant deviations during that time involve large temporary increases during the major wars: the War of 1812, the Mexican War, the Civil War, the Spanish-American War, and World Wars I and II. The only other major deviation was an exponential decline in military personnel after the Civil War and a steady state between 1878 and 1896.
>
> The data since 1940 paint a very interesting picture—a predictably huge increase in military personnel during World War II, a 70 percent decrease in personnel right afterward, and a quasi-equilibrium during the Cold War period. The data indicate very little change in military personnel during the wars in Korea and Southeast Asia (1973:98–99).

52. Wright describes a relatively small increase in the military participation ratio in the twentieth century, which is not enough to explain the sharp upsurge in casualties (1965:242). Nevertheless, more recent figures may be underestimated because of the difficulty in determining the correct absolute figure for army size in an age where the possibility of massive civilian mobilization produces accordionlike expansion and deflation.

53. Cf. Weede (1975:Ch. 6); M. Haas (1974:213, 242, 292, 461); and Rummel (1972:358).

Hibbs finds little statistical relationship between military personnel or defense expenditure, on the one hand, and domestic violence (1973:Ch. 6; cf. Rummel, 1972:App. 2; Bwy, 1971; Russett et al., 1964:269, 319).

Kegley et al. suggest that military expenditure as a percentage of GNP mediates between foreign and domestic violence.

> In militarized countries, the higher the level of civil strife, the lower the level of external conflict and, conversely . . . militarized nations experiencing low levels of domestic turmoil tend to be more conflictual in the behavior they direct toward foreign targets. . . . Only in highly militarized societies does a patterned relationship between civil strife and foreign conflict exist (1978:51; cf. Lee, 1973).

54. Dahl and Tufte report that a decade of peace is a statistically substantial predictor of low national military expenditure as a percent of GNP (1973:26).

55. There is an enormous amount of war-related art. Recent discussions of some of the literary products include Costigan (1978) and Fussell (1977).

56. The numbers of military personnel on active duty between 1879 and 1970 appear in U.S. Department of Commerce (1975:1141–43).

57. This is not a new phenomenon. Military morale, and the possibility of panic, desertion, or mutiny have been traditional problems for military commanders. During World War II, for example, American military discipline often broke down under actual battle conditions (cf. Gray, 1970; Stouffer et al., 1949). Further, World

War II produced more violations of U.S. Selective Service Acts than Vietnam (cf. Hallstrom, 1973; Cooper, 1972; Morrill, 1972; Lockham, 1971).

58. See note 7, Chapter 5.

59. The literature on this subject is enormous and fascinating. (See particularly Girard, 1977; Becker, 1976; Sagan, 1974; May, 1972; Dollard et al., 1967; Lasswell, 1965a; Battaille, 1962; Freud, 1962; Brown, 1959; Fromm, 1941. See also Gilbert, 1976; Rascovsky and Rascovsky, 1972; Sturm, 1972; Rojcewicz, 1971; Lopez-Reyes, 1971; Gray, 1970; Kisker, 1969; Meerloo, 1962; Strachey, 1957; Cantril, 1950; Pear, 1950; M. May, 1943; Durbin and Bowlby, 1939; Glover, 1933.)

CHAPTER 6

1. Alcock and Quittner (1977) use a simulation model to project civil violence, with generally longer phases and higher amplitudes during the period 1950–2000. See also Hamilton (1978).

2. Berry states (1974:19–20):

> The complete destruction of the human race appears an almost impossible task. To make intelligent life permanently extinct on this planet, it would be necessary to:
> 1. Kill every human being; if a single group of so much as fifty people of both sexes survived in one place, the operation would be futile. Our civilization could then regain its former state in as little as half a million years.
> 2. Kill all the apes and monkeys throughout the world. Branches from any one of their species could in time (a few million years) evolve into a powerful technological civilization.
> 3. Kill all squirrels, tree shrews, and all other tree-dwelling mammals. Our own ancestors are believed to have been animals of this kind some 70 million years ago.
> 4. Destroy all trees and all plant life and somehow stagnate the oceans to deprive any surviving species of oxygen.
> 5. Repeat the last operation every million years or so. Once plant life had reestablished itself, a life-giving oxygen atmosphere would soon follow.
>
> In the long run, therefore, the world appears to be almost indestructible as a habitat for life for a very long time. Provided he controls his numbers, it seems highly probable that man has an age-long future.

3. Other analyses see alternative possibilities. Thus M. Hudson (1977) discerns an emerging group that consists of Western Europe and the former colonial states in Asia and Africa. Brown (1974) imagines an evolving international polyarchy consisting of multiple coalitions.

4. Marxist ideology forecasts the eventual elimination of inequality. Lasswell is more skeptical.

> The Marx–Engels construct of universal felicity after an epoch of world war and revolution is dangerously over-sanguine, the more probable outcome being a world of ruling castes (or a single caste) learning how to maintain ascendancy against challenge by the ruthless exploitation of hitherto unapplied instruments of modern science and technology (1962:54).

5. There is substantial disagreement about the nature of crises. The following table gives an example of prototypic Western and Chinese views of crises. Our view, emphasizing the costs and dangers of crises, falls within the Western perspective. The Chinese view, which emphasizes crisis opportunities, obviously causes Westerners problems.

Western	Chinese View
1. International crises represent situations that trigger different *kinds* of coping mechanisms by social systems or individual decision-makers	1. International crises are generally extensions of the existing actor relations; they are different only in the level and intensity of actor interactions
2. They create stress and tension for the relevant systems, whether these systems represent international relations, decision units, or individual participants	2. While international crises indicate periods of stress and danger, they may also signal opportunities to advance one's interests
3. They stem from sudden, abrupt, and acute changes in systemic or situational variables	3. They are recurrent phenomena generated by long-term economic processes and are not unpredictable, sudden flares of belligerency among actors
4. They suggest anomalies, irregularities, or aberrations that depart from the routine	4. International relations are inherently competitive and antagonistic; detente arrangements, rather than overt conflict, are the exceptions to the norm
5. They have a disturbing or destabilizing impact on the order of things	5. International relations are inherently unstable, fragile, and "turbulent," and are perpetually changing
6. They indicate the danger of conflict and violence	6. International crises entail controlled use of confrontation and compromise
7. They are usually based on military-political issues and are resolved through military-political means	7. They are, at least at their initial stage of development, primarily caused by economic factors and require ultimately economic solutions; political-military crises are concomitants or consequences of economic crises
8. They imply threat from sources external to the nation state and suggest efforts to cope with the threat from abroad	8. They are, at least at their initial stage of development, primarily domestic phenomena and not foreign relations phenomena
9. They last for relatively short periods of time	9. They are protracted phenomena and take extended time to develop, and their resolution requires persistent struggle, perseverance, and patience (crisis termination could be based on nonresolution of conflict, e.g., temporary truce, partial agreement, tacit detente arrangements)

SOURCE: Bobrow et al. (1977:204). This table, drawn from "Understanding How Others Treat Crises: A Multimethod Approach" by Davis B. Bobrow et al., is reprinted from *International Studies Quarterly*, Vol. 21, No. 1 (March 1977), pp. 199–223, by permission of the International Studies Association and of the publisher, Sage Publications Inc.

6. Andriole and Young (1977) outline an early-warning method based on discontinuities in events-interaction data (cf. Singer and Wallace, 1979; Choucri and Robinson, 1978; O'Leary and Coplin, 1975; Köhler, 1974; A. Newcombe et al., 1974).

Another method might be to score nations according to variables discussed in this book under the headings of aggregation, polarization, and militarization. The numerical coefficients joining the major dimensions and their subordinate variables are not yet clear. Nevertheless, one might assume that nations scoring higher on aggregation and lower on polarization and militarization would be less likely to go to war than those scoring lower on aggregation and higher on polarization and militarization. Prospective war partners and opponents could also be deduced from the overall pattern of relationships.

Murphy and Winkler (1977) discuss the problem of subjective elements of probability in the context of weather forecasting.

7. One analyst believes that the mass media

> could increase the quantity and quality of the information that leaders and publics in each nation have about other nations; they could provide early warning of dangerous situations and could point out opportunities for strengthening international understanding; they could encourage the use of negotiation, mediation, and other mechanisms for conflict resolution, and facilitate the work of negotiators and mediators; they could help to bring about states of mind in which peaceful solutions would be more readily sought and accepted; and they could play a part in the mobilization and encouragement of individuals and organizations seeking to strengthen international understanding (Davison, 1974:6–7; cf. Luard, 1962).

8. H. Newcombe et al. (1977) report the results of a simulation of weighted voting in the U.N. General Assembly. The study found that weighted voting might tend to reduce North–South voting (cf. H. Newcombe, 1979).

9. Hoole (1977) and Etzioni (1970) take an experimental approach in attempting to evaluate the impact of international organization and arms reduction policies. (See also Axelrod, 1980; A. Newcombe, 1979; Isard and Liossatos, 1978; Caporaso and Roos, 1973.)

Snyder et al. (1976) make a proposal for a Global Monitoring System that could help evaluate experimental policy results. This proposal has been widely discussed (cf. Bertsch, 1976; Hendricks, 1976; Jordan, 1976; Naroll, 1976; Tipson, 1976; Young, 1976).

10. The Boston Study Group (1979) sets out a bold program for reducing U.S. defense spending through consolidation. It would obviously be necessary to plan conversion from military to civilian footing in order to minimize dislocations (cf. Leitenberg, 1979; Udis, 1973; U.S. ACDA, 1972; Berkowitz, 1970; Melman, 1970a; Ullmann, 1970).

11. The military draft and volunteer military forces both maintain armed forces and military participation. Nevertheless, voluntary military service is probably less harmful because it is less coercive. It is also less inegalitarian. The draft system holds military salaries down by enforcing military service. It imposes a regressive tax on the poor since the less privileged elements of society are least able to avoid the draft. In a voluntary system the military is forced to pay higher salaries based more on market criteria (cf. Garnier, 1973; Janowitz, 1973, 1972).

12. Cf. Elliott (1980); Wank (1978); Patterson (1976); Brock (1972, 1968); Allen (1971); and Mayer (1966). Quakers, Mennonites, and the Church of the Brethren have long favored allocation of such money to a World Peace Tax Fund. Bills introduced into the U.S. Senate and House of Representatives by Senator Mark Hatfield and Representative Ronald Dellums have been aimed in this direction (cf. Hyer, 1977; E. Wilson, 1963).

13. Health implies similar tradeoffs. Preservation of life may not be an individual's highest value. People may choose sickness or death rather than follow the prescriptions of modern medicine. A patient may say, "The cure is worse than the disease" or "I'd rather be dead" when asked to go on a rigorous restrictive diet or to stop smoking. If he or she does decide to comply, the patient may choose to trade off a "treat" or "splurge" against the physical consequences that are likely to result. Psychotherapy may threaten the individual with losing control of life, and he or she may decide to suffer alone, if not in silence. When he or she hears the projected size of the hospital bill, the patient may say, "Who's going to pay for it?" "I can't afford to be saved" or "Live fast, die young."

In 1973, I asked a class of ten graduate students at the University of Texas whether it would end war if the price were a loss of literacy—the ability to read and write. I repeated the question to an undergraduate class of 125 students at the University of Colorado in 1979. In both cases the students *unanimously* answered "no." Literacy was more important than peace.

14. Kenneth Boulding (1977b) referred to a "goodness function" something as follows: $G = a \pm bP \pm cW \pm dJ \pm \ldots$, where G = Goodness, P = Peace, W = Welfare, J = Justice. The rational objective is to achieve values of $P, W, J, \ldots$ so as to maximize G, or minimize B (Badness).

Hirschman (1977) suggests that Western society has concentrated almost exclusively on material welfare.

BIBLIOGRAPHY

ABERCROMBIE, C. L., III. **1977.** *The Military Chaplain.* Beverly Hills, Calif.: Sage.

ABRAHAMSSON, B. **1971.** *Military Professionalization and Political Power.* Beverly Hills, Calif.: Sage.

ABRAHAMSSON, B., and J. L. STECKLER. **1973.** *Strategic Aspects of Seaborne Oil.* Beverly Hills, Calif.: Sage.

ACCINELLI, R. D. **1977.** "The Hoover administration and the World Court." *Peace and Change,* 4(Fall):28–37.

ACDA: *See U.S. Arms Control and Disarmament Agency.*

ADAMS, C. P., and J. McCLOSKEY. **1974.** "Twice born men." In A. B. Tulipan, C. L. Attneave, and E. Kingstone, eds., *Beyond Clinic Walls.* University: University of Alabama Press. Pp. 46–60.

ADAMS, R. M. **1975.** "Machiavelli now and here: an essay for the First World." *American Scholar,* 44(Summer):365–381.

ADAMS, R. N. **1975.** *Energy and Structure: A Theory of Social Power.* Austin: University of Texas Press.

ADELMAN, I. **1967.** *Society, Politics, and Economic Development: A Quantitative Approach.* Baltimore: Johns Hopkins University Press.

——. **1961.** *Theories of Economic Growth and Development.* Stanford, Calif.: Stanford University Press.

ADELMAN, I., and C. T. MORRIS. **1973.** *Economic Growth and Social Equity in Developing Countries.* Stanford, Calif.: Stanford University Press.

ADLER, J. H. **1973.** "Development and income distribution." *Finance and Development,* 10(September):2–5.

ADORNO, T. W., et al. **1950.** *The Authoritarian Personality.* New York: Harper.

AFRICA, T. W. **1971.** "Urban violence in imperial Rome." *J. of Interdisciplinary History,* 2(Summer):3–21.

AHMAD, A., and A. S. WILKE. **1973.** "Peace and war themes in social science periodicals." *J. of Political and Military Sociology,* 1(Spring):39–56.

AKEHURST, M. **1977.** *A Modern Introduction to International Law.* London: Allen and Unwin.

ALCOCK, N. **1978.** "Cyclical analysis in global economic forecasting." *World Future Society Bull.* (March–April):7–13.

——. **1976.** "Towards a causal model of violence." *Peace Research,* 8(July):91–102.

——. **1972.** *The War Disease.* Oakville, Ontario: Canadian Peace Research Institute.

ALCOCK, N., and G. KÖHLER. **1979.** "Structural violence at the world level: diachronic findings." *J. of Peace Research,* 16(3):255–263.

ALCOCK, N., and K. LOWE. **1969.** "The Vietnam War as a Richardson process." *J. of Peace Research,* 6(2):105–112.

ALCOCK, N., and J. QUITTNER. **1977.** "Global projection of domestic compassion." *Peace Research,* 9(January):3–12.

ALCOCK, N., and C. YOUNG. **1973.** "A periodic table of peace." *Peace Research,* 5(November):68–78.

ALCOCK, N., et al. **1978.** *1982.* Oakville, Ontario: Canadian Peace Research Institute.

——. **1976.** "The limits-to-violence project: a statement of purpose." *Peace Research*, 8(January): 19–27.

——. **1970.** *Defence in the 1970's: Comments on the White Paper.* Toronto: Canadian Institute of International Affairs.

ALDCROFT, D. H. **1977.** *From Versailles to Wall Street, 1919–1929.* Berkeley: University of California Press.

ALDROUS, J., and I. TALLMAN. **1972.** "Immediacy of situation and conventionality as influences on attitudes toward war." *Sociology and Social Research*, 56(April):356–367.

ALEKSANDROWICZ, D. R. **1974.** "The psychiatrist in national emergency." *American J. of Psychoanalysis*, 34(1):85–90.

——. **1971.** "Psychoanalysis during wartime." *Psychoanalytic Rev.*, 58(Summer):245–250.

ALEXANDER, F. **1941.** "The psychiatric aspects of war and peace." *American J. of Sociology*, 46(January):504–520.

ALEXANDER, J. A. **1975.** "The twig bent: instruction on the taking of life provided in catechisms printed in America before 1800." *Peace and Change*, 3(Summer–Fall):68–77.

ALEXANDER, Y., and R. FRIEDLANDER, eds. **1978.** *Self-Determination: National, Regional, and Global Dimensions.* Boulder: Westview.

ALEXANDROWICZ, C. H. **1973.** *The European-African Confrontation: A Study in Treaty Making.* Leiden: Sijthoff.

——, ed. **1972.** *Grotian Society Papers, 1970: Studies in the History of the Law of Nations.* The Hague: Nijhoff.

——, ed. **1970.** *Grotian Society Papers, 1968: Studies in the History of the Law of Nations.* The Hague: Nijhoff.

ALGER, C. F. **1977.** "Foreign policies of U.S. publics." *International Studies Q.*, 21(June):277–318.

——. **1976.** "A world of cities." A Report to the Charles F. Kettering Foundation. Columbus, Ohio: Columbus in the World, The World in Columbus.

——. **1966.** "Interaction and negotiation in a committee of the United Nations General Assembly." *Peace Research Society (International) Papers*, 5, Philadelphia Conference, 1965.

ALKER, H. R., JR. **1977.** "A methodology for design research on interdependence alternatives." *International Organization*, 31(Winter):29–63.

——. **1964.** "Dimensions of conflict in the general assembly." *American Political Science Rev.*, 58(September):642–657.

ALKER, H. R., JR., L. P. BLOOMFIELD, and N. CHOUCRI, **1974.** *Analyzing Global Interdependence.* Vol. 3: *Methodological Perspectives and Research Implications*, by H. R. Alker, Jr., and N. Choucri. Cambridge, Mass.: Center for International Studies, MIT.

ALKER, H. R., JR., and P. G. BOCK. **1972.** "Propositions about international relations." In J. A. Robinson, ed., *Political Science Annual: An International Review.* Vol. 3. Indianapolis: Bobbs-Merrill. Pp. 385–495.

ALKER, H. R., JR., and W. J. GREENBERG. **1971.** "The UN charter: alternative pasts and alternate futures." In E. H. Fedder, ed., *The United Nations: Problems and Prospects.* St. Louis: University Center for International Studies. Pp. 113–142.

ALKER, H. R., JR., and D. PUCHALA. **1968.** "Trends in economic partnership in the North Atlantic area, 1928–1963." In J. D. Singer, ed., *Quantitative International Politics: Insights and Evidence.* New York: Free Press. Pp. 287–315.

ALKER, H. R., JR., and B. M. RUSSETT. **1965.** *World Politics in the General Assembly.* New Haven, Conn.: Yale University Press.

ALLEN, D. **1971.** *Pacifism in the Modern World.* New York: Garland.

ALLISON, G. **1971.** *Essence of Decision: Explaining the Cuban Missile Crisis.* Boston: Little, Brown.

ALLISON, P. D. **1977.** "Testing for interaction in multiple regression." *American J. of Sociology*, 83(July):144–154.

ALMOND, G. A. **1950.** *The American People and Foreign Policy.* New York: Harcourt, Brace.

ALPEROVITZ, G. **1965.** *Atomic Diplomacy: Hiroshima and Potsdam: The Use of the Atomic Bomb and the American Confrontation with Soviet Power.* New York: Simon and Schuster.

ALTFELD, M. F., and B. BUENO DE MESQUITA. **1979.** "Choosing sides in wars." *International Studies Q.*, 23(March):87–112.

ALTING VON GEUSAU, F. A. M. **1969.** *Beyond the European Community.* Leyden: Sijthoff.

AMBROSE, S. E. **1973.** *Rise to Globalism: American Foreign Policy Since 1938.* Baltimore: Penguin.

AMBROSE, S. E., and J. A. BARBER, JR., eds. **1972.** *The Military and American Society: Essays and Readings.* New York: Free Press.

AMERICAN ACADEMY OF ARTS AND SCIENCES. **1975.** "Arms, defense policy and arms control." *Daedalus*, 104(Summer):1–302.

AMIN, S. **1976.** *Unequal Development: An Essay on the Social Formations of Peripheral Capitalism.* Bruce Pearce, tr. New York: Monthly Review Press.

——. **1974.** *Accumulation on a World Scale: A Critique of the Theory of Underdevelopment.* 2 vols. New York: Monthly Review Press.

——. **1973.** *Neo-colonialism in West Africa.* F. McDonagh, tr. New York: Monthly Review Press.

AMNESTY INTERNATIONAL. **1975.** *Amnesty International Report on Torture.* New York: Noonday.

ANAND, R. P. **1972.** *New States and International Law.* Delhi: Vikas.

ANANT, S. S. **1974.** "The effect of political realignments during an armed conflict on ethnic stereotypes." *International J. of Psychology,* 9(2):139–144.

ANDEMICAEL, B., ed. **1979**. Regional International Organization and the U.N. System. Dobbs Ferry, N.Y.: Oceana.

——. **1976**. *The OAU and the UN: Relations between the Organization of Afican Unity and the United Nations.* New York and London: Africana.

ANDERSEN, R. S. **1975**. "Operation homecoming: psychological observations of repatriated Vietnam prisoners of war." *Psychiatry,* 38(February):65–74.

ANDERSON, P. **1974**. *Lineages of the Absolute State.* London: New Left Books.

ANDREANO, R. L., ed. **1974**. *Superconcentration/Supercorporation: A Collage of Opinion on the Concentration of Economic Power.* Andover, Mass.: Warner Modular Publications.

——. **1967**. *The Economic Impact of the American Civil War.* 2nd ed. Cambridge, Mass.: Schenkman.

ANDRESKI, S. **1968**. *Military Organization and Society.* Berkeley: University of California Press.

ANDREWS, C. **1974**. *Foreign Policy and the New American Military.* Beverly Hills, Calif.: Sage.

ANDRIOLE, S. J., and R. A. YOUNG. **1977**. "Toward the development of an integrated crisis warning system." *International Studies Q.,* 21(March):75–106.

ANGELL, N. **1973**. *Arms and Industry: A Study of the Foundations of International Polity.* New York: Garland.

——. **1972**. *The Great Illusion: A Study of the Relation of Military Power in Nations to Their Economic and Social Advantage.* New York: Garland.

ANGELL, R. C. **1969**. *Peace on the March: Transnational Participation.* New York: Van Nostrand, Reinhold.

ANTOLA, E. **1975**. "The roots of domestic military interventions in black Africa. *Instant Research on Peace and Violence,* 5:207–221.

ANTONOVSKY, A., et al. **1971**. "Twenty-five years later: a limited study of sequelae of the concentration camp experience." *Social Psychiatry,* 6(December):186–193.

APPLEGATE, R. **1977**. "Glaser safety slug, police-only manstopper." *American Handgunner,* 2(July–August):14–17.

ARANGO, J. L. **1970**. *The Urbanization of the Earth.* Boston: Beacon.

ARCHER, D., and R. GARTNER. **1976**. "Violent acts and violent times: a comparative approach to postwar homicide rates." *American Sociological Rev.,* 41(December):937–963.

ARDREY, R. **1970**. *The Territorial Imperative.* New York: Atheneum.

ARENDT, H. **1963**. *Eichmann in Jerusalem: A Report on the Banality of Evil.* New York: Viking.

——. **1962**. *On Revolution.* New York: Viking.

——. **1951**. *The Origins of Totalitarianism.* New York: Harcourt, Brace.

ARMACOST, M. H. **1969**. *The Politics of Weapons Innovation: The Thor–Jupiter Controversy.* New York: Columbia University Press.

ARNTZ, J. **1975**. *Der Begriff der Friedensbedrohung in Satzung und Praxis der Vereinten Nationen.* Berlin: Duncker and Humblot.

ARON, R. **1966**. *Peace and War: A Theory of International Relations.* R. Howard and A. B. Fox, trs. New York: Praeger.

——. **1955**. *The Century of Total War.* Boston: Beacon.

ART, R. J. **1973**. *The Influence of Foreign Policy on Seapower: New Weapons and Weltpolitik in Wilhelminian Germany.* Beverly Hills, Calif.: Sage.

ARX, H. J. VON. **1974**. *Atombombenversuche und Völkerrecht.* Basel: Helbing and Lichtenhahn.

ASHBY, W. R. **1956**. *Introduction to Cybernetics.* New York: Wiley.

ASHLEY, R. K. **1980**. *Political Economy of War and Peace.* New York: Nichols.

ASIMOV, I. **1952**. *Foundation and Empire.* Garden City, N.Y.: Doubleday.

ATHERTON, A. L., ed. **1976**. *International Organizations: A Guide to Information Sources.* Detroit: Gale Research.

ATKIN, S. **1971**. "Notes on motivations for war: toward a psychoanalytic social psychology." *Psychoanalytic Quarterly,* 40(October):549–583.

AUMA-OSOLO, A. **1976**. "Peace-keeping and the passions of U.N. member states." *Peace Research,* 8(April):19–24.

AUSLAND, J. C., and H. F. RICHARDSON. **1966**. "Crisis management: Berlin, Cyprus, Laos." *Foreign Affairs,* 44(January):291–303.

AXELROD, R. **1980**. "Effective choice in the prisoner's dilemma." *J. of Conflict Resolution,* 24(March):3–26.

AXLINE, W. A. **1977**. "Underdevelopment, dependence, and integration: the politics of regionalism in the third world." *International Organization,* 31(Winter):83–106.

AZAR, E. **1973**. *Probe for Peace.* Minneapolis: Burgess.

——. **1972**. "Conflict escalation and conflict reduction in an international crisis: Suez, 1956." *J. of Conflict Resolution,* 16(June):183–201.

BAADE, H. **1972**. "Individual responsibility." In C. E. Black and R. A. Falk, eds., *The Future of the International Legal Order.* Vol. 4: *The Structure of the International Environment.* Priceton, N.J.: Princeton University Press. Pp. 291–327.

BACKMAN, J., ed. **1952**. *War and Defense Economics.* New York: Rinehart.

BAGLEY, E. R. **1975**. *Beyond the Conglomerates.* New York: American Management Associations.

BAIDER, L., and E. ROSENFELD. **1974**. "Effect of parental fears on children in wartime." *Social Casework,* 55(October):497–503.

BAILEY, N. T. J. **1957**. *The Mathematical Theory of Epidemics*. London: Griffin.

BAILEY, S. D. **1977**. "Cease-fires, truces, and armistices in the practice of the UN Security Council." *American J. of International Law,* 71(July):461–473.

——. **1969**. *Voting in the Security Council*. Bloomington: Indiana University Press.

——. **1968**. "Veto in the Security Council." *International Conciliation,* No. 566(January).

BAINTON, R. H. **1978**. *Christian Attitudes Toward War and Peace: A Historical Survey and Critical Re-Evaluation*. Nashville: Abingdon.

BAIROCH, P. **1975**. *The Economic Development of the Third World Since 1900*. C. Postan, tr. Berkeley: University of California Press.

BALASSA, B. **1965**. *Economic Development and Integration*. Mexico City: Centro de Estudios Monetarios Latinoamericanos.

BALCH, R. **1978**. "The resigning of quarrels: conflict resolution in the thirteenth century." *Peace and Change,* 5(Spring):33–38.

BALDWIN, W. L. **1967**. *The Structure of the Defense Market, 1955–1964*. Durham, N.C.: Duke University Press.

BALL, R. J., and P. DOYLE, eds. **1969**. *Inflation: Selected Readings*. Baltimore: Penguin.

BALLIS, W. **1973**. *The Legal Position of War: Changes in Practice and Theory from Plato to Vattel*. New York: Garland.

BANKS, A. S. **1971**. *Cross-polity Time Series Data*. Assembled by A. S. Banks and the staff of the Center of Comparative Political Research, State University of New York, Binghamton. Cambridge, Mass.: MIT Press.

BANKS, A. S., and P. M. GREGG. **1965**. "Grouping political systems: Q-factor analysis of 'a cross-polity survey.' " *American Behavioral Scientist,* 9(November):3–6.

BANKS, A. S., and R. B. TEXTOR. **1963**. *A Cross-polity Survey*. Cambridge, Mass.: MIT Press.

BARAN, P. A. **1967**. *The Political Economy of Growth*. New York: Monthly Review Press.

BARAN, P. A., and P. M. SWEEZY. **1969**. *Monopoly Capital*. Baltimore: Penguin.

BARBERA, H. **1973**. *Rich Nations and Poor in Peace and War: Continuity and Change in the Development Hierarchy of Seventy Nations from 1913 through 1952*. Lexington, Mass.: Heath.

BARDIS, P. D. **1972**. "Violence: theory and quantification." *J. of Political and Military Sociology,* 1(Spring):121–146.

BARKUN, M. **1974**. *Disaster and the Millennium*. New Haven, Conn.: Yale University Press.

——. **1968**. *Law Without Sanctions*. New Haven, Conn.: Yale University Press.

BARNABY, F. **1976**. "Environmental warfare." *Bull. of the Atomic Scientists,* 32(May):36–43.

BARNABY, F., and R. HUISKEN. **1975**. *Arms Uncontrolled*. For the Stockholm International Peace Research Institute. Cambridge, Mass.: Harvard University Press.

BARNES, C. B. **1975**. "The partial effect of income on suicide is always negative." *American J. of Sociology,* 80(May):1454–1460.

BARNES, W., and J. H. MORGAN. **1961**. *The Foreign Service of the United States: Origin, Developments and Function*. Washington, D.C.: Historical Office Bureau of Public Affairs, Department of State.

BARNET, R. J. **1973**. *The Roots of War: The Men and Institutions Behind U.S. Foreign Policy*. New York: Penguin.

——. **1969**. *The Economy of Death*. New York: Atheneum.

——. **1968**. *Intervention and Revolution: The United States in the Third World*. New York: World.

BARNET, R. J., and R. E. MÜLLER. **1974**. *Global Reach: The Power of the Multinational Corporations*. New York: Simon and Schuster.

BAROCAS, H. A. **1970**. "Children of purgatory: reflections on the concentration camp survival syndrome." *Corrective Psychiatry and J. of Social Therapy,* 16(January):51–58.

BARRINGER, R. E. **1972**. *War: Patterns of Conflict*. Cambridge, Mass.: MIT Press.

BARTLETT, M. S. **1960**. *Stochastic Population Models in Ecology and Epidemiology*. New York: Halsted.

BARTON, J. H., and L. D. WEILER, eds. **1976**. *International Arms Control: Issues and Agreements*. Stanford, Calif.: Stanford University Press.

BAR-YAACOV, N. **1975**. *The Handling of International Disputes by Means of Inquiry*. London: Oxford University Press.

BASKIR, L. M., and W. A. STRAUSS. **1978**. *Chance and Circumstance: The Draft, the War and the Vietnam Generation*. New York: Knopf.

BATESON, G. **1936**. *Naven*. Cambridge: Cambridge University Press.

BATTAILLE, G. **1962**. *Death and Sensuality*. New York: Ballantine.

BAUGH, W. H. **1978**. "Major powers and their weak allies: stability and structure in arms race models." *J. of Peace Science,* 3(Spring):45–54.

BAUMGARTNER, J. S. **1970**. *The Lonely Warriors: The Case for the Military–Industrial Complex*. Los Angeles: Nash.

BECKER, E. **1976**. *Escape from Evil*. New York: Free Press.

BEEBE, G. W. **1975**. "Follow-up studies of World War II and Korean War prisoners, part 2: morbidity, disability and mal-adjustments." *American J. of Epidemiology,* 101(May):400–422.

BEEBE, G. W., and M. DEBAKEY. **1952**. *Battle Casualties: Incidence, Mortality and Logistic Considerations*. Springfield, Ill.: Thomas.

BEER, F. A. **1979a.** "The epidemiology of peace and war." *International Studies Q.*, 23(March):45–86.

——. **1979b.** "World order and world futures." *J. of Conflict Resolution*, 23(March):174–192.

——. **1975a.** "A methodology of world order." In L. R. Beres and H. Targ, eds., *Planning for Alternative World Futures*. New York: Praeger. Pp. 175–192.

——. **1975b.** "The structure of world consciousness." In L. R. Beres and H. Targ, eds., *Planning for Alternative World Futures*. New York: Praeger. Pp. 276–291.

——. **1974.** *How Much War in History: Definitions, Estimates, Extrapolations, and Trends.* Beverly Hills, Calif.: Sage.

——. **1972a.** "Energy, environment, and international organization." In S. L. Kwee and J. S. R. Mullender, eds. *Growing Against Ourselves: The Energy–Environment Tangle.* Lexington, Mass.: Heath. Pp. 22–31.

——. **1972b.** *The Political Economy of Alliances: Benefits, Costs, and Institutions in NATO.* Beverly Hills, Calif.: Sage.

——, ed. **1970.** *Alliances: Latent War Communities in the Contemporary World.* New York: Holt, Rinehart and Winston.

——. **1969.** *Integration and Disintegration in NATO: Processes of Alliance Cohesion and Prospects for Atlantic Community.* Columbus: Ohio State University Press.

BEER, F. A., and E. Z. WYNER. **1974.** "Drift and pluralization in international trade." *International Organization*, 28(Winter):119–125.

BEIT-HALLAHMI, B. **1972.** "National character and national behavior in the Middle East conflict: the case of the 'Arab personality.' " *International J. of Group Tensions*, 2(3):19–28.

BELDEN, T. G. **1977.** "Indications, warning, and crisis operations." *International Studies Q.*, 21(March):181–198.

BELOFF, M. **1963.** *The United States and the Unity of Europe.* Washington, D.C.: The Brookings Institution.

BENDA, J. **1969.** *The Treason of the Intellectuals.* New York: Norton.

BEN-DAK, J., ed. **1975.** *The Future of Collective Violence: Societal and International Perspectives.* Lund, Sweden: Studentlitteratur.

BENDER, L. **1953.** *Aggression, Hostility, and Anxiety in Children.* Springfield, Ill.: Thomas.

BENOIT, E. **1973.** *Defense and Economic Growth in Developing Countries.* Lexington, Mass.: Lexington Books.

——. **1966.** "Comments on papers by Weidenbaum and Karaska." *Peace Research Society (International) Papers*, 5, Philadelphia Conference, 1965.

BENOIT, E., and K. BOULDING, eds. **1963.** *Disarmament and the Economy.* New York: Harper and Row.

BENTHAM, J. **1974.** "Plan for a universal and perpetual peace." In B. W. Cook et al., eds., *Peace Projects of the Eighteenth Century.* New York: Garland. Pp. 11–44.

BERES, L. R. **1979.** *Terrorism and Global Security: The Nuclear Threat.* Boulder: Westview.

BERES, L. R. and H. TARG, eds., **1975.** *Planning for Alternative World Futures.* New York: Praeger.

BERGSTEN, C. F. **1977.** "The reform of international institutions: a rebuttal." *International Organization*, 31(Winter):149–150.

——. **1975.** *Toward a New International Economic Order: Selected Papers of C. Fred Bergsten, 1972–74.* Washington, D.C.: The Brookings Institution.

BERKOWITZ, L. **1978.** "Whatever happened to the frustration–aggression hypothesis?" *American Behavioral Scientist*, 21(May–June):691–708.

——. **1973.** "Studies on the contagion of violence." In H. Hirsch and D. Perry, eds., *Violence as Politics.* New York: Harper and Row. Pp. 41–50.

——. **1962.** *Aggression: A Social Psychological Analysis.* New York: McGraw-Hill.

BERKOWITZ, L., and J. T. ALIOTO. **1973.** "The meaning of an observed event as a determinant of its aggressive consequences." *J. of Personality and Social Psychology*, 28(November):206–217.

BERKOWITZ, M. **1970.** *The Conversion of Military-Oriented Research and Development to Civilian Uses.* New York: Praeger.

BERNARD, L. L. **1972.** *War and Its Causes.* New York: Garland.

BERNSTEIN, N. **1975.** *Validity Issues in Evaluative Research.* Beverly Hills, Calif.: Sage.

BERQUE, J., and J. P. CHARNAY. **1967.** *L'Ambivalence dans la Culture Arabe.* Paris: Editions Anthropos.

BERRY, A. **1974.** *The Next Ten Thousand Years: A Vision of Man's Future in the Universe.* New York: Mentor.

BERTELSON, J., ed. **1977.** *Nonstate Nations in International Politics: Comparative System Analysis.* New York: Praeger.

BERTSCH, G. W. **1976.** "Monitoring the effects of governments on human dignity: policy evaluation in communist party states." *International Studies Q.*, 20(December):641–646.

BÉTHUNE, M. DE (DUC DE SULLY). **1972.** "Sully's grand design of Henry IV." In B. W. Cook, ed., *Peace Projects of the Seventeenth Century.* New York: Garland. Pp. 2–56.

BETTELHEIM, B. **1969.** *Children of the Dream.* New York: Macmillan.

——. **1960.** *The Informed Heart: Autonomy in a Mass Age.* New York: Free Press.

BETTS, R. K. **1978.** "Analysis, war, and decisions: why intelligence failures are inevitable." *World Politics*, 31(October):61–89.

——. **1977.** *Soldiers, Statesmen, and Cold War Crises.* Cambridge, Mass.: Harvard University Press.

BEY, D. R. 1972. "Change of command in combat: a locus of stress." *American J. of Psychiatry,* 129(December):698–702.

BEY, D. R., and R. E. CHAPMAN. 1974. "Psychiatry—the right way, the wrong way, and the military way." *Bull. of the Menninger Clinic,* 38(July):343–354.

BEY, D. R., and J. LANGE. 1974. "Waiting wives: women under stress." *American J. of Psychiatry,* 131(March):283–286.

BEY, D. R., and V. A. ZECCHINELLI. 1971. "Marijuana as a coping device in Vietnam." *Military Medicine,* 136(May):448–450.

BIENEN, H. 1978. *Armies and Parties in Africa.* New York: Holmes and Meier.

——. 1971. *The Military and Modernization.* Chicago: Aldine Atherton.

——. 1968a. *The Military Intervenes: Case Studies in Political Development.* New York: Russell Sage Foundation.

——. 1968b. *Violence and Social Change.* Chicago: University of Chicago Press.

BIENEN, H., and D. MORELL. 1976. *Political Participation Under Military Regimes.* Beverly Hills, Calif.: Sage.

BIGELOW, R. S. 1972. "The evolution of cooperation, aggression, and self-control." *Nebraska Symposium on Motivation,* 20:1–57.

——. 1969. *The Dawn Warriors: Man's Evolution Toward Peace.* Boston: Little, Brown.

BINKIN, M., H. KANTER, and R. H. CLARK. 1978. *Shaping the Defense Civilian Work Force: Economics, Politics, and National Security.* Washington, D.C.: The Brookings Institution.

BINKIN, M., and J. SHIRLEY. 1977. *Women and the Military.* Washington, D.C.: The Brookings Institution.

BISHOP, J. W., JR. 1974. *Justice Under Fire: A Study of Military Law.* New York: Charterhouse.

BLACK, C. E., and R. A. FALK, eds. 1972. *The Future of the International Legal Order.* Vol. 4: *The Structure of the International Environment.* Princeton, N.J.: Princeton University Press.

——. 1971. *The Future of the International Legal Order.* Vol. 3: *Conflict Management.* Princeton, N.J.: Princeton University Press.

BLACK, F. W. 1975. "Unilateral brain lesions and MMPI performance: a preliminary study." *Perceptual and Motor Skills,* 40(February):87–93.

——. 1974. "Use of the MMPI with patients with recent war-related head injuries." *J. of Clinical Psychology,* 30(October):571–573.

BLACK, M. 1962. *Models and Metaphors: Studies in Language and Philosophy.* Ithaca, N.Y.: Cornell University Press.

BLAINEY, G. 1973. *The Causes of War.* New York: Free Press.

BLAIR, B. G., and G. D. BREWER. 1977. "The terrorist threat to world nuclear programs." *J. of Conflict Resolution,* 21(September):379–403.

BLANCHARD, W. H. 1962. "National myth, national character, and national policy: a psychological study of the U-2 incident." *J. of Conflict Resolution,* 6(June):143–149.

BLAU, P. M. 1977. "A macrosociological theory of social structure." *American J. of Sociology,* 83(July):26–54.

——. 1964. *Exchange and Power in Social Life.* New York: Wiley.

BLECHMAN, B. M. 1975. *The Control of Naval Armaments: Prospects and Possibilities.* Washington, D.C.: The Brookings Instutition.

BLECHMAN, B. M., et al. 1978. *Force Without War: U.S. Armed Forces as a Political Instrument.* Washington, D.C.: The Brookings Institution.

——. 1977. *The Soviet Military Buildup and U.S. Defense Spending.* Washington, D.C.: The Brookings Institution.

BLEICHER, S. A. 1971. "Intergovernmental organization and the preservation of peace." *International Organization,* 25(Spring):298–305.

BLISHCHENKO, I. P. 1975. "International treaties and their application to the territory of the U.S.S.R." *American J. of International law* 69(October):819–828.

BLOCH, H. A., and H. GEIS. 1970. *Man, Crime, and Society,* 2nd ed. New York: Random House.

BLOCH, H. S. 1970. "The psychological adjustment of normal people during a year's tour in Vietnam." *Psychiatric Q.,* 44(October):613–626.

BLOCH, J. DE. 1972. *The Future of War in Its Technical, Economic and Political Relations.* R. C. Long, tr. New York: Garland.

BLONG, C. K., R. W. MANDERSCHEID, and M. L. RUSTAD. 1976. "Militarism, religiosity and psychopathology: subjective identification vs. structural affiliation." *International Interactions,* 2(November):207–216.

BLOOM, A. 1977. "Linguistic impediments to cross-cultural communications: Chinese hassles with the hypothetical." *J. of Peace Science,* 2(Spring):205–213.

BLOOMFIELD, L. M., and G. F. FITZGERALD. 1975. *Crimes Against Internationally Protected Persons: Prevention and Punishment—An Analysis of the UN Convention.* New York: Praeger.

BLOOMFIELD, L. P., ed. 1971. *The Power to Keep Peace, Today and in a World Without War.* Chicago: World Without War Publications.

——. 1964. *International Military Forces.* Boston: Little, Brown.

BLOOMFIELD, L. P., and A. LEISS. 1969. *Controlling Small Wars: A Strategy for the 1970's.* New York: Knopf.

BLUEMEL, C. S. 1948. *War, Politics, and Insanity.* Denver: World.

BOAS, F. 1974. "Warfare in the cosmos." In P. D. Wiener and J. Fisher, eds., *Violence and Aggression in the History of Ideas.* New Brunswick, N.J.: Rutgers University Press. Pp. 3–14.

BOBROW, D. 1972. "Transfer of meaning across natural boundaries." In R. L. Merritt, ed., *Communication in International Politics*. Urbana: University of Illinois Press. Pp. 33–61.

BOBROW, D., S. CHAN, and J. A. KRINGEN. **1977.** "Understanding how others treat crises: a multimethod approach." *International Studies Q.*, 21(March):199–224.

BOCK, P. **1974.** *In Search of a Responsible World Society: The Social Teachings of the World Council of Churches*. Philadelphia: Westminster.

BODIN, J. **1955.** *Six Books of the Commonwealth*. M. J. Tooley, abr. and tr. Oxford: Oxford University Press.

BOGART, L. **1976.** *Premises for Propaganda: The United States Information Agency's Operation Assumptions in the Cold War*. A. Bogart, abr. New York: Free Press.

BOHANNAN, P., ed. **1967.** *Law and Warfare: Studies in the Anthropology of Conflict*. Garden City, N.Y.: Natural History Press.

BOLEWSKI, M. **1972.** "Neurosis, stress, and psychic load: a depth-psychological examination of late repatriates." *Zeitschrift für Psychosomatische Medizin und Psychoanalyse*, 18(January–March):48–61.

BOLTON, R. E. **1966.** *Defense Purchases and Regional Growth*. Washington, D.C.: The Brookings Institution.

BONAPARTE, M. **1947.** *Myths of War*. London: Imago.

BOND, J. E. **1974.** *The Rules of Riot: Internal Conflict and the Law of War*. Princeton, N.J.: Princeton University Press.

BOND, T. C. **1976.** "The why of fragging." *American J. of Psychiatry*, 133(November):1328–1331.

BONHAM, G. M., M. J. SHAPIRO, and T. L. TRUMBLE. **1979.** "The October war: changes in cognitive orientation toward the Middle East conflict." *International Studies Q.*, 23(March):3–44.

BONOMA, T. **1974.** *Conflict: Escalation and Deescalation*. Beverly Hills, Calif.: Sage.

BOORSTIN, D. J. **1978.** *The Republic of Technology: Reflections on Our Future Community*. New York: Harper and Row.

BORNSCHIER, V., C. CHASE-DUNN, and R. RUBINSON. **1978.** "Cross-national evidence of the effects of foreign investment and aid on economic growth and inequality: a survey of findings and a reanalysis." *American J. of Sociology*, 84(November):651–683.

BORRIE, W. D. **1970.** *The Growth and Control of World Population*. London: Weidenfeld and Nicolson.

BORUS, J. F. **1973.** "Reentry, III: facilitating healthy readjustment in Vietnam veterans." *Psychiatry*, 36(November):428–439.

BOSCH, J. **1968.** *Pentagonism: A Substitute for Imperialism*. H. R. Lane, tr. New York: Grove.

BOSERUP, A., and A. MACK. **1975.** *War Without Weapons: Non-Violence in National Defense*. New York: Schocken.

BOSMAJIAN, H. **1974.** *The Language of Oppression*. Washington, D.C.: Public Affairs Press.

BOSTON STUDY GROUP. **1979.** *The Price of Defense: A New Strategy for Military Spending*. New York: Times Books.

BOTHE, M. **1973.** *Das Volkerrechtliche Verbot des Einsatzes Chemischer und Bakteriologischer Waffen: Kritische Würdigung und Dokumentation der Rechtsgrundlagen*. Cologne and Bonn: Carl Heymanns Verlag.

BOUDET, J., ed. **1969.** *The Ancient Art of Warfare*. 2 vols. London: Barrie and Rockliff.

BOULDING, E. **1975.** "New careers and new societies: challenges for conflict and peace studies programs." *J. of World Education*, 6(Summer):4–5.

BOULDING, K. E. **1978.** *Stable Peace*. Austin: University of Texas Press.

——. **1977a.** "Peace research." *International Social Science J.*, 29(4):601–614.

——. **1977b.** Public lecture. Boulder: University of Colorado.

——. **1974.** "Defense spending: burden or boon?" *War/Peace Report*, 13(1):19–21.

——. **1973.** *The Economy of Love and Fear: A Preface to Grants Economics*. Belmont, Calif.: Wadsworth.

——, ed. **1970.** *Peace and the War Industry*. Chicago: Aldine.

——. **1965.** "War as a public health problem: conflict management as a key to survival." In M. Schwebel, ed., *Behavioral Science and Human Survival*. Palo Alto, Calif.: Science and Behavior Books. Pp. 103–110.

——. **1963a.** "Towards a pure theory of threat systems." *American Economic Rev.*, 53(May):424–434.

——. **1963b.** "The world war industry as an economic problem." In E. Benoit and K. Boulding, eds., *Disarmament and the Economy*. New York: Harper and Row. Pp. 3–27.

——. **1962.** *Conflict and Defense: A General Theory*. New York: Harper and Row.

——. **1959.** "National images and international systems." *J. of Conflict Resolution*, 3(June):120–131.

——. **1956.** *The Image: Knowledge in Life and Society*. Ann Arbor: University of Michigan Press.

BOULDING, K. E., and E. BOULDING. **1975.** "Models and data." Boulder: Lecture delivered at Institute of Behavioral Science, University of Colorado.

BOULDING, K. E., and A. H. GLEASON. **1965.** "War as an investment: the strange case of Japan." *Peace Research Society (International) Papers*, 3:1–17.

BOURNE, P. G. **1972.** "The Viet Nam veteran: psychosocial casualties." *Psychiatry in Medicine*, 3(January): 23–27.

——. **1971.** "Altered adrenal function in two combat situations in Viet Nam." In B. E. Eleftheriou and J. P. Scott, eds., *The Physiology of*

Aggression and Defeat. New York: Plenum. Pp. 265–290.

——. **1970a.** *Men, Stress, and Vietnam.* Boston: Little, Brown.

——. **1970b.** "Military psychiatry and the Viet Nam experience." *American J. of Psychiatry,* 127(October):481–488.

BOUTHOUL, G. **1970.** *Traité de Polémologie: Sociologie des Guerres.* Paris: Payot.

——. **1948.** *Huit Mille Traités de Paix.* Paris: René Julliard.

BOUTHOUL, G., and R. CARRÉRE, with J. L. ANNE-QUIN. **1976.** *Le Défi de la Guerre (1740–1974): Deux Siècles de Guerres et de Révolutions.* Paris: Presses Universitaires de France.

BOVA, S. **1972.** Il Commercio delle armi e i paesi del terzo mondo." *Quaderni di Sociologia,* 21(April–June):217–226.

BOWETT, D. W. **1958.** *Self-Defense in International Law.* New York: Praeger.

BOZEMAN, A. **1976.** *Conflict in Africa: Concepts and Realities.* Princeton, N.J.: Princeton University Press.

——. **1971.** *The Future of Law in a Multicultural World.* Princeton, N.J.: Princeton University Press.

——. **1960.** *Politics and Culture in International History.* Princeton, N.J.: Princeton University Press.

BOZEMAN, B., and T. E. JAMES. **1975.** "Toward a comprehensive model of foreign policy voting in the U.S. Senate." *Western Political Q.,* 28(September):477–495.

BRAATZ, G. A., G. K. LUMRY, and M. S. WRIGHT. **1971.** "The young veteran as a psychiatric patient in three eras of conflict." *Military Medicine,* 136(May):455–457.

BRADBURY, W., et al. **1968.** *Mass Behavior in Battle and Captivity: The Communist Soldier in the Korean War.* Chicago: University of Chicago Press.

BRADFORD, Z. B., JR., and F. J. BROWN. **1973.** *The United States Army in Transition.* Beverly Hills, Calif.: Sage.

BRAMS, S. J. **1968.** "A note on the cosmopolitanism of world regions." *J. of Peace Research,* 5(1):87–95.

BRAMSON, L, and G. GOETHALS, eds. **1968.** *War: Contributions from Psychology, Sociology, and Anthropology.* New York: Basic Books.

BRANDT, R. B. **1972.** "Utilitarianism and the rules of war." *Philosophy and Public Affairs,* 1(Winter):145–165.

BRAUDEL, F. **1973.** *The Mediterranean and the Mediterranean World in the Age of Phillip II.* Sian Reynolds, tr. New York: Harper and Row.

BREMER, S., J. SINGER, and U. LUTERBACHER. **1973.** "The population density and war proneness of European nations, 1816–1965." *Comparative Political Studies,* 6(October):329–348.

BRENNER, M. H. **1973.** *Mental Illness and the Economy.* Cambridge, Mass.: Harvard University Press.

BREWER, G. D. **1977.** "Scientific gaming: the development and use of free-form scenarios." New Haven, Conn.: Presented at annual meeting of American Political Science Association. Mimeo.

BREWER, G. D., and M. SHUBIK. **1979.** *The War Game: A Critique of Military Problem Solving.* Cambridge, Mass.: Harvard University Press.

BRIDGMAN, J. M. **1978.** "Gunpowder and governmental power: war in early modern Europe (1494–1825)." In L. L. Farrar, Jr., ed., *War: A Historical, Political and Social Study.* Santa Barbara, Calif.: ABC–Clio. Pp. 104–111.

BROCK, O. **1972.** *Pacifism in Europe to 1914.* Princeton, N.J.: Princeton University Press.

——. **1968.** *Pacifism in the United States: From the Colonial Era to the First World War.* Princeton, N.J.: Princeton University Press.

BROCH, T., and J. GALTUNG. **1966.** "Belligerence among the primitives." *J. of Peace Research,* 3(1):33–45.

BROCK, P. **1972.** *Pacifism in Europe to 1914.* Princeton, N.J.: Princeton University Press.

——. **1968.** *Pacifism in the United States: From the Colonial Era to the First World War.* Princeton, N.J.: Princeton University Press.

BRODIE, B. **1973.** *War and Politics.* New York: Macmillan.

BRODY, S. **1973.** "The son of a refugee." *Psychoanalytic Study of the Child,* 28:169–191.

BRONFENBRENNER, U. **1970.** *Two Worlds of Childhood: U.S. and U.S.S.R.* New York: Russell Sage Foundation.

——. **1961.** "The mirror image in Soviet–American relations: a social psychologist's report." *J. of Social Issues,* 17((3):45–56.

BRONOWSKI, J. **1973.** *The Ascent of Man.* Boston: Little, Brown.

BROWER, R. W. **1971.** *Hero and Saint: Shakespeare and the Graeco-Roman Heroic Tradition.* New York: Oxford University Press.

BROWN, G. S. **1976.** "Statement to the Congress on the defense posture of the United States for FY 1977." Washington, D.C.: U.S. Department of Defense.

BROWN, N. O. **1966.** *Love's Body.* New York: Random House.

——. **1959.** *Life Against Death: The Psychoanalytical Meaning of History.* Middletown, Conn.: Wesleyan University Press.

BROWN, S. **1974.** *New Forces in World Politics.* Washington, D.C.: The Brookings Institution.

BROWN, T. **1969.** *Statistical Indications of the Effect of Military Programs on Latin America.* Santa Monica, Calif.: Rand.

BROWNLEE, I. **1963.** *International Law and the Use of Force by States.* Oxford: Clarendon.

BUCHAN, A. **1974.** *Change Without War: The Shifting Structures of World Power.* London: Chatto and Windus.

BUCHANAN, A. R. **1977**. *Black Americans in World War II.* Santa Barbara, Calif.: ABC–Clio.

BUCHANAN, W., and H. CANTRIL. **1953**. *How Nations See Each Other.* Urbana: University of Illinois Press.

BUCHHEIT, L. C. **1978**. *Secession: The Legitimacy of Self-Determination.* New Haven, Conn.: Yale University Press.

BUENO DE MESQUITA, B. **1980** (in press). *The War Trap.* New Haven, Conn.: Yale University Press.

———. **1978**. "Systematic polarization and the occurrence and duration of war." *J. of Conflict Resolution,* 22(June):241–267.

———. **1975**. "Measuring systemic polarity." *J. of Conflict Resolution,* 19(June):187–216.

BULL, H. **1977**. *The Anarchical Society: A Study of Order in World Politics.* New York: Columbia University Press.

BURBECK, S. L., W. J. RAINE, and M. J. ABUDU STARK. **1978**. "The dynamics of riot growth: an epidemiological approach." *J. of Mathematical Sociology,* 6:1–22.

BURMESTER, H. C. **1978**. "The recruitment and use of mercenaries in armed conflict." *American J. of International Law,* 72(January):37–56.

BURNS, R. D. **1977**. *Arms Control and Disarmament: A Bibliography.* Santa Barbara, Calif.: ABC–Clio.

BURNS, R. D., and E. M. BENNETT, eds. **1974**. *Diplomats in Crisis: United States–Chinese–Japanese Relations, 1919–1941.* Santa Barbara, Calif.: ABC–Clio.

BURROWES, R., and B. SPECTOR. **1973**. "The strength and direction of relationships between domestic and external conflict and cooperation: Syria, 1961–67." In J. Wilkenfeld, ed., *Conflict Behavior and Linkage Politics.* New York: David McKay. Pp. 294–324.

BURSTEIN, P. **1979**. "Senate voting on the Vietnam War, 1964–1973: from hawk to dove." *J. of Political and Military Sociology,* 7(Fall):271–282.

BURSTEIN, P., and W. FREUDENBURG. **1977**. "Ending the Vietnam war: components of change in Senate voting on Vietnam war bills." *American J. of Sociology,* 82(March):991–1006.

BURT, R. R. **1977**. *Developments in Arms Transfers: Implications for Supplier Control and Recipient Autonomy.* P-5991. Santa Monica, Calif.: Rand.

BURTON, J. W. **1969**. *Conflict and Communication: The Use of Controlled Communication in International Relations.* London: Macmillan.

BUSCH, P. A. **1970**. "Mathematical models of arms races." In B. M. Russett, eds., *What Price Vigilance: The Burdens of National Defense.* New Haven, Conn.: Yale University Press. Pp. 193–234.

BUSS, A. H. **1961**. *The Psychology of Aggression.* New York: Wiley.

BUTLER, J. S. **1976**. "Inequality in the military: an examination of promotion time for black and white enlisted men." *American Sociological Rev.,* 41(October):807–818.

BUTTERWORTH, R. L. **1978a**. "Do conflict managers matter? an empirical assessment of interstate security disputes and resolution efforts, 1945–1974." *International Studies Q.,* 22(June):195–214.

———. **1978b**. *Moderation from Management: International Organizations and Peace.* Pittsburgh: Center for International Studies, University of Pittsburgh.

———. **1976**. *Managing Interstate Conflict, 1945–74: Data with Synopses.* Pittsburgh: Center for International Studies, University of Pittsburgh.

BUTWELL, R., ed. **1969**. *Foreign Policy and the Developing Nations.* Lexington: University of Kentucky Press.

BWY, D. P. **1971**. "Political instability in Latin America: the cross-cultural test of a causal model." In J. V. Gillespie and B. A. Nesvold, eds., *Macro-Quantitative Analysis.* Beverly Hills, Calif.: Sage. Pp. 113–140.

CAILLOIS, R. **1963**. *Bellone ou la Pente de la Guerre.* Brussels: La Renaissance du Livre.

CALLEO, D. **1970**. *The Atlantic Fantasy: The U.S. NATO, and Europe.* Baltimore: Johns Hopkins University Press.

CALLEO, D., and B. M. ROWLAND. **1973**. *America and the World Political Economy: Atlantic Dreams and National Realities.* Bloomington: Indiana University Press.

CAMERON, A., ed. **1978**. *Procopius: History of Wars Secret History and Building.* New York: Cyrco.

CAMPBELL, G. S. **1977**. *An Introduction to Environmental Biophysics.* New York: Springer-Verlag.

CAMPBELL, V. N. **1974**. *The Televote System for Civic Communication: First Demonstration and Evaluation.* Palo Alto, Calif.: American Institutes for Research.

CAMUS, A. **1972**. *The Plague.* S. Gilbert, tr. New York: Random House.

CANTRIL, A. H., ed. **1950**. *Tensions That Cause Wars.* Urbana: University of Illinois Press.

CANTRIL, A. H., and C. W. ROLL, JR. **1971**. *The Hopes and Fears of the American People.* New York: Universe Books.

CAPORASO, J. A. **1976**. "The external consequences of regional integration for pan-European relations: inequality, dependence, polarization, and symmetry." *International Studies Q.,* 20(September):341–392.

———. **1972**. *Functionalism and Regional Integration: A Logical and Empirical Assessment.* Beverly Hills, Calif.: Sage.

CAPORASO, J. A., and A. L. PELOWSKI. **1971**. "Economic and political integration in Europe: a time-series quasi-experimental analysis." *American Political Science Rev.,* 65(June):418–433.

CAPORASO, J. A., and L. L. ROOS, eds. **1973**. *Quasi-Experimental Approaches: Testing Theory and*

Evaluating Policy. Evanston, Ill.: Northwestern University Press.

CAPUTO, D. A. **1973**. "Public policy implications of defense and welfare expenditures in four modern democracies: 1950–1970." Denver: Presented at Graduate School of International Studies Comparative Public Policy Conference, University of Denver. Mimeo.

CAREY, O. L., ed. **1969**. *The Military–Industrial Complex and U.S. Foreign Policy.* Pullman: Washington State University Press.

CARLSMITH, L. **1973**. "Some personality characteristics of boys separated from their fathers during World War II." *Ethos,* 1(Winter):466–477.

CARLYLE, T. **1959**. *On Heroes, Hero Worship and the Heroic in History.* London: Oxford University Press.

CARNOY, M. **1974**. *Education as Cultural Imperialism.* New York: David McKay.

CARROLL, B. A. **1977**. "The outsiders: comments on Fukuda Hideko, Catherine Marshall, and Dorothy Detzer." *Peace and Change,* 4(Fall):23–27.

——. **1968**. "How wars end." Champagne–Urbana: Presented at University of Illinois. Mimeo.

CARROLL, B. A., and C. F. FINK. **1975**. "Theories of war causation: a matrix for analysis." In M. A. Nettleship, R. Dalegivens, and A. Nettleship, eds., *War: Its Causes and Correlates.* The Hague and Paris: Mouton. Pp. 55–72.

CARTWRIGHT, F. F. **1972**. *Disease and History.* New York: Crowell.

CARTWRIGHT, F. F., with M. D. BIDDISS. **1972**. *Disease and History.* New York: Crowell.

CASPARY, W. R. **1969**. "Dimensions of attitudes on international conflict: internationalism and military offensive action." *Peace Research Society (International) Papers,* 13:1–10.

——. **1967**. "Richardson's model of arms races." *International Studies Q.,* 2(March):63–90.

CATER, D., and S. STRICKLAND. **1975**. *TV Violence and the Child: The Evolution and Fate of the Surgeon General's Report.* New York: Russell Sage Foundation.

CATTELL, R. B. **1949**. "The dimensions of culture patterns and factorization of national characters." *J. of Abnormal and Social Psychology,* 44(October):443–469.

CATTELL, R. B., and R. L. GORSUCH. **1965**. "The definition and measurement of national morale and morality." *J. of Social Psychology,* 67(October):77–96.

CHAMBERS, J. W. **1977**. "The records of federal officials." *Peace and Change,* 4(Fall):47–54.

CHAN, S. **1978**. "Temporal delineation of international conflicts: Poisson results from the Vietnam war, 1963–1965." *International Studies Q.,* 22(June):237–265.

CHASE-DUNN, C. **1975**. "The effects of international economic dependence on development and inequality: a cross-national study." *American Sociological Rev.,* 40(December):720–738.

CHATFIELD, C. **1979**. "International peace research: the field defined by dissemination." *J. of Peace Research,* 16(2):163–179.

CHEN, L. F. **1974**. *State Succession Relating to Unequal Treaties.* Hamden, Conn.: Shoe String Press.

CHEN, M. K. **1976**. "A comprehensive population health index based on mortality and disability data." *Social Indicators Research,* 3(September):257–271.

CHENERY, H., et al. **1974**. *Redistribution with Growth.* London: Oxford University Press.

CHOUCRI, N. **1974a**. *Analyzing Global Interdependence.* Cambridge, Mass.: Center for International Studies, MIT.

——. **1974b**. *Population Dynamics and International Violence: Propositions, Insights and Evidence.* Lexington, Mass.: Heath.

CHOUCRI, N., and R. C. NORTH. **1975**. *Nations in Conflict: National Growth and International Violence.* San Francisco: W. H. Freeman and Company.

CHOUCRI, N., and T. W. ROBINSON, eds. **1978**. *Forecasting in International Relations: Theory, Methods, Problems, Prospects.* San Francisco: W. H. Freeman and Company.

CHRISTIANSEN, B. **1974**. *Attitudes Toward Foreign Affairs as a Function of Personality.* Westport, Conn.: Greenwood.

CHRISTIANSON, S. **1974**. "The war model in criminal justice: no substitute for victory." *Criminal Justice and Behavior,* 1(September):247–277.

CHRISTODOULOU, A. P. **1970**. *Conversion of Nuclear Facilities from Military to Civilian Uses: A Case Study in Hanford, Washington.* New York: Praeger.

CHURCHILL, R., M. NORDQUIST, and S. H. LAY, eds. **1977**. *New Directions in the Law of the Sea.* Dobbs Ferry, N.Y.: Oceana.

CIOBANU, D. **1975**. *Preliminary Objections Related to the Jurisdiction of the United Nations Political Organs.* The Hague: Nijhoff.

CLARK, C., and S. WELCH. **1972**. "Western European trade as a measure of integration: untangling the interpretations." *J. of Conflict Resolution,* 16(September):363–382.

CLARK, G. **1958**. *War and Society in the Seventeenth Century.* Cambridge: Cambridge University Press.

CLARK, G., and L. B. SOHN. **1966**. *World Peace Through World Law: Two Alternative Plans.* 3rd ed. Cambridge, Mass.: Harvard University Press.

CLARK, J. F., J. K. O'LEARY, and E. R. WITTKOPF. **1971**. "National attributes associated with dimensions of support for the United Nations." *International Organization,* 25(Winter):1–25.

CLARK, J. M. **1931**. *The Costs of the World War to the*

American People. New Haven, Conn.: Yale University Press.

CLARK, J. R. **1977**. *The Great Living System*. Pacific Grove, Calif.: Boxwood.

CLARKE, R. **1971**. *The Science of War and Peace*. New York: McGraw-Hill.

CLARKSON, J. D., and T. C. COCHRAN, eds. **1941**. *War as a Social Institution: The Historian's Perspective*. New York: Columbia University Press, for the American Historical Association.

CLAUDE, I. L. **1964**. *Swords into Plowshares*. New York: Random House.

CLAUDE, I. L., JR. **1971**. *Swords into Plowshares: The Problems and Progress of International Organization*. New York: Random House.

CLAUSEWITZ, K. VON. **1968**. *On War*. A. Rapoport, ed. Baltimore: Penguin.

CLAYTON, J. L., ed. **1970**. *The Economic Impact of the Vietnam War*. New York: Harcourt, Brace, and World.

CLEAVER, E. **1968**. *Soul on Ice*. New York: McGraw-Hill.

CLEVELAND, H. **1966**. *The Obligations of Power*. New York: Harper and Row.

CLINARD, M. B., and D. J. ABBOTT. **1973**. *Crime in Developing Countries: A Comparative Perspective*. New York: Wiley.

CLINE, R. S. **1977**. *World Power Assessment 1977: A Calculus of Strategic Drift*. Boulder: Westview.

CLINE, W. R., ed. **1979a**. *Policy Alternatives for a New International Economic Order: An Economic Analysis*. New York: Praeger.

———. **1979b**. *Proposals for a New International Economic Order*. New York: Praeger.

COBB, S. **1976**. "Defense spending and defense voting in the House: an empirical study of an aspect of the military–industrial complex thesis." *American J. of Sociology*, 82(July):163–182.

———. **1973**. "The United States Senate and the impact of defense spending concentrations." In S. Rosen, ed., *Testing the Theory of the Military–Industrial Complex*. Lexington, Mass.: Lexington Books. Pp. 157–196.

COCKCROFT, J. D. **1976**. "The transnationals, dependence, and underdevelopment." *Peace and Change*, 3(Spring):24–30.

COCKERHAM, W. **1973**. "Selective socialization: airborne training as status passage." *J. of Political and Military Sociology*, 1(Fall): 215–229.

COHEN, A. A., and J. DOTAN. **1976**. "Communication in the family as a function of stress during war and peace." *J. of Marriage and the Family*, 38(February):141–148.

COIL, G. L. **1978**. "War crimes of the American revolution." *Military Law Rev.*, 82(Autumn):171–198.

COLBACH, E. **1971**. "Marijuana use by GIs in Vietnam." *American J. of Psychiatry*, 128 (August):204–207.

COLEMAN, S. **1975**. *Measurement and Analysis of Political Systems: A Science of Social Behavior*. New York: Wiley.

COLLINS, J. N. **1973**. "Foreign conflict behavior and domestic disorder in Africa." In J. Wilkenfeld, ed., *Conflict Behavior and Linkage Politics*. New York: David McKay. Pp. 251–293.

COMBACAU, J. **1974**. *Le Pouvoir de Sanction de l'O.N.U. Etude Théorique de la Coercition Non-militaire*. Paris: Editions Pedone.

COMSTOCK, G., et al. **1978**. *Television and Human Behavior*. New York: Columbia University Press.

CONANT, M. A., and F. R. GOLD. **1978**. *The Geopolitics of Energy*. Boulder: Westview.

CONCANNON, R. J. G. **1967**. "The third enemy: the role of epidemics in the Thirty Years' War." *J. of World History*, 10(3):500–511.

CONTE, L. **1972**. "A neuropsychiatric team in Viet Nam 1966–1967: an overview." In R. S. Parker, ed., *The Emotional Stress of War, Violence, and Peace*. Pittsburgh: Stanwix House. Pp. 163–175.

COOK, B. W., ed. **1972**. *Peace Projects of the Seventeenth Century*. New York: Garland.

COOK, F. J. **1962**. *The Warfare State*. New York: Macmillan.

COOPER, K. **1942**. *Barriers Down*. New York: Farrar and Rinehart.

COOPER, M. N. **1972**. "The occurrence of mutiny in World War I: a sociological view." *International Behavioral Scientist*, 4(September):1–10.

COOPER, S. E., ed., **1974**. *Peace Projects of the Eighteenth Century*. New York: Garland.

COPLIN, W. **1968**. "The World Court in the international bargaining process." In R. W. Gregg and M. Barkun, eds., *The United Nations System and Its Functions*. Princeton, N.J.: Van Nostrand. Pp. 317–332.

COPLIN, W., and J. M. ROCHESTER. **1972**. "The Permanent Court of International Justice, the International Court of Justice, the League of Nations, and the United Nations: a comparative empirical survey." *American Political Science Rev.*, 66(June):529–550.

CORBETT, P. **1971**. *The Growth of World Law*. Princeton, N.J.: Princeton University Press.

———. **1969**. *From International to World Law*. Research Monograph No. 1. Bethlehem, Pa.: Department of International Relations, Lehigh University.

———. **1968**. "International law." In D. L. Sills, ed., *International Encyclopedia of the Social Sciences*, Vol. 7. New York: Crowell Collier and Macmillan. Pp. 547–551.

CORNING, P. A., and C. H. CORNING. **1972**. "Toward a general theory of violent aggression." *Social Science Information*, 11(June–August):7–35.

COSER, L. A. **1956**. *The Functions of Social Conflict*. Glencoe, Ill.: Free Press.

COSTIGAN, G. **1978.** "British poetry and World War I." In L. L. Farrar, ed., *War: A Historical, Political and Social Study.* Santa Barbara, Calif.: ABC–Clio.

COT, J. P. **1972.** *International Conciliation.* London: Europa.

COULTER, H. L. **1973–1977.** *Divided Legacy: A History of the Schism in Medical Thought.* 3 vols. Washington, D.C.: McGrath Publishing and Weekhawken Book.

COX, A. M. **1976.** *The Dynamics of Detente: How to End the Arms Race.* New York: Norton.

COX, R. W. **1979.** "Ideologies and the new international economic order: reflections on some recent literature." *International Organization,* 33(Spring):257–300.

——, ed. **1970.** *The Politics of International Organization.* New York: Praeger.

CRAIG, G. **1961.** *Europe Since 1815.* New York: Holt, Rinehart and Winston.

CRESPIGNY, A. DE, and J CRONIN. **1975.** *Ideologies of Politics.* New York: Oxford University Press.

CRETEKOS, C. J. **1973.** "Common psychological syndromes of the army wife." *Military Medicine,* 138(January):36–37.

CROAKE, J. W., and F. H. KNOX. **1973.** "The changing nature of children's fears." *Child Study J.,* 3(2):91–105.

CROSBY, A. W., JR. **1976.** *Epidemic and Peace: 1918.* Westport, Conn.: Greenwood.

CULYER, A. J., and P. JACOBS. **1972.** "The war and public expenditure on mental health care in England and Wales: the postponement effect." *Social Science and Medicine,* 6(February):35–56.

CUNLIFFE, M. **1968.** *Soldiers and Civilians: The Martial Spirit in America, 1775–1865.* Boston: Little, Brown.

CURLE, A. **1971.** *Making Peace.* London: Tavistock.

CURLIN, G. T., L. C. CHEN, and S. B. HUSSAIN. **1976.** "Demographic crisis: the impact of the Bangladesh civil war (1971) on births and deaths in a rural area of Bangladesh." *Population Studies,* 30(March):87–105.

CURRIE, M. R. **1976.** *The Department of Defense Program of Research, Development, Test and Evaluation, FY 1977.* Washington, D.C.: U.S. Department of Defense.

CURTIN, P. D., ed. **1971.** *Imperialism.* New York: Harper and Row.

CUTRIGHT, P. **1963.** "National political development: measurement and analysis." *American Sociological Rev.,* 28(April):253–264.

DABELKO, D., and J. M. McCORMICK. **1977.** "Opportunity costs of defense: some cross-national evidence." *J. of Peace Research,* 14(2):145–154.

DAHL, B. B., et al. **1975.** *Second Generational Effects of War-Induced Separations: Comparing the Adjustment of Children in Reunited and Non-Reunited Families:* San Diego, Calif.: Naval Health Research Center.

DAHL, R. A. **1971.** *Polyarchy: Participation and Opposition.* New Haven, Conn.: Yale University Press.

——. **1970.** *After the Revolution: Authority in a Good Society.* New Haven, Conn.: Yale University Press.

DAHL, R. A., and E. R. TUFTE. **1973.** *Size and Democracy.* Stanford, Calif.: Stanford University Press.

DALY, H. E., ed. **1973.** *Toward a Steady-state Economy.* San Francisco: W. H. Freeman and Company.

DANTE, A. **1954.** *De Monarchia. (Monarchy, and Three Political Letters.)* London: Weidenfeld and Nicolson.

DASH, J. G. **1967.** "Comments on the paper by Smoker." *Peace Research Society (International) Papers,* 7:63–65.

DAUGHERTY, W. E. **1968.** "Psychological warfare." In D. L. Sills, ed., *International Encyclopedia of the Social Sciences,* Vol. 13. New York: Crowell Collier and Macmillan. Pp. 46–49.

DAVID, A. E. **1975.** *The Strategy of Treaty Termination.* New Haven, Conn.: Yale University Press.

DAVIDSON, S. **1980.** "The clinical effects of massive psychic trauma in families of holocaust survivors." *J. of Marital and Family Therapy,* 6(January):11–22.

DAVIE, M. R. **1968.** *The Evolution of War: A Study of Its Role in Early Societies.* New York: Kennikat.

DAVIES, J. C. **1974.** "The J-curve and power struggle theories of collective violence." *American Sociological Rev.,* 39(August):607–610.

——. **1973.** "Political violence: the dominance–submission nexus." In H. Hirsch and D. Perry, eds., *Violence as Politics.* New York: Harper and Row. Pp. 52–71.

——. **1972.** "Toward a theory of revolution." In I. K. Feierabend, R. L. Feierabend, and T. Gurr, eds., *Anger, Violence, and Politics.* Englewood Cliffs, N.J.: Prentice-Hall. Pp. 67–84.

——, ed. **1971.** *When Men Revolt and Why.* New York: Free Press.

DAVIS, N. Z. **1973.** "The rites of violence: religious riot in sixteenth century France." *Past and Present,* 59(May):51–91.

DAVIS, V. **1974.** "Levée en masse, c'est fini: the deterioration of popular willingness to serve." In J. P. Lovell and P. S. Kronenberg, eds., *New Civil–Military Relations: The Agonies of Adjustment to Post-Vietnam Realities.* New Brunswick, N.J.: Transaction Books. Pp. 89–110.

DAVIS, W. W., G. T. DUNCAN, and R. M. SIVERSON. **1977.** "The dynamics of warfare: 1816–1965." Washington, D.C.: Presented at annual meeting of American Political Science Association. Mimeo.

DAVISON, W. P. **1974.** *Mass Communication and Conflict Resolution: The Role of the Information Media in the Advancement of International Understanding.* New York: Praeger.

DEAN, D. P., JR., and J. A. VASQUEZ. **1976.** "From power politics to issue politics: bipolarity and multipolarity in light of a new paradigm." *Western Political Q.,* 29(March):7–29.

DECALO, S. **1976.** *Coups and Army Rule in Africa: Studies in Military Style.* New Haven, Conn.: Yale University Press.

DECHMANN, H. B. **1972.** "Informal interaction between governments." In P. Heintz, ed., *A Macrosociological Theory of Societal Systems.* Bern: Hans Huber. Pp. 185–230.

DEDRING, J. **1976.** *Recent Advances in Peace and Conflict Research: A Critical Survey.* Beverly Hills, Calif.: Sage.

DE FAZIO, V. J. **1975.** "The Vietnam era veteran: psychological problems." *J. of Contemporary Psychotherapy,* 7(Winter):9–15.

DEITCHMAN, D., and J. SEYMOUR. **1964.** *Limited War and American Defense Policy.* Washington, D.C.: Institute of Defense Analysis.

DELACROIX, J. **1977.** "The export of raw materials and economic growth: a cross-national study." *American Sociological Rev.,* 42(October): 795–808.

DELL, S. **1963.** *Trade Blocs and Common Markets.* New York: Knopf.

DELURY, G. E., ed. **1977.** *The World Almanac and Book of Facts: 1977.* New York: Newspaper Enterprise Association.

DENENBERG, V. H., and M. X. ZARROW. **1970.** "Rat pax." *Psychology Today,* 3(May):45–47, 66–67.

DENITCH, B. **1976.** "Violence and social change in the Yugoslav revolution." *Comparative Politics,* 8(April):465–478.

DENTON, F. H. **1966.** "Some regularities in international conflict, 1820–1949." *Background,* 9(February):283–296.

DENTON, F. H., and W. PHILLIPS. **1968.** "Some patterns in the history of violence." *J. of Conflict Resolution,* 12(June):182–195.

DE RIZ, L. **1970.** "Army and politics in Uruguay." *Revista Latinoamericana de Sociologia,* 6(September–December):420–442.

DE SAUSSURE, H. **1978.** "Review of: *International Law—The Conduct of Armed Conflict with Air Operations,* by the *U.S. Air Force.* (Pamphlet 110-31, 19 November 1976.)" *American J. of International Law,* 72(January):174–176.

DEUTSCH, K. W. **1979.** *Tides Among Nations.* New York: Free Press.

———. **1978.** *The Analysis of International Relations.* 2nd ed. Englewood Cliffs, N.J.: Prentice-Hall.

———. **1976.** "Toward an interdisciplinary model of world stability and change: some intellectual preconditions." *J. of Peace Science,* 2(Spring):1–14.

———. **1975.** "On inequality and limited growth: some world political effects." *International Studies Q.,* 19(December):381–398.

———. **1974.** *Politics and Government: How People Decide Their Fate.* 2nd ed. Boston: Houghton Mifflin.

———. **1967.** *Arms Control and the Atlantic Alliance.* New York: Wiley.

———. **1966.** "Integration and arms control in the European political environment: a summary report." *American Political Science Rev.,* 60(June):354–365.

———. **1960.** "The propensity to international transactions." *Political Studies,* 8(2): 147–155.

———. **1953.** *Nationalism and Social Communication: An Inquiry into the Foundations of Nationality.* Cambridge, Mass.: MIT Press.

DEUTSCH, K. W., and A. ECKSTEIN. **1961.** "National industrialization and the declining share of the international economic sector: 1890–1959." *World Politics,* 13(January):267–299.

DEUTSCH, K. W., and W. J. FOLTZ, eds. **1966.** *Nation-Building.* New York: Atherton.

DEUTSCH, K. W., and D. SENGHAAS. **1975.** "The fragile sanity of states: a theoretical analysis." In M. Kilson, ed., *New States in the Modern World.* Cambridge, Mass.: Harvard University Press. Pp. 200–244.

———. **1973.** "The steps to war: a survey of system levels, decision stages, and research results." In P. J. McGowan, ed., *Sage International Yearbook of Foreign Policy Studies.* Beverly Hills, Calif.: Sage. Pp. 55–77.

DEUTSCH, K. W., and J. D. SINGER. **1964.** "Multipolar power systems and international stability." *World Politics,* 16(April):390–406.

DEUTSCH, K. W., et al. **1957.** *Political Community and the North Atlantic Area.* Princeton, N.J.: Princeton University Press.

DEUTSCH, M. **1973.** *The Resolution of Conflict: Constructive and Destructive Processes.* New Haven, Conn.: Yale University Press.

DE VOLPI, A. **1979.** *Proliferation, Plutonium and Policy: Institutional and Technological Impediments to Nuclear Weapons.* New York: Pergamon.

DEWEY, E. R. **1964.** "The 17.7-year cycle in war, 600 B.C.–A.D. 1957." *Research Bull.* Vol. 1964–2: (August):whole issue. Pittsburgh:Foundation for the Study of Cycles.

DEWITT, D. B. **1977.** "The dilemma of hypotheticality in research on the causes of war." Washington, D.C.: Presented at annual meeting of American Political Science Association. Mimeo.

DHOKALIA, R. P. **1970.** *The Codification of Public International Law.* Dobbs Ferry, N.Y.: Oceana.

DICKINSON, G. L. **1972.** *Causes of International War.* New York: Garland.

DICKSON, P. **1976.** *The Electronic Battlefield.* Bloomington: Indiana University Press.

DILLON, W. **1968**. *Gifts and Nations: The Obligation to Give, Receive, and Repay*. The Hague: Mouton.

DILLON, W. S. **1972**. "Anthropological perspectives on violence." In G. Usdin, ed., *Perspectives on Violence*. New York: Brunner/Mazel. Pp. 69–108.

DI MAIO, V. J. M., et al. **1974**. "Comparison of the wounding effects of commercially available handgun ammunition suitable for police use." *FBI Law Enforcement Bull.*, 43(December):3–8.

DINSTEIN, Y. **1965**. *The Defense of "Obedience to Superior Orders" in International Law*. Leyden: Sijthoff.

DIRECTOR, A., ed. **1952**. *Defense, Controls, and Inflation*. Chicago: University of Chicago Press.

DIVALE, W. T. **1973**. *Warfare in Primitive Societies: A Bibliography*. Santa Barbara, Calif.: ABC–Clio.

DIVALE, W. T., F. CHAMBERIS, and D. GANGLOFF. **1976**. "War, peace and marital residence in pre-industrial societies." *J. of Conflict Resolution*, 20(March):57–78.

DIXON, N. F. **1976**. *On the Psychology of Military Incompetence*. New York: Basic Books.

DIXON, W. J. **1977**. "Research on research revisited: another half decade of quantitative and field research in international organizations." *International Organization*, 31(Winter):65–83.

DOBBYN, R. C., W. J. BRUCHEY, JR., and L. D. SHUBIN. **1975**. *An Evaluation of Police Handgun Ammunition: Summary Report*. Washington, D.C.: U.S. Department of Justice, Law Enforcement Assistance Administration, National Institute of Law Enforcement and Criminal Justice.

DOLAN, M. B. **1975**. "The study of regional integration: a quantitative analysis of the neofunctionalist and systemic approaches." *International Studies Q.*, 19(September):285–315.

DOLLARD, J. **1944**. *Fear in Battle*. Washington, D.C.: The Infantry Journal.

DOLLARD, J., et al. **1967**. *Frustration and Aggression*. New Haven, Conn.: Yale University Press.

DOMHOFF, G. W. **1967**. *Who Rules America?* Englewood Cliffs, N.J.: Prentice-Hall.

DONELAN, M. D., and M. J. GRIEVE. **1973**. *International Disputes: Case Histories 1945–1970*. London: Europa.

DOOB, L. W. **1974**. "A Cyprus workshop: an exercise in intervention methodology." *J. of Social Psychology*, 94(December):161–178.

——, ed. **1970**. *Resolving Conflict in Africa: The Fermeda Workshop*. New Haven, Conn.: Yale University Press.

——. **1966**. *Public Opinion and Propaganda*. 2nd ed. Hamden, Conn.: Shoe String Press.

——. **1964**. *Patriotism and Nationalism: Their Psychological Foundations*. New Haven, Conn.: Yale University Press.

DORAN, C. F. **1976**. "Regional integration and domestic unrest: a comparative study in Europe and Central America." *International Interactions*, 3(2):67–82.

DÖRFER, I. **1973**. *System 37 Viggen: Arms, Technology and the Domestication of Glory*. Oslo: Universitetsforlaget.

DOUGLAS, J. D., ed. **1970**. *Deviance and Respectability: The Social Construction of Moral Meaning*. New York: Basic Books.

DROR, Y. **1971**. *Crazy States: A Counterconventional Strategic Problem*. Lexington, Mass.: Lexington Books.

DSAA: *See U.S. Department of Defense, Defense Security Assistance Agency*.

DUCENNE, D., and M. MOMDLIN, eds. **1974**. *Yearbook of International Organizations*. Brussels: Union of International Associations.

DUDDLE, M. **1973**. "An increase of anorexia nervosa in a university population." *British J. of Psychiatry*, 123(December):711–712.

DUFF, E., and J. MCCAMANT. **1976**. *Violence and Repression in Latin America: A Quantitative and Historical Analysis*. New York: Free Press.

DUFFY, G. **1977**. *Soviet Nuclear Exports*. P-6044. Santa Monica, Calif.: Rand.

DUMAS, L. J. **1977**. "Systems reliability and national insecurity." *Peace Research Rev.*, 7(November):66–85.

DUMAS, S., and K. O. VEDEL-PETERSEN. **1923**. *Losses of Life Caused by War*. Oxford: Clarendon.

DUNCAN, G. T., and R. M. SIVERSON. **1975**. "Markov chain models for conflict analysis: results for Sino-Indian relations, 1959–1964." *International Studies Q.*, 19(September):344–373.

DUPUY, R. E., and T. N. DUPUY. **1970**. *The Encyclopedia of Military History, from 3500 B.C. to the Present*. New York: Harper and Row.

DURBIN, E. F. M., and J. BOWLBY. **1939**. *Personal Aggressiveness and War*. New York: Columbia University Press.

DURFEE, H. A. **1975**. "War, politics, and radical pluralism." *Philosophy and Phenomenological Research*, 35(June):549–558.

DURKHEIM, E. **1972**. *Selected Writings*. A. Giddens, ed. Cambridge: Cambridge University Press.

——. **1966**. *Suicide: A Study in Sociology*. J. A. Spaulding and G. Simpson, trs. and eds. New York: Free Press.

——. **1964**. *The Division of Labor in Society*. George Simpson, tr. New York: Free Press.

DUVALL, R. **1980** (in press). "A formal model of 'dependencia' theory: structure and measurement." In R. L. Merritt and B. Russett, eds., *From National Development to Global Community*. London: Allen and Unwin.

DYER, M. **1959**. *The Weapon on the Wall: Rethinking Psychological Warfare*. Baltimore: Johns Hopkins University Press.

EAST, M. A. **1972**. "Status discrepancy and violence

in the international system: an empirical analysis." In J. N. Rosenau, V. Davis, and M. A. East, eds., *The Analysis of International Politics.* New York: Free Press. Pp. 229–316.

——. **1969.** "Rank-dependent interaction and mobility: two aspects of international stratification." *Peace Research Society (International) Papers,* 14:113–127.

EAST, M. A., and P. M. GREGG. **1967.** "Factors influencing cooperation and conflict in the international system." *International Studies Q.,* 11(September):224–269.

EAST, M. A., S. A. SALMORE, and C. F. HERMANN, eds. **1978.** *Why Nations Act: Theoretical Perspectives for Comparative Foreign Policy Studies.* Beverly Hills, Calif.: Sage.

EATHERLY, C. **1961.** *Burning Conscience: The Case of the Hiroshima Pilot, Claude Eatherly, told in His Letters to Gunther Anders.* London: Weidenfeld and Nicolson.

EBENSTEIN, W. E. **1973.** *Today's Issues: Communism, Fascism, Capitalism, Socialism.* Englewood Cliffs, N.J.: Prentice-Hall.

EBERWEIN, W. D., and T. CUSACK. **1980.** "International disputes: a look at some new data." Los Angeles: Presented at annual meeting of International Studies Association. Mimeo.

ECKHARDT, W. **1979.** Global compassion and compulsion," *J. of Peace Research,* 16(1):79–86.

——, ed. **1976.** "Cross-national measures of compassion." *Peace Research Rev.,* 8(October):109–114.

——. **1974.** "Primitive militarism." *Peace Research Rev.,* 6(October):63–77.

——. **1972.** *Compassion: Toward a Science of Value.* Oakville, Ontario: Canadian Peace Research Institute.

——. **1972a.** "Attitudes of Canadian peace groups." *J. of Conflict Resolution,* 16(September):341–352.

——. **1972b.** "Cross-cultural attitudes toward world government." *International J. of Group Tensions,* 2(1):31–47.

——. **1972c.** "Cross-cultural theories of war and aggression." *International J. of Group Tensions,* 2(3):36–51.

——. **1969.** "Ideology and personality in social attitudes." *Peace Research Rev.,* 3(April):1–105.

ECKHARDT, W., and R. WHITE. **1967.** "A test of the mirror image hypothesis." *J. of Conflict Resolution,* 11(September):325–332.

ECKHARDT, W., and C. YOUNG. **1977.** *Governments Under Fire: Civil Conflict and Imperialism.* New Haven, Conn.: Human Relations Area File Press.

——. **1975.** "Psychology of imperialism." *Peace Research,* 7(January):42–44.

ECKSTEIN, H. **1970.** "On the etiology of internal wars." In G. A. Kelly and C. W. Brown, Jr., eds., *Struggles in the State: Sources and Patterns*

of World Revolution. New York: Wiley. Pp. 168–195.

——, ed. **1964.** *Internal War: Problems and Approaches.* Glencoe, Ill.: Free Press.

ECONOMIST INTELLIGENCE UNIT. **1971.** *The Growth and Spread of Multinational Companies.* London: Economist Intelligence Unit.

——. **1963.** *The Economic Effects of Disarmament.* London: Economist Intelligence Unit.

EDDY, J. A. **1977.** "The case of the missing sunspots." *Scientific American,* 236(May):80–95.

EDMEAD, F. **1971.** *Analysis and Prediction in International Mediation.* New York: United Nations Institute for Training and Research.

EDWARDS, D. V. **1973.** *Creating a New World Politics: From Conflict to Coopeation.* New York: David McKay.

EFRON, B., and C. MORRIS. **1977.** "Stein's paradox in statistics." *Scientific American,* 236(May): 119–127.

EHRENKRANZ, J., E. BLISS, and M. SHEARD. **1974.** "Plasma testosterone: correlation with aggressive behavior and social dominance in man." *Psychosomatic Medicine,* 36(November–December):469–475.

EIBL-EIBESFELDT, I. **1979.** *The Biology of Peace and War.* New York: Viking.

——. **1972.** *Love and Hate.* G. Strachan, tr. New York: Holt, Rinehart and Winston.

EIDE, A. **1980.** *Human Rights in the World Society: The Commitments, the Reality, the Future.* Pine Plains, N.Y.: Earl M. Coleman.

——. **1977.** "Arms transfer and third world militarization." *Bull. of Peace Proposals,* 8(2):99–102.

EINSTEIN, A., and S. FREUD. **1971.** "Why war." *International J. for the Reduction of Group Tensions,* 1(January–March):9–25.

EISENBERG, L. **1972.** "The human nature of human nature." *Science,* 176(April):123–128.

EISENSTADT, S. N. **1963.** *The Political Systems of Empires.* New York: Free Press.

EISENSTADT, S. N., and S. ROKKAN, eds. **1973.** *Building States and Nations: Models, Analyses and Data Across Three Worlds.* 2 vols. Beverly Hills, Calif.: Sage.

EITINGER, L. **1970.** "The syndrome of concentration camps: former Norwegian prisoners of German concentration camps." *Ceskoslovenska Psychiatrie,* 66(October):257–266.

——. **1969.** "Rehabilitation of concentration camp survivors following concentration camp 'trauma.' " *Psychotherapy and Psychosomatics,* 17(1):42–49.

——. **1964.** *Concentration Camp Survivors in Norway and Israel.* New York: Humanities.

——. **1961.** "Pathology of the concentration camp syndrome." *Archives of General Psychiatry,* 5(October):371–379.

ELDRIDGE, A. F. **1979.** *Images of Conflict.* New York: St. Martin's.

ELEFTHERIOU, B. E., and J. P. SCOTT, eds. **1971.** *The Physiology of Aggression and Defeat.* New York: Plenum.

ELLIOT, G. **1972.** *The 20th Century Book of the Dead.* New York: Ballantine.

ELLIOTT, G. C. **1980.** "Components of pacifism: conceptualization and measurement." *J. of Conflict Resolution,* 24(March):27–54.

ELLIS, D. P., P. WEINIR, and L. MILLER. **1971.** "Does the trigger pull the finger? an experimental test of weapons as aggression-eliciting stimuli." *Sociometry,* 34(December):453–465.

ELLIS, J. **1974.** *Armies in Revolution.* New York: Oxford University Press.

ELLIS, L. **1973.** "Contributions to the history of psychology. XIV: Trends in peace research." *Psychological Reports,* 33(October):349–350.

ELLUL, J. **1971.** *Autopsy of Revolution.* New York: Knopf.

——. **1967.** *The Technological Society.* New York: Knopf.

EMERSON, R. **1960.** *From Empire to Nation: The Rise to Self-Assertion of Asian and African Peoples.* Cambridge, Mass.: Harvard University Press.

ENLOE, C., ed. **1979.** *Police, Military and Ethnicity: Foundations of State Power.* New Brunswick, N.J.: Transaction Books.

ENSER, A. G. S. **1979.** *A Subject Bibliography of the First World War.* Boulder: Westview.

EPSTEIN, H. **1979.** *Children of the Holocaust: Conversations with Sons and Daughters of Survivors.* New York: Putnam.

EPSTEIN, W. **1976.** *The Last Chance: Nuclear Proliferation and Arms Control.* New York: Free Press.

——. **1975.** "The Proliferation of nuclear weapons." *Scientific American,* 232(April):18–33.

ERASMUS, D. **1968.** *The Education of a Christian Prince.* L. K. Bonn, tr. New York: Norton.

ERMALINSKI, R., P. G. HANSON, and W. E. O'CONNELL. **1972.** "Toward resolution of a generation-gap conflict on a psychiatric ward." *International J. of Group Tensions,* 2(2):77–89.

ERON, L., et al. **1972.** "Does television violence cause aggression?" *American Psychologist,* 27(April):253–263.

ERSKINE, H. **1972–1973.** "The polls: pacifism and the generation gap." *Public Opinion Q.,* 36(Winter):616–627.

ESCALONA, S. **1962.** *Children and the Threat of Nuclear War.* New York: Child Study Association of America.

ETHEREDGE, L. S. **1975.** "Personality and foreign policy." *Psychology Today,* 8(March):37–42.

ETZIONI, A. **1970.** "The Kennedy experiment." In A. Etzioni and M. Wenglinsky, eds., *War and Its Prevention.* New York: Harper and Row. Pp. 215–244.

——. **1965.** *Political Unification: A Comparative Study of Leaders and Forces.* New York: Holt, Rinehart and Winston.

——. **1962.** *The Hard Way to Peace.* New York: Crowell Collier.

ETZIONI, A., and M. WENGLINSKY, eds. **1970.** *War and Its Prevention.* New York: Harper and Row.

EVANS, A. F., and J. F. MURPHY, eds. **1978.** *Legal Aspects of International Terrorism.* Lexington, Mass.: Lexington Books.

EVANS, M. D., M. FELSON, and K. C. LAND. **1980.** "Developing social indicators research on the military in American society." *Social Indicators Research,* 8(March):81–102.

FABBRO, D. **1978.** "Peaceful societies: an introduction." *J. of Peace Research,* 15(1):67–83.

FABIAN, L. L. **1976.** "Toward a peacekeeping renaissance." *International Organization,* 30(Winter):153–162.

FAGAN, S. **1970.** *Central American Economic Integration: The Politics of Unequal Benefits.* Berkeley: Institute of International Studies, University of California.

FAHEY, J. H. **1971,** *Irenology: The Study of Peace.* New York: Christophers.

FALK, R. A., ed. **1976.** *The Vietnam War and International Law.* Vol. 4: *The Concluding Phase.* Princeton, N.J.: Princeton University Press.

——, ed. **1972.** *The Vietnam War and International Law.* Vol. 3: *The Widening Context.* Princeton, N.J.: Princeton University Press.

——. **1972.** *This Endangered Planet: Prospects and Proposals for World Survival.* New York: Random House.

——, ed. **1971a.** *The International Law of Civil War.* Baltimore: Johns Hopkins University Press.

——. **1971b.** "Nuremberg: past, present, and future." *Yale Law J.,* 80(June):1501–1528.

——, ed. **1969.** *The Vietnam War and International Law.* Vol. 2. Princeton, N.J.: Princeton University Press.

——, ed. **1968a.** *Legal Order in a Violent World.* Princeton, N.J.: Princeton University Press.

——. **1968b.** "The Shimoda case: a legal appraisal of the atomic attacks upon Hiroshima and Nagasaki." In R. A. Falk, ed., *Legal Order in a Violent World.* Princeton, N.J.: Princeton University Press. Pp. 374–413.

——, ed. **1968c.** *The Vietnam War and International Law.* Vol. 1. Princeton, N.J.: Princeton University Press.

——. **1964.** "Janus tormented: the international law of internal war." In J. N. Rosenau, ed., *International Aspects of Civil Strife.* Princeton, N.J.: Princeton University Press. Pp. 185–248.

——. **1963.** *Law, Morality, and War in the Contemporary World.* New York: Praeger.

FALK, R. A., G. KOLKO, and R. J. LIFTON. **1971.** *Crimes of War: A Legal, Political-Documentary and Psychological Inquiry into the Responsibility of Leaders, Citizens, and Soldiers for Criminal Acts in Wars.* New York: Random House.

FALKOWSKI, L. S. **1978.** *Presidents, Secretaries of State, and Crises in U.S. Foreign Relations: A Model and Predictive Analysis.* Boulder: Westview.

FANON, F. **1967.** *Black Skin: White Masks.* C. L. Markmann, tr. New York: Grove.

———. **1965.** *The Wretched of the Earth.* C. Farrington, tr. New York: Grove.

FARBEROW, N. L., ed. **1975.** *Suicide in Different Cultures.* Baltimore: University Park Press.

FARER, T. J. **1977.** "The greening of the globe: a preliminary appraisal of the World Order Models Project (WOMP)." *International Organization,* 31(Winter):129–149.

———. **1971.** "Law and war." In C. E. Black and R. A. Falk, eds., *The Future of the International Legal Order.* Vol. 3: *Conflict Management.* Princeton, N.J.: Princeton University Press. Pp. 15–78.

FARLEY, P. J., S. S. KAPLAN, and W. H. LEWIS. **1978.** *Arms Across the Sea.* Washington, D.C.: The Brookings Institution.

FARRAR, L. L., JR., ed. **1978.** *War: A Historical, Political and Social Study.* Santa Barbara, Calif.: ABC–Clio.

FARRELL, J. C., and A. P. SMITH. **1967.** *Image and Reality in World Politics.* New York: Columbia University Press.

FAWCETT, J. **1977.** *International Economic Conflicts: Prevention and Resolution.* London: Europa.

FEAGIN, J. R., and H. HAHN. **1973.** *Ghetto Revolts: The Politics of Violence in American Cities.* New York: Macmillan.

FEDDER, E. H., ed. **1971.** *The United Nations: Problems and Prospects.* St. Louis: Center for International Studies, University of Missouri.

FEIERABEND, I. K. **1972.** "Systemic conditions of political aggression: an application of frustration–aggression theory." In I. K. Feierabend, R. L. Feierabend, and T. Gurr, eds., *Anger, Violence, and Politics.* Englewood Cliffs, N.J.: Prentice-Hall. Pp. 136–183.

———. **1971.** "The relationship of systematic frustration, political coercion, and political instability: a cross-national analysis." In J. V. Gillespie and B. A. Nesvold, eds., *Macro-Quantitative Analysis.* Beverly Hills, Calif.: Sage. Pp. 417–440.

———. **1969.** "Level of development and international behavior." In R. Butwell, ed., *Foreign Policy and the Developing Nations.* Lexington: University of Kentucky Press. Pp. 135–188.

FEIERABEND, I. K., and R. L. FEIERABEND. **1973.** "Violent consequences of violence." In H.

Hirsch and D. Perry, eds., *Violence as Politics.* New York: Harper and Row. Pp. 187–219.

———. **1972.** "Coerciveness and change: cross-national trends." *American Behavioral Scientist,* 15(July–August):911–927.

FEIERABEND, I. K., R. L. FEIERABEND, and T. GURR, eds. **1972.** *Anger, Violence, and Politics.* Englewood Cliffs, N.J.: Prentice-Hall.

FEIERABEND, I. K., R. L. FEIERABEND, and B. A. NESVOLD. **1969.** "Social change and political violence: cross-national patterns." In H. D. Graham and T. R. Gurr, eds., *The History of Violence in America: Historical and Comparative Perspectives.* New York: Praeger. Pp. 632–687.

FEIERABEND, I. K., and B. A. NESVOLD. **1963.** "Correlates of political stability." New York: Presented at annual meeting of American Political Science Association. Mimeo.

FEIT, E. **1973.** *The Armed Bureaucrats: Military–Administrative Regimes and Political Development.* Boston: Houghton Mifflin.

FELD, B. T., et al. **1971.** *Impact of New Technologies on the Arms Race.* Cambridge, Mass.: MIT Press.

FELD, W. J. **1976.** "The impact of nongovernmental organizations on the formulation of transnational policies." *Jerusalem J. of International Relations,* 2(Fall):63–95.

———. **1964.** *The Court of the European Communities.* The Hague: Nijhoff.

FELD, W. J., and J. K. WILGEN. **1977.** *Domestic Political Realities of European Unification: A Study of Mass Public and Elites in the European Community Countries.* Boulder: Westview.

FELDMAN, G. D. **1966.** *Army, Industry, and Labor in Germany, 1914–1918.* Princeton, N.J.: Princeton University Press.

FELDSTEIN, H. **1967.** "A study of transaction and political integration: transnational labour flow within the European economic community." *J. of Common Market Studies,* 6(September):24–55.

FERENCZ, B. B. **1979.** *An International Criminal Court: A Step Toward World Peace—A Documentary History and Analysis.* Dobbs-Ferry, N.Y.: Oceana.

———. **1975.** *Defining International Aggression: The Search for World Peace—A Documentary History and Analysis.* Dobbs Ferry, N.Y.: Oceana.

FERKISS, V. **1974.** *The Future of Technological Civilization.* New York: Braziller.

———. **1969.** *Technological Man.* New York: Braziler.

FERRERO, G. **1972.** *Militarism.* New York: Garland.

FERRIS, W. H. **1973.** *The Power Capabilities of Nation-States: International Conflict and War.* Lexington, Mass.: Heath.

FESHBACH, S., and R. D. SINGER. **1971.** *Television and Aggression: An Experimental Field Study.* San Francisco: Jossey-Bass.

FESTINGER, L. **1964.** *Conflict, Decision and Disso-*

nance. Stanford, Calif.: Stanford University Press.

FEUER, L. S. **1969.** *Conflict of Generations.* New York: Basic Books.

FIELDS, S., and W. H. SWEET. **1975.** *Neural Bases for Violence and Aggression.* St. Louis: Warren Green.

FIGLEY, C. R. **1978.** *Stress Disorders Among Vietnam Veterans: Theory, Research and Treatment.* New York: Brunner/Mazel.

FIMAN, B. G., J. F. BORUS, and M. D. STANTON. **1975.** "Black–white and American–Vietnamese relations among soldiers in Vietnam." *J. of Social Issues,* 31(4):39–48.

FINE, R. **1972.** "The stress of peace." In R. S. Parker, ed., *The Emotional Stress of War, Violence, and Peace.* Pittsburgh: Stanwix House. Pp. 92–100.

FINER, S. E. **1962.** *The Man on Horseback: The Role of the Military in Politics.* New York: Praeger.

FINK, C. F., and E. BOULDING, eds. **1972.** "Peace research in transition: a symposium." *J. of Conflict Resolution,* 16(December).

FINN, D. **1969.** *The Corporate Oligarch: An Analysis of the Men Who Head America's Largest Business Enterprises.* New York: Simon and Schuster.

FINSTERBUSCH, K., and H. C. GRIESMAN. **1975.** "The unprofitability of warfare in the twentieth century." *Social Problems,* 22(February):450–463.

FISHER, R. **1978.** *International Mediation: A Working Guide.* New York: International Peace Academy.

FITCH, J. S. **1977.** *The Military Coup d'Etat as a Political Process: Ecuador, 1948–1966.* Baltimore: Johns Hopkins University Press.

FITZGERALD, A. E. **1972.** *The High Priests of Waste.* New York: Norton.

FLAMANT, M., and J. SINGER-KERÉL. **1970.** *Modern Economic Crises.* P. Wardroper, tr. New York: Harper and Row.

FLANIGAN, W. H., and E. FOGELMAN. **1970.** "Patterns of political violence in comparative perspective." *Comparative Politics,* 3(October):1–20.

FLECK, A. C., and F. A. J. IANNI. **1958.** "Epidemiology and anthropology: some suggested affinities in theory and method." *Human Organization,* 16(Winter):38–40.

FLEMING, D. F. **1961.** *The Cold War and Its Origins, 1917–1960.* Garden City, N.Y.: Doubleday.

FONER, J. D. **1974.** *Blacks and the Military in American History: A New Perspective.* New York: Praeger.

FORCE, D. C. **1974.** "Ecology of insect host–parasitoid communities." *Science,* 184(May):624–632.

FORNARI, F. **1974.** *The Psychoanalysis of War.* A. Pfeifer, tr. Bloomington: Indiana University Press.

FORSYTHE, D. P. **1978.** "Legal-management of internal war: the 1977 protocol on non-international armed conflict." *American J. of International Law,* 72(April):272–295.

——. **1977.** *Humanitarian Politics: The International Committee of the Red Cross.* Baltimore: Johns Hopkins University Press.

——. **1976a.** "The Red Cross as transnational movement: conserving and changing the nation-state system." *International Organization,* 30(Autumn):607–630.

——. **1976b.** "Who guards the guardians: third parties and the law of armed conflict." *American J. of International Law,* 70(January):41–61.

——. **1975a.** "The 1974 Diplomatic Conference on Humanitarian Law: some observations." *American J. of International Law,* 69(January):77–91.

——. **1975b.** "The work of the ICRC [International Committee of the Red Cross]: a broader view." *Instant Research on Peace and Violence,* 5(2):109–116.

FORSYTHE, D. P., and R. MAGAT. **1978.** "Updating the rules of war: the Third World wins some symbolic victories." *Washington Post,* 101(February 12):C5.

FOSTER, J. L. **1977.** "The future of conventional arms control." *Policy Sciences,* 8(March):1–19.

FOX, J. R. **1974.** *Arming America: How the U.S. Buys Weapons.* Cambridge, Mass.: Division of Research, Harvard Business School.

FOX, R., and U. FLEISING. **1976.** "Human ethology." In B. J. Siegel, ed., *Annual Review of Anthropology.* Vol. 5. Palo Alto, Calif.: Annual Reviews. Pp. 265–288.

FOX, R. P. **1974.** "Narcissistic rage and the problem of combat aggression." *Archives of General Psychiatry,* 31(December):807–811.

——. **1972.** "Post-combat adaptational problems." *Comprehensive Psychiatry,* 13(September): 435–443.

FOX, W. T. R., ed. **1970.** "How wars end." *Annals of the American Academy of Political and Social Sciences,* 392(November):whole issue.

FRANCK, T. M. **1968.** *The Structure of Impartiality: Examining the Riddle of One Law in a Fragmented World.* New York: Macmillan.

——. **1964.** *East African Unity Through Law.* New Haven, Conn.: Yale University Press.

FRANCK, T. M., and E. WEISBAND. **1971.** *Word Politics: Verbal Strategy Among the Superpowers.* New York: Oxford University Press.

FRANK, A. G. **1978.** *World Accumulation, 1492–1789.* New York: Monthly Review Press.

——. **1977.** *On Capitalist Development.* New York: Oxford University Press.

——. **1972.** *Lumpenbourgeoisie: Lumpendevelopment; Dependence, Class, and Politics in Latin America.* M. D. Berdecio, tr. New York: Monthly Review Press.

——. **1969.** *Capitalism and Underdevelopment.* New York: Monthly Review Press.

FRANK, J. D. **1972–1973.** "Psychiatrists and international affairs: pitfalls and possibilities." *In-*

ternational J. of Social Psychiatry, 18(Winter): 235–238.

——. **1967.** *Sanity and Survival: Psychological Aspects of War and Peace.* New York: Random House.

FRANK, J. L. **1973.** "The amputee war casualty in a military hospital: observations on psychological management." *Psychiatry in Medicine*, 4(Winter):1–16.

FRANK, L. A. **1969.** *The Arms Trade in International Relations.* New York: Praeger.

FRANKEL, C. **1966.** *The Neglected Aspect of Foreign Affairs: American Educational and Cultural Policy Abroad.* Washington, D.C.: The Brookings Institution.

FRAZER, J. G. **1961.** *The Golden Bough.* Garden City, N.Y.: Doubleday.

FREEDMAN, L. **1977.** *U.S. Intelligence and the Soviet Strategic Threat.* Boulder: Westview.

FREEMAN, D. M. **1972.** "Social conflict, violence, and planned change: some research hypotheses." *Co-Existence*, 9(November):89–100.

FREI, D., ed. **1978.** *International Crises and Crisis Management: An East–West Symposium.* New York: Praeger.

FREIRE, P. **1973.** *Pedagogy of the Oppressed.* M. B. Ramos, tr. New York: Seabury.

FREUD, A., and D. T. BURLINGHAM. **1973.** *War and Children.* P. R. Lehrman, ed. Westport, Conn.: Greenwood.

FREUD, S. **1962.** *Civilization and Its Discontents.* J. Strachey, tr. and ed. New York: Norton.

FREYMOND, J. **1976.** *Guerres, Revolutions, Croix-Rouge: Réflexions sur le Rôle du Comité International de la Croix-Rouge.* Geneva: Institut Universitaire des Hautes Etudes Internationales.

FRIED, M. H., M. HARRIS, and R. MURPHY, eds. **1968.** *War: The Anthropology of Armed Conflict and Aggression.* Garden City, N.Y.: Natural History Press.

FRIEDEBERG, A. S. **1969.** *The United Nations Conference on Trade and Development of 1964: The Theory of the Peripheral Economy at the Centre of International Political Discussions.* Rotterdam: Rotterdam University Press.

FRIEDLÄNDER, S. **1975.** *Histoire et Psychoanalyse: Essai sur les Possibilités et les Limites de la Psychohistoire.* Paris: Editions du Seuil.

FRIEDLÄNDER, S., and R. COHEN. **1975.** "The personality correlates of belligerence in international conflict: a comparative analysis of historical case studies." *Comparative Politics*, 7(January):155–186.

FRIEDMAN, E. **1974.** *Backward Toward Revolution: The Chinese Revolutionary Party.* Berkeley: University of California Press.

FRIEDMAN, L., ed. **1972.** *The Law of War: A Documentary History.* 2 vols. New York: Random House.

FRIEDRICH, C. J. **1974.** *Limited Government: A Comparison.* Englewood Cliffs, N.J.: Prentice-Hall.

——. **1968.** *Constitutional Government and Democracy: Theory and Practice in Europe and America.* 4th ed. Waltham, Mass.: Blaisdell.

FRIEDRICH, C. J., and Z. BRZEZINSKI. **1956.** *Totalitarian Dictatorship and Autocracy.* Cambridge, Mass.: Harvard University Press.

FRIEDRICH, C. J., and S. E. HARRIS, eds. **1958.** *Public Policy.* Vol. 8. Cambridge, Mass.: Graduate School of Public Administration, Harvard University.

FROMM, E. **1973.** *The Anatomy of Human Destructiveness.* New York: Holt, Rinehart and Winston.

——. **1973.** *The Sane Society.* New York: Fawcett World.

——. **1971.** *The Heart of Man: Its Genius for Good and Evil.* New York: Harper and Row.

——. **1941.** *Escape From Freedom.* New York: Holt, Rinehart and Winston.

FULLER, B., J. AGEL, and Q. FIORE. **1970.** *I Seem to Be a Verb.* New York: Bantam.

FUNKENSTEIN, D. H. **1955.** "The physiology of fear and anger." *Scientfic American*, 192(May):74–81.

FURLONG, W. L. **1976.** "War and population pressures on land and food: a Central American case study." San Francisco: Prepared for annual meeting of Western Political Science Association.

FUSSELL, P. **1977.** *The Great War and Modern Memory.* New York: Oxford University Press.

GABBENESCH, H. **1972.** "Authoritarianism as a world view." *American J. of Sociology*, 77 (March):857–875.

GAIER, E. L., W. A. WATTS, and D. N. WHITTAKER. **1972.** "Demographic aspects of attitudes associated with support of civil rights and the anti-war movement." *Proceedings of the Annual Convention of the American Psychological Association*, 7(Pt. 1):163–164.

GALE, J. S., and L. J. EAVES. **1975.** "Logic of animal conflict." *Nature*, 254(April):463–464.

GALE, S., and B. GALE. **1977.** "Language and conflict: towards a semiotic theory of harmonia mundi." *J. of Peace Science*, 2(Spring):215–230.

GALLIE, W. B. **1978.** *Philosophers of Peace and War.* Cambridge: Cambridge University Press.

GALTUNG, J. **1973.** *The European Community: A Superpower in the Making.* London: Allen and Unwin.

——. **1971.** "A structural theory of imperialism." *J. of Peace Research*, 8(2):81–117.

——. **1969.** "Violence, peace, and peace research." *J. of Peace Research*, 6(3):167–191.

——. **1967.** "Two approaches to disarmament: the legalist and the structuralist." *J. of Peace Research*, 4(2):161–195.

——. **1964.** "A structural theory of aggression." *J. of Peace Research,* 1(2):95–119.

GALTUNG, J., and T. HØIVIK. **1971.** "Structural and direct violence: a note on operationalization." *J. of Peace Research,* 8(1):73–76.

GAMBLE, J. K., JR., and D. D. FISCHER. **1976.** *The International Court of Justice: An Analysis of a Failure.* Lexington, Mass.: Lexington Books.

GAMBRELL, L. **1977.** "United Nations and conflict management." *Peace and Change,* 4(Fall):47–53.

GAMSON, W. A., and A. MODIGLIANI. **1971.** *Untangling the Cold War: A Strategy for Testing Rival Theories.* Boston: Little, Brown.

GANSHOF, F. **1953.** *Le Moyen Age.* Paris: Hachette.

GANTZEL, K. J., G. KRESS, and V. RITTBERGER. **1972.** *Konflikt—Eskalation—Krise: Sozialwissenschaftliche Studien zum Ausbruch des Ersten Weltkrieges.* Düsseldorf: Bertelsmann.

GARNHAM, D. **1976a.** "Dyadic international war, 1816–1965: the role of power parity and geographical proximity." *Western Political Q.,* 29(June):231–242.

——. **1976b.** "Power parity and lethal international violence, 1969–1973." *J. of Conflict Resolution,* 20(September):379–392.

——. **1971.** "Attitudes and personality patterns of foreign service officers and the conduct of American foreign affairs." Minneapolis: University of Minnesota. Ph.D. thesis.

GARNIER, M. A. **1973.** "Some implications of the British experience with an all-volunteer army." *Pacific Sociological Rev.,* 16(April):177–191.

GARTHOFF, R. L. **1977.** "Negotiating SALT." *Wilson Q.,* 1(Autumn):76–85.

GASMAN, D. **1977.** "Is there a German pacifism?" *Peace and Change,* 4(Fall):58–61.

GAULT, W. B. **1971.** "Some remarks on slaughter." *American J. of Psychiatry,* 128(October):450–454.

GAY, A. C., and G. R. GAY. **1971.** "Haight–Ashbury: evolution of a drug culture in a decade of mendacity." *J. of Psychedelic Drugs,* 4(Fall):81–90.

GAY, M., J. FUCHS, and M. BLITTNER. **1974.** "Characteristics of the offspring of Holocaust survivors in Israel." *Mental Health and Society,* 1(5–6):302–312.

GELLNER, E. **1975.** "Cohesion and identity: the Maghreb from Ibn Khaldun to Emile Durkheim." *Government and Opposition: A Journal of Comparative Politics,* 10(Spring):203–218.

GEORGE, A. L., D. K. HALL, and W. R. SIMONS. **1971.** *The Limits of Coercive Diplomacy.* New York: Columbia University Press.

GEORGE, A. L., and R. SMOKE. **1974.** *Deterrence in American Foreign Policy: Theory and Practice.* New York: Columbia University Press.

GERBNER, G., and L. GROSS. **1976.** "The scary world of TV's heavy viewer." *Psychology Today,* 9(April):41–45.

GERTH, H. H., and C. W. MILLS. **1958.** *From Max Weber: Essays on Sociology.* New York: Oxford University Press.

GILBERT, A. N. **1976.** "Buggery and the British Navy, 1700–1861." *J. of Social History,* 10(Fall):72–98.

GILLESPIE, J. V., and B. A. NESVOLD, eds. **1971.** *Macro-Quantitative Analysis.* Beverly Hills, Calif.: Sage.

GILLESPIE, J. V., and D. A. ZINNES, eds. **1977.** *Mathematical Systems in International Relations Research.* New York: Praeger.

GILLESPIE, J. V., et al. **1980.** "Sensitivity analysis of an armaments race model." In P. J. McGowan and C. W. Kegley, Jr., eds., *Threats, Weapons and Foreign Policy.* Beverly Hills, Calif.: Sage Publications. Pp. 275–312.

——. **1977.** "An optimal control model of arms races." *Political Science Rev.,* 72(March):226–244.

GILPIN, R. **1975.** *U.S. Power and the Multinational Corporation: The Political Economy of Foreign Direct Investment.* New York: Basic Books.

GINSBERG, R. **1975.** "Confucius on ritual, moral power and war." *Peace and Change,* 3(Spring):17–21.

GINTHER, K. **1975.** *Neutralität and Neutralitätspolitik.* New York: Springer Verlag.

GIRARD, R. **1977.** *Violence and the Sacred.* P. Gregory, tr. Baltimore: Johns Hopkins University Press.

GIRARD, V., and J. M. SCHADELLE. **1975.** "The post-traumatic personality." *Revue de Medicine Psychosomatique et de Psychologie Medicale,* 17(2):135–156.

GIVEN, J. B. **1977.** *Society and Homicide in Thirteenth-Century England.* Stanford, Calif.: Stanford University Press.

GLAHN, G. VON. **1970.** *Law Among Nations: An Introduction to Public International Law.* 2nd ed. London: Macmillan.

GLASER, K., and S. T. POSSONY. **1979.** *Victims of Politics: The State of Human Rights.* New York: Columbia University Press.

GLASS, D. V., and D. E. C. EVERSLEY, eds. **1965.** *Population in History: Essays in Historical Demography.* London: E. Arnold.

GLASS, G. V. **1976.** *Evaluation Studies: Review Annual.* Vol. 1. Beverly Hills, Calif.: Sage.

GLOVER, E. **1933.** *War, Sadism, and Pacifism.* London: Allen and Unwin.

GLUCKMAN, M. **1967.** *The Judicial Process Among the Barotse of Northern Rhodesia.* Published on behalf of the Institute for Social Research, University of Zambia. Manchester: Manchester University Press.

GOBALET, J. G., and L. J. DIAMOND. **1979.** "Effects of investment dependence on economic growth: the role of internal structure characteristics and periods in the world economy." *International Studies Q.,* 23(September):412–444.

GOFFMAN, E. **1970.** *Strategic Interaction.* Philadelphia: University of Pennsylvania Press.

GOLDMAN, N. **1973.** "The changing role of women in the armed forces." *American J. of Sociology,* 78(January):892–911.

GOLDMANN, K. **1974.** *Tension and Detente in Bipolar Europe.* Stockholm: Scandinavian University Books.

——. **1973.** "East–west tension in Europe, 1946–1970: a conceptual analysis and a quantitative description." *World Politics,* 26(October):106–125.

GOLDMANN, K., and J. LAGERKRANZ. **1977.** "Neither tension nor détente: East–West relations in Europe, 1971–1975." *Cooperation and Conflict,* 12(4):251–264.

GOLDSCHMIDT, W. **1959.** *Man's Way: A Preface to the Understanding of Human Society.* New York: Holt, Rinehart and Winston.

GOLDSTEIN, J., B. MARSHALL, and J. SCHWARTZ. **1976.** *The My Lai Massacre and Its Cover-up: Beyond the Reach of Law? The Peers Commission Report with a Supplement and Introductory Essay on the Limits of Law.* New York: Free Press.

GOLOVINE, M. N. **1962.** *Conflict in Space: A Pattern of War in a New Dimension.* London: Temple Press.

GOMPERT, D. C., et al. **1977.** *Nuclear Weapons and World Politics: Alternatives for the Future.* New York: McGraw-Hill.

GOODMAN, E. R. **1960.** *The Soviet Design for a World State.* New York: Columbia University Press.

GOODRICH, C. **1967.** *The Government and the Economy, 1783–1861.* Indianapolis: Bobbs-Merrill.

GOODRICH, L. M. **1974.** *The United Nations in a Changing World.* New York: Columbia University Press.

GOODSPEED, S. S. **1959.** *The Nature and Function of International Organization.* New York: Oxford University Press.

GORDENKER, L., ed. **1971.** *The United Nations in International Politics.* Princeton, N.J.: Princeton University Press.

GORSUCH, R. L., and R. A. SMITH. **1972.** "Changes in students' evaluations of moral behavior: 1969 vs. 1939, 1949, and 1958." *J. of Personality and Social Psychology,* 24(December):381–391.

GOSOVIC, B., and J. G. RUGGIE. **1976.** "On the creation of a new international economic order: issue linkage and the Seventh Special Session of the UN General Assembly." *International Organization,* 30(Spring):309–345.

GOSS, C. F. **1972.** "Military committee membership and defense-related benefits in the House of Representatives." *Western Political Q.,* 20(June):215–233.

GOULD, J., and W. H. TRUITT. **1973.** *Political Ideologies.* New York: Macmillan.

GRAHAM, F. P. **1969.** "A contemporary history of American crime." In H. D. Graham and T. R. Gurr, eds., *The History of Violence in America: Historical and Comparative Perspectives.* New York: Praeger. Pp. 371–387.

GRAHAM, H. D., and T. R. GURR, eds. **1969.** *The History of Violence in America: Historical and Comparative Perspectives.* New York: Praeger.

GRANBERG, D. **1975.** "War expectancy: some further studies." *International J. of Group Tensions,* 5(March–June):8–23.

GRANBERG, D., and G. CORRIGAN. **1972.** "Authoritarianism, dogmatism and orientations toward the Vietnam War." *Sociometry,* 35(September):468–476.

GRANBERG, D., and N. FAYE. **1972.** "Sensitizing people by making the abstract concrete: study of the effect of 'Hiroshima–Nagasaki.' " *American J. of Orthopsychiatry,* 42(October):811–815.

GRANBERG, D., and W. MAY. **1972.** "I-E and orientations toward the Vietnam war." *J. of Social Psychology,* 88(October):157–158.

GRAND-JEAN, P. **1967.** *Guerres, Fluctuations, et Croissance.* Paris: Société d'Edition d'Enseignment Supérieur.

GRANGER, J. V. **1979.** *Technology and International Relations.* San Francisco: W. H. Freeman and Company.

GRAY, C. H., and G. W. GREGORY. **1968.** "Military spending and Senate voting: a correlation study." *J. of Peace Research,* 5(1):44–54.

GRAY, J. G. **1970.** *The Warriors.* New York: Harper and Row.

GREAVES, F. V. **1962.** "Peace in our time—fact or fable?" *Military Rev.,* 42(December):55–58.

GREEN, L. C. **1976.** *Superior Orders in National and International Law.* Leyden: Sijthoff.

GREEN, P. **1968.** *Deadly Logic: The Theory of Nuclear Deterrence.* New York: Schocken.

GREENWALD, M. W. **1975.** "Women workers and World War I: the American railroad industry, a case study." *J. of Social History,* 9(Winter):154–177.

GREENWOOD, T. **1973.** "Reconnaissance and arms control." *Scientific American,* 228(February):14–25.

GREGG, P. M., and A. S. BANKS. **1965.** "Dimensions of political systems: factor analysis of a cross-polity survey." *American Political Science Rev.,* 59(September):602–614.

GREGG, R. W., and M. BARKUN, eds. **1968.** *The United Nations System and Its Functions.* Princeton, N.J.: Van Nostrand.

GREGORY, R. J. **1974.** "Human ecology and the drug scene." *Drug Forum,* 3(Winter):193–198.

GRIEVES, F. L. **1969.** *Supranationalism and International Adjudication.* Urbana: University of Illinois Press.

GRIFFIN, K. **1974.** *The Political Economy of Agrarian*

Change: An Essay on the Green Revolution. Cambridge, Mass.: Harvard University Press.

GRIMSHAW, A. D., ed. **1969**. *Racial Violence in the United States.* Chicago: Aldine.

GROFMAN, B. N., and E. N. MULLER. **1973**. "The strange case of relative gratification and potential for political violence: the V-curve hypothesis." *American Political Science Rev.,* 67(June):514–539.

GROSS, E. **1977**. "Mayhew and Levinger's use of random models." *American J. of Sociology,* 83(July):161–164.

GROTIUS, H. **1972**. "The law of war and peace." In B. W. Cook, ed., *Peace Projects of the Seventeenth Century.* New York: Garland. Pp. 5–84.

———. **1949**. *The Law of War and Peace.* L. R. Loomis, tr. Roslyn, N.Y.: Walter J. Black.

GRUNDY, K. W. **1976**. "Intermediary power and global dependency: the case of South Africa." *International Studies Q.,* 20(December):553–580.

GRZYBOWSKI, K. **1970**. *Soviet Public International Law.* Leyden: Sijthoff.

GUETZKOW, H. **1955**. *Multiple Loyalties: Theoretical Approach to a Problem in International Organization.* Princeton, N.J.: Princeton University Press.

GULICK, E. V. **1955**. *Europe's Classical Balance of Power: A Case History of the Theory and Practice of One of the Great Concepts of European Statecraft.* New York: Norton.

GURR, T. R., ed. **1980** (in press). *Handbook of Conflict Theory and Research.* New York: Free Press.

———. **1972**. "A causal model of civil strife." In I. K. Feierabend, R. L. Feierabend, and T. Gurr, eds., *Anger, Violence, and Politics.* Englewood Cliffs, N.J.: Prentice-Hall. Pp. 184–222.

———. **1970**. *Why Men Rebel.* Princeton, N.J.: Princeton University Press.

———. **1968**. "A causal model of civil strife: a comparative analysis using new indices." *American Political Science Rev.,* 62(December):1104–1124.

GURR, T. R., and V. F. BISHOP. **1976**. "Violent nations, and others." *J. of Conflict Resolution,* 20(March):79–110.

GUTTERIDGE, W. F. **1975**. *Military Regimes in Africa.* London: Methuen.

HAAS, E. B. **1968**. *The Uniting of Europe: Political, Social, and Economic Forces, 1950–1957.* 2nd ed. Stanford, Calif.: Stanford University Press.

———. **1964**. *Beyond the Nation-State.* Stanford, Calif.: Stanford University Press.

HAAS, E. B., R. L. BUTTERWORTH, and J. S. NYE. **1972**. *Conflict Management by International Organizations.* Morristown, N.J.: General Learning Press.

HAAS, E. B., and E. T. ROWE. **1973**. "Regional organizations in the United Nations: is there externalization?" *International Studies Q.,* 17(March):3–54.

HAAS, E. B., and A. S. WHITING. **1956**. *Dynamics of International Relations.* New York: McGraw-Hill.

HAAS, E. B., M. P. WILLIAMS, and D. BABAI. **1977**. *Scientists and World Order: The Uses of Technical Knowledge in International Organization.* Berkeley: University of California Press.

HAAS, J. D., and G. G. HARRISON. **1977**. "Nutritional anthropology and biological adaptation." *Annual Rev. of Anthropology,* 6:69–101.

HAAS, M. **1974**. *International Conflict.* Indianapolis: Bobbs-Merrill.

———. **1970**. "International subsystems: stability and polarity." *American Political Science Rev.,* 64(March):98–123.

———. **1968**. "Social change and national aggressiveness, 1900–1960." In J. D. Singer, ed., *Quantitative International Politics: Insights and Evidence.* New York: Free Press.

———. **1965**. "Societal approaches to the study of war." *J. of Peace Research,* 2(4):307–322.

HAAVELSRUD, M. **1976**. *Education for Peace: Reflection and Action.* Guildford, U.K.: IPC Science and Technology Press.

———. **1972**. "Learning resources in the formation of international orientations." *Communication Rev.,* 20(Fall):229–251.

HACKETT, J., et al. **1979**. *The Third World War: August 1985.* New York: Macmillan.

HÄFNER, H., and W. BÖKER. **1972**. "Mentally deranged persons committing acts of violence in the German Federal Republic: an epidemiological investigation." *Nervenarzt,* 43(June): 215–291.

HAGUE, A. **1973**. "The mirror image hypothesis in the context of the Indo–Pakistan conflict." *Pakistan J. of Psychology,* 6(June):13–22.

HAGUE, A., and M. SABIR. **1971**. "Stereotype persistence during two wars between India and Pakistan." *Pakistan J. of Psychology,* 4(December):31–41.

HALABY, C. N. **1973**. "Hardship and collective violence in France: a comment." *American Sociological Rev.,* 38(August):495–500.

HALBERSTAM, D. **1972**. *The Best and the Brightest.* Greenwich, Conn.: Fawcett.

HALBWACHS, M. **1930**. *Les Causes du Suicide.* Paris: Felix Alcan.

HALEY, S. A. **1974**. "When the patient reports atrocities: specific treatment considerations of the Vietnam veteran." *Archives of General Psychiatry,* 30(February):191–196.

HALL, E. T. **1966**. *The Hidden Dimension.* Garden City, N.Y.: Doubleday.

HALL, L. C., and W. C. SIMMONS. **1973**. "The POW wife: a psychiatric appraisal." *Archives of General Psychiatry,* 29(November):690–694.

HALL, T., and J. D. COZEAN. **1966**. *An Annotated Bibliography on Military Civic Action.* Washington, D.C.: Center for Research in Social Systems, American University.

HALLPIKE, C. R. **1973.** "Functionalist interpretations of primitive warfare." *Man,* 8(September):451–470.

HALLSTROM, A. G. **1973.** "Problems of military panic: an overview based on literary study." *Psychological Abstracts,* 51(12045):1527.

HALPER, T. **1971.** *Foreign Policy Crises: Appearance and Reality in Decision-Making.* Columbus, Ohio: Merrill.

HALSTED, J. A. **1974.** "Severe malnutrition in a public servant of the World War II era: the medical history of Harry Hopkins." *Transactions of the American Clinical and Climatological Association,* Vol. 86.

HAMBLIN, R. L., R. B. JACOBSEN, and J. L. L. MILLER. **1973.** *A Mathematical Theory of Social Change.* New York: Wiley.

——. **1971.** *The Humanization Processes: A Social, Behavioral Analysis of Children's Problems.* New York: Wiley.

HAMBLIN, R. L., et al. **1977.** "Arms races: a test of two models." *American Sociological Rev.,* 42(April):338–354.

HAMILTON, L. C. **1978.** "Conflict variables in world simulations." *Futures,* 10(April):128–142.

HANDBERG, R. B. **1972–1973.** "The 'Vietnam analogy': student attitudes on war." *Public Opinion Q.,* 36(Winter):612–615.

HANDEL, M. I. **1977.** "The Yom Kippur War and the inevitability of surprise." *International Studies Q.,* 21(September):461–502.

HANRIEDER, W. F. **1971.** *Foreign Policies and the International System: A Theoretical Introduction.* New York: General Learning Press.

HANSBERG, H. G. **1972.** "Separation problems of displaced children." In R. S. Parker, ed., *The Emotional Stress of War, Violence, and Peace.* Pittsburgh: Stanwix House. Pp. 241–262.

HANSEN, A. H. **1932.** *Economic Stabilization in an Unbalanced World.* New York: Harcourt.

HANSEN, N. **1972** *Growth Centers in Regional Economic Development.* New York: Free Press.

HARBERT, J. R. **1976.** "The behavior of the ministates in the United Nations, 1971–1972." *International Organization,* 30(Winter):109–128.

HARBOTTLE, T. B. **1905.** *Dictionary of Battles.* New York: Dutton.

HARDACH, G. **1977.** *The First World War, 1914–1918.* Berkeley: University of California Press.

HARDIN, G. **1977a.** *Managing the Commons.* San Francisco: W. H. Freeman and Company.

——. **1977b.** *The Limits of Altruism: An Ecologist's View of Survival.* Bloomington: Indiana University Press.

HARKAVY, R. E. **1975.** *The Arms Trade and International Systems.* Cambridge: Ballinger.

HARR, J. E. **1969.** *The Professional Diplomat.* Princeton, N.J.: Princeton University Press.

HARRIS, C. K. **1977.** "Comment on 'oligarchy in human interaction.' " *American J. of Sociology,* 83(July):173–178.

HARRIS, P. **1976.** "International news media authority and dependence." *Instant Research on Peace and Violence,* 6(4):149–159.

HARRISON, R. **1975.** *Warfare.* Minneapolis: Burgess.

HART, J. **1976.** "Three approaches to the measurement of power in international relations." *International Organization,* 30(Spring):289–308.

HARTMAN, E. A., J. L. PHILLIPS, and S. G. COLE. **1976.** "Conflict and survival in triads." *J. of Conflict Resolution,* 20(December):589–608.

HARTMANN, F. H. **1970.** *The New Age of American Foreign Policy.* New York: Macmillan.

HARTUNG, J. **1978.** "Light, puberty, and aggression: a proximal mechanism hypothesis." *Human Ecology,* 6(September):273–297.

HASSOUNA, H. A. **1975.** *The League of Arab States and Regional Disputes: A Study of Middle East Conflicts.* Dobbs Ferry, N.Y.: Oceana.

HAU, T. F. **1972.** "Comparing investigations in psychosomatic adolescents born before, during, and after the war." *Praxis des Kinderpsychologie und Kinderpsychiatrie,* 21(August):193–200.

HAVENS, M. C., C. LEIDEN, and K. M. SCHMITT. **1970.** *The Politics of Assassination.* Englewood Cliffs, N.J.: Prentice-Hall.

HAWKINS, D., and L. PAULING. **1973.** *Orthomolecular Psychiatry.* San Francisco: W. H. Freeman and Company.

HAWKINS, G., and P. WARD. **1970.** "Armed and disarmed police: police firearms policy and levels of violence." *J. of Research in Crime and Delinquency,* 7(July):188–197.

HAYANO, D. M. **1974.** "Marriage, alliance, and warfare: a view from the New Guinea highlands." *American Ethnologist,* 1(May):281–293.

HAYDON, B. **1962.** *The Great Statistics of Wars Hoax.* Santa Monica, Calif.: Rand.

HAYES, C. **1960.** *Nationalism: A Religion.* New York: Macmillan.

HAYES, F. W. **1970.** "Psychiatric aeromedical evacuation patients during the TET and TET II offensives, 1968." *American J. of Psychiatry,* 127(October):503–507.

HAYTER, T. **1971.** *Aid as Imperialism.* Harmondsworth: Penguin.

HEAD, R. G., F. W. SHORT, and R. C. McFARLANE. **1979.** *Crisis Resolution: Presidential Decision Making in the Mayaguez and Korean Confrontations.* Boulder: Westview.

HECKER, M. **1971.** "Understanding aggression." *UNESCO Chronicle,* 17(October):358–363.

HEINTZ, P., ed. **1972.** *A Macrosociological Theory of Societal Systems.* Bern: Hans Huber.

HELMER, J. **1974** *Bringing the War Home: The American Soldier in Vietnam and After.* New York: Free Press.

HEMLEBEN, S. J. **1943.** *Plans for World Peace Through Six Centuries.* Chicago: University of Chicago Press.

HENDRICKS, J. W. **1976.** "The problem of outcome evaluation: a comment on the proposed global monitoring system." *International Studies Q.,* 20(December):621–628.

HENKIN, L. **1968.** *How Nations Behave.* New York: Praeger.

HENSLEY, T. R. **1978.** "Bloc voting on the International Court of Justice." *J. of Conflict Resolution,* 22(March):39–59.

——. **1968.** "National bias and the International Court of Justice." *Midwest J. of Political Science,* 12(November):568–586.

HEPBURN, J. R. **1971.** "Subcultures, violence, and the subculture of violence: an old rut or a new road?" *Criminology,* 9(May):87–98.

HERBERT, F. **1969.** *Dune Messiah.* New York: Putnam.

——. **1966.** *Dune.* London: Gollancz.

HERMANN, C. F., ed. **1972.** *International Crisis: Insights from Behavioral Research.* New York: Free Press.

——. **1969.** *Crises in Foreign Policy: A Simulation Analysis.* Indianapolis: Bobbs-Merrill.

HERMANN, M. G., and T. W. MILBURN, eds. **1977.** *A Psychological Examination of Political Leaders.* New York: Free Press.

HERNES, G. **1969.** "On rank disequilibrium and military coups d'état." *J. of Peace Research,* 6(1):65–72.

HERO, A. O., JR. **1977.** "The United States public and the United Nations." In D. A. Kay, ed., *The Changing United Nations: Options for the United States.* Proceedings of the Academy of Political Science, 32(4):17–29.

HERRELL, J. M. **1972.** "Birth order and the military: a review from an Adlerian perspective." *J. of Individual Psychology,* 28(May):38–44.

HERRERA, L. **1975a.** "Chilean economy: medicine killing the patient?" *Instant Research on Peace and Violence,* 5(1):65–74.

——. **1975b.** "The military as a link in the domination chain of Latin America." *Instant Research on Peace and Violence,* 5(4):197–206.

HERRING, E. P. **1941.** *The Impact of War: Our American Democracy Under Arms.* New York: Farrar and Rinehart.

HERZ, J. **1957.** "Rise and demise of the territorial state." *World Politics,* 9(July):473–493.

HEUER, R. J., JR., ed. **1978.** *Quantitative Approaches to Political Intelligence: The CIA Experience.* Boulder: Westview.

HIBBS, D. A., JR. **1973.** *Mass Political Violence: A Cross-National Causal Analysis.* New York: Wiley.

HILL, W. W. **1978.** "A time-lagged Richardson arms race model." *J. of Peace Science,* 3(Spring):55–62.

HILTON, G. **1977.** "The science of 'modeling through.'" In J. V. Gillespie and Zinnes, eds., *Mathematical Systems in International Relations Research.* New York: Praeger. Pp. 190–193.

HINES, S. H., M. BACHMAN, and M. STARR. **1973.** "Trial by newspaper? the cases of Charles Manson and William Calley." *Cornell J. of Social Relations,* 8(Fall):257–269.

HINSHAW, R. **1964.** *The European Community and American Trade: A Study in Atlantic Economics and Policy.* New York: Praeger.

HINSLEY, F. H. **1967.** *Power and the Pursuit of Peace: Theory and Practice in the History of Relations Between States.* Cambridge: Cambridge University Press.

HIPPLER, A. E. **1971.** "Some psychosocial aspects of army life." *J. of Human Relations,* 19(1):97–114.

HIRSCH, F. **1976.** *Social Limits to Growth.* Cambridge, Mass.: Harvard University Press.

HIRSCH, H., and D. PERRY, eds. **1973.** *Violence as Politics.* New York: Harper and Row.

HIRSCHMAN, A. O. **1977.** *The Passions and the Interests: Political Arguments for Capitalism Before Its Triumph.* Princeton, N.J.: Princeton University Press.

——. **1970.** *Exit, Voice, and Loyalty.* Cambridge, Mass: Harvard University Press.

HOAG, M. W. **1966.** *Increasing Returns in Military Production Functions: P-3309.* Santa Monica, Calif.: Rand.

HOBBS, R. **1979.** *The Myth of Victory: What Is Victory in War?* Boulder: Westview.

HOBSBAWN, E. J. **1963.** *Primitive Rebels: Studies in Archaic Forms of Social Movements in the 19th and 20th Centuries.* New York: Praeger.

——. **1962.** *The Age of Revolution, 1789–1848.* London: Weidenfeld and Nicolson.

HOBSON, J. **1965.** *Imperialism.* Ann Arbor: University of Michigan Press.

HOCHREICH, D. J. **1972.** "Internal–external control and reaction to the My Lai courts-martial." *J. of Applied Social Psychology,* 2(October):319–325.

HOEDAILLE, J. **1972.** "Pertes de l'armée de terre sous le Premier Empire, d'après les registres matricules." *Population,* 27(January–February): 27–50.

HOFFMAN, A. S., ed. **1968.** *International Communications and the New Diplomacy.* Bloomington: Indiana University Press.

HOFFMANN, S. **1976–1977.** "No choice, no illusions." *Foreign Policy,* 25(Winter):97–179.

——, ed., **1970.** *Conditions of World Order.* New York: Simon and Schuster.

——. **1968.** "Introduction," In L. Scheinman and D. Wilkinson, eds., *International Law and Political Crisis.* Boston: Little, Brown. Pp. xi–xix.

——. **1961.** "International systems and international law." In K. Knorr and S. Verba, eds., *The International System.* Princeton, N.J.: Princeton University Press. Pp. 205–238.

HOGAN, D. P., and D. L. FEATHERMAN. **1977.** "Racial stratification and socioeconomic change in the

American North and South." *American J. of Sociology,* 83(July):100–127.

HOLLING, C. S. **1973.** "Resilience and stability of ecological systems." *Annual Rev. of Ecology and Systematics,* 4:1–23.

HOLLIST, W. L. **1977.** "An analysis of arms processes in the United States and the Soviet Union," *International Studies Q.,* 21(September):503–527.

HOLMES, J. E. **1980.** "A liberal moods interpretation of American diplomatic history." Los Angeles: Presented at annual meeting of International Studies Association. Mimeo.

HOLSTI, K. J. **1966.** "Resolving international conflicts: a taxonomy of behavior and some figures on procedures." *J. of Conflict Resolution,* 10(September):272–296.

HOLSTI, O. R. **1979.** "The three-headed eagle: the United States and system change." *International Studies Q.,* 23(September):339–359.

——. **1972a.** *Crisis, Escalation, War.* Montreal: McGill–Queen's University Press.

——. **1972b.** "Time, alternatives, and communications: the 1914 and Cuban missile crises." In C. F. Hermann, ed., *International Crisis: Insights from Behavioral Research.* New York: Free Press. Pp. 58–80.

——. **1962.** "The belief system and national images: a case study." *J. of Conflict Resolution,* 6(September):244–252.

HOLSTI, O. R., R. C. NORTH, and R. A. BRODY. **1968.** "Perception and action in the 1914 crisis." In J. D. Singer, ed., *Quantitative International Politics: Insights and Evidence.* New York: Free Press. Pp. 123–158.

HOLSTI, O. R., and J. N. ROSENAU. **1980.** "Does where you stand depend on when you were born? The impact of generation on post-Vietnam foreign policy beliefs. *Public Opinion Q.,* 44(Spring):1–22.

——. **1979.** "Vietnam, consensus and the belief systems of American leaders." *World Politics,* 32(October):1–56.

HOLT, R. T., B. L. JOB, and L. MARKUS. **1978.** "Catastrophe theory and the study of war." *J. of Conflict Resolution,* 22(June):171–208.

HOLZMAN, F. D. **1975.** *Financial Checks on Soviet Defense Spending.* Lexington, Mass.: Lexington Books.

HOOLE, F. W. **1977.** "Evaluating the impact of international organizations." *International Organization,* 31(Summer):541–563.

HOOLE, F. W., and D. A. ZINNES, eds. **1976.** *Quantitative International Politics: An Appraisal.* New York: Praeger.

HOPE, M., and J. YOUNG. **1977.** *The Struggle for Humanity: Agents of Nonviolent Change in a Violent World.* Maryknoll, N.Y.: Orbis.

HOPMANN, P. T., and T. KING. **1976.** "Interactions and perceptions in the test ban negotiations." *International Studies Q.,* 20(March):105–142.

HOPMANN, P. T., and C. WALCOTT. **1976.** "The impact of international conflict and détente on bargaining in arms control negotiations: an experimental analysis." *International Interactions,* 2(4):189–206.

HORNUNG, C. A. **1977.** "Social status, status inconsistency and psychological stress." *American Sociological Rev.,* 42(August):623–638.

HOROWITZ, D. **1971.** *The Free World Colossus.* New York: Hill and Wang.

HOROWITZ, I. L. **1971.** "The treatment of conflict in sociological literature." *International J. of Group Tensions,* 1(October):350–363.

HOROWITZ, I. L., and E. K. TRIMBERGER. **1976.** "State power and military nationalism in Latin America." *Comparative Politics,* 8(January):223–244.

HORVATH, W. J. A. **1968.** "A statistical model for the duration of wars and strikes." *Behavioral Science,* 13(January):18–28.

HORVATH, W. J., and C. C. FOSTER. **1963.** "Stochastic models of war alliances." *J. of Conflict Resolution,* 7(June):110–116.

HOWARD, M. **1979.** "War and the nation-state." *Daedalus,* 108(Fall):101–110.

HSIN, K. **1972.** "A study of the 'peace' policies of Washington, Peiping and Moscow." *Issues and Studies,* 8(June):15–22.

HUDSON, D. **1977.** *The World Council of Churches in International Affairs.* Leighton Buzzard: Faith Press for the Royal Institute of International Affairs.

HUDSON, M. **1977.** *Global Fracture: The New International Economic Order.* New York: Harper and Row.

——. **1972.** *Super-Imperialism: The Economic Strategy of American Empire.* New York: Holt, Rinehart and Winston.

HUGHES, B. B. **1978.** *The Domestic Context of American Foreign Policy.* San Francisco: W. H. Freeman and Company.

HUGO, G. **1970.** *Appearance and Reality in International Relations.* London: Chatto and Windus.

HUIZINGA, J. **1954.** *The Waning of the Middle Ages: A Study of the Forms of Life, Thought, and Art in France and the Netherlands in the XIVth and XVth Centuries.* Garden City, N.Y.:Doubleday.

HUNTINGTON, S. P. **1968.** *Political Order in Changing Societies.* New Haven, Conn.: Yale University Press.

——, ed. **1962.** *Changing Patterns of Military Politics.* New York: Free Press.

——. **1958.** "Arms races: prerequisites and results." In C. J. Friedrich and S. E. Harris, eds., *Public Policy.* Vol. 8. Cambridge, Mass.: Graduate School of Public Administration, Harvard University. Pp. 41–86.

——. **1957.** *The Soldier and the State.* New York: Wiley.

HUSTON, J. A. **1966.** *The Sinews of War: Army Logis-*

tics, 1775–1953. Washington, D.C.: U.S. Army, Office of the Chief of Military History.

HUTCHINSON, M. C. **1972.** "The concept of revolutionary terrorism." *J. of Conflict Resolution,* 16(September):383–396.

HYER, M. **1977.** "Bill would ease pacifists' tax plight." *Washington Post,* 100(April 15):E6.

HYMAN, S. **1973.** "The governance of the military." *Annals of the American Academy of Political and Social Science,* 406(March):38–47.

IKEMI, Y., et al. **1974.** "Psychosomatic mechanism under social changes in Japan." *Psychotherapy and Psychosomatics,* 23(1–6):240–250.

IKLÉ, F. C. **1976.** "The prevention of nuclear war in a world of uncertainty." *Policy Sciences,* 7(June):245–250.

———. **1971.** *Every War Must End.* New York: Columbia University Press.

ILLICH, I. D. **1976.** *Medical Nemesis: The Expropriation of Health.* New York: Pantheon.

———. **1972.** *Deschooling Society.* New York: Harper and Row.

INGLEHART, R. **1970.** "Public opinion and regional integration." *International Organization,* 24(Autumn):160–191.

———. **1967.** "An end to European integration?" *American Political Science Rev.,* 61(March):91–105.

INSTITUT FRANÇAIS DE POLÉMOLOGIE. **1968.** "Periodicité et intensité des actions de guerre (1200 á 1945)." *Guerres et Paix,* 21(10):20–32.

INSTITUTO ITALO-LATINOAMERICANO. **1968.** *America Latina y la Cummunidad Economica Europea.* Milan: Giuffre.

INTRILIGATOR, M. D. **1964.** "Some simple models of arms races." *General Systems Yearbook,* 9:143–147.

INTRILIGATOR, M. D., and D. L. BRITO. **1978.** "Nuclear proliferation and stability." *J. of Peace Science,* 3(Fall):173–183.

———. **1977.** "Strategy, arms races, and arms control." In J. V. Gillespie and D. A. Zinnes, eds., *Mathematical Systems in International Relations Research.* New York: Praeger. Pp. 173–189.

ISARD, W. **1956.** *Location and Space Economy.* Cambridge, Mass.: MIT Press.

ISARD, W., and S. CZAMANSKI. **1966.** "A model for the projection of regional industrial structure, land use patterns, and conversion potentialities." *Peace Research Society (International) Papers,* 5, Philadelphia Conference, 1965.

ISARD, W., and J. GANSCHOW. **1961.** *Awards of Prime Military Contracts.* Philadelphia: Regional Science Research Institute.

ISARD, W., and G. J. KARASKA. **1961–1962.** *Unclassified Defense Contracts.* Philadelphia: World Friends Research Center.

ISARD, W., and P. LIOSSATOS. **1978.** "A formal model of big step disarmament and domino effects." *J. of Peace Science,* 3(Fall):131–146.

ISRAEL, F. L., ed. **1967.** *Major Peace Treaties of Modern History, 1648–1967.* New York: McGraw-Hill.

IVIE, R. L. **1974.** "Presidential motives for war." *Q. J. of Speech,* 60(October):337–345.

JACKMAN, R. W. **1975.** *Politics and Social Equality: A Comparative Analysis.* New York: Wiley.

JACKSON, D. C. **1975.** *The Conflict Process: Jurisdiction and Choice in Private International Law.* Dobbs Ferry, N.Y.: Oceana.

JACKSON, S., et al. **1977.** "Conflict and coercion in dependent states." Washington, D.C.: Prepared for annual meeting of American Political Science Association. Mimeo.

JACOB, P. E., and J. V. TOSCANO. **1964.** *The Integration of Political Communities.* Philadelphia: Lippincott.

JACOBSEN, K. **1978.** *The General Assembly of the United Nations: A Quantitative Analysis of Conflict, Inequality, and Relevance.* New York: Columbia University Press.

JACOBSON, A. L. **1976.** "Conflict in developing nations: a test of the interaction hypothesis." *International Interactions,* 2(August):141–150.

JACOBSON, H. K. **1979.** *Networks of Interdependence: International Organizations and the Global Political System.* New York: Knopf.

———. **1977.** "The United Nations and political conflict: a mirror, amplifier, or regulator?" *Proceedings of the Academy of Political Science,* 32(4):56–68.

JACOBY, H. **1973.** *The Bureaucratization of the World.* E. L. Kanes, tr. Berkeley: University of California Press.

JAFFE, Y., et al. **1974.** "Sexual arousal and behavioral aggression." *J. of Personality and Social Psychology,* 30(December):759–764.

JAHODA, G., and S. HARRISON. **1975.** "Belfast children: some effects of a conflict environment." *Irish J. of Psychology,* 3(Winter):1–19.

JAMES, W. **1973.** "The moral equivalent of war." In T. Maple and D. W. Matheson, eds., *Aggression, Hostility, and Violence: Nature or Nurture.* New York: Holt, Rinehart and Winston. Pp. 258–268.

JAMESON, R. T. **1978.** "The American war film." In L. L. Farrar, Jr., ed., *War: A Historical, Political and Social Study.* Santa Barbara, Calif.: ABC-Clio. Pp. 235–245.

JANEWAY, E. **1968.** *The Economics of Crisis: War, Politics, and the Dollar.* New York: Weybright and Talley.

———. **1951.** *The Struggle for Survival: A Chronicle of Economic Mobilization in World War II.* New Haven, Conn.: Yale University Press.

JANIS, I. L. **1972.** *Victims of Groupthink: A Psychological Study of Foreign Policy Decisions and Fiascoes.* Boston: Houghton Mifflin.

———. **1961.** *Air War and Emotional Stress: Psycholog-*

ical Studies of Bombing and Civilian Defense. New York: McGraw-Hill.

JANIS, I. L., and L. MANN. **1977.** *Decision Making: A Psychological Analysis of Conflict, Choice, and Commitment.* New York: Free Press.

JANOWITZ, M. **1977.** *Military Institutions and Coercion in the Developing Nations.* Chicago: University of Chicago Press.

——. **1975.** *Military Conflict: Essays in the Institutional Analysis of War and Peace.* Beverly Hills, Calif.: Sage.

——. **1973.** "The social demography of the all-volunteer armed force." *Annals of the American Academy of Political and Social Science,* 406(March):86–93.

——. **1972.** "Toward an all-volunteer military." *Public Interest,* 27(Spring):104–117.

——. **1968.** "Armed forces and society: a world perspective." In J. Van Doorn, ed., *Armed Forces and Society: Sociological Essays.* The Hague: Mouton. Pp. 15–38.

——. **1964.** *The New Military: Changing Patterns of Organization.* New York: Russell Sage Foundation.

——. **1960.** *The Professional Soldier.* Glencoe, Ill.: Free Press.

——. **1959.** *Sociology and the Military Establishment.* New York: Russell Sage Foundation.

JANOWITZ, M., with R. W. LITTLE. **1965.** *Sociology and the Military Establishment.* 3rd ed. New York: Russell Sage Foundation.

JANOWITZ, M., and J. VAN DOORN, eds. **1971.** *On Military Ideology.* Rotterdam: Rotterdam University Press.

JARHO, L. **1973.** "Korsakoff-like amnesic syndrome in penetrating brain injury: a study of Finnish war veterans." *Acta Neurologica Scandinavica,* 49(Suppl. 54).

JARVAD, I. M. **1968.** "Power vs. equality: an attempt at systematic analysis of the role and function of the International Court of Justice." In *Proceedings of the International Peace Research Association, Second Conference.* Assen: Van Gorcum. Pp. 297–314.

JASCHINSKI, H. **1975.** *Neuartige Chemische Kampfstoffe im Blickfeld des Völkerrechts: Der Einsatz nicht tödlich wirkender sowie Pflanzen schädigender chemischer Kampfstoffe in bewaffneten Konflikten und das Völkerrecht. Ein Beitrag zur Auslegung und Ermittlung kriegsrechtlicher Normen.* Berlin: Duncker and Humblot.

JASPERS, K. **1961.** *The Future of Mankind.* E. B. Ashton, tr. Chicago: University of Chicago Press.

JAURÈS, J. **1972.** *Democracy and Military Service.* G. G. Coulton, ed. New York: Garland.

JEFFERY, C. R., ed. **1979.** *Biology and Crime.* Beverly Hills, Calif.: Sage.

JEFFRIES, V. **1974.** "Political generations and the acceptance or rejection of nuclear warfare." *J. of Social Issues,* 30(3):119–136.

JELLINEK, E. M. **1960.** *The Disease Concept of Alcoholism.* New Haven, Conn.: Center for Alcohol Studies, Yale University.

JENKS, L. W. **1958.** *The Common Law of Mankind.* London: Stevens.

JENNINGS, M. K., and G. B. MARKUS. **1977.** "The effect of military service on political attitudes: a panel study." *American Political Science Rev.,* 71(March):131–147.

JENSEN, L. **1966.** "American foreign policy elites and the prediction of international events." *Peace Research Society (International) Papers,* 5, Philadelphia Conference, 1965.

JERVIS, R. **1976.** *Perception and Misperception in International Politics.* Princeton, N.J.: Princeton University Press.

——. **1970.** *The Logic of Images in International Relations.* Princeton, N.J.: Princeton University Press.

JESSOP, B. **1972.** *Social Order, Reform and Revolution: A Power, Exchange and Institutionalization Perspective.* New York: Herder and Herder.

JESSUP, P. C. **1956.** *Transnational Law.* New Haven, Conn.: Yale University Press.

JHA, B. **1972.** "Institutional neurosis: its causes and remedy." *Indian J. of Psychiatric Social Work,* 1(July):5–19.

JOB, B. L. **1977.** "Signals, triggers, and thresholds: the problem of analyzing turning points in international conflict processes." Washington, D.C.: Presented at annual meeting of American Political Science Association. Mimeo.

——. **1976.** "Membership in inter-nation alliances, 1815–1965: an exploration utilizing mathematical probability models." In D. A. Zinnes and J. V. Gillespie, eds., *Mathematical Models in International Relations.* New York: Praeger. Pp. 74–109.

JOHANSEN, R. **1979.** *The National Interest and the Human Interest: An Analysis of U.S. Foreign Policy.* Princeton, N.J.: Princeton University Press.

JOHNSON, C. **1973.** *Autopsy on People's War.* Berkeley: University of California Press.

——. **1966.** *Revolutionary Change.* Boston: Little, Brown.

JOHNSON, J. G. **1975.** *Ideology of Reason and Limitation of War: Religious and Secular Concepts.* Princeton, N.J.: Princeton University Press.

JOHNSON, J. J., ed. **1962.** *The Role of the Military in Underdeveloped Countries.* Princeton, N.J.: Princeton University Press.

JOHNSON, L. **1976.** "Political alienation among Vietnam veterans." *Western Political Q.,* 29(September):398–409.

JOHNSTON, D. M., ed. **1976.** *Marine Policy and the Coastal Community.* New York: St. Martin's.

JOHNSTON, S. W. **1974.** "Toward a supra-national criminology: the right and duty of victims of national government to seek defense through world law." *International J. of Criminology and Penology,* 2(May):133–147.

JONES, F. D., and A. W. JOHNSON. **1975.** "Medical and psychiatric treatment policy and practice in Vietnam." *J. of Social Issues,* 31(4):49–65.

JONES, J. H. **1973.** *The Economics of War and Conquest: An Examination of Mr. Norman Angell's Economic Doctrines.* New York: Garland.

JONES, R. **1951.** *A Life in Reuters.* London: Hodder and Stoughton.

JONES, S., and J. D. SINGER. **1972.** *Beyond Conjecture in International Politics: Abstracts of Data-Based Research.* Itasca, Ill.: Peacock.

JORDAN, D. S. **1972.** *War and Waste: A Series of Discussions of War and War Accessories.* New York: Garland.

JORDAN, R. S. **1976.** "United Nations General Assembly resolutions as expressions of human values." *International Studies Q.,* 20(December):647–654.

JOSSELYN, I. M. **1971.** "Value problems in the treatment of adolescents." *Smith College Studies in Social Work,* 42(November):1–14.

JOUARY, J. P. **1969.** "Typologie et périodicité du phénomène-guerre." *Guerres et Paix,* 4(13): 18–35.

JOUVENEL, B. DE. **1957.** *Sovereignty.* J. F. Huntington, tr. Chicago: University of Chicago Press.

JOYCE, J. A. **1978.** *The New Politics of Human Rights.* New York: St. Martin's.

JUDA, L. **1978.** "Negotiating a treaty on environmental modification warfare: the convention on environmental warfare and its impact upon arms control negotiations." *International Organization,* 32(Autumn):975–991.

JUDGE, A. J. N. **1978.** "International institutions: diversity, borderline cases, functional substitutes and possible alternatives." In P. Taylor and A. J. R. Groom, eds., *International Organization: A Conceptual Approach.* New York: Nichols. Pp. 28–83.

JUNN, R. S. **1980.** "Voting in the United Nations Security Council." Los Angeles: Presented at annual meeting of International Studies Association. Mimeo.

KAHN, H. **1969.** *On Thermonuclear War.* 2nd ed. New York: Free Press.

——. **1965.** *On Escalation.* New York: Praeger.

KAHN, H., W. BROWN, and L. MARTEL. **1976.** *The Next 200 Years: A Scenario for America and the World.* New York: Morrow.

KAHN, H., et al. **1977.** "The new class." *Co-Evolution Q.,* 15(Spring):8–39.

KAHN, R. L., and E. BOULDING, eds. **1964.** *Power and Conflict in Organizations.* New York: Basic Books.

KAHNERT, F., ed. **1969.** *Integration and Development.* Paris: Organization for Economic Cooperation and Development.

KÄKÖNEN, J. **1975.** "The World Bank: a bridgehead of imperialism." *Instant Research on Peace and Violence,* 5(3):150–164.

KANOVSKY, E. **1970.** *The Economic Impact of the Six-Day War: Israel, the Occupied Territories, Jordan.* New York: Praeger.

KANT, I. **1917.** *Perpetual Peace.* New York: Macmillan.

KAPLAN, A. D. J. **1964.** *Big Enterprise in a Competitive System.* Washington, D.C.: The Brookings Institution.

KAPLAN, B. H., ed. **1978.** *Social Change in the Capitalist World Economy.* Beverly Hills, Calif.: Sage.

KAPLAN, F. M. **1978.** "Enhanced-radiation weapons." *Scientific American,* 238(May):44–51.

KAPLAN, M. A. **1964.** "Intervention in internal war: some systematic sources." In J. N. Rosenau, ed., *International Aspects of Civil Strife.* Princeton, N.J.: Princeton University Press. Pp. 92–121.

——, ed. **1962.** *The Revolution in World Politics.* New York: Wiley.

——. **1957.** *System and Process in International Politics.* New York: Wiley.

KAPLAN, M. A., and N. KATZENBACH. **1961.** *The Political Foundations of International Law.* New York: Wiley.

KAPLAN, S. S. **1975.** "U.S. arms transfers to Latin America, 1945–1974: rational strategy, bureaucratic politics, and executive parameters." *International Studies Q.,* 19(December):399–431.

KARASKA, G. J. **1966.** "Interregional flows of defense-space awards." *Peace Research Society (International) Papers,* 5, Philadelphia Conference, 1965.

KARSTEN, P. **1978.** *Soldiers and Society: The Effects of Military Service and War on American Life.* Westport, Conn.: Greenwood.

KAUFMAN, R. F. **1970.** *The War Profiteers.* Indianapolis: Bobbs-Merrill.

KAUFMAN, R. P., D. S. GELLER, and H. I. CHERNOTSKY. **1975.** "A preliminary test of the theory of dependency." *Comparative Politics,* 7(April):303–330.

KAY, D. A., ed. **1977.** "The changing United Nations: options for the United States." *Proceedings of the Academy of Political Science,* 32(4).

KAY, K. **1976.** "World War I's silent killer." *Army,* 26(April):40–46.

KECSKEMETI, P. **1964.** *Strategic Surrender: The Politics of Victory and Defeat.* New York: Atheneum.

KEEHN, R. J., I. D. GOLDBERG, and G. W. BEEBE. **1974.** "Twenty-four year mortality follow-up of army veterans with disability separations for psychoneurosis in 1944." *Psychosomatic Medicine,* 36(January):27–46.

KEGLEY, C. W., JR. **1974.** "Measuring the growth and decay of transnational norms relevant to the control of violence." Chicago: Presented at annual meeting of American Political Science Association. Mimeo.

KEGLEY, C. W., JR., and P. J. McGOWAN, eds. **1979**. *Challenges to America: U.S. Foreign Policy in the 1980's.* Beverly Hills, Calif.: Sage.

KEGLEY, C. W., JR., and G. A. RAYMOND. **1980**. "International legal norms and the preservation of peace, 1860–1964: some bivariate relationships." Los Angeles: Presented at annual meeting of International Studies Association. Mimeo.

KEGLEY, C. W., JR., N. R. RICHARDSON, and G. RICHTER. **1978**. "Conflict at home and abroad: an empirical extension." *J. of Politics,* 40(August):742–752.

KEGLEY, C. W., JR., and E. R. WITTKOPF. **1979**. *American Foreign Policy: Pattern and Process.* New York: St. Martin's.

——. **1976**. "Structural characteristics of international influence relationships: a replication study." *International Studies Q.,* 20(June):261–299.

KELLEHER, C. M., ed. **1974**. *Political–Military Systems: Comparative Perspectives.* Beverly Hills, Calif.: Sage.

KELLEY, J., and H. S. KLEI. **1977**. "Revolution and the rebirth of inequality: a theory of stratification in postrevolutionary society." *American J. of Sociology,* 83(July):78–100.

KELLOG, J. C. **1964**. "A synopsis of military conflict, 1945–1964." Ann Arbor, Mich.: Presented at Bendix Systems Division, Arms Control Project Office. Mimeo.

KELLY, G. A., and C. W. BROWN, JR., eds., **1970**. *Struggles in the State: Sources and Patterns of World Revolution.* New York: Wiley.

KELLY, G. A., and L. B. MILLER. **1970**. "Internal war and international systems." In G. A. Kelly and C. W. Brown, Jr., eds., *Struggles in the State: Sources and Patterns of World Revolution.* New York: Wiley. Pp. 223–260.

KELMAN, H. C. **1977**. "The conditions, criteria, and dialectics of human dignity: a transnational perspective." *International Studies Q.,* 21(September):529–552.

——. **1973**. "Violence without moral restraint: reflections on the dehumanization of victims and victimizers." *J. of Social Issues,* 29(4):25–61.

——. **1972**. "The problem-solving workshop in conflict resolution." In R. L. Merritt, ed., *Communication in International Politics.* Urbana: University of Illinois Press. Pp. 168–204.

——, ed. **1965**. *International Behavior: A Social-Psychological Analysis.* New York: Holt, Rinehart and Winston.

KELMAN, H. C., and L. H. LAWRENCE. **1972**. "Violent man: American response to the trial of Lt. William L. Calley." *Psychology Today,* 6(June):41–45, 78–81.

KEMP, A. **1976**. "A diachronic model of international violence." *Peace Research,* 8(July):75–86.

KEMP, G., R. L. PFALTZGRAFF, JR., and U. RA'ANAN. **1975**. *The Other Arms Race: New Technologies and Non-Nuclear Conflict.* Lexington, Mass.: Lexington Books.

KENDE, I. **1978**. "Wars of ten years (1967–1976)." *J. of Peace Research,* 15(3):227–241.

——. **1977**. "Dynamics of wars, of arms trade and of military expenditure in the 'third world,' 1954–1976." *Instant Research on Peace and Violence,* 7(2):59–67.

——. **1976**. Private correspondence.

——. **1968**. *Nyolcvannyolc Haboru.* (Neo-Colonialism.) *1945–67.* Budapest: Cited in SIPRI, 1969b, p. 362.

KENNAN, G. R. **1951**. *American Diplomacy, 1900–1950.* New York: Mentor.

KENNEDY, G. **1974**. *The Military in the Third World.* New York: Scribner's.

KENNEDY, R. F. **1969**. *Thirteen Days: A Memoir of the Cuban Missile Crisis.* New York: Norton.

KENT, G. **1977**. "Pedagogy of the middle class." *Peace and Change,* 4(Fall):37–43.

——. **1967**. *The Effects of Threats.* Columbus: Mershon.

KENWOOD, A. G., and A. L. LOUGHEED. **1971**. *The Growth of the International Economy, 1820–1960: An Introductory Text.* London: Allen and Unwin.

KEOHANE, R. O., and J. S. NYE. **1977**. *Power and Interdependence: World Politics in Transition.* Boston: Little, Brown.

KEYNES, J. M. **1920**. *The Economic Consequences of the Peace.* New York: Harcourt, Brace and Howe.

KHADDURI, M. T. **1966**. *The Islamic Law of Nations: Shaybānī's Siyar.* Baltimore: Johns Hopkins University Press.

KHOKHLOV, L. K., and V. V. SYREISCHIKOV. **1972**. "The clinical picture and pathomorphosis of alcoholic psychoses according to epidemiological data." *Zhurnal Nevropatologii i Psikhiatrii,* 72(6):897–903.

KILPATRICK, S. J., JR. **1977**. "An empirical study of the distribution of episodes of illness recorded in the 1970–71 national morbidity survey." *Applied Statistics,* 26(1):26–40.

KILSON, M., ed. **1975**. *New States in the Modern World.* Cambridge, Mass.: Harvard University Press.

KIM, S. S. **1978**. *China, the United Nations, and World Order.* Princeton, N.J.: Princeton University Press.

KINDLEBERGER, C. P. **1973**. *The World in Depression, 1929–1939.* New York: Penguin.

——, ed. **1970a**. *The International Corporation: A Symposium.* Cambridge, Mass.: MIT Press.

——. **1970b**. *Power and Money.* New York: Basic Books.

——. **1967**. *The Politics of International Money and*

World Language. Essays in International Finance, No. 61. Princeton, N.J.: Department of Economics, Princeton University.

——. **1964.** *Economic Growth in France and Britain, 1851–1950.* New York: Simon and Schuster.

——. **1962.** *Foreign Trade and the National Economy.* New Haven, Conn.: Yale University Press.

KINNARD, D. **1977.** *The War Managers.* Hanover, N.H.: University Press of New England.

——. **1976.** "The Vietnam war in retrospect: the army generals' views." *J. of Political and Military Sociology,* 4(Spring):17–28.

KINTNER, W. R., and H. SICHERMAN. **1975.** *Technology and International Politics: The Crisis of Wishing.* Lexington, Mass.: Heath.

KIRK, D. **1946.** *Europe's Population in the Interwar Years.* Geneva: League of Nations.

KIRKHAM, J. F., G. LEVY, and W. J. CROTTY. **1970.** *Assassination and Political Violence.* New York: Bantam.

KIRSHNER, L. A. **1972.** "Acquiescence or change: a new look at military psychiatry." *Psychiatric Opinion,* 9(December):12–14.

KISKER, G. W. **1969.** *World Tension: The Psychopathology of International Relations.* Westport, Conn.: Greenwood.

KISSINGER, H. A. **1964.** *A World Restored.* New York: Grosset and Dunlap.

KISSINGER, H. L. **1975.** Press conference of December 9. Washington, D.C.: U.S. Department of State.

KISTIAKOWSKY, G. B. **1979.** "False alarm: the story behind SALT II." *New York Rev. of Books,* 26(March 22):33–38.

KLAASSEN, W. **1978.** "The just war: a summary." *Peace Research Rev.,* 7(September): 1–70.

KLARE, M. T. **1972.** *War Without End: American Planning for the Next Vietnams.* New York: Knopf.

KLEIN, H., and U. LAST. **1974.** "Cognitive and emotional aspects of the attitudes of American and Israeli youth towards the victims of the holocaust." *Israel Annals of Psychiatry and Related Disciplines,* 12(June):111–131.

KLINEBERG, O., ed. **1964.** *The Human Dimension in International Relations.* New York: Holt, Rinehart and Winston.

KLINGBERG, F. **1966.** "Predicting the termination of war: battle casualties and population losses." *J. of Conflict Resolution,* 10(June):129–171.

——. **1945.** *Historical Study of War Casualties.* Washington, D.C.: U.S. Secretary of War Office.

KLISE, T. S. **1974.** *The Last Western.* Miles, Ill.: Argus Communications.

KLONOFF, H., et al. **1976.** "The neuro-psychological psychiatric and physical effects of prolonged and severe stress 30 years later." *J. of Nervous and Mental Disease,* 163(October):246–252.

KNIGHT, D. E., H. W. CURTIS, and L. J. FOGEL, eds. **1971.** *Cybernetics, Simulation, and Conflict Resolution.* New York: Spartan.

KNORR, K. **1975.** *The Power of Nations: The Political Economy of International Relations.* New York: Basic Books.

——. **1956.** *The War Potential of Nations.* Princeton, N.J.: Princeton University Press.

KNORR, K., and F. TRAEGER, eds. **1977.** *Economic Issues and National Security.* Lawrence: Regents Press of Kansas.

KNORR, K., and S. VERBA, eds. **1961.** *The International System.* Princeton, N.J.: Princeton University Press.

KOCH, K. F. **1974.** *Anthropology of Warfare.* Menlo Park, Calif.: Cummings.

KÖHLER, G. **1978.** "Toward a general theory of armaments." *J. of Peace Research,* 16(2):117–134.

——. **1976.** "Imperialism as a level of analysis in correlates-of-war." *Impact of Science on Society,* 26(January–April):39–47.

——. **1975.** "Imperialism as a level of analysis in correlates-of-war research." *J. of Conflict Resolution,* 19(March):48–61.

——. **1974.** "Events data and the prediction of war: using a critical indicator method." *Peace Research Rev.,* 5(February):54–84.

KÖHLER, G. and N. ALCOCK. **1976.** "An empirical table of structural violence." Quebec: Canadian Peace Research and Education Association, Laval University. Mimeo.

KOHN, H. **1962.** *The Age of Nationalism: The First Era of Global History.* New York: Harper.

KOHN, M. L. **1976.** "Occupational structure and alienation." *American J. of Sociology,* 82(July):111–130.

KOHR, L. **1978.** *The Overdeveloped Nations: The Diseconomies of Scale.* New York: Schocken.

KOLKO, J., and G. KOLKO. **1972.** *The Limits of Power: The World and United States Foreign Policy, 1945–1954.* New York: Harper and Row.

KORANYI, E. K. **1969.** "A theoretical review of the survivor syndrome." *Diseases of the Nervous System,* 30(Suppl.)(February):115–118.

KORNHAUSER, W. **1959.** *The Politics of Mass Society.* New York: Free Press.

KOSLOW, E. E. **1977.** "An aposematic statement on nuclear war: UV radiation in the postattack environment." *Bioscience,* 27(June):409–413.

KOURVETARIS, G. A., and B. A. DOBRATZ, eds. **1977.** *World Perspectives in the Sociology of the Military.* New Brunswick, N.J.: Transaction Books.

KRASNER, S. D. **1978.** *Defending the National Interest: Raw Materials Investments and U.S. Foreign Policy.* Princeton, N.J.: Princeton University Press.

KRAUSE, L. B. **1968.** *European Economic Integration and the United States.* Washington, D.C.: The Brookings Institution.

——. **1964.** *The Common Market: Progress and Controversy.* Englewood Cliffs, N.J.: Prentice-Hall.

KRAUSS, B. J., R. D. KAPLAN, and H. H. KRAUSS. **1973.** "Factors affecting veterans' decisions to fire weapons in combat situations." *Interna-*

tional J. of Group Tensions, 3(3–4):105–111.

KREHBIEL, E. **1973.** *Nationalism, War, and Society.* New York: Garland.

KRIEGER, D. **1975.** "Terrorists and nuclear technology." *Bull. of the Atomic Scientists,* 31(June):28–34.

KRIESBERG, L., ed. **1968.** *Social Processes in International Relations.* New York: Wiley.

KRIESBERG, L., and R. KLEIN. **1980.** "Changes in public support for U.S. military spending." *J. of Conflict Resolution,* 24(March):79–111.

KRIPPNER, S. **1972.** "Marijuana and Viet Nam: twin dilemmas for American youth." In R. S. Parker, ed., *The Emotional Stress of War, Violence, and Peace.* Pittsburgh: Stanwix House. Pp. 176–225.

KRYSTAL, H., and W. G. NIEDERLAND, eds. **1971.** *Psychic Traumatization: Aftereffects in Individuals and Communities.* International Psychiatry Clinics, Vol. 8, No. 1. Boston: Little, Brown.

KUCERA, R. **1974.** *The Aerospace Industry and the Military: Structural and Political Relationships.* Beverly Hills, Calif.: Sage.

KUEHL, W. F. **1975.** "The principle of responsibility for peace and national security, 1920–1973." *Peace and Change,* 3(Summer–Fall):84–93.

KUHN, T. S. **1970.** *The Structure of Scientific Revolutions.* Chicago: University of Chicago Press.

KUKANOV, M. **1971.** *NATO—Threat to World Peace.* D. Fedlon, tr. Moscow: Progress Publishers.

KULISCHER, E. M. **1948.** *Europe on the Move: War and Population Changes, 1917–47.* New York: Columbia University Press.

KUPPERMAN, R. H., and H. A. SMITH. **1978.** "A catastrophe surface in mutual deterrence theory, arms limitation and crisis instability." *J. of Peace Science,* 3(Fall):111–122.

——. **1976.** "Formal models of arms races: discussion." *J. of Peace Science,* 2(Spring):89–96.

KWEE, S. L., and J. S. R. MULLENDER, eds. **1972.** *Growing Against Ourselves: The Energy–Environment Tangle.* Lexington, Mass.: Heath.

LA BARR, D. F., and J. D. SINGER. **1976.** *The Study of International Politics.* Santa Barbara, Calif.: ABC–Clio Press.

LAIDLAW, K. A. **1979.** "The military in the third world: a case for the convergence hypothesis?" *International Rev. of Modern Sociology,* 9(January–June):1–15.

LAMBELET, J. C. **1975.** "A numerical model of the Anglo-German dreadnought race." *Peace Science Society (International) Papers,* 24:29–48.

——. **1974.** "The Anglo-German dreadnought race, 1905–1914." *Peace Science Society (International) Papers,* 22:1–45.

——. **1971.** "A dynamic model of the arms race in the Middle East, 1953–1956." *General Systems,* 16:145–167.

LAMMERS, S. E. **1977.** "Review of J. Goldstein et al.,

The My Lai Massacre and Its Cover-Up." *Worldview,* 20(January–February):50–51.

LANDE, G. R. **1971.** "An inquiry into the successes and failures of the United Nations General Assembly." In L. Gordenker, ed., *The United Nations in International Politics.* Princeton, N.J.: Princeton University Press. Pp. 106–129.

LANE, W. C. **1976.** "Consensus, conflict, and international stratification theories of modernization: an evaluation." *Mid-American Rev. of Sociology,* 1(Winter):19–32.

LANG, G. E., and K. LANG. **1972.** "Some pertinent questions on collective violence and the news media." *J. of Social Issues,* 28(1):93–110.

LANG, K. **1972.** *Military Institutions and the Sociology of War: A Review of the Literature with Annotated Bibliography.* Beverly Hills, Calif.: Sage.

LANGBEIN, L. I., and A. J. LICHTMAN. **1978.** *Ecological Inference.* Beverly Hills, Calif.: Sage.

LAPP, R. E. **1970.** *Arms Beyond Doubt: The Tyranny of Weapons Technology.* New York: Cowles.

——. **1969.** *The Weapons Culture.* Baltimore: Penguin.

LAQUER, W., and G. MOSSE. **1970.** *Nineteen Fourteen: The Coming of the First War.* New York: Harper and Row.

LAROUI, A. **1967.** *L'Idéologie Arabe Contemporaine: Essaie Critique.* Paris: Maspero.

LARSEN, K. S. **1973a.** "Aggression and social cost." *Peace Research Rev.,* 5(January):1–104.

——. **1973b.** "Power and perception of the future." *Social Behavior and Personality,* 1(2):158–160.

——. **1972.** "Determinants of peace agreement, pessimism–optimism, and expectation of world conflict: a cross-national study." *J. of Cross-Cultural Psychology,* 3(September):283–292.

LARSON, A. D. **1974.** "Military professionalism and civil control: a comparative analysis of two interpretations." *J. of Political and Military Sociology,* 2(Spring):57–72.

LASSWELL, H. D. **1971.** *Propaganda Technique in World War I.* Cambridge, Mass.: MIT Press.

——. **1969.** *Psychopathology and Politics.* New York: Viking.

——. **1965a.** *World Politics and Personal Insecurity.* New York: Free Press.

——. **1965b.** "The world revolution of our time." In H. D. Lasswell and D. Lerner, eds., *World Revolutionary Elites.* Cambridge, Mass.: MIT Press. Pp. 29–96.

——. **1963.** *Power and Society: A Framework for Political Inquiry.* New Haven, Conn.: Yale University Press.

——. **1962.** "The garrison-state hypothesis today." In S. P. Huntington, ed., *Changing Patterns of Military Politics.* New York: Free Press. Pp. 51–70.

——. **1941.** "The garrison state." *Amer. J. of Sociology,* 46(January):455–468.

LASSWELL, H. D., and D. LERNER, eds. **1965.** *World*

Revolutionary Elites. Cambridge, Mass.: MIT Press.

LAUTERBACH, A. **1974.** *Psychological Challenges to Modernization: Emotional Factors in International Development.* Amsterdam and New York: Elsevier.

LAUTERPACHT, H., ed. **1955.** *Oppenheim's International Law.* 2 vols. London: Longmans, Green.

LAWSON, E. D., and M. GILES. **1973.** "British semantic differential responses on world powers." *European J. of Social Psychology,* 3(3):233–240.

LAYTON, C. **1966.** *Transatlantic Investments.* Boulogne-Sur-Seine: Atlantic Institute.

LEAGUE OF ARAB STATES. **1975.** *The League of Arab States and Regional Disputes: A Study of Middle East Conflicts.* Dobbs Ferry, N.Y.: Oceana.

LEAGUE OF NATIONS. **1928.** *International Health Yearbook, 1926.* Geneva: League of Nations.

LEAKEY, R. E., and R. LEWIN. **1977.** *Origins: What New Discoveries Reveal About the Emergence of Our Species and Its Possible Future.* New York: Dutton.

LeBON, G. **1968.** *The Crowd: A Study of the Popular Mind.* Dunwoody, Ga.: Berg.

LECKIE, R. **1970.** *Warfare.* New York: Harper and Row.

——. **1968.** *The Wars of America.* New York: Harper and Row.

LEE, J. R. **1973.** "Changing national priorities of the United States: budgets, perceived needs and political environments, 1945–1971." In B. M. Russett and A. Stepan, eds., *Military Force and American Society.* New York: Harper and Row. Pp. 61–105.

LEE, J. S. **1931.** "The periodic recurrence of internecine wars in China." *China J. of Science and Arts,* 14(March–April):111–115, 159–163.

LEGRAS, D. **1970–1971.** "Interest in a psychological study of the atomic phenomenon." *Bulletin de Psychologie,* 24:925–931.

LEGUM, C. **1977.** "Amin is syphilis victim, his former doctor says." *Washington Post,* 100(April 30):A16.

LEIDEN, C., and K. M. SCHMITT. **1968.** *The Politics of Violence: Revolution in the Modern World.* Englewood Cliffs, N.J.: Prentice-Hall.

LEISS, A. C., et al. **1970.** *Arms Transfers to Less Developed Countries.* Cambridge, Mass.: Center for International Studies, MIT.

——. **1967.** *The Control of Local Conflict: A Design on Arms Control and Limited War in the Developing Areas.* Prepared for U.S. Arms Control and Disarmament Agency. 4 vols. Cambridge, Mass.: Center for International Studies, MIT.

LEITENBERG, M. **1979.** "The counterpart of defense industry conversion in the United States: the USSR economy, defense industry, and military expenditure: an introduction and guide to sources." *J. of Peace Research,* 16(3):263–278.

LEITES, N. C., and C. WOLF, JR. **1970.** *Rebellion and Authority.* Chicago: Markham.

LENIN, V. I. **1966.** *On War and Peace.* San Francisco: China Books and Periodicals.

——. **1965.** *Imperialism.* San Francisco: China Books and Periodicals.

LENS, S. **1970.** *The Military–Industrial Complex.* Philadelphia: Pilgrim.

LENTZ, T. F. **1972.** *Towards a Technology of Peace.* St. Louis: Peace Research Laboratory.

——. **1955.** *Towards a Science of Peace.* New York: Bookman.

LEONTIEFF, W., A. P. CARTER, and P. PETRI. **1977.** *The Future of the World Economy: A United Nations Study.* New York: Oxford University Press.

LERNER, D. **1971.** *Psychological Warfare Against Nazi Germany: The Sykewar Campaign, D-day to VE-day.* Cambridge, Mass.: MIT Press.

——. **1965.** "The coercive ideologists in perspective." In H. D. Lasswell and D. Lerner, eds., *World Revolutionary Elites.* Cambridge, Mass.: MIT Press. Pp. 456–468.

LERNER, D., and M. GORDEN. **1969.** *Euratlantica: Changing Perspectives of European Elites.* Cambridge, Mass.: MIT Press.

LESSER, A. **1968.** "War and the state," In M. H. Fried, M. Harris, and R. Murphy, eds., *War: The Anthropology of Armed Conflict and Aggression.* Garden City, N.Y.: Natural History Press. Pp. 92–96.

LEVIE, H. S. **1979.** *Protection of War Victims: The Protocol to the 1949 Geneva Conventions.* Dobbs Ferry, N.Y.: Oceana.

——. **1969.** "Maltreatment of prisoners of war in Vietnam." In R. A. Falk, ed., *The Vietnam War and International Law.* Vol. 2. Princeton, N.J.: Princeton University Press. Pp. 361–397.

LEVIN, A. L. **1974.** *The OAS and the UN: Relations in the Peace and Security Field.* New York: United Nations Institute for Training and Research.

LEVINE, R. A. **1963.** *The Arms Debate.* Cambridge, Mass.: Harvard University Press.

LEVINE, S. V. **1974.** "American exiles in Canada: a social and psychological follow-up." *Psychiatric Opinion,* 11(November):20–31.

LEVINSON, C. **1971.** *Capital, Inflation, and the Multinationals.* New York: Macmillan.

LÉVI-STRAUSS, C. **1963.** *Structural Anthropology.* C. Jacobsen and B. Schoepf, trs. New York: Basic Books.

LEVITAN, S. A., and K. C. ALDERMAN. **1977.** *Warriors at Work: The Volunteer Armed Force.* Beverly Hills, Calif.: Sage.

LEVY, J. S. **1980.** "Historical trends in war, 1495–1975." Los Angeles: Presented at annual meeting of International Studies Association. Mimeo.

LEVY, S. G. **1970.** "The psychology of political activity." *Annals of the American Academy of Political and Social Science*, 391(September):83–96.

LEVY, S. G., and R. HEFNER. 1964. "Multi-dimensional scaling of international attitudes." *Peace Research Society (International) Papers*, 1:129–165.

LEWIN, L. 1967. *Report from Iron Mountain on the Possibility and Desirability of Peace*. New York: Dial.

LEWIS, K. N. 1979. "The prompt and delayed effects of nuclear war." *Scientific American*, 241(July):35–47.

LEWIS, R. A. 1975. "A contemporary religious enigma: churches and war." *J. of Political and Military Sociology*, 3(Spring):57–70.

LI, R. P. Y., and W. R. THOMPSON. 1978. "The stochastic process of alliance formation behavior." *American Political Science Rev.*, 72(December):1288–1303.

———. 1975. "The 'coup contagion' hypothesis." *J. of Conflict Resolution*, 19(March):63–88.

LIDER, J. 1978. *On the Nature of War*. Boulder: Westview.

LIEBER, F. 1875. *Instructions for the Government of Armies of the United States in the Field*. Cincinnati: Van Nostrand Reinhold.

LIEBERSON, S. 1973. "An empirical study of military–industrial linkages." In S. Rosen, ed., *Testing the Theory of the Military–Industrial Complex*. Lexington, Mass.: Lexington Books. Pp. 61–84.

LIESKE, J. A. 1979. "Inadvertent empirical theory: a critique of 'the J curve theory and the black urban riots.' " *Political Methodology*, 6(1):29–62.

LIFTON, R. J. 1974. " 'Death imprints' on youth in Vietnam." *J. of Clinical Child Psychology*, 3(Summer):47–49.

———. 1973. *Home from the War: Vietnam Veterans— Neither Victims nor Executioners*. New York: Simon and Schuster.

———. 1967. *Death in Life: Survivors of Hiroshima*. New York: Random House.

LINDBERG, L., and S. SCHEINGOLD, eds. 1971. *Regional Integration*. Cambridge, Mass.: Harvard University Press.

———. 1970. *Europe's Would-be Polity*. Englewood Cliffs, N.J.: Prentice-Hall.

LINDZEY, G., and E. ARONSON, eds. 1968–1969. *Handbook of Social Psychology*. 2nd ed. 5 vols. Reading, Mass.: Addison-Wesley.

LINZ, J. 1973. "Early state-building and late peripheral nationalisms against the state: the case of Spain." In S. N. Eisenstadt and S. Rokkan, eds., *Building States and Nations: Models, Analyses and Data Across Three Worlds*. Beverly Hills, Calif.: Sage. Vol. 2, pp. 36–116.

LIPPMANN, W. 1955. *Essays in the Public Philosophy*. New York: Mentor.

LIPSET, S. M. 1968. *Revolution and Counterrevolution: Change and Persistence in Social Structures*. New York: Basic Books.

LIPSEY, R. G. 1971. *The Theory of Customs Unions: A General Equilibrium Analysis*. Atlantic Highlands, N.J.: Humanities.

LIPSON, L. 1960. *The Great Issues of Politics*. Englewood Cliffs, N.J.: Prentice-Hall.

LISKE, C., J. MCCAMAUT, and W. LOEHR, eds. 1975. *Comparative Public Policy: Issues, Theories and Methods*. New York: Wiley.

LISSAK, M. 1976. *Military Roles in Modernization*. Beverly Hills, Calif.: Sage.

LITTLE, R. 1975. *Intervention: External Involvement in Civil Wars*. Totowa: Rowman and Littlefield.

———, ed. 1971. *Handbook of Military Institutions*. Beverly Hills, Calif.: Sage.

LIVINGSTON, D. 1971. "Science fiction models of future world order systems." *International Organization*, 25(Spring):254–270.

LLOYD, W. B., JR. 1958. *Waging Peace: The Swiss Experience*. Washington, D.C.: Public Affairs Press.

LOCK, P., and H. WULF. 1977. "Consequences of transfer of military-oriented technology on the development process." *Bull. of Peace Proposals*, 8(2):127–136.

———. 1975. "New trends and actors in the arms transfer process to peripheral countries: a preliminary assessment of peace research, some hypotheses and research proposals." *Instant Research on Peace and Violence*, 5(4):185–196.

LOCKHAM, A. R. 1971. "Institutional transfer and breakdown in a new nation: the Nigerian military." *Administrative Science Q.*, 16(December):387–405.

LODGAARD, S. 1977. "The functions of SALT." *J. of Peace Research*, 14(1):1–22.

LODHI, A. Q., and C. TILLY. 1973. "Urbanization, crime, and collective violence in 19th-century France." *American J. of Sociology*, 79(September):296–318.

LOEBER, D. A. 1977. *East–West Trade: A Sourcebook on the International Economic Relations of Socialist Countries and Their Legal Aspects*. Dobbs Ferry, N.Y.: Oceana.

LOFTON, J. 1972. "A perspective from the public at large." *American Psychologist*, 27(May):364–366.

LOGAN, J. R., and G. ZEITZ. 1977. "Mathematical models in the study of power: comment on Mayhew and Levinger." *American J. of Sociology*, 83(July):164–173.

LONG, F. A., and G. W. RATHJENS, eds. 1975. "Arms, defense policy and arms control." *Daedalus*, 104(Summer):whole issue.

LONGINO, C. F. 1973. "Draft lottery numbers and student opposition to war." *Sociology of Education*, 46(Fall):499–506.

LOPEZ-REYES, R. 1971. *Power and Immortality: Essays on Strategy, War Psychology, and War Control*. New York: Exposition.

LORE, R., and K. FLANNELLY. 1977. "Rat societies."

Scientific American, 236 (May): 106–116.

LORENZ, K. **1967.** *On Aggression.* M. K. Wilson, tr. New York: Bantam.

LOVELL, J. P., and P. S. KRONENBERG, eds. **1974.** *New Civil–Military Relations: The Agonies of Adjustment to Post-Vietnam Realities.* New Brunswick, N.J.: Transaction Books.

LOVINS, A. **1977.** *Soft Energy Paths: Toward a Durable Peace.* San Francisco: Friends of the Earth.

LOWTHER, M. P. **1973.** "The decline of public concern over the atom bomb." *Kansas J. of Sociology,* 9(Spring):77–88.

LUARD, E. **1972.** *The International Regulation of Civil Wars.* New York: New York University Press.

——. **1968.** *Conflict and Peace in the Modern International System.* Boston: Little, Brown.

——. **1962.** *Peace and Opinion.* London: Oxford University Press.

LUCE, D., and J. SOMMER. **1969.** *Vietnam: The Unheard Voices.* Ithaca, N.J.: Cornell University Press.

LUCIANO, D., and R. LORE. **1975.** "Aggression and social experience in domesticated rats." *J. of Comparative and Physiological Psychology,* 88(February):917–923.

LUCIER, C. E. **1979.** "Changes in the values of arms race parameters." *J. of Conflict Resolution,* 23(March):17–39.

LUMSDEN, M. **1979.** "The UN conference on inhumane weapons." *J. of Peace Research,* 16(4):289–292.

——. **1973.** "The Cyprus conflict as a prisoner's dilemma game." *J. of Conflict Resolution,* 17(March):7–32.

LUNDEN, W. A. **1967.** *Crimes and Criminals.* Ames: Iowa State University Press.

LUPSHA, P. A. **1971.** "Explanation of political violence: some psychological theories versus indignation." *Politics and Society,* 2(Fall):89–104.

LUTTWAK, E. **1974.** *The U.S.–U.S.S.R Nuclear Weapons Balance.* Beverly Hills, Calif.: Sage.

LYNCH, J. E. **1970.** *Local Economic Development After Military Base Closures.* New York: Praeger.

McCLELLAND, C. A. **1968.** "Access to Berlin: the quantity and variety of events, 1948–1963." In J. D. Singer, ed., *Quantitative International Politics: Insights and Evidence.* New York: Free Press. Pp. 159–186.

——. **1964.** "Action structures and communication in two international crises: Quemoy and Berlin." *Background,* 7(February):201–215.

McCLELLAND, D. C. **1975.** "Love and power: the psychological signals of war." *Psychology Today,* 8(January):44–48.

——. **1961.** *The Achieving Society.* Princeton, N.J.: Van Nostrand.

McCLOSKY, H. **1967.** "Personality and attitude cor-

relates of foreign policy orientation." In J. N. Rosenau, ed., *Domestic Sources of Foreign Policy.* New York: Free Press. Pp. 51–109.

MACCOBY, M. **1972.** "Emotional attitudes and political choices." *Politics and Society,* 2(Winter):209–239.

McCORMICK, J. M. **1975.** "Evaluating models of crisis behavior: some evidence from the Middle East." *International Studies Q.,* 19(March):17–45.

McCUBBIN, H. I., B. B. DAHL, and E. J. HUNTER. **1976.** *Families in the Military System.* Beverly Hills, Calif.: Sage.

McCUBBIN, H. I., E. J. HUNTER, and B. B. DAHL. **1975.** "Residuals of war: families of prisoners of war and servicemen missing in action." *J. of Social Issues,* 31(4):95–109.

MACDONALD, A. P. **1973.** "A time for introspection." *Professional Psychology,* 4(February):35–42.

McDOUGAL, M. S., and F. P. FELICIANO. **1961.** *Law and Minimum World Public Order: The Legal Regulation of International Coercion.* New Haven, Conn.: Yale University Press.

MACFIE, A. L. **1938.** "The outbreak of war and the trade cycle." *Economic History,* 3(February):89–97.

McGOWAN, P. J., ed. **1975, 1974, 1973.** *Sage International Yearbook of Foreign Policy Studies.* Beverly Hills, Calif.: Sage.

McGOWAN, P. J., and K. P. GOTTWALD. **1975.** "Small state foreign policies: a comparative study of participation, conflict, and political and economic dependence in Black Africa." *International Studies Q.,* 19(December):469–500.

McGOWAN, P. J., and C. W. KEGLEY, JR., eds. **1980.** *Threats, Weapons and Foreign Policy.* Beverly Hills, Calif.: Sage.

McGOWAN, P. J., and R. M. ROOD. **1975.** "Alliance behavior in balance of power systems: applying a Poisson model to nineteenth-century Europe." *American Political Science Rev.,* 69(September):859–870.

McGOWAN, P. J., and H. B. SHAPIRO. **1973.** *The Comparative Study of Foreign Policy: A Survey of Scientific Findings.* Beverly Hills, Calif.: Sage.

McGUIRE, M. C. **1965.** *Secrecy and the Arms Race: A Theory of the Accumulation of Strategic Weapons and How Secrecy Affects It.* Cambridge, Mass.: Harvard University Press.

McHALE, V. E., and D. PARANZINO. **1975.** "A note on the theoretical utility of elite background characteristics in predicting political longevity in the U.S.S.R." *Political Methodology,* 2(1):113–127.

MACHLUP, F. **1969.** "Cost push and demand pull." In R. J. Ball and P. Doyle, eds., *Inflation: Selected Readings.* Baltimore: Penguin. Pp. 149–176.

MACK, A. J. R. **1975.** "Why big nations lose small wars: the politics of asymmetric conflict." *World Politics,* 27(January):175–200.

McKEAN, R., ed. **1967.** *Issues in Defense Economics.* New York: Columbia University Press.

MACK-FORLIST, D. M., and A. NEWMAN. **1970.** *The Conversion of Shipbuilding from Military to Civilian Markets.* New York: Praeger.

McKINLAY, R. D., and A. S. COHAN. **1976.** "Performance and instability in military and non-military regime systems." *American Political Science Rev.,* 701(September):850–864.

——. **1975.** "A comparative analysis of the political and economic performance of military and civilian regimes: a cross-national aggregate study." *Comparative Politics,* 8(October):1–30.

McKISSACK, I. J. **1974.** "A less delinquent cohort." *British J. of Criminology,* 14(April):158–164.

McLUHAN, M. **1964.** *Understanding Media: The Extensions of Man.* New York: McGraw-Hill.

McLUHAN, M., and Q. FIORE. **1968.** *War and Peace in the Global Village.* New York: McGraw-Hill.

MacMAHON, B., et al. **1960.** *Epidemiologic Methods.* Boston: Little, Brown.

McMASTER, R. E., JR. **1970.** *Cycles of War: The Next Six Years.* Kalispell, Mont.: War Cycles Institute.

McNEIL, E. G., ed. **1965.** *The Nature of Human Conflict.* Englewood Cliffs, N.J.: Prentice-Hall.

——. **1959.** "Psychology and aggression." *J. of Conflict Resolution,* 3(September):195–293.

McNEILL, W. H. **1976.** *Plagues and Peoples.* Garden City, N.Y.: Doubleday.

——. **1969.** *History of Western Civilization.* Chicago: University of Chicago Press.

MacRAE, J. H., and D. N. BRIGDEN. **1973.** "Auditory threshold impairment and everyday speech reception." *Audiology,* 12(June):272–290.

MAGDOFF, H. **1969.** *The Age of Imperialism: The Economics of U.S. Foreign Policy.* New York: Monthly Review Press.

MAGGIOLO, W. A. **1971.** *Techniques of Mediation in Labor Disputes.* Dobbs Ferry, N.Y.: Oceana.

MAIER, N. R. F. **1949.** *Frustration: The Study of Behavior Without a Goal.* New York: McGraw-Hill.

MAILER, N. **1970.** *Of a Fire on the Moon.* Boston: Little, Brown.

MAJESKI, S. J., and D. L. JONES. **1980.** "Arms race modeling: causality analysis and model specification." Los Angeles: Presented at annual meeting of International Studies Association. Mimeo.

MAJOR, R. **1941.** *Fatal Partners: War and Disease.* Garden City, N.Y.: Doubleday.

MALINOWSKI, B. **1948.** *Magic, Science, and Religion.* Glencoe, Ill.: Free Press.

——. **1941.** "An anthropological analysis of war." *American J. of Sociology,* 46(January):521–550.

MALMGREN, H. B. **1972.** *International Economic Peacekeeping in Phase II.* New York: Quadrangle.

MANCHESTER, W. R. **1968.** *The Arms of Krupp.* Boston: Little, Brown.

MANGELSDORFF, A. D., and M. ZUCKERMAN. **1975.** "Habituation to scenes of violence." *Psychophysiology,* 21(March):124–129.

MANN, L. **1973.** "Attitudes toward My Lai and obedience to orders: an Australian survey." *Australian J. of Psychology,* 25(April):11–21.

MANNING, A., and D. A. TAYLOR. **1975.** "Effects of viewed violence and aggression: stimulation and catharsis." *J. of Personality and Social Psychology,* 31(January):180–188.

MANSBACH, R. W., Y. H. FERGUSON, and D. E. LAMPERT. **1976.** *The Web of World Politics: Non-State Actors in the Global System.* Englewood Cliffs, N.J.: Prentice-Hall.

MAPLE, T., and D. W. MATHESON, eds. **1973.** *Aggression, Hostility, and Violence: Nature or Nurture.* New York: Holt, Rinehart and Winston.

MARCUSE, H. **1964.** *One Dimensional Man: Studies in the Ideology of Advanced Industrial Society.* Boston: Beacon.

MARGIOTTA, F. D., ed. **1978.** *The Changing World of the American Military.* Boulder: Westview.

MARKHAM, J. W., C. E. FIERO, and H. S. PIQUET. **1964.** *The Common Market: Friend or Competitor.* New York University Press.

MARKOWITZ, I. **1971.** "The military mind." *Psychiatric Q.,* 45(3):440–448.

MARKS, G., and W. K. BEATTY. **1976.** *Epidemics.* New York: Scribner's.

MARSILIUS OF PADUA. **1928.** *Defensor Pacis.* C. W. Previte-Orton, ed. Cambridge: Cambridge University Press.

MARWAH, O., and J. D. POLLACK. **1978.** *Military Power and Policy in Asian States: Toward the 1980's.* Boulder: Westview.

MARWICK, A. **1974.** *War and Social Change in the Twentieth Century: A Comparative Study of Britain, France, Germany, Russia and the United States.* New York: St. Martin's.

MASARYK, T. G. **1971.** *Suicide and the Meaning of Civilization.* W. B. Weist and R. G. Batson, trs. Chicago: University of Chicago Press.

MASLOW, A. H. **1968.** *Toward a Psychology of Being.* Princeton, N.J.: Van Nostrand.

MATTELART, A. **1976.** "Cultural imperialism in the multinationals' age." *Instant Research on Peace and Violence,* 6(4):160–174.

MAUSNER, J. S., and A. K. BAHN. **1974.** *Epidemiology: An Introductory Text.* Philadelphia: Saunders.

MAX PLANCK INSTITUTE FOR COMPARATIVE PUBLIC LAW AND INTERNATIONAL LAW, ed. **1975–1978.** *Public International Law.* New York: Springer Verlag.

MAY, A. J. **1947.** *Europe and Two World Wars.* New York: Scribner's.

MAY, E. R. **1973.** *Lessons of History: The Use and Misuse of the Past in American Foreign Policy.* New York: Oxford University Press.

MAY, M. A. **1943.** *A Social Psychology of War and Peace.* New Haven, Conn.: Yale University Press.

MAY, R. **1972.** *Power and Innocence: A Search for the Sources of Violence.* New York: Norton.

MAYER, A. J. **1971.** *Dynamics of Counterrevolution in Europe, 1870–1956: An Analytic Framework.* New York: Harper and Row.

MAYER, P., ed. **1966.** *The Pacifist Conscience.* London: Penguin.

MAYHEW, B. H., and R. L. LEVINGER. **1976.** "Size and the density of interaction in human aggregates." *American J. of Sociology,* 82 (July):86–110.

MAYNE, R. J. **1970.** *The Recovery of Europe: From Devastation to Unity.* New York: Harper and Row.

MAZRUI, A. A. **1976.** "Military technology and the masculinity of war: an African perspective." *Impact of Science on Society,* 26(January–April):71–75.

———. **1975.** *Soldiers and Kinsmen in Uganda: The Making of a Military Ethnocracy.* Beverly Hills, Calif.: Sage.

———. **1971.** *The Trial of Christopher Okigbo.* New York: Third Press.

MEAD, M. **1971.** *And Keep Your Powder Dry.* West Caldwell, N.J.: Morrow.

———. **1964.** "Warfare is only an invention—not a biological necessity." In L. Bramson and G. Goethals, eds., *War: Contributions from Psychology, Sociology, and Anthropology.* New York: Basic Books. Pp. 269–274.

———. **1961.** *Cooperation and Competition Among Primitive Peoples.* 2nd ed. Boston: Beacon.

MEADE, R. D., and L. SINGH. **1973.** "Changes in social distance during warfare: a study of the India/Pakistan War of 1971." *J. of Social Psychology,* 90(August):325–326.

MEADOWS, D. H., et al. **1974.** *The Limits to Growth: A Report for the Club of Rome's Project on the Predicament of Mankind.* New York: Signet.

MEERLOO, J. A. M. **1962.** *Suicide and Mass Suicide.* New York: Dutton.

MEGURO, K. **1972.** "War neurosis: a 20-year follow-up story." *Foreign Psychiatry,* 1(Summer):165–203.

MEISEL, J. H. **1966.** *Counter-Revolution: How Revolutions Die.* New York: Atherton.

MEISSNER, W. W. **1971.** "Toward a theology of human aggression." *J. of Religion and Health,* 10(October):324–332.

MELKO, M. **1975.** "The termination of peace as a consequence of institutionalization." In M. A. Nettleship, R. Dalegivens, and A. Nettleship,

eds., *War: Its Causes and Correlates.* The Hague and Paris: Mouton. Pp. 549–558.

———. **1973.** *52 Peaceful Societies.* Oakville, Ontario: Canadian Peace Research Institute Press.

MELLETT, T. P. **1973.** "Attitudes and personal values of Vietnam veterans." *Newsletter for Research in Mental Health and Behavioral Sciences,* 15(May):4–9.

MELMAN, S. **1975.** "Twelve propositions on productivity and war economy. *Armed Forces and Society,* 1(Summer):490–497.

———, ed. **1971.** *The War Economy of the United States: Readings on Military Industry and Economy.* New York: St. Martin's.

———, ed. **1970a.** *The Defense Economy: Conversion of Industries and Occupations to Civilian Needs.* New York: Praeger.

———. **1970b.** *Pentagon Capitalism: The Political Economy of War.* New York: McGraw-Hill.

———. **1968.** *In the Name of America: The Conduct of the War in Vietnam by the Armed Forces of the United States as shown by Published Reports, Compared with the Laws of War Binding on the United States Government and Its Citizens.* New York: Clergy and Laymen Concerned About Vietnam.

———. **1965.** *Our Depleted Society.* New York: Holt, Rinehart and Winston.

MELZER, Y. **1975.** *Concepts of Just War.* Leiden: Sijthoff.

MEMMI, A. **1965.** *The Colonizer and the Colonized.* New York: Grossman.

MENDEL, J. M., and K. S. FU, eds. **1970.** *Adaptive, Learning, and Pattern Recognition Systems: Theory and Applications.* New York: Academic.

MENEGAKIS, C. **1970.** "Economic effects of military activity on states and countries, 1959–1960." In S. Melman, ed., *The Defense Economy: Conversion of Industries and Occupations to Civilian Needs.* New York: Praeger. Pp. 18–55.

MENNINGER, K. **1968.** *The Crime of Punishment.* New York: Viking.

———. **1942.** *Love Against Hate.* New York: Harcourt, Brace.

MENNIS, B., and K. P. SAUVANT. **1976.** *Emerging Forms of Transnational Community: Transnational Business Enterprises and Regional Integration.* Lexington, Mass.: Lexington Books.

MERBAUM, M. **1977.** "Some personality characteristics of soldiers exposed to extreme war stress: a follow-up study of post-hospital adjustment." *J. of Clinical Psychology,* 33 (April):558–562.

MERCER, G. **1974.** "Adolescent views on war and peace—another look." *J. of Peace Research,* 11(3):247–249.

MERKLIN, L. **1974.** *They Chose Honor: The Problem of Conscience in Custody.* New York: Harper and Row.

MERRITT, R. L. ed. **1972.** *Communication in International Politics.* Urbana: University of Illinois Press.

MERRITT, R. L., and B. RUSSETT, eds. **1980** (in press). *From National Development to Global Community.* London: Allen and Unwin.

MERSKY, R. M., ed. **1978.** *Conference on Transnational Economic Boycotts and Coercion: Papers and Documents.* Dobbs Ferry, N.Y.: Oceana.

MERTON, R. K., and P. F. LAZARSFELD, eds. **1974.** *Continuities in Social Research: Studies in the Scope and Method of the American Soldier.* New York: Arno.

MERVIN, F. S., ed. **1921.** *The Evolution of World Peace.* New York: Oxford University Press.

MESELSON, M. S., ed. **1978.** *Chemical Weapons and Chemical Arms Control: Papers and Discussion from a Conference at the American Academy of Arts and Sciences, Boston, Massachusetts, January 21–22, 1977.* New York: Carnegie Endowment for International Peace.

———. **1973.** "Chemical and biological weapons." In H. F. York, ed., *Arms Control.* San Francisco: W. H. Freeman and Company. Pp. 303–313.

MEYER, J. W. **1977.** "The effects of education as an institution." *American J. of Sociology,* 83 (July):55–77.

MEYERS, C., J. M. DONNAY, and F. DETHIENNE. **1974.** "Analysis of the present neuropsychiatric pathology of former prisoners of war, with special reference to age at onset of captivity." *Acta Psychiatrica Belgica,* 74(January):80–99.

MEYERS, W., ed. **1972.** *Conversion from War to Peace: Social, Economic and Political Problems.* New York: Gordon and Breach.

MIALE, F. R., and M. SELZER. **1975.** *The Nuremberg Mind: The Psychology of the Nazi Leaders.* New York: Quadrangle.

MICHAELY, M. **1962.** *Concentration in International Trade.* Amsterdam: North Holland.

MICHALAK, S. J., JR. **1971.** "The United Nations and the League." In L. Gordenker, ed., *The United Nations in International Politics.* Princeton, N.J.: Princeton University Press. Pp. 60–105.

MICHELS, R. **1962.** *Political Parties: A Sociological Study of the Oligarchical Tendencies of Modern Democracy.* New York: Free Press.

MIDLARSKY, M. I. **1978.** "Analyzing diffusion and contagion effects: the urban disorders of the 1960s." *American Political Science Rev.,* 72(September):996–1008.

———. **1975.** *On War: Political Violence in the International System.* New York: Free Press.

———. **1974.** "Power, uncertainty, and the onset of international violence," *J. of Conflict Resolution,* 18(September):395–431.

MIDLARSKY, M. I., and S. T. THOMAS. **1973.** "Domestic social structures and international warfare." *Proceedings of the Ninth International Congress of Anthropological and Ethnological Sciences.* Chicago: Mimeo.

MIHALKA, M. **1975.** "The measurement and modeling of arms accumulation: the Middle East as a case study." Publication C/75-8. Cambridge, Mass.: Center for International Studies, MIT.

MILBURN, T. W. **1980.** "Some limits of rewarding in international politics." Los Angeles: Presented at annual meeting of International Studies Association. Mimeo.

MILES, E., ed. **1977.** "Restructuring ocean regimes: implications of the third United Nations conference on the law of the sea." *International Organization,* 31(Spring):151–384.

MILES, I. **1975.** *The Poverty of Prediction.* Lexington, Mass.: Heath.

MILGRAM, R. M., and N. A. MILGRAM. **1976.** "The effect of the Yom Kippur war on anxiety level in Israeli children." *J. of Psychiatry.* 94 (September):107–113.

MILGRAM, S. **1974.** *Obedience to Authority: An Experimental View.* New York: Harper and Row.

MILLER, A. H., L. H. BOLCE, and M. HALLIGAN. **1977.** "The J-Curve theory and the black urban riots: an empirical test of progressive relative deprivation theory." *American Political Science Rev.,* 71(September):964–982.

MILLER, J. G. **1978.** *Living Systems.* New York: McGraw-Hill.

MILLER, L. **1972.** "Identity and violence: in pursuit of the causes of war and organised violence." *Israel Annals of Psychiatry and Related Disciplines,* 10(March):71–77.

MILLER, R. I., ed. **1975.** *The Law of War.* Lexington, Mass.: Lexington Books.

MILLS, C. W. **1959.** *The Power Elite.* New York: Oxford University Press.

MILSTEIN, J. S. **1974.** *Dynamics of the Vietnam War: A Quantitative Analysis and Predictive Computer Simulation.* Columbus: Ohio State University Press.

———. **1970.** "Soviet and American influences on the Arab–Israeli arms race: a quantitative analysis." *Peace Research Society (International) Papers,* 15:6–27.

MILSTEIN, J. S., and W. C. MITCHELL. **1969.** "Computer simulation of international processes: the Vietnam War and the pre–World War I naval race." *Peace Research Society (International) Papers,* 12:117–136.

———. **1968.** "Dynamics of the Vietnam conflict: a quantitative analysis and predictive computer simulation." *Peace Research Society (International) Papers,* 10:162–213.

MILSUM, J. H. **1966.** *Biological Control Systems Analysis.* New York: McGraw-Hill.

MILWARD, A. S. **1977.** *War, Economy and Society,*

1939–1945. Berkeley: University of California Press.

MINEAR, R. H. **1971.** *Victors' Justice.* Princeton, N.J.: Princeton University Press.

MINGST, K. A. **1976.** "Cooperation or illusion: an examination of the Intergovernmental Council of Copper Exporting Countries." *International Organization,* 30(Spring):263–289.

MINOTT, R. G. **1962.** *Peerless Patriots: Organized Veterans and the Spirit of Americanism.* Washington, D.C.: Public Affairs Press.

MIRA Y LOPEZ, E. **1943.** *Psychiatry in War.* New York: Norton.

MIRIN, S. M., and G. J. MCKENNA. **1975.** "Combat zone adjustment: the role of marijuana use." *Military Medicine,* 140(July):482–485.

MISCHE, G., and P. MISCHE. **1977.** *Toward a Human World Order: Beyond the National Security Straitjacket.* New York: Paulist Press.

MISHAN, E. J. **1967.** *The Costs of Economic Growth.* Baltimore: Penguin.

MITCHELL, E. J. **1968.** "Inequality and insurgency: a statistical study of South Vietnam." *World Politics,* 20(April):421–438.

MITCHELL, J. D. **1970.** "Cross-cutting memberships, integration, and the international system." *J. of Conflict Resolution,* 14(March):49–55.

MITCHELL, J. J. **1972.** *Human Nature: Theories, Conjectures, and Descriptions.* Metuchen, N.J.: Scarecrow.

MITRANY, D. **1966.** *A Working Peace System.* Chicago: Quadrangle.

MITSCHERLICH, A. **1971.** "Psychoanalysis and aggression in large groups." *Psyche* (Stuttgart), 25(June):463–475.

——. **1970.** *Society Without the Father: A Contribution to Social Psychology.* Eric Mosbacher, tr. New York: Schocken.

——, ed. **1969.** *Krankheit als Konflikt.* Frankfurt: Suhrkamp.

——. **1949.** *Doctors of Infamy: The Story of the Nazi Medical Crimes.* New York: Schuman.

MITSCHERLICH, A., and M. MITSCHERLICH. **1975.** *The Inability to Mourn: Principles of Collective Behavior.* B. R. Placzek, tr. New York: Grove.

MOBERG, E. **1966.** "Models of international conflicts and arms races." *Nordic Studies in International Politics,* 2:80–93.

MODELSKI, G. **1979a.** "Long cycles and U.S. strategic policy." *Policy Studies J.,* 8(Autumn):10–16.

——, ed. **1979b.** *Transnational Corporations and World Order: Readings in International Political Economy.* San Francisco: W. H. Freeman and Company.

——. **1978.** "Wars and the great power system." In L. L. Farrar, Jr., ed., *War: A Historical, Political and Social Study.* Santa Barbara, Calif.: ABC–Clio. Pp. 43–56.

——. **1974.** *Multinational Corporations and World Order.* Beverly Hills, Calif.: Sage.

——. **1964.** "The international relations of internal war." In J. N. Rosenau, ed., *International Aspects of Civil Strife.* Princeton, N.J.: Princeton University Press. Pp. 14–44.

——. **1961.** "Agraria and industria: two models of the international system." In K. Knorr and S. Verba, eds., *The International System.* Princeton, N.J.: Princeton University Press. Pp. 118–143.

MOLL, K. D., and G. M. LUEBBERT. **1980.** "Arms race and military expenditure models: a review." *J. of Conflict Resolution,* 24(March):153–185.

MONACO, P. **1974.** "The popular cinema as reflection of the group process in France, 1919–1929." *History of Childhood Q.: The J. of Psychohistory,* 1(Spring):607–636.

MONTAGU, A. **1976.** *The Nature of Human Aggression.* New York: Oxford University Press.

——, ed. **1973.** *Man and Aggression.* New York: Oxford University Press.

MONTROLL, E. W., and W. W. BADGER. **1974.** *Introduction to Quantitative Aspects of Social Phenomena.* New York: Gordon and Breach.

MOORE, B. **1966.** *Social Origins of Dictatorship.* Boston: Beacon.

MOORE, D. W. **1975.** "Repredicting voting patterns in the General Assembly: a methodological note." *International Studies Q.,* 19(June):199–211.

MOORE, J. N., ed. **1974.** *Law and Civil War in the Modern World.* Baltimore: Johns Hopkins University Press.

MORGAN, P. M. **1977.** *Deterrence: A Conceptual Analysis.* Beverly Hills, Calif.: Sage.

MORGENTHAU, H. J. **1974.** *Politics Among Nations: The Struggle for Power and Peace.* 5th ed. New York: Knopf.

MORRILL, J. S. **1972.** "Mutiny and discontent in English provincial armies, 1645–1647." *Past and Present,* 56(August):49–74.

MORRIS, D. **1970.** *The Human Zoo.* New York: Dell.

——. **1969.** *The Naked Ape.* New York: Dell.

MORRIS, J. N. **1957.** *Uses of Epidemiology.* Edinburgh and London: Livingstone.

MORRIS, R. B., and J. B. MORRIS, eds. **1976.** *Encyclopedia of American History: Bicentennial Edition.* New York: Harper and Row.

MORRISON, M. **1974.** "Television, violence and your children." *Peace Research Rev.,* 6(October):79–103.

MOSKOS, C. C., JR. **1976.** *Peace Soldiers: The Sociology of a United Nations Military Force.* Chicago: University of Chicago Press.

——. **1975.** "The American combat soldier in Vietnam." *J. of Social Issues,* 31(4):25–37.

——. **1974.** "The concept of the military–industrial complex: radical critique or liberal bogey." *Social Problems,* 21(April):498–512.

——. **1973.** "The American dilemma in uniform: race in the armed forces." *Annals of the American Academy of Political and Social Science,* 406(March):94–106.

MÖSSNER, J. M. **1972.** "The barbary powers in international law (doctrinal and practical aspects)." In C.H. Alexandrowicz, ed., *Grotian Society Papers, 1970: Studies in the History of the Law of Nations.* The Hague: Nijhoff. Pp. 197–221.

MOUNT, R. I., and R. E. BENNETT. **1975.** "Economic and social factors in income inequality." *American J. of Economics and Sociology,* 34(April):161–174.

MOUTIN, P., and M. MATHIEU. **1971.** "The doctor–patient relationship in the military environment during wartime." *Revue de Medecine Psychosomatique et de Psychologie Medicale,* 13(Winter):425–441.

MOYAL, J. S. **1949.** "The distribution of wars in time." *J. of the Royal Statistical Society,* 112: 446–458.

MOYER, W. **1973.** "House voting on defense: an ideological explanation." In B. M. Russett and A. Stepan, eds., *Military Force and American Society.* New York: Harper and Row. Pp. 106–142.

MUELLER, J. E. **1973.** *War, Presidents, and Public Opinion.* New York: Wiley.

MÜLLER, H. J. **1970.** *The Children of Frankenstein: A Preview of Modern Technology and Human Values.* Bloomington: Indiana University Press.

MUMFORD, L. **1967–1970.** *The Myth of the Machine.* New York: Harcourt, Brace.

MURPHY, A. H., and R. L. WINKLER. **1977.** "Reliability of subjective probability forecasts of precipitation and temperature." *Applied Statistics,* 26(1):41–47.

MURPHY, G. **1971.** "A note on the locus of aggression." *International J. of Group Tensions,* 1(January):55–58.

MURPHY, H. C. **1950.** *The National Debt in War and Transition.* New York: McGraw-Hill.

MURPHY, J. M. **1977.** "War stress and civilian Vietnamese: a study of psychological effects." *Acta Psychiatrica Scandinavica,* 56(2):92–108.

——. **1975.** "Psychological responses to war stress." *Acta Psychiatrica Scandinavica,* 263(Suppl.):16–21.

MURPHY, M. **1971.** "When 30,000 G.I.'s are using heroin, how can you fight a war?" *Drug Forum,* 1(October):87–98.

MUSGRAVE, P. W., and G. R. REID. **1971.** "Some measures of children's values." *Social Science Information,* 10(February):137–153.

MYRDAL, A. **1976.** *The Game of Disarmament: How the United States and Russia Run the Arms Race.* New York: Pantheon.

——. **1974.** "The international control of disarmament." *Scientific American,* 231(October):21–33.

MYRDAL, G. **1956.** *An International Economy: Problems and Prospects.* New York: Harper and Brothers.

MYTELKA, L. K. **1977.** "Regulating direct foreign investment and technology transfer in the Andean group." *J. of Peace Research,* 14(2): 155–184.

NAESS, A. **1973.** "A systematization of Ghandian ethics of conflict resolution." In T. Maple and D. W. Matheson, eds., *Aggression, Hostility, and Violence: Nature or Nurture.* New York: Holt, Rinehart and Winston. Pp. 315–337.

NAGEL, J. H. **1976.** "Erratum." *World Politics,* 28(January):315

——. **1974.** "Inequality and discontent: a non-linear hypothesis." *World Politics,* 26(July):453–472.

NAGEL, T. **1970.** *The Possibility of Altruism.* Oxford: Clarendon.

NAIDU, M. V. **1975.** *Collective Security and the United Nations: A Definition of the UN Security System.* New York: St. Martin's.

NANCE, J. **1975.** *The Gentle Tasaday: A Stone Age People in the Philippine Rain Forest.* J. Ferrone, ed. New York: Harcourt, Brace, Jovanovich.

NARDIN, T. **1976.** "Philosophy and international violence." *American Political Science Rev.,* 70(September):952–961.

——. **1971.** *Violence and the State: A Critique of Empirical Political Theory.* Beverly Hills, Calif.: Sage.

NAROLL, R. **1976.** "Toward a global monitoring system." *International Studies Q.,* 20(September):483–486.

NAROLL, R., V. L. BULLOUGH, and F. NAROLL. **1974.** *Military Deterrence in History: A Pilot Cross-Historical Survey.* Albany: State University of New York Press.

NAROLL, R., and W. T. DIVALE. **1976.** "Natural selection in cultural evolution: warfare versus peaceful diffusion." *American Ethnologist,* 3(February):97–130.

NATIONAL CANCER INSTITUTE and AMERICAN CANCER SOCIETY. **1976.** *Persons at High Risk of Cancer.* New York: Academic.

NAYAR, B. R. **1975.** *Violence and Crime in India: A Quantitative Study.* Delhi: Macmillan.

NEF, J. U. **1950.** *War and Human Progress: An Essay on the Rise of Industrial Civilization.* Cambridge, Mass.: Harvard University Press.

NELSON, J. L., and V. M. GREEN, eds. **1980.** *International Human Rights: Contemporary Issues.* Pine Plains, N.Y.: Earl M. Coleman.

NELSON, K. L., ed. **1971.** *The Impact of War on American Life: The Twentieth-Century Experience.* New York: Holt, Rinehart and Winston.

NELSON, K. L., and S. C. OLIN, JR. **1979.** *Why War?*

Ideology, Theory, and History. Berkeley: University of California Press.

NESBITT, W. A., ed. **1973.** *Human Nature and War: An Anthology of Readings.* Albany: State University of New York Press.

——, ed. **1972.** *Data on the Human Crisis.* Albany: State University of New York Press.

NESVOLD, B. A. **1971.** "Scalogram analysis of political violence." In J. V. Gillespie and B. A. Nesvold, eds., *Macro-Quantitative Analysis.* Beverly Hills, Calif.: Sage. Pp. 167–186.

NETTING, R. **1974.** "Functions of war." *Man,* 9(September):485–488.

NETTLESHIP, M. A., R. DALEGIVENS, and A. NETTLE-SHIP, eds. **1975.** *War: Its Causes and Correlates.* The Hague and Paris: Mouton.

NEUMAN, S. G., and R. E. HARKAVY, eds. **1979.** *Arms Transfers in the Modern World.* New York: Praeger.

NEWBERRY, J. V. **1977.** "Women and war in England: the case of Catherine E. Marshall and World War I." *Peace and Change,* 4(Fall):13–18.

NEWCOMBE, A. G., ed. **1979.** "GRIT." *Peace Research Rev.,* 8(January–February):1–52.

——. **1977.** "Dollars and sense of peace." *Peace Research Rev.,* 7(November):1–16.

NEWCOMBE, A. G., and J. WERT. **1972.** *An Internation Tensiometer for the Prediction of War.* Oakville, Ontario: Canadian Peace Research Institute.

NEWCOMBE, A. G., et al. **1974.** "An improved internation tensiometer for the prediction of war." *Peace Research Rev.,* 5(February):1–53.

NEWCOMBE, H. **1979.** "Reform of the U.N. Security Council." *Peace Research Rev.,* 8(May):1–104.

——. **1976a.** "Design for a better world: thirty-two theses." *Peace Research,* 8(1):1–6.

——. **1976b.** *National Patterns in International Organizations.* Dundas, Ontario: Canadian Peace Research Institute.

NEWCOMBE, H., and A. G. NEWCOMBE, eds. **1972.** "Alternative approaches to peace research." *Peace Research Rev.,* 4(February): 1–23.

——, eds. **1969.** *Peace Research Around the World.* Oakville, Ontario: Canadian Peace Research Institute.

NEWCOMBE H., M. ROSS, and A. G. NEWCOMBE. **1970.** "United Nations voting patterns." *International Organization,* 24(1):100–121.

NEWCOMBE, H., C. YOUNG, and E. SINAIKO. **1977.** "Alternative pasts: a study of weighted voting at the United Nations." *International Organization,* 31(Summer):579–586.

NEWCOMBE, H., et al. **1976.** "Patterns of nations: interactions in the United Nations, 1946–1971." *International Interactions* 2(2):83–92.

NEWMAN, A. J. **1974.** "On the desirability of conditioning for world peace." *Elementary School J.,* 75(December):138–142.

NEWMAN, A. J., M. ROSS, and A. G. NEWCOMBE. **1970.** "United Nations voting patterns." *International Organization,* 24(Winter):100–121.

NEWMAN, P. **1977.** "Malaria and mortality." *J. of the American Statistical Association,* 72(June): 257–263.

NICOLAI, G. F. **1919.** *Die Biologie des Krieges.* Zurich: Druck and Verlag.

NICOLSON, H. **1950.** *Diplomacy.* 2nd ed. London: Oxford University Press.

NIEBURG, H. **1969.** *Political Violence.* New York: St. Martin's.

NIELSON, L. J. **1971.** "Impact of permanent father loss on the intellectual level, vocational interests, personal adjustment and career plans of male war orphans." *Dissertation Abstracts International,* 32(September):1278.

NINCIC, M. **1975.** "Determinants of third world hostility toward the United States: an exploratory analysis." *J. of Conflict Resolution,* 19 (December):620–642.

NINCIC, M., and T. R. CUSACK. **1979.** "The political economy of US military spending." *J. of Peace Research,* 16(2):101–116.

NOMIKOS, E., and R. C. NORTH. **1976.** *International Crisis: The Outlook of World War I.* Montreal: McGill–Queen's University Press.

NORDLINGER, E. A. **1974.** *The Military and Political Development.* Englewood Cliffs, N.J.: Prentice-Hall.

——. **1972.** *Conflict Regulation in Divided Societies.* Cambridge, Mass.: Center for International Affairs, Harvard University.

NORMAN, J. E., JR. **1975.** "Lung cancer mortality in World War I veterans with mustard gas injury, 1919–1965." *J. of the National Cancer Institute,* 54(February):311–318.

NORTH, R., and N. CHOUCRI. **1968.** "Background conditions to the outbreak of the First World War." *Peace Research Society (International) Papers,* 9:125–137.

NORTH, R., and R. LAGERSTROM. **1971.** *War and Domination: A Theory of Lateral Pressure.* New York: General Learning Press.

NORTH, R., et al. **1963.** *Content Analysis.* Evanston, Ill.: Northwestern University Press.

NORTHEDGE, F. S., ed. **1974.** *The Use of Force in International Relations.* London: Faber and Faber.

NORTHEDGE, F. S., and M. D. DONELAN. **1971.** *International Disputes: The Political Aspects.* London: Europa.

NORTON, A. R., and M. H. GREENBERG. **1979.** *International Terrorism: An Annotated Bibliography and Research Guide.* Boulder: Westview.

NOTZ, W. W., B. M. STAW, and T. D. COOK. **1971.** "Attitude toward troop withdrawal from Indochina as a function of draft number: dissonance or self-interest?" *J. of Personality and Social Psychology,* 20(October):118–126.

NOVICOW, J. **1971.** *War and Its Alleged Benefits.* New York: Garland.

NOWAKOWSKA, M. **1973.** "Epidemical spread of scientific objects." *Theory and Decision,* 3 (March):262–297.

NUMELIN, R. J. **1950.** *The Beginnings of Diplomacy: A Sociological Study of Intertribal and International Relations.* London: Oxford University Press.

NYE, J. S. **1972.** "Regional institutions." In C. E. Black and R. A. Falk, eds. *The Future of the International Legal Order.* Vol. 4: *The Structure of the International Environment.* Princeton, N.J.: Princeton University Press. Pp. 425–447.

——. **1971.** *Peace in Parts.* Boston: Little, Brown.

NYE, J. S., and R. O. KEOHANE, eds. **1972.** *Transnational Relations and World Politics.* Cambridge, Mass.: Harvard University Press.

NYE, R. A. **1975.** *The Origins of Crowd Psychology: Gustave LeBon and the Crisis of Mass Democracy in the Third Republic.* London: Sage.

ÖBERG, J. **1977.** "The new international economic and military orders as problems to peace research." *Bull. of Peace Proposals,* 8(2):142–149.

——. **1975.** "Third world armament: domestic arms production in Israel, South Africa, Brazil, Argentina and India, 1950–75." *Instant Research on Peace and Violence,* 5(4):222–239.

O'CONNELL, D. P. **1970.** "The role of international law." In S. Hoffmann, ed. *Conditions of World Order.* New York: Simon and Schuster. Pp. 49–65.

OKIGBO, P. N. C. **1967.** *Africa and the Common Market.* Evanston, Ill.: Northwestern University Press.

O'LEARY, M. D., and W. D. COPLIN. **1975.** *Quantitative Techniques in Foreign Policy Analysis and Forecasting.* New York: Praeger.

OLIN, U. **1972.** "Population pressure and revolutionary movements." In R. S. Parker, ed., *The Emotional Stress of War, Violence, and Peace.* Pittsburgh: Stanwix House. Pp. 133–162.

OLIVER, C. T. **1976.** "Multinationals and the international legal order at the end of the Mesozoic Age of direct investment." *Peace and Change,* 3(Spring):31–34.

OLSON, M. **1971.** *The Logic of Collective Action: Public Goods and the Theory of Groups.* Cambridge, Mass.: Harvard University Press.

OLSSON, S. O. **1976.** "The documents of 'Zentrale Planung' as a basis for research on the German war economy." *Scandinavian Economic History Rev.,* 24(1):45–59.

O'MALLEY, P. **1975.** "Suicide and war: a case study and theoretical appraisal." *British J. of Criminology,* 15(4):348–359.

O'NEILL, D. J., and G. D. FONTAINE. **1973.** "Counseling for the Vietnam veteran." *J. of College Student Personnel,* 14(March):153–155.

OPPENHEIMER, M. **1969.** *The Urban Guerrilla.* New York: Quadrangle.

ORGANSKI, A. F. K., and J. KUGLER. **1980.** *The War Ledger.* Chicago: University of Chicago Press.

——. **1977.** "The cost of major wars: the Phoenix factor. *American Political Science Rev.,* 71 (December):1347–1366.

ORNSTEIN, R. **1972.** *The Psychology of Consciousness.* New York: Viking.

OSGOOD, C. **1962.** *An Alternative to War or Surrender.* Urbana: University of Illinois Press.

OSGOOD, R. E., and R. W. TUCKER. **1967.** *Force, Order, and Justice.* Baltimore: Johns Hopkins University Press.

OSTROM, C. W., JR., and J. H. ALDRICH. **1978.** "The relationship between size and stability in the major power international system." *American J. of Political Science,* 22(November):743–771.

OSTROM, C. W., JR., and F. W. HOOLE. **1978.** "Alliances and wars revisited: a research note." *International Studies Q.,* 22(June):215–236.

OSTROWER, A. **1965.** *Language, Law, and Diplomacy: A Study of Linguistic Diversity in Official International Relations and International Law.* 2 vols. Philadelphia: University of Pennsylvania Press.

OTTERBEIN, K. F. **1977.** "Warfare: a hitherto unrecognized critical variable." *American Behavioral Scientist,* 20(May–June):693–710.

——. **1976.** "Warfare, territorial expansion, and cultural evolution." *American Ethnologist,* 3(November):825–827.

——. **1970.** *The Evolution of War.* New Haven, Conn.: Human Relations Area Files Press.

OVERHOLT, W. H., ed. **1977.** *Asia's Nuclear Future.* Boulder: Westview.

OWEN, I. K. **1975.** What about dumdums?" *FBI Law Enforcement Bull.,* 44(April):3–6.

PADELFORD, N. J., G. A. LINCOLN, and L. D. OLVEY. **1976.** *The Dynamics of International Politics.* 3rd ed. New York: Macmillan.

PAIGE, G. D. **1968.** *The Korean Decision, June 24–30, 1950.* New York: Free Press.

PALGI, P. **1973.** "The socio-cultural expressions and implications of death, mourning and bereavement arising out of the war situation in Israel." *Israel Annals of Psychiatry and Related Disciplines,* 11(4):301–329.

PALMER, M., and W. R. THOMPSON. **1978.** *The Comparative Analysis of Politics.* Itasca, Ill.: Peacock.

PARENTI, M. J., ed. **1971.** *Trends and Tragedies in American Foreign Policy.* Boston: Little, Brown.

PARET, P., and J. W. SHY. **1962.** *Guerrillas in the 1960's.* 2nd ed. New York: Praeger.

PARK, T. W., F. ABOLFATHI, and M. WARD. **1976.** "Resource nationalism in the foreign policy behavior of oil exporting countries (1947–1974)." *International Interactions,* 2(November):247–262.

PARKER, R. S., ed. **1972.** *The Emotional Stress of War,*

Violence, and Peace. Pittsburgh: Stanwix House.

PARKIN, F. **1971.** *Class Inequality and Political Order: Social Stratification in Capitalist and Communist Societies.* New York: Praeger.

PARSONS, R. W., M. M. BECKWITH, and H. R. THERING. **1972.** "Surgical rehabilitation after extensive losses in the lower face from war injuries." *Plastic Reconstruction Surgery,* 49(5):533–536.

PARVIN, M. **1973.** "Economic determinants of political unrest: an econometric approach." *J. of Conflict Resolution,* 17(June):271–296.

PATTEE, H. H., ed. **1973.** *Hierarchy Theory: The Challenge of Complex Systems.* New York: Braziller.

PATTERSON, D. S. **1976.** *Toward a Warless World: The Travail of the American Peace Movement, 1887–1914.* Bloomington: Indiana University Press.

PAUST, J. J., A. P. BLAUSTEIN, and A. HIGGINS. **1977.** *The Arab Oil Weapon.* Dobbs Ferry, N.Y.: Oceana.

PEAR, T. H. **1950.** *Psychological Factors of Peace and War.* London: Hutchinson.

PEARSON, F. S., and R. BAUMANN. **1977.** "Foreign military intervention and changes in United States business activity." *J. of Political and Military Sociology,* 5(Spring):79–97.

PECK, M. J., and F. M. SCHERER. **1962.** *The Weapons Acquisition Process.* Cambridge, Mass.: Harvard University Press.

PELCOVITS, N. A., and K. K. KRAMER. **1976.** "Local conflict and UN peacekeeping: the use of computerized data." *International Studies Q.,* 20(December):533–552.

PELOWSKI, A. L. **1971.** "A quasi-experimental design in the study of international organization and war." *J. of Peace Research,* 8(3–4):279–285.

PELTON, L. **1974.** *The Psychology of Non-Violence.* New York: Pergamon.

PELZ, S. E. **1974.** *Race to Pearl Harbor: The Failure of the Second London Naval Conference and the Onset of World War II.* Cambridge, Mass.: Harvard University Press.

PENN, W. **1972.** "An essay towards the present and future peace of Europe." In B. W. Cook, ed., *Peace Projects of the Seventeenth Century.* New York: Garland. Pp. 1–21.

PENROSE, L. S. **1963.** "Pathology of group behaviour." In M. Penrose, ed., *Pathogenesis of War.* London: Lewis. Pp. 54–59.

PENROSE, M., ed. **1963.** *Pathogenesis of War.* London: Lewis.

PERKINS, M. E. **1974.** "Opiate addiction and military psychiatry to the end of World War II." *Military Medicine,* 139(February):114–116.

PERLMAN, M. S. **1975.** "Basic problems of military psychiatry: delayed reaction in Vietnam veterans." *International J. of Offender Therapy and Comparative Criminology,* 19(2):129–138.

PERLMUTTER, A. **1977.** *The Military and Politics in Modern Times: On Professionals, Praetorians, and Revolutionary Soldiers.* New Haven, Conn.: Yale University Press.

PETERSON, W. **1969.** *Population.* 2nd ed. New York: Macmillan.

PETTENGILL, J. S. **1979.** "The impact of military technology on European income distribution." *J. of Interdisciplinary History,* 10(Autumn):201–225.

PETTMAN, R. **1975.** *Human Behavior and World Politics: An Introduction to International Relations.* New York: St. Martin's.

PFISTER, J. W. **1974.** *The Compulsion to War: A Quantitative Exploration of Remote International Relations.* Beverly Hills, Calif.: Sage.

PHAN, Q. D. **1975.** "Needs of children in South Vietnam." *Carnets de l'Enfance,* 30(April–June):89–90.

PHELPS, E. S., ed. **1975.** *Altruism, Morality, and Economic Theory.* New York: Russell Sage Foundation.

PHILLIPS, N. E. **1973.** "Militarism and grass-roots involvement in the military–industrial complex." *J. of Conflict Resolution,* 17(December):625–655.

PIAGET, J., and A. M. WEIL. **1951.** "The development in children of the idea of the homeland and of relations with other countries." *International Social Science Bull.,* 3(Autumn):561–578.

PIETILA, V. **1976.** "Notes on violence in the mass media." *International Research on Peace and Violence,* 6(4):195–197.

PILISUK, M. **1966.** "Timing and integrity of inspection in arms reduction games." *Peace Research Society (International) Papers,* 5, Philadelphia Conference, 1965.

PINCUS, J. **1967.** *Trade, Aid, and Development: The Rich and Poor Nations.* New York: McGraw-Hill.

PIOTROWSKI, Z. A. **1972.** "Is permanent peace possible: how social forces can modify tendencies towards group violence." In R. S. Parker, ed., *The Emotional Stress of War, Violence, and Peace.* Pittsburgh: Stanwix House. Pp. 1–11.

PISAR, S. **1970.** *Coexistence and Commerce: Guidelines for Transactions Between East and West.* New York: McGraw-Hill.

PISZTORA, F. **1972.** "Sociocultural influences and conflict neurosis, i.e., reactive psychoses, in present-day Algiers." *Psychiatria Clinica,* 5(3):158–173.

PITCHER, B. L., R. L. HAMBLIN, and J. L. L. MILLER. **1978.** "The diffusion of collective violence." *American Sociological Rev.,* 43(February):23–25.

PLANO, J. C., and R. E. RIGGS. **1967.** *Forging World Order: The Politics of International Organization.* New York: Macmillan.

PLASCHKE, H. **1975.** "International subcontracting: on the migration of labour-intensive processing from the center to the periphery of capitalism." *Instant Research on Peace and Violence,* 5(1):88–97.

PODĚBRAD, J. Z. **1972.** *The Universal Peace Organization of King George of Bohemia: A 15th Century Plan for World Peace, 1462/1464.* Introduction by F. G. Heymann. New York: Garland.

POLACHECK, S. W. **1980.** "Conflict and trade." *J. of Conflict Resolution,* 24(March):55–78.

POMERANCE, M. **1976.** "The United States and self-determination: perspectives on the Wilsonian conception." *American J. of International Law,* 70(January):1–27.

PORTES, A. **1976.** "On the sociology of national development: theories and issues." *American J. of Sociology,* 82(July):55–87.

POTTER, E. B. **1955.** *The United States and World Sea Power.* Englewood Cliffs, N.J.: Prentice-Hall.

POWELL, E. H. **1970.** *The Design of Discord: Studies of Anomie.* New York: Oxford University Press.

PREBISCH, R. **1964.** *Towards a New Trade Policy for Development: Report by the Secretary-General of the United Nations Conference on Trade and Development.* New York: United Nations.

PRICE, T. J. **1977.** "Noncentral governments as international actors: a case study and discussion." Washington, D.C.: Presented at annual meeting of American Political Science Association.

PRINZING, F. **1916.** *Epidemics Resulting from Wars.* H. Westergaard, ed. Oxford: Clarendon.

PROSTERMAN, R. L. **1976.** " 'IRI': a simplified predictive index of rural instability." *Comparative Politics,* 8(April):339–354.

PROXMIRE, W. **1970.** *Report from Wasteland: America's Military–Industrial Complex.* New York: Praeger.

PRUITT, D. G. **1969.** "Stability and sudden change in interpersonal and international affairs." In J. N. Rosenau, ed., *Linkage Politics.* New York: Free Press. Pp. 392–408.

——. **1966.** "Reward structure and its effect on cooperation." *Peace Research Society (International) Papers,* 5, Philadelphia Conference, 1965.

PRUITT, D. G., and R. C. SNYDER. **1969.** *Theory and Research on the Causes of War.* Englewood Cliffs, N.J.: Prentice-Hall.

PRYOR, F. **1969.** *Public Expenditures in Communist and Capitalist Nations.* Homewood, Ill.: Irwin.

PUCHALA, D. J. **1973.** "Europeans and Europeanism in 1970." *International Organization,* 27(Summer):387–392.

PUGH, M. D., et al. **1971.** "Participation in anti-war demonstrations: a test of the parental continuity hypothesis." *Sociology and Social Research,* 56(October):19–28.

PURSELL, C. W., JR., ed. **1972.** *The Military–Industrial Complex.* New York: Harper and Row.

PURVES, R. **1970.** "Prolegomena to utopian inter-

national projects." In C. H. Alexandrowicz, ed., *Grotian Society Papers, 1968: Studies in the History of the Law of Nations.* The Hague: Nijhoff. Pp. 100–109.

PUSIĆ, E. **1977.** *Order and Randomness in Cooperative Systems.* Pittsburgh: International Studies Association.

QUESTER, G. H. **1973** *The Politics of Nuclear Proliferation.* Baltimore: Johns Hopkins University Press.

——. **1966.** *Deterrence Before Hiroshima: The Airpower Background of Modern Strategy.* New York: Wiley.

QUIGLEY, J. **1974.** *The Soviet Foreign Trade Monopoly: Institutions and Laws.* Columbus: Ohio State University Press.

QUINONES, M. A. **1975.** "Drug abuse during the Civil War, 1861–1865." *International J. of the Addictions,* 10(6):1007–1020.

RA'ANAN, U., R. L. PFALTZGRAFF, JR., and G. KEMP, eds. **1978.** *Arms Transfers to the Third World: Problems and Policies.* Boulder: Westview.

RAINBOLT, R. **1977.** "Women and war in the United States: the case of Dorothy Detzer, National Secretary Women's International League for Peace and Freedom." *Peace and Change,* 4(Fall):18–23.

RAMAN, K. W. **1977.** *Dispute Settlement Through the United Nations.* Dobbs Ferry, N.Y.: Oceana.

RAMAZANI, R. K. **1964.** *The Middle East and the European Common Market.* Charlottesville: University Press of Virginia.

RAMSEY, P. **1968.** *The Just War: Force and Political Responsibility.* New York: Scribner's.

RANDLE, R. F. **1973.** *The Origins of Peace: A Study of Peacemaking and the Structure of Peace Settlements.* New York: Free Press.

RANIS, G. **1975.** "Equity and growth: new dimensions of development." *J. of Conflict Resolution,* 19(September):558–568.

RAPKIN, D. P., W. R. THOMPSON, and J. A. CHRISTOPHERSON. **1979.** "Bipolarity and bipolarization in the cold war era: conceptualization, measurement, and validation." *J. of Conflict Resolution,* 23(June):261–295.

RAPOPORT, A. **1974.** *Fights, Games, and Debates.* Ann Arbor: University of Michigan Press.

——. **1969.** *Strategy and Conscience.* New York: Schocken.

——. **1966.** "Additional experimental findings on conflict and games." *Peace Research Society (International) Papers,* 5, Philadelphia Conference, 1965.

——. **1957.** "Lewis F. Richardson's mathematical theory of war." *J. of Conflict Resolution,* 1(September):249–299.

RAPOPORT, A., and A. M. CHAMMAH. **1965.** *Pris-*

oner's Dilemma: A Study in Conflict and Cooperation. Ann Arbor: University of Michigan Press.

RASCOVSKY, A., and M. RASCOVSKY. **1972.** "The prohibition of incest, filicide and the sociocultural process." *International J. of Psycho-Analysis,* 53(2):271–276.

RASER, J. R. **1966.** "Personal characteristics of political decision-makers: a literature review." *Peace Research Society (International) Papers,* 5, Philadelphia Conference, 1965.

RATHJENS, G. W., and G. B. KISTIAKOWSKY. **1973.** "The limitation of strategic arms." In H. F. York, ed., *Arms Control.* San Francisco: W. H. Freeman and Company. Pp. 201–211.

RATTINGER, H. **1976a.** "Econometrics and arms races: a critical review of some extensions." *European J. of Political Research,* 4(December):421–439.

——. **1976b.** "From war to war to war: arms races in the Middle East." *International Studies Q.,* 20(December):501–531.

——. **1975a.** "Armaments, detente, and bureaucracy: the case of the arms race in Europe." *J. of Conflict Resolution,* 19(December):571–595.

——. **1975b.** *Rustungsdynamik im Internationalen System.* Munich: Oldenbourg.

RAY, R. D. **1971.** "Psychology, aggression, and war: a survey of the literature." *Q. J. of the Florida Academy of Sciences,* 34(Suppl. 1)(March):25.

RAYMOND, G. A. **1976.** "Belief and behavior in the international system: a cliometric analysis of conflict resolution through international arbitration." Boise, Idaho: Department of Political Science, Boise State University. Mimeo.

REDICK, J. **1974.** *Military Potential of Latin American Nuclear Energy Programs.* Beverly Hills, Calif.: Sage.

REICH, W. **1971.** *The Mass Psychology of Fascism.* V. R. Carfagno, tr. New York: Farrar, Straus, and Giroux.

REID, E. **1965.** *The Future of the World Bank.* Washington, D.C.: International Bank for Reconstruction and Development.

REIK, T. **1973.** *Dogma and Compulsion: Psychoanalytic Studies of Religion and Myths.* Westport, Conn.: Greenwood.

REINHARD, M. R., and A. ARMENGAUD. **1961.** *Histoire Générale de la Population Mondiale.* Paris: Montchrestien.

RENNER, J. A. **1973.** "The changing patterns of psychiatric problems in Vietnam." *Comprehensive Psychiatry,* 14(March):169–181.

REYCHLER, L. **1979.** "The effectiveness of pacifist strategy in conflict resolution." *J. of Conflict Resolution,* 23(June):228–260.

REYNOLDS, H. T. **1977.** "Some comments on the causal analysis of surveys with log–linear

models." *American J. of Sociology,* 83(July): 127–144.

RHODES, R. I., ed. **1971.** *Imperialism and Underdevelopment: A Reader.* New York: Monthly Review Press.

RICE, E. **1965.** "Recent studies on the population of Europe, 1348–1620." *Renaissance News,* 18(Summer):180–187.

RICHARDSON, L. F. **1960a.** *Arms and Insecurity.* Pittsburgh and Chicago: Boxwood and Quadrangle.

——. **1960b.** *Statistics of Deadly Quarrels.* Pittsburgh and Chicago: Boxwood and Quadrangle.

RICHARDSON, N. R. **1978.** *Foreign Policy and Economic Dependence.* Austin: University of Texas Press.

——. **1976.** "Political compliance and U.S. trade dominance." *American Political Science Rev.,* 70(December):1098–1109.

RIKHYE, I. J., M. HARBOTTLE, and B. EGGE. **1974.** *The Thin Blue Line: International Peacekeeping and Its Future.* New Haven, Conn.: Yale University Press.

RINALDI, M. **1973.** "The olive-drab rebels: military organizing during the Vietnam era." *Radical America,* 8(May–June):17–52.

RISNER, R. **1974.** *The Passing of the Night: My Seven Years as a Prisoner of the North Vietnamese.* New York: Random House.

RITTBERGER, V. **1973.** "International organization and violence." *J. of Peace Research,* 10(3):217–226.

RIVERA, J. H. DE. **1968.** *The Psychological Dimension of Foreign Policy.* Columbus: Merrill.

RIVERS, L. M. **1969.** "House Armed Services Committee staff study reported on the floor by Chairman Rivers in 1969." *Congressional Record (Daily Edition).* Washington, D.C.: Government Printing Office.

ROBBINS, L. **1968.** *The Economic Causes of War.* New York: Fertig.

ROBERTS, M. **1962.** *The Military Revolution: 1560–1660.* Belfast: Queen's University.

ROBINS, L. N., J. E. HELZER, and D. H. DAVIS. **1975.** "Narcotic use in Southeast Asia and afterward: an interview study of 898 Vietnam returnees." *Archives of General Psychiatry,* 32(August):955–961.

ROBINSON, J. A. **1977.** "Introduction to section on 'Women, war, and resistance to war: a transnational perspective.'" *Peace and Change,* 4(Fall):8.

ROBINSON, J. A., ed. **1972.** *Political Science Annual: An International Review.* Vol. 3. Indianapolis: Bobbs-Merrill.

ROCKY FLATS ACTION GROUP. **1977.** *Local Hazard, Global Threat.* Denver: Rocky Flats Action Group.

RODBERG, L. S., and D. SHEARER, eds. **1970.** *The Pentagon Watchers.* Garden City, N.Y.: Doubleday.

ROGERS, E. M., with F. F. SHOEMAKER. **1971.** *Communication of Innovations: A Cross-Cultural Approach.* 2nd ed. New York: Free Press.

ROGERS, F. E. **1976.** "Sino-American relations and the Vietnam War, 1964–66." *China Q.,* 66(June):293–314.

ROGHMANN, K., and W. SODEUR. **1972.** "The impact of military service on authoritarian attitudes: evidence from West Germany." *American J. of Sociology,* 78(September):418–433.

ROHEIM, G. **1943.** "War, crime and the covenant." *J. of Criminal Psychopathology,* 4(April):731–753.

ROHRBAUGH, M., and G. EADS. **1974.** "Effects of Vietnam experience on subsequent drug use among servicemen." *International J. of the Addictions,* 9(1):25–40.

ROHRBAUGH, M., and S. PRESS. **1974.** "The army's war on stateside drug use: a view from the front." *J. of Drug Issues,* 4(Winter):32–43.

ROHWER, J. G. **1974.** *The Confrontation of the Superpowers in the Seas: Naval Developments and Strategy Since 1945.* Beverly Hills, Calif.: Sage.

ROJCEWICZ, S. J. **1971.** "War and suicide." *Life-Threatening Behavior,* 1(Spring):46–54.

ROKEACH, M. **1974.** "Change and stability in American value systems, 1968–1971." *Public Opinion Q.,* 38(Summer):222–238.

——. **1960.** *The Open and Closed Mind.* New York: Basic Books.

ROLFE, S. E. **1966.** *Gold and World Power: The Dollar, the Pound, and Plans for Reform.* New York: Harper and Row.

ROLFE, S. E., and W. DAMM, eds. **1970.** *The Multinational Corporation in the World Economy: Direct Investment in Perspective.* New York: Praeger.

RÖLING, B. V. A. **1960.** *International Law in an Expanded World.* Amsterdam: Djambatan.

RONFELDT, D., and C. SERESERES. **1977.** *U.S. Arms Transfers, Diplomacy, and Security in Latin America and Beyond.* Santa Monica, Calif.: Rand.

ROOS, L., JR., and J. A. CAPARASO, eds. **1973.** *Quasi-Experimental Approaches: Testing Theories and Evaluating Policy.* Evanston, Ill.: Northwestern University Press.

ROPER, M. K. **1975.** "Evidence of warfare in the Near East from 10,000–4,300 B.C." In M. A. Nettleship, R. Dalegivens, and A. Nettleship, eds., *War: Its Causes and Correlates.* The Hague and Paris: Mouton. Pp. 299–344.

ROPP, T. **1962.** *War in the Modern World.* New York: Collier.

ROSAS, A. **1976.** *The Legal Status of Prisoners of War: A Study in International Humanitarian Law Applicable in Armed Conflicts.* Helsinki: Suomalainen Tiedeakatemia.

ROSE, D. J., and R. K. LESTER. **1978.** "Nuclear power, nuclear weapons and international stability." *Scientific American,* 238(April):45–57.

ROSEBURY, T. **1971.** *Microbes and Morals: The Strange Story of Venereal Disease.* New York: Viking.

——. **1969.** *Life on Man.* New York: Viking.

——. **1949.** *Peace or Pestilence: Biological Warfare and How to Avoid It.* New York: Whittlesey.

ROSECRANCE, R. **1973.** *International Relations: Peace or War.* New York: McGraw-Hill.

——. **1963.** *Action and Reaction in World Politics: International Systems in Perspective.* Boston: Little, Brown.

ROSECRANCE, R., and A. STEIN. **1973.** "Interdependence: myth or reality." *World Politics,* 26 (October):1–27.

ROSECRANCE, R., et al. **1977.** "Whither independence?" *International Organization,* 31(Summer):425–472.

ROSEN, G. **1968.** "Public health." In D. L. Sills, ed., *International Encyclopedia of the Social Sciences.* Vol. 13. New York: Crowell Collier and Macmillan. Pp. 164–170.

ROSEN, S., ed. **1973.** *Testing the Theory of the Military–Industrial Complex.* Lexington, Mass.: Lexington Books.

——. **1972.** "War power and the willingness to suffer." In B. M. Russett, ed., *Peace, War, and Numbers.* Beverly Hills, Calif.: Sage. Pp. 167–184.

ROSEN, S., and J. R. KURTH, eds. **1974.** *Testing Theories of Economic Imperialism.* Lexington, Mass.: Lexington Books.

ROSENAU, J. N., ed. **1969.** *International Politics and Foreign Policy: A Reader in Research and Theory.* New York: Free Press.

——, ed. **1969.** *Linkage Politics.* New York: Free Press.

——, ed. **1967.** *Domestic Sources of Foreign Policy.* New York: Free Press.

——, ed. **1964.** *International Aspects of Civil Strife.* Princeton, N.J.: Princeton University Press.

ROSENAU, J. N., V. DAVIS, and M. A. EAST, eds. **1972.** *The Analysis of International Politics.* New York: Free Press.

ROSENBAUM, M., and T. NAJENSON. **1976.** "Changes in life patterns and symptoms of low mood as reported in wives of severely brain-injured soldiers." *J. of Consulting and Clinical Psychology,* 44(December):881–888.

ROSENBAUM, W. B., and L. L. ROSENBAUM. **1973.** "Changes in college student attitudes toward the Arab–Israel, India–Pakistan, and Vietnam conflicts." *J. of Psychology,* 84(May):165–171.

ROSENBERG, A. **1941.** "War and modern dictatorship." In J. D. Clarkson and T. C. Cochran, eds., *War as a Social Institution: The Historian's Perspective.* New York: Columbia University Press. Pp. 189–196.

ROSENTHAL, B. G. **1972.** "The psychology of compassion." *Human Context,* 4(Fall):600–607.

ROSENTHAL, I. **1975.** "Vietnam war soldiers and the

experience of normlessness." *J. of Social Psychology*, 96(June):85–90.

ROSTOW, E. V. **1975.** "Is peace indivisible? the role of international law in international politics." *Strategic Rev.*, 3(Summer):23–33.

ROTHSTEIN, R. L. **1978.** *Global Bargaining: UNCTAD and the Quest for a New International Economic Order.* Princeton, N.J.: Princeton University Press.

——. **1977.** *The Weak in the World of the Strong: The Developing Countries in the International System.* New York: Columbia University Press.

——. **1972.** *Planning, Prediction and Policy Making in Foreign Affairs: Theory and Practice.* Boston: Little, Brown.

ROUCEK, J. S. **1972.** "Guerrilla warfare and counterinsurgency in global politics." *Sociologia Internationalis*, 10(2):213–228.

ROUSSEAU, J. J. **1974.** "A project of perpetual peace." In S. E. Cooper, ed., *Peace Projects of the Eighteenth Century.* New York: Garland. Pp. 3–95.

ROWE, E. T. **1972.** "Financial support for the United Nations: the evolution of member contributions, 1946–1969." *International Organization*, 26(Autumn):619–658.

——. **1971.** "The United States, the United Nations, and the cold war." *International Organization*, 25(Winter):59–78.

ROWE, J. F. **1965.** *Primary Commodities in International Trade.* Cambridge: Cambridge University Press.

ROZAKIS, C. L. **1976.** *The Concept of Jus Cogens in the Law of Treaties.* Amsterdam: North Holland.

RUBIN, A. P. **1970.** "The use of piracy in Malayan waters." In C. H. Alexandrowicz, ed., *Grotian Society Papers, 1968: Studies in the History of the Law of Nations.* The Hague: Nijhoff. Pp. 111–135.

RUBINSON, R. **1976.** "The world-economy and the distribution of income within states: a cross-national study." *American Sociological Rev.*, 41(August):638–659.

RUEFF, J. **1972.** *The Monetary Sin of the West.* R. Glémet, tr. New York: Macmillan.

RUESCHEMEYER, D. **1977.** "Structural differentiation, efficiency and power." *American J. of Sociology*, 83(July):1–26.

RUGGIE, J. G. **1975.** "International responses to technology." *International Organization*, 29(Summer):557–583.

RUMMEL, R. J. **1978.** "A warning on Michael Haas's *International Conflict.*" *J. of Conflict Resolution*, 22(March):157–165.

——. **1976.** *Peace Endangered: The Reality of Détente.* Beverly Hills, Calif.: Sage.

——. **1975–1977.** *Understanding Conflict and War.* 3 vols. Beverly Hills, Calif.: Sage.

——. **1973.** "Dimensions of conflict behavior within and between nations." In J. Wilkenfeld, ed.,

Conflict Behavior and Linkage Politics. New York: David McKay. Pp. 59–106.

——. **1972.** *The Dimensions of Nations.* Beverly Hills, Calif.: Sage.

——. **1968.** "The relationship between national attributes and foreign conflict behavior." In J. D. Singer, ed., *Quantitative International Politics: Insights and Evidence.* New York: Free Press. Pp. 187–214.

——. **1967.** "Dimensions of dyadic war, 1820–1952." *J. of Conflict Resolution*, 11(June):176–183.

——. **1963a.** "Dimensions of conflict behavior within and between nations." In A. Rapoport, ed., *General Systems Yearbook*, 8:1–50.

——. **1963b.** "Testing some possible predictors of conflict behavior within and between nations." *Peace Research Society (International) Papers*, 1:101–102.

RUMMEL, R. J., and R. TANTER. **1972.** "Domestic and foreign conflict data, 1955–1960." In I. K. Feierabend, R. L. Feierabend, and T. Gurr, eds., *Anger, Violence, and Politics.* Englewood Cliffs, N.J.: Prentice-Hall. Pp. 400–414.

RUNCIMAN, W. G. **1966.** *Relative Deprivation and Social Justice: A Study of Attitudes to Social Inequality in Twentieth-Century England.* Berkeley: University of California Press.

RUNDQUIST, B. S. **1976.** "Testing a military industrial complex theory." Urbana: University of Illinois. Mimeo.

RUNDQUIST, B. S., and J. A. FEREJOHN. **1975.** "Observations on a distributive theory of policymaking: two American expenditure programs compared." In C. Liske, J. McCamaut, and W. Loehr, eds., *Comparative Public Policy: Issues, Theories and Methods.* New York: Wiley. Pp. 87–108.

RUNDQUIST, B. S., and D. E. GRIFFITH. **1976.** "An interrupted time series test of the distributive theory of military policy-making." *Western Political Q.*, 29(December):620–626.

RUSSELL, B. **1917.** *Why Men Fight: A Method of Abolishing the International Duel.* New York: Century.

RUSSELL, D. E. H. **1974.** *Rebellion, Revolution, and Armed Forces: A Comparative Study of Fifteen Countries with Special Emphasis on Cuba and South Africa.* New York: Academic.

RUSSELL, E. W. **1972.** "Factors of human aggression." *Behavior Science Notes*, 7(4):275–312.

RUSSELL, H. S. **1976.** "The Helsinki Declaration: Brobdingnag or Lilliput?" *American J. of International Law*, 70(April):242–272.

RUSSELL, R. B., et al. **1974.** *Air, Water, Earth, Fire: The Impacts of the Military on World Environment Order.* San Francisco: Sierra Club International Series.

RUSSELL, R. W. **1977.** "Governing the world's money: don't just do something; stand there."

International Organization, 31(Winter):107–129.

RUSSETT, B. M. **1978.** "The marginal utility of income transfers to the Third World." *International Organization*, 32(Autumn):913–928.

——. **1976.** Private correspondence.

——, ed. **1972.** *Peace, War, and Numbers.* Beverly Hills, Calif.: Sage.

——. **1971.** "An empirical typology of international military alliances." *Midwest J. of Political Science*, 15(May):262–289.

——. **1970a.** "Interdependence and capabilities for European cooperation." *J. of Common Market Studies*, 9(December):143–150.

——, ed. **1970b.** *What Price Vigilance: The Burdens of National Defense.* New Haven, Conn.: Yale University Press.

——. **1968.** "Is there a long-run trend toward concentration in the international system?" *Comparative Political Studies*, 1(April):103–122.

——. **1967.** *International Regions and the International System: A Study in Political Ecology.* Chicago: Rand McNally.

——. **1965.** *Trends in World Politics.* New York: Macmillan.

——. **1964.** "Inequality and instability: the relation of land tenure to politics." *World Politics*, 16(April):442–454.

——. **1962.** "Cause, surprise and no escape." *J. of Politics*, 24(February):3–22.

RUSSETT, B. M., and B. G. BLAIR, eds. **1979.** *Progress in Arms Control? Readings from Scientific American.* San Francisco: W. H. Freeman and Company.

RUSSETT, B. M., and E. C. HANSEN. **1975.** *Interest and Ideology: The Foreign Policy Beliefs of American Businessmen.* San Francisco: W. H. Freeman and Company.

RUSSETT, B. M., and J. MONSEN. **1975.** "Bureaucracy and polyarchy as predictors of performance: a cross-national examination." *Comparative Political Studies*, 8(April):5–31.

RUSSETT, B. M., and A. STEPAN, eds. **1973.** *Military Force and American Society.* New York: Harper and Row.

RUSSETT, B. M., et al. **1964.** *World Handbook of Political and Social Indicators.* New Haven, Conn.: Yale University Press.

RUSSO, A. J., JR. **1972.** "Economic and social correlates of government control in South Vietnam." In I. K. Feierabend, R. L. Feierabend, and T. Gurr, eds., *Anger, Violence, and Politics.* Englewood Cliffs, N.J.: Prentice-Hall. Pp. 314–324.

RUTLEDGE, H. W., E. J. HUNTER, and B. B. DAHL. **1979.** "Human values and the prisoner of war." *Environment and Behavior*, 11(June):227–244.

SAATY, T. L. **1968.** *Mathematical Models of Arms Control and Disarmament.* New York: Wiley.

SABROSKY, A. N **1980.** "Interstate alliances: their reliability and the expansion of war." In J. D. Singer, ed., *Correlates of War-II.* New York: Free Press. Pp. 161–198.

——, ed. **1979.** *Blue-Collar Soldiers? Unionization and the U.S. Military.* Boulder: Westview.

——. **1975.** "From Bosnia to Sarajevo: a comparative discussion of interstate crises." *J. of Conflict Resolution*, 19(March):3–21.

SAGAN, E. **1974.** *Cannibalism: Human Aggression and Cultural Form.* New York: Harper and Row.

ST. PIERRE, C. C. DE (ABBÉ DE TIRON). **1974.** "A shorter project for perpetual peace." In S. E. Cooper, ed., *Peace Projects of the Eighteenth Century.* New York: Garland, Pp. 1–61.

SAKSENA, K. P. **1974.** *The United Nations and Collective Security: A Historical Analysis.* Delhi: D. K. Publishing House.

SALE, K. **1975.** *Power Shift: The Rise of the Southern Rim and Its Challenge to the Eastern Establishment.* New York: Random House.

SALISBURY, H. E. **1970.** *War Between Russia and China.* New York: Bantam.

SALKELD, R. **1970.** *War and Space.* Englewood Cliffs, N.J.: Prentice-Hall.

SALTER, J. A. **1921.** *Allied Shipping Control: An Experiment in International Administration.* Oxford: Clarendon.

SANDERS, C. R. **1973.** "Doper's wonderland: functional drug use by military personnel in Vietnam." *J. of Drug Issues*, 3(Winter):65–78.

SANFORD, N. **1971.** "Dehumanization and collective destructiveness." *International J. of Group Tensions*, 1(January–March):26–41.

SAPOLSKY, H. M. **1972.** *The Polaris System Development: Bureaucratic and Programmatic Success in Government.* Cambridge, Mass.: Harvard University Press.

SARGENT, L. T. **1978.** *Contemporary Political Ideologies: A Comparative Analysis.* 4th ed. Homewood, Ill.: Dorsey.

SARIS, W., and C. MIDDENDORP. **1980.** "Arms races: external security or domestic pressure?" *British J. of Political Science*, 10:121–128.

SARKESIAN, S. C., ed. **1972.** *The Military–Industrial Complex: A Reassessment.* Beverly Hills, Calif.: Sage.

SARKESIAN, S. C., and T. M. GANNON. **1976.** "Military ethics and professionalism." *American Behavioral Scientist*, 19(May–June):491–664.

SAUL, L. J. **1972.** "Personal and social psychopathology and the primary prevention of violence." *American J. of Psychiatry*, 128 (June):1578–1581.

SAUVANT, K. P., and H. HASENPFLUG. **1977.** *The New International Economic Order: Confrontation or Cooperation between North and South?* Boulder: Westview.

SAVON, H. 1975. "A study on armed conflicts of the 1740–1974 period." Turku, Finland: Presented at International Peace Research Association.

SAWICKI, J. 1970. "UN reactions to unauthorized use of force in international relations." *Peace Research Society (International) Papers*, 13:47–58.

SAXONHOUSE, A. W. 1980. "Men, women, war and politics: family and polis in Aristophanes and Euripides." *Political Theory*, 8(February):65–81.

SCHAAR, J. 1961. *Escape from Authority: The Perspectives of Erich Fromm*. New York: Basic Books.

SCHAFER, S. 1974. *The Political Criminal: The Problem of Morality and Crime*. New York: Free Press.

SCHAICH, W. 1975. "A relationship between collective racial violence and war." *J. of Black Studies*, 5(June):374–394.

SCHEER, R. 1974. *America After Nixon: The Age of the Multinationals*. New York: McGraw-Hill.

SCHEINGOLD, S. 1971. *The Law in Political Integration*. Occasional Papers in International Affairs, No. 27. Cambridge, Mass.: Center for International Affairs, Harvard University.

SCHEINMAN, L., and D. WILKINSON, eds. 1968. *International Law and Political Crisis*. Boston: Little, Brown.

SCHELLING, T. C. 1966. *Arms and Influence*. New Haven, Conn.: Yale University Press.

——. 1960. *The Strategy of Conflict*. Cambridge, Mass.: Harvard University Press.

SCHEVITZ, J. 1979. *The Weaponsmakers: Personal and Professional Crisis During the Vietnam War*. Cambridge, Mass.: Schenkman.

SCHIFFER, W. 1954. *The Legal Community of Mankind*. New York: Columbia University Press.

SCHILLER, H. I. 1976. "Advertising and international communications." *Instant Research on Peace and Violence*, 6(4):175–182.

——. 1975. "Genesis of the free flow of information principles: the imposition of communications domination." *Instant Research on Peace and Violence*, 5(1):75–87.

SCHINDLER, D., and J. TOMAN, eds. 1973. *The Laws of Armed Conflict*. Leiden: Sijthoff. Geneva: Henri Dunant Institute.

SCHNEIRLA, T. C. 1971. *Army Ants: A Study in Social Organization*. San Francisco: W. H. Freeman and Company.

SCHRODT, P. A. 1978. "Statistical problems associated with the Richardson arms race model." *J. of Peace Science*, 3(Fall):159–172.

SCHUMACHER, E. F. 1973. *Small Is Beautiful: Economics As If People Mattered*. New York: Harper and Row.

SCHUMPETER, J. A. 1951. *Imperialism and Social Classes*. New York: Kelley.

——. 1939. *Business Cycles: A Theoretical, Historical, and Statistical Analysis of the Capitalist Process*. New York: McGraw-Hill.

SCHWARTZ, E. S. 1971. *Overskill: The Decline of Technology in Modern Civilization*. New York: Ballantine.

SCHWARZENBERGER, G. 1962. *The Frontiers of International Law*. London: Stevens.

SCHWEBEL, M., ed. 1965. *Behavioral Science and Human Survival*. Palo Alto, Calif.: Science and Behavior Books.

SCHWEBEL, S. M. 1971. *The Effectiveness of International Decisions*. Dobbs Ferry, N.Y.: Oceana.

SCHWIDDER, W. 1971. "On schizoid neurosis: clinical aspects and psychodynamic findings." *Zeitschrift für Psychosomatische Medizin und Psychoanalyse*, 17(January):11–20.

SCITOVSKY, T., E. SHAW, and L. TARSHIS. 1951. *Mobilizing Resources for War: The Economic Alternatives*. New York: McGraw-Hill.

SCOTT, M. P. 1958. *Aggression*. Chicago: University of Chicago Press.

SCOVILLE, H., JR. 1977. "The SALT negotiations." *Scientific American*, 237(August):24–31.

——. 1972. "Missile submarines and national security." *Scientific American*, 226(June):15–27.

SCOVILLE, H., JR., and K. TSIPIS. 1978. "Can space remain a peaceful environment?" Muscatine, Iowa: Stanley Foundation.

SECEROV, S. 1919. *Economic Phenomena Before and After War: A Statistical Theory of Modern Wars*. London: Dutton.

SEGAL, J. 1974. "Long-term psychological and physical effects of the POW experience: a review of the literature." *US Naval Health Research Center Report*, 74(January):2–29.

——. 1973. "Therapeutic considerations in planning the return of American POWs to the continental United States." *Military Medicine*, 138(February):73–77.

SEGAL, J., and B. L. CATRON. 1972. "American reactions to brain-washing in Korea." In R. S. Parker, ed., *The Emotional Stress of War, Violence, and Peace*. Pittsburgh: Stanwix House. Pp. 263–269.

SELZER, M. 1976. "Psychohistorical approaches to the study of Nazism." *J. of Psychohistory*, 4(Fall):215–224.

SELZER, R. 1976. *Mortal Lessons: Notes on the Art of Surgery*. New York: Simon and Schuster.

SERVAN-SCHREIBER, J. J. 1968. *The American Challenge*. R. Steel, tr. New York: Atheneum.

SERVICE, E. 1975. *Origins of the State and Civilization*. New York: Norton.

SEWELL, J. P. 1975. *UNESCO and World Politics: Engaging in International Relations*. Princeton, N.J.: Princeton University Press.

——. 1966. *Functionalism and World Politics: A Study Based on United Nations Programs Financing Economic Development*. Princeton, N.J.: Princeton University Press.

SHARP, G. **1973**. *The Politics of Nonviolent Action.* Boston: Porter Sargent.

——. **1963**. "The need of a substitute for war." In M. Penrose, ed., *Pathogenesis of War.* London: Lewis. Pp. 76–84.

SHATAN, C. F. **1974**. "Through the membrane of reality: 'impacted grief' and perceptual dissonance in Vietnam combat veterans." *Psychiatric Opinion*, 11(November):6–15.

——. **1973**. "The grief of soldiers: Vietnam combat veterans' self-help movement." *American J. of Orthopsychiatry*, 43(July):640–653.

SHAW, L. E. **1973**. *Modern Competing Ideologies.* Lexington, Mass.: Heath.

SHEARER, D. **1970**. "The Pentagon propaganda machine." In L. S. Rodberg and D. Shearer, eds., *The Pentagon Watchers.* Garden City, N.Y.: Doubleday. Pp. 99–142.

SHEIKH, A. **1974**. *International Law and National Behavior.* New York: Wiley.

SHERIF, M. **1966**. *In Common Predicament: The Social Psychology of Intergroup Conflict and Cooperation.* Washington, D.C.: Public Affairs Press.

SHERIF, M., and C. SHERIF. **1953**. *Groups in Harmony and Tension.* New York: Harper.

SHERRY, M. S. **1977**. *Preparing for the Next War: American Plans for Postwar Defense, 1941–45.* New Haven, Conn.: Yale University Press.

SHORTER, E., and C. TILLY. **1974**. *Strikes in France, 1830–1968.* London: Cambridge University Press.

SHUBIK, M. **1975**. *Games for Society, Business, and War: Towards a Theory of Gaming.* New York: Elsevier.

SIEGEL, B. J., ed. **1976**. *Annual Review of Anthropology.* Vol. 5. Palo Alto, Calif.: Annual Reviews.

SIGELMAN, L., and M. SIMPSON. **1977**. "A cross-national test of the linkage between economic inequality and political violence." *J. of Conflict Resolution*, 21(March):105–127.

SILLS, D. L., ed. **1968**. *International Encyclopedia of the Social Sciences.* 17 vols. New York: Crowell Collier and Macmillan.

SIMMEL, G. **1955**. *Conflict.* K. H. Wolff, tr. Glencoe, Ill.: Free Press.

SIMMONS, J. S., et al. **1944**. *Global Epidemiology: A Geography of Disease and Sanitation.* Philadelphia: Lippincott.

SIMON, J. G., C. W. POWERS, and J. P. GUNNEMANN. **1972**. *The Ethical Investor: Universities and Corporate Responsibility.* New Haven, Conn.: Yale University Press.

SIMON, S. W., ed. **1978**. *The Military and Security in the Third World: Domestic and International Impacts.* Boulder: Westview.

SIMONTON, D. K. **1976a**. "The causal relation between war and scientific discovery: an exploratory cross-national analysis." *J. of Cross-Cultural Psychology*, 7(June): 133–144.

——. **1976b**. "Inter-disciplinary and military determinants of scientific productivity: a cross-lagged correlation analysis." *J. of Vocational Behavior*, 9(August):53–62.

SINGER, J. D., ed. **1980**. *Correlates of War-II.* New York: Free Press.

——, ed. **1979**. *Explaining War: Causes and Correlates of War.* Beverly Hills, Calif.: Sage.

——. **1972**. "The 'Correlates of War' project: interim report and rationale." *World Politics*, 24(January):243–270.

——, ed. **1968**. *Quantitative International Politics: Insights and Evidence.* New York: Free Press.

SINGER, J. D., S. BREMER, and J. STUCKEY. **1972**. "Capability distribution, uncertainty, and major power war, 1820–1965." In B. M. Russett, ed., *Peace, War, and Numbers.* Beverly Hills, Calif.: Sage. Pp. 19–48.

SINGER, J. D., and T. CUSACK. **1980** (in press). "Periodicity, inexorability, and steersmanship in international war." In R. L. Merritt and B. Russett, eds., *From National Development to Global Community.* London: Allen and Unwin.

SINGER, J. D., and M. SMALL. **1974**. "Foreign policy indicators: predictors of war in history and in the state of the world message." *Policy Sciences*, 5(September):271–296.

——. **1972**. *The Wages of War, 1816–1965: A Statistical Handbook.* New York: Wiley.

——. **1968**. "Alliance aggregation and the onset of war, 1815–1945." In J. D. Singer, ed., *Quantitative International Politics: Insights and Evidence.* New York: Free Press. Pp. 247–286.

——. **1966**. "The composition and state ordering of the international system." *World Politics*, 18(January):236–282.

SINGER, J. D., and M. D. WALLACE, eds. **1979**. *To Augur Well: Early Warning Indicators in World Politics.* Beverly Hills, Calif.: Sage.

——. **1970**. "Intergovernmental organization and the preservation of peace, 1816–1964: some bivariate relationships." *International Organization*, 24(Summer):520–547.

SINGER, M. **1972**. *Weak States in a World of Powers: The Dynamics of International Relationships.* New York: Free Press.

SINGH, I. S. **1977**. *A New International Economic Order: Toward a Fair Redistribution of the World's Resources.* New York: Praeger.

SIPES, R. G. **1973**. "War, sports and aggression: an empirical test of two rival theories." *American Anthropoligist*, 75(February):64–86.

SIPRI. **1979a**. *Armaments or Disarmament? The Crucial Choice.* Stockholm: SIPRI.

——. **1979b**. *Nuclear Energy and Nuclear Weapon Proliferation.* London: Taylor and Francis.

——. **1979c**. *Postures for Non-Proliferation: Arms Limitation and Security Policies to Minimize Nu-*

clear Proliferation. London: Taylor and Francis.

———. **1979d.** *Warfare in a Fragile World: Military Impact on the Human Environment.* London: Taylor and Francis.

———. **1978a.** *Anti-Personnel Weapons.* London: Taylor and Francis.

———. **1978b.** *Armaments or Disarmament? The Crucial Choice.* London: Taylor and Francis.

———. **1978c.** *Arms Control: A Survey and Appraisal of Multilateral Agreements.* London: Taylor and Francis.

———. **1978d.** *Outer Space—Battlefield of the Future?* London: Taylor and Francis.

———. **1978e.** *Tactical Nuclear Weapons: European Perspectives.* London: Taylor and Francis.

———. **1978f.** *SIPRI Yearbook of World Armaments and Disarmament, 1978.* London: Taylor and Francis.

———. **1977a.** *Strategic Disarmament: Verification and National Security.* London: Taylor and Francis.

———. **1977b.** *Weapons of Mass Destruction and the Environment.* London: Taylor and Francis.

———. **1976a.** *Armaments and Disarmament in the Nuclear Age.* London: Taylor and Francis.

———. **1976b.** *Ecological Consequences of Second Indochina War.* London: Taylor and Francis.

———. **1976c.** *The Law of War and Dubious Weapons.* Stockholm: Almqvist and Wiksell.

———. **1976d.** *Medical Protection Against Chemical-Warfare Agents.* London: Taylor and Francis.

———. **1976e.** *SIPRI Yearbook of World Armaments and Disarmament, 1976.* Cambridge, Mass.: MIT Press.

———. **1975a.** *Chemical Disarmament: New Weapons for Old.* London: Taylor and Francis.

———. **1975b.** *Delayed Toxic Effects of Chemical-Warfare Agents.* London: Taylor and Francis.

———. **1975c.** *The Problem of Chemical and Biological Warfare, 1971–75.* Vols. 1–6. London: Taylor and Francis.

———. **1974a.** *Force Reductions in Europe.* London: Taylor and Francis.

———. **1974b.** *Nuclear Proliferation Problems.* Cambridge, Mass.: MIT Press.

———. **1974c.** *SIPRI Yearbook of World Armaments and Disarmament, 1974.* Cambridge, Mass.: MIT Press. Stockholm: Almqvist and Wiksell.

———. **1973.** *Chemical Disarmament: Some Problems of Verification.* London: Taylor and Francis.

———. **1972a.** *The Near-Nuclear Countries and the NPT.* London: Taylor and Francis.

———. **1972b.** *Reesources Devoted to Military Research and Development: An International Comparison.* London: Taylor and Francis.

———. **1971.** *The Arms Trade with the Third World.* Stockholm: Almqvist and Wiksell.

———. **1969a.** *Seismic Methods for Monitoring Underground Explosions.* London: Taylor and Francis.

———. **1969b.** *SIPRI Yearbook of World Armaments and Disarmament, 1968/69.* New York: Humanities.

SISSON, R. L., and R. L. ACKOFF. **1966.** "Toward a theory of the dynamics of conflict." *Peace Research Society (International) Papers,* 5, Philadelphia Conference, 1965.

SIVARD, R. L. **1976.** *World Military and Social Expenditures, 1976.* Leesburg, Va.: WMSE Publications.

SIVERSON, R. M., and G. T. DUNCAN. **1976.** "Stochastic models of international alliance initiation, 1885–1965." In D. A. Zinnes and J. V. Gillespie, eds., *Mathematical Models in International Relations.* New York: Praeger. Pp. 110–131.

SIVERSON, R. M., and J. KING. **1980.** "Attributes of national alliance membership and war participation, 1815–1965." *American J. of Political Science,* 24(February):1–15.

SJOBERG, G. **1960.** "Contradictory functional requirements and social systems." J. of Conflict Resolution, 4(June):198–208.

SKINNER, B. F. 1971. *Beyond Freedom and Dignity.* New York: Bantam.

SKJELSBAEK, K. **1979.** "Militarism, its dimensions and corollaries: an attempt at conceptual clarification." *J. of Peace Research,* 16(3):213–230.

———. **1972.** "Peace and the structure of the international organization network." *J. of Peace Research,* 9(4)315–330.

———. **1971.** "Shared memberships in intergovernmental organizations and dyadic war, 1865–1964." In E. H. Fedder, ed., *The United Nations: Problems and Prospects.* St. Louis: Center for International Studies, University of Missouri. Pp. 31–62.

———. **1970.** "Development of the systems of international organizations: a diachronic study." In *Proceedings of the International Third General Conference. Vol. 2: The International System.* IPRA Studies in Peace Research No. 4. Assen, Netherlands: van Gorcum and Comp. N.V.

SLATER, P. E. **1971.** *The Pursuit of Loneliness: American Culture at the Breaking Point.* Boston: Beacon.

SMALL, M., and J. D. SINGER. **1979.** "Conflict in the international system, 1816–1977: historical trends and policy futures." In C. W. Kegley, Jr., and P. J. McGowan, eds., *Challenges to America: U.S. Foreign Policy in the 1980's.* Beverly Hills, Calif.: Sage. Pp. 89–115.

SMELSER, N. **1963.** *Theory of Collective Behavior.* New York: Free Press.

SMIRNOV, A. A. **1975.** "Soviet psychologists in the defense of the motherland during the great patriotic war." *Voprosy Psikhologii,* 2(March–April):13–30.

SMITH, D. D. **1979.** *Space Stations: International Law and Policy.* Boulder: Westview.

SMITH, J. M., and G. R. PRICE. **1973.** "The logic of animal conflict." *Nature*, 246(November):15–18.

SMITH, M. **1976.** "The League of Nations and international politics." *British J. of International Studies*, 2(October):311–323.

SMITH, M. B., J. S. BRUNER, and R. W. WHITE. **1956.** *Opinions and Personality*. New York: Wiley.

SMITH, P. M. **1970.** *The Air Force Plans for Peace, 1943–1945*. Baltimore: Johns Hopkins University Press.

SMITH, T. **1977.** "Changing configurations of power in North–South relations since 1945." *International Organization*, 31(Winter):1–27.

SMITH, T. C. **1976.** "Arms race instability and war: preliminary findings." *International Studies Notes*, 3(4):41–46.

SMOKE, R. **1977.** *War: Controlling Escalation*. Cambridge, Mass.: Harvard University Press.

SMOKER, P. **1969.** "A time series analysis of Sino–Indian relations." *J. of Conflict Resolution*, 13(June):172–191.

———. **1967a.** "The arms race as an open and closed system." *Peace Research Society (International) Papers*, 7:41–62.

———. **1967b.** "Nation state escalation and international integration." *J. of Peace Research*, 4(1):61–74.

———. **1966.** "The arms race: a wave model." *Peace Research Society (International) Papers*, 4:151–192.

———. **1964.** "Fear in the arms race: a mathematical study." *J. of Peace Research*, 1(1):55–64.

SNELL, J. L. **1967.** *War and Totalitarianism*. Lexington, Mass.: Heath.

SNIDERMAN, P. M., and J. CITRIN. **1971.** "Psychological sources of political belief, self-esteem and isolationist attitudes." *American Political Science Rev.*, 65(June):401–417.

SNITCH, T. H. **1980.** "Assassinations and political violence, 1968–1978: an events data approach." Los Angeles: Presented at annual meeting of International Studies Association. Mimeo.

SNYDER, D. R., and W. R. KELLY. **1976.** "Industrial violence in Italy, 1878–1903." *American J. of Sociology*, 82(July):131–162.

SNYDER, D. R., and C. H. TILLY. **1974.** "On debating and falsifying theories of collective violence." *American Sociological Rev.*, 39(August):610–613.

———. **1973.** "How to get from here to there." *American Sociological Rev.*, 38(August):501–504.

———. **1972.** "Hardship and collective violence in France, 1830–1960." *American Sociological Rev.*, 37(October):520–532.

SNYDER, G. H., and P. DIESING. **1977.** *Conflict Among Nations: Bargaining, Decision Making, and System Structure in International Crises*. Princeton, N.J.: Princeton University Press.

SNYDER, J. L. **1977.** *The Soviet Strategic Culture: Im-*plications for Limited Nuclear Operations. Santa Monica, Calif.: Rand.

SNYDER, R. C., H. W. BRUCK, and B. SAPIN, eds. **1962.** *Foreign Policy Decision-Making: An Approach to the Study of International Politics*. New York: Free Press.

SNYDER, R. C., C. F. HERMANN, and H. D. LASSWELL. **1976.** "A global monitoring system: appraising the effects of government on human dignity." *International Studies Q.*, 20(June):221–260.

SOCIETY OF FRIENDS, AMERICAN FRIENDS SERVICE COMMITTEE. **1963.** *The War Within Man*. Beyond Deterrence Series, Peace Education Department. Philadelphia: American Friends Service Committee.

SODEUR, W., and K. ROGHMANN. **1972.** "Autoritarismus und dogmatismus im militar." *Soziale Welt*, 23(3):269–283.

SOLNIT, A. J., and B. PRIEL. **1975.** "Scared and scarred: psychological aspects in the treatment of soldiers with burns." *Israel Annals of Psychiatry and Related Disciplines*, 13(September):213–220.

SOLOV'EV, N., ed. **1972.** "Divorce, its factors, internal and external causes." In *Psychological Abstracts*, 48(00807):92.

SOLZHENITSYN, A. **1974.** *The Gulag Archipelago*. T. P. Whitney, tr. New York: Harper and Row.

SONNENBERG, S. M. **1974.** "Children of survivors." *J. of the American Psychoanalytic Association*, 22(1):200–204.

SOROKIN, P. A. **1975.** *Hunger as a Factor in Human Affairs*. E. P. Sorokin, tr.; T. L. Smith, ed. Gainesville: University of Florida Press.

———. **1937.** *Social and Cultural Dynamics*. Vol. 3: *Fluctuation of Social Relationships, War, and Revolution*. New York: American Book.

———. **1925.** *The Sociology of Revolution*. Philadelphia: Lippincott.

SOROOS, M. **1977.** "Behaviour between nations." *Peace Research Rev.*, 7(April):1–105.

SOUTHARD, S. **1969.** "The southern soldier-saint." *J. for the Scientific Study of Religion*, 8(Spring):39–46.

SPEIER, H. **1969.** *Force and Folly: Essays on Foreign Affairs and the History of Ideas*. Cambridge, Mass.: MIT Press.

———. **1952a.** "International political communications: elite vs. mass." *World Politics*, 4(April):305–317.

———. **1952b.** *Social Order and the Risks of War: Papers in Political Sociology*. New York: Stewart.

SPERO, J. E. **1977.** *The Politics of International Economic Relations*. New York: St. Martin's.

SPIRO, H., and R. B. BARBER. **1970.** "Counter-ideological uses of 'totalitarianism.' " *Politics and Society*, 1(November):3–22.

STAGNER, R. **1967.** *Psychological Aspects of Interna-*

tional Conflict. Belmont, Calif.: Brooks/Cole.

STALEY, E. **1967**. *War and the Private Investor*. New York: Fertig.

STANLEY, S., and H. H. KITANO. **1973**. "Stereotypes as a measure of success." *J. of Social Issues*, 29(2):83–98.

STANLEY, T. W., et al. **1977**. *Raw Materials and Foreign Policy*. Boulder: Westview.

STARKE, J. G. **1968**. *An Introduction to the Science of Peace (Irenology)*. Leyden: Sijthoff.

STARR, H. **1977**. "Physical variables and foreign policy decision making: daily temperature and the pre–World War I Crisis." *International Interactions*, 3(2):97–108.

——. **1975**. *Coalitions and Future War: Dyadic Study of Cooperation and Conflict*. Beverly Hills, Calif.: Sage.

——. **1972**. *War Coalitions: The Distributions of Payoffs and Losses*. Lexington, Mass.: Lexington Books.

STARR, H., and B. A. MOST. **1978**. "A return journey: Richardson's frontiers and wars in the 1946–1965 era." *J. of Conflict Resolution*, 22 (September):441–467.

——. **1976**. "The substance and study of borders in international relations research." *International Studies Q.*, 20(December):581–620.

STARR, J. M. **1975**. "Religious preference, religiosity, and opposition to war." *Sociological Analysis*, 36(Winter):323–334.

——. **1974**. "The peace and love generation: changing attitudes toward sex and violence among college youth." *J. of Social Issues*, 30(2):73–106.

STARR, P. D. **1975**. "How the Arabs see themselves after the war." *New Society*, 31(January):186–187.

STAVRIANOS, L. S. **1976**. *The Promise of the Coming Dark Age*. San Francisco: W. H. Freeman and Company.

STAW, B. M., W. W. NOTZ, and T. D. COOK. **1974**. "Vulnerability to draft and attitudes toward troop withdrawal from Indochina: replication and refinement." *Psychological Reports*, 34(April):407–417.

STEFFLRE, V. **1974**. "Long-term forecasting and the problem of large-scale wars." *Futures*, 6 (August):302–308.

STEGENGA, J. A. **1973**. "Peacekeeping: postmortems or previews?" *International Organization*, 27(Summer):373–385.

——. **1972**. "Personal aggressiveness and war." *International J. of Group Tensions*, 2(4):22–36.

STEHR, U. **1977**. "Unequal development and dependency structures in Comecon." *J. of Peace Research*, 14(2):115–128.

STEIBER, S. R. **1979**. "The world system and world trade: an empirical exploration of conceptual conflicts." *Sociological Q.*, 20(Winter):23–36.

STEIN, A. A. **1976**. "Conflict and cohesion: a review of the literature." *J. of Conflict Resolution*, 20(March):143–172.

STEIN, A. A., and B. RUSSETT. **1980** (in press). "Evaluating war: outcomes and consequences." In T. R. Gurr, ed., *Handbook of Conflict Theory and Research*. New York: Free Press.

STEIN, Z., et al. **1975**. *Famine and Human Development: The Dutch Hunger Winter of 1944–1945*. New York: Oxford University Press.

STEINER, B. **1973**. *Arms Races, Diplomacy, and Recurring Behavior: Lessons from Two Cases*. Beverly Hills, Calif.: Sage.

STEINER, J. **1963**. "The control of war-preparing behaviour." In M. Penrose, ed., *Pathogenesis of War*. London: Lewis. Pp. 35–41.

STEINER, M. **1979**. "Conceptions of the individual in the world order models project (WOMP) literature." *International Interactions*, 6(1):27–41.

STENGER, C. A. **1973**. "Life style shock: the psychological experience of being an American prisoner of war in the Vietnam conflict." *Newsletter for Research in Mental Health and Behavioral Sciences*, 15(May):1–4.

STEPAN, A. C. **1971**. *The Military in Politics: Changing Patterns in Brazil*. Princeton, N.J.: Princeton University Press.

STERN, E. A. **1978**. "The military–industrial–academic–congressional complex." In L. L. Farrar, Jr., ed., *War: A Historical, Political and Social Study*. Santa Barbara, Calif.: ABC–Clio. Pp. 181–186.

STERN, E. P., ed. **1977**. *The Limits of Military Intervention*. Beverly Hills, Calif.: Sage.

STERN, F. M. **1957**. *The Citizen Army: Key to Defense in the Atomic Age*. New York: St. Martin's.

STERNBACH, O. **1974**. "The pursuit of happiness and the epidemic of depression." *Psychoanalytic Rev.*, 61(Summer):283–293.

STEVENS, J. D. **1973**. *From the Back of the Foxhole: Black Correspondents in World War II*. Journalism Monographs, No. 27. Lexington, Ky.: Association for Education in Journalism.

STEVENSON, J. R., and B. H. OXMAN. **1975**. "The third United Nations conference on the law of the sea: the 1974 Caracas session." *American J. of International Law*, 69(January):1–30.

STEWART, L. H. **1977**. "Birth order and political leadership." In M. G. Hermann and T. W. Milburn, eds., *A Psychological Examination of Political Leaders*. New York: Free Press. Pp. 206–236.

STICE, J. W. **1974**. "Verbal aggression in State of the Union messages during wartime and nonwartime." *Dissertation Abstracts International*, 34(April):6786.

STILLMAN, R. J., II. **1968**. *Integration of the Negro in the U.S. Armed Forces*. New York: Praeger.

STINCHCOMBE, A. **1973**. "Comment on 'the impact

of military service on authoritarian attitudes.' " *American J. of Sociology*, 79(July):157–159.

STIX, A. H. **1974.** "Chlordiazepoxide (Librium): the effects of a minor tranquilizer on strategic choice behavior in the prisoner's dilemma." *J. of Conflict Resolution*, 18(September):373–394.

STOBAUGH, R. B., and D. YERGIN. **1979.** *Energy Future: A Report of the Energy Project at the Harvard Business School*. New York: Random House.

STOCKHOLM INTERNATIONAL PEACE RESEARCH INSTITUTE: *See* SIPRI.

STOESSINGER, J. **1978.** *Why Nations Go to War*. New York: St. Martin's.

STOHL, M. **1976.** *War and Domestic Political Violence: The American Capacity for Repression and Reaction*. Beverly Hills, Calif.: Sage.

STOMMEL, H., and E. STOMMEL. **1979.** "The year without a summer." *Scientific American*, 240 (June):176–186.

STONE, J. **1958.** *Aggression and World Order: A Critique of United Nations Theories of Aggression*. Berkeley: University of California Press.

STORR, A. **1973.** "Possible substitutes for war." In T. Maple and D. W. Matheson, eds., *Aggression, Hostility, and Violence: Nature or Nurture*. New York: Holt, Rinehart and Winston. Pp. 306–314.

——. **1968.** *Human Aggression*. New York: Atheneum.

——. **1963.** "Is conflict inevitable?" In M. Penrose, ed., *Pathogenesis of War*. London: Lewis. Pp. 65–75.

STOUFFER, S., et al. **1949.** *The American Soldier*. Princeton, N.J.: Princeton University Press.

STRACHEY, A. **1957.** *The Unconscious Motives of War*. London: Allen and Unwin.

STRACK, H. R. **1978.** *Sanctions: The Case of Rhodesia*. Syracuse, N.Y.: Syracuse University Press.

STRANGE, R. E., and D. E. BROWN. **1970.** "Home from the war: a study of psychiatric problems in Viet Nam returnees." *American J. of Psychiatry*, 127(October):488–492.

STRAVINSKY, I. **1956.** *Poetics of Music in the Form of Six Lessons*. A. Knodel and I. Dahl, trs. New York: Vintage.

STRAYER, R., and L. ELLENHORN. **1975.** "Vietnam veterans: a study exploring adjustment patterns and attitudes." *J. of Social Issues*, 31 (4):81–93.

STROMBERG, R. **1977a.** "On 'cherchez le financier': comments on the economic interpretation of World War I." *History Teacher*, 10(May):435–443.

——. **1977b.** "Revising the revisionists: remarks on the cold war as an anti-capitalist plot." *Peace and Change*, 4(Fall):58–61.

STRUENING, E. L., and M. GUTTENTAG. **1975.** *Handbook of Evaluation Research*. Beverly Hills, Calif.: Sage.

STURM, I. E. **1972.** "The emotional satisfactions of war." In R. S. Parker, ed., *The Emotional Stress of War, Violence, and Peace*. Pittsburgh: Stanwix House. Pp. 117–121.

STUYT, A. M. **1972.** *Survey of International Arbitrations, 1974–1970*. Leiden: Sijthoff.

SUBBARAO, A. V. **1978.** "The impact of binding interest arbitration on negotiation and process outcome: an experimental study." *J. of Conflict Resolution*, 22(March):79–103.

SUCHMAN, E. **1968.** "Epidemiology." In D. L. Sills, ed., *International Encyclopedia of the Social Sciences*, Vol. 5. New York: Crowell Collier and Macmillan. Pp. 97–102.

SUE, S., and H. H. KITANO. **1973.** "Stereotypes as a measure of success." *J. of Social Issues*, 29(2):83–98.

SUEDFELD, P., and Y. M. EPSTEIN. **1973.** "Attitudes, values, and ascription of responsibility: the Calley case." *J. of Social Issues*, 29(4):63–71.

SUEDFELD, P., and P. TETLOCK. **1977.** "Integrative complexity of communications in international crises." *J. of Conflict Resolution*, 21(March):169–171.

SUEDFELD, P., P. E. TETLOCK, and C. RAMIREZ. **1977.** "War, peace, and integrative complexity: U.N. speeches on the Middle East problem, 1947–1976." *J. of Conflict Resolution*, 21(September):427–442.

SUH, I. R. **1969.** "Voting behavior of national judges on international courts." *American J. of International Law*, 63(April):224–236.

SULLIVAN, D. F. **1966.** "Conceptual problems in developing an index of health." U.S. Department of Health, Education, and Welfare, USPHS Pub. No. 1000, Series 2, No. 17. Washington, D.C.: U.S. Government Printing Office.

SULLIVAN, M. P. **1978.** "International organizations and world order: a reappraisal." *J. of Conflict Resolution*, 22(March):105–120.

SULLIVAN, M. P., and W. THOMAS. **1972.** "Symbolic involvement as a correlate of escalation: the Vietnam case." In B. M. Russett, ed., *Peace, War, and Numbers*. Beverly Hills, Calif.: Sage. Pp. 185–212.

SUSSER, M. **1973.** *Causal Thinking in the Health Sciences: Concepts and Strategies in Epidemiology*. New York: Oxford University Press.

SUTER, K. D. **1976.** "Reforming the international Red Cross movement." *Instant Research on Peace and Violence*, 6(3):120–129.

——. **1974.** "The work of the ICRC in Vietnam: an evaluation." *Instant Research on Peace and Violence*, 4(3):121–132.

SVENNILSON, I. **1954.** *Growth and Stagnation in the European Economy*. Geneva: United Nations Economic Commission for Europe.

SWANN, D., and D. L. MCLACHLAN. **1967.** *Concentration or Competition: A European Dilemma?* London: Royal Institute of International Affairs.

SWANSON, J. R. **1972.** "The superpowers and multipolarity: from pax Americana to pax Sovietica?" *Orbis,* 15(Winter):1035–1050.

SWOMLEY, J. M., JR. **1964.** *The Military Establishment.* Boston: Beacon.

SYLVAN, D. A. **1976.** "Consequences of sharp military assistance increases for international conflict and cooperation." *J. of Conflict Resolution,* 20(December):609–636.

TAAGEPERA, R., and J. P. HAYES. **1977.** "How trade/GNP ratio decreases with country size." *Social Science Research,* 6(March):108–132.

TANAY, E. **1976.** "The dear John syndrome during the Vietnam war." *Diseases of the Nervous System,* 37(March):165–167.

TANTER, R. **1974.** *Modeling and Managing International Conflict: The Berlin Crisis.* Beverly Hills, Calif.: Sage.

——. **1970.** "Toward a theory of conflict behavior in Latin America." In R. W. Cox, ed., *The Politics of International Organization.* New York: Praeger. Pp. 153–179.

——. **1969.** "International war and domestic turmoil: some contemporary evidence." In H. D. Graham and T. R. Gurr, eds., *The History of Violence in America: Historical and Comparative Perspectives.* New York: Praeger. Pp. 550–569.

——. **1966.** "Dimensions of conflict behavior within and between nations, 1958–1960." *J. of Conflict Resolution,* 10(March):41–64.

TANTER, R., and M. MIDLARSKY. **1967.** "A theory of revolution." *J. of Conflict Resolution,* 11 (September):264–280.

TASCHNER, K. L., and K. WANKE. **1973.** "Social causes of drug consumption in young persons." *Psychiatrie, Neurologie und Medizinische Psychologie,* 25(April):208–215.

TAX, S., ed. **1975.** *World Anthropology.* The Hague and Paris: Mouton.

TAYLOR, A. J. P. **1961.** *The Origins of the Second World War.* London: Hamilton.

TAYLOR, C. L., and M. C. HUDSON. **1972.** *World Handbook of Political and Social Indicators.* 2nd ed. New Haven, Conn.: Yale University Press.

TAYLOR, I., and J. KNOWELDEN. **1958.** *Principles of Epidemiology.* Boston: Little, Brown.

TAYLOR, P., and A. J. R. GROOM, eds. **1978.** *International Organization: A Conceptual Approach.* New York: Nichols.

TAYLOR, R. K. **1977.** *Blockade: A Guide to Non-violent Intervention.* Maryknoll, N.Y.: Orbis.

TAYLOR, T. **1970.** *Nuremburg and Vietnam.* Chicago: Quadrangle.

TEFFT, S. K., and D. REINHARDT. **1974.** "Warfare regulation: a cross-cultural test of hypotheses among tribal peoples." *Behavior Science Research,* 9(2):151–172.

TERHUNE, K. W. **1965.** "Nationalistic aspiration, loyalty, and internationalism." *J. of Peace Research,* 2(3):277–287.

TERRELL, L. M. **1977.** "Attribute differences among neighboring states and their levels of foreign conflict behavior." *International J. of Group Tensions,* 7(1–2):89–108.

TEXTOR, R. B. **1967.** *A Cross-cultural Summary.* New Haven, Conn.: Human Relations Area Files.

THAYER, C. W. **1959.** *Diplomat.* New York: Harper.

THAYER, G. **1969.** *The War Business: The International Trade in Armaments.* New York: Simon and Schuster.

THEE, M. **1977.** "Arms control: the retreat from disarmament, the record to date and the search for alternatives." *J. of Peace Research,* 14(2):95–114.

THIESSEN, D. D. **1976.** *The Evolution and Chemistry of Aggression.* Springfield, Ill.: Thomas.

THOMAS, A. V. W., and A. J. THOMAS, JR. **1956.** *Nonintervention: The Law and Its Import in the Americas.* Dallas: Southern Methodist University Press.

THOMAS, K. **1976.** "Epidemic man." *New York Rev. of Books,* 23(September 30):3–4.

THOMAS, S. T. **1975.** "War, domestic violence, and instability." Seattle: Presented at annual meeting of Western Political Science Association. Mimeo.

THOMLINSON, R. **1965.** *Population Dynamics: Causes and Consequences of World Demographic Change.* New York: Random House.

THOMPSON, D., and B. JACOBS. **1973.** *A Photographic Essay of Apache Clothing, War Charms, and Weapons.* Vol. 2, Part D. Tuscon: Bureau of School Services, University of Arizona.

THOMPSON, K. S., A. C. CLARKE, and S. DINITZ. **1974.** "Reactions to My-Lai: a visual–verbal comparison." *Sociology and Social Research,* 58 (January):122–129.

THOMPSON, W. R. **1975.** "Regime vulnerability and the military coup." *Comparative Politics,* 7 (July):459–487.

THOMPSON, W. R., and J. A. CHRISTOPHERSON. **1979.** "A multivariate analysis of the correlates of regime vulnerability and proneness to the military coup." *J. of Political and Military Sociology,* 7(Fall):283–289.

THOMPSON, W. R., and G. MODELSKI. **1977.** "Global conflict intensity and great power summitry behavior." *J. of Conflict Resolution,* 21(June):339–370.

THOMSON, D. **1962.** *Europe Since Napoleon.* New York: Knopf.

THORSON, T. L. **1970**. *Biopolitics*. New York: Holt, Rinehart and Winston.

TIGER, L., and R. FOX. **1971**. *The Imperial Animal*. New York: Holt, Rinehart and Winston.

TILLICH, P., et al. **1965**. *To Live as Men: An Anatomy of Peace*. Santa Barbara, Calif.: Center for the Study of Democratic Institutions.

TILLY, C., ed. **1975**. *The Formation of National States in Western Europe*. Princeton, N.J.: Princeton University Press.

——. **1973**. "The chaos of the living city." In H. Hirsch and D. Perry, eds., *Violence is Politics*. New York: Harper and Row. Pp. 98–124.

——. **1964**. *The Vendée*. Cambridge, Mass.: Harvard University Press.

TILLY, L., and R. TILLY. **1975**. *The Rebellious Century: 1830–1930*. Cambridge, Mass.: Harvard University Press.

TIMASHEFF, N. S. **1965**. *War and Revolution*. New York: Sheed and Ward.

TINBERGEN, J. **1965**. *International Economic Integration*. 2nd ed. Amsterdam: Elsevier.

TINBERGEN, J., and J. J. POLAK. **1950**. *The Dynamics of Business Cycles: A Study in Economic Fluctuations*. London: Routledge and Kegan Paul.

TIPSON, F. S. (1976). "Toward a GMS 'archipelago': a case of ocean policy." *International Studies Q.*, 20(December)635–640.

TITMUSS, R. M. **1971**. *The Gift Relationship: From Human Blood to Social Policy*. New York: Pantheon.

——. **1962**. *Income Distribution and Social Change: A Study in Criticism*. London: Allen and Unwin.

TOCQUEVILLE, A. DE. **1956**. *Democracy in America*. H. Reeve, tr. New York: Mentor.

——. **1955**. *The Old Regime and the French Revolution*. G. Stuart, tr. New York: Doubleday.

TOFFLER, A. **1970**. *Future Shock*. New York: Random House.

TOLKIEN, H. **1965**. *The Lord of the Rings*. 3 vols. Boston: Houghton Mifflin.

TOLLEY, H. **1973**. *Children and War: Political Socialization to International Conflict*. New York: Teachers College Press.

TOLSTOY, L. N. **1957**. *War and Peace*. R. Edwards, tr. Harmondsworth, Middlesex: Penguin.

TOMLIN, B. W., and M. A. BUHLMAN. **1977**. "Relative status and foreign policy: status partitioning and the analysis of relations in Black Africa." *J. of Conflict Resolution*, 21(June):187–216.

TOOKE, J. D. **1965**. *The Just War in Aquinas and Grotius*. Naperville, Ill.: Allenson.

TORACH, E., et al. **1974**. *The Four Horsemen: Racism, Sexism, Militarism, and Social Darwinism*. New York: Behavioral Publications.

TOULMIN, S., and A. JANIK. **1973**. *Wittgenstein's Vienna*. New York: Simon and Schuster.

TOYNBEE, A. J. **1950**. *War and Civilization*. New York: Oxord University Press.

TRETIAK, D. **1970**. "Political assassinations in China, 1600–1968." In J. F. Kirkham, G. Levy, and W. J. Crotty, eds., *Assassination and Political Violence*. New York: Bantam. Pp. 635–671.

TRIMBERGER, E. K., ed. **1978**. *Revolution from Above: Military Bureaucrats and Developments in Japan, Turkey, Egypt, and Peru*. New Brunswick, N.J.: Transaction Books.

TRISKA, J. F., and D. D. FINLEY. **1965**. "Soviet–American relations: a multiple symmetry model." *J. of Conflict Resolution*, 9(March):37–53.

TROOBOFF, P. D., ed. **1975**. *Law and Responsibility: The Vietnam Experience*. Chapel Hill: University of North Carolina Press.

TROUT, B. T. **1977**. "Arms competition and naval conduct: the external pacer hypothesis." Washington, D.C.: Presented at annual meeting of American Political Science Association. Mimeo.

TRUMBO, D. **1970**. *Johnny Got His Gun*. New York: Stuart.

TSIPIS, K. **1977**. "Cruise missiles." *Scientific American*, 236(February):20–29.

TUCHMAN, B. **1971**. *The Guns of August*. New York: Dell.

TUCKER, R. W. **1977**. *The Inequality of Nations*. New York: Basic Books.

——. **1966**. *The Just War and Vatican Council: A Critique*. New York: Council on Religion and International Affairs.

TULIPAN, A. B., C. L. ATTNEAVE, and E. KINGSTONE, eds. **1974**. *Beyond Clinic Walls*. University: University of Alabama Press.

TULLOCK, G. **1974**. *The Social Dilemma: The Economics of War and Revolution*. Blacksburg: University Publications, Virginia Polytechnic Institute.

TUOMI, H. **1975**. "The food power: the position of main exporting countries in world food economy." *Instant Research on Peace and Violence*, 5(3):121–137.

TUNKIN, G. E. **1974**. *Theory of International Law*. W. E. Butler, tr. Cambridge, Mass.: Harvard University Press.

TURBAYNE, C. M. **1970**. *The Myth of Metaphor*. Columbia: University of South Carolina Press.

TURK, H., and R. L. SIMPSON, eds. **1971**. *Institutions and Social Exchange: The Sociologies of Talcott Parsons and George C. Homans*. Indianapolis: Bobbs-Merrill.

TURNBULL, C. **1974**. *The Forest People*. London: Cape.

——. **1972**. *The Mountain People*. New York: Simon and Schuster.

TURNER, R. H. **1977**. "Reply to Phillip Wexler." *American J. of Sociology*, 83(July):185–187.

TURNEY-HIGH, H. H. **1971.** *Primitive War: Its Practice and Concepts.* Columbia: University of South Carolina Press.

TWAIN, M. **1968.** *The War Prayer.* New York: Harper and Row.

TYRRELL, C. M. **1970.** *Pentagon Partners: The New Nobility.* New York: Grossman.

UDIS, B., ed. **1973.** *The Economic Consequences of Reduced Military Spending.* Lexington, Mass.: Lexington Books.

UDRY, J. R. **1977.** "The importance of being beautiful: a reexamination and racial comparison." *American J. of Sociology,* 83(July):154–161.

UGBOAJAH, F. O. **1976.** "Nigerian mass media behaviour on development issues of conflict." *Instant Research on Peace and Violence,* 6 (4):183–194.

ULLMANN, J. E., ed. **1970.** *Potential Civilian Markets for the Military–Electronics Industry: Strategies for Conversion.* New York: Praeger.

UNCTAD. **1964.** *Proceedings of the United Nations Conference on Trade and Development, Geneva, 23 March–16 June, 1964; Trade Expansion and Regional Groupings.* Vols. 6 and 7. New York: United Nations.

UNION OF INTERNATIONAL ASSOCIATIONS, ed. **1977.** *Yearbook of International Organizations.* Brussels: Union of International Associations.

UNITED NATIONS. **1980.** Private correspondence.

——. **1978a.** *Statistical Yearbook, 1977.* New York: United Nations.

——. **1978b.** *Yearbook of International Trade Statistics, 1977.* New York: United Nations.

——. **1978c.** *Yearbook of National Accounts Statistics, 1977: Individual Country Data.* Vol. 1. New York: United Nations.

——. **1975a.** *Demographic Yearbook, 1974.* New York: United Nations.

——. **1975b.** *A New United Nations Structure for Global Economic Cooperation.* E/AC62/9. New York: United Nations.

——. **1971.** *Yearbook of International Trade Statistics, 1969.* New York: United Nations.

——. **1969.** *A Study of the Capacity of the United Nations Development System,* 2 vols. DP/5. Geneva: United Nations.

UNITED NATIONS ASSOCIATION. **1976.** *Controlling the Conventional Arms Race.* New York: United Nations Association.

UNITED NATIONS CONFERENCE ON TRADE AND DEVELOPMENT: *See* UNCTAD

U.S. ARMS CONTROL AND DISARMAMENT AGENCY. **1978.** *World Military Expenditures and Arms Transfers, 1967–1976.* Washington, D.C.: U.S. Government Printing Office.

——. **1977.** *World Military Expenditures and Arms Transfers, 1966–1975.* Washington, D.C.: U.S. Government Printing Office.

——. **1974.** *Documents on Disarmament.* Publication #76. Washington, D.C.: U.S. Government Printing Office.

——. **1972.** *The Economic Impact of Reductions in Defense Spending.* Washington, D.C.: U.S. Government Printing Office.

U.S. DEPARTMENT OF THE AIR FORCE. **1976.** *International Law: The Conduct of Armed Conflict and Air Operations.* Washington, D.C.: U.S. Department of the Air Force.

U.S. DEPARTMENT OF COMMERCE. **1977.** *Statistical Abstract of the United States, 1977.* Washington, D.C.: U.S. Department of Commerce.

——, BUREAU OF THE CENSUS. **1975.** *Historical Statistics of the United States: Colonial Times to 1970.* Bicentennial ed. Washington, D.C.: U.S. Department of Commerce.

U.S. DEPARTMENT OF DEFENSE. **1977.** *Selected Manpower Statistics.* Washington, D.C.: OASD (Comptroller), Directorate for Management Information Operations and Control, U.S. Department of Defense.

——, DEFENSE SECURITY ASSISTANCE AGENCY. **1978.** *Foreign Military Sales and Military Assistance Facts.* Washington, D.C.: U.S. Department of Defense.

U.S. GOVERNMENT PRINTING OFFICE. **1978.** *SALT and American Security.* Washington, D.C.: U.S. Government Printing Office.

U.S. HOUSE OF REPRESENTATIVES, COMMITTEE ON INTERNATIONAL RELATIONS. **1976.** *United States Contributions to International Organizations.* Twenty-third Annual Report—Communication from the Secretary of State—Transmitting the Annual Report on United States Contributions to International Organizations for Fiscal Year 1974, Pursuant to Section 2 of Public Law 806, 81st Congress. Washington, D.C.: U.S. Government Printing Office.

U.S. SENATE, COMMITTEE ON FOREIGN RELATIONS. **1976.** *U.S. Military Sales to Iran: A Staff Report to the Subcommittee on Foreign Assistance.* Washington, D.C.: U.S. Government Printing Office.

UNIVERSITY OF CALIFORNIA COMMITTEE ON INTERNATIONAL RELATIONS. **1937.** *Problems of War and Peace in the Society of Nations.* Freeport, N.Y.: Books for Libraries Press.

URLANIS, B. **1971.** *Wars and Populations.* L. Lempert, tr. Moscow: Progress Publishers.

USDIN, G., ed. **1972.** *Perspectives on Violence.* New York: Brunner/Mazel.

USHIODA, S. C. **1977.** "Women and war in Meiji Japan: the case of Fukuda Hideko (1865–1927)." *Peace and Change,* 4(Fall):9–13.

USLANER, E. M. **1976.** "The pitfalls of per capita." *American J. of Political Science,* 20(February):125–133.

UTTER, G. H. **1976.** "The ICRC and conflict:

post–World War II experience." *Instant Research on Peace and Violence*, 6(3):111–119.

VACCA, R. **1974**. *The Coming Dark Age: What Will Happen When Modern Technology Breaks Down?* J. S. Whale, tr. Garden City, N.Y.: Doubleday.

VAGTS, A. **1959**. *A History of Militarism*. New York: Free Press.

VAN DOORN, J. **1975**. *The Soldier and Social Change: Comparative Studies in the History and Sociology of the Military*. Beverly Hills, Calif.: Sage.

——, ed. **1969**. *Military Profession and Military Regimes: Commitments and Conflicts*. The Hague: Mouton.

——, ed. **1968**. *Armed Forces and Society: Sociological Essays*. The Hague: Mouton.

VAN PUTTEN, T., and W. H. EMORY. **1973**. "Traumatic neuroses in Vietnam returnees: a forgotten diagnosis?" *Archives of General Psychiatry*, 29(November):695–698.

VARIS, T. **1976**. "World information order." *Instant Research on Peace and Violence*, 6(4):143–147.

——. **1975**. "The impact of transnational corporations on communication." Research Report No. 10. Finland: Tampere Peace Research Institute.

VASQUEZ, J. A. **1976**. "Statistical findings in international politics: a data-based assessment." *International Studies Q.*, 20(June):171–218.

VAUGHAN, T. R., and G. SJOBERG. **1970**. "The social construction of legal doctrine: the case of Adolf Eichmann." In J. D. Douglas, ed., *Deviance and Respectability: The Social Construction of Moral Meaning*. New York: Basic Books. Pp. 160–191.

VAYDA, A. P. **1974**. "Warfare in ecological perspective." *Annual Rev. of Ecology and Systematics*, 5:183–193.

——. **1968a**. "Hypotheses about functions of war." In M. H. Fried, M. Harris, and R. Murphy, eds., *War: The Anthropology of Armed Conflict and Aggression*. Garden City, N.Y.: Natural History Press. Pp. 85–91.

——. **1968b**. "Primitive war." In D. L. Sills, ed., *International Encyclopedia of the Social Sciences*. Vol. 16. New York: Crowell Collier and Macmillan. Pp. 468–472.

VÄYRYNEN, R. **1979**. "Economic and military position of the regional power centers." *J. of Peace Research*, 16(4):349–370.

VÄYRYNEN, R., and L. HERRERA. **1975**. "Subimperialism: from dependence to subordination." *Instant Research on Peace and Violence*, 5(3):165–177.

VELIKOVSKY, I. **1955**. *Earth in Upheaval*. New York: Dell.

VELLINGA, M. L. **1976**. "The military and the dynamics of the Cuban revolutionary process." *Comparative Politics*, 8(January):245–269.

VERNANT, J. P. **1974**. *Mythe et Pensée chez les Grecs: Etudes de Psychologie Historique*. Paris: Maspero.

VERNANT, J. P., and P. VIDAL-NAQUET. **1972**. *Mythe et Tragédie en Grèce Ancienne*. Paris: Maspero.

VERNON, R. **1971**. *Sovereignty at Bay: The Multinational Spread of U.S. Enterprises*. New York: Basic Books.

VERWEY, W. D. **1972**. *Economic Development, Peace, and International Law*. Atlantic Highlands, N.J.: Humanities.

VESZY-WAGNER, L. **1973**. "Destructiveness against individuals and groups." *Dynamische Psychiatrie*, 6(6):414–426.

VIETNAM VETERANS AGAINST THE WAR. **1972**. *The Winter Soldier Investigation: An Inquiry into American War Crimes*. Boston: Beacon.

VIGOR, P. H. **1975**. *The Soviet View of War, Peace and Neutrality*. London: Routledge and Kegan Paul.

VINCENT, J. E. **1978**. "Empirical studies of behavioural patterns at the United Nations." *Peace Research Rev.*, 7(4–5).

——. **1976a**. *Predicting Conflict and Cooperation in the International Relations System*. Boca Raton: Florida Atlantic University Press.

——. **1976b**. "Reinterpreting 'repredicting voting patterns in the General Assembly.' " *International Studies Q.*, 20(June):325–330.

——. **1972**. "An application of attribute theory to General Assembly voting patterns, and some implications." *International Organization*, 26(Summer):551–582.

——. **1971**. "Predicting voting patterns in the General Assembly." *American Political Science Rev.*, 65(June):471–498.

——. **1969**. "The convergence of voting and attitude patterns at the United Nations." *J. of Politics*, 31(November):952–983.

——. **1968**. "National attributes as predictors of delegate attitudes at the United Nations." *American Political Science Rev.*, 62 (September):916–931.

VINCENT, R. J. **1974**. *Nonintervention and International Order*. Princeton, N.J.: Princeton University Press.

VINER, J. **1966**. *Dumping: A Problem in International Trade*. New York: Kelley.

——. **1950**. *The Customs Union Issue*. New York: Carnegie Endowment for International Peace.

VIRKKUNEN, M., A. NUUTILA, and S. HUUSKO. **1976**. "Effect of brain injury on social adaptability: longitudinal study of frequency of criminality." *Acta Psychiatrica Scandinavica*, 53(March):168–172.

VLADIMIROV, S., and L. TEPLOV. **1977**. *NATO: A Bleak Picture*. V. Batishchev, tr. Moscow: Progress Publishers.

VOEVODSKY, J. **1972**. "Crisis waves: the growth and

decline of war-related behavioral events." *J. of Psychology*, 80(March):289–308.

——. **1971.** "Modeling the dynamics of warfare." In D. E. Knight, H. W. Curtis, and L. J. Fogel, eds., *Cybernetics, Simulation, and Conflict Resolution*. New York: Spartan. Pp. 145–170.

——. **1969.** "Quantitative analysis of nations at war." *Peace Research Rev.*, 3(5):1–63.

VVAW: *See Vietnam Veterans Against the War*.

WAIN, H. **1970.** *A History of Preventive Medicine*. Springfield, Ill.: Thomas.

WAINHOUSE, D. D., et al. **1973.** *International Peacekeeping at the Crossroads: National Support—Experience and Prospects*. Baltimore: Johns Hopkins University Press.

——. **1966.** *International Peace Observation: A History and Forecast*. Baltimore: Johns Hopkins University Press.

WAITE, R. G. L. **1977.** *The Psychopathic God: Adolf Hitler*. New York: Basic Books.

WAKIN, M. M., ed. **1979.** *War, Morality, and the Military Profession*. Boulder: Westview.

WALKER, S. G. **1977.** "The interface between beliefs and behavior: Henry Kissinger's operational code and the Vietnam War." *J. of Conflict Resolution*, 21(March):129–168.

WALLACE, A. R. **1973.** *Contributions to the Theory of Natural Selection: A Series of Essays*. New York: AMS Press.

WALLACE, M. D. **1980.** "Accounting for superpower arms spending." In P. J. McGowan and C. W. Kegley, Jr., eds., *Threats, Weapons and Foreign Policy*. Beverly Hills, Calif.: Sage. Pp. 259–274.

——. **1979.** "Arms races and escalation: some new evidence." *J. of Conflict Resolution*, 23 (March):3–16.

——. **1975.** "Clusters of nations in the global system: some preliminary evidence, 1865–1964." *International Studies Q.*, 19(March):67–89.

——. **1973a.** "Alliance polarization, cross-cutting, and international war, 1815–1964: a measurement procedure and some preliminary evidence." *J. of Conflict Resolution*, 17(December):575–604.

——. **1973b.** *War and Rank Among Nations*. Lexington, Mass.: Heath.

——. **1972.** "Status, formal organization and arms levels as factors leading to the onset of war, 1820–1964." In B. M. Russett, ed., *Peace, War, and Numbers*. Beverly Hills, Calif.: Sage. Pp. 49–69.

——. **1971.** "Power, status, and international war." *J. of Peace Research*, 8(1):23–35.

WALLACE, M. D., and J. D. SINGER. **1971.** "The use and abuse of imagination: a reply to Samuel A. Bleicher." *International Organization*, 25 (Autumn):953–957.

——. **1970.** "Intergovernmental organization in the global system, 1815–1964: a quantitative description." *International Organization*, 24(Spring): 239–287.

WALLACE, M. D., and J. M. WILSON. **1978.** "Nonlinear arms race models." *J. of Peace Research*, 15(2):175–192.

WALLENSTEEN, P. **1973.** *Structure and War: On International Relations, 1920–1968*. Stockholm: Rabén and Sjögren.

WALLERSTEIN, I. **1972.** *The Modern World System: Capitalist Agriculture and the Origins of the European World-Economy in the Sixteenth Century*. New York: Academic Press.

WALSH, M. N. **1962.** "Psychoanalytic studies on war." *Philadelphia Association for Psychoanalysis Bull.*, 12(3):129–131.

WALTON, R. J. **1972.** *Cold War and Counter-Revolution: The Foreign Policy of John F. Kennedy*. New York: Viking.

WALTZ, K. N. **1967.** *Foreign Policy and Democratic Politics: The American and British Experience*. Boston: Little, Brown.

——. **1959.** *Man, the State, and War: A Theoretical Analysis*. New York: Columbia University Press.

WALZER, M. **1977.** *Just and Unjust Wars: A Moral Argument with Historical Illustrations*. New York: Basic Books.

WAN, T. **1973.** "Effects of social status and status inconsistency on morbidity for the poor and nonpoor: a binary variable multiple regression analysis." *Social Biology*, 20(June):196–202.

WANGH, M. **1972.** "Some unconscious factors in the psychogenesis of recent student uprisings." *Psychoanalytic Q.*, 41(April):207–223.

WANK, S., ed. **1978.** *Doves and Diplomats: Foreign Offices and Peace Movements in Europe and America in the Twentieth Century*. Westport, Conn.: Greenwood.

WANNAMAKER, B. B., and A. J. HEIN. **1974.** "Categorization of seizure disorders in combat zone evacuees." *Military Medicine*, 140(May):380–383.

WARD, S. R., ed. **1975.** *The War Generation: Veterans of the First World War*. Port Washington, N.Y.: Kennikat.

WASHBURN, M. A., and C. BEITZ. **1974.** *Creating the Future: A Guide to Living and Working for Social Change*. New York: Bantam.

WAYMAN, F. **1974.** *Military Involvement in Politics: A Causal Model*. Beverly Hills, Calif.: Sage.

WEBSTER. **1970.** *New World Dictionary of the American Language*, 2nd college ed. New York: World Publishing.

WEDDERBURN, D., ed. **1974.** *Poverty, Inequality and Class Structure*. Cambridge: Cambridge University Press.

WEEDE, E. **1976.** "Overwhelming preponderance as a pacifying condition among contiguous Asian dyads, 1950–1969." *J. of Conflict Reso-*

lution, 20(September):395–411.

——. **1975.** *Weltpolitik und Kriegsursachen im 20. Jahrhundert: Eine quantitativ-empirische Studie.* Munich and Vienna: Oldenbourg.

WEHR, P. **1979.** *Conflict Regulation.* Boulder: Westview.

WEHR, P., and M. WASHBURN. **1976.** *Peace and World Order Studies: Teaching and Research for the Growth of Peace Systems.* Beverly Hills, Calif.: Sage.

WEIDENBAUM, M. L. **1974.** *The Economics of Peacetime Defense.* New York: Praeger.

——. **1966.** "Shifting the composition of government spending: implications for the regional distribution of income." *Peace Research Society (International) Papers,* 5, Philadelphia Conference.

WEINSTEIN, B. **1976.** "Francophonie: a language-based movement in world politics." *International Organization,* 30(Summer):485–508.

WEINSTOCK, U. **1964.** *Das Problem der Kondratieff-Zyklen.* Berlin: Duncker and Humblot.

WEISMAN, A. **1971.** "Is suicide a disease?" *Life-Threatening Behavior,* 1(Winter):219–231.

WEISS, E. B. **1975.** "Weather control: an instrument for war?" *Survival* (Great Britain), 17(March–April):64–68.

WEISS, H. K. **1963.** "Stochastic models for the duration and magnitude of a 'deadly quarrel.'" *Operations Research,* 11(January–February): 101–121.

WEISS, P. A., ed. **1971.** *Hierarchically Organized Systems in Theory and Practice.* New York: Hafner.

WEISS, W. **1969.** "Effects of the mass media of communication." In G. Lindzey and E. Aronson, eds., *Handbook for Social Psychology.* Vol. 5. Reading, Mass.: Addison-Wesley. Pp. 77–195.

WELCH, C. E., JR., and A. K. SMITH. **1974.** *Military Role and Rule: Perspectives on Civil–Military Relations.* North Scituate, Mass.: Duxbury.

WELCH, R. E., JR. **1977.** "Détente and its analysts." *Peace and Change,* 4(Fall):3–8.

WELCH, W. **1970.** *American Images of Soviet Foreign Policy: An Inquiry into Recent Appraisals from the Academic Community.* New Haven, Conn.: Yale University Press.

WELLS, L. E., and G. MARWELL. **1975.** *Self-Esteem: Its Conceptualization and Measurement.* Beverly Hills, Calif.: Sage.

WEN, C. P. **1974.** "Secular suicidal trend in postwar Japan and Taiwan: an examination of hypotheses." *International J. of Social Psychiatry,* 20(Spring–Summer):8–17.

WEPPNER, R. S. **1972.** "Drug abuse patterns of Vietnamese war veterans hospitalized as narcotic addicts." *Drug Forum,* 2(Fall):43–54.

WESLEY, J. P. **1962.** "Frequency of wars and geo-graphical opportunity." *J. of Conflict Resolution,* 6(December):387–389.

WESSON, R. G. **1967.** *The Imperial Order.* Berkeley: University of California Press.

WETTER, J. G. **1979.** *The International Arbitral Process: Public and Private.* Dobbs Ferry, N.Y.: Oceana.

WEXLER, P. **1977.** "Comment on Ralph Turner's 'the real self: from institution to impulse.'" *American J. of Sociology,* 83(July):178–185.

WHALEN, R. E., ed. **1974.** *The Neuropsychology of Aggression.* New York: Plenum.

WHEELER, H. **1976.** "Choosing war and peace: the effects on industrial growth, 1860–1965." San Francisco: Presented at annual meeting of Western Political Science Association. Mimeo.

——. **1975.** "The effects of war on industrial growth, 1816–1970." Ann Arbor: University of Michigan. Ph.D. thesis.

WHEELER, J. H., ed. **1973.** *Beyond the Punitive Society.* San Francisco: W. H. Freeman and Company.

WHITE, R. K. **1968.** *Nobody Wanted War: Misperception in Vietnam and Other Wars.* Garden City, N.Y.: Doubleday.

——. **1966.** "Misperception and the Vietnam War." *J. of Social Issues,* 22(July):1–164.

WHITE, R. K., and R. LIPPITT. **1960.** *Autocracy and Democracy.* New York: Harper.

WHITING, A. S. **1960.** *China Crosses the Yalu: The Decision to Enter the Korean War.* Stanford, Calif.: Stanford University Press.

WIEGELE, T. **1973.** "Decision-making in an international crisis: some biological factors." *International Studies Q.,* 17(3):295–333.

WIENER, P. D., and J. FISHER, eds. **1974.** *Violence and Aggression in the History of Ideas.* New Brunswick, N.J.: Rutgers University Press.

WIGHT, M. **1978.** *Power Politics.* H. Bull and C. Holbraad, eds. New York: Holmes and Meier.

——. **1960.** "Why is there no international theory?" *International Relations,* 2(April):35–48, 62.

WILHELMSEN, F. D., and J. BRET. **1970.** *The War in Man: Media and Machines.* Athens: University of Georgia Press.

WILKENFELD, J. **1975.** "A time-series perspective on conflict in the Middle East." In P. J. McGowan, ed., *Sage International Yearbook of Foreign Policy Studies.* Beverly Hills, Calif.: Sage. Pp. 177–212.

——. ed. **1973a.** *Conflict Behavior and Linkage Politics.* New York: David McKay.

——. **1973b.** "Domestic and foreign conflict." In J. Wilkenfeld, ed., *Conflict Behavior and Linkage Politics.* New York: David McKay. Pp. 107–123.

——. **1972.** "Models for the analysis of foreign conflict behavior of states." In B. M. Russett, ed., *Peace, War, and Numbers.* Beverly Hills, Calif.: Sage. Pp. 275–298.

——. **1968.** "Domestic and foreign conflict behavior of nations." *J. of Peace Research,* 5(1):56–69.

WILKENFELD, J., and D. ZINNES. 1973. "A linkage model of domestic conflict behavior." In J. Wilkenfeld, ed., *Conflict Behavior and Linkage Politics*. New York: David McKay. Pp. 325–374.

WILKINS, M. 1974. *The Maturing of Multinational Enterprise: American Business Abroad from 1914 to 1970*. Cambridge, Mass.: Harvard University Press.

———. 1970. *The Emergence of Multinational Enterprise: American Business Abroad from the Colonial Era to 1914*. Cambridge, Mass.: Harvard University Press.

WILKINS, W. L. 1972. "Psychiatric and psychological research in the Navy before World War II." *Military Medicine*, 137(June):228–231.

WILKINSON, D. 1980. *Deadly Quarrels*. Berkeley: University of California Press.

WILLIAMS, W. A. 1962. *American Diplomacy*. New York: Dell.

WILLRICH, M. 1975. *Energy and World Politics*. New York: Free Press.

———, ed. 1973. *International Safeguards and Nuclear Industry*. Baltimore: Johns Hopkins University Press.

WILLRICH, M., and T. TAYLOR. 1974. *Nuclear Theft: Risks and Safeguards*. Cambridge: Ballinger.

WILSON, A. W. 1972. "Magic in contemporary life and in psychoanalysis." *Psychoanalytic Rev.*, 59(Spring):5–18.

WILSON, B. R. 1973. *Magic and the Millennium: A Sociological Study of Religious Movements of Protest Among Tribal and Third-World Peoples*. New York: Harper and Row.

WILSON, E. O. 1975. *Sociobiology: The New Synthesis*. Cambridge, Mass.: Belknap.

WILSON, E. 1963. *The Cold War and the Income Tax: A Protest*. New York: Farrar, Straus.

WILSON, L. 1964. *Catalogue of Cycles: Part I–Economics*. Pittsburgh: Foundation for the Study of Cycles.

WILSON, L. C. 1980. "The practice and status of intervention and non-intervention in contemporary international law." Los Angeles: Presented at annual meeting of International Studies Association. Mimeo.

WINKLER, A. M. 1978. *The Politics of Propaganda: The Office of War Information, 1942–1945*. New Haven, Conn.: Yale University Press.

WINKLER, H. Z., R. MOSES, and M. OSTOW. 1973. *Psychological Bases of War*. New York: Quadrangle.

WINTER, J. M., ed. 1975. *War and Economic Development*. Cambridge: Cambridge University Press.

WITTKOPF, E. R. 1973. "Foreign aid and United Nations votes: a comparative study." *American Political Science Rev.*, 67(September):868–888.

WOHLSTETTER, A. 1976–1977. "Spreading the bomb without quite breaking the rules." *Foreign Policy*, 25(Winter):88–96.

———. 1974. "Rivals, but no 'race.' " *Foreign Policy*, 16(Fall):48–82.

WOHLSTETTER, A., V. GILINSKY, and G. WOHLSTETTER. 1979. *Nuclear Policies: Fuel Without the Bomb*. Cambridge: Ballinger.

WOHLSTETTER, R. 1962. *Pearl Harbor: Warning and Decision*. Stanford, Calif.: Stanford University Press.

WOLF, C. 1972. "The logic of failure: a Vietnam 'lesson.' " *American Behavioral Scientist*, 15(July):929–937.

———. 1967. *United States Policy and the Third World: Problems and Analysis*. Boston: Little, Brown.

———. 1965. "The political effects of military programs: some indications from Latin America." *Orbis*, 8(Winter):871–893.

WOLF, E. R. 1969. *Peasant Wars of the Twentieth Century*. New York: Harper and Row.

WOLFE, M. 1972. *The Economic Causes of Imperialism*. New York: Wiley.

WOLFENSTEIN, M., and G. KLIMAN, eds. 1965. *Children and the Death of a President*. Garden City, N.Y.: Doubleday.

WOLFERS, A. 1962. *Discord and Collaboration*. Baltimore: Johns Hopkins University Press.

WOLFF, K. H. 1976. *Surrender and Catch: Experience and Inquiry Today*. Boston: Reidel.

WOLFSON, M. 1968. "A mathematical model of the cold war." *Peace Research Society (International) Papers*, 9:107–123.

WOLIN, S. 1960, *Politics and Vision*. Boston: Little, Brown.

WOLPIN, M. D. 1977. "Military dependency versus development in the third world." *Bull. of Peace Proposals*, 8(2):137–141.

———. 1973. *Military Aid and Counterrevolution in the Third World*. Lexington, Mass.: Lexington Books.

WOOD, D. 1968. *Conflict in the Twentieth Century*. Adelphi Paper No. 48. London: Institute for Strategic Studies.

WOODS, F. A., and A. BALTZLY. 1915. *Is War Diminishing? A Study of the Prevalence of War in Europe from 1450 to the Present Day*. Boston: Houghton Mifflin.

WORLD HEALTH ORGANIZATION. 1976. *World Health Statistics Annual, 1973–1976*. Geneva: World Health Organization.

WRIGHT, H. T. 1977. "Recent research on the origin of the state." *Annual Rev. of Anthropology*, 6:379–397.

WRIGHT, Q. 1965. *A Study of War*. 2 vols. Chicago: University of Chicago Press.

———. 1955. *The Study of International Relations*. New York: Appleton Century Crofts.

WULF, C., ed. 1974. *Handbook on Peace Education*. Frankfurt/Main and Oslo: International Peace Research Association.

WYNNER, E., and G. LLOYD. 1946. *Searchlight on*

Peace Plans: Choose Your Road to World Government. New York: Dutton.

YAGER, J. **1976.** "Postcombat violent behavior in psychiatrically maladjusting soldiers." *Archives of General Psychiatry,* 33(November): 1332–1335.

——. **1975.** "Personal violence in infantry combat." *Archives of General Psychiatry,* 32 (February):257–261.

YANARELLA, E. J. **1977.** *The Missile Defense Controversy: Strategy, Technology and Politics, 1955–1972.* Lexington: University Press of Kentucky.

——. **1975.** "The 'technological imperative' and the strategic arms race." *Peace and Change,* 3(Spring):3–16.

YARMOLINSKY, A. **1970.** *The Military Establishment: Its Impacts on American Society.* New York: Harper and Row.

YARROW, C. H. M. **1978.** *Quaker Experiences in International Conciliation.* New Haven, Conn.: Yale University Press.

YESELSON, A., and A. GAGLIONE. **1974.** *A Dangerous Place: The United Nations as a Weapon in World Politics.* New York: Grossman.

YORK, H. F., ed. **1973a.** *Arms Control.* San Francisco: W. H. Freeman and Company.

——. **1973b.** "Military technology and national security." In H. F. York, ed., *Arms Control.* San Francisco: W. H. Freeman and Company. Pp. 188–200.

——. **1973c.** "The great test ban debate." In H. F. York, ed., *Arms Control.* San Francisco: W. H. Freeman and Company. Pp. 294–302.

YOUNG, N. **1975.** "The nation-state and war resistance." Bradford, England: University of Bradford. Mimeo.

YOUNG, O. R. **1967.** *The Intermediaries: Third Parties in International Crises.* Princeton, N.J.: Princeton University Press.

YOUNG, R. A., ed. **1977.** "International crisis: progress and prospects for applied forecasting and management." *International Studies Q.,* Special Issue 21(March).

——. **1976.** "Toward a global monitoring system: some comments and suggestions." *International Studies Q.,* 20(December):629–634.

ZAMPAGLIONE, G. **1973.** *The Idea of Peace in Antiquity.* Notre Dame, Ind.: University of Notre Dame Press.

ZARTMAN, I. W. **1971.** *The Politics of Trade Negotiations Between Africa and the European Economic Community: The Weak Confront the Strong.*

Princeton, N.J.: Princeton University Press.

ZASLAVSKY, V. **1980.** "Socioeconomic inequality and changes in Soviet ideology." *Theory and Society,* 9(March):383–407.

ZEEMAN, E. C. **1977.** *Castastrophe Theory: Selected Papers, 1972–1977.* Reading, Mass.: Addison-Wesley.

——. **1976.** "Catastrophe theory." *Scientific American,* 234(April):65–83.

ZIMMERMAN, E. **1975.** "Dimensions of internal and international conflict: a critical inventory of attempts to use factor analysis in researching large-scale conflict." *Politische Vierteljahresschrift,* 16(September):343–408.

ZINNES, D. A. **1976.** *Contemporary Research in International Relations: A Perspective and a Critical Appraisal.* New York: Free Press.

——. **1968.** "The expression and perception of hostility in prewar crisis: 1914." In J. D. Singer, ed., *Quantitative International Politics: Insights and Evidence.* New York: Free Press. Pp. 85–122.

ZINNES, D. A., and J. V. GILLESPIE, eds. **1976.** *Mathematical Models in International Relations.* New York: Praeger.

ZINNES, D. A., J. V. GILLESPIE, and P. A. SCHRODT. **1976.** "The Arab–Israeli arms race: an empirical examination." *Jerusalem J. of International Relations,* 2(Fall):28–62.

ZINNES, D. A., J. V. GILLESPIE, and G. S. TAHIM. **1978a.** "A formal analysis of some issues in balance of power theories." *International Studies Q.,* 22(September):323–353.

——. **1978b.** "Modeling a chimera: balance of power revisited." *J. of Peace Science,* 3(Spring):31–44.

ZINSSER, H. **1935.** *Rats, Lice, and History.* Boston: Little, Brown.

ZIV, A., and R. ISRAELI. **1973.** "Effects of bombardment on the manifest anxiety level of children living in the kibbutzim." *J. of Consulting and Clinical Psychology,* 40(April):287–291.

ZIV, A., A. W. KRUGLANSKI, and S. SHULMAN. **1974.** "Children's psychological reactions to wartime stress." *J. of Personality and Social Psychology,* 30(July):24–30.

ZORGBIBE, C. **1975.** *La Guerre Civile.* Paris: Presses Universitaires de France.

ŽOUREK, J. **1974.** *L'Interdiction de l'Emploi de la Force en Droit International.* Leiden: Sijthoff

ZUCKERMAN, S. **1966.** *Scientists and War: The Impact of Science on Military and Civil Affairs.* New York: International Publications.

ZURCHER, L. A., and G. HARRIES-JENKINS, eds. **1978.** *Supplementary Military Forces: Reserves, Militias, Auxiliaries.* Beverly Hills, Calif.: Sage.

INDEX OF NAMES

INDEX OF TOPICS